2nd International Conference on Language and Cultural Communication (ICLCC 2024)

SHS Web of Conferences Volume 185 (2024)

Sanya, China
19 – 21 January 2024

Editors:

D. Pandya
E. Marino
S.F. Syed Mohammed
N.R. Ghlamallah

ISBN: 978-1-7138-9557-2

Printed from e-media with permission by:

Curran Associates, Inc.
57 Morehouse Lane
Red Hook, NY 12571

Some format issues inherent in the e-media version may also appear in this print version.

For additional information, please contact EDP Sciences – Web of Conferences
at the address below.

EDP Sciences – Web of Conferences
17, Avenue du Hoggar
Parc d'Activité de Courtabœuf
BP 112
F-91944 Les Ulis Cedex A
France

Phone: +33 (0) 1 69 18 75 75
Fax: +33 (0) 1 69 28 84 91

contact-edps@webofconferences.org

Additional copies of this publication are available from:

Curran Associates, Inc.
57 Morehouse Lane
Red Hook, NY 12571 USA
Phone: 845-758-0400
Fax: 845-758-2633
Email: curran@proceedings.com
Web: www.proceedings.com

TABLE OF CONTENTS

RESEARCH ON LANGUAGE TEACHING AND TEXT READING

TRADITIONAL CULTURAL INHERITANCE AND INTERCULTURAL COMMUNICATION

BRAND MANAGEMENT AND MARKETING STRATEGY ANALYSIS

Preface

International Conference on Language and Cultural Communication (ICLCC) was motivated to bridge the scientists, experts, practitioners, and students in the scientific forum through sharing ideas and issues about theoretical and practical knowledge in fields of language and cultural communication.

The 2024 2nd International Conference on Language and Cultural Communication (ICLCC 2024) took place via hybrid form from January 19th to 21st, 2024 in Sanya, China, bringing together about 80 attendees nationally and internationally. As an annual conference, ICLCC has been held in China starting from 2023 and will continue to be held every year in the future. With strong organization team, committee members domestically and internationally (more than half of them from abroad), dependable reputation and wide sponsors globally, ICLCC 2024 was even more successful than previous one.

The keynote speeches were provided especially to show the contributions of scholars and experts around the world working in the fields related to language and cultural communication towards research experience and knowledge sharing. We had four keynote speakers (Assoc. Prof. Chew Fong Peng from University of Malaya (UM), Malaysia, Prof. Budsaba Kanoksilapatham from Silpakorn University, Thailand, Prof. Yongjun Feng from Shaanxi Normal University, China, and Prof. Junfeng Diao from Hainan Normal University, China). They made keynote speeches on: Factors Influencing the Students' Learning of the Malay Language in Malaysia Independent Chinese Secondary Schools, Academic Writing Culture of Research Articles: Deciphering The Conclusion Section Using Linguistic Analysis, Using Education Big Data to Select and Evaluate the New Round of " World first-class" Universities in the Context of Chinese-style Modernization, and Research on Standard and Training Implementation for Dual Professional Vocational Teachers' Teaching Competency in the Information Age.

The Proceedings of ICLCC 2024 involves various accepted excellent papers around topics including Chinese/Foreign Languages and Literature, Research on Classroom Teaching Method, Translation & Writing, Journalism and Communication, Network and New Media, Advertising Photography, etc. The selected papers were checked through a rigorous peer review process, and are published in the present volume. Reviews were conducted by expert referees to the professional and scientific standards expected of SHS Web of Conferences.

We would like to thank the Conference Committee members for their great support and suggestion provided in every aspect to make the Conference successful and the members of reviewers for their kind assistance in reviewing the manuscripts submitted. We would also extend our best gratitude to the keynote speakers for their invaluable contribution and worthwhile ideas shared in the Conference. Last but not the least is our appreciation to SHS Web of Conferences for every process its members conducted to make this Proceedings published.

The Committee of ICLCC 2024

Committee Member

Conference General Chair
Prof. Zhu Shoutong, University of Macau, Macau, China

Technical Program Committee Chair
A. Prof. Mohd Farid Mohd Sharif, Universiti Sains Malaysia, Malaysia

Publication Chair
Prof. Dr. Digvijay Pandya, Parul University, India
A. Prof. Elisabetta Marino, University of Rome "Tor Vergata", Italy
A. Prof. Dr. Sharifah Faizah Syed Mohammed, Universiti Teknologi MARA, Malaysia
A. Prof. Nahed Rajaa GHLAMALLAH, University of Oran 2 – Mohamed Ben Ahmed, Algeria

International Technical Program Committee
Prof. Hui Ding, Central South University, China
Prof. Andrea L. Baldini, Alliance University, Bengaluru, India
Prof. Fengxia Cao, Guangdong University of Technology, China
A. Prof. Sikandar Ali Qalati, Jiangsu University, Pakistan
A. Prof. Jordan Yan, JiaYing University, Taiwan, China
A. Prof. Bootheina Majoul, ISLT- University of Carthage, Tunisia
A. Prof. Jasni Sulong, Universiti Sains Malaysia, Malaysia
A. Prof. Chuanjun Zhao, Shanxi University of Finance and Economics, China
Dr. Purrie Pui-Yee NG, Beijing Normal University-Hong Kong Baptist University United International College (UIC), China

Statement of Peer review

In submitting conference proceedings to *Web of Conferences*, the editors of the proceedings certify to the Publisher that

1. They adhere to its **Policy on Publishing Integrity** in order to safeguard good scientific practice in publishing.
2. All articles have been subjected to peer review administered by the proceedings editors.
3. Reviews have been conducted by expert referees, who have been requested to provide unbiased and constructive comments aimed, whenever possible, at improving the work.
4. Proceedings editors have taken all reasonable steps to ensure the quality of the materials they publish and their decision to accept or reject a paper for publication has been based only on the merits of the work and the relevance to the journal.

Title, date and place of the conference

The 2nd International Conference on Language and Cultural Communication （ICLCC 2024）
January 19-21, 2024
Sanya, China

Proceedings editor(s):

Digvijay Pandya, Parul University, Vadodara, Gujarat, India
Elisabetta Marino, University of Rome “Tor Vergata”, Italy
Sharifah Faizah Syed Mohammed, Universiti Teknologi MARA, MalaysiaNahed Rajaa GHLAMALLAH, University of Oran 2 – Mohamed Ben Ahmed, Algeria

Date and editor’s signature

Digvijay Pandya

Elisabetta Marino

Sharifah Faizah Syed Mohammed

Nahed Rajaa GHLAMALLAH

An Action Research on Phonetics Instruction in College-level English Education

Yuan Pang*

General Ability Teaching Department, Beijing Information Technology College, Beijing, China

Abstract. The deficiency in knowledge of English phonetics constitutes a significant contributing factor to the lower proficiency observed among college students in terms of their listening and speaking skills in English. By implementing a communicative approach, an action research study was conducted with the aim of enhancing students' pronunciation and intonation within speech flow, thereby effectively improving their ability to communicate in English. This investigation suggests that incorporating phonetic instruction into college-level English education can augment language acquisition accuracy and enhance students' linguistic proficiency when expressing themselves, ultimately facilitating successful communication in the English language.

1. Introduction

There are various factors that impact the English listening and speaking proficiency of college students, including insufficient vocabulary and grammar knowledge. Additionally, inadequate understanding of English phonetics is a significant contributor to lower levels of English listening and speaking ability among college students. To address this issue, action research methodology is employed to conduct reflective teaching experiments in practice. Through adopting a communicative approach, this study aims to enhance the pronunciation and intonation skills of college students in speech flow, thereby improving their accuracy in acquiring language information and ultimately achieving effective communication in English.

2. Overview of Action Research Theory

Action research was initially proposed by social psychologist Lewin in the 1940s and has been introduced to China for numerous years[1]. Various scholars have provided their own definitions of action research from diverse perspectives. The most widely accepted definition characterizes action research as a form of self-reflection, enabling social workers and educators to enhance their understanding and evaluation of the social or educational initiatives they are involved in, as well as their work processes and environments. The fundamental essence of action research lies in the integration of action and research. Key elements encompass inquiry, reflection, action, collaboration, change, and professional development[2]. The process of action research follows a spiral deepening developmental trajectory that comprises four interconnected and interdependent stages: planning, action, observation and reflection[3]. Lewis contends that the integration of teaching and research engenders an unprecedented fervor for pedagogy among educators, bolstering their self-esteem and fostering a heightened sense of confidence[4]. Based on this premise, teachers can enhance their efficiency in implementing action research by proactively reflecting on teaching issues and actively seeking solutions. Consequently, not only can teachers elevate their professional standards but also improve student achievement[5].

Action research was introduced into foreign language teaching in China during the 1990s[6]. Wang provides a comprehensive and systematic exposition of action research theory in her book *Action Research for English Teachers*. Furthermore, she offers guidance to English teachers in China on how to effectively implement action research in their own teaching practices[7]. Her work has had a profound impact on the advancement of action research in China. Meng employs bibliometric analysis as a research method, utilizing databases such as CNKI, core journals from Peking University and Nanjing University, to conduct an extensive data analysis on various topics related to action research in foreign language teaching between 2011 and 2021. The findings reveal that approximately 85.7% of the literature focuses on action research pertaining to English listening, speaking, reading, writing, and translation, however, phonetic instruction within college-level English is not extensively explored[8]. Specifically searching through CNKI using keywords such as phonetic teaching and action research within the scope of advanced search for college-level English from 2013 to 2023 yielded only a total of 14 papers. This indicates that there is limited scholarly attention given to action studies concerning phonetics instruction within college-level English education in China.

*Corresponding author's mail: pangy@bitc.edu.cn

3. Action Research in English Phonetic Teaching

This study involved 58 second-grade Business English major students from 2 classes who participated in a one-year comparative teaching experiment, with two courses (*Business Listening* and *Oral English for Business Negotiation*) serving as experimental interventions. A communicative approach was employed to facilitate the development of students' pronunciation and intonation within the context of speech flow, which is characterized by native speakers' sequential production of multiple sounds rather than articulating each word in isolation. Merely engaging in mechanical practice of single phonemes does not effectively contribute to language learning, therefore, it is recommended that learners actively participate in more authentic language communication environments. The two courses specifically designed for business English majors provide ample opportunities and content for learners to acquire and apply phonological knowledge within the natural context of speech flow.

3.1. Identifying the Problem and Formulating Hypotheses

Through early classroom observations and interviews with students and teachers in both classes, the author discovered that a significant number of students exhibited limited understanding of fundamental phonetic knowledge. Specifically, their comprehension of English phonetic alphabets was frequently inaccurate, hindering their ability to effectively read and memorize numerous college-level English words. Furthermore, these students encountered difficulties in grasping essential English phonetic rules such as stress, linking, reduction, explosion, assimilation, and rhythm.

These aforementioned factors have resulted in a decline in interest and confidence among students when it comes to furthering their proficiency in the English language. In both speaking and listening classes, students demonstrated subpar performance with the majority still struggling. For these reasons mentioned above, the author devised a course questionnaire and conducted English listening and phonetic tests in both classes. These measures led to the identification of issues which formulated a hypothesis: namely that phonetic knowledge constitutes one of the crucial factors influencing students' proficiency in English listening and speaking skills. Phonetic training can enhance students' accuracy in expressing themselves in English as well as their ability to comprehend language information ultimately facilitating effective communication. Consequently, an intervention plan for action research was designed by selecting the class with lower scores on initial tests as the experimental group for implementing said plan.

3.2. Revising and Executing Action Plans

The action plan consisted of two distinct stages. The initial stage encompassed the acquisition of phonetic knowledge, which required approximately 4 class hours for completion. Subsequently, the second stage involved intensive phonetic training in two courses. Throughout the entire academic year, a communicative approach was utilized to improve students' pronunciation and intonation in their speech flow.

3.2.1. The first stage

In the initial phase of the study, the teacher employed an engaging English phonetic alphabet teaching approach to introduce English phonetic alphabets in 2 class hours. By means of categorization and comparison with Chinese pronunciations, each phonetic symbol was assigned a vivid Chinese name. Through association, homophony and other techniques, students were able to acquire and proficiently grasp English phonetic alphabets in just 2 class hours. Subsequently, following the completion of the phonetics instruction, an additional 2 class hours were dedicated to elucidate concepts pertaining to hyperphonology encompassing stress patterns, intonation variations, rhythmic elements, weak forms usage as well as linking and reduction phenomena.

3.2.2. The second stage

In the second phase of the study, the communicative approach was employed to facilitate phonetic training in speech flow within the experimental group. Taking into account both language characteristics and students' proficiency levels in this particular class, a series of meticulously designed classroom activities were implemented, encompassing syllable training, simulation exercises, free expression and role play. These activities were strategically sequenced from simpler tasks to more demanding ones without necessitating significant adjustments.

During syllable training, students were guided in the process of reading and memorizing challenging words by systematically dissecting them into individual syllables during listening or oral English classes. This pedagogical approach not only facilitated accurate word recognition but also enhanced the ability to effortlessly decode unfamiliar words with longer spellings, thereby enabling students to improve their orthographic skills based on phonetic segmentation.

In the simulation training, students should engage in repetitive simulation exercises based on the phonological characteristics present in the oral and listening learning materials. This enabled them to develop familiarity with pronunciation and intonation, thereby ensuring accuracy and fluency in their spoken language.

In the sessions of free expression and role-play, the author meticulously curated topics to facilitate unrestrained discussions among students, while also imposing a requirement for them to deliver spontaneous speeches lasting approximately 2 minutes on these subjects. Following each speech, both the teacher and fellow students actively engaged by posing inquiries or offering suggestions pertaining to language usage or content. Subsequently, after the conclusion of the free expression activity, the author devised specific scenarios and criteria aligned with the learning objectives, prompting students to assume designated roles within a predetermined time frame. Furthermore, various forms of extracurricular activities were intricately designed by the teacher to further augment students' listening and speaking skills beyond regular class hours.

3.3. Evaluating and Reflecting of Action Plans

Following implementation of intervention plans, an extensive evaluation and reflection were conducted using questionnaires, interviews, and classroom observations. Subsequently, a comparative analysis was carried out between the experimental class and the comparison class regarding pre- and post-experiment phonetic/oral English tests as well as listening tests based on language test score data analysis. Furthermore, within the experimental class itself, vertical comparisons were made by examining pre- versus post-experiment test scores. The final outcomes undeniably revealed substantial improvements in students' English listening and speaking proficiency resulting from integrating phonetic training with a communicative approach to speech flow (see Table 1-3 for statistical data analysis).

The students from both classes underwent phonetic and listening tests at the beginning and end of the initial semester, followed by listening and speaking assessments at the end of the second semester. Subsequently, utilizing SPSS software, the data obtained from these three evaluations were meticulously organized and subjected to rigorous statistical analysis. The ensuing comparisons are presented as follows.

3.3.1. Horizontal Comparison

The horizontal comparison involves assessing the scores of the experimental and comparison classes in the initial and final tests, respectively, to ascertain whether there is a statistically significant improvement in the scores of the experimental class compared to the comparison class following implementation of the action plans.

Table 1. Horizontal comparisons between 2 classes.

Test time	Test	Class	Class size	Lowest score	Highest score	Average score	Standard deviation
The beginning of semester 1	Phonetic test scores	Comparison class	28	31.00	85.00	50.7143	15.90215
		Experimental class	30	31.00	81.50	48.2667	12.92267
	Listening test scores	Comparison class	28	71.00	93.00	84.5357	5.75733
		Experimental class	30	75.00	92.00	83.1333	4.45462
The end of semester 1	Phonetic test scores	Comparison class	28	32.00	88.00	50.8214	14.27521
		Experimental class	30	32.00	89.00	58.2667	13.64307
	Listening test scores	Comparison class	28	65.00	90.00	80.6429	6.51616
		Experimental class	30	75.00	94.00	84.0333	3.76447
The end of semester 2	Oral test scores	Comparison class	28	65.00	90.00	76.8214	7.15983
		Experimental class	30	77.00	95.00	84.2667	4.52528
	Listening test scores	Comparison class	28	73.00	89.00	75.5521	7.89045
		Experimental class	30	76.00	96.00	84.4738	5.90577

The initial tests in the first semester revealed similar scores between the two classes, as indicated by Table 1. However, during consecutive semesters' final assessments, the experimental class outperformed the comparison class in both phonetic/oral English tests and listening tests. The significance of this disparity can be further elucidated through an independent sample T-test.

Table 2. T-test scale of the final test scores in semester 1 and 2 between the 2 classes.

Independent sample test										
		Variational Levene test		T-test for mean equation						
		F	Sig.	t	f	Sig. (bilateral)	Mean difference	Standard error value	95% confidence interval for the difference	
									Lower limit	Upper limit
The phonetic scores at the end of semester 1	Suppose variance Equal	.688	.410	-2.031	56	.047	-7.44524	3.66601	-14.78913	-.10135
	Suppose variance Not equal			-2.028	55.264	.047	-7.44524	3.67183	-14.80297	-.08751
The listening scores at the	Suppose variance Equal	4.988	.030	-3.890	56	.000	-3.38048	1.38573	-8.16643	-2.61452

end of semester 1	Suppose variance Not equal			-3.822	42.593	.000	-3.38048	1.41025	-8.23531	-2.54564
The oral scores at the end of semester 2	Suppose variance Equal	11.577	.001	-4.767	56	.000	-7.44524	1.56167	-10.57365	-4.31683
	Suppose variance Not equal			-4.696	45.055	.000	-7.44524	1.58538	-10.63825	-4.25222
The listening scores at the end of semester 2	Suppose variance Equal	4.347	.042	-2.726	56	.009	-8.9217	1.82203	-8.61663	-1.31670
	Suppose variance Not equal			-2.699	49.912	.009	-8.9217	1.84015	-8.66288	-1.27046

The T-test scale in Table 2 presents the final test scores of the phonetic/oral and listening courses for two semesters in both classes. As this comparison involves two independent samples, an independent sample t-test was employed. Analysis of Table 2 reveals that at the end of both semesters, there were probability values indicating significant differences between phonetic/oral scores and listening scores in both classes: 0.047, 0.000, 0.000, and 0.009 respectively.

At the end of semester1, with a probability value of 0.047 falling within range of 0.01 to 0.05, it demonstrates a significant difference between these classes, whereas all other values are less than <0.01, indicating extremely significant differences.

The negative t-value in this table is attributed to the utilization of SPSS software, where data from the comparison class is designated as group one, while the experimental class is assigned as group two during the inspection and calculation procedures.

These findings indicate that after implementing communicative approach to enhance pronunciation and intonation skills among college students in speech flow context, the experimental class achieved higher scores compared to their counterparts in both phonetic/oral and listening tests.

3.3.2. Longitudinal Comparison

The longitudinal comparison involves evaluating the test scores of multiple assessments to determine whether there is any discernible improvement subsequent to the implementation of action plans in the experimental class, thereby facilitating an assessment of the efficacy of the instructional approach.

Table 3. Longitudinal comparisons in experimental class.

Test	Test time	Lowest score	Highest score	Average score	Standard deviation
Phonetic/ Oral test scores	The beginning of semester 1	31.00	81.50	48.2667	12.92267
	The end of semester 1	32.00	89.00	58.2667	13.64307
	The end of semester 2	77.00	92.00	84.2667	4.52528
Listening test scores	The beginning of semester 1	75.00	92.00	83.1333	4.45462
	The end of semester 1	75.00	94.00	84.0333	3.76447
	The end of semester 2	76.00	96.00	84.4738	5.90577

The results presented in Table 3 demonstrate a statistically significant improvement in the average scores of phonetic/oral and listening performance following the implementation of the action plans, as observed at the culmination of both semesters.

Table 1-3 reveal a significant enhancement in English phonetic/speaking and listening test scores for the experimental group after implementing the action plans over two semesters, as compared to the comparison group within an equivalent time frame.

After the implementation of action intervention plans, a significant improvement in classroom teaching effectiveness was observed. Through student interviews, it was revealed that the majority favored this phonetic training method due to its enjoyable approach towards acquiring English phonetics. They believed that this engaging pedagogy facilitated rapid comprehension of phonetic knowledge, boosted their confidence in spoken English, and prevented them from being subjected to ridicule for mispronunciations. Consequently, their interest in learning English substantially increased. In the post-experiment questionnaire survey, 87% of students expressed support for employing a communicative approach to train phonetic knowledge in speech flow. By actively participating in activities such as word spellings, simulations, free expressions, and role-plays during class time, they gradually improved their pronunciation and intonation skills while unconsciously enhancing their listening and speaking proficiency in English. In contrast to the experimental class, the comparison group exhibited significantly lower levels of enthusiasm towards learning English as well as reduced engagement in classroom activities and interactions between teachers and students.

4. Conclusion

After implementing action plans for one academic year, this study suggests that employing a communicative approach to phonetic training within the speech flow can significantly enhance students' motivation to learn English phonetics, bolster their confidence in speaking English, transform the learning atmosphere and outcomes of English listening and speaking classes, ultimately leading to improved accuracy in students' expression of the English language and acquisition of linguistic information.

In the interim, it is imperative to acknowledge a crucial aspect of this study. The present action research was conducted within two classes, encompassing a mere 58 participants, thereby rendering the sample size insufficiently substantial. Consequently, investigations involving larger cohorts of students are warranted to further delve into the pivotal roles played by phonetic knowledge in English listening and speaking proficiency. Furthermore, it should be noted that this study solely relied on the discernment of a solitary researcher who undertook the action research. Incorporating additional researchers would have facilitated an enhanced point of comparison.

References

1. Shuping Han, *Grow in action research.* China Education Daily. 4,5 (2009)
2. Kemmis, S., McTaggart, R. *The Action Research Planner* M. Geelong, Victoria: Deakin University Press (1982).
3. Anne, B. *Doing Action Research in English Language Teaching: A Guide for Practitioners* M. Foreign Language Teaching and Research Press. Beijing, China (2011)
4. Lewis, C. How do teachers learn during lesson study? A. In Wang-Iverson, P.&Yoshida, M. (eds). *Building Our Understanding of Lesson Study.* Philadelphia: Research for Better Schools, 77-84 (2005)
5. Fishman, J., Marx W., Best, S, et al. Linking teacher and student learning to improve professional development in systemic reform. J. Teaching and Teacher Education, **19**, 6 (2003)
6. Z. Liu, X. Li, *Action research on college English teaching in China* J. Overseas English, **12**, 3-6 (2022)
7. Qiang Wang, Hong Zhang. *Action Research for English Teachers* M. Foreign Language Teaching and Research Press. Beijing, China (2020)
8. Y. Meng, *An overview of action research on foreign language teachers in China in recent ten years*, J. Overseas English, **24**,11-14 (2022)

A Feminist Study of the English Translation of Can Xue's *The Gloomy Mood of Ah Mei on a Sunny Day*

He Ling*

School of Humanities and Education Science, Foshan University,528225, Foshan, China

Abstract: From the perspective of feminist translation, this study makes an analysis of the English version of Can Xue's *The Gloomy Mood of Ah Mei on a Sunny Day* translated by Ronald R. Janssen and Zhang Jian. The conclusion shows that the translators adopt the two feminist translation strategies—supplementing and hijacking—in the process of translation. By these means, Ah Mei's feelings, thoughts, and attitude to marriage are revealed. The translated works not only reproduces feminism presented in the source text, but also makes the implied feminist consciousness of the author obviously conveyed. It shows the creative rewriting of the translators, which enhances the value of the English translation and benefits its dissemination and acceptance in the English world.

1.Introduction

Can Xue, a Chinese female writer, has good reputation in the English- speaking world. This is not only reflected in the fact that her works have been continuously translated into English for nearly three decades, but also in the fact that Can Xue was nominated or even won several important literary awards in English-speaking countries. Since 2015, the number of the researches on the English translation of Can Xue's works in China has gradually increased, and they are mostly conducted in the following three dimensions. Firstly, many studies focus on the overall introduction to the overseas dissemination and acceptance of Can Xue's works as well as the reasons for her success, such as Wang Wenqiang and Guo Enhua [1], Liu Chengcai[2], Liu Kun[3], Yang Liu[4], Xin Xiaoxiao [5]. Secondly, some studies analyze the success of the English translations of her masterpieces. For example, Sun Huijun and Zheng Qingzhu[6] analyzed that *The Yellow Mud Street* has won the favor of western readers due to its remarkable modernist features; Cen Qunxia[7] discussed the reasons for the successful translation of *The Last Lover* from the perspectives of sociology. Thirdly, quite a few studies probe into the features of the English translation of her works from the linguistic perspective. Especially, in the past two years, with the application of corpus in translation studies, some scholars, like Zhang Lizhu[8][9]discussed the unique spatio-temporal narration of Can Xue's works from the perspective of corpus translation stylistics.

However, few scholars interpret her English translations from the perspective of feminist translation although many of Can Xue's works have very distinct feminist characteristics. In Can Xue's works, the most outstanding and successful characters are a group of different women, with male characters playing a foil role or even downplayed. Besides, Can Xue's greatest contribution to contemporary female literature lies in the fact that she destroys and subverts the perception system and discourse system of the complete set of procedures formed under the patriarchal system, and she also deconstructs the traditional ethical and moral relations of modern families and subverts the self-image of women[10] These features coincide with "the purpose of subverting the culture of patriarchal hegemony of translation"[11] in feminist translation studies. Therefore, this paper makes a case study of the English translation of Can Xue's short story *The Gloomy Mood of Ah Mei on a Sunny Day*[阿梅在一个太阳天里的愁思](hereinafter referred to as *The Gloomy*)from the perspective of feminist translation, and thus reveal its manifestations of feminism.

2. Theoretical Framework: Feminist Translation Studies

Western feminism rose along with the second wave of western women's movement in the 1960s. Snell Hornby[12] put forward the "cultural shift" in the study of translation, with the historical, cultural and political factors of translation activities being included in the research scope, and translation was no longer regarded as a simple and mechanical language transformation. In this context, Feminist Translation Studies (FTS) was brought about by Canadian feminist translators in the late 1970s, providing a new perspective for translation studies. The main contributors to FTS are Barbara Godard (1984), Sherry Simon (1996), Luise von Flotow(1991)and Susanne de Lotbinière-Harwood, etc. The chief features and focuses of FTS are pursuing the gender equality in literature and translation, eliminating discrimination against women in

*Correspondence author's mail: heling527@163.com

translation studies, and displaying the subjectivity of translators.

FTS advocates an interference approach in translation, and intends to "womanhandle" the text[13].It is "a method of translating the focus on and critique of 'patriarchal language' by feminist writers"[14].To this end, the feminist translator adopts several feminist translation strategies, such as supplementing, prefacing and footnoting, as well as hijacking, as discussed by Flotow (ibid).In terms of supplementing, "the ST(source text) is supplemented by its translation, matured, developed, and given an afterlife"(ibid). In prefaces and footnotes, the feminist translators indicate their presence and promote their feminist consciousness. With respect to hijacking, the translator makes extreme interference in the translation process by hijacking the source text.The research objects of FTS ranges from translating women writers' work, feminist works, to challenging patriarchal translation of the women's texts [15].

FTS was introduced into China in the late 1990s. Up to now, Chinese scholars has conducted considerable theoretical explorations, such as Xu Lai(2004)[16], Zhang Jinghua(2004)[17], and Jiang Xiaohua(2004)[18]. Many case analyses have been made as well, for example, Wu Jing(2012)[19], Lv Xiaofei & Dai Guiyu(2017)[20], and Xiang Ping(2018)[21]. Summarizing from these studies, we found that novels are one of the most important research objects in the application of FTS, especially those written or translated by women and those full of female characters. For example, Wu Jing(2012)[21] conducted a study of Pearl S. Buck's translation of the female figures in *Shui Hu Zhuan* from the feminist perspective; He Hongli(2015)[22] analyzes the mild translation strategies of harmonization adopted by Eileen Chang; Cen Qunxia(2019)[23] made a feminist study of the English translation of *Hong Lou Meng* translated by Florence and Isabel McHUGH. These studies are good examples to show that feminist translation strategies are adopted in the English translation, and may even enhance the feminism implied in the original text. However, the researches on the English translation of Can Xue's works have been just conducted in the past ten years and there are few studies based on feminist translation. Therefore, this paper attempts to enrich the studies of Can Xue's works and the application of FTS.

3. A Brief Introduction to *The Gloomy* and its Translation

As a female writer, Can Xue shows her great concerns about and reflections on women in her works. Her creation highlights the extremely distinct and unique feminist characteristics for her works focus on women's survival and emotions, inquiring after their happiness or unhappiness, while challenging the traditional concepts applied to them. Her short story *The Gloomy Mood of Ah Mei on a Sunny Day*(hereinafter referred to as *The Gloomy*), along with the other two short novels published in 1986, embodied the typical factors of Can Xue's works[24]. It was originally written in Mandarin Chinese and published in *Tianjin Literature Journal* in June,1986. As soon as it came out, it attracted wide attention in Chinese literary critics.

This short story is about Ah Mei's reminiscence of her marriage with Old Li. Ah Mei, the main character, lived together with her mother but they were on bad terms. Old Li often came to visit them and chatted happily with Ah Mei's mother. Then, Ah Mei was arranged by her mother to marry with Old Li. Their life was not happy because their marriage was not based on love but on a ridiculous reason that Ah Mei's mother owning a house. The next day of their wedding, Old Li moved to the attic, and left her three months later. After the birth of their son Da-gou, Old Li returned home but stayed all day with their son and Ah Mei's mother. When Da-gou was five years old, Old Li never came back. Due to his leaving, her mother disliked her more than before. In this story, the relation between mother and daughter and that between wife and husband are very indifferent and weird. Ah Mei and her mother are described to be ugly and unpleasant. This is the typical writing style of Can Xue. She usually uses the deformed figures to challenge the traditional concepts of family and women, and arouse the readers' attention to their inner world.

Shortly after its appearance, *The Gloomy* was translated by the sinologist Ronald R. Janssen and the Chinese scholar Zhang Jian into English. It is also included into Can Xue's short story collection *Dialogues in Paradise* published by Northwest University Press in 1989, which is the first separate edition of Can Xue's novels translated in English. It is compiled as the first short story among the 13 ones in this volume. Due to its significance in Can Xue's works, this paper attempts to analyze the English translation of *The Gloomy*.

4. Analysis of Feminist Translation Strategies in *The Gloomy*

In this section, this study focuses on the English version of *The Gloomy* from the perspective of FTS. The examples will be given to show that the translators often deploy the feminist translation strategies of supplementing and hijacking to (re-)construct the female characters and reproduce the feminist consciousness in their translation.

4.1. Examples of Supplementing

Supplementing, which has the "compensation" function, is the most common feminist translation strategy[25]. In FTS, supplementing means that on the basis of respecting the source text the translator reasonably adds the feminist consciousness in the target text. In *The Gloomy*, Ronald R. Janssen and Zhang Jian adopt this strategy to show Ah Mei's personal traits and the family relationship. Here are some examples.

Example 1:

Chinese ST:三年来，老李渺无音信，我再也没有在大街上看见过他。在我的想象中，他现在已经变成了一个精干的、漂亮的小个子男子汉，走起路来又轻松又精神。[26]

English TT: For the past three years nothing has been heard of Old Li, and I have not seen him in the street. I imagine he has become a capable, handsome, short but "manly" man, relaxed and high-spirited in his walk. [27]

Example 1 is about Ah Mei's imagination of Old Li after his leaving home for 3 years. In the English TT, the translators translated "男子汉" into "manly man", by supplementing the word "manly" with quotation marks to describe Old Li. This is an emphasis and also an irony of Old Li's image. It shows that Ah Mei was contemptuous of the arranged marriage and it is also an irony to the traditional concept of marriage. Thus, the implied feminist thoughts in ST are obvious in TT.

Example 2:

Chinese TT: 隔了一会儿，鞭炮又在屋后什么地方大响，吓得我心脏"怦怦"直跳。后来我进了屋，从抽屉里找出一点棉花，把耳朵紧紧地塞上了。[26]

English TT: Minutes later, I hear firecrackers exploding somewhere at the rear of the house. My heart pounds, and I go into my room and stuff my ears with cotton which I find in a drawer. [27]

Example 2 describes Ah Mei's reaction to her son Dagou setting off firecrackers. In Chinese ST, the clause "鞭炮又在屋后什么地方大响" is just an objective expression of the sound of firecrackers. However, the translators add "I hear" before it. Thus, the whole paragraph is made up of a serious of Ah Mei's reactions to the firecrackers from "hear" to "go" and to "stuff" by keeping the same subject "I" in the two sentences. Moreover, through Ah Mei's actions, readers may understand that Ah Mei is very timid and her relations with her son is not intimate and friendly.

4.2. Examples of Hijacking

For a long time, women's inner consciousness, psychology, emotion, etc. have lost their discourse power due to women's fate in writing. In order to reveal them, when translating *The Gloomy*, the translators Ronald R. Janssen and Zhang Jian hijack the ST and creatively rewrite it by changing the agents or the recipients of the actions to Ah Mei. By this means, Ah Mei is set in the obvious place in the sentence. In this way, her thoughts and feelings are stressed, and the feminist consciousness in the ST are strengthened. Here are some examples.

Example 3:

Chinese ST: 那一天我到厨房舀水，他冷不防就进来了，我正打算溜走，没想到他开口讲起话来了。

"喂，你，对我有什么意见？"

"……"

然后他对我说，愿不愿意马上跟他结婚？他说话的当儿脸色发灰，一身抽搐得怪难受的。[26]

English TT: I was in the kitchen fetching water. All of a sudden he entered. Before I could escape, he started talking.

"Hey, you, any comment to make about me?"

"……"

Then he asked if I was willing to marry him immediately. His face turned gray and his body twitched, making me feel most uncomfortable while he spoke. [27]

Example 3 is a dialogue between Old Li and Ah Mei. Although Old Li visited her home now and then before their marriage, he always chatted and chuckled with Ah Mei's mother. At that day, he suddenly stopped Ah Mei and proposed to her in the kitchen. In Chinese ST, "他说话的当儿脸色发灰，一身抽搐得怪难受的" is a clause describing Old Li's painful looks on the face and the twitches of his body when he made the proposal. But in English TT, the translators rewrote the sentence into "making me feel most uncomfortable while he spoke". By hijacking the ST, the translator emphasized the inner world the Ah Mei, providing the reader with the a better understanding of the fact that Ah Mei did not like Old Li and even felt very uncomfortable while Old Li spoke. It created a strong conflict with the following reversal that Ah Mei accepted Old Li's proposal.

Example 4:

Chinese ST: 我们结婚的那天他脸上紫疱涨成了黑色，红鼻头象蜡烛一样又硬又光，他的又短又小的身体紧紧地裹在新衣服里面，让人看了有一种很伤心的想法。[26]

English TT: On our wedding day, all his pimples swelled into blackheads. His red nose was hard and bright like a candle. Seeing his short, small body wrapped tightly in new clothes, I couldn't help feeling misery and regret.[27]

Example 4 is the description of Old Li in their wedding day. In Chinese ST, the clause "他的又短又小的身体紧紧地裹在新衣服里面，让人看了有一种很伤心的想法" literally means "his short and small body was wrapped tightly in new clothes, making people feel sad". The subject of this sentence is Old Li. The character "人", a general word, means "people", without telling clear who feels sad when seeing Old Li. In English TT, the translators rewrite it in two ways. First, they changed the subject to "I", and in this novel "I" refers to Ah Mei. Second, the translated sentence "I couldn't help feeling misery and regret" makes it clear that it was Ah Mei who felt sad. By hijacking the ST, the translators change the angle of the description from Old Li to Ah Mei, stressing the inner world and the emotions of women.

The similar examples are also found in the translation, for example "这种情形一直延续到大狗生下之后" is translated into "He stayed away until I gave birth to Dagou". Here, "这种情形", which literally means "this situation" in English, is translated to be "he stayed away" so that it repeatedly tells readers Old Li's leaving home. The subject of the clause "大狗" is changed to "I", which refers to Ah Mei. Through the change, the indifferent attitude of Old Li to Ah Mei and the disappointment of Ah Mei are expressed.

5. Conclusion

From the above analysis, it is found that Ronald R. Janssen and Zhang Jian take full advantage of the two feminist translation strategies—supplementing and hijacking—in the process of translating *The Gloomy Mood of Ah Mei in a Sunny Day*, which not only reproduced the feminism presented in the source text, but also made the implied feminist consciousness obviously conveyed. It is the creative rewriting of the translators, which results in the improvement of the value of the English translation and its dissemination and acceptance in the English world. Compared with the previous traditional translation theories, feminist translation studies have many advantages, such as allowing the translators to add personal interpretations to the source text, giving translators more creative space, and affirming the translator's subjectivity, etc. However, with the collision and integration with different theories, feminist translation studies should be revised, improved and developed in order to be better applied to the translation practice and studies.

Funding

This work is supported by the Philosophy and Social Science Projects of Guangdong Province (No.:GD20XWY18; Title: The Actor Network of Dissemination and Reception of Can Xue's Novels in the English-speaking World).

References

1. W. Wang, E. Guo. *A study of overseas translation and spreading of Can Xue's works*. Foreign Studies.4.03(2016):67-73+107.
2. C. Liu. *Can Xue, Avant-garde Literature and the Narration of Chinese Story: Based on the Canxue's Overseas Acceptance of Investigation*. Research of Chinese Literature. 03(2018):145-151.
3. K. Liu. *Can Xue in Western Readers' Horizon*. Journal of Social Sciences. 05 (2017):185-191.
4. L. Yang. *The translation and acceptance of Can Xue's works in the United States*. Contemporary Literary Criticism. 03(2022):43-449
5. X. Xin. *Dissemination and Reception of Can Xue's Fictions in the English-speaking World*. Foreign Languages and Translation. 30.02(2023):42-49+98.
6. H. Sun, Q. Zheng. *The Translation and Reception of Can Xue's Fiction in the English World—with The Yellow Mud Street as a case study*. Journal of Yanshan University (Philosophy and Social Science Edition).16.03(2015):72-77.
7. Q. Cen. *The Sociological Analysis of Can Xue's Interference in the English Translation and Acceptance of The Last Lover*.Shandong Foreign Language Teaching. 39.03(2018):115-122.
8. L. Zhang. Unique Spatio-Temporal Narration: A Corpus-Based Stylistic Study of Can Xue's Fiction in English Translation. Journal of PLA University of Foreign Languages. 45.04(2022):96-104.
9. L. Zhang. *A Cognitive Stylistic Study on the Spatio-Temporal Narration of Can Xue's Fictions in Different English Translations*. Foreign Languages Research. 40.03(2023):74-80.
10. Y. Yao. *On the female narrative of Can Xue's novels*. Jiangxi Social Sciences. 02(2004):118-120.
11. I. Irshad, M. Yasmin. *Feminism and literary translation: A systematic review*. Heliyon. 8.3(2022).
12. M. Snell-Hornby. *Linguistic transcoding or cultural transfer? A critique of translation theory in Germany*. In: S. Bassnett, A. Lefevere (Eds.), Translation, History and Culture. Printer Publisher, London & New York (1990).
13. B.Godard.*Theorizing Feminist Discourse/translation*. Tessera. (1989) Retrieved from https://tessera.journals.yorku.ca/index.php/tessera/article/view/23583.
14. L.V.Flotow. *Feminist translation: contexts, practices and theories*. TTR. 4.2(1991):69–84.
15. S.Simon. *Gender in Translation: Cultural Identity and the Politics of Transmission*. Routledge, London (1996).
16. L. Xu. *"Rewriting" in the Name of Feminie—The Significance of the Feminism Translation Theory in the Study of the Translator's Subjectivity*. Chinese Translators Journal.04(2004):18-21.
17. J. Zhang. *On the Contributions and Limitations of Feminist Translation Theory*. Chinese Translators Journal.04(2004):22-27.
18. X. Jiang. *Influences of Feminism upon Translation Theory*. Chinese Translators Journal.04(2004):12-17.
19. J. Wu. *A Study of Pearl S.Buck's Translation of the Female Figures in Shui Hu Zhuan from the Feminist Perspective*. Journal of Guangzhou University (Social Science Edition). 11.11(2012):92-96.
20. X. Lv, G. Dai. *An Exploration of Three Chinese Versions of The Bell Jar from the Perspective of Feminist Translation Studies*. Foreign Language and Literature Research.3.04(2017):76-83.
21. P. Xiang. *A Corpus-Based Study of Feminism in M. Pearson's English Translation of The Original I Ching*. Technology Enhanced Foreign Language Education. 04 (2018):91-96.
22. H. He. *Beauty of Harmonization: Oriental Features in Eileen Chang's Feminist Translation Poetics*. Foreign Languages and Literature. 31.02(2015): 122 -126.
23. Q. Cen. *A Feminist Study of the English Translation of Hong Lou Meng by Florence and Isabel McHUGH*. Chinese Culture Research. 02(2019) :161 -170.
24. J. Zhuo. *Can Xue Studies*. Changsha: Hunan Literature and Art Press (2012).
25. X. Sui, X. Song. *A Study on Feminist Translation Strategies in Chinese-English*. Shanghai Journal of Translators.04(2019):42-47.
26. X. Can. *Collected works of Can Xue (Volume 1)*. Changsha: Hunan Literature and Art Press (1998).
27. R.R. Janssen, J. Zhang. *Dialogues in Paradise*. Northwest University Press (1989).

Metaphorical Analysis of the Concepts of "Zhu Yan" and "Hong Yan"

Guo Yang*

Nanning Normol Universite, Chinese language Department, Nanning, Guangxi, China

Abstract. "Zhu Yan", "Hong Yan" by the color morphemes, most readers think that these two are synonyms, the text can be arbitrarily replaced, but this is not the case. Although the two are similar in certain contexts, tracing them back to their roots reveals that there are differences between them. In recent years, with the progress of the society and the innovation of theories, many researchers have found that there is a great connection between metaphors and color words, which can enrich the connotation of each other if they are studied together. In this paper, on the basis of traditional exegesis, we find the literature and combine it with the theory of metaphor to analyze the "Hong Yan" and "Zhu Yan", in order to reveal the similarities and differences between the two.

1.Introduction

In the world of language, color words play an extremely important role as a unique medium for expressing emotions, portraying images, and transmitting cultural values, and we seem to be able to smell the emotions and cultural deposits welling up in them. [1]Zhu Yan and Hong Yan are both related to color and appearance, but deeper into the text and in context they are found to imply a deeper understanding of life, beauty, and gender roles. Cognitive linguistics provides a new perspective for examining linguistic phenomena through conceptual metaphors, through which we can deeply analyze the similarities and differences between "Zhu Yan" and "Hong Yan" in literary works, character depictions, and the use of idioms, and trace the unique interpretations of color-word metaphors in the society in order to try to reveal the latent cultural perceptions and social concepts behind the differences.[2]

2.Linguistic color and Cultural Exploration of Zhu Yan and Hong Yan

In the rich and varied universe of language, color vocabulary plays a mysterious and fascinating role. Among them, "Zhu Yan" and "Hong Yan", as representatives of colors, seem to be intertwined in our perception. However, when we delve deeper into these two terms, we find that they are not as simple as they seem. This is the subtle and profound relationship between "Zhu Yan" and "Hong Yan", a linguistic feast of colors, beauty, and gender roles, full of literary emotions and cultural deposits.

In the traditional conception, "Zhu Yan" and "Hong Yan" are often regarded as interchangeable synonyms, both of which imply the image of red color, and seem to differ only slightly in the way they are expressed. However, this thesis will take the reader through the boundaries of the text and delve into the conceptual metaphors of the two, revealing their subtle similarities and differences in context.[3]By crawling through the foundations of traditional exegesis and combining it with the theory of conceptual metaphor in cognitive linguistics, we will reveal the more profound cultural connotations underlying these two terms. Color vocabulary carries a wealth of cultural symbols in language and serves as a bridge between emotion, literature and culture." Zhu Yan" and "Hong Yan" have gained attention precisely because they are not just words that describe colors, but also carry a unique understanding of life, beauty and gender roles. In this linguistic arena, each of their letters seems to tell a story of love, joy and sorrow. The importance of color words in language, mentioned in the introduction, is not only a tool for describing colors, but also a unique medium for expressing emotions, portraying images, and conveying cultural values. Among them, "Zhu Yan" and "Hong Yan" are like an artist's palette, through which we can get a glimpse of the author's insights into life, beauty and gender. However, these two are not simply color descriptions; they are the art of metaphor in literature, a profound reflection on language.

Conceptual metaphor, as an important theory of cognitive linguistics, provides us with a new perspective to examine linguistic phenomena. In this perspective, we will no longer only see "Zhu Yan" and "Hong Yan" as representations of the color red, but will understand them in a broader cultural context. Through an in-depth analysis of these two terms, we will explore their similarities and differences in literary works, characterization and idiomatic usage, and try to reveal the cultural perceptions and social concepts behind them.The words "Zhu Yan" and "Hong Yan" play colorful roles in

*1390411607@qq.com

literary works, and they are unique linguistic elements that shape the image of characters. Through a comparative study of the two, we can have a more comprehensive understanding of their evolution and application in different works. This comparison is not only a contrast of language forms, but also a collision of literary ideas, a refraction of the changing times and changing social concepts. Through this layer-by-layer analysis, we will enter into the literary world of "Zhu Yan" and "Hong Yan", and appreciate the profound connotations contained therein.[4]

In this opening journey, we will follow the mysterious words "Zhu Yan" and "Hong Yan" through the time and space of words, tracing their origins and analyzing their connotations.As the paper progresses, we will reveal the uniqueness of these two words in literature, language and culture. This is an exploration of color and metaphor, and a profound reflection on human cultural perceptions.[5]

3.The original meaning of "Zhu Yan" and "Hong Yan"

From the point of view of word formation, "朱颜" and "红颜" consist of "朱" and "红" plus "颜" to form a noun, which are synthetic words. "朱" and "红" as a definite article modifying "颜", a paratactic structure, with "朱" and "红" at the center of the paratactic. Therefore, the focus of the study should also be on "朱" and "红", "颜" as the center of the face meaning. The word "Hong Yan" first appeared in Han Shu. "Zhu Yan" first appeared in *Chu Ci*.

Table 1. The following is a tabular list of the interpretations of Zhu Yan and Hong Yan in the *Hanyu Da Cidian* as an example:

Zhu Yan	Hong Yan
1.A rosy and beautiful face	1.Refers to the rosy cheeks of the young。
2.indicate youthfulness	2.Refers to juveniles.
3.Beauty; beautiful women.	3.Referring to a beautiful woman.
4.And a pleasant face. Expresses affectionate trust.	4.It refers to a woman's beautiful face.
5.Blush. Describes a drunken face.	
6.Blush.Blushing color.	

A comparison of the two denotations in Table1 shows that: "Zhu Yan" has a slightly larger number of meanings than "Hong Yan", Horizontal comparison shows that the first three meanings of "Zhu Yan" and "Hong Yan" are the same or similar, roughly having the meaning of rosy and beautiful face, young and beautiful women. Longitudinal comparisons show that the fourth and third denotative terms of "Hong Yan" are highly correlated and work directly in the female role. The fourth denotation of "Zhu Yan" is weakly related to its first three denotations, and the fifth and sixth denotations are only different in the emotional process of causing blushing but the result is the same, which is weakly related to the first four denotations.

The traditional Chinese character for "红" is "紅". From its font we can tell that "紅" is both a morpheme and an ideogram. Left-right structure, polyphonic, with the left being a righteous symbol meaning silk fabric, and the right working epithet.The earliest appearance of the glyphs in simple silks of the Chu. According to the Zhou Li records, the Zhou Dynasty palace workshops with a full-time official "dyeing people", in charge of silk and silk dyeing. At that time, the dyeing process has been quite developed, people not only invented the mordant dyeing method, but also mastered the set dyeing process. As a result of a large number of fabrics of various colors, the natural color has sought to name the need. "縓","纁","绀","缁","绿","紫","红","绛","缊","缇"and so on in *Shuo Wen Jie Zi*.All of them are monikers for the color of "bo"(帛) that appeared in the Zhou and Qin Dynasties. Among them, "绿", "紫" and "红" soon acquired a generalized meaning of color. As we can see from the above, the original meaning of "Hong" is to refer to the item - light red silk, silk is a general term for silk fabrics, the main use of red to indicate the color of the silk, not to indicate that the item of silk. Later, with the development of society and culture, "Hong" gradually gained the meaning of general color.[6]

4.The target domains of "Zhu Yan" and "Hong Yan" from a metaphorical perspective

Besides, Chinese people have long been influenced by ancient traditional thinking, and tend to use indirect communication for some sensitive, erotic and vulgar matters, so Chinese people often exude a cryptic style in their lines and conversations. In literary works authors are more inclined to use the target domain to implicitly express their views or opinions on events and express their true inner feelings, rather than directly listing the source domain on the paper.[7]The terms "Zhu Yan" and "Hong Yan" are typical examples of the clever use of this perspective.

4.1. A Metaphorical Study of "Zhu Yan" and "Hong Yan"

In cognitive linguistics, metaphor is not only a rhetorical method, but also a basic tool for cognizing the world. *In Metaphors We Live By,* Lecov and Johnson put metaphors into the cognitive world for research, and argued that the essence of metaphors is mapping across conceptual domains, that is, following the principle of constancy, selective mapping from the source domain to the target domain, and recognizing the source domain through the target domain,and that metaphors are used subconsciously, which is also a way commonly used by human beings to recognize and understand other abstract concepts.[8] Metaphor sees "Zhu" and "Hong" as a kind of archetypal meaning - the source domain, the color domain is an important domain of human cognitive world, it is an important domain of linguistic cognition along with the domain of emotion, the domain of value, the domain of the h uman body, a nd s o on, a nd t he m echanism o f reference metaphors is an important way to push forward the t ransformation o f t he o riginal m eaning o f t he c olor words i nto t he ar chetypal s emantics of t he non-color words. "Zhu", "Hong" is a color word of the same color system, c olor w ords, i n a ddition t o t heir o wn c olor meaning, b ut also a l arge n umber of " Yan" o utside t he meaning, "Yan" outside the meaning is often used in the sense of m apping other meanings, a nd t his m eaning i s often derived from metaphors.

4.2. Mapping to historical and cultural domains

Sapir once said that c ulture lies behind l anguage. Vocabulary i s t he part o f the l anguage system t hat changes most frequently and cannot exist independently of cu lture. Early m an reflected natural p henomena o nly through c olor words, a nd i n pr imitive s ocieties n atural phenomena a ssociated with t he c olor r ed were worshipped or f avored by c ertain tr ibes, s uch a s blood, sun and fire. "Rites three positive record" said: "summer Shang black, Yin S hang white, Z hou S hang red, t his i s called t he t hree u nity." " Spring a nd Autumn Ann als - Yuan life package" and "music latitude - Jiyaojia" cloud: "the week in N ovember for t he pos itive, the r est of the trigrams subject to the resumption of the color is still red, to the middle of the night for the first day of the month." Can be s een on the Z hou Dynasty, there has be en " still red" said. L ate Paleolithic Z houkoudian S handingdong site ex cavated o chre powder-dyed s tone be ads, the Shandingdong people's habit of sprinkling ochre powder on the bodies usually when burying clan members. It can be l argely c onfirmed t hrough t he e fforts o f p hilologists and a rchaeologists that the e arliest n atural pigment used by humans w as usually r ed.[9] The r eason wh y h uman beings used red more frequently in the early days was that it w as e asier a nd more c onvenient t han other c olors i n terms o f production process a nd ingestion of raw materials. With t he development of t he t imes a nd t he needs of h uman s ocial pr ogress, th e m eaning e xpressed by color words is not only limited to color, but also has a deeper cultural connotation, which has different changes in different times. Human beings often have two levels of cultural c onnotations for c olor words, on t he one ha nd, they consider this type of color as positive and active, and on the other hand, they consider it as vulgar and gloomy, for example, red is considered as a symbol of good luck and celebration on the one hand, but on the other hand, it has the meanings of blood and violence.

In addition to this, the ancient ceremonial music law is num erous a nd c omplicated i n process, and t he c olor culture formed mainly by color words is an important part of the national culture, so the colors are subjected to the ancient culture in learning and living. The concepts of five colors, f ive e lements, five p ositions, e tc. w ere also nurtured one after another in this environment.

4.3. Mapping to the Literature Domain

"Zhu Yan" and "Hong Yan" are high-frequency words in literary creation. People's fondness for different red color words va ries f rom person to pe rson, wi th "Zhu Yan" emphasizing health, vi tality, a nd a uspiciousness, a nd "Hong Y an" e mphasizing b eauty, go od fortune, and celebration. With the loss and transfer of the positive red meaning o f t he ch aracter "C hi （赤） ", i ts s tatus a s a positive c olor w as c hallenged by c olor words s uch a s "Hong" an d " Zhu", e specially d uring t he Middle T ang Dynasty w hen a l arge number o f p oems e merged, t he character "H ong" an d "Z hu". T he number o f t imes "Hong" an d " Zhu" w ere u sed i n t he l iterature i ncreased and gradually replaced "Chi", so in the late development of "C hi" a nd "Zhu". Therefore, t he b oundary between "Chi", "Zhu" and "Hong" tends to be blurred, of course, this change is also related to the ambiguity of the red color words themselves. Because of the early influence of the concepts of five c olors and positive c olors, " Zhu" generally on ly appears i n m ore s erious a nd formal occasions, while "Hong Yan" lacks this solemn color.

From the perspective of mapping "Zhu" and "Hong", we can further d iscover t he d ifferences b etween " Zhu Yan" a nd " Hong Yan". Before the T ang and S ong dynasties, due to the influence of the five colors and the concept of positive color, "Chi", "Chi Se", "Zhu", "Zhu Yan" is used more frequently than "Hong", "Hong Yan", and its positive red meaning has not been transferred, and has always occupied t he dominant position i n t he r ed color words. From the Tang Dynasty onwards, the rapid social a nd e conomic development l ed t o c ontinuous changes i n the cultural industry, a nd "Hong" w as gradually changed from "Fen Hong" to "red", and "Chi" and "Zhu" gradually lost the meaning of red, and it was used to depict women's beauty and charisma, which was reflected in many cultural works of the same period. Fu Yi's *WuFu* of the Han Dynasty: "The appearance is smart and wonderful wi th de monic c ompulsion, a nd t he r ed color yeh its Yanghua." The term "Hong Yan" here refers to a woman's beautiful face. With the development of the times, the meaning of "Hong Yan" is gradually enriched, and its m eaning is n ot onl y the depiction of be autiful appearance, but a lso implies the m eaning of s hort-lived beauty a nd i ll-fated, s uch as Hong Yan Bo Ming,Hong Yan Yi Lao and so on. The evolution of "Zhu Yan" and "Hong Yan" is not only an evolution of language, but also a true reflection of the outside world. In ancient literature, the t erm "H ong Y an" i s m ore often us ed t o de pict t he beauty of a woman's face, and this beauty often carries a hint of fugitive, fleeting meaning.[10] Cao Zhi's *Jing Si Fu*: "What a beautiful woman is a rotten demon, and her red face is bright and flowing with light." In *Hong Lou Meng*: "Once the spring is over, the red face grows old, and the flowers fall and the people die without knowing it." In all these places, the term "Hong Y an" i s used to r efer to a woman's p erishable face. In a ddition, similar t o " Hong Yan", there ar e a lso "Y u R ong"(玉容)and " Yu Y an"(玉颜), etc., which are often m apped to a w oman's face o r beauty. For example, Bai Juyi's *Chang Hen Ge* says: "In the m ud u nder Mawei s lope, I don't see t he j ade f ace dying."

4.4. Mapping to the gender role field

The terms "Zhu Yan" and "Hong Yan" are not only widely mapped in the literary domain, but are also influential in the gender roles domain. "Zhu Yan" is mostly used to depict women's youth and health, symbolizing vitality, optimism, positive attitude and outlook on life. "Hong Yan" is used to depict the beauty of women as well as to praise beauty. Meng Jiao's "Spring colors do not choose the plants next to the tomb, but the red faces and white colors go away in the spring." In Du Anshi's *Yu Meiren*, "The red face and green temples make people grow old. When will the world come to an end?" All of these verses reflect the idealized expectations of women in ancient societies that women should remain youthful, beautiful, healthy and energetic. However, the target domain of "Hong Yan" has gradually been given deeper connotations, including the contemplation of women's looks and destiny, as well as cultural connotations relevant to the development of the times, and the metaphorical phenomenon has been shifted and transformed, which, however, is more relevant to reflecting the sorrow and pessimism of the ancient society towards the miscarriages of fortune of beautiful women. Although "Hong Yan" still has the meaning of praising a woman's appearance, But the creation of phrases such as "the red face ages easily" and "the red face has a thin life" It reflects people's concern and thinking about the status of women. It shows the complex emotions and understanding of women in ancient society, and at the same time influences today's understanding of women's images and roles. The difference between the two reflects the different understanding and feelings of ancient and modern societies about women, their looks and destiny, and is an important reference for understanding the cultural values and social concepts of ancient Chinese society. *Ci Yuan* explains "Zhu Yan" as the reddish face, which also refers to the beautiful face of a young person. The rosy cheeks have no obvious gender modifiers and can refer to both men and women. According to Sun Weilan, for example, Song Yu's *Zhao Hun* contains the line "The beauty is drunk and her face is flushed", which describes the drunken demeanor of the king of Chu during the court banquet, and is intended to reveal the inner reasons for the decline of the state of Chu.

In addition to the female character domain, "Zhu Yan" and "Hong Yan" can also be mapped to the male character domain to refer to the appearance of a male, as well as to the appearance of a young person or the time of youth. *Ci Yuan* explains "Zhu Yan" as "rosy cheeks", which also refers to the beautiful face of a young man. There is no obvious gender modification in the meaning of "rosy cheeks", which can refer to both men and women. According to Sun Weilan, for example, Song Yu's *Zhao Hun* contains the line "The beauty is drunk and her face is flushed", which describes the drunken demeanor of the king of Chu during the court banquet, and is intended to reveal the inner reasons for the decline of the state of Chu.*Li Sao* also often uses "beauty" as a metaphor for the king of Chu, such as "The sun and the moon are not flooded, and I fear that the beauty will be late". Li Bai's *Shu Dao Nan* "The road to Shu is more difficult than going up to the sky, making people wither their faces when they listen to it." Here the hyperbole is used to emphasize the difficulty of the road to Shu, and "Zhu Yan" should refer to the face of a man. Feng Yansi's *Que Ta Zhi* "I am always sick in front of the flowers day after day, and my face is thin in the mirror". The main character mentioned in the sentence is the lyricist herself, who is "sick and drunk every day", and who is "thin in the mirror" as a result of drinking to drown her sorrows. The same phenomenon occurs with the term "Hong Yan", The Dictionary defines "Hong Yan" as "the rosy cheeks of a young man." Liu Yuxi's *Dai Bei Bai Tou Weng*, which reads: "This weng has a pitiful white head, and I used to be a beautiful young man with a red face", uses the word "Hong Yan" to map out the appearance of the Weng who has a vicissitude of life and is full of white hair, but his demeanor is young and energetic, which is a contrasting image. The contrasting image of youthfulness and vigor. Li Bai, Tang Dynasty, *Liu Ye Lang Zeng Xin Pan Guan*"Are you willing to fall behind others in terms of style? I am a young man with a red face." In ancient times, Fu Zi often referred to young adult men, and "Hong Yan" was used as a predicate after Fu Zi, so "Hong Yan" here obviously refers to a man's appearance.

4.5. Mapping to the Idiom Domain

The words "Zhu Yan" and "Hong Yan" are not only used in poems and songs, but also in idioms. In the cultural connotation of idioms, "hong" can be mapped to flowers in addition to colors,For example, Lv Fei Hong Shou(绿肥红瘦);Hong Xiu Tian Xiang(红袖添香)can be mapped to a beautiful young woman; Deng Hong Jiu Lv(灯红酒绿)can be mapped to a bustling scene. The cultural connotations of "Zhu" are as follows: the first refers to a large red color, such as "Hao Chi Zhu Chun"(皓齿朱唇); the second refers to rouge or a woman with a pretty face, such as "Shi Zhu Fu Fen"(施朱傅粉); and the third, as mentioned above, denotes a person of wealth or high status, such as "Zhu Men" or "Zhu Que"."Hong Yan Bai Fa" (红颜白发)is interpreted as a robust old man or a red-faced girl and a white-haired old man. Although the robust old man and the white-haired old man are older and have white hair, their temperament is young, their pace is light, and their face is rosy and no different from that of a young man; therefore, Zhu Yan is used to describe the rosy face, reflecting the youthfulness of the atmosphere.

5. Conclusions

In conclusion, this paper, under the background of cognitive linguistics, through the metaphorical cross-conceptual domain mapping, the study of "Zhu Yan" and "Hong Yan" found that we can not only understand how the ancient literati constructed the mood and expressed their emotions through language, but also vertically penetrate into their unique insights into life, women's image and beauty. "Zhu Yan" is mainly used to describe women's health and vitality, showing a passionate admiration for life, a characteristic that makes Zhu Yan often used to depict optimistic and positive situations. Due to the influence of the ancient concept of positive color, "Zhu" is often used in formal and serious occasions. In contrast, "Hong Yan" focuses more on the depiction and praise of beautiful women, especially on the sentiment of the transience of beauty and the impermanence of life, as well as the expression of mourning and negative attitudes towards life, and is therefore more often used in certain deep and mournful contexts. This is also the result of the shift in the metaphorical meaning of "Hong" as a color word. The differences between the two words lie in their hidden socio-cultural values, which not only help us to understand the word differences accurately, but also reveal to us the aesthetic concepts and the way women were portrayed in the ancient Chinese society, and enable us to have a deeper understanding of Chinese culture and history. At the same time, through the in-depth analysis and comparison of "Zhu Yan" and "Hong Yan", we can better understand and appreciate the language art and emotional expression of the ancient literati, which also has an important revelation and influence on literary creation, metaphor derivation, and cultural research.

In this in-depth exploration of the terms "Zhu Yan" and "Hong Yan", we are unraveling the mystery of these two terms as if we were tracing the vein of time, layer by layer. This is not just a linguistic interpretation, but also an examination of cultural diversity and the depth of human cognition.[11]By analyzing the conceptual metaphors of these two terms, we find that they carry cultural connotations that go far beyond our superficial understanding. The terms "Zhu Yan" and "Hong Yan" are not simply descriptions of colors, but a profound reflection on life, beauty and gender roles. This is not only reflected in their use in literature, but also in their insights into human emotions and social concepts. In a comparative study, we traverse the variations of these two in different periods and literary works. They may be a celebration of female appearance in ancient poetry, while they may carry more complex social concepts in modern literature. This contrast is not only a comparison of vocabulary forms, but also a reflection of literary ideas and social changes. Through this in-depth excavation, we can see more clearly the multi-faceted nature of "Zhu Yan" and "Hong Yan" on the literary stage. The use of conceptual metaphors provides us with a new perspective on the phenomenon of language. Through this new perspective, we see that "Zhu yan" and "Hong yan" go beyond the superficial color to become a broader cultural symbol. This transcendence enables us to understand more deeply the power of language and the unique contribution of color words in literary expression.

In the end, when we look back on this thesis, the mystery of "Zhu Yan" and "Hong Yan" does not end here, but opens up to more profound thinking. This is just the beginning of a journey of discovery, and the fascination of these two terms will continue to shine through academic research and literary creation." "Zhu Yan" and "Hong Yan"will always shine in our forest of thoughts, providing us with never-ending revelations.[12]Perhaps this paper can inspire more scholars and researchers to pay deeper attention to language, literature and culture. Perhaps, it can become an opportunity for more in-depth research on color vocabulary and cultural symbols in the future. "Zhu Yan" and "Hong Yan" tell not only the story of color, but also a mystery of intertwined literature, language and culture, waiting for us to unravel. In this vast ocean of culture, the journey of exploration of "Zhu Yan" and "Hong Yan" will continue forever, bringing us new thoughts and revelations.

References

1. Yao,X.,(1998) A Review of the Theory of Basic Color Tones--An Introduction to the Evolutionary History of Basic Chinese Color Words. Foreign Language Teaching and Research.,1988(01):19-28+80
2. Liu,C.,(2012) Cultural Connotation Differences between English and Chinese Basic Color Words. Liaoning Normal University.,20-21
3. Zhou,A.,Xu,D.,(2002) "Zhu Yan" ≠ "Beauty"--An Annotated Query *Yu Meiren*. Multilingualism.,04:22
4. Zhou,J.,(2005) What's the meaning of the word "Zhu Yan"?. language learning., 307(01):30-31
5. Xu,J.,Yu,T.,Wang,E.,(2023) Emotional Metaphors for Different Colors. Journal of Hefei Normal University., 41(01):101-103+128
6. Zhang,J.,(2022)A Comparative Study of Color Metaphors in Chinese and English: A Comparative Study of "黄" and "yellow". Culture of Chinese Characters.,No.306(08):144-145.
7. Zhang,D.,(2023) An Analysis of the Metaphorical Meaning of Basic Chinese Color Words. Culture of Chinese Characters., No.346(22):14-16.
8. Lakoff G ,Johnson M .(1980)Metaphors we live by. University of Chicago Press,Chicago
9. He,T.,(2023) A preliminary study on the teaching of color words in junior high school language. Secondary school language., No.988(32):118-119.
10. Wang,J.,(2023) Cultural Connotation Differences between Chinese and English Color Words. Imago Creative., No.190(46):128-130.
11. Raymond W.(2008)What about Metaphor.Gibbs,JR. (Eds)., The Cambridge Hand-book of Metaphor and Thought,Cambridge University Press,Cambridge, pp. 233, 239.
12. Langacker,R.W.(1987)Roundations of Cognitive Grammar: Theoretical Prerequistites.Stanford University Press,Palo Alto.

SHS Web of Conferences **185**, 01004 (2024) https://doi.org/10.1051/shsconf/202418501004
ICLCC 2024

A Review of the Current Status of AI Research in Handwritten Chinese Character Recognition

Kim Ye-eun*

School of Chinese Language and Literature, Beijing Normal University, Haidian District, Beijing, China.

Abstract. With the continuous development of artificial intelligence technology, there have been attempts to utilize AI in the field of linguistics. In this context, research and development in AI-based Chinese character recognition technology has spanned 40 years, with its outcomes attracting significant attention. However, in the field of Chinese character recognition, the research into offline handwritten recognition technology is particularly challenging due to the unique characteristics of handwritten Chinese characters. The main issue in current research is the significant decrease in accuracy for characters composed of similar components or characters with similar overall shapes. The focus of research solutions has been on modern mechanical programming and other engineering aspects, while research that integrates the inherent characteristics of Chinese characters themselves has been relatively overlooked. The author believes that combining engineering technology research with a deeper understanding of the nature of Chinese characters can solve many of the current problems. This paper reviews the current state of related domestic and international research to identify areas with significant potential for improvement and progress in research, and finally proposes directions for future research.

1. Introduction

As Artificial Intelligence (AI) technology continues to evolve, its contributions are evident in various aspects of modern life. In the field of linguistics, these include voice recognition, translation tools, text recognition in dictionaries and lexicons, and image-based text recognition capabilities. Among these applications, the author believes that the field with the greatest potential for improvement is the study of Handwritten Chinese Character Recognition (HCCR). There is a considerable history of research on online handwritten Chinese character recognizer, with significant achievements in methods and accuracy. However, recent dictionaries and translators, in addition to online input and translation, have gradually acquired the capability to extract and recognize text from images, and many people also employ camera-based direct translation features. In this context, the recognition accuracy for English characters or other phonetic scripts, as well as printed Chinese characters, is comparatively high. Nevertheless, the recognition of handwritten Chinese characters continues to be a crucial area of research that requires further enhancement. The primary reason for this is the issue of the sheer number of characters. The 'Table of General Standard Chinese Characters', which includes commonly used Chinese characters, contains 8,105 characters. The actual number of Chinese characters exceeds 50,000, with a particularly high number of categories. Additionally, many characters feature complex structures and similar shapes. Coupled with the varied writing habits of individuals, these results in an extremely broad data range. These factors contribute to the phenomenon where the accuracy of handwritten Chinese character recognition remains comparatively lower than other languages and scripts. This study aims to summarize the current state of research in this area, providing a theoretical background and suggesting directions for future improvements.

2. Analysis of Domestic and International Research Status

In researching relevant literature, the author discovered that there is extensive research on English character recognition, while the research on Chinese character detection and recognition in natural scenes is relatively limited and presents more unresolved challenges. The following is a review of relevant literature that is valuable in terms of theory, viewpoints, or research methods:

2.1. Research on Chinese Character Recognition

"A Comprehensive Review of the Application of Deep Learning in Handwritten Chinese Character Recognition" (Jin Lianwen, Zhong Zhuoyao, Yang Zhao, Yang Weixin, Xie Zecheng, Sun Jun, 2016) provides a comprehensive overview of the methods, principles, technical details, and performance indicators of Chinese character recognition, summarizing the overall developments in the field to date. [1] In the 1960s, IBM in the United States began research on pattern recognition of

*Corresponding author's mail: kyee93@naver.com

printed Chinese characters, successfully recognizing 1,000 printed characters using template matching by 1996. Handwritten Chinese Character Recognition (HCCR) was initially explored by Japan. In the 1980s, China started its own research on handwritten Chinese characters. Since Chinese characters are predominantly used in China and the country has the most comprehensive understanding of their types, connotations, and principles of character formation, China's research in this field is particularly thorough. The in-depth research on handwritten Chinese character recognition is mainly focused in China. Handwritten Chinese character recognition can be divided into two categories: "offline recognition" and "online recognition". Online handwritten Chinese character recognition involves writing characters online using physical devices such as digital pens, digital writing pads, or touch screens. Offline handwritten text recognition is achieved by capturing images through scanners or cameras. Generally speaking, the former contains information arranged in a chronological sequence, while the latter lacks stroke order information. Furthermore, digitization can introduce noise interference due to different factors such as varying lighting, resolution, and writing paper. Hence, offline handwritten text recognition poses greater challenges compared to online handwritten text recognition. The paper discusses the difficulties and problems in machine learning for Chinese character handwriting recognition, such as the arbitrary and non-standardized writing styles, the complexity at the character level, the similarity in appearance that leads to confusion, and the challenges in collecting training data. However, these challenges can be seen as opportunities for significant progress and research value. The recent developments in deep learning are well-suited to meet the demands of handwritten Chinese character recognition and are expected to enhance recognition accuracy.

The paper also lists the application methods and types of algorithms of deep learning in Chinese character recognition. The authors highlight that among the deep learning models and methods, Deep Reinforcement Learning (DRL) deserves special attention. For example, the Deep Q-Network (DQN) proposed by Google DeepMind team in 2015 demonstrates exceptional performance in simulating human intelligence and online reinforcement learning. Finally, the paper summarizes unresolved and research-worthy topics, outlining the following topics that require attention from the academic community. Firstly, the types of characters that can be recognized are primarily based on the 3755 categories of Chinese characters in the National Standard First Level Character Set, with a low recognition rate for characters beyond this set. Beyond the training data, there will eventually be a need to input all Chinese characters. How can one develop a deep learning-based solution that not only processes data rapidly but also remains practical with minimally sized model parameters? The process of constructing ultra-large-scale datasets, developing rapid algorithms for various deep learning models, and finding techniques for compressing parameters in deep learning models presents challenges that require continued exploration and resolution by researchers. The second area of focus is the recognition of content in ancient manuscripts and handwritten documents. The character categories in Chinese ancient texts exceed 30,000, with numerous variant and similar characters. Addressing the issue of insufficient training samples and designing classifiers for extremely large categories are both questions worthy of attention. Thirdly, there is the research on the application of new deep learning models in handwritten Chinese character recognition, as well as the study of the interrelationships and integrated applications of various deep learning models.

Zhang Bin and Jin Lianwen (2017) discussed in their paper titled *"Handwritten Chinese Similar Characters Recognition Based on AdaBoost"* the factors that pose challenges to the improvement of recognition rate in comparison to recognition in other languages. [2] Firstly, the extensive number of Chinese characters with numerous categories (3755 characters in the National Standard First Level and 3008 in the Second Level, exceeding Western characters by two orders of magnitude) hinders the direct application of many established recognition methods and patterns. Furthermore, there are a significant number of visually similar characters within the Chinese character set. Experimental evidence indicates that the errors of traditional distance classifiers mainly arise from distinguishing these visually similar characters. This is more prominent in handwritten Chinese character recognition because handwriting involves deformations, resulting in a greater number of visually similar characters compared to printed characters. Therefore, the paper advocates that improving the recognition rate of visually similar characters can enhance the overall recognition rate of Chinese characters. Since the number of categories within the visually similar character set is relatively small, a new integrated Chinese character recognition system can be proposed through detailed analysis of visually similar handwritten Chinese characters and their components. This paper primarily addresses the limitations and elements of Chinese character recognition and conducts research on improving these limitations using the AdaBoost algorithm. Experimental results demonstrate that this algorithm enhances the recognition rate of visually similar characters compared to traditional distance classifiers.

The paper *"On-line Handwriting Chinese Character Recognition; Comparison and Improvement to Japanese Kanji Recognition"* (1998), published by Japanese scholars in Australia, marked the beginning of active research in Chinese character recognition.[3] It analyzed the differences between handwritten Chinese characters in China and Japan and represents an initial research effort in exploring methods to improve recognition accuracy. While this paper is a relatively early study in online recognition, its descriptions of stroke shape classification and transformation methods aimed at improving accuracy hold academic value. For example, statements such as "A connected stroke is better to be divided into the original strokes. Some feature points are helpful for analysis, such as the end point and break point," represent these valuable insights. (Figure 1)

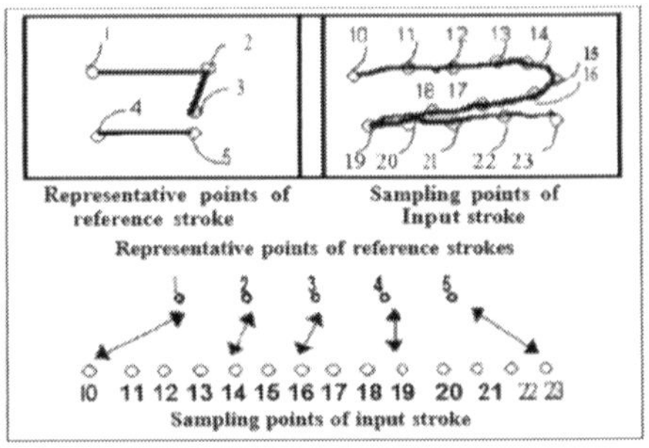

Fig. 1. Example of Stroke Transformation.

2.2. Research on the Image and Structure Analysis of Chinese Characters

In the study *"On-line Handwriting Chinese Character Recognition for PDA Using a Unit Reconstruction Method,"* South Korean scholar Chin Won and Kim Kidoo (2002) conducted a survey on the accuracy and speed of online handwriting recognition for 1,800 basic Chinese characters taught in South Korean middle and high schools. [4] This research, relevant for PDAs (including smartphones, tablets, handheld gaming devices, and other handheld computers), is not only scientifically significant but also valuable in the field of humanities, such as the categorization of Chinese character strokes. It involves the analysis of features of the targeted Chinese characters and the average error rate in stroke order among the surveyed characters. The paper defines the basic unit of writing as a "stroke," categorizing them into basic and special strokes. Basic strokes are linear and come in five types, while special strokes include more than one segment of angle turns and are categorized into seven types. (Figure 2) Generally, strokes are distinguished using seven types, but to enhance the recognition of similar characters, the paper classified strokes into twelve different forms. (Figure 3)

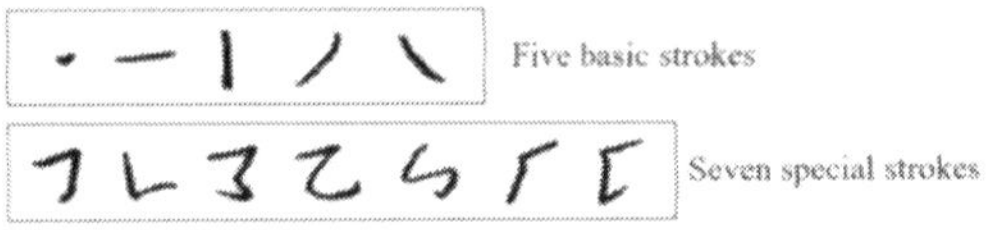

Fig. 2. Classification of Strokes.

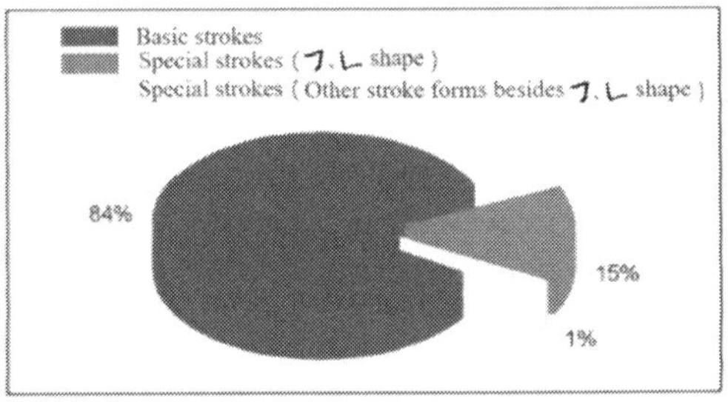

Fig. 3. Proportion of Stroke Forms.

In the paper *"Similar Pattern Discriminant Analysis for Improving Chinese Character Recognition Accuracy"* (2013), authors Wang Yanwei, Liu Changsong, and Ding Xiaoqing focused on developing a method for analyzing and distinguishing similar Chinese characters. [5] They employed a modified quadratic discriminant function (MQDF) in conjunction with Linear Discriminant Analysis (LDA) and Similar Pattern Discriminant Analysis. This approach resulted in a 15.59% lower error rate compared to the Compound Mahalanobis Function (CMF) method. In their research, they calculated the number of recognition errors and created a confusion matrix to illustrate the similarities between two similar characters. They compared the accuracy of LDA and SPDA for similar character combinations, leading to the following results. The variable 'n' represents the number of Chinese characters in the training data. (Table 1)

Table 1. Comparison of Accuracy between LDA and SPDA.

n	LDA(%)	SPDA(%)
128	95.06	96.00
200	95.75	96.28
320	96.39	96.98
400	96.63	97.22
600	97.10	97.55

The authors then presented the structure and procedures of the Modified Quadratic Discriminant Function (MQDF) using charts and compared two distinct approaches: (a) and (b). Structure (a) involves selecting the maximum value between MQDF1 and MQDF2, while structure (b) applies MQDF2 classification to the two characters with the highest probability from MQDF1 when the MQDF1 result is not satisfactory. The results show that the highest accuracy for structure (a) is 98.62%, while the accuracy for structure (b) is 98.15%. (Figure 4)

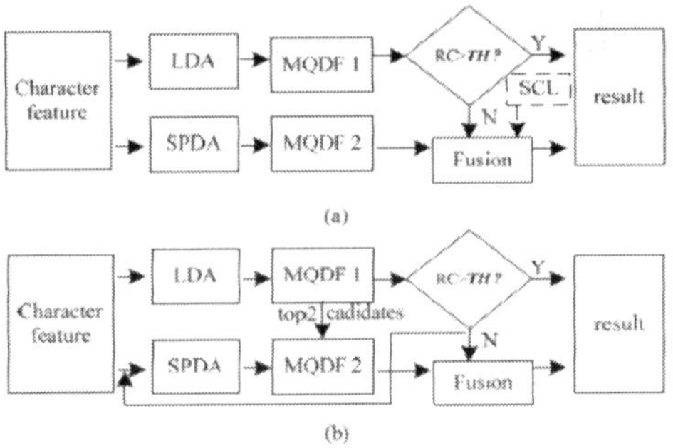

Fig. 4. Structures and procedures of Two Types of Cascade MQDF.

Finally, the authors confirm that the accuracy of the algorithm combining MQDF with CMF (98.62%) is slightly higher than that of using MQDF alone (98.53%).

Yang Chen, Wang Qing, Du Jun, Zhang Jianshu, Wu Changjie, Wang Jiaming (2021) introduced an advanced method in Chinese character recognition using a transformer-based radical analysis network, emphasizing improvements in recognizing complex and low-frequency characters. [6] A transformer-based radical analysis network is a type of neural network architecture used in machine learning, particularly in the field of Chinese character recognition. This network leverages the transformer model, which is known for its effectiveness in handling sequential data, like language. In the context of Chinese characters, the network analyzes the radicals, which are the building blocks of Chinese characters. This approach differs from traditional character recognition methods by emphasizing the underlying structure and components of the characters, leading to improved accuracy and efficiency in recognition tasks. By focusing on these radicals, the network can more effectively learn and recognize the vast array of characters, and this approach can address the challenges of recognizing characters that appear less frequently and have more complicated structures. The integration of a dense encoder and a transformer decoder was a key innovation, enhancing the model's ability to interpret a wide range of character styles and contexts, particularly in difficult scenarios like character occlusion and distortion. The authors' comprehensive experimental validation highlighted the model's superior performance in various datasets, demonstrating a significant leap in the field of Chinese character recognition technology, especially in terms of adaptability and accuracy.

Kim Woo-jeong and Choi Ji-yeon (2023) introduced a three-step process—'Character Analysis,' 'Character Review,' and 'Character Confirmation'—in the Database Management System of the Han-Character Education Research Institute, affiliated with Dankook University. [7] They also classified the types of errors in Chinese character recognition identified during the data verification process as follows:

1) Cases where the Chinese character image is not fully extracted: Mainly occurs in Chinese characters that include components which are also used as independent characters.

2) Cases where adjacent, different Chinese characters are additionally extracted.

3) Cases of mistaking noise for Chinese characters.

4) Cases involving poor printing quality.

5) Cases where character shapes are similar.

6) Cases where artificial intelligence training is not progressing well due to insufficient training data.

2.3. Applied Research of Various CNN Architectures in Chinese Character Recognition

"DenseRAN for Offline Handwritten Chinese Character Recognition" (2018) is an applied research of the DenseRAN algorithm in offline handwritten Chinese character recognition. [8] This paper introduces a novel radical analysis network based on the DenseRAN algorithm, which can analyze the radicals and their two-dimensional structures within Chinese characters. In traditional methods, the process of handwritten Chinese character recognition typically includes image normalization, feature extraction, data dimensionality reduction, and classifier training. With the advancement of deep learning, the Multi-Column Deep Neural Network (MCDNN) emerged as the first convolutional neural network (CNN) used for handwritten Chinese character recognition.

However, these algorithms can only recognize Chinese characters that have appeared in the training dataset. Moreover, they treat each character as a whole, without considering the similarities and sub-structures between characters. The distinctive aspect of this paper is its identification of Chinese characters as logograms composed of basic radicals. Previous research largely treated each character as a whole, without explicitly considering the internal two-dimensional structure and component radicals of the characters. Unlike the algorithms mentioned above, DenseRAN employs an attention-based encoder-decoder model to automatically learn and detect the segmentation of radicals. [9] Here, 'attention' refers to the concept of assigning more 'weighted value' to specific parts (components) in the image. The primary idea behind DenseRAN is to decompose Chinese characters into 'descriptors' that detail the radicals and their structure. When these descriptors match with the actual data, handwritten Chinese characters are successfully recognized.

Compared to the vast number of Chinese characters, the total number of radicals is limited. According to the GB13000.1 standard published by the Working Committee for National Language and Text, nearly 500 radicals form over 20,000 Chinese characters. The following presents thirteen common spatial structures of Chinese characters along with corresponding examples, as provided by the author. (Figure 5)

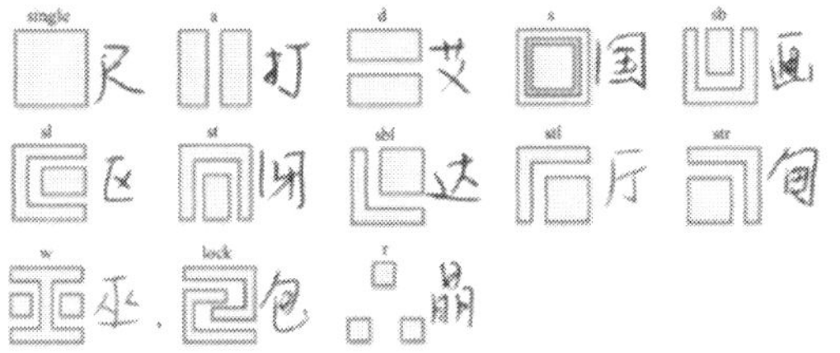

Fig. 5. Thirteen Common Spatial Structures of Chinese Characters and Their Examples.

Then, the author used images to provide a detailed description of how DenseRAN recognizes Chinese characters. (Figure 6), (Figure 7)

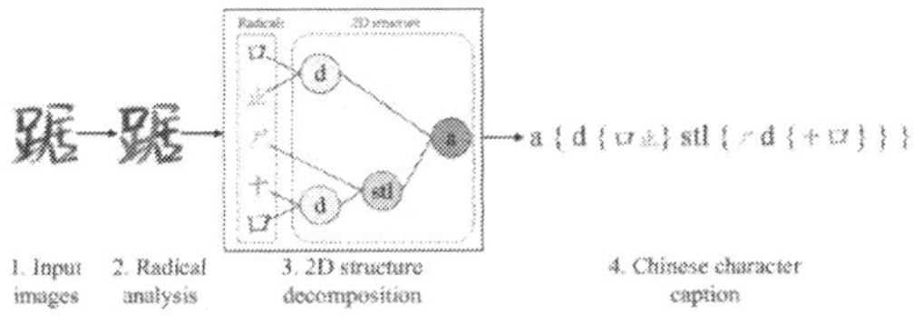

Fig. 6. Illustration of DenseRAN to recognize Chinese characters by analyzing the radicals and two-dimensional structures.

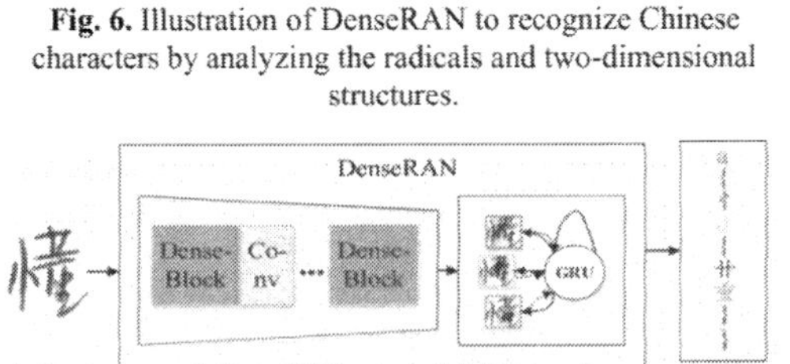

Fig. 7. The overall architecture of DenseRAN for HCCR.

Pavlo Melnyk, You Zhiqiang, Li Keqin (2020) introduced a novel deep CNN architecture for offline handwritten Chinese character recognition, focusing on enhancing network interpretability. [10] The authors developed a CNN with bottleneck layers, reducing computational demands while preserving expressiveness. They innovated with Global Weighted Output Average Pooling (GWOAP) to calculate class activation maps (CAMs), highlighting crucial input character image regions. This approach led to a 0.83% error reduction and a 49% parameter reduction compared to existing methods, without increasing computational costs. Their comprehensive experiments and comparisons showcased the model's superior recognition accuracy and interpretability, marking a significant advancement in the field of HCCR.

"Deep matching network for handwritten Chinese character recognition" (2020) introduced a Deep Matching Network that employs features from template character images, mimicking the human approach to learning Chinese characters. [11] Feature extraction is achieved through CNNs, which map these template images to a feature space. The network utilizes local softmax regression with a subset of template images for each training iteration, enhancing focus and efficiency. A significant advantage of this method is its ability to generalize to new characters by generating template images for characters not included in the training set. The architecture is compact yet effective, featuring several convolutional and pooling layers tailored for both image batches and template image processing. This approach marks a significant advancement in HCCR, particularly in terms of generalization and template-based feature extraction.

Nina Aleskerova and Aleksei Zhuravlev (2020) presented a novel two-stage hierarchical Convolutional Neural Network (CNN) for recognizing handwritten Chinese characters. [12] As mentioned above, one of the major challenges in the study of Chinese character recognition is the extensive quantity of patterns associated with Chinese characters. This method with two-stage hierarchical Convolutional Neural Network (CNN) is designed to effectively manage a large number of target classes, a significant challenge in Chinese character recognition due to the extensive character set. The model involves dividing training samples into clusters, with each cluster representing a subset of character classes. A first-level classifier identifies the cluster, and a second-level classifier, trained specifically on that cluster, performs the final recognition. This hierarchical approach results in improved accuracy and efficiency compared to traditional single-network CNN methods.

"Zero-shot Handwritten Chinese Character Recognition with hierarchical decomposition embedding" (2020) focused on encoding the hierarchical structure of Chinese characters into a semantic vector space for recognizing a large vocabulary of characters, their complex hierarchical structures, various writing styles, and the scarcity of training samples for uncommon characters. [13] This innovative approach involves decomposing characters into smaller components, such as radicals and strokes, and then embedding this decomposed structure hierarchically. By doing so, HDE captures the essence of Chinese character formation, which is not just about the individual strokes but also about how these strokes are combined to form meaningful units. This detailed decomposition and embedding enable the model to understand and recognize characters it has never seen before, by leveraging its learned knowledge of character structures and components. This method is particularly effective for characters that are rare or have few training samples, as it relies on structural understanding rather than rote memorization of character appearances.

Shi Pingping, Lou Yuansheng and Xia Rui (2023) presented a novel approach with character segmentation and classification. [14] Character segmentation uses a morphology-based algorithm for character enhancement and segmentation. It involves steps like binarization, centerline extraction, adaptive dilation, central line erosion, geometric center calculation for positioning, and adaptive bounding box segmentation. These steps are designed to effectively separate adhesive characters and improve the clarity of segmented characters. Character classification employs a pre-trained ResNet101 model, leveraging transfer learning for feature extraction and classification. The use of pre-trained weights, data augmentation techniques like label smoothing and Mixup, and the efficient architecture of ResNet101 contribute to the high accuracy in character recognition.

The specific recognition methods and test results of this study will be elaborated in the next section.

2.4. Research on Handwritten Chinese Character Recognition Methods and Algorithms

Chin Won and Kim Kidoo's (2002)[4] paper introduces the preprocessing steps for recognition data:

1) Smoothing: A filtering process to eliminate discontinuities in the data caused by hand tremors or writing surface issues.

2) Dehooking: The process of removing traces unrelated to strokes, such as traces of pen pressure, incorrect writing habits, or intentionally hooked strokes.

3) Distance filtering

4) Size normalization

Therefore, in the data preprocessing phase of online recognition, some aspects are also essential for offline recognition, rendering research in offline recognition a valuable reference. The author also mentions common stroke classification methods, including the use of neural networks, fuzzy functions, elastic matching, and dynamic programming matching. However, these methods are not well-suited for devices such as PDAs, whose central processing units (CPUs) are slower than those of PCs, due to their high computational demands. Thus, further research is necessary to analyze which algorithms are appropriate for specific functionalities and which are not suitable for certain circumstances.

When reconstructing text into units, it is necessary to represent the positional relationship parameters within the text domain. This is a characteristic of offline handwritten recognition data. However, in this paper, a method was developed and utilized to lessen the computational burden, rather than focusing on the precision of domain feature parameters, due to issues related to computational capacity. Since this research pertains to PDA mobile devices, it prioritizes computational capacity and processing speed over positional parameters. Yet, this aspect is an important part of offline handwritten recognition and should not be overlooked. Furthermore, the author anticipates that processing unhandled similar characters could significantly improve the average recognition rate. The final experimental results are as follows (Table 2):

Table 2. Recognition Experiment Results.

Five DB set	Average recognition rate	Average speed of recognition	
		First experiment	Second experiment
JJH	92.32	0.009	0.164
KJY	93.59	0.009	0.164
WON	96.65	0.009	0.162
JYS	94.70	0.009	0.168
SKB	94.19	0.009	0.163
Average	94.29	0.0088 sec	0.164 sec

Additionally, the experimental results from the paper *"DenseRAN for Offline Handwritten Chinese Character Recognition"* (2018)[8] are as follows: When training with 500 Chinese characters (356,553 handwritten character images) and testing with 1,000 characters, the accuracy was only 1.70%. With 1,000 characters (712,254 handwritten character images) used for training data, the accuracy rate tested with the ICDAR 2013 COMPETITION dataset was 8.44%. Training with 3,755 characters (2,674,784 handwritten character images) resulted in an accuracy of 40.82%. The results show that accuracy increases with the number of Chinese characters used in training. However, the accuracy remains low for characters that were not included in the training set. (Table 3)

Table 3. Test Results for Untrained Data.

Train set	Train class	Train samples	Test set	Test class	Accuracy
HWDB 1.0+1.1	500	356553	ICDAR 2013	1000	1.70%
	1000	712254		1000	8.44%
	1500	1068031		1000	14.71%
	2000	1425530		1000	19.51%
	2755	1962529		1000	30.68%
HWDB 1.0+1.1	3755	2674784	HWDB 1.2	3277	40.82%

The author also demonstrated how the DenseRAN algorithm recognizes radicals and two-dimensional structures, and analyzed examples of recognition errors through the visualization of weighted values. (Figure 8)

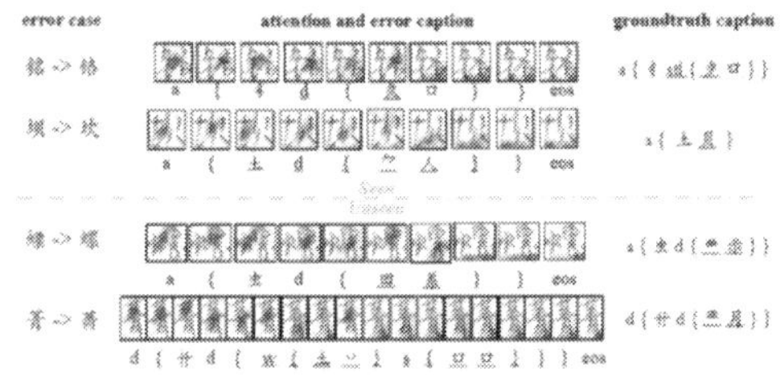

Fig. 8. Examples of Recognition Errors Visualized through Weighted Values.

"Fast and Robust Online Handwritten Chinese Character Recognition with Deep Spatial and Contextual Information Fusion Network" (2022) introduces advanced models for recognizing online handwritten Chinese characters.[15] The Vanilla Compositional Network (VCN) and the Deep Spatial & Contextual Information Fusion Network (DSCIFN) stand out for their methodological approach. DSCIFN employs a transformer-based autoregressive framework combined with multi-layer fusion modules. This approach effectively handles complex character recognition tasks, including characters that are poorly written or have missing strokes. DSCIFN model operates by intricately combining the spatial attributes of handwritten Chinese characters with their preceding contextual information. Spatial features include aspects like stroke order and character shape. The model analyzes these to understand each character's unique structure. Simultaneously, it considers the characters that come before the current one, acknowledging that their meanings and forms can influence the character in question. This dual approach, merging physical attributes (spatial features) with linguistic context (previous contextual information), significantly enhances the model's accuracy in character recognition.

"Chinese character recognition with radical-structured stroke trees" (2023) introduces a unique method for recognizing Chinese characters by first breaking them down into radicals using a Feature-to-Radical Decoder, and then further decomposing these radicals into strokes through a Radical-to-Stroke Decoder. [16] This process forms a structure known as the Radical-Structured Stroke Tree (RSST). The RSST is then interpreted by a Tree-to-Character Translator that employs a Weighted Edit Distance algorithm, enabling the system to effectively handle complex scenarios like zero-shot cases and visual distortions, such as blurring or occlusion, which challenge traditional single-level character recognition methods.

"A Novel Multilevel Stacked SqueezeNet Model for Handwritten Chinese Character Recognition," (2023) introduces model with multilevel stacked feature group extraction to analyze data at different scales, enhancing the model's ability to understand complex character structures. [17] Down-sampling is utilized to reduce feature map dimensions, maintaining essential information while lowering computational demands. Channel amplification is applied to highlight critical features and suppress less relevant ones, aiding in distinguishing similar characters. Lastly, feature information refinement is conducted to ensure only the most pertinent and distinct features are

considered, thereby improving recognition accuracy. These techniques collectively enhance the model's efficiency and precision in recognizing diverse handwritten Chinese characters within computational constraints.

"Characters as graphs: Interpretable handwritten Chinese character recognition via Pyramid Graph Transformer" (2023) presents a novel approach for recognizing handwritten Chinese characters by representing them as skeleton graphs and processing them with a Pyramid Graph Transformer (PyGT). [18] This method integrates the benefits of Transformers and graph convolutional networks, capturing global information through graph attention and local adjacency structures with graph convolutions. The first graph construction process for Chinese characters is transforming the strokes of a character into a graph structure. Each stroke is represented as a node, and the connections between strokes are represented as edges. The process focuses on accurately capturing the spatial relationships and structural characteristics of the strokes within each character. This graph representation forms the basis for the Pyramid Graph Transformer (PyGT) to analyze and recognize the characters. The PyGT is shown to be superior in interpretability and robustness compared to existing methods like 2D-CNN, RNN/1D-CNN, and Vision Transformer (ViT). It achieves state-of-the-art performance for online handwritten Chinese character recognition and is extendable to offline recognition and text recognition.

In conclusion, the accuracy comparison of studies within the last 5 years is as follows (Table 4):

Table 4. Performance comparisons of Chinese character recognition models over the last 5 years.

Dataset	Method	Accuracy (%)
ICDAR2013	**FewshotRAN (Wang et al., 2019)** [19]	96.97
	Template + Instance (Xiao et al., 2019) [20]	97.45
	SAE (Chen et al., 2023)[21]	97.19
	Hierarchical CNN (Aleskerova et al., 2020)[12]	92.10
	HDE (Cao et al., 2020)[13]	97.14
	Melnyk-Net (Melnyk et al., 2020)[10]	97.61
	Chen et al. (2021)[22]	96.74
	ACPM (Zu et al., 2022)[23]	97.80
	RSST (Yu et al., 2023)[16]	96.05
CASIA-HWDB+ ICDAR2013	**ROA (Wang et al., 2021)**[24]	95.77
	PageNet (Peng et al., 2022)[25]	92.19
	SON (Xu et al., 2022)[26]	93.45
	HHCR (Huang et al., 2022)[27]	94.87
	SqueezeNet (Du et al., 2023)[28]	98.65
CASIA-HWDB	**ResNet101 + transfer learning (Shi et al., 2023)**[14]	92.61

The current accuracy of online handwritten Chinese character recognition and offline printed Chinese character recognition is already relatively high. However, offline handwritten Chinese character recognition, due to certain inherent features, has the lowest accuracy in Chinese character recognition systems. Therefore, it is essential to identify the Chinese characters that current CNN algorithms misrecognize along with the various reasons for these errors. This includes analyzing deformations during handwriting, stroke features of similar characters, and the cognitive processes of the human brain in recognizing these characters. Subsequently, integrating these principles into the current algorithms can help improve and develop more accurate algorithms for handwritten Chinese character recognition.

3. Conclusions

Although the study of handwritten Chinese character recognition (HCCR) has a history of over 40 years, the author has identified several shortcomings and unresolved issues in the course of reviewing the literature on this subject. First, while online handwritten Chinese character recognition has achieved a certain level of accuracy, the accuracy of offline handwritten character recognition remains low. Second, the author believes that specialized research is needed for the analysis of the form and structure of Chinese characters specifically for HCCR. Third, the issue of discriminating between similar-looking characters has not been sufficiently resolved. The academic community should address these existing deficiencies to explore how artificial intelligence (AI) can more accurately and effectively learn and recognize handwritten Chinese characters. The author suggests that current Chinese character recognition algorithms and theories of text recognition in other languages can be referenced and integrated with ontological research in Chinese character studies, such as theories on Chinese character structure, stroke order, and analysis of radicals and components, thereby developing more effective and sophisticated recognition methods. [29] Additionally, insights can be gained from artificial intelligence-based image recognition systems, as their engineering designs for image recognition are currently more intricate and specialized. There have been many algorithms used for image recognition in the past. Among them, the recently utilized Convolutional Neural Network (CNN) algorithm for image recognition takes the pixel values of an image as input data. It recognizes images through feature maps calculated by filters. Currently, research involving the use of Convolutional Neural Networks (CNNs) is being conducted across various fields. This research has demonstrated considerable performance in numerous areas of image recognition and continues to improve through a variety of methods. The author believes that research in this area could consider the principles of Chinese characters and the structure of handwritten characters to enhance the accuracy of handwritten Chinese character recognition.

The author intends for this paper to contribute a theoretical basis to AI Chinese character recognition research and also aims to inspire studies that seek to enhance offline Chinese character recognition capabilities.

References

1. Jin, L.W., Zhong, Z.Y., Yang, Z., Yang, W.X., Xie, Z.C., Sun, J. (2016) Applications of Deep Learning for Handwritten Chinese Character Recognition: A Review. Acta Automatica Sinica, 42(8): 1125−1141.
2. Zhang, B., Jin, L.W. (2017) Handwritten Chinese Similar Characters Recognition Based On AdaBoost. Proceedings of the 26th Chinese Control Conference.
3. Nambu, H., Kawamata, T., Maruyama, F., Yoda, F. (1998) On-line Handwriting Chinese Character Recognition; Comparison and Improvement to Japanese Kanji Recognition. In: International Conference on Pattern Recognition. IEEE Computer Society.
4. Chin, W., Kim, K. (2002) On-line Handwriting Chinese Character Recognition for PDA Using a Unit Reconstruction Method. Journal of the Institute of Electronics Engineers, 39(1): 97-107.
5. Wang, Y.W., Liu, C.S., Ding X.Q. (2013) Similar Pattern Discriminant Analysis for Improving Chinese Character Recognition Accuracy. International Conference on Document Analysis & Recognition. IEEE.
6. Yang, C., Wang, Q., Du, J., Zhang, J.S., Wu, C.J., Wang, J.M. (2021) A Transformer-based Radical Analysis Network for Chinese Character Recognition. In: 25th International Conference on Pattern Recognition (ICPR). Milan, Italy. 3714-3719.
7. Kim, W.J., Choi, J.Y. (2023) Current Status and Prospects of Chinese Character Recognition Models in Korea. The Society for Korean Language & Literary Research, 51(4): 313-341.
8. Wang, W.C., Zhang, J.S., Du, J., Wang, Z.R., Zhu, Y.X. (2018) DenseRAN for Offline Handwritten Chinese Character Recognition. IEEE, 16: 104-109.
9. Xu, Q., Bai, X., Liu, W. (2019) Multiple Comparative Attention Network for Offline Handwritten Chinese Character Recognition. 2019 International Conference on Document Analysis and Recognition (ICDAR). 2019.6.
10. Melnyk, P., You, Z.Q., Li, K.Q. (2020) A high-performance CNN method for offline handwritten Chinese character recognition and visualization. soft computing, 24(11), 7977-7987.
11. Li, Z., Wu, Q., Xiao, Y., Jin, M., Lu, H. (2020) Deep matching network for handwritten Chinese character recognition. Pattern Recognition, 107, 107471.
12. N. Aleskerova, A. Zhuravlev (2020) Handwritten Chinese Characters Recognition Using Two-Stage Hierarchical Convolutional Neural Network. In: 2020 17th International Conference on Frontiers in Handwriting Recognition (ICFHR). Dortmund, Germany. 343-348.
13. Cao, Z., Lu, J., Cui, S., & Zhang, C. (2020) Zero-shot Handwritten Chinese Character Recognition with hierarchical decomposition embedding. Pattern Recognition, 107, 107488.
14. Shi, P., Lou, Y., & Xia, R. (2023) Handwritten Chinese Character Recognition Based on Morphology and Transfer Learning. In 2023 International Conference on Intelligent Perception and Computer Vision (CIPCV), IEEE, 47-51.
15. Li, Y.X., Yang, Q., Chen, Q.C., Hu, B.T., Wang, X.L., Ding, Y.X., Ma, L. (2022) Fast and Robust Online Handwritten Chinese Character Recognition with Deep Spatial & Contextual Information Fusion Network. IEEE Transactions on Multimedia.
16. Yu, H., Chen, J., Li, B., & Xue, X. (2023) Chinese character recognition with radical-structured stroke trees. Machine Learning, 1-21.
17. Du, Y.K., Liu, F.Q., Liu, Z.L. (2023) A novel multilevel stacked SqueezeNet model for handwritten Chinese character recognition. Computer Science and Information Systems, (00), 30-30.
18. Gan, J., Chen, Y.Y., Hu, B., Leng, J.X., Wang, W.Q., Gao, X.B. (2023) Characters as graphs: Interpretable handwritten Chinese character recognition via Pyramid Graph Transformer. Pattern Recognition, 137, 109317.
19. Wang, T.W., Xie, Z.C., Li, Z., Jin, L.W., Chen, X.L. (2019) Radical aggregation network for few-shot offline handwritten Chinese character recognition. Pattern Recognition Letters, 125: 821-827.
20. Xiao, Y., Meng, D., Lu, C., & Tang, C. K. (2019) Template-instance loss for ofine handwritten Chinese character recognition. In 2019 International Conference on Document Analysis and Recognition (ICDAR), 315–322.
21. Chen, Z., Yang, W., Li, X. (2023) Stroke-based autoencoders: Self-supervised learners for efcient zeroshot Chinese character recognition. Applied Sciences, 13(3), 1750.
22. Chen, J., Li, B., & Xue, X. (2021) Zero-shot Chinese character recognition with stroke-level decomposition. In Proceedings of the Thirtieth International Joint Conference on Artifcial Intelligence.
23. Zu, X., Yu, H., Li, B., Xue, X. (2022) Chinese character recognition with augmented character profle matching. In Proceedings of the 30th ACM International Conference on Multimedia, 6094–6102.
24. Wang, Y., Yang, Y., Ding, W., et al. (2021) A residual-attention offline handwritten Chinese text recognition based on fully convolutional neural networks," IEEE Access, Vol. 9, 132301-132310.
25. Peng, D., Jin, L., Liu, Y., et al. (2022) PageNet: Towards End-to-End Weakly Supervised Page-Level Handwritten Chinese Text Recognition. International Journal of Computer Vision, Vol. 130, No. 11, 2623-2645.

26. Xu, X., Yang, C., Wang, L., et al. (2022) A sophisticated offline network developed for recognizing handwritten Chinese character efficiently. Computers and Electrical Engineering, Vol. 100, 107857.
27. Huang, G., Luo, X., Wang, S., et al. (2022) Hippocampus-heuristic character recognition network for zero-shot learning in Chinese character recognition. Pattern Recognition, Vol. 130, 108818.
28. Zhou, Y.C., Tan, Q.H., Xi, C.L. (2021) Offline Handwritten Chinese Character Recognition of SqueezeNet and Dynamic Network Surgery. Journal of Chinese Computer Systems, 42(3), 556-560.
29. Zhang, J.S., Du, J., Dai, L.R. (2020) Radical analysis network for learning hierarchies of Chinese characters. Pattern Recognition, 103: 1-13.

SHS Web of Conferences 185, 01005 (2024) https://doi.org/10.1051/shsconf/202418501005
ICLCC 2024

Promoting Language and Literature in Colleges and Universities for the Development of International Chinese Language Education Professionals

Li Meng[1], Wang Pan[2*]

[1]Faculty of Letters, Heilongjiang University, National Language and Literature Promotion Base (Heilongjiang University), Heilongjiang China
[2]College of Arts and Letters, Heilongjiang University, Heilongjiang China

Abstract. In order to better promote the language and writing system in colleges and universities, the State Language Commission has established national language and writing system promotion bases in many colleges and universities, and now the bases have become the basic positions to make full use of the characteristic advantages, and to demonstrate and guide the work of the national common language and writing system. This paper mainly discusses the current situation of language and writing work in colleges and universities, the effective way of language and writing work in colleges and universities to promote the professional development of international Chinese education, and the impact of language and writing work in colleges and universities on the development of international Chinese education, with the aim that colleges and universities can better cultivate more and more excellent international Chinese education talents.

1. Introductory

Schools are an important position for carrying out language and writing work, in which colleges and universities play a major role. From 2019 to now, the State Language Commission has set up projects to build 122 national language and writing promotion bases (hereinafter referred to as the "bases") in two batches, of which 108 are colleges and universities, and 14 are primary and middle schools, language associations, institutions, and so on, which have become important platforms for integrating talents and resources to carry forward and disseminate Chinese excellent language and culture. The bases have become a basic position for giving full play to their special advantages, demonstrating and leading the work on national common language and writing system, and an important platform for integrating talents and resources, as well as inheriting, promoting and spreading the excellent Chinese language and culture. In the face of the new deployment and requirements of the work on national common language and writing system in the context of the new journey of comprehensively building a socialist modernization country, colleges and universities should deeply study and understand the important exposition of General Secretary Xi Jinping on education and language and culture, and implement the decision-making and deployment of the CPC Central Committee and the State Council, as well as the spirit of the National Conference on Work on Language and Writing System, and have in mind the "two big situations", and the "greatness of the country". With "two big situations" and "the greatness of the country" in mind, they should strengthen the construction of bases and show their due commitment and unique style in promoting the high-quality development of national language and writing work and helping the development of the Party and the country.

Since the founding of the country, the Chinese government has always been steadfast in promoting language and writing, and the Party has always insisted on its leading responsibility for language and writing and language and culture work, pointing out the direction for the development of the country's language and writing working. In the report of the 20th Party Congress, for the first time, education, science and technology, and talents were integrated and deployed in a trinity, clearly stating that education, science and technology, and talents are the basic and strategic support for the comprehensive construction of a socialist modernized country, emphasizing that adherence to the priority development of education, self-reliance of science and technology, and leadership of talents drive education to play an important pivot in science and technology and human resources innovation, and that it is important to strengthen the construction of basic, emerging, and intersectional subjects, and increase the construction of national common languages and cross-disciplinary construction, increasing the promotion of the national common language and writing system, and building superior disciplines with Chinese characteristics and world-class quality.

*Corresponding author's email: 1873668509@qq.com

As a base for training international Chinese language education professionals, actively promoting all language and writing work in colleges and universities will help to build a high-quality international Chinese language education team, disseminate the excellent traditional Chinese culture, and promote the development of the international Chinese language education profession[1].

2. Current situation of language and writing work in colleges and universities

Schools are the basic position for language and writing work, and colleges and universities play an important role in it. In 2020, the General Office of the State Council issued the Opinions on Comprehensively Strengthening Language and Writing Work in the New Era, which puts forward the idea of "insisting on taking schools as the foundation of national common language and writing education"[2], and organically integrates the language and writing work with the cultivation of talents in colleges and universities, scientific research, social service, cultural inheritance and innovation, and international exchanges and cooperation, scientific research, social service, cultural heritage and innovation, and international exchange and cooperation. The report of the 20th CPC National Congress emphasized "increasing the promotion of the national common language and writing system, improving the school management and education evaluation system, and perfecting the mechanism for nurturing people in schools, families and society".

In recent years, the state has increased its attention to language and writing work, and many universities have established language and writing bases. In 2020, the Department of Language and Writing Application Management of the Ministry of Education (Office of the State Language Commission) established the first batch of 60 national language and writing promotion bases. Of these, 83.61% are located in colleges and universities, and 16.39% are non-colleges and universities, colleges and universities are already the main position of language and writing promotion bases, Colleges and universities have incorporated the cultivation of students' awareness of the standardized use of language and writing and of the traditional promotion of Chinese outstanding language and culture into their personnel training programme; established Putonghua testing sites to conduct Putonghua proficiency tests; offered university language, oral expression, and set up bases for the promotion of language and writing and set up language and writing columns to organize activities for studying the standardization of language and writing through the bases radiating across the entire campus. A series of activities in colleges and universities have achieved the purpose of cultivating students to standardize the use of national common language and writing and laid the foundation for the rapid development of language and writing work. However, the variety of forms makes the language and writing work face more challenges, which at the same time brings barriers to the international Chinese teaching students in promoting Chinese language to foreign countries.

According to the incomplete statistics of the Ministry of Education, since the development of international Chinese language education, the number of people learning Chinese abroad has exceeded 25 million, and the cumulative number of people learning and using Chinese is nearly 200 million. Due to the development of teaching platforms and force majeure factors, colleges and universities to promote the development of international Chinese language education mode has changed dramatically, online teaching platforms or blended teaching platforms have been developed as a common mode of teaching, for more committed to the international promotion of Chinese language students in colleges and universities to bring a certain degree of opportunity. However, the establishment of a high-quality international Chinese language teaching system in colleges and universities and the improvement of the language and writing skills of school students have raised higher requirements.

3. Effective Paths for Language and Writing Work in Colleges and Universities to Contribute to the Development of International Chinese Language Education

3.1 Adhering to the Ideology of Socialism with Chinese Characteristics in the New Era and Promoting the Development of the Language and Writing Project

The report of the 20th Party Congress pointed out that we should always adhere to the leadership of the Party Central Committee with Comrade Xi Jinping as the core, adhere to the Xi Jinping Thought on Socialism with Chinese Characteristics in the New Era, and accelerate the pace of reform of the language and writing business, and that colleges and universities should adhere to the self-confidence and self-improvement, and resolutely take the road of language and writing development with Chinese characteristics[3].The road of language and writing development in New China has laid a solid foundation for information communication and cultural improvement for all people on the road to socialist modernization. Whether in the past or at present, we should always adhere to the leadership of the Party, start from the actual situation of China and universities, positively respond to internal and external challenges, continue to create a path of development of the language and writing business that is suitable for China's basic national conditions, continue the Party's great achievements of the century-long struggle, pass on the excellent language and culture, promote the self-confidence and self-reliance of culture, and promote the development of language and writing business.

3.2 Adhering to the principle of observance and innovation and realizing the innovative development of language and writing

For a long time, we have been comprehensively implementing the Party's guidelines and policies, promoting the State common language and writing system in primary and secondary schools, colleges and universities as well as remote areas across the country, scientifically protecting the languages and writing systems of various ethnic groups, and respecting and safeguarding the learning and use of minority languages and writing systems. Nowadays, the new round of scientific and technological revolution and industrial revolution are advancing in depth, real and virtual spaces co-exist, and the form of language and writing work has changed significantly. We should keep up with the pace of the times, vigorously promote the digitization and intelligent construction of language and writing, combine language and writing innovations in universities and international Chinese language education majors, and make use of existing technology to actively explore new ideas of digital empowerment.

3.3 Improvement of rules and regulations to raise the awareness of teachers and students in the use of the national general language and writing system

Colleges and universities can make full use of platforms such as school magazines, college websites, public numbers of bases, and jitterbugs to vigorously publicize national policies and laws and regulations on language and writing, such as the Opinions on Comprehensively Strengthening the Work of Language and Writing in the New Era issued by the General Office of the State Council, and the Opinions on Strengthening the Services of Higher Education Institutions for the High-quality Promotion and Popularization of the National Common Language and Writing Systems issued by the Ministry of Education and the State Language Commission, to improve teachers' and students' overall knowledge of language and writing. Colleges and universities can integrate the requirements for standardization of the language and writing system into all relevant systems, and establish a system of responsibility management, with layers of management and responsibility. In addition, the language and writing bases of universities can make use of the relevant associations on campus to promote language and writing and enhance their influence. Improving the rules and regulations related to language and writing in colleges and universities not only promotes the development of language and writing, but also enhances international Chinese education.

3.4 Fulfilment of the role of the classroom position and the development of professionalism

Colleges and universities are first and foremost to educate people and cultivate talents, to promote language and writing on campus, to strengthen students' ability to use language and writing, to improve the level of Putonghua, and to create a group of talented people with a high level of professional knowledge as well as professional competence. We will offer courses on the standardized use of the national common language and writing system, strengthen the teaching ability of international Chinese majors in the basic aspects of character pronunciation and stroke order, and incorporate the basic requirements of the use of standardized language and writing system and academic writing into the mandatory public courses; we will offer special cultural classes to pass on the excellent Chinese culture, strengthen the efforts of students in spreading the excellent Chinese culture, and actively participate in the "Chinese Classics Recitation, Writing and Speaking Competition", "Red Chinese Classics Recitation, Writing and Speaking Competition We will also actively participate in the "Red Classics in the Countryside" thematic activities, so that students can develop the habit of standardizing the use of language and writing and improve their ability to pass on their culture; increase the proportion of practical courses, improve the new type of teaching methodology, and cultivate "digital" professionals, and improve the international standard of academic writing. "digital" professionals, enhance the digital and informatization teaching ability of teachers and students of international Chinese majors, and cultivate new types of international Chinese education talents.

4. The Impact of Language and Writing Work in Colleges and Universities on International Chinese Language Education

4.1 Support for the development of professionalism and the building of a high-quality teaching workforce

General Secretary Xi Jinping pointed out that the promotion of the national general language and writing, and efforts to cultivate party-loving and patriotic builders and successors of the socialist cause. Colleges and universities play an irreplaceable role in building a professional talent team. Firstly, create a team of teachers with expertise in international Chinese language education, and make use of scientific research platforms to improve professional teaching ability; secondly, create a multi-dimensional integrated education system of classroom teaching, social practice and cultural activities to strengthen the use of the national general language and writing skills of students at different levels in undergraduate and postgraduate studies of this programme; finally, attract more overseas Chinese language teachers to study master's and build a three-dimensional and diversified international Chinese language education teachers and volunteers[4].

4.2 Conducive to the promotion of the dissemination of Chinese language and culture

It is an important task to strengthen China's international communication capacity building to tell China's story, disseminate China's voice, and show a real, three-dimensional and comprehensive China. The promotion of language and writing in colleges and universities is not just about the language itself, but more importantly, it is about passing on and carrying forward the excellent traditional Chinese culture behind the language and writing[5]. International Chinese language teachers can bring the activities of universities to carry out Chinese classics recitation, poetry relay recitation by teachers and students, and the classics-run-the-countryside programme to Chinese language classrooms overseas, to promote the dissemination of Chinese culture overseas as well as exchanges and collisions with different cultures, and to stimulate the interest of foreign students in Chinese culture and to promote the development of Chinese culture.

4.3 Contributing to the International Chinese Language Education System

Give full play to the function of colleges and universities as an important position for discipline construction, increase scientific research investment, integrate professional resources, and make use of the scientific research platforms of colleges and universities to build a more scientific and targeted discipline system. Under the standard of building a modern socialist country in a comprehensive manner, high-quality development is of primary importance. Universities should make full use of their advantages to promote the state common language and writing system in high quality, especially the international Chinese language education programme, so as to cultivate high-quality and all-rounded talents. System practitioners and cultural communicators in universities can continue to promote the standardization and standardization of language and writing work, deepen their efforts in international Chinese language education, and help build a community of human destiny[6].

4.4 It is conducive to attracting international students to China and enhancing the international status and influence of the Chinese language.

Since the development of international Chinese language education, Confucius Institutes have been opened all over the world, however, they have been affected to a certain extent due to the epidemic. Nowadays, colleges and universities are promoting language and writing work, which not only attracts more international students with strong interest in Chinese language, but also cultivates professional talents, and lets these talents and teachers go to the front line overseas to promote the international communication ability of Chinese language and tell the Chinese story well. In this process, colleges and universities should pay attention to the mechanism of articulation, improve the quality and demonstration of leadership, improve the institutional mechanism of language and writing work, do a good job in scientific research, serve the community to inherit the culture and international communication and dissemination, and enhance the Chinese language's international status and influence, under the basis of improving the students' language competence and literacy and advancing the excellent traditional Chinese culture.

5. Final comments

General Secretary Xi Jinping has shown that mastering a language is mastering the key to a country's culture. As a cross-discipline, international Chinese language education not only teaches more foreign students Chinese, but also serves as a bridge between China and the world. As the basic position of language and writing promotion, universities should always pay attention to language and writing education, use science and technology to deepen language and writing research, pass on the excellent traditional Chinese culture, and combine with international Chinese language education to cultivate new types of digitized professionals and enhance the international status and influence of language and writing culture.

Acknowledgments

This paper is the stage results of the Philosophy and Social Science Research Planning Project of Heilongjiang Province in 2021 (21YYC248), the stage results of the Special Project of Basic Research Operating Costs of Colleges and Universities in Heilongjiang Province in 2022 (2022-KYYWF-1138), and the stage results of the High Quality Construction Project of Curriculum Civics and Politics of the Province of Heilongjiang Provincial Department of Education for the Study of the Province of Heilongjiang in 2022.

References

1. C. Peng, Research on Innovation Path of Language and Literature Work in Colleges and Universities [J]. Gansu Education Research,2022(09):60-64.
2. Starting a New Journey of Reform and Development of Language and Writing Career--The person in charge of the Ministry of Education and the State Language Commission answered reporters' questions on the Opinions of the General Office of the State Council on Comprehensively Strengthening Language and Writing Work in the New Era[J]. Language and Translation,2022(01):8-10.
3. Opinions of the General Office of the State Council on Comprehensively Strengthening Language and Writing Work in the New Era[J]. Language and Translation,2021(04):5-7.

4. X.S. (Andy) Gao & H. Zhu (2021) Experiencing Chinese education: learning of language and culture by international students in Chinese universities, Language, Culture and Curriculum, 34:4, 353-359, DOI: 10.1080/07908318.2020.1871002
5. Jiani, M.A. Why and how international students choose Mainland China as a higher education study abroad destination. High Educ 74, 563–579 (2017). https://doi.org/10.1007/s10734-016-0066-0
6. Diao WH. & Liu HY. (2021). Starting College, Quitting Foreign Language: The Case of Learners of Chinese Language during Secondary-Postsecondary Transition. Journal of Language, Identity & Education (2), 75-89.

The Interference of Native Language on English Writing Syntax Errors of High School Students

Ren Xiaoling*, Huang Ting, Liu Yue

Maoming No.10 Middle School, 525000 Maoming, China

Abstract. This paper discusses the common syntactic errors in Chinese senior high school English writing, explores the causes of their English expression errors, and proposes a writing enhancement plan for senior high school students. Based on the theory of error analysis and the analysis of writing materials, this paper collects relevant data, analyzes the types of transfer errors and interference patterns in writing, and tries to explain the causes of interference syntactic errors in students' English writing. Although the reasons for the negative transfer of senior high school students are complex and diverse, the efforts of teachers and students can still effectively avoid the formation of negative transfer of English thinking reduction. In English teaching, teachers should strengthen students' syntactic discrimination ability and syntactic structure through comparative analysis, encourage students to overcome the interference of mother tongue thinking, and cultivate students' English thinking ability.

1. Introduction

Due to the interference of the mother tongue, the problems caused by the negative transfer of the mother tongue of senior high school students can be directly reflected in their English writing. Therefore, how to help senior high school students reduce the negative transfer errors of their mother tongue in English writing, improve the efficiency of English learning, develop the habit of English thinking, and improve their language expression ability has become one of the main topics gradually explored and concerned in the field of English teaching.[1,2] In the process of writing, learners are influenced by the unconscious of their mother tongue. Speak Chinese instead of English in English class. Nor do they have the opportunity to speak English outside the classroom. When writing in English, most students are mechanically translating words into English according to Chinese ideas. They also translate Chinese grammar into English sentences using Chinese forms, meanings, and conventions of expression. In the teaching process, the imitation paper is the main tool to teach English writing, which is a very simple subject. Writing is a very difficult skill to master when learning English, because it requires both a solid foundation and the ability to organize the text. However, the examination of sentences and speech in teaching is often neglected by teachers. They ignore the problem of students' native language interfering with written English. L1 interference is not the latest development in second language acquisition (SLA) research, but it is a key aspect to be taken into account when guiding English writing.[3]

2. Error Analysis Method

Error analysis, initially proposed by Corder[4], holds that the classification and analysis of errors made by second language learners during the translation of source language to target language should be a primary focus of empirical research. To understand the nature and root causes of language errors and develop strategies to prevent or reduce them, error analysis studies and examines the mistakes made by people learning a second language. He also pointed out that learners' errors can provide researchers with information about the methods and strategies used in language learning; teachers regularly assess students' language errors to determine the extent to which learners have not achieved their goals and what they still need to learn. For scholars and teachers engaged in language teaching research, the development of error analysis theory in the SLA (Second Language Acquisition) field provides a new perspective. The four steps in error analysis are error identification, error description, error interpretation, and error correction.

3. Research Design

3.1. Research Questions

The aim of this study is to investigate the interference of L1 on high school students' writing errors, and explore possible strategies to help them improve their writing level. Specifically, it aims to answer the following questions:

* Corresponding author's mail: mmrxl@qq.com

1) What are the syntactic errors found in the participants' writing output?

2) What are the reasons for L1 interference in the participants' writing output?

3.2. Research Participants

This study selected 150 high school students from a school in Guangdong, as shown in Table 1. They were not randomly chosen. Their English scores were at an intermediate level. Divided by grade, they were grouped into three categories: 50 students in the first grade, 50 students in the second grade, and 50 students in the third grade. The selection of male and female participants was balanced within each grade.

Table 1. Participant Information.

Grade	mm	Male	Female	Age	Length of study
First Grade	50	30	20	15	6
Second Grade	50	18	32	16	7
Third Grade	50	22	28	17	8
Total	150	70	80		

3.3. Research Instruments

In the examination, students were required to complete two types of writing tasks, such as descriptive and narrative. They were advised to write an introduction, body paragraphs, and a conclusion. Additionally, students were given 40 minutes to write a paragraph (minimum of 100 words and maximum of 150 words). The English writing materials were selected from the simulated high school entrance examination questions. The topics were familiar to students, focusing on spending the Chinese New Year holiday and doing housework on weekends. The essay prompts provided writing points, word counts, and specific instructions to be mindful of.

3.4. Research Steps

1) The author conducted error statistics on the 300 essays collected using YouDao software, and analyzed the grammatical errors in the corpus. These essays reflect both common issues in high school students' English writing and the writing level of most ordinary high school students.

2) To analyze the error data, they were checked using YouDao software, errors were classified, and then summarized and analyzed by at least two English teachers to ensure reliability.[5]

3) After analyzing the articles, this study used text analysis to sort and annotate these samples based on different error types and dimensions. Each component was encoded, and each narrative essay was ranked from N1 to N150, while each descriptive essay was ranked from D1 to D150. The data was then analyzed to objectively understand the common types of errors in students' essays and the distribution of errors in students' essays, and examples of some error types were extracted, providing a wealth of material for future analysis of the reasons behind these errors. All data was obtained from student exams and represents accurate and objective data, providing a reliable basis for subsequent analysis.

3.5. Data Collection

Participants will be required to take a writing test, and writing samples will be collected from the students. The data collected from the test will be organized, categorized, analyzed, and interpreted in written form. Then, the information will be compiled into tables, and charts designed to include error types and performance patterns will be created to calculate the frequency of errors.

4. Data Analysis

Chinese English learners often make syntax and expression-related errors when writing in English due to the organizational style and thinking patterns of their native language.[6, 7] Most of the errors in students' English writing are related to sentence structure and sentence form. Table 2 lists the types of syntactic errors, performance patterns, and frequency.

Table 2. Types, patterns, and frequencies of syntactic errors.

Error Type	Performance Pattern	Frequency
Missing components	Missing subject or predicate in the main or subordinate clause.	486
Predicate misuse	A simple sentence containing two predicate verbs and above sentence pattern.	336
Clause misuse	Omissions, repetitions, or lack of conjunctions, or redundancy.	175
Word order errors	Chinese word order.	112
Improper placement of Attributive and adverbial	Attributive or adverbial placed in an incorrect position relative to the word it decorates.	87

The analysis of syntactic error data is divided into three steps.

Step 1: Calculate the proportion of syntactic errors used in the thinking process of each student's essay, and then identify and classify them. The total number of errors was counted without excluding repeated words.

Step 2: Find examples of each type of sentence in each student's essay to analyze and describe the reasons for the errors. The process of establishing categories is time-consuming and laborious because it requires repeated revision and verification.

Step 3: Analyze the differences between English and Chinese based on the established categories, and infer the reasons for the negative transfer of the mother tongue in the foreign language writing process.

5. Results and Discussion

The results primarily address the following two questions: The first question examines the types of syntactic errors that participants encountered in their writing. The second question explores the patterns of L1 interference observed in the participants' writing output.

5.1. Manifestations of Syntactic Errors

5.1.1. Missing components

D116: Before the festival will clean the room, paste the spring festival couplets and hang lanterns.

D75: When you finish doing laundry, fold the clothes before putting them away.

N108: We all like doing housework because make us relaxed.

N131: I full and warm after doing the housework.

N65: I help my parents do housework, so they happy and rest.

5.1.2. Predicate misuse

N84: Last Friday, my parents was went out shopping.

N57: I help my parents do the housework, which making them very happy and rest.

D124: The older will giving the children red packets.

D141: We watch a program name spring festival gala.

D84: People wear new clothes visit their relatives.

5.1.3. Clause misuse

D33: Because the Spring Festival is the most important festival in China, so it is celebrated by people all over the country.

D46: Before the Spring Festival, we clean the house, stick the couplets, hang all kinds of lanterns .

N63: Because the room is too messy, so I need to clean it.

N58: Although I am tired, but I feel very successful.

N75: I always clean the kitchen, so it is always spotless.

5.1.4. Word order errors

D49: On the first day of the new year, people will wear new clothes, when meeting others will say good wish for others.

D67: Eat the New Year's Eve dinner is a very important tradition of the Spring Festival.

D81: One of the most important activities during the Spring Festival is family reunion, usually a New Year's Eve dinner at night.

N112: A big meal together would have on New Year's Eve.

N13: Before the Spring Festival, cleaning the room is my family always do.

5.1.5. Improper placement of attributive and adverbial

N66: I very much like do housework.

N84: After cleaning, we have been tiredly in the bed.

N56: I told my parents what I perfectly have done.

D24: I'll share interesting something with you.

D46: People wear new clothes cotton during the festival.

5.2. The Reason for the Interference of Native Language in Sentence Pattern Recognition

The influence of the native language on Chinese high school students' English writing is a phenomenon that cannot be ignored.[8] This influence can be explored mainly from two perspectives.

First, we can look at the influence of the native language's expressive habits on high school students' writing. In their native language, students have developed ways of using specific sentence structures and expressions that are deeply ingrained and form their language thinking patterns. When they try to write in English, these native language expressive habits are likely to be transferred to English writing, leading to confusion between native and target languages in understanding and expression. This confusion may sometimes even affect their grammatical structures and expressions, making their English writing show clear traces of the native language.

Second, the influence of native language thinking is also an important factor in high school students' English writing. There are many differences in syntax between the native language and the target language, which poses a significant challenge for Chinese high school students. When they are learning a second language, they often need to use translation and substitution from their native language to understand the target language. However, this method easily roots deep in their thinking habits, so when writing in English, they may unconsciously use their native language thinking patterns, leading to grammatical interference in the writing process.

Overall, the influence of the native language on Chinese high school students' English writing is multifaceted, including not only the expressive habits of the native language but also the influence of native language thinking. These factors make it difficult for them to write in English, such as confusion between native and target languages, and interference from their native language thinking patterns. Therefore, for English writing teaching, helping students overcome the influence of the native language and improving their English writing skills is a crucial task.

6. Writing Enhancement Plan

English writing is an important reflection of language proficiency in high school English core literacy. Therefore, writing plays a crucial role in high school English teaching. Writing requires students not only to correctly apply the vocabulary and grammar they typically learn, but also to have a higher level of language organization and expression. With the reform and deepening of education, this reflects the need for continuous innovation in high school English teaching methods, exploring effective strategies to reduce the interference of the mother tongue and promote high school English writing teaching. These teaching strategies require teachers to effectively improve students' English writing literacy and writing abilities.

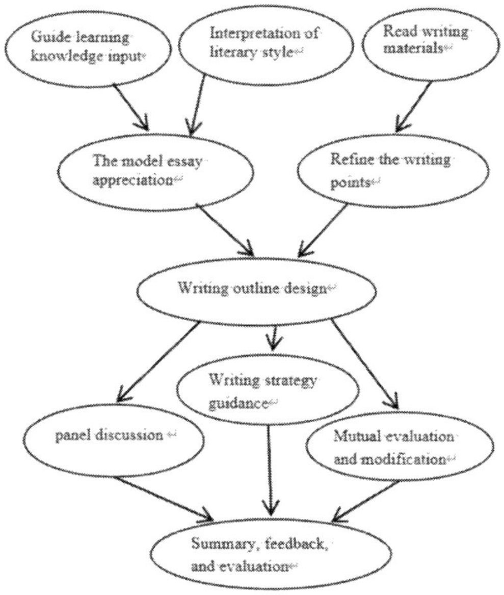

Fig. 1. The design concept of the entire writing teaching reform model

For high school English writing, the learning objectives are aimed at the personal abilities and qualities developed by students during the process of learning English, including language ability, learning ability, thinking quality, and cultural quality. Language differences are an objective reality, and the interference of the mother tongue affects various levels of students' English writing. Teachers can take measures to minimize this interference and guide students to express ideas fluently in English. In practice, teachers can adopt various teaching strategies and methods to help students improve their English writing abilities. Designing high school English writing teaching models as the mainstay, taking students' actual needs as the main reference, and using English writing strategy training as an auxiliary means, fully leveraging the teaching resources and means of modern educational technology, optimizing the writing teaching process, improving the evaluation mechanism for composition, and stimulating students' enthusiasm for participation in writing.

The process-oriented teaching method is a writing teaching method based on communication theory that emerged in the late 20th century. It emphasizes the writing process of students and emphasizes that during the writing process, teachers help them analyze, discover, and solve problems. The key is to guide students through their writing process and writing abilities, fully developing their thinking abilities. The design concept of the entire writing teaching reform model is illustrated in Figure 1.

The teaching plan in this proposal aims to promote English writing teaching in high school. The baseline data results of this teaching plan are as follows: students' evaluation of the teaching content, strategies, evaluation, and materials; students' ability to solve problems based on the process writing theory through logical processes; teachers' teaching practices; and difficulties, questions, and suggestions raised by both students and teachers to facilitate writing acquisition for high school students.

7. Conclusion

In summary, there is a mother tongue interference phenomenon at the syntax level when students practice English writing. In order to improve students' writing abilities, teachers should consciously compare the differences at various levels of syntax between English and Chinese and help students master the syntactic patterns in English that are formed due to different ways of thinking and cultural backgrounds. It is also important to enhance students' understanding of English cultural background knowledge and cultivate English thinking habits. Additionally, teachers should regularly encourage and guide students to read extensively and memorize English model essays to develop a sense of English language. Only by overcoming mother tongue interference through multiple approaches can students' English writing skills be effectively improved.

Acknowledgment

This paper is one of the accomplishments of the "Enhancing the Research Capacity of Primary and Secondary School Teachers" project in Guangdong Province, titled "The Manifestations and Countermeasures of Native Language Interference in High School English Writing" (2023YQJK630).

References

1. R. Budiharto. Indonesian EFL Journal, 5, 107-116 (2019)
2. J. Cai, J. Li. Foreign Language Teaching, 4, 43-50 (2016)
3. L. Dong, M. Shen, N. Li. Overseas English language(24), 1-2 (2016)
4. Corder. International Review of Applied Linguistics, 5, 161-170 (1967).
5. M. Hu, B. Wu. Overseas Eng. Language, 8, 4-6 (2022)
6. Richards. English Language Teaching, 3, (1971)
7. Richards. New frontiers in second language learning, 32-53, (1974)
8. G. Jia. Theory and Practice of Foreign Language Teaching(01),30-35 (2017)

An Analysis of English Teaching Strategies in Higher Vocational Technical College

Yutong Jiang*

Yingkou Vocational and Technical College, Xishi District, Yingkou City, Liaoning Province, China

Abstract: English teaching in higher vocational techcial colleges has certain particularity, so the English teaching mode of exam-oriented education should not be used. It should not imitate the college English teaching model of undergraduate colleges as well. It is necessary to pay more attention to students' actual English level and employment needs to formulate vocational college English teaching methods. Based on the analysis of the current situation of students' English learning and the common problems in English teaching in higher vocational technical colleges, this thesis explores some practical strategies for English teaching in higher vocational technical colleges and provides some new methods to improve the quality of English teaching and cultivate comprehensive English talents for English teachers in higher vocational colleges.

1. Introduction

Higher vocational technical colleges mainly train vocational talents for the society. The revised Vocational Education Law of the People's Republic of China in 2022 clearly states that "vocational education is a type of education with the same important status as general education." [1]That is also standardizes the development of higher vocational technical education.

With the continuous development of China's economy, the trade and economic exchanges between China and the other countries in the world are becoming more and more frequently. This not only brings more employment opportunities for job seekers, but also puts forward higher requirements for them. [2]Today's society no longer only needs a language translator, but needs the comprehensive English talents who understand the language, rules, management, vocational skills and so on.

Therefore, it is necessary to change traditional English teaching model to meet the growing needs of society and students. English teaching in higher vocational technical colleges should be social demand-oriented and provide versatile talents who understand both professional and English.

2. Current situation of English learning in higher vocational technical colleges

2.1. Students pay less attention to English learning

Most of the students in higher vocational technical colleges have lower admission scores and lower enthusiasm for learning. Especially for English learning, many students do not have enough confidence to learn English well. There are also some students who can't understand the content of the English class, then begin to give up on themselves. They are not interested in learning English, have no motivation to learn English. They feel that their major has nothing to do with English. They do not realize its importance to their future life and work. So many students show a lack of concentration in English class. They just want to learn a special skill that will help them earn a living.

2.2. Weak basic English skills and poor language learning environment

Most of the students in higher vocational technical colleges have less English vocabulary and grammar. Their listening and speaking skills in English are very limited as well. Because they used to study English mainly to cope with various examinations and ignore the importance of oral communication.

In vocational technical college, students usually receive English instruction for only 2-4 hours per week, so students do not have enough time to study English. In order to take care of the students' general English level, teacher can not always speak English in whole course, so students have very limited time to practice English communication. Students seldom learn English on their own initiative after English class.

Therefore, the phenomenon of "can not understand" and "can not speak" English has become more and more common among higher vocational students.

* jytls@126.com

3. Problems of English teaching in higher vocational technical colleges

3.1. The traditional English teaching model can not meet the requirements of learners

Teachers continue to use the traditional English teaching mode in the teaching process, which is difficult to stimulate students' interest in English learning. The English cultivating of students in higher vocational technical colleges mainly stays in the teaching mode of exam-oriented and passing English grade, which leads to the mentality of most students to learn English by taking the exam. [3]Teachers are used to focus on the cultivating of students' English, especially on reading, writing, translation, reciting words and so on, especially in the teaching process, teachers will spend a lot of time to lead students to learn English grammar knowledge, and learning grammar has become the key points to learn English well for many students. However, teacher do not have enough time to cultivate students' listening and speaking ability. In addition, the traditional final exam system has led students to hold a "pass long live" mentality, thus, the status of traditional English teaching mode is more deeply rooted, making students lose the purpose and focus of language learning - communication.

3.2. English teachers and teaching equipments are relatively backward

In recent years, higher vocational technical colleges continue to expand enrollment, while the number of teachers basically unchanged, resulting in a serious imbalance between the number of teachers and students. College English teaching gradually becomes "co-class teaching", with more than 50 students in each class. As a result, it is difficult for English teachers to have enough time to carry out whole-class English speaking and listening training.[4] In addition, the teaching equipments can not keep up with the teaching and students' needs, so many English teachers only rely on portable tape recorders for listening training. Therefore, English teaching quality can hardly be guaranteed.

3.3. English textbooks are out of line with students' majors

Teaching materials are the main basis for teachers to teach, so the appropriate teaching materials will benefit students, and vice versa. At present, the college English textbooks used by higher vocational colleges have unity, that is, no matter what major you are, you should use the same English textbook. This results in a disconnect between students' English knowledge and their major. Students can not use English to correspond to some key words of their own major. In the process of job hunting or employment in the future, if students need English for professional business communication, there will still be language barriers.

At present, English teaching materials which commonly used in higher vocational technical colleges still focus on vocabulary and grammar learning, and there are also many repeated contents in primary and secondary school textbooks, which is not conducive to the expansion of English knowledge of higher vocational technical students.[5] In addition, the English level of students in vocational technical colleges is uneven, and it is difficult for teachers to teach students according to their aptitude in the teaching process.

Therefore, the difficulty of choosing English teaching materials is generally medium, which leads to those students with weak English foundation, can not understand the teaching materials, and lack of confidence in learning English, however, students with good basic English skills will find the textbooks too simple and it is difficult to further improve their English level.

3.4. Lack of cross-cultural communication ability training for students

In the process of English teaching, teachers mainly teach language knowledge, and seldom cultivate students in cross-cultural communication knowledge. Even if there is, it is only a few minutes to talk about superficial comments, so very few students can realize the importance of learning cross-cultural communication. Language learning that ignores social background and humanistic etiquette is incomplete. If English teachers do not impart knowledge of Western culture and intercultural communication etiquette to students, it will inevitably lead to communication bottlenecks in real work exchanges in the future, and even cause cultural conflicts, which will affect the feelings of both Chinese and foreign parties.

4. Strategies of English teaching in higher vocational technical colleges

4.1. Clarify the purpose of English teaching in higher vocational technical colleges

Both teachers and students should change the traditional concept of English teaching and learning, and make it clear that the real purpose of learning English is to serve employment during the higher vocational technical colleges. All the English teaching activities should be employment demand-oriented. Teaching emphasis should focus on improving English language communication skills.[6] Only when students change their traditional test-oriented learning concept, truly realize the social needs and historical opportunities of English talents, and clearly realize that the actual English communication ability will affect their employment competitiveness, they can change their learning attitude, stimulate their learning interest and initiative, and grasp the essence of language training, and then transform the former "paper English language" ability into a language communication ability.

At the same time, teachers should encourage students to constantly expand their Enghish knowledge, combine language with vocational skills, and become a versatile talent who understands both English and majors.

4.2. Teach students according to their aptitude and make targeted teaching plans

As early as two thousand years ago, Confucius put forward the teaching concept of teaching students according to their aptitude. It means that according to the actual situation of students, teaching at different levels, promoting strengths and avoiding weaknesses[7], and carrying out targeted teaching activities, so that students can achieve all-round development to the maximum extent. Therefore, according to the English proficiency is uneven, we can make students carry out a survey test at the beginning of entering the school, then according to the test results, English courses can be divided into advanced classes, basic classes and zero-basic classes.

The advanced class mainly cultivates compound talents who are proficient in English and professional; the basic class mainly cultivates applied talents who can understand English materials and carry out daily oral English communication; zero-basic classes can start with simple English letters, cultivate students to regain their confidence in learning English, and develop students' ability to learn English independently as the goal.

In addition, it is necessary to adjust the capacity of students in English classes, which also helps teachers carry out whole-class English practical training, so that each student can get professional guidance, so as to ensure the effect of English teaching.

4.3. Update the curriculum and offer a variety of English teaching activities

English basic theory teaching aims at application, providing a variety of English teaching activities, and strengthening the pertinence and practicability of applied English teaching. The curriculum of higher vocational techcial colleges can get rid of the college English teaching mode of using unified textbooks[8], and there is no necessary to learn the public English teaching mode of undergraduate colleges. Therefore, vocational English curriculum can take into account the actual situation of regional economy and carry out targeted professional English teaching. Such as hotel English, aviation English and tourism English can be set up to meet students' future employment needs. It is also necessary to choose appropriate English textbooks according to different courses, and it is not necessary to unify the content and progress of college English teaching for all majors. Colleges can also set up college English test training courses, which can be divided into different levels of classes to meet the actual needs of students.

4.4. Choose the right English textbook and optimize the teaching content

Conventional English textbooks can no longer stimulate students' interest in English learning. Vocational English teaching materials should be different from the structure of primary and secondary school English teaching materials, and practice training should be the leading line of English teaching materials. At the same time, it is also necessary to combine the students' major and life, and incorporate the simulated scenario training into the English textbook.

Only to reform of English teaching materials thoroughly, English teaching content can be transformed from the traditional "word explanation + text translation + grammar analysis + after-class practice" completely. Only to make English teaching materials based on vocational needs, English teaching content can be tilted towards vocational skills, so that students can establish a strong sense of vocational role during college period. Only to make English teaching materials fit students' major and their life, English teaching content can stimulate students' interest in English learning and make students attach importance to English learning.

Vocational English teaching materials should fully reflect their practical application and professional pertinence, so that students can combine their major with English, apply what they have learned, and meet the development needs of the industry, and cultivate students to become comprehensive talents who understand both English and majors.

4.5. School-enterprise cooperation to cultivate precise English talents

"School-enterprise cooperation" is the main mode of vocational education personnel training and an effective way to cultivate vocational skilled talents. Usually, students learn professional theoretical knowledge in the first two years at school, and carry out internship training in the enterprise in the last year.

During the period of school, teachers can focus on developing students' ability to use English language and integrate vocational skills. At the same time, it is necessary to cultivate students' awareness of law-abiding, responsibility, integrity, quality and professionalism, and carry out professional quality education for students.[9] And then to improve students' ability to withstand pressure and frustration, and cultivate students' ability to communicate and cooperate with others.

During the internship period, students should focus on strengthening the core English communication skills, expanding vocational skills, stimulating the vocational potential, and cultivating professional ethics and innovative spirit. Professional internship should have both clear learning tasks and production tasks. English learning should be combined with production, and production should be linked with students' English learning. It is necessary to cooperate with enterprises to strengthen students' English knowledge and other vocational and technical abilities required for jobs, improve students' English level, so as to improve their employability.

4.6. Reform English teaching assessment model

It is very necessary to establish a new assessment standard for college English courses and to change the traditional assessment method based on final examination results.[10] In order to ensure that students can develop better skills and acquire English language, the assessment of English courses should include written, oral and listening tests and the proportion of process assessment should be increased. Teachers should lead students to learn English in new directions and make them pay more attention on English communication. Meanwhile to urge students stay in a continuous state of study, rather than cram for final exam results.

4.7. Construction of "double-qualified" English teachers

The progress of students cannot be separated from the guidance of good teachers.If we want to train students to become compound talents of "English + major", we should strengthen the construction of "double-qualified" English teachers. Students' English practice level is closely related to teachers' social practice ability. Colleges should encourage and support English teachers to improve their academic qualifications and vocational skills, especially strengthen teachers' practical teaching guidance ability, encourage English teachers to practice in enterprises or learn other professional skills, and obtain relevant vocational qualifications to improve their "English + other major" level.

In addition, the college can also hire professional from various industries to have lectures or trainings, specially cultivate English teachers to have other professional skills, and recommend English teachers to go to enterprises for field visits or short-term learning.

Strengthening the construction of "double-qualified" teachers will certainly help to train students to become English application-oriented talents and improve their employment competitiveness.

5. Conclusion

Most students in higher vocational colleges generally have negative emotions when learning English. If we want to reverse this situation, the first task is to change the traditional English teaching mode, make students have a new understanding of English, clarify the importantance of learning English for their future life and work, so as to stimulate students' initiative in learning English. At the same time, English teaching in higher vocational colleges should focus on English practice communication, so that students can carry out simple oral and written communication in the daily activities of foreign communication and various business activities, instead of blindly participating in the grade training and examination. Vocational English teachers should constantly update and improve their English teaching methods, keep pace with The Times, combine English knowledge with students' professional knowledge, and cultivate students to be comprehensive talents who understand both English and majors.

Therefore, we should pay high attention to English teaching strategies in higher vocational technical colleges, we should constantly innovate in exploration, and make continuous progress in innovation, so as to accurately transport valuable "English + professionals" talents for the society.

References

1. Fu, C.X. (2023) A Study on Exploration and Integration of Ideological-political Elements in College English Teaching—Taking New Horizon College English Reading and Writing 2 (3rd Edition) as an Example. Journal of Educational Research and Policies., 11:112-116.
2. Yan, Z. (2021) Exploration of English Teaching Strategies in Higher Vocational Colleges under the Background of NLA. In: 2021 International Conference on Modern Education, Management and Social Science Research. Chengdu. pp. 225-229.
3. Antonia, R. (2018) On Language Teaching. Journal of Classics Teaching., 19:53-57
4. Jiang, Y. (2022) Strategies of English Teaching in Higher Vocational Colleges Based on Different Dimensions of Kaplan Matrix. In: 2022 International Conference on Educational Innovation and Multimedia Technology. Hangzhou. pp. 556-565.
5. Xiaoli, H. (2023) Research on Strategies of Integrating Traditional Chinese Culture into Vocational English Teaching under the Background of Curriculum-based Ideological-politiccal Education. Journal of Social Science Humanities and Literature.,6: 161-164.
6. Shang, D. (2021) Exploration of Combining College English Teaching with Traditional Chinese Culture in Vocational Colleges. Journal of Jiamusi Vocational College.,10:170-171
7. Ron, D., Bonny, N. (2023) Investment and motivation in language learning: What's the difference?. Journal of Language Teaching., 56:29-40.
8. Wang, J. (2023) The role of college English teaching reform in overcoming students' learning anxiety disorders. CNS Spectrums., S2:47-47.
9. Yuko, G.B. (2023) Self-assessment in second language learning. Journal of Language Teaching.,1:1-15.
10. Asad, U.R (2020) Teachers' Teaching Reading Strategies at Public Elementary Schools in Haripur District. Journal of Creative Education.,11:468-478.

Reform of College English Vocabulary Teaching with the" Vocabulary Handout" as the Core from the Perspective of the Levels of Processing Theory

Hao Shen*

Shenyang Aerospace University, School of Foreign Languages, Shenyang, Liaoning Province, 110000 China

Abstract: Under the theoretical framework of Levels of Processing, this study designs and implements a university English vocabulary teaching model with the "Vocabulary Handout" at its core. This innovative vocabulary teaching model is driven by two testing sessions, selects vocabulary based on students' recent learning needs, and applies the Levels of Processing Theory to conduct shallow processing, deep processing, and elaborative processing on target words. The scientific design and implementation of university English vocabulary instruction have positively influenced the teaching and learning of vocabulary in the university context.

1. Introduction

In the absence of grammar, very little can be conveyed, but without vocabulary, nothing can be conveyed (Wilkins, 1972)[8]. This highlights the importance of English vocabulary in English learning. However, in the curriculum of non-English majors in universities, English vocabulary teaching is not an independent subject or course; it is merely an organic component of college English teaching (Huangbin, 2013)[5]. In many cases, due to the heavy workload and limited class hours of college English courses, English vocabulary teaching is often greatly compressed. Additionally, traditional English vocabulary teaching is often dull and students can hardly connect vocabulary they learnt with practical usage, leading to students' lack of interest in learning English vocabulary and teachers' being confronted with time-consuming but inefficient teaching dilemma. In light of this, many domestic scholars have conducted extensive research on English vocabulary teaching from different perspectives. Zhang Yingqiu (2005)[11] approached the study from the perspective of metacognition in science and technology and college English vocabulary teaching, Zhang Ping (2010)[9] studied the contrast of mental lexicon association patterns among English learners in China, and Gao Xiang (2013)[4] focused on traditional linguistic research on vocabulary, mainly examining the extension and change of word meanings from a diachronic perspective. However, in order to truly improve the effectiveness of vocabulary teaching and enhance students' learning interest, English vocabulary instruction needs to consider how to meet students' immediate learning needs and improve their vocabulary memory effects (Zhang & Wu, 2005)[10]. Therefore, this study is under the theoretical framework of Levels of Processing and designs college English vocabulary teaching from the perspective of memory processing.

This project is guided by the Levels of Processing Theory of cognitive psychology, which aims to propose a processing framework for memory. Since the beginning of the 21st century, second language acquisition has started to incorporate the research findings of contemporary cognitive psychology, and memory has been an important research topic in cognitive psychology (Luo & Zhao & Xing, 2016)[6]. Cognitive psychologists divide the memory process into three stages: information encoding, information storage, and information retrieval.(Atkinson & Shiffrin, 1968)[1]. Under the influence of the quality of second language input, learner's internal factors and task demands, information encoding (or information processing) affects the quality of information storage or the effectiveness of memory (Skehan, 1998)[7]. Information storage is further divided into three stages: sensory memory, short-term memory, and long-term memory. In order to improve memory effectiveness, based on the views of Atkinson and Shiffrin , Craik and Lockhart (1972)[2] proposed the Theory of Levels of Processing, which includes form-based processing and semantic-based processing, namely, shallow and deep processing. The former mainly involves reciting the pronunciation of words and copying words, while the latter goes through three stages: contextual processing, non-contextual processing, and re-contextual processing. Craik and Lockhart pointed out that the duration and effectiveness of memory retention depend on the different processing methods and the depth of processing. Building on the theoretical framework of Levels of Processing, Craik and Tulving (1975)[3] further proposed elaborative encoding strategies.

*103558969@qq.com

2. Methodology

2.1 Research Material

Participants: This study was conducted at a comprehensive university with 16 colleges and 50 majors. The university implements a stratified teaching approach for college English, dividing students into three levels (A, B, C) based on their performance in the College English Test Band 4. The research consisted of two rounds of teaching practices. In the first experimental teaching phase, the researcher applied the brand new model of college English vocabulary teaching to all students. In the second experimental teaching phase, two classes (501 and 520) were selected from the three A-level classes. The number of students in these two classes is similar and the students exhibited no significant differences in both the College English Test Band 4 scores and the previous semester's final English exam scores ($p > 0.05$). Class 501 was designated as the control group, while class 520 was assigned as the experimental group.

Textbooks: Throughout the study, *New Theme College English Integrated Course* Book Three and Book Four were used. This books were published by Changchun Publishing House and edited by university faculty members. Specifically, the third book of the series was employed during the experimental teaching phase, and the fourth book was utilized during the second experimental teaching phase. Each unit of the textbooks consisted of three sections: Section A, Section B, and Section C. Following the school's academic plan, the teaching process focused only on Section A of each unit and its key vocabulary. Section A articles from the first, third, fifth, sixth, and seventh units of the third book were selected, while Section A articles from the second, fourth, fifth, sixth, and seventh units of the fourth book were chosen. Each article in the textbooks was accompanied by numerous new words and phrases; however, the vocabulary list lacked cognitive fixation points, leading students to often overlook vocabulary learning.

2.2 Experimental Design

Research Questions: Under the guidance of the Levels of Processing Theory, this study conducted shallow, deep, and elaborative processing of English vocabulary. Corresponding vocabulary handouts were created for each unit taught in the reading class. Vocabulary instruction revolved around these handouts, overturning the traditional approach of randomly selecting vocabulary for classroom teaching. The study attempted to answer the following questions:

(1) How should vocabulary instruction be designed within the framework of Levels of Processing, considering the characteristics of English courses for non-English major students and their English proficiency?

(2) Does vocabulary instruction based on the Levels of Processing Theory have a positive impact on vocabulary learning?

Vocabulary Instruction Design

The vocabulary instruction in this study involved two teaching modes: traditional vocabulary instruction and vocabulary instruction centered around vocabulary handouts.

(1) Traditional Vocabulary Instruction:

The researcher selected unfamiliar words that could potentially affect students' reading comprehension based on previous teaching experience. The instruction included explanations of word roots, affixes, definitions, parts of speech, collocations, example sentences, and derived words. An immediate test was administered one week after students learned the vocabulary. The test consisted of memory-based questions and productive tasks, totaling 15 questions with a maximum score of 40. The memory-based questions assessed vocabulary definitions, word roots and affixes, synonyms and antonyms, and alternative words. A retention test was conducted two weeks after vocabulary learning, using the same test format and scoring system as the immediate test. The retention test retained the questions with lower scores from the immediate test and included some other new questions.

(2) Vocabulary Handout Mode:

Design of Vocabulary Handouts: This innovative college English vocabulary teaching mode, guided by the Theory of Levels of processing, centered around vocabulary handouts. The design of the handouts took into consideration students' recent learning needs. The handouts covered shallow, deep, and elaborative processing of key vocabulary, and included two tests as task requirements to actively engage students in vocabulary learning.

Target Words: The vocabulary handouts highlighted the key vocabulary (i.e., target words) from Unit Section A of the course text (Table 1), based on students' recent learning needs. The researcher taught Class A students at the A-level, and their recent learning needs were focused on preparing for the College English Test Band 6 (CET-6). Therefore, the selection of vocabulary for the handouts was based on words that belong to the CET-6 vocabulary, with a preference for high-frequency words in the past five years of CET-6 exams (frequency indicated in the upper right side of each word). The design of target words took into consideration students' learning needs, aiming to draw their attention to vocabulary and stimulate their enthusiasm for learning.

Table 1 Vocabulary Handout (Excerpt)

	outset[1]	**bully**[3]	**potent**[1]	**initiative**[9]1
Word-building	out-: outside set: to put		-pot-: capable of -ent: *adj.* ending	
Word in context	I made it clear right from the outset that I disapproved.	1. That's a bully idea for reviving the town's retail center. 2. the school bully	1. a potent force 2. a potent tea	1. a United Nations peace initiative 2. She did it on her own initiative.

<table>
<tr><td></td><td></td><td>3. My son is being bullied at school.</td><td></td><td></td></tr>
<tr><td>Definition</td><td></td><td></td><td></td><td></td></tr>
<tr><td>Word form</td><td></td><td></td><td></td><td></td></tr>
<tr><td>Synonym/antonym</td><td></td><td></td><td></td><td></td></tr>
<tr><td>Collocation</td><td></td><td></td><td></td><td></td></tr>
<tr><td>Alternative word</td><td>×</td><td>n.</td><td>n.</td><td>n.</td></tr>
<tr><td colspan="5"><u>Definition:</u>
1. very effective and powerful
2. at/from the beginning of sth
<u>Synonym & antonym</u>
1.robust/rich/strong/concentrated/heady/mild/weak/light/thin/delicate/powerful/influential/significant/impotent/weak/powerless/insignificant/feeble/unimportant
2.[a.] great/terrific/excellent/wonderful/prime/awesome/superb/fabulous/fantastic/vile/terrible/awful/bad
[n.]intimidator/abuser/harasser/hector [v.]abuse/oppress/mistreat/injure/care for/foster/nurture/cherish
<u>Collocation</u>
1.[n.]big ~/real ~/class ~/school ~/playground ~
[v.]~ sb into doing sth/~ sb into sth
2.at/from the ~ of sth.</td></tr>
</table>

Utilization of vocabulary handouts: Firstly, the vocabulary handouts provided target words, pronunciation symbols, and example sentences. Students were required to infer the part of speech of the target words based on the example sentences. The English definitions, synonyms, and antonyms, as well as common collocations of the target words, were arranged in a random order, and students needed to analyze and fill in the blanks. These designs took into consideration reducing students' academic burden and avoiding students resorting to searching for unauthoritative knowledge content online. Secondly, other elements such as word roots, affixes, and cognates required students to consult dictionaries and filled in the information themselves. This design aimed to stimulate students' subjective initiative. The vocabulary handouts were in full English version, avoiding students' excessive reliance on Chinese in English learning.

Test Mode: The tests consisted of immediate tests and retention tests. The immediate test was conducted one week after students have studied the vocabulary handouts. The test included memory-based questions and productive tasks, totaling 15 questions with a maximum score of 40. The memory-based questions assessed vocabulary definitions, word roots and affixes, synonyms and antonyms, and alternative words. Among them, definitions, word roots and prefixes, and synonyms and antonyms were multiple-choice questions, where students selected the correct definition, vocabulary, or affix from four options provided. The alternative words question was a subjective question that required students to spell words based on the question's requirements.

The retention test was conducted two weeks after students have studied the vocabulary handouts. The test format and scoring system were the same as the immediate test. The retention test retained the questions with lower scores from the immediate test and included additional new questions.

Teaching Process: The teaching process of the new English vocabulary instruction mode was as follows: One week before teaching a new unit, the vocabulary handouts were distributed to students for self-study and preview. In the first class, the researcher used Rainclass platform to administer an immediate test based on the vocabulary handouts. The researcher gave lecture on vocabulary which students didn't grasp well. After class, the answer to the vocabulary handouts was provided. In the second class, the researcher continued to use Rainclass platform to administer a retention test based on the vocabulary handouts, keeping the questions with lower scores from the first test and adding new questions. The researcher provided further classroom explanations for the vocabulary with lower scores in the test. The researcher reflected on the vocabulary instruction.

Research Procedure: This study went through two rounds of teaching practices: an exploratory teaching phase (first round) and an experimental teaching phase (second round). In the exploratory teaching phase, the researcher employed the college English vocabulary instruction mode centered around vocabulary handouts, guided by the Theory of Levels of Processing levels, in all the A-level classes. At the end of the phase, students' opinions and suggestions were collected to guide the next round of teaching. In the experimental teaching phase, the researcher further refined the new college English vocabulary instruction mode based on the feedback received in the previous phase. One control class and one experimental class were selected from the classes taught. The control class followed the traditional teaching mode, where key vocabulary was selected for classroom instruction based on the teacher's experience. The experimental class adopted the college English vocabulary instruction mode centered around vocabulary handouts. Vocabulary tests were regularly conducted for both classes, and at the end of the semester, an independent samples t-test was performed to compare the average scores of all vocabulary tests conducted throughout the semester, aiming to evaluate the instructional effectiveness of the two vocabulary teaching modes.

2.3 Data Collection

Data collection was divided into two phases, lasting for two semesters. The first phase was the exploratory teaching phase, primarily using questionnaire surveys to extensively collect students' acceptance, opinions, and suggestions regarding the new vocabulary teaching mode centered around vocabulary handouts. This data served as support and guidance for the second phase of experimental teaching. The second phase was the experimental teaching phase, which involved conducting immediate tests and retention tests throughout one semester in both the control class (501) and the experimental class (520) for five teaching units. The average scores of these tests were subjected to an independent samples t-test to observe the teaching effectiveness of the new vocabulary teaching mode and provided guidance for subsequent vocabulary instruction.

2.4 Data Analysis

Exploratory Teaching Phase: During this phase, a computer program called "Wenjuanxing" was used to collect extensive opinions from students. The researcher created a satisfaction survey questionnaire specifically for the new vocabulary teaching mode centered around vocabulary handouts. The questionnaire consisted of five multiple-choice questions and one open-ended question. The overall satisfaction of students with the new vocabulary teaching mode centered around vocabulary handouts reached 93.55%. Regarding the design of various parts of the vocabulary handouts, including the selection criteria for target words based on recent learning needs, matching of synonyms and antonyms, vocabulary collocation, and satisfaction with the all-English mode, the satisfaction rates were 93.55%, 83.87%, 83.87%, and 64.51% respectively. In addition, the participating students provided many constructive opinions and suggestions. For example, student 16 suggested "providing memory techniques for vocabulary in the handouts," student 67 suggested "increasing the number of target words in the handouts," and student 134 suggested "adding example sentences in the vocabulary collocation section."

Experimental Teaching Phase: During this phase, the researcher used SPSS software to perform an independent samples t-test on the average scores of all immediate tests and retention tests conducted throughout one semester in the control class (501) and the experimental class (520). Firstly, a comparison was made between the average scores of the control class (501) and the experimental class (520) in the immediate tests and retention tests to examine whether there were differences in teaching effectiveness between the traditional vocabulary teaching mode and the new vocabulary teaching mode (Table 2). Then, a separate comparison was made between the immediate test scores and retention test scores of the control class (501) (Table 3) and the experimental class (520) (Table 4) to determine which teaching mode, traditional or new, was more conducive to vocabulary retention.

Table 2 Comparison between the average scores of the control class and the experimental class

Test Variable	Class	Number of Cases	Average Value	Standard Deviation	t	Sig.
Immediate Test	501	38	29.95	6.920	-3.984	0.000162
	520	35	35.43	4.461		
Retention Test	501	38	26.26	8.526	-4.826	0.000008
	520	35	34.06	4.485		

Table 3 Comparison between the immediate test scores and retention test scores of the control class

Test Variable	Class	Number of Cases	Average Value	Standard Deviation	t	Sig.
Immediate Test	501	38	29.95	6.920	2.068	0.042
Retention Test	501	38	26.26	8.526		

Table 4 Comparison between the immediate test scores and retention test scores of the experimental class

Test Variable	Class	Number of Cases	Average Value	Standard Deviation	t	Sig.
Immediate Test	520	35	35.43	4.461	1.283	0.204
Retention Test	520	35	34.06	4.485		

3. Research Results

Based on the results of the survey questionnaire collected during the first round of exploratory teaching, students show a high level of satisfaction with the new university English vocabulary teaching model, which focuses on vocabulary handouts, with a satisfaction rate of 93.55%. Students generally recognize the role of vocabulary handouts in stimulating vocabulary learning motivation and interest, with 96.78% of students believing that they are effective. This provides support and a foundation for the sustainable development of the vocabulary teaching model centered around vocabulary handouts in future English teaching, including the next round of experimental teaching. Additionally, after experiencing the first round of teaching, students provide many suggestions and recommendations for the new vocabulary teaching model. Based on these suggestions, the researchers make modifications to the vocabulary handouts, including: 1) increasing the number of target words from 15 to 20 from the first round of teaching; 2) incorporating the method of memorizing word roots and affixes into the vocabulary handouts. The researchers provided commonly used word roots and affixes related to the target words in the vocabulary handouts; 3) adding a large number of example sentences with Chinese translations in the vocabulary collocation section to help students better understand the usage of vocabulary.

Based on the test results calculated through SPSS software after the second round of experimental teaching, over the course of one semester, in vocabulary tests for five teaching units, the experimental class (520) consistently outperform the control class (501) in both immediate and retention tests. From a two-tailed perspective, the control class (501) shows a significant difference between immediate and retention test scores, with immediate test scores being much higher than retention test scores, indicating that students' English vocabulary retention was not ideal. The experimental class (520) shows no significant difference between immediate and retention test scores, with immediate test scores only slightly higher than retention test scores, indicating that students' English vocabulary retention was relatively solid and lasting. According to the results of independent samples t-tests, the traditional vocabulary teaching model is not effective in helping students learn and retain vocabulary. On the other hand, the new vocabulary teaching model centered around vocabulary handouts is far more effective than the traditional vocabulary teaching model in helping students master vocabulary usage and improve vocabulary retention. It plays a positive role in students' English vocabulary learning.

4. Discussion

The traditional university English vocabulary teaching model mainly relies on teachers' teaching experience as the main reference for selecting target words, which does not align well with students' learning needs. As a result, students lack clear goals and motivation for vocabulary learning. Moreover, the traditional vocabulary teaching methods predominantly involve teacher-centered vocabulary lectures, and students are mostly passive recipients of knowledge, without actively participating in the learning process. As a result, students have poor vocabulary usage and retention.

The new university English vocabulary teaching model, with vocabulary handouts as its core, incorporates two tests after each unit, namely immediate and retention tests, which effectively encourage students to study and process vocabulary information seriously. By selecting target words based on students' recent learning needs, the model greatly enhances students' emphasis on vocabulary, thereby improving their learning motivation. The vocabulary handouts contain information such as word roots, affixes, definitions, synonyms, antonyms, and collocations, which require students to consult dictionaries for learning and fill in the tables in the handouts. The teacher provides accurate and reasonable choices, thereby maximizing students' subjective initiative and cultivating their autonomous learning ability. The handouts cover various aspects of vocabulary processing, including shallow and deep processing, as well as elaborative processing, which comprehensively help students understand, use, and remember vocabulary. The vocabulary teaching model centered around vocabulary handouts adopts a pre-class distribution and preview, in-class tests and focused vocabulary explanations, and post-class review mode, effectively addressing the problem of time-consuming and inefficient vocabulary teaching.

It is worth noting that the university English vocabulary teaching model centered around vocabulary handouts emphasizes student autonomous learning, with teacher explanations serving as guidance and assistance. During the implementation of the research, the researchers found that some students lacked autonomy in their independent learning and were dependent on the classroom environment. Therefore, in future teaching, it may be beneficial to encourage students to engage in group learning, where students with different levels of autonomy are grouped together. Students can work collaboratively in groups before the class, with the aim of promoting collaborative learning and progress, and enhancing the effectiveness of vocabulary learning.

5. Conclusion

This study applies the Levels of Processing Theory to analyze students' language learning and memory processes, focusing on the relationship between vocabulary and cognition, as well as vocabulary and psychology. From the perspective of enhancing vocabulary memory through cognitive processing, the researchers scientifically design and implement English vocabulary teaching, aiming to maximize students' vocabulary size within the limited teaching time, improve students' motivation for vocabulary learning, and enhance their vocabulary retention. The study has had a positive impact and driving force on the teaching and learning of university English vocabulary.

References

1. Atkinson, R. C. & R. M. Shiffrin. Human Memory: A Proposed System and Its Control Process[M]/ /In W. K. Spence & J. T.Spence. The Psychology of Learning and Motivation: Advances in Research and Theory (Vol. 1). New York: Academic Press, 1968.
2. Craik, F. I. M. & R. S. Lockhart. Levels of Processing: A Framework for Memory Research [J]. Journal of Verbal Learning and Verbal Behavior, 1972(11): 671-684.
3. Craik, F. I. M. & E. Tulving. Depth of Processing and the retention of Words in Episodic Memory. [J] Journal of Experimental Psychology:General Vol.104,1975.
4. Gao Xiang. On the Vocabulary Acquisition from a Cognitive Perspective [J]. Journal of Central South University of Forestry & Technology (Social Sciences), 2013 (4): 131-134.
5. Huangbing. College English Vocabulary Teaching Based on Information Processing Theory. [J]. Journal of Hubei University for Nationalities (Philosophy and Social Sciences),2013(3):150-153.
6. Luo Shaoqian, Zhao Haiyong, Xing Jiaxin. English Vocabulary Teaching [M]. Nanning: Guangxi Education Publishing House. 2016.
7. Skehan P. A Cognitive Approach to Language Learning [M]. Oxford: Oxford University, 1998.
8. Wilkins D. Linguistics in Language Teaching [M]. London: Edward Arnold, 1972: 111.
9. Zhang Ping. A Comparative Study of Mental Lexicon and Association Patterns of Chinese English Learners [J].Foreign Language Teaching and Research, 2010(1): 9-15.

10. Zhang Qingzong, Wu Xiyan. Cognitive Processing Levels and Foreign Language Vocabulary Learning -- Vocabulary Cognition Direct Method learning [C]. Hu Wenzhong. Essays on Excellent English Teaching in China (1). Beijing: Foreign Language Teaching and Research Press, 2005: 166-182.
11. Zhang Yingqiu. Metacognition in Science and Technology and English Vocabulary Teaching in College [J]. Foreign Languages and Foreign Language Teaching, 2005(6): 26-28.

A Correlation Study of Individual Differences Factors and Oral Chinese Learning Strategies: A Survey Based on Sri Lankan Learners

Bo Yu*

International College of Chinese Language and Culture, Chongqing Normal University Chongqing, China

Abstract. Individual differences of learners will affect foreign language learners' use of learning strategies. This study focuses on Chinese learners in Sri Lanka, and analyzes the correlation between their age, gender, length of time and oral language learning strategies. The results showed that there was no significant difference in the use of learning strategies among learners of different genders; with the increase of age, the frequency of overall use of strategies showed a downward trend; the frequency of use of cognitive strategies, compensation strategies and affective strategies increased with learning length while increasing, the frequency of use of meta-cognitive strategies, memory strategies and social strategies decreased with the increase of learning length.

1. Introduction

In foreign language learning, individual and social factors jointly affect learners' learning behavior or learning strategies, which in turn affect foreign language learning effects (Ellis, 1994). The study of individual differences of learners helps to reveal the nature of language acquisition and helps to discover which individual differences of learners are related to the achievement of language acquisition. Vermetten et al. (2001) believed that individual differences in the use of learning strategies were affected by factors such as personality traits, learning styles, learning concepts, and learning motivations[1]. Generally speaking, the individual factors of learners are relatively stable and not easy to change, such as age, gender, personality, attitude and motivation. By carefully understanding the individual differences of learners, foreign language teachers can better teach according to the characteristics of students to improve the level of teaching. This research focuses on learners who learn Chinese as a foreign language to discuss the correlation between their individual differences and strategies for learning oral Chinese.

2. Literature review

There have been many research results on the influence of individual differences on learning strategies. For example, children mostly use simple strategies for specific learning tasks, while adults often flexibly use complex general strategies (O'Malley &Chamot, 1990); Learners with language potential are better at describing their own strategies (Skehan, 1989); Learning style is also closely related to learning strategies, and the strength of learning motivation is directly related to the number of learning strategies used (Oxford, 1989); Extroverted learners tend to adopt affective and visual strategies and are better than introverted learners in acquiring basic interpersonal skills (Ehrman 1990). In the field of Learning Chinese as a foreign language, Jiang Xin (2000) investigated the correlation between students' natural characteristics and the use of Chinese learning strategies[2]. Xu Ziliang (2006) specifically studied the differences in the use of learning strategies among Chinese learners with different cognitive styles[3]. The correlation analysis of individual factors and learning strategies mentioned above is not comprehensive enough. Li Qiang et al. (2011) discussed the correlation between Chinese learners' gender, age, mother tongue, duration of Learning, Chinese proficiency and Chinese learning strategies. The results showed that age was the main individual factor affecting the overall use of Chinese learning strategies, the use of direct strategies was affected by gender and Chinese level, the use of indirect strategies was mainly affected by Chinese level, and other individual factors have no significant impact on the use of learning strategies [4].

In recent years, there have been some Master's thesis studies on the oral learning strategies of Chinese learners from different countries, such as Wu Xuan (2021), Zeng Andi (2019), Zhang Ruonan (2019) etc. In other journal papers, there are mainly studies on learning strategies of Central Asian countries [5], American learners[6] and Thai learners[7]. There are few researches on oral Chinese learning strategies of South Asian learners. Yu Wenbo et al. studied the oral Chinese learning strategies of South Asian students studying Chinese in Yunnan [8].

* Corresponding author's email: 20130496@cqnu.edu.cn

In terms of research methods, the existing research is generally quantitative research, or the combination of quantitative and qualitative research. In recent years, qualitative research has also become active, and many aspects of oral strategy learning research have been carried out [9].

There is a boom in Chinese learning in the world, and the demand for oral Chinese learning is also relatively strong. The strategies for oral Chinese learning are also limited to regions or countries where Chinese teaching and research are widely carried out, such as Southeast Asia, Europe and the United States, some African countries. This research hopes to take Sri Lankan Chinese learners as the research object, to investigate the correlation between gender, age, learning length and oral Chinese learning strategies, and to enrich the content of country-specific research in this field.

3. Methodology

3.1. Participants

Participants of this study were 50 Sri Lankan learners studying Chinese at the Confucius Institute in University of Kelaniya, Sri Lanka. There were 19 males and 31 females. The youngest of the participants was 16 years old, the oldest was 60 years old, and the ages were mainly concentrated between 16 to 22. They study Chinese for 1 to 12 months. Among them, there are 38 learners who study for 2 to 3 months, accounting for 76%.

3.2. Research Question

This research mainly discussed the influence of three individual factors of gender, age, and length of study on the oral learning of elementary-level Chinese learners in Sri Lanka.

3.3. Instruments

The research mainly adopts Strategy Inventory for Language Learning (SILL, v5.1) compiled by Oxford (1990). SILL has been recognized as a standard scale with good reliability and validity [10].

SILL was modified in this study. In order to make the scale more suitable for Chinese learners, topics irrelevant to oral Chinese learning were deleted and 60 strategy questions were finally obtained. For statistical convenience, each strategy is replaced by a different letter, see Table 1. (use simplified letters instead of strategies).

The options of the questionnaire use a five-point scale, and the results of the questionnaire are mainly analyzed by SPSS software.

Table 1 Item distribution

Strategy	alternate letters	number of items
meta-cognitive strategies	A	15
cognitive strategies	B	16
memory strategies	C	9
social strategies	D	7
compensation strategies	E	6
affective strategies	F	7
Total		60

4. Data collection and analysis

4.1. Correlation between gender and strategy use

In the present study, the independent sample T test was used to compare the gender differences in six learning strategies. The T test is to compare the means of different data to investigate whether there is a significant difference between the two data sets. The results of this test are shown in the table 2.

Table 2 Frequency of strategy selection by gender

Strat egy	Male		Female		T	p
	Mea n	Standard deviation	Mea n	Standard deviation		
A	3.63	0.69	3.55	0.61	0.393	0.6 96
B	3.30	0.69	3.46	0.49	-0.967	0.3 38
C	3.46	0.87	3.47	0.70	-0.044	0.9 65
D	3.36	0.80	3.26	0.76	0.436	0.6 65
E	3.46	0.80	3.39	0.78	0.301	0.7 65
F	3.08	0.88	3.12	0.80	-0.184	0.8 55

From the test results, it is identified that there was no gender difference in the scores of the six learning strategies, $p > 0.05$. Although there are no significant differences, there are still differences in strategy choices between male and female.

The results were ranked by average scores, from highest to lowest, to show subtle differences between the sexes in the use of different strategies. The ranks of male using learning strategies are: meta-cognitive strategies, memory strategies, supplementary strategies, social strategies, cognitive strategies, and affective strategies. Female use slightly different strategies. (see table 3)

Table 3 Ranking by frequency of gender use strategies

Male	Strate gy	A	C	E	D	B	F
	Mean	3.62 8	3.45 6	3.45 6	3.36 1	3.29 9	3.07 5
Fema le	Strate gy	A	C	B	E	D	F
	Mean	3.55 4	3.46 6	3.46 1	3.38 7	3.26 3	3.12 0

Male and female used meta-cognitive strategies and memory strategies the most, used affective strategies the least often. Male were slightly different from female.

Male were more likely to use compensation strategies than female, and female were more likely to use cognitive strategies than male.

4.2. Correlation between age and strategy use

According to the age distribution of Chinese learners in Sri Lanka, they were divided into three groups: 16 to 19 years old; 20 to 30 years old ; over 31 years old.

The six types of strategies used by participants at different ages are shown in the table 4 :

Table 4 Strategies used by learners of different ages

Age group	A	B	C	D	E	F
16-19 (N=15)	3.599	3.045	3.341	3.42	3.433	3.03 3
20-30 (N=28)	3.614	3.393	3.642	3.275	3.488	3.27 8
over31 (N=7)	3.476	3.143	3.00	3.124	3.071	2.52

According to the average score, the use strategies of each age group are arranged from high to low as follows table 5:

Table 5 Frequency ranking of different age groups

Age group	frequency ranking					
16-19	A	E	D	C	B	F
20-30	C	A	E	B	F	D
over31	A	D	B	C	E	F

The results showed that the frequency of using affective strategies was lower in different age groups, especially those over 31 years old. Meta-cognitive strategy scores were higher in all age groups, especially in the 16 to 19 age group. From the changes in the mean value, the frequency of strategy use tends to decrease with age. For example, the mean value of social strategy is 3.42 for the group aged 16 to 19, 3.275 for the group aged 20 to 30, and 3.124 for the group aged over 31, indicating that social strategy will decrease with age. The group of 20 to 30 years old used learning strategies most frequently. Learners in this age group have strong learning awareness and can use various strategies to learn Chinese.

4.3. Correlation between learning length and strategy use

Participants were divided into two groups: learning Chinese for 1 to 3 months; learning time for 4 months to 1 year.

In this study, the two groups of learners who have studied for different length have different frequency of using various strategies. The frequency of use of cognitive strategies, compensation strategies and affective strategies increased with the increase of learning time, while the frequency of use of meta-cognitive strategies, memory strategies and social strategies decreased with the increase of learning time.

Participants in the first group (1-3 months) used meta-cognitive strategies the most and affective strategies the least. Participants in the second group (4months to 1 year) used compensation strategies the most and social strategies the least. As show in table 6:

Table 6 Use of strategies for different learning length groups

Learning length	A	B	C	D	E	F
1-3 months (N=39)	3.64 4	3.38 4	3.50 9	3.35 8	3.39 7	3.07 3
4 months To 1 year (N=11)	3.36 3	3.45 4	3.29 2	3.09 0	3.46 9	3.20 8

5. Conclusion

There was no significant difference in the use of six types of oral learning strategies among learners of different genders. This result is consistent with the research of Jiang Xin (2000), Li Jiang (2007), etc., but it is inconsistent with the results of some second language learning studies. For example, Politzer (1983) found that gender is related to the use of learning strategies. Female use learning strategies more often than male, especially social strategies. Female college students participate in extra-curricular second language social activities more than male of the same age, and they also use social strategies more frequently[11]. Wen Qiufang and Wang Lifei (2004) surveyed on the relationship between gender and learning strategies showed that women were more likely to use social strategies than men, and men were more likely to use compensation strategies than women. Their research showed that men tend to be field-independent, and they preferred to think independently and solve problems on their own; instead, women were more field-dependent, and they liked to find and solve problems in communication and exchange[12]. It can be seen that this study has similar conclusions to other studies, but also has different conclusions.

In this study, meta-cognitive strategies were used more frequently in all age groups, especially in the 20 to 30 age group. Affective strategies were used less frequently in different age groups, especially those over 31 years of age. With the increase of age, the frequency of overall use of the strategy had a downward trend, such as social strategies, indicating that social strategies will decrease with age. The 20 to 30 age group used learning strategies most often. It can be seen that learners in this age group have a strong sense of learning and can use various strategies to learn Chinese.

Jiang Xin (2000) believed that there was a significant correlation between Chinese learning time and cognitive strategies. After about one year of study, students' use of cognitive strategies began to increase, but the use of other strategies remained unchanged. In this study, the use frequency of various strategies of the two groups of learners who studied at different length was different. The use frequency of cognitive strategy, compensation strategy and affective strategy increased with the increase of learning length, but the use frequency of meta-cognitive strategy, memory strategy and social strategy decreased with the increase of learning length. The difference in results may be due to the fact that Jiang xin's study highlighted a gap in learning time of more than a year, while this study mainly examined changes in learners within a year.This may also be caused by the difference between target language environment and non-target language environment, which is worth further study. YE Wanlin and Tan Dingliang (2020) concluded that learners use learning strategies selectively in different learning stages. Within a certain time span, Chinese learning strategies develop nonlinearly. Learners' strategy use is closely related to cognitive level and problem context. It is concluded that understanding learners' choice and development of Chinese learning strategies in different learning periods and carrying out targeted strategic interventions can reduce learners' cognitive load and improve the effectiveness of Chinese learning and teaching[13].

In the process of foreign language learning, learners should correctly use learning strategies to achieve ideal results. When teaching oral Chinese, Chinese teachers should pay attention to helping students use memory strategies reasonably and memorize new words and texts quickly. It is necessary to correctly guide students to use compensation strategies to help students form correct oral study habits. In addition, Sri Lankan elementary-level learners did not pay much attention to the use of affective strategies in the process of oral Chinese learning, and did not have a good way to overcome the nervousness of direct communication with native speakers. Teachers should create opportunities for students to speak more in oral classes.

Learners need to gradually improve their use of cognitive strategies. They should actively communicate with native Chinese speakers to create conditions for the use of social strategies. Meta-cognitive strategies should be full use, which can help learners arrange and adjust their learning process effectively.

Acknowledgment

Many thanks to the students who participated in this study, whose cooperation made the data collection go smoothly. It was supported by Chongqing Normal University [grant number 23XWB013]; Center for Language Education and Cooperation, Ministry of Education of the People's Republic of China [grant number 22YH15C].

References

1. Vermetten, Y. J. , Lodewijks, H. G. , & Vermunt, J. D . (2001). The role of personality traits and goal orientations in strategy use. *Contemporary Educational Psychology,* 26(2), 149-170.
2. Jiang Xin. (2000). A preliminary study on Chinese as a second language learning strategy. *Language Teaching and Linguistic Studies*.(1):61
3. Xu Ziliang.(1999).A cognitive psychological analysis of foreign students' Chinese learning strategies. *Chinese teaching in the world*,(4):75-85
4. LiQiang,Yao Yiru,Liu Naizhong. (2011). A Correlation Study of Chinese Learning Strategies and Individual Factors. *Language teaching and linguistic studies*.(1):41-47R. Nicole, "Title of paper with only first word capitalized," J. Name Stand. Abbrev., in press.
5. Zhang Li-rui& Wan ying.(2019).On the Chinese Learning Strategies Employed by Foreign Students from Five Central Asian Countries. Chinese Language Learning.(02):94-104
6. Li Na.(2021).Strategies for US University Students'Chinese Language Learning as a Foreign Language.Journal of Yichun University.(43):68-74
7. Yu Xiao yu.(2020).An Investigation and Analysis on Chinese Learning Strategies of Thai Government Officials in China. Journal of Huaqiao University(Philosophy & Social Sciences).(04):53-62
8. Yu Wen-bo, Naimul, DU He, ZHANG Ming-lei, SUN Wen-jie.(2019).Investigation and Research on the Strategies of Foreign Students Learning Spoken Chinese in South Asian Countries.Management & Technology of SME.(07):68-69
9. Liu Hong-ying.(2020).A Qualitative Study of Learning Strategies of Advanced Oral Language Adopted by Foreign Students.Journal of Zhejiang Business Technology Institute.(19):69-71
10. Oxford, R. and Nyikos, M. (1989). Variables Affecting Choice of Language Learning Strategies by University Students. *Modern Language Journal*, 73, 291-300.
11. Politzer, & Robert, L. . (1983). An exploratory study of self reported language learning behaviors and their relation to achievement. Studies in Second Language Acquisition, 6(01), 54-68.
12. Wen, Q.F. & Wang Lifei.(2004).Review of Various Factors Affecting the Operation of Foreign Language Learning Strategy System. *Foreign languages and their teaching*.(9):28-32
13. Ye Wanlin,TAN Dingliang.(2022).Dynamic Selection and Development of Strategies in Learning Chinese as a Second Language:A longitudinal Study.(02):65-75

Statistical analysis of Bach's Well-tempered Clavier

Gen-Fang Chen*

Zhejiang Conservatory of Music, Hangzhou, Zhejiang Province, 310024, China

Abstract: Bach's Well-tempered Clavier is the greatest work of Bach keyboard music, it contains 48 preludes and fugue, it is one of Bach's representative works of music creation. This paper firstly inputs MIDI data of Bach's Well-tempered Clavier, and then constructs the analysis model of Bach's Well-tempered Clavier. The experimental results show that the envelope of the number of occurrences of each musical note is in the shape of a double hump, indicating that the statistical number of musical notes played by the right hand or the left hand should be in the shape of a single camel peak in the musical range.

1. Introduction

The best known of Bach's clavier works is the famous set of preludes and fugues called The Well-Tempered Clavier. Part I was completed at Cöthen in 1722, and Part II was completed at Leipzig around 1740. Each part consists of twenty-four preludes and fugues, one prelude and one fugue in each of the twelve major and minor keys.

Bach's Well-tempered Clavier stands at the core of baroque keyboard music and has been a model and inspiration for performers and composers ever since it was written. It contains 48 preludes and fugues, it is the peak of Bach's musical creation, the work has an important position in the western music world[1], commonly known in English as the 48 preludes and fugues, are at the centre of European civilisation, and are the beloved property of generations of people all over the world. Hans Guido Von Bullow likened it to the musical "Old Testament bible"[2].

The Well-tempered Clavier is a collection of two pieces written by Bach for keyboard instruments, the first of which was completed around 1722 and was mainly used for teaching purposes. The second was assembled in Leipzig in 1740. Each episode has 24 preludes and fugues in 24 major and minor keys. Each prelude is in the same key as the fugue, but the theme is not related. The prelude is free in form and the fugue shows Bach's superb contrapuntal creation skills. the Well-tempered Clavier confirmed the superiority of the Well Temper, further established the western mode of large and small, for the creation of the equal temperament, set up a model, its influence is extremely far-reaching.

Due to its outstanding status in the field of music and art, the research on Bach's Well-tempered Clavier has been a hot topic with abundant research results and materials. As of June 2022, known in China online (www.cnki.net) queries to related to the average of the piano theme 132 papers, which involved the texts of Bach's Well-tempered Clavier fugue related with 50 references, prelude to related with 45 references, the average law related with 22 references, and works BWV849 related with 13 references, There are 13 literature related to polyphonic music, 11 literatures related to piano music, 11 literatures related to keyboard instruments, 8 literatures related to duotemperament, 6 literatures related to homophonic music, 5 literatures related to polyphonic works, and many literatures related to other topics. At the research level, basic research accounted for the majority, with 94 and 24 literary works.

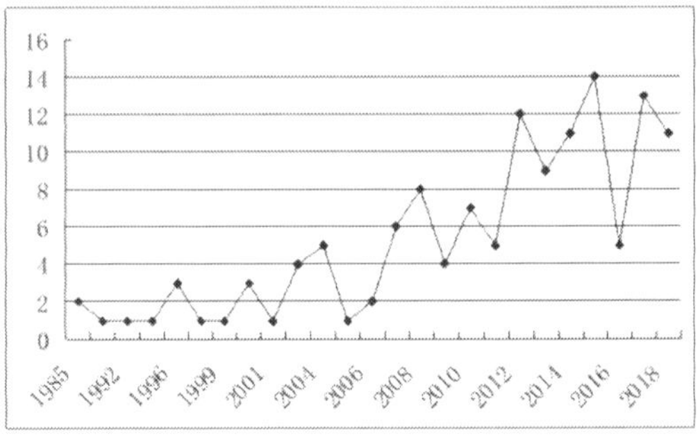

Figure 1. The number of documents of Bach's Well-tempered Clavier by CNKI in recent 35 years.

In www.cnki.net, the most recent 35 years the average piano album in related research results shows the tendency of increase year by year, visible Figure 1 the research achievements of the average of the piano, increasing in number, from the nineties of the 20th century random single digits, research achievements to the 21st century in the past ten years, In the past ten years, the annual number of achievements reached about ten pieces, and the researchers' research enthusiasm for Bach's Well-tempered Clavier increased with each passing day.

*Corresponding author's email: genfangchen@163.com

In the research literature about Bach's Well-tempered Clavier, the researchers have studied the historical influence, creation techniques, performance techniques, educational methods, fugue, prelude and so on. Pan Jie [3] expounded the rigor and accuracy of fugue structural thinking, as well as the historical origin and social background of the formation of such thinking mode through the analysis of fugue in Bach's Well-tempered Clavier. It shows that the fugue in the baroque period is the concentrated embodiment of the rationalist thinking mode of European music.

In terms of influence, Ye Dongying [4] believes that Bach's great influence on later generations is self-evident in western classical music. It is no exaggeration to call him the father of music. Although Beethoven has "music saint", but in his later years, Beethoven increasingly revered Bach, in the works more and more frequent use of fugue and other polyphonic techniques, showing traces of imitation of Bach. From Polish piano poet Frederic Chopin, German composer Johann Hindimith to Russian master Sergei Shostakovich, musicians of different nationalities and backgrounds all followed Bach's 48 pieces to write masterpieces out of respect for Bach. 48 can be regarded as a model for later generations in terms of musical form, composition techniques and emotional expression. Of course, these later imitations are by no means pure imitations, but fully show the composer's own individuality, originality, nationality and characteristics of their own times. Bach is like a fertile soil, from which the composers of later generations have absorbed rich nutrition and produced fruitful results.

In terms of performance, Cui Xiufeng [5] believes that the works has strong artistic charm, and proves the feasibility of Well Temper from the perspective of practice, creating an artistic conception full of beauty and expressing delicate and moving emotions. In order to better deduce the connotation and emotion of the works, in the process of playing, a lot of attention to the relevant elements. Attention should be paid to the level of voice parts, rhythm and touch keys, rational use of pedals, grasp the sense of structure, and experience religious meaning.

In terms of teaching, Li Yifan [6] believes that learning Bach's Well-tempered Clavier is of special significance for improving polyphonic playing techniques. Therefore, there is no dispute today about whether to learn Bach polyphonic works for non-piano major students with poor foundation and late contact with piano in the music department of normal universities, which can be clearly seen in the piano teaching syllabus of normal universities. Although students majoring in piano in the music department of normal university, Bach's set has become a must-play textbook. And points out some practice methods: 1. Play each part separately to understand the overall layout of the tune and the development of each detail. 2. Determine the correct fingering. 3. It is also a good practice to practice two parts in a group. 4. Sing one part with your mouth and play another part on the instrument. 5. Take turns to highlight a part as you play the whole piece.

In the study of polyphonic techniques, Zou Shu [7] believes that The Collection of the Well-tempered Clavier is a representative work of Bach's polyphonic music. There are 48 preludes and fugues in the two volumes, all of which are arranged in 24 semitones. In fugue with the same tonality and standard form, Bach adopts different polyphonic techniques, and his ability to control the technique is unique. In this paper, two fugues in C minor in the works are taken as objects, and the characteristics of polyphonic thinking are compared from four aspects: theme form, tonality, counterpoint and interposition.

In terms of aesthetic influence, Wang Site [8] thought for a long time many people believe that Bach's Well-tempered Clavier feat only on the practical application and the music form of Well Temper, but on the average of the piano music structure and contents of the analysis we can see, the people think that is the most limited form of fugue, Bach gives their largest free, show the endless changes, and includes a variety of genres, the expression of the most basic human emotions and humanistic spirit. This unique spirit of innovation made Bach not understood by his contemporaries. Bach uses fugue, the most formal music genre, to express the full and distinct musical image. He innovates the form to enrich the connotation. His inspiration is like a spring gushing, and in turn requires the development and breakthrough of the form. This non-acoustic factor refers to the spiritual connotation in music works, and Bach's Well-tempered Clavier can be regarded as a classic for hundreds of years, because of its immortal spiritual content, expressing the rich emotions of human beings and expressing the essence of humanistic spirit.

2. Data and methodology

Musical Instrument Digital Interface (MIDI) is a standard to transmit and store music, originally designed for digital music synthesizers. MIDI does not transmit recorded sounds. Instead, it includes musical notes, timings and pitch information, which the receiving device uses to play music from its own sound library. MIDI was proposed in the early 1980s to solve the communication problem between electroacoustic instruments. MIDI is one of the most popular digital music formats in the music industry. Almost all music software supports MIDI, which uses digital control signals of musical notes to record music.

Bach's Well-tempered Clavier is one of the most widely circulated piano works, and the music information contained in it can be expressed by MIDI information. In order to facilitate the intelligent analysis of the music information of Bach's Well-tempered Clavier, the complete MIDI file of Bach's Well-tempered Clavier should be obtained first. The MIDI file set of the works is obtained by using the score set of the works published by authoritative music publishing house through manual input, which provides data for the intelligent analysis of the works.

If the analysis model is implemented in MATLAB language, then the MIDI data interface corresponding to MATLAB is required. The data interface can read MIDI file data and convert it to the required data type. Here, the MIDI data type is converted to matrix data. The matrix data structure is shown in Table 1:

Table 1. Converted MIDI data structures.

Serial No.	Duration	MIDI channel	MIDI pitch	intensity	Time serial number	Time duration
0	0.9000	1.0000	64.0000	82.0000	0	0.5510
1.0000	0.9000	1.0000	71.0000	89.0000	0.6122	0.5510

Each row in the table contains seven columns of data, and each row represents the information of a musical note. The first column represents the start of the note in the metronomic ordinal number, the second column represents the duration of the musical note in the metronomic value, and the third column represents the MIDI channel (the value is: 1-16), the fourth column represents the MIDI pitch, where the central C (C4) is 60, and the fifth column describes the speed of the key at which the note is pressed, in other words, the volume at which the note is played (0-127). The last two columns correspond to the first two (start of beat, duration of beat), except that seconds are used instead of beats.

Beat ordinal numbers starting from 0, pat the number according to the piece a clap, if music is a quarter notes or duration longer music, then its ordinal number is an integer, if music is a quaver, then its ordinal number is 0.5 for the mantissa, if music is semiquaver, then its ordinal number is 0.25 for the tail, so on, demisemiquaver, the mantissa is 0.125, 64 minutes of music, the mantissa is 0.0625, and so on.

When analyzing data, analysis model needs to be designed according to certain analysis purpose, and the information exchange between analysis model and data needs to design specific software interface. Software interface is a method of information exchange provided by software for a specific application. In the design of intelligent analysis model of the works, because its data type is MIDI data, it is necessary to design the specific data interface of the language used in the analysis model.

3. Statistical results

Tables and figures are commonly adopted methods for presenting specific data or statistical analysis results. Figures can be used to display characteristics and distributions of data, allowing for intuitive understanding through visualization and thus making it easier to interpret the statistical results.

Using the designed MIDI data interface, statistical analysis can be carried out on the music of Bach's Well-tempered Clavier according to the analysis model. Figure 3 below is the statistical result of the music of the Fugue in C major.

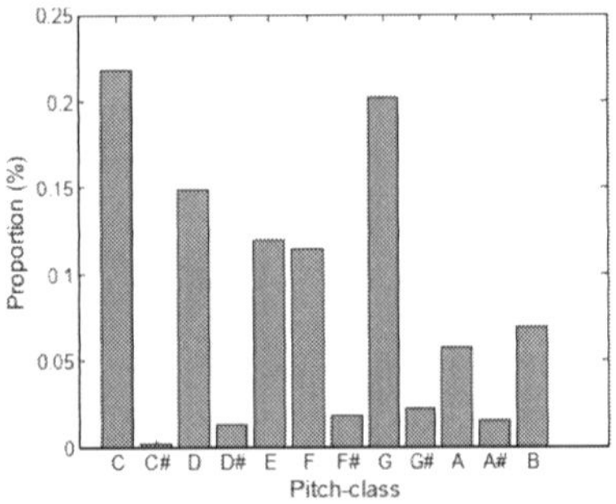

Figure 2. Pitch Distribution bar chart (Fugue in C major).

As shown in Figure 2, note C is used the most times, which is consistent with the tonality of this note. Meanwhile, note G occupies the second place, which is the pure fifth of note C.

The piano function displays traditional piano notes, because it's intuitive to use it to show the progression of musical notes under the music's timeline. Figure 3 is the piano curtain music illustration of a fugue in C major.

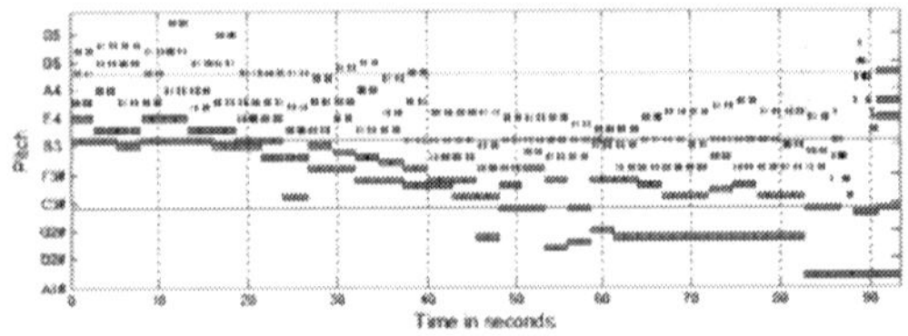

Figure 3. Music Illustration under piano Curtain (Fugue in C major).

Table 2 and Figure 4 show the statistics and diagrams of various musical sounds in the works. X-axis in Figure 4 shows the names of musical notes, and Y-axis shows the frequency of occurrence of corresponding musical notes. As shown in Table 2, #g1 appears most frequently, followed by # a. The range of these musical notes are from great A to small c.

Table 2. Statistics are made on the various musical sounds in Bach's Well-tempered Clavier.

Note	Times	Note	Times	Note	Times
a1	1	#d3	1901	a4	2620
#a1	0	e3	1887	#a4	2783
b1	1	f3	2119	b4	2583
c2	58	#f3	2015	c5	2643
#c2	62	g3	2314	#c5	2554
d2	123	#g3	2318	d5	2234
#d2	162	a3	2133	#d5	2113
e2	216	#a3	2295	e5	1735

f2	272	b3	2057	f5	1452
#f2	330	c4	2312	#f5	1314
g2	549	#c4	2002	g5	948
#g2	599	d4	2238	#g5	785
a2	726	#d4	2368	a5	534
#a2	938	e4	2220	#a5	349
b2	1066	f4	2679	b5	208
c3	1275	#f4	2322	c6	96
#c3	1414	g4	2732	#c6	2
d3	1709	#g4	2910		

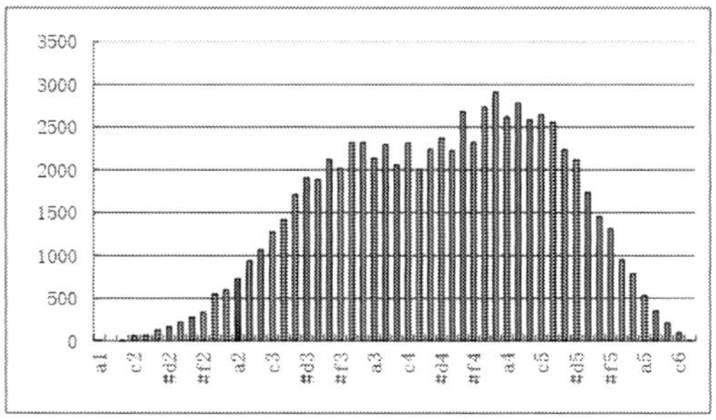

Figure 4. The number of occurrences of all notes in Bach's Well-tempered Clavier.

Piano music is played with the left hand and the right hand, all in Figure 4 the emergence of various music is both statistics, Figure 4 occurrences of the envelope is bimodal hump shape, separate the right hand or left hand play the music of count in a tone should be in the range in camel peak shape, the total after the bimodal hump shape.

4. Discussion

The music practice in Europe has experienced a process of change from monophonic music to multi-voice music, from Pythagorean tuning to just intonation and then to the 12-tones equal temperament. Bach was living in the era of the rise of the Well-temper. The emergence of Bach's Well-tempered Clavier established the position of the Well-temper to a certain extent, and the homophonic music was gradually accepted by composers.

This paper makes data visualization and statistical analysis on MIDI data of Bach's Well-tempered Clavier, and uses these MIDI data to analyze tonality and musical form in the future.

Acknowledgments

This work was financially supported by the Humanities and Social Sciences Foundation of the Ministry of Education in China (19YJAZH004), the Key Project of Humanities and Social Science Research Program at universities in Zhejiang Province (2021GH043), the cultural innovation team of Zhejiang Province, the Scientific Research Start-up Fund from Zhejiang Conservatory of Music of China, the Zhejiang provincial first-class undergraduate program in "Art and Technology," the Zhejiang provincial first-class undergraduate program in "Computer Applications," and the Zhejiang provincial virtual experiment/simulation project on "AI simulation experiments for music composition" in China.

References

1. Thomas Christensen, "the Cambridge history of Western music theory", Cambridge University Press,UK(2002).
2. Murray Barbour J., "Tuning and Temperament", Dover Publication, Inc, Mineola, New York, USA(2004).
3. Pan, J., "Structural thinking of Fugue in Baroque period from Bach's Well-tempered Piano Works," Journal of Nanjing University of the Arts, 03, 62-64(2004).
4. Ye, D. Y. "From Bach to Shostakovich — On the Influence of Well-tempered Piano Works on later piano music," Piano Art,04,23-26(2000) .
5. Cui, X. F. "Several Elements to be paid attention to when playing Bach's well-tempered clavier," Art Research,02,192-194(2015).
6. Li, Y. F., "On piano teaching of Bach's well-tempered clavier," Journal of Shanghai Normal University,02,87-90(1997).
7. Zou, S., "Comparison of the Characteristics of Polyphonic Thinking in Bach's Two Fugues in C Minor," Music Exploration,04,56-60(2007).
8. Wang, S.T., "The Spiritual Connotation and Aesthetic Tendency of Bach's well-tempered clavier," Journal of Nanjing University of the Arts,02,60-63(2003).

A Study on Foreign Language Teaching and Intercultural Education in the English Newspaper Course

Meng Fan*

School of Foreign Languages, East China Jiaotong University, Nanchang, China

Abstract. This paper discusses the blended teaching practice of foreign language teaching and intercultural education in the English newspaper course deploying the reading and writing integrated teaching model. It firstly explores the relationship between intercultural education and reading teaching of English news in Chinese higher education, then expounds the teaching objectives and curriculum design of this course, and also discusses the construction and application of the blended teaching in the context of new media. The study conducts teaching experiments in two classes (control class and experimental class) of English majors in a university in China for one semester (16 weeks), and utilizes questionnaires to gain insights into students' perspectives on this course. The results show that the reading and writing integrated teaching model in the blended teaching class can better raise students' learning interest, develop English comprehensive competence, enhance information literacy, promote critical thinking ability and improve the practical competence of intercultural communication.

1 Introduction

The English newspaper course is a language skill course for English majors in universities in China, aiming at cultivating students' ability to read English publications and improving their English proficiency and overall quality. Based on the survey of this course, there are two main problems currently: one is that the textbooks are outdated, as traditional paper textbooks contain fewer articles and fixed content, which cannot fully reflect the timeliness of this course; the other is the traditional teaching method is mostly teacher-centered, with just a focus on interpreting texts. Thus, students passively receive knowledge and are lack of opportunities to independently obtain information, conduct research, and solve problems [1].

According to the National Standards for the Quality of Teaching in Foreign Languages and Literature [2], intercultural communication competence refers to the appropriate and effective behavior of communicators in an intercultural context, which is an essential skill for English majors. The features of English publications include strong timeliness, large amount of information, and diverse types, reflecting various levels of society in English speaking countries. Some researchers have conducted in-depth research on cultivating students' intercultural competence in the English newspaper course, pointing out that using materials from English newspapers in the teaching process can stimulate students' interest, develop information searching skills, improve thinking skills, and promote intercultural communication practice [3-5]. Therefore, from an intercultural perspective, the English newspaper course has been given new requirements and urgently need to be reformed to meet the needs of cultivating intercultural competence.

In recent years, the number of research on blended teaching in English classes in China has significantly increased. However, there are few empirical studies on such form for the English newspaper course from an intercultural perspective. Without the constraints of classroom hours, the use of blended teaching brings a new direction for the teaching reform in cultivating intercultural competence. As innovating intercultural education is one of the important tasks in foreign language teaching in China today, applying the reading and writing integrated teaching model, the study constructs and verifies the blended teaching in the English newspaper course, attempting to promote foreign language teaching and intercultural education.

2 Intercultural Education and Curriculum Design

Newspapers are closely related to culture [6]. The essence of the English newspaper course is to use newspapers as a carrier of cultural dissemination, allowing students to understand the world through exposure to the language and culture of the target language, conduct cultural comparative analysis, and ultimately enhance intercultural communication competence. Thus, the teaching objectives of this course are: (1) to understand domestic and foreign current affairs, broaden international perspectives, enhance cultural literacy, and cultivate intercultural competence by reading English newspapers and magazines; (2) to expand English vocabulary in various contexts, and improve

*532754535@qq.com

overall English proficiency; (3) to develop critical thinking skills through analyzing reading materials. This course uses "Reading English Newspapers" [7] as the textbook, and "China Daily" to supplement the teaching. New media is a new type of carrier for information storage, transmission, and expression, such as text, audio, and images, with strong expressive power, large capacity, and excellent interactivity. Therefore, the course can choose appropriate new media materials to assist multi-dimensional teaching of cultural knowledge.

The blended teaching deploying the reading and writing integrated teaching model was designed as shown in Figure 1. The feature is to highlight student-centered learning, with a focus on cultivating English comprehensive competence and intercultural competence. The difficulty lies in effective interaction, and the operating point is the appropriate use of new media in the context of the blended teaching.

(1) Pre-class (online learning): students search materials related to unit topics before the class, discuss and prepare for presentations.

(2) In class (classroom teaching): On the basis of understanding news articles, various viewpoints on social hot topics can be set up for students to have small debates. Through the continuous exchange of ideas and viewpoints, students can gradually improve their language competence and accumulate intercultural competence.

(3) After class (online learning): As an extension of classroom teaching, students are required to write a reading report after class, explaining the causes and consequences of the event, outlining the government and public responses, and providing personal evaluations. In addition, teachers and students can express their opinions on a news event online in English. News events happen anytime and anywhere, and so does the blended teaching.

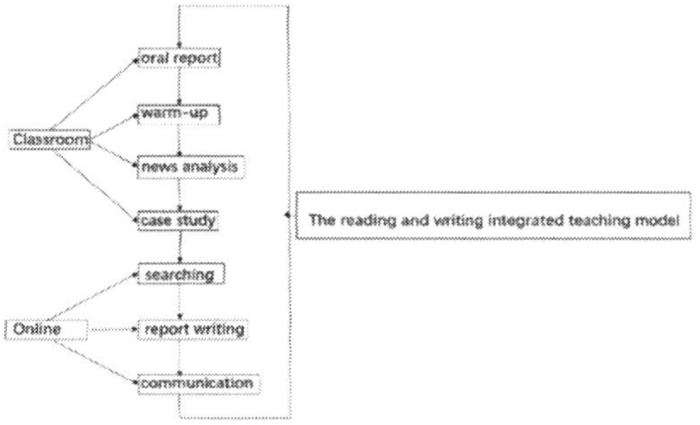

Fig. 1. The reading and writing integrated teaching model

3 Research Methods and Results

The study explores the construction and application of the blended teaching that integrates reading and writing in the English newspaper course, with a focus on cultivating students' intercultural competence. The study selected two classes of sophomores majoring in English in a university in China. One was an experimental class (28 students, 6 male and 22 female), using the blended teaching, and the other was a control class (30 students, 4 male and 26 female), using a traditional teacher-centered classroom teaching approach. A teaching experiment was conducted for one semester (16 weeks), with the same teacher teaching both classes.

Before the experiment, students from two classes took the College English Test Band 6 (CET 6) in June 2021. An independent sample t-test on the scores of two classes was conducted by SPSS 26. The results are shown in Table 1. Although the experimental class had slightly higher average scores than the control class, there was no significant difference in the scores of each individual item of CET 6 between the two classes, indicating that the initial English competence of the two classes was similar.

After the experiment, students from two classes participated in CET 6 in December 2021, and the average scores of each item in both classes improved (Table 2). Paired sample t-tests were conducted on the scores of each item in the former and latter CET 6 test before and after the experiment (Table 3). After using the blended teaching approach with the reading and writing integrated teaching model, the latter scores of the CET 6 test in the experimental class were significantly improved ($p=0.002$ for listening, $p=0.000$ for reading, and $p=0.000$ for writing and translation). Under the traditional teaching model, Table 4 shows that there was a significant improvement in the reading, writing, and translation scores of CET-6 in the control class ($p=0.006$ for reading, $p=0.048$ for writing and translation). The results indicate that after one semester's learning, the overall English proficiency of students has improved.

Independent sample t-tests were conducted on the scores of each item in the latter CET 6 test for two classes (Table 2). The experimental class had significantly higher scores in reading, writing, and translation than the control class ($p=0.000$ for reading, $p=0.022$ for writing and translation), and there was no significant difference in listening scores between the two classes ($p=0.6$). The results indicate that although both classes have improved their overall English proficiency after one semester's learning, the improvement level of the control class is not as significant as that of the experimental class. Therefore, from the overall empirical results, it can be seen that the teaching effect of the blended teaching that integrates reading and writing from an intercultural perspective is significant.

This study used two times of CET 6 scores as pre- and post-tests. Although it cannot fully indicate that the improvement of individual scores is only related to the English newspaper course, through this semester the course plays an important role in reading training, and CET 6 is a relatively objective test with similar difficulty levels former and latter. From this perspective, the study chose CET 6 scores as the pre- and post-test data.

After the completion of the course, a questionnaire (the Likert's 5 scales) was administrated to students in both classes to investigate their satisfaction of the teaching approaches, from the perspectives of improving English skills, intercultural competence, learning interest, information literacy, critical thinking ability, etc. There were a total of 58 students in two classes, and a total of 58 questionnaire responses were received. Three untrustworthy responses were excluded. SPSS 26 was used and

Cranbach's α was 0.918, indicating that the questionnaire design had high reliability. Table 5 shows the independent sample t-test results of questionnaires from two classes.

There is a significant difference in the evaluation of English listening and speaking ability, intercultural ability, learning interest, information literacy ability, critical thinking ability, and learner autonomy between the two classes, and students in the experimental class more agree with the improvement of these abilities, indicating that the blended teaching classroom has more advantages compared to traditional teaching and is conducive to the development of students' comprehensive literacy.

Table 1. Independent sample t-test of the former CET 6 of the two classes

Item	Mean	SD	F	T	P
Listening	Exp-class 155.54 Con-class 146.67	27.269 31.959	1.184	1.133	.262
Reading	Exp-class 179.54 Con-class 167.73	24.663 27.202	.185	1.727	.090
Writing & Translation	Exp-class 145.43 Con-class 136.43	29.191 18.776	4.650	1.405	.165

Table 2. Independent sample t-test of the latter CET 6 of the two classes

Item	Mean	SD	F	T	P
Listening	Exp-class 168.43 Con-class 162.07	27.189 58.224	1.198	.527	.600
Reading	Exp-class 201.68 Con-class 174.10	22.303 30.994	1.936	3.865	.000
Writing & Translation	Exp-class 155.00 Con-class 140.63	26.992 19.182	3.200	2.349	0.022

Table 3. Paired sample t-tests of the former and latter CET 6 in the Exp-class

Item	Mean	T	P
Listening	-12.893	-3.432	0.002
Reading	-22.143	-7.801	0.000
Writing & Translation	-9.571	-4.603	0.000

Table 4. Paired sample t-tests of the former and latter CET 6 in the Con-class

Item	Mean	T	P
Listening	-15.400	-1.457	.156
Reading	-6.367	-2.992	.006
Writing & Translation	-4.200	-2.064	.048

Table 5. The independent sample t-test of questionnaires from two classes

Items	F	T	P
Improved my listening ability	.446	2.691	.010
Improved my speaking ability	4.951	2.642	.011
Improved my reading ability	.062	.458	.649
Improved my writing ability	2.220	1.476	.146
Improved my intercultural ability	1.418	2.948	.005
Improved my learning interest	.951	2.845	.006
Improved my information literacy	7.739	5.546	.000
Improved my critical thinking	.824	2.341	.023
Improved my learner autonomy	.161	2.752	.008

4 Discussion

Reading is a psychological cognitive activity in which readers decode the language and sentence structure of written materials, in order to understand their ideological content, while writing is the process of coding one's thoughts through word selection and sentence construction. Therefore, the reading and writing integrated teaching model has emerged, which is different from the traditional model of setting reading and writing as two independent subjects in foreign language teaching. In this research, students in the experimental class selected a newspaper article and wrote a reading report after class. This integrated reading and writing task design further exercised students' abilities in reading, summarizing, and elaborating arguments. At the same time, selecting articles can also exercise students' ability to independently seek information and evaluate the value of information.

In addition, the teaching design also required the students in the experimental class to complete an oral report during the semester, either in the form of the class presentation or micro-video sent to the class online platform. This task was designed to developing students' ability to extract, summarize and evaluate information, and to express themselves orally. The results of this teaching experiment show that the students' reading, writing, listening and speaking skills were improved through reading reports and oral tasks, and of which were more obvious in the experimental class. These two tasks were designed to help students understand that reading with purpose can quickly improve the speed and effectiveness of reading, and holistic language teaching based on reading can also exercise listening, speaking, and writing skills [8] and cultivate the ability of self-directed learning of English.

Pre-class searches, class discussions, after-class extensions, and online platform exchanges are all speculative activities carried out on the basis of reading English newspaper articles, so that students can understand the cultural differences between Chinese and foreign ways of thinking, communication methods, values, historical background, social structure, etc. At the same time, it integrates ideological and political education, strengthening the input of traditional Chinese culture, analyzing cross-cultural misunderstandings and conflict cases, and realizing two-way cultural import. In the end, students will establish a cross-cultural consciousness and a cross-cultural personality, and form an ideology that can master English, tell Chinese stories well, shape China's image, and contribute to China's socialist modernization, as well as the spirit that can not only tolerate the advanced Western culture but also safeguard the fine traditions and national characteristics of the Chinese. Therefore, the English newspaper course is an activity to explore and study culture in the process of teaching and implementation, while the behavior practice of cross-cultural education cultivates students to understand the differences between different cultures and their own cultures from specific case discussions, and to achieve the ultimate goal of effective cross-cultural communication by consciously establishing a multi-dimensional way of thinking and enhancing the acceptance and judgment of different cultures.

This research shows that the blended teaching in the context of Internet plus provides electronic English news materials such as audios, videos and pictures, including many topics of interest to students, which will accumulate students' intercultural knowledge. Peer interaction or teacher-student communication online or in the class is beneficial for helping students establish thinking habits that consider problems from multiple perspectives. During the communication process, students become aware of cultural differences, thereby further regulating their intercultural communication activities.

5 Conclusion

To conclude, the fundamental purpose of intercultural education is to broaden students' global perspectives and enable them to engage in more effective intercultural communication with people from different cultural backgrounds. This study indicates that the teaching practice of the English newspaper course is a process of gradually implementing intercultural education in foreign language teaching. With the development of the modern information technology in the context of new media, especially the wide application of intelligent terminals (mobile phones), a large number of rich, timely and authentic reading materials have been brought to newspaper reading. The blended teaching with the reading and writing integrated teaching model established in this study cannot only be applied to English-major reading courses in universities, but also to non-English majors. It can also provide references for foreign language writing courses, improving students' overall language skills, expanding their knowledge of current events, enhancing their thinking ability, and promoting intercultural competence.

Acknowledgment

Funded by Jiangxi Province Education Planning and Research Program 20YB055; Jiangxi Province Educational Reform in Higher Education Program JXJG-19-5-15.

References

1. Yu, J.X., Su, A.Y. (2019) Research on the teaching-aided platform serving for selected readings of British and American newspapers. Modern Educational Technology, 29(09):73-79. DOI: CNKI:SUN:XJJS.0.2019-09-012
2. National Standards for the Quality of Teaching in Foreign Languages and Liter- ature (2018). https://www.sohu.com/a/227935754_507486
3. Akdemir, A.S., Barin, M., Demiroz, H. (2012) Broadsheet English: Teaching speaking through newspaper articles. Procedia-Social and Behavioral Sciences, 46:3967-3971. DOI: 10.1016/j.sbspro.2012.06.180
4. Doganay, Y., Ashirimbetova, M., Davis, B. (2013) Making culture happen in the English language classroom. English Language Teaching, 6(10):11-16. DOI:10.5539/elt.v6n10p11
5. Yan, L.J. (2018) Practice and reflection on foreign language teaching and inter cultural education: Taking the English newspaper course as an example. Foreign Language World, 3:18-23. DOI: CNKI:SUN:WYJY.0.2018-03-004
6. Wilson, S.L.R. Mass Media /Mass Culture: An Introduction. New York: McGraw-Hill,1995.
7. Wang, Z.H., Ma, Y.L. (2009) Reading English newspapers. Higher Education Press, Beijing. https://www.hep.com.cn/book/show/8ef63873-b297-4df1-a8af-6bee1feeb7d6
8. Goodman, K. S. What's whole in whole language? Portsmouth, NH: Heinemann,1986.

Corpus-based Translation Studies: Examining Media Language through a Linguistic Lens

Jie Ding*

Central South University, Changsha, Hunan, China

Abstract: This paper delves into the multifaceted world where translation studies converge with corpus linguistics, casting a spotlight on the dynamic domain of media language. By harnessing the power of a corpus-based methodology, our research meticulously dissects the intricate process of translating and adapting media texts within a panoply of linguistic landscapes and cultural contexts. The core objective of the study is to excavate and analyze the pantheon of linguistic attributes and the repertoire of tactics translators wield in the realm of media, unlocking a treasure trove of understanding pertaining to cultural subtleties and the nuanced art of translation practices. Our exploration traverses a broad spectrum of media genres, encompassing the rigor of news journalism, the creative complexity of television programming, and the viral nature of digital content, to construct a comprehensive understanding of the translation phenomena at play. The findings illuminate the myriad ways in which media narratives are reconfigured and presented to global audiences, ultimately enriching the discourse on how translation shapes and is shaped by the currents of worldwide communication. This study, therefore, serves as a crucial beacon for academics, professionals, and enthusiasts poised at the crossroads of linguistics and cultural exchange, guiding them through the labyrinth of media translation and its profound influence on international dialogues and perceptions.

1. Introduction

In an increasingly interconnected world, media language constitutes a fundamental vein through which cultures communicate, clash, and coalesce. In this juncture, the interplay between translation studies and corpus linguistics emerges as a potent analytical tool to dissect the complexities of media language as it traverses linguistic boundaries. This paper seeks to explore the nuances of meaning conveyed in translated media texts, examining the role of translation in shaping public discourse and cultural perception on a global scale. By leveraging the empirical strengths of corpus linguistics, this study aims to offer a systematic, data-driven investigation into the patterns and peculiarities of translated media language. Employing a meticulously constructed corpus comprising various media texts, our analysis will underscore the intersection of translation choices and cultural nuances, delving into questions of how translation strategies maintain or alter message impact and the extent to which semantic shifts occur across cultural contexts [1]. The objectives of this investigation are thus twofold: to illuminate the intricacies of media translation processes and to contribute to broader understanding of cross-cultural communication in the media sphere. In pursuit of these goals, the study will harness corpus methodologies such as concordance analysis, frequency counts, and collocation patterns, enabling a comprehensive exploration of the linguistic landscape sculpted by the interplay of translation studies and corpus linguistics in the domain of media language.

2. Linguistic Features in Media Translation

2.1. Lexical Choices

The selection of words in the translation of media content is a complex endeavor, where translators must juggle the directness of language with the rich tapestry of cultural subtexts [2]. These lexical choices are pivotal in determining how the audience perceives the translated material. While addressing connotations, translators strive to find words in the target language that evoke similar sentiments and associative meanings without distorting the source's intent. Collocations present another hurdle as word pairings that sound natural in one language may come across as awkward or unidiomatic in another. Translators have to be keenly aware of these linguistic partnerships and the effect they have on fluency and comprehension. Register, the level of formality or informality in language, also plays a critical role in media translations. The translator must choose lexicon that aligns with the tone of the original media text, whether it be formal, casual, or technical. Delineating the correct register ensures that the translation resonates in the same way as the source with its target audience. Navigating through these lexical choices, translators reveal patterns in

*Corresponding author's email: 2482516799@qq.com

their approach—some may favor a more literal translation, while others might prioritize the cultural subtleties of the target language. Maintaining fidelity to the source material often requires creative solutions to encapsulate its essence in culturally relevant ways.

2.2. Syntactic Structures

Syntactic structures in media translation require meticulous consideration as they can profoundly influence the readability and comprehension of a text. Translators confront multifaceted decisions when adapting sentence structures, seeking to replicate the original's rhythm while ensuring syntactic coherence in the target language. Sentence complexity often needs reworking, with translators potentially breaking down long, intricate sentences of the source text into shorter, simpler ones or vice versa, to accommodate the linguistic preferences of the target audience. There is also a dance with passive and active voice constructions; a translator must decide whether to retain the source's voice or shift it to better fit the target language's stylistic norms and clarity standards. Occasionally, translators might diverge from source-language syntax in favor of conforming to the syntactic conventions of the target language, which could enhance the translated text's fluency. Nevertheless, such deviations are carefully deliberated to avoid diluting the original's nuances. Overall, these syntactic choices are pivotal in preserving the author's voice while making the text accessible to the target audience [3].

2.3. Pragmatic Functions

The subtleties of pragmatic functions play a major role in the translation of media texts due to their reliance on context, cultural norms, and tacit social rules. When translating speech acts, the challenge lies in conveying not just the literal meaning but also the intended action or response provoked by the original text. Politeness strategies are particularly nuanced and must be translated in a manner that mirrors the social etiquette of the target culture while maintaining the interaction dynamics intended by the source. Moreover, context-specific references—including idioms, cultural allusions, and regional humor—require a deep understanding of both the source and target cultures to achieve a translation that is equivalent in impact and comprehension. Translators often have to decide between a direct translation, which may be meaningless to the new audience, and a more localized adaptation that carries the same weight and effect. These pragmatic adaptations are critical, as they significantly influence how the translated media is received by the audience. The subtlety in conveying the intended pragmatics can mean the difference between a translation that engages and resonates with the audience and one that falls flat or is misunderstood.

3. Cultural Adaptation in Media Translation

3.1. Localization Strategies

In the intricate process of media translation, the art of localization strategies stands as a cornerstone for transforming content to resonate profoundly with a target audience's unique cultural nuances. Translators are tasked with the hefty endeavor of bridging wide cultural divides, meticulously tailoring cultural references, idioms, humor, and more to ensure that none of the original flavor is lost amidst the transition from one culture to another. This often manifests in the careful replacement of local metaphors or region-specific jokes—for instance, a humorous remark deeply rooted in the nuances of American baseball culture might be reimagined to tap into the collective consciousness and appreciation for cricket or soccer in another area of the world [4]. The goal is to preserve the hilarity and impact of the content in a way that is both authentic and relatable to the new audience.

A successful localization strategy is one that strikes a harmonious balance between fidelity to the source material and the creative alterations necessary for the content to truly strike a chord in the hearts and minds of the international audience. This requires not only a thorough understanding of the source language and culture but also an intimate knowledge of the target audience's societal values, slang, popular culture, and historical context. Transitioning comedic material, allegories, and culturally ingrained narratives can be akin to tightrope walking—requiring meticulous precision and unwavering attention to the subtleties of linguistic and cultural interplay.

Nevertheless, the process is not without its challenges and potential pitfalls [5]. Overzealous or misguided localization efforts can sometimes lead to the destruction of the very essence that gave the original content its charm, or worse, introduce clichés and stereotypes that may perpetuate misunderstandings or even cause offense. These challenges highlight the nuanced expertise of translators who walk the fine line between two cultural realities, underlining the necessity for translators to possess a sensitive and informed approach to their craft.

The measure of successful localization lies in its invisible nature—when a piece of media resonates so well with the audience that the translation becomes transparent, creating an illusion of originality within the target culture. It is this seamless integration that marks the summit of the translator's endeavor [6]. Through effective localization, the once foreign piece of media metamorphoses into something innately familiar and effortlessly comprehensible, thereby expanding its reach and fostering cross-cultural connections that might otherwise have been lost in the chasm between languages and societies. In doing so, skilled translators don't merely translate words; they reinterpret and weave content into the fabric of a different cultural reality, enabling stories and messages to transcend borders and echo with universal appeal.

3.2. Audience Reception

Understanding the reception of translated media by different cultural audiences is an essential measure of the success of localization strategies. This part involves an in-depth analysis of audience feedback, including reviews and ratings, that provides direct insights into how well the translation resonates with viewers or readers. Positive reception often suggests that the translation has successfully catered to the cultural nuances and expectations of the target audience, while negative feedback can indicate a disconnect, perhaps due to cultural misunderstandings or an inability to capture the source material's essence. The audience's perception of the translated media is influenced by a myriad of factors, including cultural identity, social norms, and individual preferences. This analysis highlights the importance of a translator's role in understanding the audience and creating a translation that maintains the source material's integrity and fosters meaningful cross-cultural connections [7].

3.3. Ethical Considerations

Cultural adaptation in media translation goes beyond linguistic accuracy; it also encompasses significant ethical considerations. In this complex landscape, translators must grapple with the responsibility of preserving the original message and intent of the source material while navigating the potential risks of distorting or diluting minority voices and perspectives. The ethical implications include avoiding cultural stereotyping or misrepresentation, which can perpetuate harmful biases. Additionally, translators face the challenge of deciding how to handle content that might be controversial or sensitive in different cultural contexts. The translator's work is a balancing act of respect for the source material, its creator's vision, and the target audience's culture and values. By embodying ethical principles and cultural competence, translators play a pivotal role in fostering cross-cultural understanding and ensuring that adaptations are not only accurate but also culturally respectful and inclusive.

4. Technological Advancements in Translation

4.1. Machine Translation and AI

Machine translation, powered by Artificial Intelligence, has dramatically transformed the landscape of media translation by enabling the processing of vast quantities of content swiftly. Earlier forms of machine translation relied on rigid rule-based systems until the advent of statistical models that utilized large bilingual corpora to predict translations. Presently, neural machine translation models represent the frontier, employing deep learning algorithms to produce translations that are more fluent and attuned to linguistic subtleties. With neural networks, the technology has made leaps in understanding idiomatic expressions and cultural nuances, though AI still struggles with context-dependent connotations, sarcasm, and humor, necessitating human intervention to fine-tune and verify the translation output for quality assurance and cultural sensitivity.

4.2. Digital Tools and Resources

The landscape of media translation has been enriched by an array of digital tools and resources that have become integral to the process. Translators now have at their disposal expansive online databases and digital corpora that provide immediate access to a wealth of parallel texts and contextual usage examples, vastly improving the accuracy of translations. Translation management software streamlines workflow and ensures consistency across projects by tracking progress and applying translation memories. Additionally, the advent of collaborative online platforms has ushered in an era of greater connectivity among translators, enabling them to pool their knowledge and linguistic expertise, thus fortifying the sense of community and shared purpose within the global translation profession.

4.3. The Future of Translation Technology

The trajectory of translation technology is poised for further innovation, with neural machine translation at the helm, promising even more intricately nuanced translations that grasp the essence of the original content with higher contextual awareness. Augmented reality holds promise for the future of translation, potentially allowing for instantaneous translation overlays on media content to enhance viewer accessibility and engagement. Moreover, the role of AI is expanding in the realm of predictive translation, which could revolutionize efficiency by suggesting contextually appropriate translations in real-time, really embedding itself in the workflow by learning from historical translation data and ongoing patterns of linguistic usage [8]. Such advancements hint at a future where digital translation aids are not only reactive but proactive participants in the translation process, heralding a blend of technology and human expertise to meet the dynamic demands of global communication.

5. Professional and Ethical Responsibilities

5.1. Translator's Role and Identity

In the realm of media translation, the translator has become an indispensable cultural intermediary, bridging diverse cultures and fostering cross-cultural communication by transcending mere linguistic barriers. The contemporary translator's mandate extends beyond literal translation to encompass an intricate comprehension of cultural connotations, colloquialisms, and societal contexts. This newfound identity as cultural mediators means translators must grapple with ethical dilemmas, striking a delicate equilibrium between maintaining faithfulness to the source material and honoring the cultural sensitivities and idiomatic expressions of the target audience. The incursion of advanced technology, specifically artificial intelligence and sophisticated machine translation tools, introduces an additional layer of complexity to the translator's vocation, demanding a skill set that blends linguistic finesse with technological savvy. By marrying the art of language with digital proficiency, translators ensure that the spirit and nuance of the original text are preserved while adapting to the linguistic tastes and cultural expectations of an evolving global audience [9].

5.2. Standards and Best Practices

In the specialized practice of media translation, a stringent adherence to industry standards and best practices is indispensable. This adherence is the bedrock of ethical and professional integrity, which requires translators to balance the faithful rendition of the source's message with an acute awareness of the target culture's sensibilities. Ethical codes and guidelines, often championed by professional translation organizations and regulatory bodies, serve as a compass, directing translators toward practices that uphold authenticity, cultural relevance, and audience receptivity. These bodies frequently extend certifications and provide ongoing education to consolidate the translators' ability to navigate the complexities of media translation. As a result, translations emanating from professionals within this framework are not only linguistically precise but also culturally resonant, ensuring that the message conveyed respects and reflects the cultural mosaic of the target demographic.

5.3. Challenges in Maintaining Professional Integrity

Media translators routinely encounter a labyrinth of ethical quandaries and professional obstacles that threaten to compromise their integrity [10]. The landscape of media is often beset with issues such as censorship demands, the imposition of bias, and the pressure to manipulate content to serve political agendas or mollify commercial interests. Confronting these challenges requires a steadfast commitment to a strong ethical paradigm coupled with robust support from fellow translators and professional alliances. By steadfastly clinging to the pillars of accuracy, impartiality, and cultural deference, translators navigate through these tumultuous waters, ensuring that their translations remain true to the source and do not distort or bias the message. It is this unwavering dedication to these core values that fortifies the integrity of the translated content, and, by extension, the integrity of the source and target cultures' representation in the media.

6. Conclusion

In conclusion, our exploration of the intersection between translation studies and corpus linguistics within the realm of media language has illuminated the intricate and significant role of translation in shaping global communication. The study underscores the complex interplay of linguistic choices, syntactic considerations, and pragmatic functions that translators navigate in adapting content across diverse cultural landscapes. It reveals the artistry and ethical responsibilities entrenched in media translation practices, emphasizing the critical need for cultural competence, and balances linguistic precision with audience receptivity. The advent of AI and advanced digital tools has been acknowledged as both an asset and a challenge, propelling the field towards a technologically integrated future that nevertheless reaffirms the irreplaceable value of human expertise. As media continues to evolve and reach across borders, this research underscores the enduring impact of translation in crafting media narratives that resonate internationally, bridging differences, and fostering a more interconnected, empathetic world.

Reference

1. Schäffner, Christina. "Translation studies." Handbook of pragmatics. John Benjamins, 2022. 1412-1426.
2. Usmonova, Zarina Khabibovna. "The Main Peculiarities of Translation Studies: Tranlator's Skill." Conference on Applied and Practical Sciences. 2023.
3. Lin, Phoebe, and Svenja Adolphs. "Corpus linguistics." The Routledge Handbook of Applied Linguistics. Routledge, 2023. 296-308.
4. Aarts, Jan, and Willem Meijs. "Corpus linguistics: recent developments in the use of computer corpora in English language research." (2022).
5. Vosiljonov, Azizbek. "Basic theoretical principles of corpus linguistics." Academicia Globe 3.02 (2022): 173-175.
6. Ruziev, Kh B. "Proverbs and corpus linguistics." Актуальные проблемы гуманитарных и естественных наук 6 (2020): 64-67.
7. Rustamov, Ilhom. "TEACHING ENGLISH AS A FOREIGN LANGUAGE." Журнал иностранных языков и лингвистики 4.4 (2022).
8. Hutton, John S., et al. "Associations between screen-based media use and brain white matter integrity in preschool-aged children." JAMA pediatrics 174.1 (2020): e193869-e193869.
9. Müller, Martin, Marcel Salathé, and Per E. Kummervold. "Covid-twitter-bert: A natural language processing model to analyse covid-19 content on twitter." Frontiers in Artificial Intelligence 6 (2023): 1023281.
10. Anderson, Nina J., et al. "Linking quality and quantity of parental linguistic input to child language skills: A meta-analysis." Child Development 92.2 (2021): 484-501.

Evolution of Poetic Composition Theories from *Shilin Shihua* to *Chengzhai Shihua*

Huiling Chen*

College of Humanities and Law, South China Agricultural University, Guangzhou, Guangdong 510642

Abstract: Ye Mengde, a well-known Chinese poet and poetry critic in the Song Dynasty, advocated the concept of implicit naturalness in his work, *Shilin Shihua (Shilin's Remarks on Poetry)*. He emphasized that the use of allusions in poetic composition should not be far-fetched and demanded that words and sentences be refined and hammered. Based on Ye's insights, Yang Wanli, another famous Chinese poet in the Southern Song Dynasty, further developed the theory. In *Chengzhai Shihua (Chengzhai's Remarks on Poetry)*, he proposed that the essence of poetry lies in "poems being concluded while the taste remains eternal," paid attention to the skillful integration of idioms and allusions, advocated the importance of creating "stunning verses" in writing poetry, and practiced what he preached by actively engaging in poetic composition. He shattered the traditional conventions of the late Jiangxi School of Poetry, created the unique "Chengzhai Style" characterized by freshness and liveliness, and injected a vibrant "poetic taste" into poetry, enhancing the role of poetic composition theory in guiding poetry creation practices.

1. Introduction

"The tradition of offering commentaries on poetry had its origin in the Song Dynasties."[1] Since the creation of Ouyang Xiu's *Liuyi Shihua* in the Northern Song Dynasty, the style of shihua (remarks on poetry) was born and gained significant momentum thereafter. As a new style of poetry commentaries, it spread like wildfire and was quickly in vogue. The *Shilin Shihua* was compiled by Ye Mengde at the turn of the Northern and Southern Song Dynasties. Its poetics stemmed from the Jiangxi School of Poetry, which no longer focused on discussing poetry and poetic activities for casual conversation but took a theoretical turn. This shift represents a transition of Shihua in the Song Dynasty from "centered on activities"[1] to "striking a balance between poetic activity discussion and verse analysis,"[1] marking a significant milestone in bridging the past and the future. Yang Wanli, in the Southern Song Dynasty, also drew inspiration from the Jiangxi School of Poetry in his early years. However, he later experienced a moment of enlightenment and decided to get rid of the rigidity of the Jiangxi School of Poetry, creating the distinctive "Chengzhai Style" featuring freshness, liveliness, and rich spiritual interest. He emphasized the "taste" of poetry and articulated his views in the work titled *Chengzhai Shihua*. Both authors were influenced by the Jiangxi School of Poetry from the outset, but they later dismissed its influence and forged their own distinct styles. Although their theories on poetry were both fragmentary, Yang Wanli, delving more deeply than his predecessor, had engaged in specific arguments and discussions about poetry instead of mere subjective judgments.

Many researchers have delved into the *Shilin Shihua* from diverse perspectives. For instance, the *Shilin Shihua and Jiangxi School of Poetry* written by Xia Yuandong, the *Research on Ye Mengde's Shilin Shihua* by Ying Zi, the *Research on the Potic Thoughts of Ye Mengde's Shilin Shihua* by Bi Zhentao and the *Discussion on Shilin Shihua* by Deng Guojun explored the literary thoughts and poetics it encapsulated. Pan Shuxian's work, *Poetic Cases and the Political and Cultural Ecology of People in the Song Dynasty: The Mirror Image of Wang Wei in the Shilin Shihua*, and Rong Mo's work, *Poetic Theory Features and Selections of Poetry Paradigms in the Period of Nandu of Song Dynasty—Discussion on the "Intentional Disparagement of Yuanyou Poetics" in the Shilin Shihua*, on the other hand, examined the connection between the *Shilin Shihua* and political factions. Furthermore, Xu Mengmeng conducted a detailed analysis of the editions of *Shilin Shihua*, and Yu Qinghui, in her research titled *Acceptance of Liu Zongyuan's Poetry in the Song Dynasty—A Glimpse from Shilin Shihua,* incorporated the reception theory to shed light on the influence of Liu Zongyuan's poetry.

On the contrary, the research on *Chengzhai Shihua* mainly revolves around its poetic ideology, time of completion, and philological significance. For example, Li Guoping's *Exploration of Poetics in Chengzhai Shihua* studied Yang Wanli's poetics of "fictitious and realistic comparison" and "seven-character line expressing three meanings." Wei Xiangxue, in his study *A Brief Discussion on Chengzhai Shihua*, summarized Yang Wanli's poetic spirit of learning from predecessors, advocating innovation and individuality, and emphasizing the

* Lavender5688@163.com

importance of preserving "lingering poetic tastes." In another study, Yang Xuedong explored the poetics, four-six style, and miscellaneous discussions of Yang Wanli. Additionally, Hu Jiansheng's *Textual Research on the Writing Time of Chengzhai Shihua* defined the time of completion and examined the poetic ideology of the work. Meng Dan, in her research titled *Investigating the Philological Significance of the Annotated Catalog of the Complete Library of the Four Treasuries through its Annotations of Chengzhai Shihua*, explored the philological significance of the work.

Currently, the comparative study of *Shilin Shihua* and *Chengzhai Shihua* is underreported. To bridge the gap, this paper attempts to conduct a detailed comparative analysis of the poetics contained in the two works by leveraging the systematic analysis method and macro comparison method, exploring the evolution of poetic composition theories from *Shilin Shihua* to *Chengzhai Shihua.*

2. Artistic Style: From Implicit Naturalness to Eternal Poetic Taste

Ye Mengde pursues a style of poetry that is restrained, implicit, and natural, and praises Zhang Jingxiu's poems in *Shilin Shihua* as "elegant and plain, with plenty of beautiful lines." Meanwhile, he strongly appreciates Du Fu's "The spring colors of Brocade River come to Earth and Heaven, drifting clouds over Jade Fort Mountain transform through present and past" and "I hear drear horns and drums announce the dawning day, mirrored in the Three Gorges, shivers the Milky Way," which are majestic, powerful, as well as profound and reserved in aesthetic conception, such that he laments "nobody is capable of creating such verses afterward." In contrast, he criticizes Wang Anshi's "All the people are anticipating the pouring rain, yet unaware if the dragon meanders here," "Amid lush and verdant leaves lies a lone red flower, this touch of red is enough to brighten the spring scenery," and "Cleansing the impurities of the mundane world with boundless merits, nourishing the scorched land with extraordinary talents" for being over straightforward and candid, thus losing the beauty of implicitness. Ye advocates that "Thoughts and words should be melded seamlessly, with words shifting in harmony with the changes of mind; the two are naturally intertwined."[3] Such a proposition is aimed at converting the long-standing dull formalistic style of poetry caused by the sharp increase of argumentation and excessive reasoning in poetic composition during the Song Dynasties by calling for a clear and plain style. Although he has proposed an implicit and natural style of poetry by commenting on predecessors' poems, he has not specifically explained the methods through which poets can achieve the effect of "carved without leaving a trace" and "ingenious yet natural."

Upon the pursuit of the implicit nature of poetry, Yang Wanli seeks a "poetic taste." [4] He inherits the theory of "taste beyond the taste" proposed in Sikong Tu's *Twenty-Four Styles of Poetry*, eulogizing "poems being concluded while the taste remains eternal" and insisting that poetry should have "infinite taste." He praised Tao Yuanming and Liu Zongyuan's five-character poems for being "elegant and profound" and proposed that poetic composition should be euphemistic and implicit, expressing "taste beyond the taste" and "meaning beyond the textual descriptions." In this regard, he provides detailed arguments and discussions in *Chengzhai Shihua*:

Chapter 5:

"In the *Golden Needle Method*, it is stated that 'In an eight-line regulated poem, the closing line should be like a rolling stone down a high mountain, never to return.' I disagree with that. I believe 'poems being concluded while the taste remains eternal' is the most ideal. As Du Fu wrote in the poem *The Double Ninth*: 'I wonder who would still be around in next year's get-together, in inebriety I look carefully at a cornel leaf.' In *Declining an Invitation from Minister Li in Summer*, he expressed: 'It's not that I disregard the appointment with you, but the wild snow in Shanyin impedes the visit.' Such instances can also be found in Tang poems: 'Immersing Sword Gan Jiang in the Ge River, the sound of apes is heartbreaking.' In *Fishing Pier*, it is mentioned: 'Still there are anglers fishing in this river, who sell the fish in exchange for money.' And in *Nagato Complain*, it has 'Wrongly using gold to buy poetry, Sima Xiangru himself is a heartless person.' Cui Daorong commented: 'Now I envy Sima Xiangru's wealth, who at least resides within a four-wall room of the mundane world. '"[2]

Chapter 6:

"There are poems with three meanings in a seven-character line. Du Fu says: 'I face my meal, take a bite, and then I can take it no more.' Han Yu says: 'Before arriving at the destination, I already contemplate returning.' There are also poems with two meanings in a five-character line. Chen Shidao says: 'Illness prevents solace in alcohol; internal coldness is already anticipated as the weather turns cold.' There are even poems without explicit words within the line but with implicit meanings beyond. In *Xiang Bo*, Su Gong rebukes Bo Gong's false accusations. Thus, he questions, 'As two travel together, who ultimately brings about this calamity?' Du Fu says: 'Dispatching someone to the market on credit for fragrant rice, calling his wife out of the kitchen to prepare a meal for me himself.' The previous sentence mentioned his poverty, hence the use of 'she'; later, it mentioned he has no one to command, thus the use of 'qin.' In another poem, 'Coming back from the east, I yearned for the road, but now I feel it is hard; about to part, I mount my horse, my body lacks all strength,' The previous sentence implies mutual connection without explicit mention, while the next sentence carries a lingering reluctance to parting without expressing it out. And in 'Gathering daily in joy for friendship and ale, this old fellow understands now for the first time,' he mocks himself for being left alone. Then, in *Declining an Invitation from Minister Li in Summer*, he says, 'Wild snow in Shanyin impedes the visit,' which explicitly mentions the hot weather but implies it." [2]

In Chapter 5, Yang Wanli begins by refuting the assertion in the *Golden Needle Method* regarding the closing line in eight-line regulated poems, advancing the proposition that "poems being concluded while the taste remains eternal" is the most ideal, which means an exceptional poem should achieve the state where the lines are completed, yet the poetic taste endures. Subsequently, he provides several exemplary poems, such as *The Double Ninth* and *Declining an Invitation from Minister Li in Summer*, to illustrate his point. Moving on to Chapter 6, he provides a more detailed supplement to the concept mentioned in Chapter 5 by enumerating verses that exemplify enduring poetic tastes and categorizes them into three forms: those with three meanings in a seven-character line, those with two meanings in a five-character line, and those without explicit words within the line but with implicit meanings beyond. He further interprets these examples, elucidating to the reader what constitutes the "taste beyond the taste."

In terms of artistic style, *Shilin Shihua* mainly centers on the artistic ideas of implicitness, blending sentiment with scenery, and naturalness, while Yang Wanli's *Chengzhai Shihua* directs more attention to the eternal poetic taste, namely the enduring meaning, apart from implicit naturalness.[5] Yang emphasizes aesthetic perception and value beyond the verses in poetry, highlighting the perfect unity of words, meanings, and poetic tastes. He also provides specific instances to guide the analysis of the implicit meanings in the beautiful lines of predecessors, holding specific guidance for creative endeavors beyond the evaluation and appreciation of poetry.

3. Syntactic Skills: From "Refined Verses" to "Stunning Verses"

Within the spectrum of poetic syntax, Ye Mengde was influenced by predecessors' remarks on poetry, demanding that words and sentences be refined and hammered, preferring the use of unique words, reduplicated words, lively words, and other language forms, and pursuing the conformity of words, sentiments, and sceneries. Chapter 15 of *Annotated Notes on Shilin Shihua* says:

"The craftsmanship of a poet often manifests in a single word, a fact long recognized by people. Only in the verses of Du Fu does one find a myriad of changes, which are nearly elusive. Take the line 'Standing amid the mountains and waters of Bashu region, with its buildings tracing back to the Qi and Liang Dynasties' for instance. Thousands of miles and hundreds of years are condensed into the two words 'you' and 'zi.' Yet, with these simple words, the poem is imbued with a spirit that can conquer mountains and rivers and a broad mind that embraces both ancient and modern times, all subtly revealed beyond the textual descriptions. In the *Pavilion of Prince Teng*, he says, 'The pink wall still retains the hue of bamboo, from the empty pavilion, the sound of pine echoes.' If the words 'you' and 'zi' are not used, the remaining eight words can employed for any pavilion, without the necessity of Tengwang. All these verses are spectacular to the extreme, beyond the reach of ordinary human effort. Only Du Fu, with ease and leisure, achieved this out of naturalness, without a hint of strain. Many contemporary poets blindly imitate the words he used, falling into rigid and unchanging patterns. They seem unaware of the subtleties of blending sentiment with scenery; as long as they touch upon the crucial points, any words can be employed." [3]

From the very outset, Ye Mengde has explicitly pointed out that "The craftsmanship of a poet often manifests in a single word." He then cites two couplets of Du Fu's poems as an example, elucidating that with the use of only two common empty words, the poet manifests a spirit that can conquer mountains and rivers and a broad mind that embraces both ancient and modern times. The verses "The pink wall still retains the hue of bamboo, from the empty pavilion, the sound of pine echoes" also employ empty words to describe objective scenes, highlighting the unique features of the Pavilion of Prince Teng. In addition to the use of unique words, Ye further elaborates on the use of reduplicated words, as seen in Chapter 21 of the *Annotated Notes on Shilin Shihua*:

"The most challenging aspect of poetry composition lies in the use of 'reduplicated words.' It is imperative to ensure that the spirit and vitality of seven-character and five-character poems are fully encapsulated within two reduplicated characters, so as to be considered ingenious. The claim that the phrase 'Above the paddy fields, a line of white egrets glides through the sky; in the grove, the melodious cries of yellow orioles resonate' was stolen by Wang Wei from Li Jiayou, as asserted by people of the Tang Dynasty, is not accurate. The brilliance of these two lines lies in the addition of the words 'mo mo' and 'yin yin.' These four words were skillfully added by Wang Wei after being inspired by Jiayou, demonstrating his appreciation for the poetic nuances. This is akin to Li Guangbi leading the army of Guo Ziyi, issuing a single command, and enhancing the brilliance several times over. Otherwise, the original verses are merely a description of scenery, something an ordinary person could compose. In a word, only sentences like Du Fu's 'Endless trees shed their leaves that descend in the whistling wind, unending, the long river comes on churning' and 'The river sky spreads far and wide, birds go off in pairs, in wind and rain always the dragon hums' can be considered extraordinary. Modern verses such as Wang Anshi's 'The new frost resembles the fair beauty by the water, pure and white; as night approaches, the distant mountain ranges ofter appear green,' and Su Shi's 'The rich scent of the stove has just begun to diffuse in the night, the gently swaying flower shadows intensify the spring sentiments,' can also be considered complementary to the earlier examples. [3]

Ye Mengde first points out that the most challenging aspect of poetry composition lies in the use of "reduplicated words." He cites exemplary lines from Wang Wei, Du Fu, Wang Anshi, and Su Shi that employ reduplicated words to show that when reduplicated words are appropriately used, they can not only capture the external features of the landscape but also reflect the poet's senses and sensibilities. What's more, reduplicated words will contribute to the harmony of words and sounds in poetry, adding beauty to sound and rhythm. Therefore, Ye believes that when reduplicated words are properly used in poetry, it brings about a "spirit and vitality" to the poem, achieving the effects of being "exquisitely crafted," "transcendent," and "rivaling earlier works."

From the two chapters above, it is evident that Ye Mengde emphasizes the refinement of words in poetic syntax. To illustrate the opinions that "the craftsmanship of a poet often manifests in a single word" and "the most challenging aspect of poetry composition lies in the use of reduplicated words," he systematically summarizes and elaborates on the refining of words and sentences in the works of predecessors. This reveals his recognition of meticulous craftsmanship in poetic syntax. Yang Wanli delves deeper on the basis of evaluating works by predecessors. From these evaluations, he deduces and extracts specific writing methods. In Chapter 7 of *Chengzhai Shihua*, for example, he first points out what constitutes a "stunning verse":

"Poetry has stunning verses. In Du's *A Folding Screen Painted with Landscapes*, he says, 'In a hall where maples shouldn't grow, A strange sight, the mist below the mountain goes aloft.' Again, in another poem, he says, 'If the cassia tree in the moon is cut down, the emitting limpid light should be brighter.' Bai Juyi says, 'Feeling sorry for the lone cassias bloom in distant heavens, I ask Heng'e if she wants to plant more. Fortunately, there are idle fields in the moon palace; why not plant two trees in the center?' In Han Ju's *A Painting of Mount Heng*, he says, 'A friend hails from Tianzhu Peak in Mount Heng, with hands, he carries the Shilin Peak and Zhurong Peak. Two peaks stretch for hundreds of miles; how can they fit in the modest luggage space?' This is inspired by Su Shi's 'I bring this stone back with me, in my sleeve lies the East Sea,' Du Mu's 'I would like to summon the giant from the east Longbo Kingdom, to reach the heavens and grasp the Big Dipper,' 'Standing atop Penglai, I scoop up the ocean, until the sea is dried and the bottom surfaces,' and Li He's 'Where Nüwa tempers stones to repair the sky, the stones break, Heaven in shock, and tickle the autumn rain.'[2]

Here, Yang Wanli enumerates representative poems with fantastical and peculiar qualities. He not only elucidates what constitutes "stunning verses" but also provides examples illustrating that the "stunning" points lie in the poetry's unique imagination and unusual collocation. Examples include bold imaginations like "In my sleeve lies the East Sea" and "To reach the heavens and grasp the Big Dipper," as well as the use of novel collocation such as "If the cassia tree in the moon is cut down, the emitting limpid light should be brighter" and "Fortunately, there are idle fields in the moon palace, why not plant two trees in the center?" How can there be fields in the middle of the moon? These verses employ unique imagination to render ordinary things unfamiliar and unusual, creating the "stunning" effect. Apart from citing and commenting on "stunning verses," Yang also subtly explains how aspiring poets can create such verses.

Hence, in Chapter 12 of *Chengzhai Shihua*, he further analyzes the peculiarity of predecessors' poems:

"Regulated poems in the Tang Dynasty consist of eight lines with seven characters each. In a single poem, every line is remarkable, and within each line, every character is extraordinary, which is difficult for both ancient and modern authors. I once discussed this matter with Lin Guangchao, and he earnestly remarked, 'In our poetry collections, we should not refrain from composing several pieces.' For example, Du Fu's *The Double Ninth* says: 'As I age, I grieve over autumn and force myself to relax; a good mood comes on me today, and I have a full measure of delight with you.' The first line of this poem features perfect symmetry. Moreover, it undergoes an instant transformation, initially expressing a sense of autumnal sorrow, then suddenly followed by self-comfort. The use of 'zi' in contrast to 'jun' is particularly poignant, where 'jun' refers to the other party, and 'zi' denotes the author. 'Embarrassed that with this thinning hair, my hat would be again blown off; one might ask a bystander to tease me, so I straighten up my cap' is reversing one thing into a couplet. Meng Jia's mishap of losing his hat is deemed graceful, whereas Du Fu's not losing the hat is also considered elegant. Reversing all the ancient poetry cases is the most ingenious technique. The third couplet is 'The Lan River comes from afar, falling from a thousand mountain streams, Jade Mountain's height matches the paired peaks in the cold.' When most poets reach this point, their vigor often wanes. Yet, this poem remains vigorous and erect, evoking the spirit of the entire piece; such achievement wouldn't be possible without extraordinary vigor of strokes. 'I wonder who would still be around in next year's get-together, in inebriety I look carefully at a cornel leaf,' on the other hand, is endowed with a profound and enduring meaning." [2]

Here, Yang Wanli cites examples of seven-character, eight-line regulated poems in the Tang Dynasty. Through the perspective of Lin Guangchao, he analyzes where the "extraordinary" lies in Du Fu's poetry and what makes this "extraordinary" so enchanting. He then proposes that "reversing all the ancient poetry cases is the most ingenious technique" and gives a detailed discourse on how to compose "extraordinary" poetry and stunning verses, holding great theoretical guidance implications.

In terms of poetic syntax, *Shilin Shihua* emphasizes the refinement of words and characters. By citing and summarizing the subtle use of "unique words" and "reduplicated words"[3] in the verses of predecessors, Ye Mende expresses his pursuit of refining characters and making sentences that "blend sentiment with scenery." [3] On the other hand, Yang Wanli, in *Chengzhai Shihua*, introduces the concept of "stunning verses"[2] in poetry. He not only critiques the masterpieces of predecessors but also distills from them two poetic composition methods: the "reversal" method and the "inversion" method. Moreover, he puts these methods into practice, applying the technique of inversion in his own poetic creations, such as "Spring arrives abruptly on the morrow, winter fades as midnight comes" in *Two Poems on the Eve of Start of Spring* and "Last year's grassroots, reborn in spring's gentle breeze; a path unseen in the past year is newly trodden to the desolate grave" in *Tomb-sweeping* on *Cold Food Festival*. This not only offers theoretical guidance to future poets but also constitutes practical poetic composition experiments.

4. Imitating Ancient Poets and Using Allusions: From "Not Being Far-fetched" to "Skillful Integration"

In *Shilin Shihua*, it is stated: "Having read the poems of predecessors extensively, when encountering phrases that bring delights, one tends to memorize them repeatedly, and over time, inadvertently misappropriates them as one's own." [3] Ye Mende cites examples of Wei Yingwu and Wang Anshi, highlighting the phenomenon of similarities between verses of predecessors and successors. In contrast, *Chengzhai Shihua* explicitly states, "Those who are new to poetry must study the good verses of ancient poets" and "some good verses of successors accidentally resemble those of ancient poets, while others are intentionally passed down by later generations."[2] Yang Wanli provides examples illustrating instances where some predecessors surpass their predecessors, and some successors do not match their predecessors. He encourages aspiring poets to study the works of ancient poets, saying, "Those learning poetry can benefit from seeking excellent verses in the poems of Li Bai, Du Fu, Su Shi, and Huang Tingjian. By reciting and immersing themselves in these verses with deep understanding, they will have their own creativity naturally emerge when putting pen to paper."

The poetic theories of *Shilin Shihua* are embedded in its records and in dealing with the poetry of ancient poets. By listing ancient poems and commenting on them, Ye expresses his own poetic and literary thoughts. This is exemplified in Chapter 30 of *Annotated Notes on Shilin Shihua:*

"Du Fu's poems, *Sick Cypress, Sick Orange Trees, Withered Palms, and Withered Nanmu Tree,* all lament the events of the time. *Sick Cypress* seems to be composed for Emperor Ming of Tang, sharing a theme with *The Cuckoo: A Ballad. Withered Palms* employs analogy to portray the hardships of the people, as expressed in the text itself. In *Withered Nanmu Tree*, it says, 'It still holds provision for rafter and beam, Though its goals to reach wispy heights are gone.' This poem is likely written for individuals like Prime Minister Fang Guan. Only in *Sick Orange Trees* does Du Fu begin by saying, 'Too bad, indeed, that their fruits are so small, sour and sharp as the wild pear,' and in the end, he mentions the hardship people suffered for lychees, likely referring to those who have encountered setbacks. Since the Han and Wei periods, poets have demonstrated profound intentions while maintaining the classical style. Du Fu, in particular, goes beyond the confines of refining language, embodying this tradition." [3]

This commentary evaluates four poems of Du Fu, *Sick Cypress, Sick Orange Trees, Withered Palms, and Withered Nanmu Tree,* believing that these poems all reflect real-life experiences, expressing Ye's praise for Du Fu's poetry and affirming the poetic ideology based on social life. However, Ye Mengde also criticizes Du Fu's *Eight Laments*, as stated in Chapter 23 of *Annotated Notes on Shilin Shihua:*

"However, the *Eight Laments* are not masterpieces created concentratedly, yet many people refrain from discussing them out of reverence and a lack of understanding and appreciation. The shortcomings probably lie in the excessive verbosity. For example, in the poems lamenting Li Yong and Su Yuanming, there are many excessively verbose sentences. I have once ruthlessly edited them, retaining only half, in an effort to achieve perfection. Nevertheless, such words cannot be spoken by those who are unaware of these problems." [3]

Ye Mengde points out the "excessive use of verbose sentences" in the two poems that lament Li Yong and Su Yuanming, criticizing them for not achieving conciseness and beauty. From these two examples, it can be observed that *Shilin Shihua*, while admiring the poetic styles of ancient poets, confines its commentaries to the author's perspectives on poetry creation and critiques of earlier poets. It does not offer guidance on how beginners should study ancient poetry and engage in poetry composition. In contrast, Yang Wanli, in *Chengzhai Shihua*, provides specific arguments and discussions on how to learn from ancient poets, serving as an exemplary work for aspiring poets. An example can be found in Chapter 8 of *Chengzhai Shihua*:

"The five-character regulated poem, praising merits and virtues, demands utmost elegance and grandeur. For instance, Du Fu wrote: 'Phoenix calendar, Xuanyuan's time calculations, the dragon has taken flight for forty years. To the encircling wilds was opened a realm of long life, the Single Force turned the Great Potter's Wheel.' Another example from Du Fu is: 'Its sapphire tiles lie outside the first chill, its golden pillar is beside the One Vapor. Mountains and river support finely wrought windows, sun and moon come close to its carved beams.' Li Shangyin also states: 'The emperor established the capital, and immortals opened up a celestial palace. With outstanding individuals upholding truth, the essence of Heaven and Earth draws down the very night.' As for seven-character regulated poems praising merits and virtues, Du Fu and Jia Zhi jointly compose *Dawn Court at Daming Palace*, which also embodies elegance and grandeur. Among those who responded to this poem, Cen Shen's verses, 'The colors of flowers intertwine with the gleam of the sword, with morning stars just faded away, banners lightly brush against willow branches, with dewdrops lingering on the branches' stand out as the best." [2]

Chapter 9:

"Seven-character long regulated poems, such as Du Shaoling's *Song of a Painting, Pictures of Horses by General Cao*, and *Song for the Painted Landscape Screen of Liu Dan, Sheriff of Fengxian*, are majestic and grand and difficult to capture. Those learning poetry can benefit from seeking excellent verses in the poems of Li Bai, Du Fu, Su Shi, and Huang Tingjian. By reciting and immersing themselves in these verses with deep understanding, they will have their own creativity naturally emerge when putting pen to paper." [2]

Chengzhai Shihua points out what characteristics different poetic forms should possess. For example, five-character long regulated poems should be elegant and profound, which can draw inspiration from the works of Du Fu and Li Shangyin. Seven-character long regulated poems should be majestic and grand, which can refer to the above three poems by Du Fu. Ye encourages aspiring poets to seek out these characteristics in the poetry of Li Bai, Du Fu, Su Shi, and Huang Tingjian, thoroughly reading and deeply appreciating the nuances. By doing so, they are able to produce excellent works when composing poetry.

Regarding allusions, Ye Mengde emphasizes in Chapter 26 of *Annotated Notes on Shilin Shihua* that "the use of allusions should not be far-fetched; they must be used only when necessary." He compares verses from Su

Shi and Wen Tingyun, stating that Su Shi's "Unintentionally, the sun slants after the year of Gengzi, suddenly, I'm startled to find the year has reached Sichen" is adorned with allusions without artificial embellishment, displaying a natural and innate beauty. On the other hand, Ye Mengde criticizes Wen Tingyun's thought that "Sitting in quiet meditation throughout the night with the ascetic, I often hear urgent matters emanating from the west" for appearing contrived in its use of allusions. Ye Mengde cites examples of allusion usage in poems, expressing his own judgment on whether the allusions are employed well or not. However, he does not provide theoretical guidance on how to use allusions.

Yang Wanli attaches great importance to the skillful integration of idioms and allusions in poetry, proposing that "Utilizing the language of ancient predecessors rather than adhering strictly to their intended meanings is the most ingenious technique." He points out that the use of allusions should be flexible and adaptable, thus avoiding rigidity. He further categorizes the methods into "reversal" and "inversion." He believes that the "reversal" method can make poetry more subtle and enchanting, considering it as a technique that poets should master in the study of poetry.

As for the method of "reversal," Yang also presents multiple clear examples in his work. In Chapter 12, for instance, he states, "Embarrassed that with this thinning hair, my hat would be again blown off; one might ask a bystander to tease me, so I straighten up my cap' is reversing one thing into a couplet.' Meng Jia's mishap of losing his hat is deemed graceful, whereas Du Fu's not losing the hat is also considered elegant. Reversing all the ancient poetry cases is the most ingenious technique." In Chapter 15, he cites Huang Tingjian's "Heaven and Earth serve as the canopy and bumper" and "Unable to produce two or three volumes" and Su Shi's "The carriage canopy need not be tilted" and "A whip is available but unused, opting instead for a papyrus whip" as examples of transforming allusions. He cites Su Shi's adding the phrase "why bother" before Du Fu's "At once I recall the past, how autumn wells caved in," explaining how to "utilize the language of ancient predecessors rather than adhering strictly to their intended meanings." Finally, he concludes with Liu Jingming's poetry as a successful case for learning the "reversal" method. In Chapter 13, he points out that "inversion" is a particularly ingenious technique for poets, providing several examples such as "The snow-white tea froths swirl when boiling, pouring it resembles the wild wind in a pine forest," "Sweet-smelling rice, pecked the last, for parrots, the grains; sapphire tung trees, perch of old, the phoenix's branches," and "With an empty stomach, though, I am unable to drink three bowls; sitting here, I listen to the long and short night watchman's bells in the mountainous city." These examples illustrate the charm of inversion, allowing readers to savor the infinite flavors of this technique.

Regarding imitating ancient poets and allusion usage, Ye Mengde, in *Shilin Shihua*, expresses his poetics by citing examples of ancient poetry, briefly illustrates his views on ancient poetry and allusions, and makes commentaries. In comparison, Yang Wanli's *Chengzhai Shihua*, building upon the evaluation of ancient poetry, delves deeper into exploring how to study the poetic composition methods of ancient poets. In addition, he systematically summarizes the ancient poets' ingenious techniques for employing allusions with illustrative examples and detailed analysis, serving as critical guidance for novice poets. [7]

5. Conclusion

From the perspective of artistic characteristics of poetry, Shilin Shihua has delved into some critical theoretical issues of poetic composition, including the relationship between content and form, as well as the artistic mindsets and rules of poetry. However, it primarily conveys the author's personal poetics or critiques of poetry by giving examples. By contrast, Yang Wanli's *Chengzhai Shihua* is more instructive and exploratory. Building upon the poetic theoretical foundation of *Shilin Shihua*, it digs more deeply into exploring how to learn the poetic style of ancient poets and elevates the artistic style of poetry from implicit naturalness to the level of "eternal poetic taste. "Additionally, it puts forward that poetry should have "stunning verses" and "utilize the language of ancient predecessors rather than adhering strictly to their intended meanings," and provides guiding specific suggestions for beginners on how to write poetry. Yang Wanli himself also breaks the shackles of the Jiangxi School of Poetry and creates the "Chengzhai Style"[6] characterized by its freshness and liveliness, reflecting a valuable spirit of exploration in summarizing predecessors' poetic composition experience, inheriting the traditions predecessors' poetics, and researching poetry theories.

References

1. Cai,Z.C.(2001)The History of Chinese Shihua, Revised Edition [M]. Changsha: Hunan Literature and Art Publishing House.
2. Yang,W.L.(1998)YangWangli Shihua.In:Wenzhi,W.(Editor). The Complete Compilation of Song Shihua [M]. Nanjing: Jiangsu Ancient Books Publishing House.
3. Ye,M.D.(2011) Annotated Notes on Shilin Shihua [M]. Beijing: People's Literature Publishing House.
4. Liang,Y.N.(2019) Viewing Yang Wanli's Poetic Thoughts from Cheng Zhai Shi Hua [D]. Soochow University. 10.27351/d.cnki.gszhu.2019.001297
5. Li Zhi-Zhu. (2019). The development and characteristics of Naturalism in Song Dynasty Poetics. 한국중어중문학 우수논문집, 107-123.
6. Li, E. (2020). Beyond the City Walls: Photographic Seeing and the Longing for Wilderness in Yang Wanli's Nature Poems. Journal of Chinese Literature and Culture, 7(2), 313-338.
7. Du, F. (2020). Poetry as Epistemology: The Naïve Poet Yang Wanli (1127-1206) in the Age of Learning (Doctoral dissertation).https://nrs.harvard.edu/URN-3:HUL.INSTREPOS:37368941

Enhancing English Writing Proficiency in TESOL: Integrating Traditional and Technological Approaches for a Multifaceted Learning Experience

Jianing Wang[1], Weiwei Li[2], Ming Lu[3], Yu Chen[4*]

[1] Southeast University, Nanjing, China
[2]University of York, York, UK
[3]Guangdong University of Science and Technology, Guangdong, China
[4]University of Edinburgh, Edinburgh, Scotland

Abstract: This scholarly article delves into the latest advancements within the Teaching English to Speakers of Other Languages (TESOL) arena, specifically concentrating on their impact on teaching English writing. The study critically analyses a variety of pioneering methods, tactics, and tools currently employed in TESOL, with a special emphasis on refining students' English writing capabilities. It explores the intersection of traditional and modern pedagogical techniques, highlighting how blended approaches can significantly enhance the writing skills of learners. The paper provides in-depth insights into how these innovative strategies not only improve writing proficiency but also foster a deeper understanding of the English language among students. It argues that the effectiveness of these teaching methodologies is pivotal in equipping students with the skills necessary to excel in English writing, thereby contributing to their overall academic success. The research emphasizes the role of tailored instruction, feedback mechanisms, and the integration of digital tools in creating an engaging and effective learning environment.

1. Introduction

Recent advancements in TESOL have profoundly impacted English writing pedagogy, emphasizing the need for more inclusive and adaptable teaching methods. These developments recognize the diverse linguistic backgrounds of learners and the varying contexts in which English is used globally. There is a growing focus on communicative competence, where the emphasis is not just on grammatical accuracy but also on the ability to use language effectively in different social and cultural contexts. This shift has led to the incorporation of digital tools and multimedia resources in teaching, making learning more interactive and engaging. Additionally, there is an increasing emphasis on learner-centered approaches, where instruction is tailored to meet the individual needs, interests, and learning styles of students. Teachers are now equipped with a range of strategies to help students develop a more nuanced understanding of the English language, encouraging critical thinking and creativity in their writing. This holistic approach not only improves writing skills but also builds confidence and motivation among learners, preparing them for various challenges in a multilingual world.

2. Strategies for effective english writing instruction

2.1. Integrated Skills Approach

The integrated skills approach in TESOL, by intertwining the four core language skills—listening, speaking, reading, and writing—creates a more dynamic and engaging learning environment. This method mirrors the natural way languages are learned and used in real life, where these skills are rarely isolated. For example, a lesson might begin with a reading activity where students explore a text, followed by a group discussion to express their understanding and perspectives. This discussion serves as a springboard for a writing task, where students are encouraged to articulate their thoughts in writing, integrating new vocabulary and grammatical structures encountered in the reading and speaking activities [1]. This multifaceted approach not only reinforces language learning but also enhances critical thinking skills, as students are required to analyze, interpret, and express complex ideas across different modalities. It also fosters a deeper understanding and retention of the language, as students see how various linguistic elements work together in different contexts.

Furthermore, the integrated skills approach is highly adaptable to different learning styles and needs. By

*Corresponding author's email: 2482516799@qq.com

incorporating a variety of activities, it caters to students who may excel in one particular skill while providing support and development opportunities in others. For instance, a student who is a strong reader but struggles with speaking can benefit from discussions that build confidence in oral expression, while the written reflections allow them to showcase their analytical skills. This approach also offers numerous opportunities for creative and authentic language use. Teachers can incorporate real-world materials such as news articles, podcasts, and videos, making the learning experience more relevant and interesting. Students learn not just to understand and produce language, but also to use it effectively in diverse situations, from formal academic writing to casual conversations. By engaging with the language in its entirety, students develop a more rounded and practical proficiency, better preparing them for the complexities of real-world communication.

2.2. Genre-Based Writing

In TESOL, the genre-based writing approach has been refined to cater to the varied needs of learners across different proficiency levels. This approach involves teaching the conventions and structures of specific genres, such as argumentative essays or business reports, by using authentic examples. It helps students understand the purpose and audience of different types of texts, enabling them to adapt their writing style accordingly. Teachers often use a variety of texts as models and engage students in analyzing these texts to identify key features and stylistic elements [2]. This method not only improves students' ability to write in different genres but also enhances their reading and analytical skills. By understanding the nuances of various genres, learners become more versatile writers and are better equipped to handle different writing tasks in academic and professional settings.

2.3. Process Writing

In the realm of TESOL, the process writing approach has increasingly embraced digital tools and platforms to enhance its effectiveness. These technologies provide dynamic and interactive ways for students to engage in each stage of the writing process. For example, online collaborative platforms allow for real-time brainstorming and idea sharing, where students can collectively develop concepts and outlines. This digital integration also enables students to receive immediate, iterative feedback from instructors and peers, not only on written drafts but also on their brainstorming and planning stages. Such tools often come with features that track changes and suggest improvements, making the revision process more comprehensive and insightful. Additionally, these platforms often include resources like grammar and style checkers, which aid students in self-editing their work. This tech-forward approach in process writing not only develops writing skills but also digital literacy, preparing students for a world where digital communication is increasingly prevalent [3].

Furthermore, the expanded view of process writing in TESOL also involves a greater emphasis on reflective practices. After completing a writing assignment, students are encouraged to engage in self-reflection and analysis, considering what they have learned during the process and identifying areas for future improvement. This reflective stage is crucial as it helps learners internalize the skills they have acquired, leading to a deeper and more personal understanding of their writing journey. Teachers may also incorporate various forms of feedback, including individual conferences, written comments, or group discussions, to provide personalized guidance and support. This reflective approach ensures that the learning extends beyond the specific assignment, fostering long-term writing development. It cultivates a mindset of continuous learning and adaptation, crucial for students in an ever-evolving linguistic landscape. Through this comprehensive and reflective process writing approach, learners are not only improving their writing skills but are also becoming more self-aware and autonomous writers, capable of navigating and adapting to different writing contexts and demands.

3. Technological Advancements in English Writing Instruction

3.1. Online Writing Platforms

The surge in online learning environments has led TESOL educators to integrate online writing platforms into their curricula, revolutionizing the way writing skills are taught and practiced. These platforms, characterized by their user-friendly interfaces and accessibility, offer a dynamic space for learners to engage in various writing activities. They facilitate collaborative writing projects, allowing students from diverse geographical locations to work together, thereby fostering a global perspective in writing. These platforms often come equipped with tools for real-time feedback and editing, enabling students to refine their writing with immediate guidance. Additionally, they provide access to a vast array of resources, including writing templates, sample essays, and interactive tutorials, which cater to different proficiency levels and learning styles [4]. By promoting learner autonomy and engagement, online writing platforms have become indispensable in contemporary TESOL practices, significantly enhancing the learning experience and outcomes in English writing instruction.

3.2. Automated Writing Assessment

The advent of automated writing assessment tools in TESOL has significantly transformed the landscape of English writing education. These advanced tools, powered by sophisticated algorithms and natural language processing technologies, are capable of providing nuanced analysis of student writing. Beyond basic grammar and vocabulary checks, they assess aspects like sentence structure, argument strength, and coherence, offering a more holistic evaluation of a student's writing ability. This level of detailed analysis is particularly beneficial in identifying specific areas where a student may struggle, such as the use of passive voice, varied sentence lengths, or the clarity of thesis statements. By highlighting these areas, students receive targeted feedback that directly addresses their individual needs, fostering a more effective and personalized learning experience. Additionally, the instantaneous nature of this feedback accelerates the learning cycle, allowing students to immediately apply the suggestions and improve their subsequent writing attempts.

Moreover, the integration of these tools into TESOL has broader implications for curriculum development and instructional strategies. With access to comprehensive data on student performance, educators can identify trends and common challenges within a class or across different cohorts [5]. This data-driven approach enables teachers to refine their teaching methodologies, focusing on areas that require more attention or introducing new topics that cater to the evolving needs of their students. For instance, if a significant number of students struggle with persuasive writing, teachers can allocate more time to teaching persuasive techniques and structuring arguments. Furthermore, these tools often allow for customization, enabling teachers to set specific criteria based on their curriculum goals or the proficiency level of their students. This adaptability ensures that the assessment aligns with the learning objectives and the overall educational context. In essence, automated writing assessment tools not only enhance the efficiency and effectiveness of individual learning but also contribute to the continuous improvement of TESOL programs, ensuring they remain relevant and responsive to the needs of diverse learners in a rapidly changing world.

3.3. Multimedia and Multimodal Writing

Multimedia and multimodal writing in TESOL classrooms is transforming the way English is taught and learned. This approach goes beyond the conventional focus on text by incorporating a variety of media, such as videos, podcasts, infographics, and interactive presentations. By doing so, it aligns more closely with the multifaceted nature of communication in the digital era, where messages are often conveyed through a blend of text, images, and sound. For students, this method of learning is not only more engaging but also more reflective of the real-world scenarios in which they are likely to use English. For example, a project might involve creating a video blog, designing a digital poster, or recording a podcast, tasks that combine language skills with digital creativity. These activities encourage learners to think critically about how different modes of expression can be used to convey meaning effectively [6]. They also provide a platform for students to showcase their individual talents and preferences, catering to diverse learning styles and interests. This variety ensures that each student can find a mode of expression that resonates with them, increasing motivation and participation.

In addition, the integration of multimedia elements in writing tasks prepares students for the demands of the modern, digital workplace. As the global economy becomes increasingly interconnected, the ability to communicate effectively across different platforms becomes crucial. By engaging in multimodal writing activities, students develop not just language proficiency, but also digital literacy and media skills. They learn to critically evaluate and select appropriate media for different purposes, understand the nuances of digital communication, and become adept at using technology to enhance their messages. This kind of training is invaluable in a world where digital communication is ubiquitous, giving students a competitive edge in both academic and professional settings. Moreover, by exposing students to a range of digital tools and platforms, educators are helping to bridge the digital divide, ensuring that all learners have the opportunity to develop the skills necessary to thrive in a digitally driven future. As such, multimedia and multimodal writing in TESOL is more than just an innovative teaching strategy; it is an essential component in preparing learners for the complexities and opportunities of the 21st century.

4. Challenges and Considerations

4.1. Addressing Access to Technology and Digital Literacy

One of the primary challenges in integrating technological advancements into English writing instruction is ensuring equitable access to technology. Not all learners have the same level of access to digital devices or stable internet connectivity, which can create disparities in learning opportunities. TESOL educators must be mindful of these digital divides and seek to implement strategies that mitigate their impact. This might involve offering blended learning options that combine online and offline resources, ensuring that students without regular internet access can still participate effectively in the learning process. Additionally, there's the challenge of digital literacy among learners. Students from different backgrounds may have varying levels of familiarity and comfort with digital tools, necessitating the need for initial training or support. TESOL programs must incorporate digital literacy as a fundamental component, equipping students with the necessary skills to navigate and utilize technology efficiently in their learning journey [7].

4.2. Embracing Learner Diversity and Professional Development

The diversity in learner backgrounds in TESOL presents both opportunities and challenges for educators. Students come from a wide array of cultural contexts, each bringing their own unique experiences and perspectives to the English learning process. This cultural richness can greatly enhance the learning environment, providing a tapestry of viewpoints and experiences that enrich discussions and understanding. However, it also requires educators to adopt a more nuanced and sensitive approach to teaching. They must be adept at navigating cultural nuances and avoiding a one-size-fits-all approach to instruction. This involves not only being aware of cultural differences but also incorporating these diverse perspectives into the curriculum. For instance, incorporating texts and materials that reflect a variety of cultures and experiences can make learning more relatable and engaging for students from different backgrounds. Moreover, understanding and accommodating various learning styles is crucial. While some students may thrive in collaborative and interactive settings, others may prefer more structured and individualized learning experiences. TESOL educators need to design their courses in a way that caters to these varied learning preferences, ensuring that each student has the opportunity to learn in an environment that suits their individual needs [8].

Professional development plays a critical role in equipping educators with the skills and knowledge required to meet these challenges. Continuous training and development opportunities are essential for teachers to stay abreast of the latest educational technologies, pedagogical strategies, and cultural competencies. This ongoing education should not just be about integrating technology into the classroom; it should also focus on how to use these tools in culturally sensitive and pedagogically sound ways. For example, training sessions might cover topics like leveraging digital tools to create more inclusive and engaging learning experiences or using multimedia resources to address different learning styles and cultural contexts [9]. Additionally, professional development should encourage reflection and self-assessment, helping educators recognize their own biases and assumptions and understand how these might impact their teaching. By committing to lifelong learning and adaptability, TESOL educators can better balance the integration of innovative technologies with traditional teaching methods, creating a more dynamic, inclusive, and effective learning environment for their diverse student populations [10].

5. Conclusion

This article has explored the dynamic and evolving landscape of TESOL, with a particular focus on the advancements in English writing instruction. Throughout, we have seen how innovative pedagogical approaches, underpinned by the integration of technology, are reshaping the way English writing skills are taught and learned. The implementation of strategies such as the integrated skills approach, genre-based writing, and process writing, complemented by the use of online platforms, automated writing assessment tools, and multimedia elements, exemplifies a modern, holistic approach to language instruction. These methods not only enhance the effectiveness of teaching English writing but also cater to the diverse needs and learning styles of students, making education more inclusive and accessible.

However, the incorporation of these technologies and methods is not without its challenges. Issues of digital divide, cultural diversity, and the necessity for continuous professional development for educators are critical considerations that need addressing to ensure the success of these innovative approaches. As TESOL continues to adapt to the demands of a globalized and digital world, it is imperative that educators and institutions remain sensitive to these challenges, striving to provide equitable access to resources and tailoring teaching methods to embrace the rich diversity of learners.

In conclusion, the future of English writing instruction in TESOL is promising, marked by a shift towards more interactive, learner-centered, and technologically integrated approaches. These advancements are pivotal in equipping learners with the necessary skills and competencies to excel in English writing, ultimately contributing to their broader academic and professional success. As the field continues to evolve, it is essential that educators and stakeholders remain committed to innovation, inclusivity, and continuous improvement, ensuring that TESOL remains responsive to the ever-changing educational landscape and the diverse needs of learners around the world.

Reference

1. Consoli, Sal. "Life capital: An epistemic and methodological lens for TESOL research." Tesol Quarterly 56.4 (2022): 1397-1409.
2. Yazan, Bedrettin, Luis Javier Penton Herrera, and Doaa Rashed. "Transnational TESOL practitioners' identity tensions: A collaborative autoethnography." TESOL quarterly 57.1 (2023): 140-167.
3. McKinley, Jim. "Evolving the TESOL teaching–research nexus." Tesol Quarterly 53.3 (2019): 875-884.
4. Aghai, Laila, et al., eds. Envisioning TESOL through a translanguaging lens: Global perspectives. Springer International Publishing, 2020.
5. Rose, Heath, et al. Global TESOL for the 21st century: Teaching English in a changing world. Vol. 81. Multilingual Matters, 2020.
6. Kuyyogsuy, Sirikarn. "Promoting Peer Feedback in Developing Students' English Writing Ability in L2 Writing Class." International Education Studies 12.9 (2019): 76-90.
7. Saragih, Mandra, and Novimariono Novimariono. "An Experimental Study of The Effectiveness PEOW MODEL Through Applying Quartet Card in Teaching English Writing." Indonesian Journal of Education, Social Sciences and Research (IJESSR) 1.1 (2020): 32-40.
8. Karaca, Mehmet, and Hacer Hande Uysal. "The development and validation of an inventory on English writing teacher beliefs." Assessing writing 47 (2021): 100507.
9. Rahman, Ayuni Madarina Abdul, Mohd Nazri Latiff Azmi, and Isyaku Hassan. "Improvement of English writing skills through blended learning among university students in Malaysia." Universal Journal of Educational Research 8.12A (2020): 7694-7701.
10. Alghazo, Khitam Mohameed, and Mohamed Khaliefah Alshraideh. "Grammatical Errors Found in English Writing: A Study from Al-Hussein Bin Talal University." International Education Studies 13.9 (2020): 1-9.

A Study on Translation of Numbers in *the Analects of Confucius* from the Perspective of Cultural Translation Theory—— a Case study of the Translation Version by Gu Hongming

Ying LI[1,*], Rui Xiang[1], Shuxin Xiu[2], Weiwei Qu[1]

[1]Research and Teaching Institute of College Foreign Languages, Bohai University, Jinzhou Liaoning, 121013, China
[2]School of Foreign Languages, Northeast Normal University, Changchun, Jilin, 130024, China

Abstract: The language of the *Analects of Confucius* is concise, rich in connotation and highly abstract, so the problem of lack of meaning or semantic insufficiency is very obvious, and the numerical meaning is one of the most obvious examples. Based on Susan Bassnett view of cultural translation, this paper analyzes Gu Hongming's translated version of *Analects* and finds that there are great cultural differences between Chinese and Western numerals in terms of definite reference and vague reference. In addition to definite reference, Chinese numbers also have the function of vague reference; In English, numbers are mostly used in definite reference, and vague reference is mostly based on larger numbers. This increases the difficulty for translators and readers to understand the original work. In addition to having a solid bilingual foundation, the translator should have a profound bilingual cultural knowledge to realize the translation of cultural information behind the language. The theory of cultural translation has certain feasibility in guiding the translation of Chinese classics into English, which can promote the foreign translation of Chinese classics and has certain practical significance in promoting the transmission of Chinese culture to the world.

1.Introduction

At present, cultural diversity has become the mainstream of global development. In this context, China has attached great importance to carry forward its soft power especially its culture. We should tell Chinese stories to promote the international exchange of Chinese culture. Excellent literary translation can promote mutual learning of civilizations and people-to-people exchanges, thus building quality language services and enhancing the national image[1].The translation of Chinese classics is exactly a kind of literary translation[1].Relying on the translation and introduction of classics to let Chinese culture go global, we let more people better know about Chinese sinology, and enhance the correct understanding of China in the international community. It laid the foundation for the West to better understand China in the future[2].The Analects of Confucius is one of the classical cultural classics in China, which plays an important role in ancient Chinese civilization and attracts the attention of people all over the world. Its English version can better play its function of intercultural exchange. With Susan Bassnett's cultural translation theory as the guidance, Gu Hongming's English translation of *the Analects of Confucius* as the corpus, this study analyzes the translation methods in numbers of Gu's translation, and explores these methods under the guidance of cultural translation theory, in the hope that the methods can be applied to other English translations of classics. There are great differences between Chinese and Western cultures, so are numbers. Therefore, how to better translate numbers of classical Chinese into English is a great question which is worth exploring and studying. Gu Hongming frequently adopts the domestication translation strategy, that is, he tries his best to convert the information in the original work into the scope of knowledge understood by the readers. Therefore, his translation has been deeply praised by the other translators with the characteristics of that time.

2.Culture and number

2.1 Number is part of the culture

Number is a part of language, which not only has the function of counting, but also carries the historical and cultural information of a nation. The East and the West have different geographical locations, different cultures, religions, social customs, etc., so the interpretation of number is also different. Due to the cultural differences between English and Chinese, the specific number preferred in English and Chinese are not exactly the same. By comparing the different interpretations of numbers by Chinese and Western nationalities, it is helpful to understand the differences between Chinese and Western cultures and analyze their different social psychology,

*Corresponding author's mail: 773325428@qq.com

which is of great significance for cross-cultural communication. Chinese and English belong to different language families in the East and the west, and the different cognition of numbers in the two languages also reflects the different cultural connotations of the East and the West.

For example, the number "three" has different cultural connotations in Chinese and Western cultures. Three is a number that Westerners respect and love, symbolizing holiness, fullness and auspiciousness. Christianity advocates the trinity of the Father, the Son and the Holy Spirit; The Pythagoreans believed that the three represented birth, life and death, the past and present and the future, men, women and children. Three also means good luck. There is a saying in English "All things come in threes. " In the eyes of Westerners, three is a lucky and auspicious number, representing a perfect and stable triangle.

The number "three" in Chinese culture mostly comes from ancient philosophical theories and thoughts. In the Tao Te Ching, it is said: "From Tao there comes one, from one there comes two, from there comes there, from three there comes all things". That everything in the world is derived from the number three. In Chinese culture, there are also symbols of fullness and holiness. Like the three spirits of heaven, earth and man. However, because "three" has the similar pronunciation to the word "scattered" which is full of unlucky meaning, some festive occasions will avoid fall on a date with the number three. In addition, in ancient Chinese, the words "three" mostly represent the concept of quantity. It can be used for both definite and vague reference, but three is only used for definite reference in English, without vague reference function. This requires more attention in Chinese-English translation to faithfully translate the full text.

2.2 Numbers are also influenced by culture

Due to cultural differences between English and Chinese, the specific numbers preferred in English and Chinese are not exactly the same. There are great cultural differences between Chinese and western numerals in terms of definite and vague reference. In Chinese, the vague number refers to "one" to "ten", "hundred", "thousand", "million" and other numbers, while in English, it refers to a large number of numbers, such as a hundred and one, not in a hundred year and so on [3]. The extended meaning of numbers in ancient Chinese goes far beyond the numbers themselves. This is called vagueness in semantics. Zhang Rulun once said that both the lack of meaning and the excess of meaning produce inconsistency between the form and content of meaning [4]. The language of ancient Chinese classics is concise and rich in connotation, which often shows a lack of meaning, so that later generations cannot grasp their meaning. The concise and abstract language of the *Analects of Confucius* leads to the obvious problem of insufficient semantic meaning, among which the number meaning in ancient Chinese is the most obvious example. Numbers carry a lot of Chinese cultural connotations. In the process of translating numbers into English, it is more important to interpret the cultural meaning of numbers. The various peoples do not use the same systems of hypernyms, so the translation, beyond the literal meaning, is likely to brand itself of erroneous meanings[5].There are two kinds of numbers in the *Analects of Confucius*: definite and vague reference. For some numbers, literal translation according to its literal meaning can also be understood by the target readers, and literal translation can better convey the content and form of the source language. For some vague numbers, which cannot be translated literally, translators need to use free translation or ellipsis translation methods to translate them.

3.Cultural translation theory

Translation has a long history. Since the 1970s, translation has gone from being a marginal subject that was ignored like Cinderella to being incorporated into the field of study by linguists, and then scholars have noticed that translation is closely related not only to linguistics, but also to literature, philosophy and even sociology, psychology and other disciplines. Research is being conducted in the aesthetic, philosophical, psychological, linguistic, physiological, and sociological areas[6]. This long process has pushed translation studies to new heights again and again. In the 1980s, translation studies ushered in a new stage: cultural translation.

The cultural turn of translation studies is a major breakthrough in the field in recent years. Susan Bassnett, as the first translation theorist who put forward the view of cultural translation, argues that culture should be regarded as the basic unit of translation. She believes that translation should take culture as the unit of translation, and translation is not a simple code-recombination process, but more importantly a communication behavior. Translation should not be limited to the description of the source text, but should focus on the functional equivalence in the target language culture.

In other words, translation is a kind of cross-cultural exchange. Freedom is also connected to creativity, which is another motivating factor mentioned by translator[7]. Since language is an inseparable part of culture, translators should master the two cultures behind the two languages while having a good command of the two languages they translate. Translation, in essence, is a kind of cross-cultural behavior. Susan Bassnett's cultural translation theory breaks the traditional concept of translation studies, brings translation studies to a new stage, provides a new theoretical perspective for translation studies, and has far-reaching significance for translation practice and research.

4.Translation strategies of numbers under the guidance of cultural translation theory

4.1 Definite reference

Numbers precisely refer to the aspects mentioned, and it is best to keep these numbers in English translation to convey the original information truthfully and accurately. Regarding these numbers, literal translation could be adopted to make the lexical meaning of the translation as similar as possible to the original text. Take a sentence for example."曾子曰:'吾日三省吾身，为人谋而不忠乎，与人交而不信乎，传不习乎?'"（篇一）As for this sentence, Gu's translation: "A disciple of Confucius remarked, 'I daily examine into my personal conduct on three points:--First, whether in carrying out the duties entrusted to me by others, I have not failed in conscientiousness; Secondly, whether in intercourse with friends, I have not failed in sincerity and trustworthiness; Thirdly, whether I have not failed to practice what I profess in my teaching.'" In this example, there are several interpretations of "three", one is the triple check; The second is to examine from three aspects; Third, multiple inspections. Since it is followed by three aspects of "seeking advice for others", "communicating with others" and "passing on", Gu Hongming regards this as the definite reference and adopts the literal translation method to translate it into "three points", so as to make the translation reproduce the style of the original text and accurately convey the original content.

4.2 Vague reference

The concise language of ancient Chinese classics often shows a lack of meaning, which makes it impossible for future generations to grasp its meaning. Numbers carry many cultural connotations, so it is more important to interpret the vague numbers from the cultural significance of the numbers. Due to cultural heterogeneity, "it is not easy to find appropriate equivalents[8].In the process of translation, it is necessary to use liberal translation instead of literal translation. Liberal translation means smoothly expressing the meaning of the source text without keeping the form of the target text.claims that liberal translation emphasizes the conveying of the actual meaning of the words of the source text in a specific context. Take this sentence as an example."子曰：'回也其心三月不违仁，其余则日月至焉而已矣。'"（篇六）Gu's translation: "Confucius remarked of his disciple, the favourite Yen Hui, saying, 'For months he could live without deviating from a pure moral life in thought as in deed. With other people, the utmost is a question of a day or a month.'" In this sentence, "three" is also a vague reference, "march" refers to a long time. Corresponding to "sun and moon" in the following clause, "sun and moon" here means "short time". This sentence means that Yan Hui's heart can not leave benevolence for a long time, and the rest of the students can only achieve benevolence for a short time. Therefore, Gu Hongming did not use literal translation in translation, but used free translation to translate "march" as "for months."

In ancient China, the number nine was the symbol of the emperor. The height of the three main halls of the Forbidden City is nine feet nine; Tian 'anmen rostrum is nine rooms wide; The doornails on the palace and the gates were nine rows across and nine rows up; The steps in the palace are nine, or a multiple of nine; Because the homophonic sound of "nine" is "long", it represents a long time, and also symbolizes the rule of the ancient emperors can last forever. In the following example taken from *The Analects of Confucius*, the translation of "九" to English needs paying much attention."子欲居九夷。或曰：'陋，如之何？'"（篇九）Translation by Gu Hongming："On one occasion Confucius said he would go and live among the barbarous tribes in the East:, 'You will there,' remarked somebody,'feel the want of refinement'." The "九夷" here is the general name for the Eastern minority in ancient China. Therefore, Gu Hongming also adopted the liberal translation strategy when translating "九夷"into "barbarous tribes in the East". In some ancient Chinese, the word "九州" is also common, and here it is also a vague reference, short for ancient China. Therefore, it is often translated as "China".

5.Perspective on Gu's translation of *the Analects of Confucius* through cultural translation theory

Through the above analysis of the definite and vague reference of the numerical translation examples, it can be seen that Basnett's cultural translation theory is reasonable as a guide for the translation theory of the Analects. Translation, as a language communication activity, is not only the conversion of one language into another, but also the exchange between different cultures. Although any communication is achieved in the process of decoding and transcoding information, Basnett believes that translation is not a simple process of decoding and transcoding. In the process of converting two languages, translators should fully understand the unique culture contained in the two languages and realize the communication between language and culture.For example, "八佾" in the Court" in the third chapter of the Analects , "Eight Yiwu" is indeed its actual meaning, that is, 64 people, but it contains cross-cultural information behind it is the content that should be most passed on to the reader. According to *The Book of Changes*, only the emperor of Zhou Dynasty can use "八佾",六佾, 四佾 and 二佾 namely for vassal, officials and scholars. However, Ji Shi, he illegally used the "八佾" , so this is an unforgivable transgression. Gu Hongming's translation not only translated the actual meaning of numbers, but also translated the cultural information behind them with simple and concise notes of "an Imperial prerogative", which not only enhanced the comprehensibility of the translation, but also avoided the loss of cultural information. In addition, the translation of the same number in different contexts is also a major translation difficulty for translators. For example, "one" has three meanings in Chinese thought, one is the origin of all things, that is, "Tai one" in Taoist thought, the second is the chaotic state of heaven and earth, and the third is the unity between the objects that are opposite to "many" and "two". "one" is a unique ideological concept in Chinese culture. In the Western philosophical world, there is no first and second meaning, only a third meaning, that is, the numeral one. In order to distinguish it from the numeral, the term is translated as the one, but different translations are still used for terms containing "one" in different contexts. For instance, in the following sentence, "一",

mentioned twice, should not be translated into one: "父母之年，不可不知也。一则以喜，一则以忧". So this translation is better: A son should always keep in mind the age of his parents,as a matter of thankfulness as well as for anxiety.

6.Conclusion

The numbers in the *Analects of Confucius* carry rich connotations of Chinese culture. In the process of translation, the cultural translation theory can be used as a guide to convey their cultural significance more accurately and vividly. The study of Gu Hongming's translation activities is of great practical significance for promoting Chinese cultural classics to the world, enhancing the soft power of Chinese culture and shaping the image of Chinese culture. Translation is inherently a difficult task. Yan Fu once said that the three difficulties of translation namely faithfulness, expressiveness and elegance. The difficulties of translation are not only reflected in the understanding and expression of the original text, but also in the understanding and mastery of culture and background knowledge. It can be seen that the translator's cultural knowledge reserve plays an important role in translation work. Therefore, in order to convey the culture behind the language in the translation of abstract and rich cultural classics, the translation should be based on culture as the translation unit, rather than just from the linguistic level to achieve lexical, syntactic and textual equivalence. Bassnett's cultural translation theory provides a theoretical basis for this study. There is a great cultural difference between the definite reference and the vague reference in Chinese and western numerals. In English, numbers are mostly used for definite reference, and vague reference is mostly based on larger numbers. Therefore, in the process of translation, the translator should not only master the bilingual language ability, but also have a good bilingual cultural background knowledge, actively spread Chinese culture and show the Chinese cultural heritage.

References

1. Li Z.S.,(2020). Literary translation contributes to the construction of China's image. http://sscp.cssn.cn/xkpd/tbch/tebiecehuaneirong/202004/t20200417_5115274.html
2. Zheng J.N. (2020) Study, translation and others of the *Art of War*-- Interview with Professor An Lezhe.Foreign Language Research,(1) : 1– 6, Roger T.Ames.
3. Gu G.(2007)Foreign language and cultural Studies.Tianjin University Press,Tianjin.
4. Zhang R.L.(1986)An inquiry into Meaning -- Contemporary Western Hermeneutics.Liaoning People's Publishing House,Shenyang.
5. L.C.Piccinini,T.F.M.Chang,G.Tubaro,M.Taverna.Rezekne, Latvia,22-23,5(2015)
6. V.Kincāns.Society,Integration,Education, **2**,5(2013)
7. M. Marin-Lacarta, M. Vargas-Urpi.(2020)Translators as publishers: exploring the motivations for non-profit literary translation in digital initiative. Meta Journal des traducteurs, 3(2020)
8. Sun L.Han C.H.(2021)The English translation of culture-loaded words in Folding Beijing -- from the perspective of ecological translation. Shanghai Journal of Translators,(4) : 90 - 94.

Interpreting Studies: A Comprehensive Analysis

Jianing Wang*

Southeast University, Nanjing, China

Abstract: This article provides a comprehensive analysis of Interpreting Studies, a field that plays a pivotal role in bridging linguistic and cultural gaps in today's globalized world. It explores the key concepts, methodologies, challenges, and future prospects within this dynamic discipline. By examining the history, evolution, and various approaches in Interpreting Studies, this article aims to shed light on its significance and potential contributions to cross-cultural communication.

1. Introduction

Interpreting Studies is a vital discipline facilitating cross-cultural communication. This article explores its history, methodologies, challenges, and future prospects. Interpreters bridge language gaps, conveying messages accurately in diverse settings. Historically, Interpreting Studies has evolved, and pioneers like Eugenio Coseriu made significant contributions. Methodologies encompass linguistic analysis, ethnographic approaches, and technological advancements, enabling effective interpretation. Challenges include ethical dilemmas, cultural sensitivity, and training needs. As the demand for interpreters grows, maintaining professionalism becomes paramount. Interpreting finds application in diplomacy, healthcare, and legal fields. Its future promises automation through AI, virtual interpretation environments, and interdisciplinary collaborations. In conclusion, Interpreting Studies plays a critical role in our globalized world. This article aims to provide readers with a comprehensive understanding of its importance and the complexities involved, shedding light on its potential to shape the future of cross-cultural communication.

2. Historical evolution

2.1. Origins of Interpretation

Interpretation, in its most primitive form, can be traced back to the dawn of human communication. In ancient societies, interpreters played crucial roles in facilitating trade, diplomacy, and the exchange of ideas between different linguistic and cultural groups. These early interpreters often relied on their linguistic skills and cultural knowledge to bridge communication gaps. This rudimentary form of interpretation laid the foundation for the complex practice we know today [1]. The origins of interpretation can be traced back to the dawn of human civilization when communities with diverse languages and cultures began to interact. In these early societies, interpreters emerged as indispensable individuals who facilitated communication and understanding between groups that spoke different languages. Whether it was in the context of trade, diplomacy, or cultural exchange, these interpreters played a pivotal role in bridging linguistic and cultural gaps. These early interpreters operated in a world without the sophisticated tools and technologies available to contemporary interpreters. Instead, they relied on their linguistic prowess and cultural sensitivity to convey messages accurately and effectively. They were often bilingual or multilingual individuals who had an innate understanding of the nuances of language and culture. One can imagine the challenges they faced in an era where dictionaries, language courses, and interpreting equipment were non-existent [2]. Yet, their ability to mediate between languages and cultures paved the way for the development of interpretation as a formal discipline.

2.2. Pioneers in Interpreting Research

Pioneers like Eugenio Coseriu and Danica Seleskovitch made pioneering contributions to the development of interpreting research. Coseriu, for instance, emphasized the importance of linguistic analysis in interpreting, which remains a fundamental aspect of the field today. Their work laid the groundwork for modern interpreting studies and helped elevate interpretation from a practical skill to an academic discipline [3]. Eugenio Coseriu, a linguist of great influence, made significant contributions to the field of interpretation. He stressed the importance of linguistic analysis within the practice of interpretation. Coseriu's insights into language structures, idiomatic expressions, and discourse patterns have had a lasting impact on how interpreters approach their work. Coseriu's emphasis on linguistic analysis serves as a cornerstone of interpretation methodology. Interpreters today continue to delve into language structures, syntax, semantics, and pragmatics to ensure accurate and effective communication. By dissecting the intricacies of language, interpreters can navigate the challenges of conveying messages between

*Corresponding author's email: wangjianingphdapply@outlook.com

languages with precision [4]. Danica Seleskovitch is another luminary in the world of interpreting studies. Her work focused on interpreting in the context of international organizations and conferences. Seleskovitch's research and contributions helped raise the profile of interpretation as a profession. Her efforts shed light on the complexities of interpretation in high-stakes settings and underscored the need for rigorous training and professionalism among interpreters. Both Coseriu and Seleskovitch's pioneering work contributed to the recognition of interpretation as a specialized field of study. Their insights continue to guide interpreters in their quest for accuracy and excellence in cross-cultural communication.

2.3. Significant Milestones in the Field

Interpreting Studies has reached several significant milestones over the years. The establishment of professional organizations, such as AIIC (International Association of Conference Interpreters), in the mid-20th century marked a turning point for the field. These organizations have played vital roles in setting standards, providing training, and fostering collaboration among interpreters. Additionally, the integration of technology, such as computer-assisted interpretation tools, has transformed the way interpreters work, making their tasks more efficient and accessible. The mid-20th century brought about a significant transformation in the field of Interpreting Studies with the establishment of professional organizations, most notably the International Association of Conference Interpreters (AIIC). These organizations played a pivotal role in unifying interpreters worldwide and elevating the standards of the profession. AIIC, founded in 1953, brought together interpreters from diverse linguistic backgrounds and provided them with a platform to collaborate, share best practices, and advocate for the profession. It set forth a code of professional ethics and standards that continue to guide interpreters in their work. This development not only enhanced the professionalism of interpreters but also contributed to a greater recognition of their role in facilitating cross-cultural communication [5]. Moreover, the integration of technology into the field of interpretation has been a game-changer. Computer-assisted interpretation tools, such as speech recognition software and terminology databases, have significantly improved the efficiency and accuracy of interpreters. These tools have become indispensable aids, especially in high-pressure settings like conferences and diplomatic negotiations, where interpreters must convey information rapidly and accurately. The use of technology has also expanded the reach of interpretation services. Remote interpretation, made possible through video conferencing and telecommunication technologies, has made interpretation accessible in a wide range of contexts, including healthcare, legal proceedings, and international conferences. As Interpreting Studies continue to evolve, it is this significant milestone, such as the establishment of professional organizations and the integration of technology that has paved the way for a more standardized, efficient, and accessible practice of interpretation. These developments reflect the field's ongoing commitment to excellence and its adaptation to the changing demands of our globalized world.

3. Methodologies in interpreting studies

3.1. Linguistic Analysis in Interpretation

Linguistic analysis is fundamental in interpretation. It involves a detailed examination of language structures, idiomatic expressions, and discourse patterns. Interpreters must understand syntax, semantics, and pragmatics to navigate complex linguistic terrain accurately. Interpreters dissect sentence structure, word order, and grammatical nuances to ensure the faithful transfer of meaning. They also delve into the semantic meanings of words and phrases in both source and target languages. Pragmatics, understanding language use in context, is crucial for grasping subtle cues and cultural nuances. Linguistic analysis demands continuous language skill refinement to stay current with evolving usage and cultural context [6]. This enables interpreters to bridge linguistic divides effectively.

3.2. Ethnographic Approaches to Interpretation

Ethnographic approaches enhance cultural competence in interpretation. Immersing oneself in the cultural context is crucial to understand communication nuances. These approaches go beyond linguistic analysis to grasp cultural meanings, unspoken cues, and context-specific norms [7]. Ethnography encourages interpreters to become cultural insiders through participant observation and cultural immersion. It helps interpreters recognize nonverbal communication, gestures, body language, and tone of voice. Understanding cultural nuances is vital as cultural differences can manifest in various ways [8]. Interpreters who use ethnographic approaches can provide culturally respectful and effective interpretations.

3.3. Technological Advancements in Interpretation

Technology has revolutionized interpretation. Speech recognition software aids in transcription, terminology databases assist with specialized vocabulary, and remote interpretation is facilitated through video conferencing and telecommunication. Speech recognition software provides rapid and accurate transcriptions, especially in fast-paced settings. Terminology databases ensure precise translations of technical terms. Remote interpretation extends interpretation services' reach, especially when interpreters cannot be physically present [9]. While technology enhances interpretation, skilled and culturally competent interpreters remain central to ensuring accurate and culturally sensitive interpretations. These tools are most effective when in the hands of experienced professionals who can navigate language complexities and culture while leveraging technology's benefits.

4. Challenges in interpreting studies

4.1. Ethical Considerations in Interpretation

Ethical dilemmas are a common and complex aspect of interpretation, often arising when interpreters are confronted with sensitive information or moral quandaries. Maintaining ethical standards is paramount, but it can be challenging to strike a balance between the principles of confidentiality, impartiality, and the need for accuracy. Confidentiality is a fundamental ethical principle in interpretation. Interpreters are privy to sensitive information in various contexts, such as medical consultations, legal proceedings, or confidential diplomatic discussions. Upholding the confidentiality of this information is essential to maintain trust between all parties involved. However, interpreters may find themselves in situations where they must grapple with the tension between safeguarding confidentiality and ensuring that the message is accurately conveyed. Striking this balance requires careful judgment and adherence to ethical guidelines and codes of conduct specific to interpretation. Impartiality is another crucial ethical principle that interpreters must uphold. Interpreters are expected to remain neutral and not favor any party involved in the communication [10]. This impartiality ensures that interpretations are unbiased and objective, essential in contexts like legal or diplomatic proceedings. Nevertheless, interpreters may encounter situations where their own beliefs or emotions come into play, making it challenging to maintain complete impartiality. Ethical considerations dictate that interpreters must navigate these personal biases and emotions professionally, always prioritizing the integrity of the interpretation. Ethical training and ongoing dialogue within the interpreting community also play a vital role in helping interpreters navigate the intricate ethical landscape they encounter.

4.2. Cultural Sensitivity and Bias

Cultural sensitivity and the avoidance of bias are paramount in interpretation to ensure that interpretations are impartial, respectful, and inclusive. Interpreters must maintain cultural sensitivity by being aware of their own cultural perspectives and biases, which can inadvertently influence their interpretations. Cultural sensitivity involves recognizing and respecting cultural differences in communication styles, norms, and values. Interpreters must be attuned to the subtleties of cross-cultural communication, including nonverbal cues, gestures, and tone of voice. Failure to do so can lead to misunderstandings, misinterpretations, or even offense. In contexts like healthcare, legal proceedings, or diplomacy, where cultural diversity is the norm, cultural sensitivity becomes particularly crucial. Moreover, interpreters must be vigilant about their own cultural biases, which can unconsciously seep into their interpretations. Maintaining cultural sensitivity and avoiding bias is an ongoing journey for interpreters. It requires a commitment to self-awareness, continuous learning, and humility. By embodying these principles, interpreters can navigate the complexities of cultural diversity while upholding the highest standards of professionalism and impartiality.

4.3. Professional Training and Development

The demand for skilled interpreters continues to grow in our globalized world, underscoring the significance of comprehensive training and continuous professional development. Rigorous training programs, mentorship, and certification processes are instrumental in preparing interpreters to meet the diverse needs of their clients and ensure high-quality interpretations. Professional training serves as the foundation upon which interpreters build their expertise. These training programs typically encompass linguistic skills, interpreting techniques, and ethical standards. Linguistic proficiency is fundamental, as interpreters must master the languages they work with, including vocabulary, grammar, and specialized terminology relevant to their chosen fields. Interpreters also acquire essential skills related to interpreting modes, such as simultaneous, consecutive, or sight translation. These techniques enable interpreters to adapt to various settings, whether it's a fast-paced conference or a one-on-one medical consultation. Moreover, ethical training is a crucial component of professional development. Interpreters must navigate complex ethical dilemmas while upholding confidentiality, impartiality, and accuracy [11]. Training equips interpreters with the ethical framework and decision-making skills needed to address these challenges effectively.

5. Interpreting studies in practice

5.1. Diplomatic Interpretation

Diplomatic interpretation stands as a pinnacle within the field, where interpreters navigate high-stakes scenarios, facilitating communication between nations, international organizations, and diplomatic delegations. This demanding and critical role places accuracy, neutrality, and confidentiality at the forefront, as diplomatic interpreters play instrumental roles in negotiations, treaty signings, and international dialogue. In the world of diplomacy, interpreters often work behind the scenes, their voices heard only by a select few. Yet, their contributions are immeasurable, as they ensure that discussions between parties from different linguistic backgrounds proceed smoothly and effectively. The stakes are often high, with the potential for international relations, peace agreements, and global security hanging in the balance. Diplomatic interpreters must possess not only linguistic mastery but also a deep understanding of diplomatic protocols, cultural sensitivities, and the intricacies of international relations. Their ability to convey messages accurately, without bias or distortion, is paramount. Any miscommunication or misunderstanding could have far-reaching consequences. Moreover, diplomatic interpreters often operate in situations where confidentiality is paramount. They are privy to sensitive information and must uphold strict ethical standards. This includes safeguarding classified discussions and maintaining the highest level of discretion and professionalism. In diplomatic circles, interpreters are trusted allies who ensure that diplomatic exchanges proceed with clarity, precision, and a commitment to peaceful resolutions.

5.2. Medical and Legal Interpretation

In healthcare and the legal system, interpreters bridge language gaps, ensuring equitable access to vital services. Medical interpreters operate within healthcare, facilitating patient-provider communication when language barriers exist. Their presence is crucial for accurate diagnoses and treatment plans. Beyond translation, they convey empathy and cultural sensitivity, enhancing patient well-being. Medical interpreters navigate intricate medical terminology, ensuring precise communication and patient confidentiality. Their role extends to ensuring patients fully comprehend their conditions and treatment options, emphasizing clarity in healthcare. Legal interpreters aid individuals with language barriers in accessing justice. They assist in understanding rights, navigating legal procedures, and participating in legal proceedings, including court hearings and client-attorney consultations. They actively contribute to fairness, safeguarding due process and overcoming linguistic obstacles. Both medical and legal interpreters operate in high-stakes contexts, where miscommunication can have severe consequences. They maintain impartiality, uphold ethical standards, and possess specialized knowledge [12]. Their contributions promote equity in accessing essential services and justice, fostering fairness and healthcare equality.

5.3. Community Interpreting

Community interpreting, often underestimated, bridges language gaps in local communities, promoting social inclusion. These interpreters work in various settings, ensuring linguistic diversity doesn't hinder participation in society. In educational settings, they assist students and families during conferences, meetings, and assessments, ensuring an understanding of educational progress and needs. Within social services, they facilitate communication, guaranteeing access to critical services for immigrants and refugees. Community interpreters also aid newcomers' integration, helping them understand local customs and cultural norms, and reducing isolation [13]. Their impact extends to public institutions like libraries. These interpreters are more than just language experts; they are community builders, fostering access to resources for diverse populations.

6. Conclusion

Interpreting studies emerges as an ever-evolving and essential discipline, it remains dynamic, addressing the demands of our interconnected world. This exploration has traced its evolution, methodologies, challenges, applications, and future prospects. From its roots in early communication, Interpreting Studies matured, thanks to pioneers like Eugenio Coseriu and Danica Seleskovitch. Methodologies encompass linguistic analysis, ethnography, and technology integration. Challenges persist, necessitating ethical standards, cultural sensitivity, and professional training. Applications span diplomacy, healthcare, legal settings, and community inclusion. In summary, Interpreting Studies fosters understanding across linguistic and cultural frontiers.

Reference

1. Pöchhacker, Franz. Introducing interpreting studies. Routledge, 2022.
2. Pöchhacker, Franz. "Issues in interpreting studies." The Routledge companion to translation studies. Routledge, 2009. 142-154.
3. Gile, Daniel. "Interpreting studies: a critical view from within." (2009).
4. Salevsky, Heidemarie. "The distinctive nature of interpreting studies." Target 5.2 (1993): 149-167.
5. Jacobson, Holly E., and Claudia V. Angelelli. "Testing and assessment in translation and interpreting studies." Testing and assessment in translation and interpreting studies (2009): 1-392.
6. Jacobson, Jenna, and Brooke Harrison. "Sustainable fashion social media influencers and content creation calibration." International Journal of advertising 41.1 (2022): 150-177.
7. Gerver, David, ed. Language interpretation and communication. Vol. 6. Springer Science & Business Media, 2013.
8. Brown, Peter F., et al. "A statistical approach to language translation." Coling Budapest 1988 Volume 1: International Conference on Computational Linguistics. 1988.
9. Neubert, Albrecht. "Competence in language, in languages, and in translation." Benjamins Translation Library 38 (2000): 3-18.
10. Gardner, George H. "Cross cultural communication." The Journal of social psychology 58.2 (1962): 241-256.
11. Smith, Larry, ed. English for cross-cultural communication. Springer, 1981.
12. Gudykunst, William B. Cross-cultural and intercultural communication. Sage, 2003.
13. Mead, Richard, and Colin J. Jones. "Cross-cultural communication." The Blackwell Handbook of Cross-Cultural Management (2017): 283-291.

Resisting Trauma: Exploring Queer Emotional Narratives in *Madame* from the Perspective of Cultural Politics of Emotion in Chinese Context

Junyi Qian*

College of Arts and Media, Tongji University, Shanghai, China

Abstract: This paper delves into the documentary *Madame*, examining the intricate emotional narrative of Qihui Fan within the Chinese cultural framework using Sara Ahmed's Cultural Politics of Emotion. By analyzing Fan's experiences, encompassing childhood strife, youth prostitution, and grappling with a sense of nothingness in middle age, the exploration delves into his emotional journey and the construction of his queer identity. Employing Ahmed's framework, it dissects how emotions, notably pain and pleasure, interplay within Fan's narrative. Through resisting societal norms and embracing a persona—madame "BILAN DE LINPHEL," Fan navigates pleasure as a form of rebellion against heteronormativity. However, this pleasure is fleeting, entangled in a cycle of despair, as his narrative oscillates between self-empowerment and trauma-driven despair. The analysis uncovers Fan's struggle for recognition in a society with limited tolerance for queer identities. It scrutinizes the performance of emotions, the role of pleasure in resistance, and the narrative's performative nature. Ultimately, this examination unravels the complex interplay of emotions, societal control, and identity struggles within the context of Chinese queer culture, shedding light on the challenges and nuances faced by individuals like Fan.

1.Introduction

Filmed towards the end of 2009, the documentary *Madame* stood out with its unique format, featuring a one-man oral drama centered on protagonist Qihui Fan. It intertwined his personal narrative with stage performances, spotlighting his self-identity exploration and the challenges of being queer within the societal landscape of that time. Covering three decades of a transvestite's identity evolution, the documentary offered a profound and inclusive examination of queer experiences, setting itself apart from narrative-driven films and documentaries.

Despite homosexuality being officially removed from China's list of mental illnesses in 2001 and a gradual increase in social tolerance, the mainland environment remained largely closed to queer communities. Limited spaces were designated for their existence, with queer individuals still being associated with a sense of disease. Discussions around sexuality predominantly revolved around risk behaviors and diseases, highlighting the persistent marginalization of queer individuals in Chinese society, despite improving discourse (Huang, 2020).[1]

However, recent years witnessed a shift toward broader attention and depth regarding queer groups, aligning domestic public opinion with international voices. Though official media began focusing on events related to domestic queer communities, it remained within the tolerance and permissions set by mainstream heterosexual norms (He, 2018).[2] The voices within the queer community lacked extensive representation, limiting their discourse power and government incorporation. In the late 1990s and early 2000s, queer-themed movies and television gained traction, primarily in Hong Kong and Taiwan. Mainland China, on the other hand, showcased a diverse underground cinema, offering a wider spectrum of representations for queer individuals in visual media (Zhang, 2016).[3] While mainstream movies progressively transitioned from negative stereotypes to more positive depictions, breaking away entirely from heteronormative norms remained a challenge.

Madame, through the lens of the character Qihui Fan's personal narrative, provided an honest portrayal of the myriad obstacles faced by the queer community over the past thirty years. This authenticity elevated its research value above many other director-driven films, television productions, and event-centered documentaries. Therefore, this study aims to delve deeply into how Qihui Fan interprets and defines his identity within the documentary, examining his struggle against societal oppression and exclusion of queer individuals. Focusing on his emotional journey from a cultural research perspective offers insights into the societal contradictions faced by queer communities, unveiling their concealed acceptance and struggle amidst identity dynamics and discourse power.

*raffaeloqian@163.com

2.Chinese LGBTQ+ Culture in the Film and Television Industry

The ongoing debate between homosexual essentialism and constructivism has been a cornerstone of discussions since the public became aware of homosexuality. Homosexual essentialism, while advocating for the equality of rationality within the homosexual community akin to the nature of life, has faced criticism for overlooking the cultural and historical dimensions of the issue (Byne ,1997).[4] The intricate nature of sexual orientation and identity has made it challenging to establish a scientific basis for essentialism, leading to its critique for insufficient evidence (Wang, 2017).[5] Consequently, the constructivist viewpoint, inspired by Alfred Kinsey's work, has gained traction, asserting that "gay-straight" isn't polar opposites but rather the ends of a sexual continuum. Butler's perspective on gender orientation directly opposes essentialism, viewing gender identity as fluid. She draws from Foucault's theory, contending that gender operates as a primary cultural agent shaping concepts like masculinity/femininity and heterosexual/homosexual identities (Butler, 1990).[6]

While this theory has gained global attention, its integration in China has been relatively recent compared to Western societies. Yinhe Li (2001) introduced the concept, gradually gaining acceptance over the past two decades.[7] Wang Jinling defines gender constructivism as a process of gender socialization involving the influence of social norms and an individual's internalization of these norms related to gender (Wang, 2011).[8] Surveys indicate that around 20% of domestic college students hold a constructivist view on sexuality, while a larger percentage believe in a mix of nature and nurture influencing sexuality (Liu et al., 2017).[9] This diversity in views indicates that the issue remains unresolved in China, with some in the gay community still holding onto essentialist perspectives.

Constructionists have examined the social factors shaping homosexual identity, forming the basis for a minority-like community and politics (Seidman, 1994).[10] Constructivism, while highlighting sexual identity and politics, paradoxically categorizes homosexuals as a "minority," complicating gay identity politics itself (Wang, 2018).[11] However, Eve Kosofsky Sedgwick shifted the debate focus to minority versus universalization, exploring how homosexuality becomes the constitutive "other" of the heterosexual hegemonic structure (Du, 2015).[12]

China's government historically adopted a "nonposition" stance toward LGBT individuals, neither approving nor disapproving, leading to marginalization (Moreno-Tabarez et al., 2014).[13] Yet, the visibility of queer films has increased domestically and internationally in recent years, presenting diverse and straightforward representations of queer identities. These films, including *Madame*, explore cross-dressing during a time predating China's full embrace of the internet and coincide with the development of queer theory in the country. The documentary features Qihui Fan, probing the connection between queer issues and the broader gender composition of society, challenging prevailing sexual and gender norms that shaped the emergence of queer theory in China (Ding, 2022).[14]

Documentaries delving into queer themes experienced renewed restrictions post-2016, particularly in television series. The General Regulations on Television Content Production categorized homosexuality as abnormal, effectively re-closeting queer films. This repressive environment refocused attention on domestic queer theories, with most underground films openly expressing queer identities but having limited public impact (Zhang, 2016).[3] However, *Madame* emerged as a standout on domestic video platforms, gaining popularity for its portrayal of queer characters amidst China's social transformations over three decades. The documentary's unique aspect lies in its extensive interviews spanning time and geography, distinguishing it from other Chinese productions. The director employed a special narrative strategy, spotlighting the character's background to illuminate queer identity within the social context.

Drawing from Stijn Deklerck's (2017) reference to Lisa Rofel's 'nomadic activism,' Chinese queer documentary filmmakers navigate and maneuver within the diverse powers shaping subjectivities, social structures, political beliefs, and economic inequalities in China.[15] In a landscape of stringent regulations and limited public visibility for queer art, innovative strategies shedding light on changing times become crucial. This approach not only circumvents censorship but also highlights the regional and epochal qualities of queer art, grounding the queer community within the cultural context of the times—a vital resource for comprehensive studies of queer theories in China.

Amidst numerous studies exploring identity in queer documentaries, *Madame* stands apart due to its distinctive form, housing a wealth of interviews conducted over an extensive period. Spanning 30 years, the film resonates with strong regional and timely elements. Analyzing its narrative text offers insights into how different eras, locations, and cultures have influenced attitudes and the formation of queer identity since the Cultural Revolution.

3.A unique perspective: the cultural politics of emotion

The cultural politics of emotion, as proposed by Sara Ahmed (2015), redefines emotion as a social-cultural practice rather than an individual psychological state. Emotions, in this context, are not confined to subjects or objects but are produced through the circulation of impressions. Ahmed delves into the intricate relationship between emotion, the body, and discourse, emphasizing how emotions assign value to the body and create societal "others" through marginalization. Emotions thus serve as a gateway to the social and material world, forging political and social alliances and shaping national identities. Ahmed focuses on the dynamics of emotions, analyzing how they "move," "stick," and "circulate" in terms of influence and function, shaping our bodily reactions (p. 4).[16]

Her analysis explores emotions' role in public texts and social phenomena, offering insights into the concept of the cultural politics of emotion. This paper aims to employ Ahmed's framework to further dissect the documentary *Madame*. The focus lies in protagonist Qihui Fan, a member of a marginalized queer community, aligning with Ahmed's proposition that emotion plays a crucial role in societal marginalization. The documentary, predominantly comprising Fan's interviews and cross-dressing performances, overtly elicits emotions in the audience, making visible the work of emotions, providing a valuable case study for analyzing emotional dynamics through Ahmed's lens.

Moreover, the film captures Fan's emotional connection to China's social changes post the Cultural Revolution. His emotions are deeply entwined with the shifting cultural landscape, making the concept of cultural politics of emotion pertinent to understanding how these transformations impact marginalized groups. The documentary chronicles Fan's life, shaped by tumultuous experiences— a challenging childhood marred by family conflicts, involvement in youth prostitution, and grappling with the disillusionment of middle age. Throughout, Fan navigates a spectrum of emotions, from pessimism and bitterness to a yearning for happiness as a queer individual. This analysis aims to delve into the depths of his emotional journey, exploring both pain and distorted excitement, illuminating the challenges queer individuals encounter in society and their resilient efforts in shaping their identities.

4.Circulation of pain: The struggle of queer identity

The documentary *Madame* presents a comprehensive view of Qihui Fan's life across eight acts, primarily focusing on three pivotal experiences he narrates. Throughout, he candidly expresses secular desires while navigating ongoing trauma and discrimination from others. I aim to delve deeper into these experiences, elucidating how pain circulated and contributed to shaping his queer identity.

Qihui Fan's upbringing during the waning days of the Cultural Revolution was marred by his father's absence, fostering an estrangement between his parents that left him with childhood insecurities. According to Ahmed's interpretation of impressions, emotional experiences have a bidirectional effect, forming impressions that transpire from one object to another's surface (Ahmed, 2015, p. 6). Consequently, the disharmony within his family left a painful impression on Qihui Fan, shaping his perception of family dynamics as distant and adverse, making family discussions a subject he avoided. The pain he experienced manifested as "the effect of impressions" (p. 8), arising from the conflict within his family and contrasting sharply with traditional notions of familial tolerance.[16] This familial pain further contributed to the marginalization of his body as an emotional subject. As he aged, his consciousness of this pain grew, consolidating the surface of his body (p. 24) and compelling him to distance himself from his family. Moreover, "the pain recalls us to the body surface" (p. 26), reinforcing his awareness of physical presence and enhancing his ability to introspect about a missing sense of identity from his past, ultimately aiding in the establishment of a unique identity at a young age.[17]

Continuing trauma prompted Qihui Fan to leave Beijing for Guangzhou, leading to his involvement in prostitution. This decision not only served as an escape from past emotional turmoil but also facilitated the development of a distinct self-identity within a broader social context. Ahmed's explanation of sensations immediately influencing emotions through impressions elucidates why similar emotions from past experiences are rekindled upon encountering mediated sensations (Ahmed, 2015, p. 25).[17] Despite his attempt to evade it, the sensation of pain persisted. When he failed to find love in Guangzhou, it reawakened painful emotions as impressions, stemming from the perception that his identity was not accepted. These painful emotions traversed from childhood family trauma through emotional setbacks, ultimately contributing to the dismantling of his self-construction.

The memories of childhood disappointment and lost love compel a revisit to painful experiences, intensifying the sensation of pain and deeply embedding it as a palpable presence (Ahmed, 2015, p. 24). Reinterpreting this pain prompts Qihui Fan to contemplate the attribution of his "bodily surface", reshaping his body and crafting new impressions through the narrative of pain (p. 25).[17] He condensed his anguish into an on-stage identity, embodied in "Madame BILAN DE LINPHEL," thus reconstructing his sense of self. By externalizing the emotion of pain through symbolic representation, he encapsulated his impressions. However, in perpetuating this symbol of pain, he continually revisited and relived the process of reconnecting with these feelings, establishing a direct link between emotional anguish and an unfulfilled psychological void. Thus, he struggled to "gradually withdraw from the object and hence denies the other through forgetting its trace" (p. 159), ensnaring himself in a cyclical agony, perpetuating self-torment.[18]

Hence, I posit that Qihui Fan's recurrent circulation of painful emotions stems from trauma continually interpreted and internalized into his mental state. Consequently, the self-identity he forges evokes past impressions upon facing setbacks, fortifying his anguish and unraveling his subjectivity. This disintegration echoes in his construction of "Madame BILAN DE LINPHEL," initially as a queer self-empowerment but ending in a struggle and failure.

This analysis also explores how Qihui Fan shapes his queer identity, particularly examining the role of societal culture and the emotion of pain in this process. Ahmed highlights that "emotions are not 'in' either the individual or the social, but produce the very surfaces and boundaries that allow the individual and the social to be delineated as if they are objects" (Ahmed, 2015, p. 10).[16] This assertion resonates in Qihui Fan's formation of his queer identity, where perceiving pain defines the boundaries of his emotions. His queer identity emerges from symbolic representations of traumatic experiences, such as his mother's depression and his involvement in prostitution. Since the 1980s, increasing acceptance and tolerance of queer identity within our culture have influenced Qihui Fan's own identity. Despite the anguish accompanying this journey, he seeks acknowledgment from others and selectively absorbs positive societal influences, fortifying his self-perception. Presently, his subjectivity assumes a self-appointed authority, resisting aesthetics and gender norms under heterosexual standards during self-construction, while grappling to find solace within the societal construct's informational sphere.

5.A performed emotion of pleasure: The building and falling of queer joy

However, Qihui Fan didn't allow painful emotions to consume him entirely. These emotions surfaced not just in recounting trauma but also in acknowledging the aftermath of his struggle against it. Therefore, analyzing Qihui Fan's emotions should encompass not only the pain he endured as a queer individual but also his efforts to resist. His discourse in the documentary is concise yet vivid, challenging societal norms by embodying madame "BILAN DE LINPHEL" and deriving self-empowerment. This verbal resistance offers satisfaction, aiding in expressing and resolving his traumatic experiences, termed as a form of "detoxification" (Ahmed, 2015, p. 164).[18] Pleasures, as Ahmed notes, open bodies to the world, a proclamation of existence for queers, described as "dispersing poison."

Qihui Fan finds pleasure in being queer and in the outcome of his defiance against heterosexual norms. He rebels against the heteronormative system by openly discussing his experiences in prostitution and non-reproductive sexual pleasure. Over nearly three decades, the country gradually allowed space for open discussions on homosexuality, albeit controlled. Fan's rebellion surfaces through recounting experiences, cross-dressing, and embracing non-conventional sexual intimacy. Joyful emotions actively participate in challenging the dogmatic norms of heterosexual intimacy, forming a part of Fan's acceptance of the outcomes of his struggle. Pleasure serves not only as a result of his rebellion but also as an investment to maintain a connection with the audience. It acts as a driving force in his narrative, adopting a flirtatious and assertive tone, positioning himself as the subject of desire while positioning the audience as the object, maintaining a dynamic power status during the struggle process and sustaining his construction of a queer identity.

Qihui Fan narrates his life story uniquely, employing a simple yet detailed language style. He often adopts an objective viewpoint, analyzing his behavior and language. This perspective might stem from childhood trauma, potentially heightening sensitivity to social interactions and threat perception, imprinting painful impressions on his body. Thus, he tends to focus on avoiding threatening information and evading potential oppression. However, in the societal context of China, physical escape from uneasy familial relationships is deemed challenging. Nevertheless, it doesn't hinder the orientation of his thoughts and feelings, leading to an intuitive self-examination perspective. This perspective isn't solely rooted in painful experiences but also serves as a narrative strategy to convey his emotions and experiences outwardly, connecting with others. In expressing his trauma, this perspective becomes a means of self-empowerment, challenging norms and culminating in a queer declaration of liberation from original trauma, empowering him to critique and resist the constraints of heteronormativity (Ahmed, 2015, p. 164).[18]

However, pleasure within him remains fleeting throughout the narrative process. His emotions tend to veer towards despair and pain after he dissects his own thoughts and views. This emotional cycle creates a unique narrative effect through repetition, lending a performative quality to the ostensibly joyful narrative (Ahmed, 2015, p. 92). Qihui Fan employs power relations metaphorically between body and space (Ahmed, 2015, p. 89) through ironic humor.[19] He bifurcates himself into two identities: madame "BILAN DE LINPHEL," exuding freedom and pride before the audience, and the talkative queer man, the tailor, haunted by solitude and trauma backstage. While the emotion of happiness fortifies the protagonist's powerful stance, it clashes with the unstable power dynamics during introspection due to identity shifts, recognizing the challenge of acknowledging the construction of a queer identity in the outside world. Thus, as he returns to reality, trauma-induced introspection fragments the facade of happily resisting heterosexual norms. The expression of happiness loses its essence, identities splinter, and the outward expansion of the body diminishes. The occupied space of the body decreases (Ahmed, 2015, p. 164), emotions reverting to reliving traumatic experiences woven into the memories of the joyous resistance narrative and lamenting the loss of that pleasure.[18] Consequently, this joyful emotion assumes an inherently transient nature, inseparable from his narrative strategy's performance.

This portrayal of happiness in this context is queer, reflecting self-acceptance amidst stigmatization and resistance, employing non-traditional discourse and imagery, showcasing disdain for what Qihui Fan himself terms as "tristesse." Even if transiently stimulating and offering a form of "detoxification," it also presents a potent rebellion and a "negative model of freedom" (Ahmed, 2015, p. 164) against societal norms of heterosexuality and patriarchy. However, unlike the swift rise of queer politics in the West where queer discourse power and non-transcendental hope can coexist (Ahmed, 2015, p. 165), in the Chinese context, despite having space and voice, low social tolerance restricts survival and outward expression of queer bodies in pleasure. Consequently, the formation of diverse impressions through forbidden contact by queer individuals is constrained, compromising the purity of queer pleasure. Furthermore, Qihui Fan's frequent shifts in identities, both on and offstage, heighten his understanding of the dichotomy between public norms and queer freedom. However, upon re-entering mainstream social settings, expressing these feelings becomes arduous. Thus, his performance of joy and excitement during resistance is deprived. Heterosexual culture's dominance and control over the living space of queer individuals (Ahmed, 2015,

p. 164) lead to the deprivation of this joyful emotion in daily life, deepening the impression of his queer identity and intensifying his struggle with maintaining a stable identity orientation.[18]

6.Conclusions

In the documentary, Qihui Fan grapples with the emotion of pain, repeatedly internalizing this agonizing impression into emotional fortitude, forging it into a supportive self-construction. Through this process, he seeks to resist societal prejudices as a queer individual, finding glimpses of joy amid resistance. This emotional flux stems from his interpretation of his own queer identity, shaping his performance and expression of self. However, the loss of joy as a focal point and the perpetual cycle of painful emotions erode his grasp on identity. He withdrew from social interactions post-filming and tragically took his own life shortly after the documentary's release. This transition from pain to a somewhat supportive yet stimulating happiness might have foretold the eventual faltering of his struggle. Despite increasing tolerance towards queer individuals in China at that time, their freedom of expression and identity status remained curtailed. The disillusionment and powerlessness experienced in this struggle accelerated the emotional schism within his identity transformation, rendering his resistance unable to be fully acknowledged and comprehended. Consequently, this form of resistance born from pain reflects his personal ethos but lacks a definitive goal in the queer struggle, perpetually separating his identity as one recognized by society. This could explain the uniqueness and representativeness of his image, vividly illustrating the practical hardships faced by queer individuals in Chinese society during that era, portraying their intricate internal battles and transformations.

Nevertheless, the portrayal of the character in the documentary is curated and selected, still subject to the director's narrative control, potentially constrained within the confines of China's mainland censorship mechanisms. Despite documentaries offering a more authentic perspective due to their reliance on real events and characters, their depth often falls short compared to thorough field investigations. The exploration of the documentary's formal expression and its alignment with the cultural milieu of that time, as well as the comprehensive examination of the queer community within China's social context during that period, remains underdeveloped. This warrants further in-depth research to delve into and enrich our understanding of these facets in future studies.

References

1. Huang, Y. (2020) Sex Change: Combing and thinking about sex in the 40 years since the reform and opening up. Sociological Review of China,2020,8(02):28-46. https://kns.cnki.net/KXReader/Detail?invoice=bAXDJZMCYlHiVq5CQeMeWDJXeLDKxUVqSBXPMFyfxrD9CbD%2FeDNCehE2%2FrcKHsKkWSmqbno9TFMdeJCNrDH2sOX59pmZpoLTWDmaVrrj28GbolYwL4215mEElroOIh2kGUkxdZMzJjU6%2BDsTMk1wxG5gS2UiBlraFqj0w5M2U1Y%3D&DBCODE=CJFQ&FileName=SHPL202002006&TABLEName=cjfdlast2022&nonce=301BC8C4C12B4ED986EF7AE6F5767EB8&TIMESTAMP=1700907018638&uid=
2. He, L. (2018) An analysis of homosexual discourse in 11 media official microblogs. https://kns.cnki.net/kcms2/article/abstract?v=O0ap_2NIr0889zxmM8VJH6r_z7zzsPuVn5OfROVb_QiMqV5DoMeuBRcNr-ZjLPFpxJ-9BSbZmOZaeffWVXXI-oUTbXqQTsU9IHByuP2PF9dfkYMoh4AWD2MrF1ugGqT5k4SkQBcQlPI=&uniplatform=NZKPT&language=CHS
3. Zhang, L. (2016) Video in the Closet: Discourse Dilemmas and Development Trends of Queer Films in China,https://kns.cnki.net/kcms2/article/abstract?v=ohXIcpZjJKwkgP2fKt2MV43T42xgnzvGW6d3fWuBzVN61ZEV-qbTpWsVNMJXlRq4pPdaji4kx-XjLeTCGMQQu9f8k4axtFL4MXB5wCwkyX2d5ov7w2hq3wJsWirziggW94SxrsdK8L66GPNJh64ykg==uniplatform=NZKPTlanguage=CHS
4. Byne, W. (1997) Why We Cannot Conclude That Sexual Orientation is Primarily a Biological Phenomenon. Journal of Homosexuality, 34(1): 73-80. DOI: 10.1300/J082v34n01_07
5. Wang, Q. (2017) Debate on the paradigm of homosexual studies: Essentialism and constructivism. Academic Forum,40 (05): 62-69. doi:10.16524/j.45-1002.2017.05.009.
6. Butler, J. (1990) Gender Trouble: Feminism and the Subversion of Identity. Routledge, New York, 33. http://www.jstor.org/stable/3809989
7. Li, Y. (2002) Every Aspect of Queer Theory. Social Sciences Abroad (02):23-29. https://kns.cnki.net/kcms2/article/abstract?v=ohXIcpZjJKwWy-fiUXspCRAgi2td5lJbNWfC_9yvz-ru47tDl21YiOKgtVUeQ0rDYEZD1INJrmB_MBIRIrxGPLl9Wwgee_qFhNqvawKXDIrMQn6c9VwSaIukF9_yh5m7&uniplatform=NZKPT&language=CHS
8. Wang, J. (2011) Individual Gender Socialization and Gender Role Performance.J. Journal of Yunnan Minzu University (Social Sciences). 28(05): 107-111. DOI: 10.13727/j.cnki.53-1191/c.2011.05.039.
9. Liu, B., Guo, Y., Chen, J., Lu, L. (2017) Investigation on Homosexuality Among College Students. Journal of Chifeng University (14), 157-160. DOI: 10.13398/j.cnki.issn1673-260x.2017.14.067.

10. Seidman, S. (1994) Queer-Ing Sociology, Sociologizing Queer Theory: An Introduction. Sociological Theory, 12(2): 166-177. https://doi.org/10.2307/201862
11. Wang, Q. (2018) Research in homosexuality theory: from label-interactivity theory, Constructivism to queer theory. Journal of Yanshan University, 19(03): 17-23. DOI: 10.15883/j.13-1277/c.20180301707.
12. Du, L. (2015) Is Queer Theory Equal to Gay and Lesbian Studies? Theoretical Studies in Literature and Art, 35(6): 185-191. https://tsla.researchcommons.org/journal/vol35/iss6/9
13. Moreno-Tabarez, U., Chávez, K. R., Leonelli, S. J., Huang, A., Deklerck, S., & Rother, C. (2014) Queer Politics in China: A Conversation with "Western" Activists Working in Beijing. QED: A Journal in GLBTQ Worldmaking, 1(3): 109–132. https://doi.org/10.14321/qed.1.3.0109
14. Ding, L. (2002) The Transformation of Body Language in Queer Cinema, https://link.cnki.net/doi/10.27264/d.cnki.gqdhc.2022.000780doi:10.27264/d.cnki.gqdhc.2022.000780.
15. Deklerck, S. (2017) Bolstering queer desires, reaching activist goals: practicing queer activist documentary filmmaking in Mainland China, Studies in Documentary Film, 11(3): 232-247, DOI: 10.1080/17503280.2017.1335564
16. Ahmed, S. (2015) Introduction: Feel Your Way. The Cultural Politics of Emotion (NED-New edition, 2). Edinburgh University Press. pp. 1-19. http://www.jstor.org/stable/10.3366/j.ctt1g09x4q
17. Ahmed, S. (2015) The Contingency of Pain. The Cultural Politics of Emotion (NED-New edition, 2). Edinburgh University Press. pp. 20-41. http://www.jstor.org/stable/10.3366/j.ctt1g09x4q
18. Ahmed, S. (2015) Queer Feelings. The Cultural Politics of Emotion (NED-New edition, 2). Edinburgh University Press. pp. 144-167.http://www.jstor.org/stable/10.3366/j.ctt1g09x4q
19. Ahmed, S. (2015) The Performativity of Disgust. The Cultural Politics of Emotion (NED-New edition, 2). Edinburgh University Press. pp. 82-100.http://www.jstor.org/stable/10.3366/j.ctt1g09x4q

A Comparative Analysis of Female Consciousness through the Avenging Female Figures in Western and Chinese Literature – A Case Study of Medea and He Hongyao

Zhenni Zhang*

School of Literature, Chongqing Three Gorges University, Wanzhou, Chongqing, China

Abstract. Classical female figures like Medea and He Hongyao are prevalent in Western and Chinese literary tragedies. Despite their distinct literary backgrounds, these avenging women face diverse destinies. This paper focuses on analyzing the fate, outcomes, and the representation of female consciousness and tragic reasons in these two avenging female characters to delve deeper into the differences in female consciousness in Western and Chinese literature.

1.Introduction

Throughout history, women in male-dominated societies often find themselves in challenging circumstances. By examining gender issues as an independent entry point, hidden truths behind the "silent majority" may come to light.[2] This paper explores the divergent female representations of the Greek mythological figure Medea and Jin Yong's character He Hongyao, both deviating from traditional female images. The goal is to uncover the nuances of female consciousness beneath their tragic destinies.

2.Similar Trajectories from Love to Revenge

In Greek mythology, Medea was originally a young and beautiful princess. Under the arrangement of Cupid's golden arrow and fate, she fell in love at first sight with Jason, who came to the island to search for the golden wool. She helped him steal the golden wool, killed his flesh and blood brothers, betrayed her father and country, abandoned her princess identity, and ultimately became a homeless criminal. Later, Jason moved on to another love, and Medea grew hateful from love. She killed Jason's new lover with a poison robe and also killed her two sons.

Medea, from Greek mythology, and He Hongyao, from Jin Yong's "The Sword Stained with Royal Blood", share a similar fate trajectory, transitioning from love to betrayal and eventually revenge. Both unfortunate women, unable to escape the consequences of love, face tragic ends.

Like Medea, He Hongyao comes from a noble background and is the second expert of the Five Poisons Sect. Later, Xia Xueyi fell in love at first sight and helped him steal treasures from the Five Poisons Cult. After Xia Xueyi succeeded, he disappeared without a trace. However, He Hongyao accused Xia Xueyi of violating religious rules and was bitten by countless snakes, resulting in her appearance being completely destroyed. After years of searching for Xia Xueyi's whereabouts, she finally found his burial spot and saw him holding another woman's golden hairpin in his mouth. So she wanted to burn everything, but Xia Xueyi had already set a trap, and in the end, He Hongyao was buried in the cave.

3.Different Destinies Fated by Life and Death

The differences in social background and ideological consciousness between the two female characters destined them to have different fates. In the end, Medea and He Hongyao chose different ways of revenge based on the consistent characteristics of Chinese and Western literature, life and death were already predetermined.

Medea faces a powerful society that sees her husband's infidelity as a common occurrence. At the same time, the atmosphere of promoting freedom and individuality advocated in Western society also leaves a certain space for female images to survive and resist. So when Medea learned that Jason had betrayed her, she chose to kill her own son and witnessed the heartless person suffer the pain of losing their child. The best way to make a person suffer is to see them destroyed as treasures. So Medea didn't even let go of her and Jason's children after killing the enemy. Medea is referred to by some scholars as the wicked woman of Europe in this matter, but the so-called wicked woman only does what men can do within the framework of patriarchal society. The final outcome is presented to readers with a mechanical surrendering artistic effect, where Medea rides in a dragon carriage carrying the corpses of her two

*Corresponding author's mail: 1271818946@qq.com

sons, waiting for her to embark on a brand new life. This is a manifestation of Medea's step-by-step detachment of patriarchal thinking from her own background in that era. Her personality, which is not bound by any constraints, has always been advocated as "individualism" in Western society. It can be said that "Greek Mythology" is, in a sense, a reference and leader used by primitive Western society to guide public consciousness.

Unlike Medea's resolute opposition to welcoming new life, He Hongyao's ending conforms to the stereotypical impression of women in Chinese literature. In ancient China, the value of women was mainly reflected in their loyalty to love. As the saying goes, "one lifetime, one couple" is largely for women. In ancient times, it was common for emperors to have three thousand harems, and in history, the only one who truly achieved one life, one life, one pair of people was Emperor Xiaozong Zhu Youjian. When Empress Wu Zetian faced the issue of the harem, she was often criticized for having a chaotic private life. It can be seen that China places much higher demands on women than men in terms of loyalty in love. So even though He Hongyao knew he was unfaithful, he still chose to strive to get closer.

As a master of the Five Poisons Cult, she couldn't understand that it was a trap set by her lover. She wanted to die with her, but all she had to do was breathe in the scent of poison, willingly let her life pass, and ultimately achieve an inseparable ending. Perhaps even at the last moment, she was still deceiving herself.

From the name He Hongyao, it already foreshadows her final ending. "Red medicine" comes from Jiang Kui's "Yangzhou Slow". "The Twenty Four Bridges are still here, with the waves swaying in the heart and the cold moon silent. Remembering the red medicine by the bridge, who is it born for every year?" The Twenty Four Bridges are still there, and the waves in the river below the bridge are vast and the desolate moonlight is silent everywhere. Sighing at the annual red peony by the bridge, do you know who it blooms and thrives for? "Red medicine" is peony, and peony also has a nickname called "Jiangli". In addition, in the feudal society of China, the traditional concept of women's "clear aspirations, clear chastity, and clear love through death" also foreshadowed the outcome of He Hongyao.

4.The Implied Female Consciousness of "Avenging Women" in Different Contexts

Whether in China or Western countries, the fate of women seeking revenge often ends in tragedy. They use their thoughts to compete with reality, attempting to break the lens of the Philese center[9], but ultimately leave behind a bloody image of a poisonous woman. "The loss of humanity" often becomes the evaluation of women by the world, and revenge, destruction, and subversion have become the ultimate destination for this type of women. Even in such extreme behaviors, female consciousness belonging to both the East and the West has been injected, resulting in diversity in the final revenge outcomes.

Medea's revenge may be cruel, but it shows us that women can make different choices when oppressed. After experiencing betrayal, she regained consciousness and realized that she was still in a position without a voice. She realized that her tragic fate was caused by the times and society. Therefore, she used violent revenge methods and her divine skills to fight against fate, refusing to become a helpless victim under the tragedy of fate. She interpreted a sobering and rebellious character that was different from many traditional female images. A researcher praises Medea as a woman who has been insulted and harmed, and her strong resistance reflects the awakening of female self-awareness. From the perspective of tragic aesthetics, she uses evil to resist the reality that harms her, creating a beautiful side of this character in the collision of evil and good.

Medea has a strong personal will unique to Western individualism that is not bound by social morality. She opposed the entire patriarchal society with her own strength, even though she knew that her resistance was "killing a thousand enemies and losing eight hundred", she was unwilling to swallow her anger. In the Greek Mythology, one's own value can be reflected by resisting authority, so many researchers believe that the Greek Mythology encourages people to dare to oppose or even confront authority. One reason for opposing authority is to uphold one's own beliefs. Just like Medea's fate, at the beginning she believed in love, She was willing to resist and obstruct her "patriarchal power" for the sake of her love, killing her own flesh and blood brothers and betraying her father and country. Later, she believed in herself, so she used cruel revenge to kill her enemies and also killed her two sons. In a patriarchal society, sons are the continuation of fathers, and she wants to sever such connections. In this regard, Beauvoir wrote in "The Second Sex": "If childbirth is always connected to death, then death is also connected to childbirth. Death that is hated appears like rebirth, so it is also blessed." Children have always been associated with their mothers, but in ancient Greece at that time, it was believed that the father was the one who gave birth. So Medea must sever this connection, remove the marks left by patriarchal beliefs in her life, and her revenge realizes women's rebellion against patriarchal society and a male dominated worldview.

In He Hongyao's poignant love, she sacrificed her body for her lover and betrayed the sect, then was ruthlessly abandoned, and ultimately died tragically in his tomb. In most Chinese literature, women often have tragic endings in love. The outcome of female roles also depends on the spatial framework that allows women to survive and develop, as well as the culture and morality that are appropriate to the social conditions. In traditional Chinese society, there is a saying that goes, "The heart of love is determined by a woman's life and death." Women always play the role of love first. This is also a manifestation of a patriarchal society. "What is love in the world? It teaches people that life and death are intertwined." Most of them are used to describe women. The mourning for the deceased wife in Song Ci is "ten years of life and death, two vast expanses". Even if one's heart and blood are exhausted, it can still be considered as a matter of life and death. A man mourns his deceased wife and sheds a few tears, which always evokes sorrow. But after losing her loved one, a woman always hopes to make a promise of life and death.

In traditional society, due to the constraints of society and the unequal feudal system, coupled with the lack of career support for women, they were firmly bound to their husbands like canaries. Therefore, "women devoted all their emotions and even their entire lives to the so-called love.".[4] Under such a concept, even if He Hongyao had the idea of revenge, he ultimately chose to be buried with Xia Xueyi due to love, and even to his death, he chose to "endure forever and sometimes, this hatred will last forever.". He Hongyao's revenge remained in her own inner world's resistance against patriarchy. Even though she suffered from the deception and betrayal of her lover, in the social context of that time, she could only examine herself in the end and chose to use her own life to achieve ideological revenge. This revenge method is too pale in the face of reality, just as Chen Xiaoming said, "Does this resistance method mean are acceptance of male/female hierarchy?".

5.Causes of Female Tragedy in Western and Chinese Literature Backgrounds

5.1 Physiological Factors

Male and female destinies differ significantly in terms of "the construction of the body."

Firstly, there is a substantial physiological difference between males and females, a factor that greatly influences gender perceptions. As Butler stated in "Gender Trouble," "A girl is not born as a girl but becomes one at birth or before, based on whether she possesses a penis or a vagina. And this difference is arbitrary, gendered body parts are invested with meaning." [8] From the perspective of reproductive organs, male genitalia are external appendages, usually seen as subordinate to the subject, distinguishing them from others. This establishes a sense of agency in males from birth. In contrast, female reproductive organs are hidden within the body, existing as objects. In the process of sexual intercourse, men play the role of the aggressor, engaging in an attacking role, while women are invaded, playing the role of the receiver. This physiological structure creates a consciousness: women are subordinate to men.

Secondly, the difference in physical strength between men and women also contributes to their unequal social status. Women are often unable to perform many physically demanding and dangerous tasks, leading to an inability to achieve the same output as men in the workforce. From the primitive stages of society, where the womb of women was necessary for the continuation of life, and the high physical strength of men was needed for hunting, the societal division of labor emerged: "men outside, women inside."

The physiological vulnerabilities of women give men a privileged position in society. Men play the role of attackers in physiology, conquerors in love, and leaders in society, while women perpetually exist in a passive relationship. Through these physiological differences, women are consistently placed in a subordinate position.

5.2 Ideological Factors

For most women, even if granted independence, they still tend to choose attachment to love because there exists a difference in ideological consciousness regarding love between men and women.

It is observable that, for women, love is inseparable from loyalty. In China over two thousand years ago, women expressed their unwavering commitment to love by swearing to the heavens: "I desire to know you, may we live a long life without decay. The mountains have no end, the rivers will dry up. Thunder rumbles in winter, rain and snow fall. Heaven and earth unite, and then I dare not part from you."[5]. In the poem "Méng," it is said, "For a gentleman, indulgence is permissible and may be spoken of. For a woman, indulgence is not permissible and may not be spoken of!" Once a man changes his heart, he can abandon a woman without hesitation, but it is challenging for a woman to break free from love. It can be seen that men and women have different attitudes towards love loyalty. "People close a woman in the kitchen or in the boudoir, but they are surprised at her limited vision; people break her wings, but they lament that she can't fly."[6] Society seems to expect women to be loyal to love, sacrificing themselves for men, fulfilling male desires, but this does not necessarily earn women the respect they deserve. It may lead to being labeled as an "abandoned woman" or a "resentful woman." Society seems to believe that the word "loyalty" is unique to women, while men can be forgiven for their waywardness. In many folk stories, it is a woman's duty to mourn for the deceased and accompany her husband in death, as death is considered her creation. Traditionally, society has assigned women the destiny of dependence on men.[7]

In western literature, men and women also have great injustice to love. Take Greek mythology as an example. Although Zeus is the God of the universe, it does not affect his emotional madness and neglect. It is summed up in two words: cheating and possession. But women are full of unlimited romance and fantasy to love. Simone de Beauvoir, in "The Second Sex," explicitly stated, "'Love' is one of the roots of a serious misunderstanding that divides men and women: this is a serious misunderstanding." Lord Byron, in "Anna Karenina," said, "Love in a man's life is just a pastime, but it is a woman's life itself." Nietzsche, in "The Gay Science," expressed a similar viewpoint: "The word 'love' means something different for men and women. Women's understanding of love is quite clear: this is not only loyalty, this is the dedication of body and soul, without reservation or consideration for anything else. It is this unconditional commitment that makes their love a kind of faith, a unique faith they possess." [1] For women, love is as important as faith.

5.3 Historical and Cultural Factors

In Greek mythology, the patriarchal society imposes certain ideologies on individuals within the temporal framework through mythological figures.[3] Male mythological characters are often portrayed as heroes, whether it's the Western Zeus or the Eastern Emperor. The emergence of female myths is primarily due to male fantasies about female images within a specific historical context. Figures like the Snail Girl represent the male desire for women to silently contribute and be virtuous and diligent. The imagery of characters like Meng Jiangnu embodies the male wish for women to remain faithfully devoted. These female myths are constructed from a male-centered perspective, dictating what women should be.

Throughout history, political power has consistently rested in male hands, creating a male-dominated society. Even in the Western context, with figures like Eve, the mother of all living beings, her existence is not autonomous. She is created by taking a rib from Adam, and when Adam says to her, "Bone of my bones, and flesh of my flesh," women are once again objectified. In China, despite historical figures like Empress Wu Zetian breaking gender norms by appointing female officials, it did not signify a gradual shift towards gender equality or an improvement in the status of women. Following her era, the rise of Neo-Confucianism during the Song and Ming dynasties further restricted women. Women became entirely subordinate to men, and feudal ethics became the biggest obstacle for women. As Simone de Beauvoir said, even if a country is ruled by a queen, it does not change the overall low social status of women.

"From primitive civilization to today, people have always believed that for women, the marital relationship is a form of 'service.' Men express gratitude to women through gifts or assure to support them, but the service implies giving oneself a master; in this relationship, there is no mutuality." [6]Terms like "service" and "master" inherently imply an unequal relationship. In ancient China, the term "concubine" was used to refer to women married outside the main wife, and originally, "concubine" meant a female slave. In primitive societies, women were used as slaves or objects for exchange between tribes. Women have never had an equal status with men.

In conclusion, the causes of female tragedy in both Western and Chinese literature backgrounds stem from a combination of physiological and ideological factors. Physiologically, the differences in reproductive organs and physical strength contribute to the subordinate status of women. Ideologically, societal expectations regarding love, loyalty, and women's role in relationships further reinforce their disadvantaged position.

6.Conclusion

Examining the tragic destinies of Medea and He Hongyao, we can observe differences in female consciousness between Western and Chinese literature. In Chinese literature, due to prolonged constraints from feudal systems, most women still exhibit a passive acceptance of love, even hoping for a perfect and happy ending, even if it means "living and dying together." Therefore, He Hongyao willingly steps into the trap to fulfill her unwavering love for Xia Xueyi. In Western literature, while the status of women is consistently inferior to men, female consciousness is awakening, enabling them to resist male dominance through their efforts. Medea, for instance, can kill her own children for revenge, demonstrating a rebellion against patriarchal society and male moral values. Western values emphasize the individual's struggle for personal interests, a stark contrast to the ethical and moral focus in traditional Chinese culture, highlighting the divergence in female consciousness between the two cultures. However, both in China and Western countries, the existence of vengeful women is often seen as incompatible with the expected traits of femininity. Women are expected to be pure, gentle, and, even with the demons hidden within, forced to become the "other," helpless, and dependent. Despite the rise of female consciousness, the plight of vengeful women remains challenging to change in both Chinese and Western literature.

References

1. [Germany]Nietzsche.F, *The Gay Science*. Central Compilation & Translation Press, CCTP ,The Beijing.(2007)
2. Y.R.Wang,Analysis of the Image of the Resisting Female Medea and He Xiaoyu. Journal of Henan Normal University (Philosophy and Social Sciences Edition), 39,3:229-231.(2012)
3. C.X.Heng, Analysis of Self-consciousness of People in Greek Mythology. Journal of Xinyang Normal University,21,1:9-12,25-26. DOI:10.3969/j.issn.1003-0964.2001.01.003. (2001)
4. Y.N.Song, Entering the Female World in Jin Yong's Works: On Jin Yong's Female View. Science and Technology Information, 6:102-103. DOI:10.3969/j.issn.1001-9960.2009.06.083.(2009)
5. Q.Wang, Female Consciousness in Chinese Traditional Literature. Language Teaching and Research,10:73-78. DOI:10.3969/j.issn.1004-0498-B.2010.10.033.(2010)
6. [France]S.De.Beauvoir, *The Second Sex*. Shanghai Translation Publishing House, The Shanghai.(2011)
7. C.H.Cui, Blood and Tears Struggle for the Same Grief——On the Female Tragic Spirit in Ancient Chinese Tragedies. Qufu Normal University,DOI:10.7666/d.Y448791.(2002)

https://doi.org/10.1051/shsconf/202418501018

8. [America]J.Butler, *Gender Troubles: Feminism and Identity Disruption.* Shanghai Sanlian Bookstore, The Shanghai.(2009)
9. X.K.Pan, Ontological Construction of Revengeful Women in Chinese Literature under the Mirror Theory. Journal of Southwest Agricultural University (Social Science Edition), 11(1):80-85.(2013)

Urban Women's Writing in the Revolutionary Wave—a Counter-Reading of the "Eclipse" Trilogy and "Song of Youth"

Zhexi Li*

Qingdao University of Science and Technology, Qingdao, Shandong, 266061, China

Abstract. There are obvious differences between the left-wing literature of the 1930s and the revolutionary literary works after the founding of New China in the 1950s. Among the many works, the "Eclipse" trilogy and "Song of Youth" are the few works that develop plots with women as the center. By reading these two works, we can have a more comprehensive understanding of the revolutionary trends in the 1930s and 1950s, and it is also conducive to studying the status of women and the development of female literature in the two periods.

1. Introduction

With the outbreak of the Revolution of 1911 and the May Fourth Movement, China began to awaken and innovate in various fields, and women were no exception. It can be said that the feminist movement and the Chinese revolution were carried out almost at the same time. However, with the failure of the revolution, the feminist movement was also marginalized, and female revolutionary leaders turned to cooperate with the more revolutionary party-the Communist Party of China. The Chinese Communist Party was also keenly aware of the importance of women's liberation. Therefore, Women's activities during the Great Revolution and beyond were not purely feminist movements, but more of an accessory to China's new democratic revolution. [1,10]

Mao Zedong classified intellectuals and other classes that occupied a small amount of the means of production as the petty bourgeoisie. They were the centrists and targets of China's new democratic revolution. Therefore, compared with the workers and peasants, the petty bourgeoisie's own contradictions make literary works centered on them more dramatic. Urban women such as Lin Daojing and Ms. Jing are representative images of petty bourgeois intellectuals.[4]

2. Different Perspectives of Male and Female Writers

In the "Eclipse" trilogy, due to the male identity of the author Mr. Mao Dun, it is naturally inevitable to "other" women. The women in the work are not only the vassals of the revolution, but also the vassals of men. In "Shake", the ambiguity between Sun Wuyang and Fang Luolan is to highlight the weakness of Fang Luolan's petty bourgeoisie and the wavering caused by the revolutionary process. Zhang Qiuliu's passion is a trend and fashion popular during the May Fourth period, and it is just to show the sinking and confusion of progressive young people after the failure of the Great Revolution. As for Ms. Hui, who claims to be passionate in order to take revenge on men, in the final analysis, she is also helpless after being molested by men.[5]

The female images in the "Eclipse" trilogy are often divided into two types. One is the traditional conservative female image, represented by Mrs. Fang. They are naturally the ideal images of women imagined and written by male writers. They are weak, beautiful, considerate, and have almost perfect qualities, but they are always the vassals of men. The other type is the progressive women represented by Sun Wuyang, Zhang Qiuliu and Ms. Hui. They no longer stick to feudal etiquette and dogma, but strive to put themselves on an equal footing with men. However, these progressive women resist The means and goals of patriarchy are to imitate men and become men, which is completely different from the truly independent women described by female writers.

In "Song of Youth", Lin Daojing's relationship with three men successively puts the subject on the woman herself, with the men only guiding and helping. When Lin Daojing was in poverty, Yu Yongze solved her food and clothing problem; when Lin Daojing faced a crisis of faith, Lu Jiachuan guided her to the road of revolution; after Lu Jiachuan was arrested and sacrificed, Jiang Hua took over as the revolutionary guide Responsibility eventually cultivated Lin Daojing into an excellent revolutionary fighter.

On the one hand, at the beginning of the story, Lin Daojing's melody was "escape". She escaped from her feudal family. After receiving help from Yu Yongze, she found that she still had not escaped from Yu Yongze's shackles, so she chose to escape again. Lin Daojing's "escape" is a resistance to the reality of women being oppressed. Similarly, Ms. Hui in "Disillusionment" also encounters obstacles on the road to independent survival. Lin Daojing's resistance and Ms. Hui's sinking

*Corresponding author's email: lizhexi29@163.com

compromise form a distinct contrast. Later, with the help of Lu Jiachuan and Jiang Hua, Lin Daojing embarked on the road of revolution and successfully led the revolution. Although Lin Daojing escaped from the cruel old society, she still could not avoid the guidance and help of men on the road to true independence.

3. Similarities and Differences in Female Images

Different from contemporary feminist literature by writers such as Wang Anyi and Tie Ning, the female images in the "Eclipse" trilogy and "Song of Youth" ultimately serve the revolution. The only female perspective narrative in the trilogy is "Disillusionment", in which Ms. Jing has many similarities and differences with Lin Daojing. Although the two were caught up in the wave of the May Fourth Movement, they still could not escape the oppression of their patriarchal families. Ms. Jing's mother told her to stay safe, and she became even more worried after hearing Ms. Hui's rumors; Lin Daojing's parents were standard feudal parents who objectified women, and all their training for her was to sell her at a good price.

Mao Dun and Yang Mo are completely different in their handling of relationships with men. Ms. Jing admires Qiang and is subordinate to men. When faced with the strong officer who takes pleasure in war, she tries to use love to change his pleasure. Lin Daojing did not surrender to other men. Yu Yongze saved her life, but she was still unwilling to be controlled by Yu. Lu Jiachuan and Jiang Hua redeemed her spirit and led her to the road of revolution. She worked hard to learn and progress, just for Being able to stand with the two of them equally.

Regarding sexual concepts, male writers also showed misunderstandings of female sexual concepts. Mao Dun describes how when Ms. Jing discovers Bao Su's true identity, she suffers from the fact that her virginity has been tarnished. Lin Daojing and Yu Yongze lived together and then broke up. She was only angry at Yu Yongze's hypocrisy, but did not mention a word about her chastity. Another example is Ms. Shafei written by Ding Ling, Wang Qiyao in "Song of Everlasting Sorrow"; and many female writers' female images, which do not emphasize or care about the so-called "chastity".[3]

Beauvoir believes that an important reason for women to become the "second sex" is economic independence. [2,11] In the "Eclipse" trilogy and "Song of Youth", the author has noticed this keenly. After Ms. Hui returned from studying abroad, she encountered obstacles in finding a job. Her brother took pleasure in her misfortune and was happy to support her sister; Lin Daojing never gave up the idea of financial independence after living together with Yu Yongze, even though Yu Yongze opposed and obstructed her many times. Without financial resources, it is far more difficult for women to join the revolution than for men.

In the "Eclipse" trilogy and "Song of Youth", there is a negative typical female image respectively. Lu Meili in "Shake" is gentle, virtuous, and dedicated to playing the role of Mrs. Fang. She has been in love with Fang Luolan since childhood, and they have a deep relationship as husband and wife. However, this traditional female image was completely defeated by the progressive woman Sun Wuyang. After Fang Luolan met Sun Wuyang, she left Lu Meili behind. After the May 4th Movement, traditional women like Lu Meili were destined to be eliminated by the times. In "Song of Youth", Bai Liping was once a progressive young man who actively participated in the student movement and was aggrieved by the September 18th Incident. However, when Lin Daojing saw Bai Liping again, she had become a social butterfly in the dance hall. He mingled among the so-called upper class society and even wanted to introduce Lin Daojing to other dignitaries. The two female figures, Lu Meili and Bai Liping, stand on opposite sides of the two identities of progressive women during the May Fourth period. Lu Meili stood on the opposite side of women - men, while Bai Liping stood on the opposite side of revolution - reactionary. This also shows once again that whether it is from the front or the back, the two identities that the women in the two works have at the same time - women and revolutionaries are equally important.

4. Love, Revolution, Gender

Beauvoir once commented on the female images of many male writers. Although they are extremely beautiful and are everything to men, they are not themselves.[2] These women are all vassals of men. As a male writer, Mr. Mao Dun naturally cannot escape his narrow prejudice against women. There are two types of female images in the "Eclipse" trilogy. One is passionate women like Sun Wuyang, Ms. Hui, and Zhang Qiuliu, and the other is women like Ms. Jing who try to break the shackles of tradition and find her own direction in life. They were revolutionary and progressive, but in the end they were still restrained by men.

The appearance of Sun Wuyang was to promote the conflict between Fang Luolan and Mrs. Fang. As a typical representative of progressive young women during the May Fourth period, she was progressive, open-minded, and devoted to the revolution, which formed a clear contrast with Mrs. Fang's traditional family-centered woman image. Compared. But Sun Wuyang still cannot get rid of the female image portrayed by male stereotypes. Similar to Flaubert's Emma and Tolstoy's Anna, they are both wandering between an increasingly open and inclusive world and the traditional old forces in the era of bourgeois revolution. contradictory images. Mrs. Fang, on the other hand, is a standard image of a family woman in traditional feudal society who abides by women's ethics and obeys the three obediences and four virtues. This is the standard and perfect woman favored by male writers.

Ms. Hui showed mercy at all times, just to take revenge on the men who had hurt her. In Mr. Mao Dun's "Eclipse" trilogy, the portrayal of women is still inseparable from the description of male love and female love, and this kind of male love and female love is often under the male perspective. Ms. Hui was hurt by a man because of emotional inequality; when she took revenge on a man, she also took advantage of the gender inequality between men and women. Even though she longs to be independent, she still finds it difficult to move forward without being dependent on a man. The tragedy of Ms. Hui lies in the male trap that she can never escape from.

Zhang Qiuliu was intoxicated in the love between men and women, but ended up suffering from illness. As the only woman among the many failed revolutionaries in "The Pursuit", she chose to indulge in the love between men and women to escape reality. But for male revolutionaries, love is just a seasoning that comes and goes away. For Zhang Qiuliu, once he falls in love, he can no longer escape and is trapped by his feelings for life, ending up like this.

Ms. Jing is different from the first three. On the one hand, she pursues revolution, but on the other hand, she is willing to submit to men. At school, she opposed the student movement that only talked empty words and longed to do something practical, but she could not refuse the pursuit of her classmates. After being disappointed by her classmates, she devoted herself to the revolution, but fell in love with a soldier again. After the soldiers left, she once again joined the revolution. In the end, both the dream of love and the dream of revolution came to disillusionment.

Therefore, the women in Mr. Mao Dun's works serve the revolution and men, but have lost the charm of women themselves.

The heroine Lin Daojing in "Song of Youth" has distinct feminist liberation characteristics while pursuing revolution. She escapes twice in the novel, one is to escape from her family by taking a train, and the other is to escape from Yu Yongze's control and join the revolution. Lin Daojing's first escape is very similar to the escape of "Nora" in various Chinese and foreign works. They yearn for freedom and have the courage to practice it. They are representatives of bourgeois progressive women. Lin Daojing's second escape was a classic question that has troubled literati since the May Fourth Movement - what happened to Nora after she left, and she gave her own answer.[6] After escaping from the new shackles, Lin Daojing chose to join the revolution, liberating herself and liberating more people. As a revolutionary novel with a clear political stance, "Song of Youth" finally leads the issue of women's liberation to the issue of revolution.[9]

When Yang Mo himself portrayed Lin Daojing's image, he also focused on describing her characteristics as a woman.

"Jing, I have grown up so much - I am twenty-nine years old. This is the first time that I am good to you. Except when I was a child, my mother is like you... So, I am willing to use my heart and my feelings I came to make you happy, to make you happy... But, I'm sorry for you, I feel very uneasy, I gave you too little."

The relationship between Jiang Hua and Lin Daojing has always been interpreted as (party) father/daughter, (male) initiate/initiate. However, looking at Jiang Hua's dependence on Lin Daojing's motherhood after being injured, not only Not only Jiang Hua's paternal guidance to Lin Daojing, but also the brilliance of Lin Daojing's maternal nature. The image of Lin Daojing is not in a low position like the women described by traditional male writers, but she and men support each other and make progress as equals.[7]

5. Revolutionary literature with women as the theme

"Song of Youth" was created in a special literary stage - the seventeen-year period. At the beginning of the work's birth in 1958, many proletarian critics criticized Lin Daojing's female identity and petty bourgeois intellectual identity in the text. Guo Kai believes that it is full of petty bourgeois personal sentiments and self-expression, but weakens the revolutionary content and lacks the bridge between workers and peasants. After the reform and opening up in the 1980s, with the introduction of feminism, liberalism and avant-garde literature, critics' attitudes towards "Song of Youth" also changed. They believed that Lin Daojing's pursuit of revolution was succumbing to revolution. It betrays female identity and "is the deconstruction and denial of female liberation." Therefore, in two different periods, the 1950s and 1960s and the 1980s and 1990s, the attitudes towards female writing in "Song of Youth" were also completely different.

The "Song of Youth" we see now is a revised version after criticism by Guo Kai and others. Mr. Yang Mo added that Lin Daojing successfully led the peasant movement in Ding County, Hebei under the guidance of "Aunt" and Jiang Hua. Lin Daojing's own femininity has been further weakened. She is no longer a woman, but a daughter, a party member, and a proletarian revolutionary. Lin Daojing's resistance and escape as a woman in the first half of the novel are ignored, replaced by reconciliation and cooperation with the peasant class, and her struggle for the liberation of the proletariat.

At the beginning of the birth of "Song of Youth", its female narrative was to serve the revolution. Lin Daojing's resistance and growth as a woman actually reflects the growth of the Chinese revolution. After the novel was revised, its female independence part was almost completely erased, replaced by Lin Daojing's understanding of the revolution and serving the revolution in the second half of the work. This triggered dissatisfaction and criticism of "Song of Youth" by a new group of critics and feminist writers after the reform and opening up.

Lin Daojing's two escapes provided an answer to the new democratic revolution for a key issue in old China - "What happens after Nora leaves?" Lin Daojing's first escape was from her family and the shackles of patriarchal and feudal patriarchal systems. However, after escaping from her family, she quickly fell into Yu Yongze's patriarchal trap. Although Lin Daojing was determined to become financially independent, she was hit by both her husband and society. In the end, she chose to escape for the second time, that is, to escape from her husband's power. When the question came to "what happens after Nora leaves?", Mr. Yang Mo chose the path of proletarian revolution for Lin Daojing, using Lin Daojing's identity as a farmer's daughter to pave the way for her to integrate into the revolution and resist class oppression.

We cannot absolutely say that Lin Daojing's tragedy of female identity is a foil to the revolutionary narrative, because revolution has in turn become one of Lin Daojing's solutions to escape male oppression. After the revision of "Song of Youth", it obviously highlights the status of revolution, but the author also potentially provides a unique solution to the issue of female independence, that is, joining the revolution and contributing to the liberation of all mankind.

In the "Eclipse" trilogy, the only female perspective narrative is Ms. Jing in "Disillusionment". Putting aside her weak female character, Ms. Jing's attitude towards revolution is not much different from Fang Luolan in "Shake" or Zhang Manqing in "Pursuit". The three people were unwilling to join forces with the reactionary forces, but they were helpless in the face of the failure of the revolution. Ms. Jing is different from Lin Daojing. Mr. Yang Mo's description of Lin Daojing has relatively clear female characteristics, although she always follows in the footsteps of men. Mr. Mao Dun almost ignored the femininity of Ms. Jing as a revolutionary, eliminated her gender characteristics, and almost equated her with a male revolutionary.

6. The contradiction between personal narrative and collective narrative

As a novel with a revolution as the background, especially a work with a proletarian revolutionary theme, the author's understanding of how to deal with the relationship between the individual and the collective and how to revolutionize and collectivize individual intellectuals was an extremely important issue of that era.

In this regard, Lin Daojing in "Song of Youth" is a woman who longs for independence. Her escape from the family and the process of revolution is her personal choice. After the revision, when Lin Daojing chose a path, her female gender characteristics were covered up, and the core of the novel became the story of how oppressed women awakened and turned over. When looking at "Song of Youth" from the perspective of a feminist novel, the narrative of Lin Daojing's transformation from an oppressed woman and a petty-bourgeois intellectual to revolution is particularly eye-catching, simply because the subject matter is so novel and prominent. After the revision, the emphasis on depicting the peasant and student movements made the work stand out from the crowd.

As for the "Eclipse" trilogy, which is set before and after the Great Revolution, it does not emphasize collectivist narratives. Young intellectuals do not reject their petty bourgeois identity, and naturally they cannot escape the wavering and weakness of petty bourgeois revolutionaries. They threw themselves into the revolution with enthusiasm, but when the revolution reached its lowest ebb, they became confused and hesitant, not knowing where to go.

7. Characteristics of the petty bourgeoisie

As Mao Zedong said in "Analysis of the Classes in Chinese Society", the petty bourgeoisie wavers in the revolution. When the revolutionary situation is good, they often join the revolution. When the revolution falls into a low ebb, they fall into confusion and even become reactionary. They are both won over by the revolution and favored by the reactionaries.[4] Therefore, when Mao Dun wrote the "Eclipse" trilogy, he was at the low ebb of the failure of the Great Revolution, and his characters were naturally at a loss. Ms. Jing's disillusionment again and again, Fang Luolan's wavering, and Zhang Manqing's decline are all symbols of the wavering of the petty bourgeoisie. When Yang Mo wrote "Song of Youth", New China had been born, China's new democratic revolution had been victorious, and the petty bourgeoisie naturally had an optimistic attitude towards the revolution, even though the background of the novel was still soberingly depressed.

Not only that, the pursuit of revolution by young intellectuals in the "Eclipse" trilogy and "Song of Youth" are completely different. Mao Dun created the "Eclipse" trilogy around the time of the Great Revolution. Intellectuals naturally strive for the interests of the bourgeoisie themselves. What troubles them is not only the shackles of the times and the weakness of the petty bourgeoisie themselves, but also the limitations of the social system. Mao Dun Disheartened after the failure of the Great Revolution, he wrote about the confusion and uncertainty of the petty bourgeoisie in the revolution based on his personal experience during the revolution. "Song of Youth" was created in the 1950s after the founding of New China. Lin Daojing was bound to move towards the path of new democratic revolution. The most fundamental difference between Lin Daojing and many intellectuals in the "Eclipse" trilogy also determines their different paths - Lin Daojing is not only from a petty bourgeois background, but also a victim of the comprador class and feudal landlord family. More importantly, her farmer mother and grandfather gave her a natural affinity for the proletariat. Therefore, the revolutionary path chosen by Lin Daojing is aimed at liberating the proletariat. She helped the proletariat along the way and received much help from proletarian revolutionaries, eventually reconciling with the proletariat and joining them.[8]

8. Summary

In general, the "Eclipse" trilogy and "Song of Youth" are more revolutionary novels than women's novels. Women's narratives often serve the revolution. As far as the revolution is concerned, they emphasize the role of the petty bourgeoisie in the revolution. One is pessimistic and the other is optimistic, which proves the weakness and wavering of the petty bourgeois revolution. As far as women are concerned, although they have improved their status in literary works to a certain extent, it is still difficult to change the dominant position of men; they overemphasize revolution, weaken women themselves, ignore women's desires and needs, and regard women as A vehicle for revolutionary narrative.

On the other hand, "Song of Youth", as a work by a female writer, also implies a way out for women's liberation in the revolutionary narrative - joining the revolution. Only by breaking the cage of class can gender equality be achieved.

References

1. Kristeva, J.(2021) Chinese Women. Tongji University Press, Shanghai
2. Beauvoir, S.(2019) The Second Sex. Shanghai Translation Publishing House, Shanghai
3. Ran, X. (2004) The construction of female self: the subject presentation and connotation of contemporary women's writing. Journal of South Central University for Nationalities (Humanities and Social Sciences Edition), (05): 125-128.
4. Mao, Z.(1994) Selected Works of Mao Zedong Volume 1. People's Publishing House, Beijing
5. Lu, W.(1994) On Mao Dun and Women's Literature. Journal of Shenyang Normal University (Social Science Edition), (02): 28-31
6. Qian, S.(2022) Seeing "Gender" in "Revolution" - Reinterpretation of "Song of Youth" . Humanities, 8(02): 239-256.
7. Guo, K.(1959) A Brief Discussion on the Shortcomings in the Description of Lin Daojing—A Comment on Yang Mo's Novel "Song of Youth". China Youth" (02): 37-40.
8. Zhang, J.(2022) Text production" and its female discourse in "Song of Youth" . Journal of Tianshui Normal University, 42(03):94-99.
9. Song, J and Liu, D(2008) Reargument of "Song of Youth". Novel Review 143(05):59-65.
10. Showalter, E.(2012) A Literature Of Their own. Zhejiang University Press, Hangzhou
11. Moi, T. (1992) Sexuality and the politics of Text Feminist Literary Theory. Times Literature and Art Publishing House, Changchun

Research on the Digital Inheritance and Protection of Yue Embroidery Under the Meta-cosmic Technology

Yuying Wang, Huiyang Huang, Xiaochen Li, Wenkun Yang, Haoyuan Li, Min You*

Guangdong Institute of Technology, Zhaoqing, Guangdong

Abstract. With the rise of meta-cosmic technology and the increasing importance of intangible cultural heritage protection and inheritance, the integration of digitalization and intangible cultural heritage protection has become one of the hot spots in contemporary research. Taking Yue embroidery as the research object, this paper first introduces the characteristics of Yue embroidery and the current situation of its digital protection, then analyzes the application of meta-universe technology in intangible heritage protection, including the presentation of virtual exhibitions, real-time teaching of embroidery skills and the establishment of digital archives, and discusses the digital protection and inheritance methods of Yue embroidery under the meta-universe technology in detail. Integrate Cantonese embroidery culture with modern science and technology, put forward a new development direction, and promote the inheritance and innovation of Cantonese embroidery.

1. Introduction

Yue embroidery, also known as Guang embroidery and Chao embroidery, is one of the four famous embroideries in China with a long history. Yue embroidery often features full and intricate composition, neat and exaggerated patterns, vivid and contrasting colors, and diverse and variegated needlework. Due to its high requirements, it often requires skilled male workers and embroiderers and consumes a lot of time and effort, resulting in high prices and costs that deter prospective learners. Moreover, changes in the aesthetic preferences of contemporary youth and the acceleration of life pace have led to a decrease in demand for Yue embroidery, making its development and survival increasingly difficult in terms of limited space, disconnection from reality, and difficulties in inheritance. However, with the rapid development of technology, including the widespread use of 5G technology, human-machine interaction, virtual reality technology, big data, and cloud computing, non-material cultural heritage has found a new opportunity in the metaverse.

The "metaverse" is a virtual world where humans surpass reality and achieve virtual and real-world interactions based on the mapping of the real world using existing digital technologies. As a new form of digital communication, it is gradually changing people's lives. It features high immersion, open-source creation, closed-loop economic system, and sustainable development[1]. It provides a new solution for non-material cultural heritage faced with problems such as space limitation and low attraction, allowing non-material cultural heritage to rejuvenate in the metaverse.

2. Characteristics of Yue embroidery and the significance of digital protection

2.1 Artistic value and cultural significance of Yue embroidery

As a representative embroidery craft in Guangdong, Guangdong embroidery is full of Lingnan characteristics from artistic style to creative thinking. In the image performance, the composition is full, golden and brilliant, focusing on the coordination of light and shadow, coupled with rich and exquisite stitching and bright and rich colors, highlighting the noble and elegant temperament, known as the magnificent "treasure of South Lingnan", with high technical value and cultural aesthetic value. Under the inheritance of Chen Shaofen and others, the needlework technique of Guangdong embroidery has undergone continuous development and innovation, and has become more modern value. Cantonese embroidery masters made good use of white painting techniques to produce, and applied color techniques on the basis of white painting, and extended the selection of materials to the categories of portraits, and used the expression techniques of traditional Chinese painting and oil painting to form a new style of "modern Canton embroidery", which ushered in the peak of Cantonese embroidery art.

After thousands of years of inheritance, exploration, absorption and innovation, Guangdong embroidery has formed a unique art form, showing deep and long historical and cultural accumulation. While inheriting the characteristics of traditional embroidery techniques, it has unique regional technological characteristics, and it has

*Corresponding author's mail: 10150129@qq.com

been developing continuously. At the same time, Guangdong embroidery adopts the paintings of Lingnan school painters, with lychee, cotton, flowers and birds and other Lingnan characteristics as the main theme, which not only carries the essence of Lingnan culture, but also integrates the Western painting style, absorbing Western painting lines, light and shade changes, making the works look very three-dimensional and ornamental. Therefore, Guangdong embroidery not only has a deep historical and cultural foundation in China, but also enjoys a high reputation in the world, showing the excellent artistic talent and exquisite craftsmanship of the Chinese nation.

2.2 The important role of digital protection in the inheritance of Guangdong Embroidery

Due to the emergence of mechanized production and computer embroidery machines, the traditional craft has been impacted by modern production methods, and few people are willing to learn the needle-line skills. Relying on the local environment, Guangdong embroidery is difficult to further open the market and is facing the danger of being lost and forgotten. With the development of modern science and technology, industrial digital transformation is being actively and steadily promoted.

On the one hand, the social informatization caused by science and technology threatens the living environment of intangible cultural heritage; On the other hand, the traditional protection of intangible cultural heritage has brought great changes due to the rapid development of digital technology represented by information technology, virtual reality and communication technology, which provides a broad space for the classification, preservation, display and dissemination of intangible cultural heritage resources[2]. Moreover, information technology, as the representative, has played a great role in promoting the far-reaching spread of Chinese culture.

In recent years, China has paid more and more attention to the digital protection of intangible cultural heritage. Digital technology has significant advantages in storage, dissemination, application and display, etc. It provides a way to overcome the situational limitations of intangible cultural heritage, display and inherit intangible cultural heritage in the most authentic way, and also creates conditions for the construction of new protection and inheritance methods of intangible cultural heritage. For Yue embroidery, digital protection can effectively preserve its traditional skills and artistic style. Through digital technology, the production process, pattern design, stitch skills and other details of Yue embroidery can be recorded to form digital archives. In this way, even if the traditional production methods are gradually lost, future generations can still learn and study the skills of Cantonese embroidery through digital materials to ensure the continuation of its traditional skills.

3. The development status of Guangdong embroidery and the exploration of digital path

3.1 Difficulties and challenges of traditional Cantonese embroidery inheritance

With the continuous development of social economy and the improvement of people's living standard, people's demand for spiritual and cultural life is also growing. Under this background, traditional Cantonese embroidery has been unable to meet the needs of modern people's pursuit of both material and spiritual culture. At the same time, it has gradually lost its practical value in modern life and is facing a severe situation of declining day by day. The shortage of inheriting talents is an urgent problem to be solved. With the development of modern science and technology and the change of people's lifestyle, young people often choose other emerging professions, and the inheritance of traditional Cantonese embroidery is facing a serious talent gap. In addition, with the diversified development of contemporary people's needs, traditional Cantonese embroidery products have been unable to meet the market demand and lack of innovation, which is crucial to the innovation of traditional Cantonese embroidery. Improving market demand is also one of the important links to protect and promote Guangdong embroidery.

Due to the variety of similar products, similar products to meet the needs of the people and the increasingly fierce market competition, traditional Guangdong embroidery products continue to be squeezed by the market, the market share is also declining. In addition, traditional Cantonese embroidery has high requirements for artisans, and the high cost leads consumers to prefer cheaper alternative crafts

To solve this series of problems, we need to increase the intensity of technology research and development, improve the quality and design level of products. How to protect and carry forward the intangible cultural heritage in the rapid development and modernization of modern life, so as to continue the local spirit is a creative problem worth thinking about. On the way of protecting and developing Yue embroidery, we must face many difficulties and hardships. We should deal with the relationship between inheritance and innovation, and strive to protect and develop this traditional handicraft with a long history and rich cultural connotation - Yue embroidery.

3.2 Exploration and application of digital inheritance methods of Cantonese embroidery

Because of the traditional handicrafts often have more demanding requirements on their technology and materials, it is difficult for traditional handicrafts to achieve innovation and breakthrough to adapt to contemporary needs. The rise of digital technology can skillfully solve this problem.

Such as the use of three-dimensional scanning technology, 3D printing, virtual reality technology and other ways to display and spread the digital Guangdong embroidery. In the inheritance of Yue embroidery skills, digital technology can be used to introduce new materials, techniques and design concepts, so as to further expand the creative space of Yue embroidery. Just as the product design through the computer, mobile phone, tablet and other tools, and then import it into the machine, so as to print 3D Guangdong embroidery model;

Another example is the three-dimensional scanning of Cantonese embroidery works, the use of virtual reality technology and specific equipment to show people its details and the full picture. Among these new ways of inheritance and development, the technical application achievements of virtual Reality technology (Virutual Reality, referred to as VR) are particularly remarkable. For example, the Guangfu Temple Fair in Guangzhou breaks through the limitations of time and space, and vividly displays Guangdong intangible cultural heritage through digital modeling and unreal engine technology, including embroidery workshops and Cantonese embroidery techniques, which are re-engraved in front of the audience in a new way, allowing the audience to instantly cross the ancient and modern times and have a "dialogue" with historical time and space, so as to revitalize this ancient art.

The application of virtual reality technology makes Yue embroidery break through the limitation of space. The audience can watch through VR, so as to achieve the immersive effect, and then make the audience feel the exquisite embroidery technology of the craftsman and the pursuit of beauty. This new digital display not only provides a more convenient and efficient learning platform for the audience, but also provides more possibilities for the inheritance and development of Guangdong embroidery.

4. Yue embroidery digital protection and inheritance under the meta universe technology method

4.1 Application of meta universe technology in digital protection of intangible heritage Basics

The meta-universe is a new virtual-real Internet application and social form based on the integration of new technologies such as extended reality, digital twin, cloud computing, and blockchain[3]. The application of meta-cosmic technology in the protection of intangible cultural heritage can effectively cater to the characteristics of The Times, regionalism, culture and embodiment of intangible cultural heritage through the construction of pseudo-real space and surreal space. In addition, it can also promote the evolution of intangible cultural heritage projects from traditional ways such as mentoring and family inheritance to "spatial reconstruction", so as to solve the current problems such as space loss and shrinking inheritance groups in non-genetic inheritance. For example, in March this year, the Gansu Provincial Department of Culture and Tourism, together with Taobao Life, promoted Dunhuang culture with meta Universe digital technology, and fully re-carved more than 10 classic Dunhuang murals of the Sui and Tang dynasties in 3D ancient style, creating and opening the first online tourist attraction - Meta Universe Dunhuang Museum.

At present, the rapid development of 5G technology has made the intangible cultural heritage more closely integrated with modern science and technology. The basic technologies of the meta-universe include blockchain and NFT, which can provide strong technical support for the digital preservation and dissemination of intangible cultural heritage. As a distributed ledger technology, blockchain technology has the characteristics of decentralization, immutability, transparency and so on[4]. It can ensure the information security of intangible cultural heritage projects, thereby preventing unauthorized tampering and forgery. NFT is a digital asset based on blockchain technology, which has the characteristics of uniqueness, scarcity and tradability[5]. Converting intangible cultural heritage projects into NFT can give them unique value and become an asset that can be traded in the market, thus improving the realization mechanism of intangible cultural heritage and opening up the economic closed loop. To this end, in the creation of digital assets of Yue embroidery, embedding NFT with unique, verifiable and traceable characteristics can improve the collection value of Yue embroidery artworks, provide new ideas for the digital innovation of Yue embroidery cultural creations, and further improve the current cash mechanism.

From this point of view, in the digital protection of intangible cultural heritage, the meta-universe technology has an important application basis and value, enabling the transformation of intangible cultural heritage data and intelligence, while realizing effective communication, it can also improve the intangible cultural heritage industry chain, help the innovation of intangible cultural heritage products "live", and make the intangible cultural heritage more in line with the development of the new era.

4.2 Digital protection and display of Yue embroidery art works based on virtual reality

Previous display methods were based on two-dimensional planes, and Cantonese embroidery works were limited to rigid display and exhibition, so they could not be effectively disseminated. Adding elements that appeal to the audience is the way to make the intangible cultural heritage spread effectively. The meta-universe, with its advantages of immersion and interaction, brings the audience a multi-angle perception experience. The core of the meta-universe construction is to expand the technology, using the technology to create a virtual space, such as establishing an art exhibition with the theme of Cantonese embroidery, by displaying three-dimensional models of Cantonese embroidery works in this virtual space, to provide users with an immersive viewing experience. At the same time, users can also feel the real atmosphere of the exhibition through virtual reality technology, and can freely roam, enlarge details, and understand the historical and cultural background of the work, so as to improve the immersion of the exhibition.

The Meta Universe exhibition Hall is not only a display platform, but also has the function of social interaction. Users enter the virtual space through the brain-computer interface to participate in intangible cultural heritage ceremony activities remotely, achieve remote group gathering, and create an interactive ritual chain[6]. Experiencers can share common emotions or emotional experiences in the process of exploring different exhibition areas in the virtual space. At the same time, users can also get to know more people who are interested in Yue embroidery through the social platform of virtual space and expand their social circle. Not only that, the use of meta-universe technology through 1:1 replica VR digital exhibits can avoid the loss of cultural relics due to improper protection of various factors, especially some special materials of cultural relics are easy to react with the external environment. In the case of Cantonese embroidery, due to the difficulties of hand embroidery and the restrictions of exhibition venues, it is impossible to display the same product in different exhibition halls at the same time.

Moreover, if the art gallery is overcrowded, it will cause two problems: First, the size of the venue is limited, and the high passenger flow makes the daily maintenance of the art gallery a large workload, which is not convenient for closed maintenance. Secondly, during peak periods, tourists may not be able to fully appreciate the charm of Cantonese embroidery. Therefore, the role of Yue Embroidery virtual reality exhibition hall project has been highlighted. People can experience the charm of Yue embroidery exhibition at home by scanning codes, feel the heritage of China's intangible cultural heritage, broaden their personal vision, and improve aesthetic appreciation and participation.

4.3 Real-time inheritance and assisted learning of Cantonese embroidery skills based on augmented reality

Augmented reality technology (AugmentedReality) is A new technology that can simulate human vision, hearing, smell, touch and other senses and output them again, superimpose information generated by computers in real time into the real world[7], so as to enhance the real world and provide people with experiences beyond the real world. Compared with VR technology, which only provides a completely virtual experience, AR technology can retain the user's perception and interaction ability of the real world, and solve the dilemma of VR technology's lack of realism by combining virtual-real scenes.

At present, there are many cases in which AR technology is applied to non-genetic inheritance. For example, Fengning Paper-cutting Culture uses AR technology to transform it into 3D animation, and projects intangible cultural paper-cutting techniques into real objects in the mobile APP for dynamic display; Pingjiang Shadow Play created an AR game with shadow play characters as game characters and combined with the real environment, and deepened the cognition of the cultural connotation of Pingjiang shadow play through interesting interaction.

For the innovative inheritance of Yue embroidery, the use of augmented reality technology as a new media can break the limitations of the communication mode of Yue embroidery and improve user participation. If this technology can be used to design a real-time inheritance and guidance system for Cantonese embroidery skills. Compared with the traditional face-to-face teaching method, AR technology provides interactive animation for the stitching details of Guangdong embroidery technique, including patterns, colors and stitching, etc. By simulating the real production process of Guangdong embroidery, users can intuitively understand all aspects of Guangdong embroidery technique with rich visual effects. In addition, the brain waves in the AR system can also accept real-time neurofeedback, and the system will provide real-time guidance and suggestions according to the movements and progress of learners in the process of using the AR device to operate Guangdong embroidery. If the learner makes a mistake or is not proficient in a certain link, the system will immediately give corresponding tips and correction methods. Such an augmented reality inheritance and guidance system for Cantonese embroidery skills can undoubtedly improve learning efficiency and interaction, help learners to master Cantonese embroidery skills faster, thus reducing the threshold and learning cost of understanding Cantonese embroidery culture, and narrowing the distance between people and intangible cultural heritage.

5. Limitations of digital means in inheritance and protection of Cantonese embroidery

At present, the meta-universe has penetrated into many industries, fully activating the value of data elements in the management of various industries with the application orientation of multiple digital technologies, and has a wide range of application scenarios. As a new generation of Internet applications and social forms, it has set off a wave of innovation in the cultural industry. Although digital means provide a new way for the inheritance and development of Cantonese embroidery, and can increase the diversity of its content creation, preservation, dissemination and utilization, there are still many problems.

5.1 The conversion quality and precision of Cantonese embroidery figures need to be improved

The technical problems such as image distortion and color deviation are difficult to avoid in the digital conversion of Cantonese embroidery under the current situation of technology. If these problems are not solved, they will affect the audience's experience and sense of Cantonese embroidery. Therefore, we should increase research and development efforts, further improve digital conversion technology, overcome difficulties, in order to improve the quality and accuracy of digital conversion of Guangdong embroidery.

5.2 The reality of virtual reality technology is still lacking

Although virtual reality technology can enable the audience to appreciate Cantonese embroidery more directly and comprehensively, due to the lack of technology, the audience will have a certain sense of dizziness, weightlessness and other adverse reactions. At the same time, virtual reality technology can not completely restore the true touch and details of Yue embroidery, making it difficult to further restore Yue embroidery. This is very important for traditional handicrafts. To this end, we still need to further explore and develop virtual reality technology or create more advanced ways to improve the reality of virtual display.

5.3 The intellectual property system needs to be improved

With the popularization and application of digital technology, the reproduction and dissemination of Cantonese embroidery works has become easier. Therefore, it may induce and aggravate the phenomenon of original works being plagiarized and infringed, resulting in the threat to the creative rights and interests of original Cantonese embroidery craftsmen, and the difficulty of protecting data property rights, which will affect the development of Cantonese embroidery in the field of digital cultural creation. To this end, we should vigorously advocate the establishment and improvement of relevant legal systems and data property rights mechanisms to ensure that the legitimate rights and interests of Guangdong embroidery handicraft producers can be protected, starting from the construction and deepening of resource holding rights, processing rights, and product management rights, by protecting the legitimate rights and interests of digital asset owners to regulate digital copyright[8]. Improve creative freedom and commercial flexibility to promote the creation and dissemination of high-quality digital content, so that data property rights in a more standardized way to profit, so as to stimulate the creative power of the digital cultural and creative field.

Although digitization brings new opportunities for the development of Yue embroidery, traditional skills are still the core and soul of Yue embroidery. To this end, the digital development of Guangdong embroidery should also be combined with traditional skills, not only to retain the unique charm of traditional skills, but also to give play to the advantages of digital Guangdong embroidery. Only through the organic combination of traditional handicraft technology and modern digital technology can we better promote the inheritance and development of Guangdong embroidery in this era.

6. Conclusion

The emergence of the meta-universe has brought new possibilities for the inheritance of the intangible cultural heritage of Guangdong embroidery. With the support of the meta-universe technology, the original ecological soil of Yue embroidery can be completely reproduced, which can intuitively reproduce the full picture of the traditional production scene of Yue embroidery, and its embroidery skills have been permanently retained, bringing more convenience and flexibility to the creation conditions, learning inheritance and realization mode of Yue embroidery, and helping to inherit and protect this intangible cultural heritage. However, the application of science and technology also needs to pay attention to the protection and inheritance of the traditional essence of Guangdong embroidery. It is not only necessary to consolidate the traditional foundation of the intangible cultural heritage, but also to make full use of the advantages of emerging science and technology, expand innovative thinking and inheritance paths, strengthen the connection between the intangible cultural heritage and people[9], and avoid the impact of technology on traditional culture. Only on the basis of preserving the tradition can modern technology bring greater value to the inheritance and development of Guangdong embroidery.

Fund project

[1] 2023 Guangdong University Student Innovation and Entrepreneurship Project (project number: S202313720023)

[2] 2023 Guangdong University Student Innovation and Entrepreneurship Project (project number: S202313720009)

References

1. Zhang Haoran. Thinking on Promoting the Development of intangible cultural heritage in Shaanxi with meta-cosmic technology [J]. New West,2022(07):64-65.
2. Tan Guoxin, Zhang Lilong. Discussion on digital protection and inheritance of intangible cultural heritage [J]. Library,2019(04):79-84.
3. Zhan Qi. Intangible Element Universe: Empowerment, Integration and Immersion [J]. Today Media,2022,30(09):101-103.
4. Nguyen C D ,Pathirana N P ,Ding M , et al.Blockchain for 5G and beyond networks: A state of the art survey[J].Journal of Network and Computer Applications,2020,166(prepublish):
5. Sajjad A ,Amin S ,Arash M , et al.A network analysis of the non-fungible token (NFT) market: structural characteristics,evolution,and interactions[J].Applied Network Science,2023,8(1):
6. Han Xuan, Hu Hu Liu. Research on the application of blockchain in the network trust system [J]. Information Security and Communication Confidentiality, 2021 (09): 100-114.

7. Yadav N ,Sinha A .Augmented Reality and its Science[J].International Journal of Education and Management Engineering(IJEME),2022,12(6):33-44.
8. Hemley M .Playwrights bid to tackle Wild West' of digital rights[J].The Stage,2021,(38):1-1.
9. Wu Chengdu, Wang Ying. Let the intangible "live" : yuan universe and development of China's national intangible new thought [J]. Journal of jiang, reading 2022, 14 (3) : 148-157. The DOI: 10.13878 / j.carol carroll nki yjxk. 20220424.001.

The Impact of International Students' Social Media Use on Their Intercultural Adaptation: Insights from In-depth Interviews

Siqi Sun*

University of Edinburgh, UK

Abstract: The existence of social media provides a convenient chance for people to communicate with their families or make new friends without the limitation of time and space, which facilitates the process of globalization to some extent. Recent research has demonstrated that many international students use social media to adapt to their new lives in foreign countries because it can help them connect with families and friends back home and in their host countries. This essay aims to explore the impact of international students' social media use on their intercultural adaptation and provide valuable implications for language teaching and learning.

1. Introduction

Currently, social media is an integral part of our daily life. According to Sawyer & Chen, social media such as Facebook and YouTube transcends geographic barriers and cultural differences[2]. For international students, social media is crucial because it provides them convenient means to connect with their families at home and their classmates in host countries[9], which is beneficial for their intercultural adaptation. Regarding the definition of intercultural adaptation, it means a process of changing some ways of life and communication patterns to meet the requirements of new environment, which involves increasing understanding through interaction[2]. As more and more students leave their own countries and go to study abroad, it is necessary to research the relationship between social media and intercultural adaptation in order to provide more practical implications for educators and learners.

This essay aims to explore the impact of social media use on intercultural adaptation based on an in-depth interview of an international student. The first part reviews prior research on the relationship between social media and intercultural adaptation. Then, my own case study will be presented and analysed critically, including its methodology, methods, data analysis and findings. Last, I describe connections between previous research and provide some practical implications for language teaching and learning.

2. Literature Review

Given the significance of social media, scholars heavily researched the relationship between social media and intercultural adaptation and proved the existence of a strong correlation. In the study by Chen, he chose some mainland Chinese immigrants in Singapore through a nationwide telephone survey[2]. As quantitative research, this study applied Ward and Kennedy's Sociocultural Adaptation Scale (SCAS)[10] to measure the participants' feelings when they were in a foreign country. The result demonstrated that social media significantly impacted the participants' intercultural adaptation. In addition, social media helped them strengthen their relationships with their families or friends and establish the sense of community and belonging.

Furthermore, some scholars carried out their studies in more detail. They divided social media into ethnic media and host media. Ethnic media plays a vital role in promoting intercultural adaptation, especially when people first arrive in a foreign country. In the study of Lee and Tse, they examined the social media use among Hong Kong immigrants in Canada. They found that recent migrants use more ethnic media in their daily lives compared with long-term residents[6]. Similarly, Park argued that immigrants are willing to read the newspapers in their language because it can meet their demand to express themselves in their mother tongue[7]. However, depending on ethnic media alone is not enough for intercultural adaptation. As Kim pointed out, long term reliance on ethnic media among migrants impedes their adaptation because it only helps with immediate or initial environmental adaptation[4].

Meanwhile, host media can provide a good platform for international students to improve their host language in the host country, which is a prerequisite for effective communication with locals. According to Bennett et al., there is a relationship between people's host language proficiency and intercultural adaptation; the more proficient someone is in a host language, the more likely they are to adapt[2].

*E-mail: sunsiqi202109@163.com

In addition, some scholars studied the role of both ethnic and host media. Walker found that ethnic media has some positive influence on first-year immigrants' adaptation only when they use some host media at the same time[11]. Therefore, for immigrants, using ethnic and host media simultaneously can promote better their intercultural adaptation process.

Although many scholars have studied the relationship between immigrants' social media use and intercultural adaptation, some limitations necessitate further research. Most studies focused on general immigrants, with only a few studies involving international students. As temporary immigrants, international students are unique because they are studying abroad, functioning under high life and study pressure[12]. Moreover, most studies focused on communication competence, such as host language proficiency, when exploring the relationship between social media and intercultural adaptation. Only a few studies paid attention to the perspective of culture and identity. According to Belay, social media can form people' s new cultural identity, challenging their original identity to some extent[1]. Similarly, Phinney argued that cultural identity is dynamic and fluid instead of fixed[8]. Therefore, future research can connect more culture and identity and intercultural adaptation.

3. A Case Study

In order to explore the impact of international students' social media use on their intercultural adaptation, a case study is introduced and analyzed critically in this part. The following questions guided this study:

What intercultural adaptation challenges do the international students encounter?

How does the international students' intercultural adaptation process be impacted by their social media use?

3.1 Methodology

This qualitative research used interviewing as the method for data collection. According to Kvale, compared with questionnaires, interviewing is more suitable for eliciting narrative data and exploring participants' views and feelings in more depth[5]. Therefore, in this study, choosing to interview is beneficial for analysing participants' feelings of using social media and adapting to their new environment.

3.2 Participant

Considering this was a mini project, two participants were interviewed to gather in-depth data, although the small sample limits the study' s transferability. There was one female and one male participant. Both are Chinese international students. Among the two participants, one was a female approximately 23 years old (Interviewee A) and the other a male around 26 years of age (Interviewee B). They had been in the UK for almost seven months.

3.3 Procedure

The participants were recruited by email. During the interviewing, participants were answered open-ended questions about their social media use and intercultural adaptation. Questions included but were not limited to social media's purpose and influence, intercultural adaptation challenges, and the impact of social media on their transition. In addition, participants provided consent for their interviews to be recorded and transcribed. Both interviews were approximately 40 minutes and were conducted in English.

3.4 Results

Regarding the data analysis, the study applies thematic analysis. According to Guest et al., thematic analysis is an effective method to analyse qualitative data[3]. In this study, through organising the participants' transcripts and reading through them, the researcher found some repeated characteristics. Later, the researcher searched for themes, reviewed themes and defined themes. This section presents an analysis of the participants' interview responses to questions about social media use and intercultural adaptation, organised by theme. A whole discussion will be presented in the next section.

3.4.1 Use of Social Media

Both participants use social media almost every day. For interviewee A, she thinks social media is very convenient and useful in her daily life because social media lets her communicate with others. She described using social media to connect with others by attending local activities and learning about the area. Interviewee B shared how he uses social media to message and socialise with family and friends. In addition, he uses it for learning and foreign language acquisition. The following are the excerpts from the participants' answers:

"Actually, I almost use social media every day because it really plays an important role in my daily life. I use WeChat to connect with my families and friends in China. I use Facebook to attend many interesting activities. Social media can provide me much convenience and bring me much happiness in my spare time." (Interviewee A)

"I like using social media to send some messages to my families or friends. Sometimes, I watch some language learning videos from YouTube, which are very interesting and easy to understand." (Interviewee B)

3.4.2 Intercultural Adaptation Challenges

Both participants experienced some challenges when studying in the UK regarding the intercultural adaptation challenges. Interviewee A struggled with foreigners' accents and adjusting to the local' s eating habits. At the same time, Interviewee B found the different teaching and learning styles between China and the UK difficult. The following are some excerpts from their answers:

"I indeed met some intercultural adaptation challenges especially in the beginning time when I came to the UK I could not fully understand the local people's meaning when I went to buy something because many of them speak so fast and have some accents." (Interviewee A)

"I met some intercultural adaptation challenges when I came to the UK. I was surprised to find that there are many differences of learning styles between China and the UK. It was difficult for me to adapt to this teaching pattern at the first time." (Interviewee B)

3.4.3 The Positive Impact of Social Media on Intercultural Adaptation

Regarding the impact of social media, both participants think that social media use positively influences their intercultural adaptation. Interviewee A chose to communicate with her friends through social media. Interviewee B watched some videos on YouTube and learned many discussion skills. Below are some excerpts from their answers:

"When I met some challenges on intercultural adaptation, I talked it to my friends through social media. Gradually, I can communicate with local people fluently and enjoy the local food very much." (Interviewee A)

"I tried to adapt to this different class atmosphere. I watched many videos on group discussion from YouTube and learned many discussion skills. Later, I began to enjoy discussing with my group members because I think it is a good chance to share our ideas and learn from each other." (Interviewee B)

3.4.4 Ethnic Media and Host Media

Regarding the preference of ethnic media and host media, the answers of two participants are a little different. Interviewee A tends to use ethnic and host media to communicate with her family and friends. Furthermore, compared with host media, she prefers ethnic media because it is more related to her ethnic identity. Interviewee B also uses ethnic media to communicate with his family, but he often uses host media such as YouTube to learn. Compared with ethnic media, he prefers to use host media because he thinks it is more practical and can help him adapt to foreign life better. As Interviewee A and Interviewee B mentioned,

"In my daily life, I tend to use ethnic such as WeChat to connect with my families and use host media such as Facebook to communicate with my foreign friends. Actually, compared with host media, I prefer to use ethnic media. I feel that ethnic media is related to my ethnic identity because when I type my mother tongue, I have more sense of belongings." (Interviewee A)

"I use both ethnic media and host media in my life. I use ethnic media to communicate with my parents. In addition, I like watching videos from YouTube. Compared with ethnic media, I prefer to use host media because it can help me adapt to the foreign life better." (Interviewee B)

3.4.5 Advantages and Disadvantages of Social Media

Both participants think social media is a double-edged sword with advantages and disadvantages. They recognize that social media can connect people regardless of distance and provide a source of information. However, the participants acknowledge the presence of limitations and drawbacks. People can easily become addicted to social media, causing them to lose precious time. The following are the excerpts from the two participants:

"Social media has many advantages, which can avoid the limitation of space and distance and provide a convenient life for us. To be honest, there are indeed some disadvantages. For example, sometimes I cannot be concentrated on my study because of social media and I am easy to spend much time watching some interesting videos." (Interviewee A)

"I think social media can link the people who are in different places, which is an amazing thing. It can provide much information and resources for us. But it is a double-edged sword. People are easy to be addicted to it and waste much time. Therefore, I think it is important to use social media reasonably." (Interviewee B)

3.5 Discussion

This case study shows that international students' social media use positively influences their intercultural adaptation. International students experience many challenges upon arriving in their host country, ranging from communication barriers to lifestyle changes, which can cause much stress. These students are also pursuing academic studies in their host country alone, having left their friends and family at home. Therefore, international students benefit from opportunities that provide language learning, communication, and relationship building while adapting to their new home and lifestyle, which participants explained that social media could provide. There were three main findings.

First, social media use positively influences intercultural adaptation by providing a platform for communication and relationships. International students are still learning the language of their host country. They can use social media to expand their vocabulary to improve communication with locals since social media provides a platform for communication and relationship building. This study found that social media use reduced some of their anxiety.

Second, ethnic media is associated with developing a sense of belonging and helping them adapt to their new environment because it is related to their ethnic identities. Third, host media provides a wealth of knowledge and valuable information. From host media, international students can learn about the culture of their foreign country, which helps facilitate adaptation. Overall, using ethnic and host media can promote international students' intercultural adaptation process. However, through interviews, the disadvantages of social media are also acknowledged, mainly that social media can easily become addictive, costing these students valuable time for studying and socialization.

This case study presents some practical implications for educators and learners. In order to promote international students' intercultural adaptation, educators should guide them to gradually adapt to the new teaching pattern and give them some suggestions for group discussion. In addition, educators should encourage international students to express their ideas bravely and focus on the meaning instead of accents when they communicate with others. For international students, they should have a positive attitude towards cultural differences. Then, they can make full use of social media. Through social media, they can seek suggestions from their parents and friends, which help them reduce stress and anxiety. Moreover, they can also gain much knowledge and information from social media to better adapt to the new environment.

4. Conclusion

This essay focuses on the relationship between international students' social media use and intercultural adaptation. Through a case study, the findings demonstrate that international students' social media use positively impacts their intercultural adaptation from the perspective of communication, ethnic identity, and knowledge. Therefore, international students should utilise social media when studying abroad. However, they must balance their time on social media with their other priorities to minimise the potential drawbacks of social media, namely overuse and overreliance.

References

1. Belay, G. The (re) construction and negotiation of cultural identities in the age of globalization. *Interaction & identity*, *5*(1996)
2. Chen, R. T. H., Bennett, S., & Maton, K. The adaptation of Chinese international students to online flexible learning: Two case studies. *Distance Education*, *29*(2008)
3. Guest, G., MacQueen, K. M., & Namey, E. E. *Applied thematic analysis*. (Sage Publications, 2011)
4. Kim, Y. Y. Communication patterns of foreign immigrants in the process of acculturation. *Human Communication Research*, *4*(1977)
5. Kvale, S. *The psychoanalytical interview as inspiration for qualitative research*. (American Psychological Association, 2003)
6. Lee, W. N., & Tse, D. K. Changing media consumption in a new home: Acculturation patterns among Hong Kong immigrants to Canada. *Journal of Advertising*, *23*(1994)
7. Park, R. E. *The immigrant press and its control* (Harper & Brothers,1922)
8. Phinney, J. S. Ethic identity and acculturation. In K. M. Chun, P. Balls Organista, & G. Marín (Eds.), *Acculturation: Advances in theory, measurement, and applied research* (American Psychological Association, 2003)
9. Trebbe, J. Types of integration, acculturation strategies and media use of young Turks in Germany. *Communications: The European Journal of Communication Research*, *32*(2007)
10. Ward, C., & Kennedy, A. The measurement of sociocultural adaptation. *International Journal of Intercultural Relations*, *23*(1999)
11. Walker, D. The media's role in immigrant adaptation: How first-year Haitians in Miami use the media. *Journalism & Communication Monographs*, *1*(1999)
12. Yeh, C. J., & Inose, M. International students' reported English fluency, social support satisfaction, and social connectedness as predictors of acculturative stress. *Counselling Psychology Quarterly*, *16*(2003)

Exploring the Delivered Value and Sustainable Development of the Intangible Cultural Heritage, Xiaolan Chrysanthemum Exhibition

Delphine Ya-Chu Chan[1,*], Zihao He[2], Chumiao Zhang[3]

[1]School of Management, University of Electronic Science and Technology of China, Zhongshan Institute, 528402 Guangdong, China
[2]Marketing Department, Majesty holdings Co., Ltd, 528437 Zhongshan, Guangdong, China
[3]Marketing Department, Anshi Pharmaceutical (Zhongshan) Inc., 528437 Zhongshan, Guangdong, China

Abstract. Intangible cultural heritage (ICH) is a result of human wisdom and civilization around the world and should be guarded and inherited by all people. Xiaolan Chrysanthemum Exhibition, as one of China's national ICH folk activities, represents chrysanthemum culture. Taking the Xiaolan Chrysanthemum Exhibition as a case study, we aim to explore the relationship among ICH delivered value, emotional identity, and sustainable development. We collected 587 questionnaires, 495 of which are valid, achieving a valid sample rate of 84.33%. After that, IBM SPSS 22.0 and AMOS 26.0 were used for empirical analysis. The results show that perceived cost does not have a notable impact on ICH sustainable development while social value and educational value can pose a positive impact on ICH sustainable development through emotional identity. Notably, economic value can pose both direct and indirect impacts on ICH sustainable development through emotional identity.

1. Introduction

In the United Nations Educational, Scientific and Cultural Organization's (UNESCO) Convention for the Safeguarding of the Intangible Cultural Heritage (ICH), ICH encompasses the practices, representations, expressions, knowledge, and skills, as well as the instruments, objects, artifacts, and cultural spaces that communities, groups, and individuals recognize as integral components of their cultural heritage. It is emphasized that world heritage conservation should involve participants at multiple levels, including the government, local communities, civil society organizations, and even individual citizens. Additionally, the contribution and leading role of cultural heritage in promoting economic, social, environmental protection, and other sustainable development should be recognized and valued. As of December 2023, China has a total of 43 items inscribed on UNESCO's ICH list, ranking first in the world. This not only reflects the fact that China has done a systematic job of inheriting and preserving ICH, but plays an important role in promoting traditional Chinese national culture. As one of the initial entries in China's national ICH list, the history of the Xiaolan Chrysanthemum Exhibition can be traced back to the 1782 large-scale Chrysanthemum Exhibition. This event, characterized by a diverse array of flower stands and captivating drama performances, was originally organized as a gathering for friends. The grand chrysanthemum exhibition took place annually during the year of the Wood Dog (which occurs every 60 years), while a smaller-scale exhibition was held once every decade. Located in the middle of China's Pearl River Delta, Xiaolan is a major town in Zhongshan City, Guangdong Province. The people of Xiaolan have excellent chrysanthemum-potting skills. When chrysanthemums are in full bloom, the villagers will set up various kinds of chrysanthemums for evaluation and competition, which further developed into chrysanthemum exhibitions lasting for several days, covering various activities, including appreciation, race, poetic creation, painting, tasting, and opera performance concerning chrysanthemum. The exhibition spans 10 kilometers, showcasing 1,568 varieties of chrysanthemums, and drawing more than 6 million visitors from over 20 countries worldwide [1]. The Xiaolan Chrysanthemum Exhibition has a high added value for refining one's character, improving personal cultural literacy, and promoting international exchanges. It has a profound significance for the sustainable development of ICH in terms of continuously passing on and promoting chrysanthemum culture, strengthening cultural confidence and identity, and allowing more people to appreciate the beauty of Chinese culture.

Thanks to technological advances and new media campaigns, cultural traveling has become a modern leisure option. The effective integration of the ICH, travel, and sustainable development requires a further understanding of tourists' attitudes towards ICH cultural travel. However, relatively few studies have explored the sustainable development of ICH cultural tourism. Therefore, this study aims to empirically investigate the

* Corresponding author's mail: yachuchan@zsc.edu.cn

delivered value, emotional identity, and sustainable development of China's ICH, Xiaolan Chrysanthemum Exhibition. As a result, this study will not only facilitate similar ICH folk activities in acquiring a comprehensive understanding of tourists' perceptions and attitudes but also put forward countermeasures for the future development of ICH cultural tourism, ultimately fostering its sustainable growth.

2. Literature review

2.1. ICH delivered value and sustainable development

2.1.1. ICH perceived value

Delivered value consists of perceived value and perceived cost. Customer perceived value, proposed by Zeithaml (1988), refers to the consumer's overall assessment of the utility of a product based on what is received and what is given [2]. Sheth, Newman, and Gröss (1991) proposed the theory of consumption values, explored perceived value from an interdisciplinary perspective, and categorized it into social value, emotional value, functional value, epistemic value, and conditional value [3]. Notably, these five types of value are independent of each other and cannot be substituted for one another. Moreover, even the difference in the situations where customers make choices will lead to different perception values. The importance of perceived value is widely recognized in ICH research, but the dimensional features of perceived value are perceived differently [4]. Williams et al. (2017) continued the value framework of Sweeney and Soutar (2001) to explore the tourism customer value and classified it into functional value, price value, emotional value, social value, and novelty value [5-6]. It is found that customer value has a positive impact on both satisfaction and behavioral intention. Qiu et al. (2019) explored non-heritage tourism from the perspective of value-cognitive attitude and found that ICH value could be classified into four values: aesthetic value, educational and spiritual value, social and economic value, and historical value [4]. Besides, ICH values can positively affect tourism intention through emotional attitude. In other words, ICH value has multiple dimensions and affects tourists' attitudes and behavioral intentions.

Based on the theories of customer perceived value, this paper combines the perceived value research in culture and tourism and chooses five dimensions of perceived value for measurement: historical value, social value, aesthetic value, educational value, and economic value. Among them, historical value refers to the unique culture and historical inheritance of ICH for its long history [4]; social value refers to the social recognition, personal image enhancement, lifestyle, and taste achieved through the ICH activity experience and communication [4-8]; aesthetic value refers to the fact that ICH can convey a sense of art and allow visitors to perceive the unique style and beauty of ICH in appreciation [4, 7, 9]; educational value refers to the new knowledge and skills tourists learned in ICH cultural tourism, as well as the awareness enhancement of ICH protection, inheritance and development [4]; and economic value refers to the economic benefits derived from ICH through marketization and commercialization combined with the customer needs, which may even lead to the development of local employment as well as the local economy. In summary, we can obtain the following hypotheses:

H1: The (a) historical value, (b) social value, (c) aesthetic value, (d) educational value, and (e) economic value of perceived values have a positive impact on ICH sustainable development.

2.1.2. ICH perceived cost

Zeithaml (1988) argues that perceived cost consists of product/service quality, and external and internal attributes, which means that monetary price paid and non-monetary prices (energy, effort, and time) constitute perceived cost [2]. Gallarza and Saura (2006) categorized perceived cost into three dimensions in their study of college student group travel: perceived monetary cost, perceived risk, and time and effort spent. They found that time and effort spent have a significantly negative relation to perceived value, which in turn affected travel attitude (satisfaction and loyalty) [7]. Concerning the above two studies, we classify ICH's perceived cost into three dimensions, namely monetary cost, energy, and time. Among them, monetary cost refers to the money paid for participating in ICH activities, including admission fees, transportation fees, accommodation fees, activity experience fees, and cultural- and creative-related product fees; energy refers to all the energy spent for the ICH activities from information collection, itinerary preparation, touring or experiencing to the end of the activity and return journey; and time refers to all the time spent for the ICH activity from the preparation, the actual tour experience, and the round-trip transportation. Based on the above analysis, the following assumptions were obtained:

H2: The perceived costs of (a) monetary cost, (b) energy, and (c) time have a negative impact on ICH sustainable development.

2.2. The mediating effect of emotional identity

Cultural identity reflects the self-perception and self-construction of individuals in a specific cultural context [10]. Previous studies show that in the consumption of non-heritage, cultural identity is an identity attitude that carries national attribute cognition and emotional interplay. It is not only affected by the ICH value but also by the intention of tourists [4, 11]. Therefore, we define emotional identity as an individually positive emotional response after perceiving comprehensive cultural attributes conveyed by ICH, including affirmation, fondness, empathy, and recognition, which can lead to behaviors such as support, and advocacy towards it. Consequently, this paper proposes the following hypothesis:

H3: Emotional identity has a positive impact on ICH's sustainable development.

H4: The (a) historical value, (b) social value, (c) aesthetic value, (d) educational value, and (e) economic value of perceived values have a positive impact on emotional identity.

H5: The (a) monetary cost, (b) energy, and (c) time of perceived costs have a negative impact on emotional identity.

H6: Emotional identity has a mediating impact on the effect of perceived value on ICH sustainable development.

H7: Emotional identity has a mediating impact on the effect of perceived cost on ICH sustainable development.

In summary, we conclude that ICH's delivered value affects consumers' emotional identity. Especially, perceived value has a positive impact on emotional identity and perceived cost has a negative impact on emotional identity. Additionally, emotional identity is found to pose a mediating effect between delivered value and ICH sustainable development.

3. Methodology

3.1. Questionnaire design and measurement

The questionnaire is designed in three parts. The first part is about tourists' knowledge of ICH and the Xiaolan Chrysanthemum Exhibition. Certain samples were filtered based on their responses to two initial questions "Do you know about ICH?" and "Do you know about the Xiaolan Chrysanthemum Exhibition?". Respondents who answered negatively were considered invalid samples and were excluded from the questionnaire. Those who were considered valid samples were then asked about their information sources for the events, interested activities, their impressions of the events, and the people they wished to be their partners. The second part of the survey is about questions on ten variables, covering dimensions of perceived value including historical value, social value, aesthetic value, educational value, and economic value; dimensions of perceived cost including monetary cost, energy cost, and time cost; as well as emotional identity and ICH sustainable development. Notably, all the questions are designed regarding matured scales and scholars' and experts' suggestions using the Likert 5-scale for measurement. Lastly, the third part is about the basic information of the respondents, including gender, age, education level, and monthly disposable income.

3.2. Sampling and data collection

To ensure the quality of the instrument and process of the survey, we first conducted a preliminary survey inviting 30 consumers to fill in the questionnaire. The preliminary test results showed that the Cronbach's α value of all variables reached 0.70, indicating that the survey instrument had exemplary reliability and could be used for formal research. The formal research was carried out during the Xiaolan Chrysanthemum Exhibition in November-December 2021, and 587 questionnaires were collected. After removing the invalid samples of those who did not know about ICH or the Xiaolan Chrysanthemum Exhibition, there were 495 valid samples, with an effective response rate of 84.33%.

4. Empirical results

4.1. Descriptive analysis

The demographic analysis of the sample is as follows: in terms of gender, 66.67% of them are female and 33.33% of them are male; in terms of age, the respondents are predominantly 20-39 years old (62.63%), with 27.67% respondents over 40 years old and 9.70% under 20 years old; in terms of educational level, mostly are university graduates (78.79%), with 18.38% high school graduates, and 2.83% master's graduates; in terms of monthly disposable income, 42.42% of them are less than RMB 3500, 28.69% fell within the range of RMB 3500-6000, and 28.89% indicated monthly incomes exceeding RMB 6000.

In addition, visitors indicated that the main sources of information about the ICH Xiaolan Chrysanthemum Exhibition are the Internet (27.91%), television media (26.91%), and friends and relatives (25.31%), with print media and other sources accounting for 19.87%. In terms of the items of interest to the Xiaolan Chrysanthemum Exhibition, chrysanthemum art display is the most popular item (30.27%), followed by food and leisure support (26.26%) and chrysanthemum knowledge popularization (25.82%), while other items accounted for a total of 17.65%. Regarding the impression of the Xiaolan Chrysanthemum Exhibition, 37.10% of the visitors thought it had a cultural connotation, 29.83% found it to be creative, 23.06% considered it to be novel, and the remaining impressions accounted for a total of 10.01%. In terms of those who wished to travel with companions, 66.26% of the tourists wished to go with their families, 23.23% indicated a preference for traveling with their friends, and the remaining answers accounted for 10.51%.

4.2. Reliability and validity

The reliability tests of the scales were analyzed using IBM SPSS 22.0 and the results are shown in Table 1. From Table 1, it can be seen that the Cronbach's α of the 10 variables ranged from 0.930 to 0.959, together with the corrected item-total correlation (CITC) > 0.50, which indicates that the scales of the study have qualified internal consistency; the factor loading value of all the questions exceeded 0.70, and the composite reliability (CR) is over 0.80, with average variable extraction (AVE) over 0.50, indicating that the scale also has excellent validity.

Table 1. Reliability and validity.

Construct & item		Reliability		Convergent validity		
		Cronbach's α	CITC	Factor loading	CR	AVE
Historical Value (HV)	prominent	0.954	0.866	0.953	0.967	0.88
	historic		0.876	0.944		
	culturally unique		0.897	0.931		
	historic		0.914	0.924		
Social Value (SV)	help make more friends	0.946	0.860	0.938	0.961	0.86
	show taste		0.886	0.932		
	show lifestyle		0.858	0.921		
	A good way to enhance people's positive impression		0.877	0.921		
Aesthetic Value (AV)	striking	0.959	0.881	0.950	0.970	0.89
	literary		0.910	0.950		
	fancy		0.909	0.941		
	a fusion of color and installation art		0.894	0.933		
Educational Value (EDV)	learn about science	0.946	0.840	0.945	0.961	0.86
	learn about the types of chrysanthemums		0.896	0.943		
	familiarize oneself with the uses of chrysanthemums		0.899	0.915		
	appreciate related works of ornamental chrysanthemum		0.849	0.909		
Economic Value (ECV)	revitalize local economic development	0.950	0.886	0.939	0.965	0.87
	lead to local employment opportunities		0.869	0.936		
	increase the added value of goods (chrysanthemums)		0.882	0.935		
	increase the value of services (chrysanthemum exhibition)		0.887	0.926		
Monetary cost (MC)	ticket fees	0.930	0.825	0.871	0.909	0.71
	transportation fees		0.845	0.842		
	boarding and lodging fees		0.869	0.841		
	gift fees		0.827	0.826		
Energy (EN)	prepare for a trip can take a lot of energy	0.956	0.927	0.907	0.918	0.79
	the day of the tour will take a lot of energy		0.932	0.891		
	make one tired after the tour.		0.947	0.866		
Time (TI)	travel information collection time	0.957	0.929	0.917	0.931	0.77
	travel itinerary planning time		0.933	0.887		
	transportation and accommodation time		0.855	0.864		
	visiting time		0.878	0.844		
Emotional Identity (EI)	willingness to allocate time for engagement in activities	0.947	0.868	0.938	0.962	0.86
	willingness to share discussion activities with others		0.861	0.936		
	affirmation of the cultural image of this non-heritage activity		0.881	0.925		
	recognize the national significance of this non-heritage activity		0.884	0.920		
Sustainable Development of ICH (SD)	scale up advocacy	0.955	0.886	0.952	0.967	0.88
	increase in the number of active projects		0.912	0.936		
	integrate with policy development		0.886	0.936		
	continue the legacy		0.875	0.930		
Metrics		**≥0 .70**	**≥0 .50**	**≥0 .70**	**≥0 .80**	**≥0 .50**

Note: CITC = corrected item-total correlation; CR = composite reliability; AVE = average variable extraction

4.3. Structural equation model

According to H1 to H7, delivered value was used as the independent variable, emotional identity as the mediator variable, and ICH sustainable development as the dependent variable to build a structural equation model and conduct fit test using AMOS 26.0, as shown in Fig.1. The results show that $\chi 2/df$ = 3.191, RMSEA = 0.067 (<0.08), PGFI = 0.668 (>0.50); NFI = 0.916, IFI = 0.941, TLI = 0.933, CFI = 0.941 whose coefficients are all higher than the fit criterion of 0.90, indicating a strong fitting performance for the theoretical model [12]. However, the impacts of the two perceived values—historical value and aesthetic value—and the three perceived costs—monetary cost, energy, and time—did not attain a significant influence on either emotional identity or sustainable development. Therefore, the hypotheses H1(a), H1(c), H2, H4(a), H4(c), H5, H7 are not supported. The effect of social value and education value on sustainable development is also not significant, so H1(b) and H1(d) are not supported.

Since the above five concepts (historical value, aesthetic value, monetary cost, energy, and time) have no impact on the mediator and dependent variables, i.e., they do not play a real role in the model. For the consideration of the degree of parsimony of the structural equation model, we exclude these concepts re-fit and modify the model, and get the final impact path relationship as shown in Fig. 2.

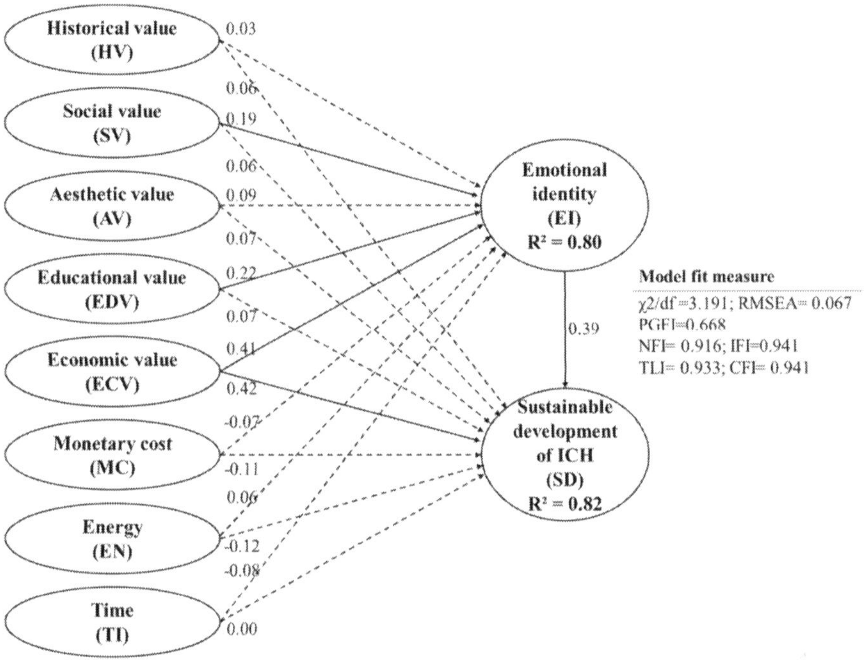

Fig. 1. Results of the proposed model.

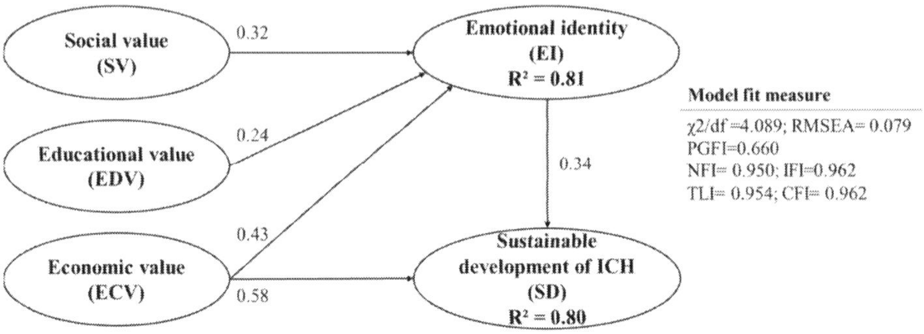

Fig. 2. Results of the revised model.

The fit of the modified structural equation model shows that $\chi2/df = 4.089$, RMSEA = 0.079 (<0.08), PGFI = 0.660 (>0.50); NFI = 0.950, IFI = 0.962, TLI = 0.954, CFI = 0.962, all of which are higher than the fit criterion of 0.90. The critical criterion for $\chi2/df$ is typically considered to be less than 0.50 when the sample size is large, and the other fit values are higher than the initial model. Consequently, the modified theoretical model demonstrates a better fit [12]. In addition, the path coefficients show that economic value and emotional identity have a significant positive impact on sustainable development, and social value, education value, and economic value also have significant positive impacts on emotional identity. Hence, H1(e), H3, H4(b), H4(d), H4(e) are supported. In addition, the modified model shows that social value and education value can only indirectly affect sustainable development through emotional identity while economic value not only has a positive direct impact on sustainable development but also has an indirect impact on sustainable development through emotional identity. In other words, emotional identity has a mediating effect on the impact of perceived value on ICH sustainable development, and thus H6 is supported.

5. Conclusion and suggestion

Xiaolan Chrysanthemum Exhibition has a long history, and some of the chrysanthemum species have been lost so far, which also reflects the predicament of the global ICH inheritance in terms of sustainable development. We aim to understand the feelings of tourists towards ICH's delivered value and emotional identity, as well as the impact path of ICH's sustainable development through practice and surveys, putting forward suggestions for ICH's inheritance and development. The results of the study show that perceived cost has no significant impact on the impact of delivered value on emotional identity and ICH sustainable development. This finding indicates that, from the perspective of delivered value, perceived value is the most important effecting factor for emotional identity and ICH sustainable development. Among them, economic value is the most direct factor in predicting the sustainability of ICH, which also has an indirect impact on it through emotional identity. In other words, if ICHs are rich in economic value that can enhance the added value of goods and services, revitalize the local economy, and provide employment opportunities, they will not only be recognized and shared by tourists but be beneficial to the publicity and heritage of the ICHs in the future. Moreover, it is suggested that ICH management can develop more memorable design projects through industry-academia cooperation projects or competitions to produce cultural and creative commodities or organize cultural and tourism activities, including souvenirs integrating elements of non-heritage, souvenirs, experiential activities, and taking pictures in the attractions. These are conducive to the tourists' reminiscence memory, the publicity and recommendation of the attractions, and the increase in economic income. Besides, it is also recommended that the corresponding planning of the neighboring attractions and food and accommodation businesses nearby also be included, continuously improving local economic development. In addition, the study shows that emotional identity can also help predict the sustainable development trend of ICH. Emotional identity represents the tourists' affirmation of the cultural image and national significance of ICH activities after experiencing the ICH activities. Thus, the activity design needs to be elevated and promoted with distinguished stories of its history to prevent tourists from missing the emotional resonance caused by a swift overview of the ICH.

Given the origin of the Xiaolan Chrysanthemum Exhibition, this study was conducted in Zhongshan City, located in Guangdong Province, China. The local respondents possess extensive knowledge and aesthetic appreciation for chrysanthemums and thus do not have strong perceptions of the perceived costs in terms of money, energy, and time spent. This may partly contribute to the insignificant predictive effect. Consequently, it is suggested that future research could expand the investigation scope or study other types of ICH to explore and compare the differences in delivered value and impact path, providing more detailed recommendations for the conservation, inheritance, and development of ICH globally.

Acknowledgment

This study was funded by the 2020 disciplinary co-construction project "Research on the delivered value of intangible cultural heritage and sustainable development under the background of rural revitalization" under the "13th Five Year" Plan of Philosophy and Social Sciences in Guangdong Province (Project No.: GD20XGL37)

References

1. Chinese Intangible Cultural Heritage Digital Museum. (2024) Representative List of National Intangible Cultural Heritage: Xiaolan Chrysanthemum Exhibition. https://www.ihchina.cn/Article/Index/detail?id=15002
2. Zeithaml V. A. (1988) Consumer perceptions of price, quality, and value: a means-end model and synthesis of evidence. *The Journal of Marketing*, 52: 2-22. doi: 10.1177/002224298805200302
3. Sheth J. N., Newman B. I., and Gröss B. L. (1991) *Consumption Values and Market Choice*, South Western Publishing, Cincinnati, OH.
4. Qiu Q., Zheng T., Xiang Z., Zhang M. (2019) Visiting intangible cultural heritage tourism sites: from value cognition to attitude and intention. *Sustainability*, 12: 132-152. doi: 10.3390/su12010132
5. Williams P., Soutar, G., Ashill, N. J., and Naumann E. (2017) Value drivers and adventure tourism: a comparative analysis of Japanese and Western consumers. *Journal of Service Theory and Practice*, 27: 102-122. doi: 10.1108/JSTP-05-2015-0116
6. Sweeney J. C., Soutar G. N. (2001) Consumer perceived value: the development of a multiple item scale. *Journal of Retailing*, 77: 203-220. doi: 10.1016/S0022-4359(01)00041-0
7. Gallarza M. G., Saura I. G. (2006) Value dimensions, perceived value, satisfaction and loyalty: an investigation of university students' travel behaviour. *Tourism Management*, 27: 437-452. doi: 10.1016/j.tourman.2004.12.002
8. Liu, H. (2021) Perceived value dimension, product involvement and purchase intention for intangible cultural heritage souvenir. *American Journal of Industrial and Business Management*, 11: 76-91. doi: 10.4236/ajibm.2021.111006
9. Heredia-Carroza, J., Palma Martos, L., & Aguado, L. F. (2021). How to measure intangible cultural heritage value? The case of flamenco in Spain. *Empirical Studies of the Arts*, 39: 149-170. doi: 10.1177/0276237420907865

10. Schwartz, S.H., Cieciuch, J., Vecchione, M., Davidov, E., Fischer, R., Beilerlein, C., Ramos, A., Verkasalo, M., Lönnqvist, J.E., Demirutku K., Dirilen-Gumus O., and Konty M. (2012) Refining the theory of basic individual values. *Journal of Personality and Social Psychology*, 103: 663-688. doi: 10.1037/a0029393
11. Zhang M., Guo X., Guo X., Jolibert A. (2023) Consumer purchase intention of intangible cultural heritage products (ICHP): effects of cultural identity, consumer knowledge and manufacture type. *Asia Pacific Journal of Marketing*, 35: 726-744. doi: 10.1108/APJML-11-2021-0831
12. Hooper D., Coughlan J., Mullen M. R. (2008) Structural equation modelling: guidelines for determining model fit. *Electronic Journal of Business Research Methods*, 6: 53-60. doi: 10.3109/03005364000000039

German-Albanian Intercultural communication and interaction in the workplace

Fiona Hoti*, Jürgen Huber

Department of Communication Design, Hochschule für Technik und Wirtschaft, Berlin, Germany

Abstract. Remote work has brought societies and cultures more together than ever. The workplace has been taken to another level and understanding the cultures and behaviours of different countries has become essential, so that there can be a harmonious working environment. Different ways of conveying the information in the same situation and context but at the same time in two different cultural environments, often lead to inconsistencies or problems in different situations in everyday life. In this thesis, German-Albanian communication and interaction in the workplace is observed from a cultural point of view. Communication in the workspace environment has quite a high influence on the working atmosphere, satisfaction, productivity of the employees or companies worldwide management success. The field of study focuses on the workspace since the reason why many Albanian citizens stay in Germany or have work relations with German companies is the offer of a working contract with higher income possibilities. The purpose of this study is to achieve understanding from both sides of the cultures or even let other cultures understand them both at the same time. Beside the theoretical solution of this problem, an illustrated book with funny and simple illustration has been designed to bring better understanding for the cultural differences independent from their age, gender or intellectual level.

1. Introduction

1.1. Subject and purpose of the study

Communication problems of foreign employees in Germany as well as intercultural communication has been an interesting field of study for many researchers. The following observation is going to highlight both topics from a point of view which has been considered as little observed. In the past few years, Germany has become a country, in which many immigrants from different countries seek for a better life with higher incomes and standards in the fields of economy, education, and health. One of them are also Albanian citizen. They are a part of almost every area of everyday life and in constant contact and interaction with German citizens. They are present for instance in the workplaces, schools, recreational spaces. Finding themselves in encounter with each other, both these cultures make an exchange of information with or without them being aware of their doing. Different ways of conveying the information in the same situation and context but at the same time in two different cultural environments, often lead to inconsistencies or problems in different situations in everyday life.

In this thesis, German-Albanian communication and interaction in the workplace is observed from a cultural point of view. The field of study focuses on the workspace since the reason why many Albanian citizens stay in Germany is the offer of a working contract. Through practical examples, intercultural communication problems are easier to study. The other reason is that through this study an understanding can be developed from both sides of the cultures, since the communication in the workspace environment has quite a high influence on the working atmosphere, satisfaction, and productivity of the employees, which, in a business, is relevant to the company's management.

This study is pilot research, meaning that „ ...first limited attempt to address a relatively under-researched subject area "[1] (Jin 1994, pg. 1; Keinem u.a. 1982:12). It is based on 13 individual interviews on a range of jobs: construction area, medical area, development and software engineering, educator, truck driver, executive employees, project manager.

The purpose of the study is to find verbal and nonverbal communication styles from both cultural groups, similarities and differences as well as determine communication difficulties and misunderstanding. At the same time, to support the employees and employers of both cultures in the intercultural communication processes so that the working space atmosphere and productivity can be improved.

1.2. Questions

"Communication between members of different ethnic in Alaska and northern Canada, as elsewhere, frequently

*Corresponding author's email: hoti.fiona1999@gmail.com

results in confusion, misunderstanding and conflict." [1] (Jin, 1994, pg. 7) Can this saying be said for the everyday interaction between Germans and Albanians as well? Can this prevent a successful cohabitation in the working environment now or in the future?

Returning to everyday life, Albanians themselves notice some incompatibilities on the behaviour with German citizens, without taking in consideration the different point of view of the cultures. Therefore, they raise the questions: "Why are Germans so cold? Why do they not want to hug or show affection to us when we meet? Why do they interpret or see the world so differently from us? Why do they react differently in these occurrences from us?

These questions and other ones similar to these seem to be raised without having the understanding that each group of culture reacts and acts with each other based on their cultural patterns. The same questions or situations that are found in everyday life are repeated quite often in the workplace of the individuals. Most Albanians living in Germany find their job a very important part of their life, because their wage labour is a way they are allowed to continue to stay in Germany. Since they spent more than half of the day at their job and value it as a main motive of holding on to the opportunity to maintain the possibility of a residence in Germany, their relationship to their colleagues and supervisors does not only affect their work satisfaction, but also their psychological behaviour. This influences them in the quality of the productivity as well as the atmosphere it is created from both parties automatically indicating on the results and economy of the company.

Mutual behaviour of employees and their superiors influence - positively or negatively - the work atmosphere, which is felt during everyday communication, in that the manner or intensity and effectiveness of communication reflects the work situation there. Communication in the workplace must therefore focus on both groups of stakeholders: [2] (Kartaı, 1997, 9 / vgl. Müller 1993: 27-52)

Based on the aspects mentioned above the following questions are raised:

- What communication styles are used by the Germans and Albanians at the workplace?
- In which communication situations do the contacts between Germans and Albanians happen?
- How do Albanians work and live in this host country? How do Germans think and react to Albanians in the workplace?
- Which factors affect the cultural integration of the individual into a foreign environment?
- Can better language knowledge (German and Albania) ensure better intercultural communication? If not, what are the difficulties in the German-Albanian communication?
- What can visual communication contribute to solving communication problems?

2 Theory: The cultural differences between both countries

2.1 Intercultural communication

Going back in history, the way we dealt with cultural differences sides more with a response of an avoidance. If an avoidance of this confrontation was not possible or unsuccessful, then a conversion of beliefs, values and the way of thinking was implied. Politics, economics and religion were used as "tools" to impose on others the beliefs of a culture. A more extreme reaction to the other cultures was to "kill" them by having in mind that if people had a more similar way of thinking between each other, it would be easier to be around. On one hand, the monocultural way of thinking says that "... similarities generally allow people to predict the responses of others to certain kinds of messages and to take for granted some basic shared assumptions about the nature of reality." [5] (ff. Bennett, 1998, pg.1).

Augmenting that differences might represent the conflicts and misunderstandings in a society. On the other hand, intercultural communication cannot accept that and encourages understanding, appreciation, and respect of each culture's differences, as important values to create harmony and open-minded societies.

Whenever the theme of cultural difference comes up in the society, not rarely is a culture associated with a stereotype. (…) To avoid these stereotypes and anticipate the culture of another country or group, people often turn to history, art, literature, movies, music and dance. By this action they are participating in gaining knowledge about that culture, which is referred to as the objective culture. Part of the objective culture are also the systems of politics, economics, society and linguistics. (…) Understanding objective culture may create knowledge, but it doesn't necessarily generate competence. [5] (vgl. Bennett, 1998, pg.1-4)

2.2 The cultural differences

Many scholars have developed arguments based on the idea that in the future the decisive consequence in many aspects of global developments will no longer be conflicts between states, between peoples or ideologies, but between cultures, confrontations between civilizations [3] (Zydi Dervishi, Veshtrime te kryqezuara ne det, 2021, S.101). According to social scientist Dervish, it is argued that such predictions are based primarily on several factors that lead to disagreements and conflicts between people of different cultures.

Conflicting attitudes and perceptions of people about the relationships between individuals, man and God, social groups and state structures, etc. These differences in the mentality of cultures have crystallized over the centuries and have been imposed on the characteristics of cultures, languages and religious beliefs of civilizations, leading to conflicts when two or more cultures with their different views meet.

The intensification of multiple interactions of peoples of different civilizations increases the possibility of mutual interactions of their cultures by increasing the transition of cultural elements from one culture to another. These elements do not obscure the distinctive features between cultural systems, but provoke opposing attitudes and reactions. „Experience shows that differences between cultures of the same civilization are generally more tolerable than differences between cultures of different civilizations.“

The two opposing tendencies of cultures, such as the Western culture compared to the culture of the Balkan regions, is one of the factors that influence the conflicts of civilizations, because they attempt to influence each other. On the one hand, there is the desire to increase the influence of Western countries on other civilizations and cultures, especially in the fields of science, politics, and technology. On the other hand, non-Western civilizations seek to preserve and develop their original cultural characteristics, as well as to Westernize themselves by increasing their influence on a global scale. [3] (cf. Zydi Dervishi 2012, 103-104)

3. Formal communication

During the interviews the answer of the Albanian employees when asked for their relationship with their German colleges, most of them answered as having mainly a good correlation, despite some differences. The same answer came from the German employees. (…)

An issue that was mentioned quite often from the interviewees, was the tidiness in the working place. Some of the interviewees complained about the behaviour of the Albanian employees related to the motivation of them to constantly keep their working area clean. They took it as a lack of interest. Germans were referred to maintain their working area as quite dissent. They see the maintenance of their office or their workspace as their responsibility. Observations show that Germans, before they leave their workplace, they start to put their things in order and make sure that everything is put in its place. This routine they do voluntarily. Albanians, during the interviews were characterized as not willingly taking the responsibility of cleaning their place by the end of a working day. They do not see "the cleaning of their working area" as part of their profession. It was explained as not being a necessity, since the companies do hire cleaning employees that are expected to maintain the areas at the company clean. (…) … this way of mindset doesn't necessarily create conflicts, but creates confusion of the employer toward this kind of behaviour. Based on observations, Albanians perceive the idea of cleaning, which they were not hired for, as a substandard work for which they are being pushed to do without their will. (…)

In Germany rules and regulations are strictly followed, preventing the people from being able to have spontaneous solutions for the problems that occur at the workplace. An example is the construction branch, which sometimes requires a spontaneous under-standing and response toward the problem. Albanians, being raised in a country, where the facilities are not invested as much as in Germany, tend to be more practical and find quicker solutions within a shorter time. (…)

Just as much as an advantage, it can also lead to the disadvantage of not having the patience to deal with the details of a job that has to be done in the same amount of time. The lack of patience with the details and requirements that a work in the german standards might require, has put Albanians into a difficult position, where sometimes Germans stay unsatisfied with the job.

Germans are mostly very time oriented when it comes to their working hours. They expect to have the ability to leave at the actual time the working hours have been done for the day. Compared to the German employees, Albanians were specified as being more willing to do after office hours if the work had to be done at a shorter period of time or even to not have a problem getting a call after the working hours were over. It was claimed that if the chef would ask them to stay for a longer period at work, they would not oppose him.

In the German mentality, the individual's health care is more important than finishing a project or work in a shorter period. A work, which couldn't be done by the end of the day, can be continued on the following day, which means that Germans no longer wish to talk after the working hours about work issues. This behaviour of Germans is not always received in the best way from Albanians point of view.

An Albanian working as a group leader at a company was found in a situation where while working with a german coworker, this theme was turned to a conflict. As the leader of the group, he was responsible for the project that was being undertaken. While talking to his coworkers about the situation they were in, he had tried to explain the necessity of them to be working longer on that day, since a deadline set by the end of the day had to be met. (…) The German employer, even though was aware of the hard situation, where the work had to be done by the time it had been set, did withstand his group leader's wish (…). This conflict made the supervisor go to further conclusions, where he thought that the german employee was assaulting him, because of him being a foreigner and having a higher position than the German employee. (…) (Based on the Interview, Person M) In another situation, where Albanians are in the position of the employee, they seem to have very pleased superiors with the work and amount of time they put into it. However, Albanians seem to have a different opinion on this matter, where their thought about it is that "the readiness that we provide, the Germans use very well" (Based on the Interview, Person F).

The example presented above proclaims also that Germans often separate work from their free time. Many declared that it is hard to create friendships with their german coworkers outside of the workplace, since they define very clearly the line between a coworker relationship and that of a friendship. (…) Albanians define friendship as a state of respect which follows with the terms of trust and support between two or more individuals and is presented as a high value in the society. Among Albanians, friendship at the workplace, presents a better understanding and easier cooperation between people, because being trustworthy and supportive are high principles that are followed at the workplace too. As a matter of fact, they find it important to create friendships at the workplace (…).

4. Conclusion and First Conceptual Thoughts for Praxis

In this paper it has been studied the communication problems at the workplace between Albanian and German employees and their supervisor.

It has been based on empiricism and literature research methods. Since the first phase of the research, it has been defined that the interviews will be undertaken with employees of different fields of the economy, with the purpose to have a more inclusive point of view of the Albanian culture and difficulties that Albanian foreigners encounter every day at the workplace.

Both cultural groups are quite satisfied with the intercultural relationship they have, but during the interviews it has been augmented, that they have cultural as well as communication differences, which might interfere with the working atmosphere. Through this comparative analysis has been noticed, that both cultural groups have shown interest into having a better understanding of each other's culture and increase the chances of stronger cooperation in the working place.

The formal communication during the working hours is rather more dominant than the informal one. The perspective of the way Albanian see the relationship with their coworkers has an indication in the other cultural group, who also is sometimes unclear about the behaviour Albanians show with each-other or even with their German colleagues.

It turns out that Albanian are a very collectivistic society, that put a lot of value into friendships and relationships they built at the workplace. Their relationship indicates the successful process of cooperation and atmosphere created between employees, which is followed from further accomplishments of an operation. In the research it has also been noticed the role that informal communication plays in the progress inside a business. In the Albanian mentality, closeness between employees can be developed through spending more time to get to know the individuals at the workplace. Germans underestimate the impact informal communication has in building group harmony and readiness to work together. They pay more attention to their qualifications and not to their socio-cultural roles.

After the important cultural and communicative differences have been pointed out, from this research have been given the following solutions: To increase the chances of better communication and understanding, it is required for both cultural groups to invest into this issue. On one side is the influence and offerings of the government and social investments in the education possibilities for the foreigners, who are trying to adjust in the German culture. (…) On the other hand, they should accept each other 's cultural standards and not exclude or refuse them. There should exist the interest of both cultures in understanding and adjusting their behaviour toward each other.

Based on the last point, a compendium will be developed in the format of a small book to orientate both cultures on the differences that they have. It will have explanations in the simplest forms of design, by using simple and funny pictogram illustrations – A pictogram needs to capture user's attention (users need to see the pictogram), to improve user's comprehension of warnings (users need to attend to it), and it also needs to increase their awareness of risk, generally by serving as an „instantaneous memorandum "of a risk [4] (Tijus, Barcenilla, Cambon de Lavalette, Meunier, 2007: Otsubo, 1988). – to allow all people, independent from their knowledge of language, to understand the main concept of this handbook. (…)

References

1. Xiufang Jin: Kontakte, Konflikte und Kompromisse: Interkulturelle Kommunikation zwischen Deutschen und Chinesen in einem Joint-Venture, 1994, Saarbrücken
2. Kartaı, Asker, 1997, Deutsch-türkische Kommunikation am Arbeitsplatz: Zur interkulturellen Kommunikation zwischen türkischen Mitarbeitern und deutschen Vorgesetzten in einem deutschen Industriebetrieb, München
3. Dervishi, Zyhdi, 2012, Vështrime të kryqëzuara në det, Shtëpia botuese "Emal", Tiranë
4. Charles Tijus1, Javier Barcenilla2, Brigitte Cambon de Lavalette3 and Jean-Guy Meunier 4: The Design, Understanding and Usage of Pictograms, 2007: http://www.cognition-usages.org/chart/dmdocuments/inrets22.pdf
5. Bennett, Milton, J.: Intercultural communication: A current perspective. In Milton J. Ben¬nett (Ed.), Basic concepts of intercultural communication: Selected readings. Yarmouth, ME: Intercultural Press, 1998: https://www.researchgate.net/publication/246501677_Intercultu-ral_Communication_A_Current_Perspective

Language and cultural communication —— Smart media has become a bridge for cross-cultural communication

Jiaqi Lu*

Department of Foreign Affairs and Foreign Affairs Management, China Foreign Affairs University, Shahe, Changping, Beijing, China

Abstract: Language and culture are two indispensable elements of human society. They interweave and influence each other, and jointly constitute the diversity and uniqueness of human society. As a tool of communication, language not only transmits information, but also is a carrier of culture. This paper aims to explore the importance and mutual influence of language and culture on cross-cultural communication in the era of intellectual media. Through the analysis of related literature review, this paper puts forward in the era of intellectual media, can to a certain extent, break the barriers between cultural communication and cross-cultural language communication, "cross language and cross-cultural" the humanities social important proposition, make the communication activities of "language", "culture", "communication" three elements maximum transmission efficiency, make based on intellectual media multimodal culture communication and language communication more affinity and story.

1. Foreword

Language is a tool of human communication and a part of a culture. Culture is embodied, transmitted, and preserved through language. At a time when global cultural exchanges and interactions are becoming more frequent and deepening, language and culture are the necessary guarantee for countries in the world to continue to maintain economic development and cooperation, follow up cultural export, dissemination and promote communication and communication. The "barrier" of cross-language communication is that people speak the same language with different cultural identities. The common obstacle of cross-cultural communication is that people live in the same cultural circle, but the language barrier leads to the failure of cross-cultural communication. As a result, the language communication is superficial, the cultural background is very different, and the lack of deep communication and interaction, leading to the weakening of the communication effect. This paper aims to build a bridge for culture in the cross-language communication in the era of intellectual media, and pave the way for language in the cross-cultural communication, so that language and culture can join hands to build the civilization process of international communication. In addition, this paper discusses the application and challenges of language and cultural communication in the process of internationalization, and makes some suggestions.

2. Cross-linguistic and cross-cultural concepts and meanings

2.1 The connection between language and culture

Culture, being tangible yet boundless, means that cultural production and reproduction are never and can never be exact reproductions or reinforcements. If cultures exist in isolation, there would be no notion of cultural "interactions" because they would be severed. And if each culture does not have its own "gateway," there would be no possibility of multiple cultures in the world, as they would be indistinguishable. As a constantly evolving complex system, culture operates in a tendency towards chaos and converges within that chaos. Each culture is both a link in the chain of inheritance and an emerging form within the flow of communication and fusion. Cultural heritage continues through the transformation of its types.[1] This results in the process of cultural meaning, which cannot be placed on a final foundation because it is constantly influenced by random and unique occurrences. The rootlessness of meaning allows each meaning to be embedded in a history of meanings.[2]

Language, as a symbol, is the carrier of human civilization and the medium of cultural travel. To a certain extent, language reflects culture and contains profound cultural connotation. Culture is the specific content conveyed by language. The development of culture and the dissemination of culture are inseparable from language, which is inextricably linked with language. Therefore,

*Corresponding author's email: ljq2004ljq@126.com

language and culture use communication to make this mutual promotion between them more effective.

"The reason why human communication ability is particularly strong is that the important means of language, which makes the content of communication have great potential in scope and depth."[3] It can be seen that communication promotes the communication and progress of human civilization. In the process of realizing language and cultural communication, there are often two important connotations: cross-linguistic cultural communication and cross-cultural language communication.

Language mainly relies on the audio language, and through the orderly and scientific combination and arrangement, the cultural connotation and essence of the language itself are transmitted outward. The communication media used in the transmission will affect the communication characteristics of language and culture to a certain extent, and even bring diversified cultural impact to the audience, and it will also show the cultural characteristics in the process of language communication.

2.2 Cross-language and cross-cultural significance

Translation and interpretation are the typical and direct ways to facilitate cross-cultural and cross-linguistic understanding. They aim to convey information from one language and culture to another, increasing the likelihood of correct understanding by the recipient, establishing connections between input and background information, and enhancing the availability of shared background information. In other words, sharing information through translation and interpretation increases the passive understanding of another culture and enhances the possibility of mutual positive understanding.

To some extent, machine translation can also achieve translation and interpretation through automated translation programs like Google Translate. However, the most successful automatic translation programs, such as deep learning software, do not rely on true understanding but rather search for matching patterns in the corresponding language databases to complete translation tasks. Therefore, automatic translation still requires additional human correction, editing, and translation to be useful.[4]

In the field of translation and interpretation, individuals with multilingual and multicultural abilities are valuable resources. They act as bridges between different languages, as well as between different concepts and worldviews, serving as sources of mutual understanding between languages and cultures. They can also train others to become such resources.[5]

In today's increasingly frequent international communication, language, as the main communication tool, is playing an increasingly important role. Ostler points out: " If language makes us truly human, then it also makes us superhuman. Once a human group learns a language, this language can convey infinite knowledge and belief: when we think, listen, speak, read, and write, it is an intangible wealth that can give us strength, allowing us to stand on the shoulders of our ancestors' thoughts and emotions. Language makes us a continuum of culture, connecting us to history and transmitting our ideas to later speakers of language... language, as the banner and symbol of the human community, also defends our common memory."[6] This shows that language is like a symbol carrying the" collective memory ", connecting the history, reality and the future. Some scholars believe that: "Language is a sensitive indicator that can indicate cultural changes, although it is not just a simple reflection."[7] Especially in the communication activities, we need to think about the" cross-language " problem of cultural communication.

First of all, since the generation and development of language is inseparable from the geographical, ethnic, humanities and other people who use language,

If the communication between people once out of this category, there will be communication and communication problems between different languages, which requires mastering different languages of different nationalities, different regions or different countries, in order to achieve the purpose of international communication. Secondly, cross-language cultural communication is mainly based on applied language, with translation as the bridge and cross-cultural communication as the purpose. Because of the need of communication, contact between different languages, communication, collision, running, also contribute to influence between each other, penetration, absorption, fusion, gradually also let people use different languages began to accept other languages, so there are two or more languages in parallel use, but also influence each other, promote each other, this kind of phenomenon is across the language of culture.

"Language is not only a tool of communication, it also carries specific cultural information, because language is the product of society... the understanding and mastery of language is only the first step of cross-cultural communication, and at the same time having a thorough understanding of the cultural meaning contained in the deep layers of language."[8] Cultural communication, as a unique phenomenon, transmits and spreads the information between various cultures and cultures, and is attached to the language. Without language, culture will lose the carrier of transmission. On the contrary, without transmission, the culture loses its vitality. Therefore, "language, as a conventional symbol system and the carrier of culture, is the most important 'filter' in the process of cross-cultural communication" [9]. Cross-language communication and cross-cultural communication are the expression of the concept of "fusion", which belong to the intersection of interdisciplinary knowledge system. They mainly express the different meanings between the cultures transmitted by different languages and the languages represented by different cultures in the international communication.

3. Cross-language cultural communication and problems

3.1 Communication builds a bridge between different languages and different cultures

In the process of communication, language will bring new doubts and uncertainties to people in different regions and different Spaces. Therefore, the function, status and significance of language in cross-cultural communication are always important issues in the study of cross-cultural communication. In the "New Trends of Cultural Communication: the Fourth Conference of The People" held in 2018-2021, a consensus was reached that " cross-linguistic cultural communication is a new mode of cultural communication in the new era. Cross-linguistic and cultural communication will be conducted among multilingual, multi-ethnic and multicultural without linguistic information barriers. Break the language information barrier, let different civilizations convey the charm of the nation. Contributors to the industrial chain of cross-language and cultural communication should gather cross-border wisdom and build win-win results to promote the progress of a community with a shared future for mankind."[10] Furthermore, cross-language cannot be separated from the promotion of cross-culture, and is more conducive to the expansion of cross-cultural development, which is also the significance of the study of" cross-language and cross-cultural ", a major proposition of humanities and social sciences.

Because of the language, we can inherit the civilization and wisdom of our predecessors. If language is missing or blocked, cross-cultural communication is out of the question. As the scholar Levi-Strauss said: " Language behavior is also a condition of culture, because the construction of culture is very similar to the construction of language. Both are established through antagonistic relationships and associations, in other words, by logical relationships. Therefore, we can regard language as a foundation designed to withstand structures that, though sometimes more complex than it, belong to the same type as its own structure, which correspond to cultures that we view from different sides." [14]

The essence of the language relationship is the interaction between information and information, that is, the communication relationship. The relationship between people

To activity, considered in the human social system, especially the interaction between information and information in the specific communication environment analysis, this is the spread of marxism —— spiritual communication theory brings us important enlightenment, also we study language phenomenon, investigate social information, spread the starting point of human civilization. The five basic principles of communication proposed by the Palo Alto School all emphasize the important role of language in communication relations: " It is impossible for people not to communicate, conversations contain content information and relationship information, communicators integrate interactions into meaningful patterns, and people use digital analogy for two codes

Message pairing and message capture in broadcasting and interaction."[15] Language is a means of knowledge communication and an important carrier of human cultural communication, while cross-cultural communication is an open cultural platform with language as a tool to deep development. Thus, through close academic connection, language and cross-cultural communication form common research interests in context, meaning, language structure, language rules, language effect, discourse analysis, discourse structure, discourse characteristics and other aspects, and the two are mixed to form a interdependent relationship.

3.2 Problems facing cross-linguistic and cross-cultural situations

Language " is a key to the core of a culture. It has a strong, obvious symbolism, so it is very important to racial and nationalist sentiments, it is a core symbol, with cohesion " [11]. If the language deviates from the normal expression track, the effect of cross-cultural communication will be greatly reduced. What causes this discount is the basic medium of the —— language

Or a problem with the language translation. The reasons are as follows: first, the differences of the language itself. "The use and style of language can reflect a person's personality, and similarly, it can also reflect the personality of a culture."[12] Because language arises from social practice and historical phenomena, it records the development trajectory and changes of human society. Secondly, translation plays an important role in the cultural communication system." Translation is the activity of the interconversion between different languages, and this transformation necessarily involves the language."[13] However, due to the huge differences in different languages, translation is difficult, and improper translation of words will cause serious consequences. As the scholar Xu Junyan said, " Translation is not only a purely linguistic activity, but also an important cultural practice."[14] Therefore, the cultural translation theory has elevated the translation practice to a higher level. Third, language not only reflects reality, but it also distorts reality. There is no lack of negative language in cross-cultural communication, such as language trap, language hegemony, language violence and so on. This requires the establishment of a language barrier to safeguard national security in international discourse. People in the scope of activities, communication, language dissemination and circulation.

4. Intelligent media for the "cross-language" and "cross-cultural" communication brought about changes

Discussion above are two core issues of "cross-language" and "cross-cultu ral" in cross-cultural communication activities. So, are there any means to eliminate or reduce the "language" and "cultural" barriers in the communication activities? The answer is yes. With the development of science and technology and the progress of society, the media presents the characteristics of intelligence.

Intelligent media has many characteristics, such as cross-regional, virtual, immediacy and cheap, which has brought great convenience to information diffusion and has become a new way of cultural communication. Today, "contributors to cross-language cultural communication are far beyond language workers, but also product designers, developers, media practitioners, cultural planners and AI robots to boost cultural communication" [16]. As a communication platform or communication channel, the Internet has broken the restrictions of traditional media and is a cross-media communication platform that integrates various advantages, such as colorful pictures, vivid scenes, and flexible and diverse expressions. Based on the theory of multimodal linguistics, combined with the translation and communication theory of cross-cultural communication construction, for intellectual media era of excellent cultural cross-cultural communication provides new ideas, new ideas and new means, help to improve the cultural communication ability and effect, realize the effective combination of information technology industry and language services and perfect docking.

4.1 The Impact of Intelligent media on Intercultural Communication

Intelligent media, with its distinct characteristics, has both influenced the form and content of information and how people understand each other in human communication, especially among those from different cultural or ethnic groups.

Essentially, the new culture incubated from Intelligent media creates a continuity gap between tradition and innovation in culture. Before the emergence of Intelligent media, traditional and innovative values coexisted in a dynamically synchronized manner in human society. However, the speed and impact of Intelligent media communication has caused traditional values to fall behind the new cultural values generated by Intelligent media. This cultural difference creates difficulties in understanding or communication between generations or within the same culture.

Intelligent media has also given rise to communication gaps between different cultural and ethnic groups. The fragmentation of Intelligent media has created new patterns in traditional cultural grammar, themes, or cultural maps, resulting in the loss of traditional cultural logic. The rearrangement or recombination of cultural patterns or worldviews requires members of a culture to readjust their communication behavior within their own community and learn new ways to interact with people from different cultures. Intelligent media has nurtured a new culture in human society, where the level of ambiguity and uncertainty has been reshuffled to its highest point, especially in the process of intercultural communication. Adapting to this new situation and enabling mutual understanding among different cultural groups during the chaotic phase of cultural transition has become a significant challenge faced by academia in everyday life and research interaction. It is in this context that more and more scholars are beginning to focus on the relationship between Intelligent media and intercultural communication.

4.2 The Impact of Intelligent media on Intercultural Interactions

The influence of Intelligent media on various aspects of intercultural interactions has attracted increasing attention from scholars in the field of intercultural communication. In a global context, Intelligent media has three common impacts on intercultural interactions: cross-cultural relationships, cross-cultural adaptation, and cross-cultural conflicts.

4.2.1 Cross-Cultural Relationships

Intelligent media, particularly social media platforms such as Facebook, blogs, MySpace, YouTube, Twitter, and iPhone, enable people from all over the world to showcase themselves in a specific way and stay connected in the online space. Clearly, the flexibility of information presented and shared in Intelligent media will directly impact the development of cross-cultural relationships in virtual communities, whether positive or negative.

Furthermore, Elola and Oskoz (2009) found that the use of blogs in foreign language and study abroad contexts not only had a positive impact on the development of cross-cultural relationships but also enhanced participants' intercultural communication competence. In addition to interpersonal cross-cultural relationships, social media also contributes to the establishment of international business relationships. However, Intelligent media can also have negative effects on intercultural communication.

Lastly, McEwan and Sobre-Denton (2011) proposed that mediated communication through computers can foster and develop virtual cosmopolitanism and virtual third culture. They noted that by constructing a third cultural space, a new hybrid culture is created where interactants from different cultures can gather cultural and social information, build online communities, and form cross-cultural relationships.

4.2.2 Cultural Adaptation

As Intelligent media allows individuals from around the world to exchange information in order to understand people from different cultures, it has become popular for migrants or immigrants to use Intelligent media to communicate with their friends, classmates, relatives, or family members in their home country and host country during their learning process or everyday life. The longer immigrants reside in the host country, the more frequently they engage in communication with the host country nationals through Intelligent media, while the frequency of browsing websites from their home country decreases (Chen, W., 2012). Chen also found that the use of Intelligent media has a significant impact on the cross-cultural adaptation process of immigrants. In other words, social interactions conducted by immigrants through Intelligent media have been proven to be a key factor in determining their successful adaptation to the host country.

Furthermore, Sawyer and Chen (2011) investigated how international students use social media and how social media influences their cross-cultural adaptation. The authors found that social media provides international students with an environment to connect with people from their home country and the host country, which in turn helps them strengthen personal relationships and develop a sense of belonging to the host country's culture. The use of Intelligent media clearly aids international students in overcoming cultural barriers during the process of cross-cultural adaptation. The study also found that due to the impact of culture shock, sojourners tend to rely on social media more during the initial stages.

4.2.3 Cross-Cultural Conflicts

Intelligent media provides a powerful tool for individuals and governments to construct their own image, define and redefine the meaning of information, set media agendas, or create news or information. However, cultural differences result in different manifestations of media at the individual or governmental level. Due to the potential order, perspectives, and practices of media in any society being based on its cultural value orientations, different forms of media representation often reflect the asymmetry of cross-cultural communication and inevitably lead to interpersonal, group, and national-level conflicts or confrontations.[19]

5. The spread of intelligent media to the masses

Language culture through audio language to the public has its cultural essence and connotation, communicators according to their own characteristics, life perception, aesthetic cognition and culture connotation choose the appropriate media, to provide the public with clear thinking logic, unique aesthetic style, profound cultural connotation of excellent language culture works, cause the resonance of the public, make more audience involved in the language culture communication, common creation, to reach their own thinking space.

5.1 Multiple spatial expression of language and cultural communication in the context of intellectual media

In the context of intelligent media, the audience also hopes that these language and cultural works will have clear logical thinking, high aesthetic level and rich cultural connotation when accepting various forms of language and cultural communication. At the same time, the context of intellectual media enables more members of the public to participate in the communication of these languages and cultures, and jointly create these language and cultural works, and then extend and transcend the space of spirit and thinking. In the process of perceiving language and culture, the public constantly deepens and interprets these languages and cultures in an interesting way. In general, the language and culture in the society have great influence, and in the context of intellectual media, the communication process of language and culture presents a strong field, public and space.

5.1.1 Sound and picture to communicate together

Wisdom media is superior to other media form mainly because intellectual media pay more attention to network technology research, using cloud computing, big data and other advanced network technology, intelligent push according to user demand, and use the voice and picture to communicate restructuring of language culture communication process, through the visual and sensory information symbol to realize the transmission process, and the emotional interaction between the audience and atmosphere rendering [6]. Voice and picture is an important mode of transmission of language culture works, intellectual media context language culture can control the speed, adjust the tone, rendering tone, rich picture to create atmosphere, give a person a kind of immersive feeling, really feel the unique artistic and aesthetic characteristics of language culture, to achieve the purpose of spreading language culture in the form of art.

5.1.2 Recognition and communication of aesthetic understanding

Language and culture can disseminate literature works or literature and art to the public in a diversified way through the use of Internet intelligent media. Implemented in a more advanced aesthetic form will language culture in front of the public, and the public in the reception of the language culture art, understanding, and the process of appreciation, perceive the language surface outside the deep connotation, gradually have a new understanding of aesthetic, subtly improve the aesthetic level, form the advanced aesthetic feeling.

5.1.3 The transmission of emotional resonance in the spiritual world

The characteristic of public space is that it can expand the breadth and dimension of language and culture. Use the intelligent media context to expand the existing communication field and space of language and culture communication, and reflect the humanistic feelings and internal emotions [10] contained in the works in different dimensions. To integrate the audience into the language and cultural works and have emotional resonance with them, this process can be called perfect aesthetic perception and aesthetic experience, which improves the level of public aesthetic perception.

5.1.4 Promote the coordinated development of many media

Media in the context of intelligent media is the optimization and extension of traditional media, and the inevitable product of the development of The Times and science and technology. It keeps the dynamic development mode of continuous update, provides a broader means of communication for the innovation and upgrading of language and cultural products, and meets the public's demand for media screening when receiving cultural information. The efficient communication of language and cultural products depends on the synchronous media support of sound and picture, so as to fully display the emotional connotation of cultural products themselves. According to the different content of cultural information, different media transmission are selected, which reflects the functional distinction of media and meets the public's demand for innovation and change of media. Through the different choices of media by the public and the feedback to the received information, various media are effectively debugging and optimized, combined with various media communication technologies, showing innovative and diversified communication effects, and improve the communication efficiency and quality of language and cultural products [17]. Therefore, in the future development path of media, it is an inevitable trend for many media to develop together and complement their advantages and disadvantages, so as to improve the comprehensive development level of media.

5.2 Provide a public space for harmonious interaction for the public

Through the public space in the context of intellectual media, the public can participate in the cultural works, feel the information and emotions conveyed by the cultural works, optimize and sublimate the received information according to their own understanding and appreciation, and interact and communicate with the author. In this interactive process, on the one hand, it improves the public's aesthetic ability and cultural understanding ability, and on the other hand, it also promotes the public to form a good ability to receive active cultural information. Thus, it also provides a new direction for the creation and conception of language culture, and promotes language culture to continuously optimize its own communication mode and improve its own communication content.

5.3 Public space to effectively maintain and promote the development of language and cultural communication

Use the publicity and sharing of public space to closely connect the implication expressed by individuals and language and cultural works, and establish a field and space [18] with high-level aesthetic characteristics. Language and culture uses its unique form of artistic expression to create cultural works leading the new fashion of The Times, bringing the audience visual, auditory and even spiritual and emotional shock, and making the audience more willing to accept the communication mode of language and culture in the context of intellectual media, so as to maintain and promote the communication and development of language and culture.

5.4 Public art space effectively promotes the dissemination of language and culture to achieve aesthetic transcendence

In the process of spreading language and culture in public space, seeking new aesthetic phenomena in a wider communication space is not only to meet the public's demand for innovative language and culture, but also the sublimation process of language and culture itself, from which the far-reaching influence brought by language and culture communication can be explored.

Under the influence of intelligent media context, language and culture communication realizes the purpose of rapid communication through the mobile intelligent terminal service system under 5G technology. At the same time, the communication of language and culture is not limited to language expression, but can also be transmitted through a variety of video methods. For example, VR panoramic video, high-definition video, short video, etc., all play an important role in the dissemination of language and culture. This is a new development direction for the communication mode of language and culture, refreshes the cognition of language and culture communication, innovates the development way of language and culture communication, so as to make the mode of language and culture communication develop steadily and rapidly.

6. Mode of transmission and its principles

6.1 Video communication and principles

The general use of video communication mode has the following principles. One is to understand the rules of the platform culture communication. Each video platform has different requirements for language and cultural works, so the creators should first understand the creative requirements and communication characteristics of each platform, so as to create excellent cultural video content in line with the characteristics of the platform. Second, to understand the needs of the audience. The audience is the ultimate recipient of language and culture communication, so the audience's acceptance of the communication content determines the communication efficiency of language and culture under the video communication mode. Therefore, it is a very necessary link to investigate the audience's language and culture cognition, preference and recognition of the video communication mode. Only by fully understanding the audience can better language and culture videos be created. Third, to ensure the quality of video content.(1) The dissemination of cultural videos should follow the characteristics of fragmentation and diversification of information received by the public, and be disseminated in the simplest form of expression, so that the audience can understand the rich cultural content in a short time through cultural videos.(2) Classify the theme, content and theme of cultural videos, and formulate personalized video content to push to the corresponding audience, so as to improve the audience's recognition of cultural videos.(3) language culture communication to the positive attitude of life, and correct life values, combined with the new mode of transmission, derived more interesting cultural video content, to attract more audience involved, interaction, interactive communication, the positive attitude and values passed through language culture, increase the appeal of language culture spread.

6.2 Immersive communication and principles

To improve the audience's ability to improve empathy and immerse them in the language and cultural content is the means to fundamentally improve the communication efficiency. Immersive communication mode uses VR technology to break through the boundary between the virtual space and the real world, provides the audience with more real cultural information with the help of "acoustic images", and enhances the interaction of the communication of language and cultural information in the public space. The effective combination of language and culture content and VR technology can continuously improve the communication effect of language and culture. The specific operation is divided into the following points.(1) Discover the deeper connotation and implication of language and culture, boldly innovate the content of language and culture, and combine VR technology to make the audience feel the content of language and culture in the corresponding situation, and can fully experience the internal implication of language and culture.(2) Language and cultural communication to use the immersive communication mode should stimulate the scene interaction. That is to say, in the process of language and culture communication, the corresponding situation is set, so that the audience can fully interact and communicate with the scene in the process of receiving the language and culture, so as to deepen the impression of the language and culture.(3) In the context of intellectual media, adding strong emotional elements to the language and cultural content can enable the audience to appreciate the language and cultural works, touch the heart, resonate, and deepen the love for language and culture [12].(4) Using immersive communication mode, on the one hand, improve the audience and language through the use of intelligent media.

The close connection between culture, through the high-quality language and culture, and the audience to establish a good acceptance and appreciation relationship; on the other hand, enhance the interaction of the audience in the public space and language culture, the high quality language culture of cultural knowledge in the process of language and culture communication, therefore, high-quality language culture and the audience to build a good atmosphere of communication space and field, then make the audience interest in language culture, improve the quality of language and culture communication.

Language and cultural communication play an important bridge role in the process of internationalization. Language plays an important role in international communication and intercultural cooperation, in promoting communication, enhancing understanding and building trust. Cultural communication can help people understand and respect other cultures and promote cultural diversity and cultural exchanges.

7. Conclusion and suggestion

Effective and efficient cross-cultural communication in the Internet era cannot be separated from new technologies such as intelligent media. Digitalization, big data, hypertext, hyperlink, multimedia, multimodal, virtual simulation and other technologies are becoming more mature, and the impact on cross-language communication activities is comprehensive and profound. The multi-modal language environment built by intelligent media provides elastic media for language learning, cultural contact and the elimination of cultural shock. Make full use of artificial intelligence technology of natural language processing, intelligent search, machine learning, knowledge acquisition, pattern recognition, artificial life, complex system technology, with multilingual jointly create multimodal culture form, make the abstract content, make cold words alive, make single-dimensional picture, will greatly strengthen the cross-cultural transmission force. Communication between different cultures is often in a certain "hidden subconscious" state. The multimodal cultural presentation helps to activate this hidden subconscious mind and stimulate the willingness and enthusiasm of the public to understand the foreign cultures. The cross-cultural communication platform built by intelligent media makes the original abstract communication content more and more concrete, visualized and civilian.

Good cross-cultural communication activities are the organic integration of language, communication and translation. In the cross-cultural communication activities, only paying attention to the language and ignoring the cultural connotation will lead to the failure of the cross-cultural communication. The complexity and particularity of language communication, as well as the abstraction and simplicity of cultural communication, all need a kind of "adhesive", which can reduce the complexity of language communication and reduce the abstraction of cultural communication. And the intelligent media can create a good interface and interface for the better interaction between the two. Using smart media, we will create a multi-modal closeness and story text based on artificial intelligence, and the language and culture in cross-cultural communication will also have more nutrients and vitality.

Reference

1. Hollenstein, M. (2019). Self-Understanding: Self-Consciousness, Intersubjectivity, Cross-Cultural Understanding. (X. Xianjun, Trans.). Beijing: Commercial Press.
2. Walden, or Life in the Woods. Translated by Sheli Min. Beijing: Commercial Press, 2020.
3. Chen Weixing. Concept of communication (revised version) [M]. Beijing: People's Publishing House, 2008:8.
4. NÉMETH G D.Machine translation: a short overview| EB/OL].(2019-10-18)[2021-11-12].ht-tps://towardsdatascience.com/machine-translation-a-sh hort-overview-91343ff39c9f.

5. Shan Bo (2023) Intercultural Communication Studies, Communication University of China Press, Beijing.
6. Ostler. The Language Empire: The Language History of the World [M]. Zhang Lu, et al. Shanghai: Shanghai People's Publishing House, 2009: Preface 1-2.
7. Burke. Cultural history of languages: languages and communities in early modern Europe [M]. Li Xiaoxiang, et al. Beijing: Peking University Press, 2007:1.
8. Chen Lidan. Intercultural communication of languages and non-language [J]. Southeast transmission, 2017(3):22-25.
9. Wang Xiaoyue. Language: a "filter" for cross-cultural communication [J]. Hubei radio According to the university Journal, 2009 (1): 108-109.
10. The conference promotes the integration of cross-linguistic and cultural communication to explore the symbiosis between human and technology

    Born [EB /OL].(2019-12-19).https://baijiahao.baidu.
11. Xu Jun. Introduction to Translation (revised version) [M]. Beijing: Foreign Language Teaching and Research Press, 2020:29.
12. Claude Levy-Strauss. Structural anthropology [M]. Zhang Zujian, translation. Beijing: China Renmin University Press, 2006:73-74.
13. EdwardsJ.Language,Society,andIdentity[M].Oxford: Blackwell,1985:15.

    [EB/OL].(2019-12-19).https://baijiahao.baidu.com/s?id=1653246143225343047&wfr=spider&for=pc.
14. Sommerwa, Porter. Cross-cultural transmission [M].6 Edition. Min Huiquan, et al. Beijing: China Renmin University Press, 2013:158.
15. Zhang Zheng. An Introduction to Translational Science [M]. Beijing: Tsinghua University Press, 2018:105.
16. John Steven, Jr. Communication theory [M]. Chen Demin, Ye Xiaohui, translated. Beijing: China Social Sciences Press, 1999:452-457.
17. Zheng Hongyan. Create intelligent media to enhance the communication power —— The way to improve the traditional media communication power in the era of all media [J]. Propagation power study, 2019.
18. Liu Liangmo. Research on the path of new government media participation in community governance in the era of intelligent media [J]. China Journal of Radio and Television, 2022 (5).
19. Tian Dexin, Yu Hongliang (2022) Intercultural Communication Studies, Xi'An Jiaotong University Press, Xi'An.

An Empirical Study on Cultural Image, Perceived Value, and Purchase Intention: A Case of Chinese Intangible Cultural Heritage "Gambiered Canton Gauze"

Delphine Yachu Chan[1,*], Zicheng Pan[2]

[1]School of Management, University of Electronic Science and Technology of China, Zhongshan Institute, 528402 Guangdong, China
[2]School of Management, Macau University of Science and Technology, 999078 Macau, China

Abstract. Gambiered Canton gauze is a unique double-sided silk product in Guangdong Province, China, securing its status as one of the national intangible cultural heritages (ICH) due to its exceptional yarn finishing techniques. Despite the implementation of China's rural revitalization policy, gambiered Canton gauze did not seize the opportunity to enhance its live transmission. Instead, it encountered a small consumer market because of its high prices and weak publicity. To better inherit and promote ICH products, this study explores the relationship between their cultural images, perceived values, and purchase intention from the perspective of cultural values. The results demonstrate that the cultural images of ICH products, such as practical reason, nostalgic inheritance, and face images, exert a significantly positive impact on purchase intention. Notably, the face images conveyed by ICH products are the key factor affecting the purchase intention. In the above relationship, functional values and social values serve as intermediary factors.

1. Introduction

Since China joined the UNESCO Convention for the Safeguarding of Intangible Cultural Heritage in 2004, it has continuously explored protection measures and inheritance practices for intangible cultural heritage (ICH). ICH encompasses various traditional cultural expressions, such as practices, performances, knowledge systems, and skills, as well as related objects and places, which are regarded as cultural heritage by all ethnic groups. Currently, ICH projects across Chinese provinces actively engage in cultural and creative construction and tourism development through rural revitalization policies, aiming to secure a position among global ICH and achieve sustainable development goals. Gambiered Canton gauze, a unique traditional fabric with dual-sided colors and environmentally friendly features in Guangdong Province, China, has earned national ICH status for its distinctive plant dyeing and finishing process. However, after 1970, the continuous development of science and technology led to the emergence of numerous new and low-cost textile fiber products, which made the gambiered Canton gauze industry, characterized by prolonged production time, high costs, and limited color options, face a gradual decline in market demand. From the perspective of cultural functionalism, ICH has a multi-dimensional and dynamic value, serving as a gem that embodies the local history and characteristics. Therefore, a comprehensive understanding of ICH values and the factors influencing purchase intention is crucial for guiding the scientific development of ICH products and holds practical significance for the sustainable development of ICH. Overall, based on the value theory, this paper conducts an empirical study on the cultural images, customer values, and purchase intention of Chinese ICH gambiered Canton gauze. It aims to deeply comprehend consumer attitudes towards ICH products, help gambiered Canton gauze merchants master the needs and sentiments of consumers, and put forward countermeasures and suggestions for the future development of ICH products to promote their sustainable development.

2. Literature review

2.1. ICH cultural Image and purchase intention

Pan et al. (2014) constructed a consumer values scale based on Chinese culture and found that cultural values with multiple dimensions, such as practical reason and face images, will affect consumers' product perception. Cultural values refer to the values formed by a society or a group in a certain historical period [1], and the image and cultural connotations conveyed by the product will also affect its purchase intention. Similarly, Guo and Sun (2016) observed in the consumption research of cultural values that the perception of inheritance and nostalgia aesthetics will influence purchase intention [2]. Therefore, this paper divides ICH's cultural images into three dimensions: practical reason, nostalgic inheritance, and face images. Among them, "practical reason" reflects an enterprising and pragmatic life attitude, where consumers perceive ICH products as practical and make rational judgments and choices when purchasing [1]. In "nostalgia

*Corresponding author's mail: yachuchan@zsc.edu.cn

inheritance", nostalgia involves respecting and embracing old or retro products, while inheritance represents the cultural values influenced by ancestors and their continuation or promotion [2]. In other words, ICH products feature designs with nostalgic and retro elements or convey cultural images worthy of transmission to future generations. "Face image" refers to the emphasis on personal images, being rich in cultural self-confidence, or even garnering respect from others [1]. In essence, ICH products are rich in cultural connotations and images, which can effectively highlight users' tastes. Given the limited availability of special cultural and creative products, purchasing limited edition ICH items enhances consumers' sense of prestige. To sum up, the following hypothesis is derived:

H1: The (a) practical reason, (b) nostalgic inheritance, and (c) face images of ICH culture images exert a positive impact on purchase intention.

2.2. The mediating effect of perceived value

By analyzing cultural heritage in Western European states, Vecco (2010) proposed a shift from tangible to intangible definitions of cultural heritage and highlighted that the discourse on ICH should evolve from pure norms and protective appeals to discussions that awaken values. As a result, research and development approaches towards ICH in different countries have gradually diversified [3]. Perceived values refer to the evaluation of the overall utility made by customers when purchasing products or services by weighing the proportion between perceived benefits and sacrifices [4]. Qiu et al. (2019) discussed the value cognition, attitude, and tourism intention in ICH tourist attractions, and categorized ICH values into aesthetic values, educational spiritual values, socio-economic values, and historical values. It is found that ICH values have multiple dimensions that influence consumers' attitudes and behavior intention [5]. Heredia-Carroza, Martos, and Aguado (2020) explored ICH value measurement from Flamenco's music and dance art in Spain and extracted three values—the emotional value, aesthetic value, and cognitive value—through exploratory factor analysis [6]. In line with Sweeney and Soutar (2001), this paper divides ICH's perceived values into two dimensions: functional values and social values [7]. "Functional values" denote the practical attributes of products to meet the efficacy, providing a sense of economic benefits and value for money. On the other hand, "social values" refer to the effect that customers link with other social groups through products, conveying benefits such as culture, identity, social responsibility, and personal images. In summary, the following hypotheses are obtained:

H2: The (a) practical reason, (b) nostalgic inheritance, and (c) face images of ICH cultural images exert a positive impact on functional values.

H3: The (a) practical reason, (b) nostalgic inheritance, and (c) face images of ICH cultural images have a positive impact on social values.

H4: Functional values serve as an intermediary factor in the impact of (a) practical reason, (b) nostalgic inheritance, and (c) face images on purchase intention.

H5: Social values serve as an intermediary factor in the influence of (a) practical reason, (b) nostalgic inheritance, and (c) face images on purchase intention.

Overall, this study believes that when consumers encounter ICH products, their perceived cultural images and perceived values of the products will positively influence their purchase intention. The research framework is shown in Fig. 1.

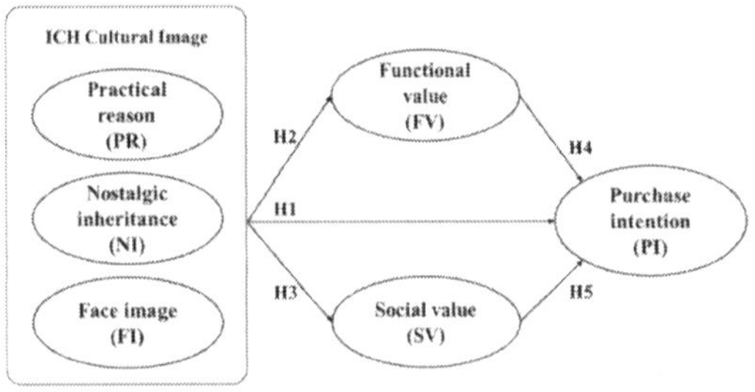

Fig. 1. Research framework.

3. Research method

3.1. Questionnaire design and measurement

The questionnaire is divided into three parts. The first part focuses on the consumer group's awareness of ICH products and gambiered Canton gauze. Initially, respondents are filtered using the screening question "Have you ever bought ICH products? (e.g., Ru porcelain, embroidery, clay sculpture, pyrography, paper-cutting, etc.)" to ensure the inclusion of valid samples. Subsequent inquiries delve into their purchase frequency, types, and budgets. The second part comprises variable items, including six latent variables: ICH cultural images (e.g., practical reason, nostalgia inheritance, and face images), perceived values (e.g., functional values and social values), and purchase intention. All the items are designed with reference to self-maturity scales and expert opinions and measured by the Likert 5-scale. The third part gathers basic information about the subjects, encompassing gender, age, education level, and monthly disposable income.

3.2. Sampling and data collection

To ensure the quality of survey tools and the survey process, this study first invited 30 consumers to participate in a pre-survey questionnaire. The pretest results revealed a Cronbach's α of 0.70 for all variables, indicating signifying favorable reliability of the survey tool and readiness for the formal investigation. The formal investigation commenced in March 2020, targeting tourists in Foshan, Guangzhou, Zhongshan, and Chaoshan District of Guangdong Province. A total of 385 questionnaires were collected, and all samples were deemed valid, achieving a 100% effective recovery rate. The findings indicate that consumers who have purchased

ICH are mostly women (71.69%), primarily aged between 19 and 25 years old (82.82%), with a predominant education level of university/junior college (84.38%). Their monthly disposable income is concentrated in RMB 2000 and below (76.62%). Furthermore, 68.89% of consumers have only purchased ICH products once or twice. The ICH products of interest predominantly fall within the creative life and clothing series categories (40.52%), among which clothing ranks highest (18.75%) as the most preferred product for purchase, followed by bags (17.94%).

4. Empirical results

4.1. Reliability and Validity

The reliability and validity of the research scale are analyzed using IBM SPSS 22.0, with the results presented in Table 1 and Table 2. Table 1 demonstrates that the Cronbach's α of the six variables (practical reason, nostalgia inheritance, face images, functional values, social values, and purchase intention) ranges from 0.848 to 0.948, with the corrected item-total correlation > 0.50, indicating excellent internal consistency of the scale. The factor loading of six constructs ranges from 0.756 to 0.923, and the acquisition percentage of explained variation exceeds 80%, which reveals minimal information missing and good convergent validity of the scale [8]. Additionally, Table 2 indicates that the square root of AVE for constructs exceeds the correlation coefficient between constructs, demonstrating excellent discriminant validity [9].

Table 1. Reliability and validity.

Construct & Item		Reliability		Convergent validity	
		Cronbach's α	CITC	Factor loading	KMO (APEV)
Practical reason	PR1: I like to "shop around" when choosing products.	0.855	0.751	0.877	0.758 (83.271%)
	PR2: I purchase ICH products according to my daily needs.		0.751	0.907	
Nostalgic inheritance	NI1: I am willing to accept retro items.	0.848	0.713	0.756	
	NI2: I like ICH products with retro elements.		0.765	0.890	
	NI3: I am willing to collect ICH products if I have enough ability.		0.688	0.848	
Face image	FI1: Purchasing limited ICH products makes me feel prestigious.	0.893	0.761	0.845	
	FI2: Using ICH products makes people feel that I have cultural depth.		0.865	0.903	
	FI3: Using ICH products brings about compliments and instills confidence.		0.748	0.890	
Functional value	FV1: It can reduce environmental pollution.	0.948	0.867	0.843	0.911 (85.268%)
	FV2: It is value for money.		0.855	0.847	
	FV3: It is beneficial to the sustainable development of society.		0.879	0.878	
	FV4: It can enhance the environmental awareness of self and others.		0.894	0.892	
Social value	SV1: It makes a good impression on others.	0.934	0.868	0.827	
	SV2: I can gain more people's recognition.		0.861	0.841	
	SV3: It makes people feel that I have a sense of social responsibility.		0.808	0.873	
	SV4: It establishes a good personal image.		0.845	0.845	
Purchase intention	PI1: I will purchase/use gambiered Canton gauze ICH products.	0.920	0.774	0.871	0.832 (80.750%)
	PI2: I would like to recommend gambiered Canton gauze ICH products for my friends.		0.817	0.899	
	PI3: I am willing to pay a higher price for ICH products.		0.820	0.900	
	PI4: I have a good chance of purchasing/using ICH products.		0.857	0.923	
Metrics		≥0 .70	≥0 .50	≥0 .70	≥0 .50

Note: CITC=corrected item-total correlation; APEV= accumulation percentage of explained variance

Table 2. Discriminant validity.

	Mean	SD	PR	NI	FI	FV	SV	PI
PR	3.994	0.854	**0.892**					
NI	3.936	0.732	0.481**	**0.833**				
FI	3.331	0.818	0.367**	0.398**	**0.880**			
FV	3.684	0.798	0.380**	0.591**	0.571**	**0.830**		
SV	3.507	0.778	0.236**	0.378**	0.600**	0.689**	**0.815**	
PI	3.440	0.799	0.364**	0.504**	0.630**	0.773**	0.781**	**0.898**

Note: * $p \leq 0.05$, ** $p \leq 0.01$; the diagonal values in bold represent the square roots of AVE for each construct

4.2. Hypothesis test

To examine the impact of ICH products' cultural images such as practical reason, nostalgic inheritance, and face images, on consumers' perceived values and purchase intention, this study employs regression analysis to test the hypothesis, with the results shown in Table 3.

Table 3. Results of regression analysis.

Model	*β*	*t*	*Adjusted* R^2	*F-value*
(1) PR→PI	0.364***	7.660	0.131	58.676
(2) NI→PI	0.504***	11.414	0.252	130.272
(3) FI→PI	0.630***	15.867	0.395	251.766
(4) PR→FV	0.380***	8.030	0.142	64.475
(5) NI→FV	0.591***	14.334	0.347	205.464
(6) FI→FV	0.571***	13.621	0.325	185.531
(7) PR→SV	0.236***	4.749	0.053	22.551
(8) NI→SV	0.378***	7.980	0.140	63.685
(9) FI→SV	0.600***	14.680	0.358	215.506
(10) PR→FV→PI	0.083*	2.381	0.602	291.374
(11) NI→FV→PI	0.072	1.796	0.599	288.334
(12) FI→FV→PI	0.279***	7.572	0.649	355.673
(13) PR→SV→PI	0.191***	6.083	0.643	346.839
(14) NI→SV→PI	0.243***	7.572	0.660	372.936
(15) FI→SV→PI	0.251***	6.656	0.649	356.202
Results: Hypothesis 1 ~ Hypothesis 5 are supported				

Note: *$p \leq 0.05$; **$p \leq 0.01$; ***$p \leq 0.001$

Models (1) to (3) in Table 3 show that the three culture images, PR, NI, and FI, exhibit a significantly positive impact on PI. This indicates that consumers perceive a stronger cultural image conveyed by ICH products, correlating with higher predicted purchase intention, which supports H1. Similarly, Models (4) to (9) demonstrate that PR, NI, and FI exert a significantly positive influence on both FV and SV. This signifies that consumers attributing a stronger cultural image to ICH products tend to have higher perceived functional values and social values, thereby supporting H2 and H3.

This paper examines the mediating effect of perceived values by referring to Baron and Kenny (1986) [10]. It can be found in Model (10) of Table 3 that after FV is added to the relationship between PR and PI, the influence coefficient of PR on PI decreases compared with Model (1), but it remains significant. Therefore, it is determined that FV has a partial mediating effect in the influence relationship between PR and PI. Similarly, in Model (12), after introducing FV into the relationship between FI and PI, the influence coefficient of FI on PI decreases compared with Model (3), but it remains significant. This indicates that FV also has a partial mediating effect in the influence relationship between FI and PI. In particular, Model (11) shows that after adding FV into the relationship between NI and PI, the influence coefficient of NI on PI not only decreases but becomes insignificant compared with Model (2), so it is determined that FV plays a complete intermediary role in the influence relationship between NI and PI. In other words, when consumers perceive a stronger cultural image conveyed by ICH products, it not only enhances their perceived functional values but also positively influences their purchase intention, which supports H4.

Models (13) to (15) in Table 3 show that after adding SV, the influence coefficients of the three ICH cultural images on PI all decrease but remain significant. Therefore, it is determined that SV has a partial mediating effect in the influence relationship between the three ICH cultural images and PI. In other words, the stronger consumers feel the cultural image conveyed by ICH products, the higher their perceived social values are, positively reinforcing their purchase intention. Thus, H5 is supported.

5. Conclusion and suggestion

ICH represents a life philosophy encompassing the coexistence of human beings, society, and nature. Through practical investigation, this paper delves into consumers' real sentiments regarding ICH's cultural images and their influence on their perceived values and purchase intention and then proposes some suggestions for the sustainable development of ICH. The findings reveal that the robustness of the three ICH cultural images—practical reason, nostalgic inheritance, and face images—positively correlates with heightened perceived values and purchase intention among consumers. Notably, face images are the key factor in predicting the social values and purchase intention of ICH products. Nostalgic inheritance plays a crucial role in predicting the perceived functional values of ICH, with functional values serving as a complete intermediary between nostalgic inheritance and the purchase intention of ICH. Therefore, this paper puts forward the following suggestions for ICH product development and future research:

5.1. ICH product development suggestions

The results demonstrate that the face images conveyed by ICH positively influence consumers' perceived social values and purchase intention. This implies that consumers consider purchasing ICH products with high-end categories and cultural connotations, such as gambiered Canton gauze, as a means to improve their social status, garner praise, and boost confidence. Hence, it is suggested that ICH product development focuses on strengthening its unique cultural elements. For example, gambiered Canton gauze can integrate various Lingnan ICH elements such as Cantonese embroidery, pearl embroidery, and Chaozhou embroidery by utilizing its distinctive colors and traditional handicrafts. This integration aims to further form Lingnan's profound cultural heritage and aesthetics into a unique style, enhance its allure through craftsmanship and texture, endow consumers with cultural confidence, and drive their purchasing power.

Moreover, the research highlights that the nostalgic inheritance conveyed by ICH is a crucial factor in triggering perceived functional values, and, in turn, functional values can promote consumers' purchase intention. Therefore, it is recommended that ICH makes good use of the protection and inheritance policies implemented by various countries to promote its sustainable development. For instance, ICH gambiered Canton gauze can establish a related process inheritance base. By aligning with China's current rural revitalization policy and the integration of culture and tourism, it can perpetuate the traditional production technology and environmentally friendly materials through a scientific layout of industrial clustering and cross-border integration. This approach can promote the green value of sustainable development and healthy living while embracing retro elements, aiming to stimulate local economic income and showcase the unique charm of local ICH to the world.

5.2. Future research

First, the investigation scope of this study is limited to Guangdong Province, China, owing to the origin of gambiered Canton gauze. It is suggested that future research can broaden its scope to explore or compare potential differences in perceived values. Second, since this paper takes gambiered Canton gauze, one of China's ICH process categories, as a representative case, the follow-up study is recommended to compare whether cultural images and perceived values of other ICH products are different in dimension and variable relationship. Therefore, it is possible to put forward more concrete recommendations for the protection, inheritance, and development of global ICH.

Acknowledgment

This study was funded by the 2020 disciplinary co-construction project "Research on the delivered value of intangible cultural heritage and sustainable development under the background of rural revitalization" under the "13th Five Year" Plan of Philosophy and Social Sciences in Guangdong Province (Project No.: GD20XGL37)

References

1. Pan Y., Gao L., Zhang X., Wan Y. (2014) A study on consumer values in the context of Chinese culture: scale development and comparison. *Management World*, 4: 90-106. doi: 10.19744/j.cnki.11-1235/f.2014.04.010
2. Guo Y., Sun M. (2016) The impact of cultural values on purchase intention of nostalgia products: the mediating effect of nostalgic aesthetics. *Journal of Zhejiang Gongshang University*, 138: 53-64. doi: 10.14134/j.cnki.cn33-1337/c.2016.03.008
3. Vecco M. (2010) A definition of cultural heritage: from the tangible to the intangible. *Journal of Cultural Heritage*, 11: 321-324. doi: 10.1016/j.culher.2010.01.006
4. Zeithaml V. A. (1988) Consumer perceptions of price, quality, and value: a means-end model and synthesis of evidence. *The Journal of Marketing*, 52: 2-22. doi: 10.1177/002224298805200302
5. Qiu Q., Zheng T., Xiang Z., Zhang M. (2019) Visiting intangible cultural heritage tourism sites: from value cognition to attitude and intention. *Sustainability*, 12: 132-152. doi: 10.3390/su12010132
6. Heredia-Carroza J., Martos L. P., Aguado L. F. (2020) How to measure intangible cultural heritage value? The case of flamenco in Spain. *Empirical Studies of the Arts*, 1: 1-22. doi: 10.1177/0276237420907865
7. Sweeney J. C., Soutar G. N. (2001) Consumer perceived value: the development of a multiple item scale. *Journal of Retailing*, 77: 203-220. doi: 10.1016/S0022-4359(01)00041-0
8. Hair J. F., et al. (2010) *Multivariate data analysis: a global perspective (7th ed.)*. Pearson Prentice Hall, Upper Saddle River, NJ.
9. Fornell C., Larcker D. F. (1981) Evaluating structural equation models with unobservable variables and measurement error. *Journal of Marketing Research*, 18: 39-50. doi: 10.2307/3151312
10. Baron R. M., Kenny D. A. (1986) The moderator–mediator variable distinction in social psychological research: conceptual, strategic, and statistical considerations. *Journal of Personality and Social Psychology*, 51: 1173-1182. doi: 10.1037/0022-3514.51.6.1173

A Comparison of Folk Printmaking in China and the West

Yuan Wei*

School of Fine Art, Northwest Minzu University, Lanzhou, 730000, China

Abstract: Chinese and Western popular printmaking art share common roots in primitive art. Deeply ingrained in the daily lives of the masses, Chinese and Western folk printmaking art, with its vibrant artistic energy, has become an integral part of people's lives. This paper presents a comprehensive overview of popular printmaking in both regions, encompassing its history, representative works, and materials. The development of Chinese art can be broadly categorized into official art and folk art. Chinese popular printmaking art, as an art form directly derived from the people, possesses the characteristics of originality and authenticity. However, throughout Chinese art history, class status and artistic status were intertwined, leading to popular art being often as low-level and vulgar, rather than being recognized as art. In contrast, Western folk printmaking art did not harbor such hierarchical distinctions, instead directly acknowledging the originality and origins of art.

1. Introduction

In China, research on the development of world printmaking is still in its infancy, with only a handful of books dedicated to the subject. Among these, "World Printmaking History" and "Western Printmaking History" are notable contributions, yet they do not provide a comprehensive overview of the development of popular printmaking worldwide [1]. Moreover, there is a lack of scholarly discourse on popular printmaking in China, and most studies on ancient printmaking focus on works intended for the elite rather than the masses.

The decline of traditional forms of popular art in both the East and the West is a holistic phenomenon, and popular printmaking is no exception. The constantly evolving society is increasingly altering the "primitive ecological environment," which has shaken the practical foundation for the inheritance of ancient public printmaking art, leading to its decline today. Fortunately, many ancient folk traditions and simple laboring communities still exist in modern China [2]. The life of traditional woodcut printmaking art stubbornly persists and continues within these folk customs, presenting a diverse and complex developmental landscape. It is, therefore, meaningful to return to the original source and infuse our contemporary printmaking content with this vital energy.

A comparative study of the originality of Chinese and Western popular printmaking is, on the one hand, a process of organizing and supplementing the integrity of printmaking. On the other hand, it involves reflecting on the specific existence and value of popular printmaking, which cannot be ignored in the development of printmaking. By comparing Chinese and Western popular printmaking, we can discover and illuminate more characteristics of originality. This is highly significant and pressing, as it allows us to reflect on the aesthetic form, technical form, and lifestyle of popular printmaking. In seeking a connection between the public and printmaking, we must not allow them to become disconnected. In the current context, we should focus on cultivating the art market for printmaking and consider strategies to transform the current state of printmaking art, enabling it to truly become the art of the people [3].

This study conducted a comparative analysis of Chinese and Western popular printmaking using representative figures from the time period, such as Du Le and Chen Hongshou, as examples. First, it compared the originality of Suzhou printmaking with Western printmaking. Second, it compared the printmaking themes and styles of Chinese and Western popular printmaking by analyzing the works themselves. The study explored the characteristics of originality in these works and presented them intuitively in charts, which further enriched the content of the paper. The results provide a deeper understanding of the concept and art of popular printmaking. Popular printmaking art not only has its own unique artistic form but also embodies the cultural and spiritual connotations of the people's lives. By analyzing the primary artistic beauty of popular printmaking art from cultural and daily perspectives, this study explores the rich cultural heritage of Chinese folk printmaking art and delves into the essence of local popular printmaking.

*18693082318@163.com

2. Comparison of Chinese and Western Popular Printmaking Art

2.1. Regional differences in popular printmaking art between the East and the West

Throughout the long history of Chinese and Western painting, distinct characteristics have emerged in each tradition due to varying influences, such as painting concepts, tools and materials, political and cultural backgrounds, religious beliefs, local philosophy, and aesthetic tastes. These factors have contributed to the formation of two distinct painting systems. Numerous works have analyzed and interpreted the differences between Chinese and Western painting from various perspectives. Among these, the differences between Chinese painting and oil painting have been extensively discussed, while systematic and rigorous comparative studies of woodblock painting between the East and the West remain scarce [4].

The production of woodblock prints involves plate making and printing, emphasizing the aesthetics of material language and the direct expression of the painting process. These characteristics distinguish woodblock prints from direct painting methods. Traditional painting theory and practice encompass various aspects, but they generally maintain the stability and directness of materials and production. Art forms with strong production and high craftsmanship requirements have not gained acceptance among mainstream aesthetic elites. Traditional Chinese sculpture has largely developed in a folk and anonymous state, contrasting with the status of Western sculptors and the recognition accorded to art history. The close relationship between Western painting, printmaking, and sculpture stems from the artist's preference for production. Consequently, the lack of true printmakers in ancient China can be attributed to regional and cognitive differences between the East and the West.

2.2. The Historical Background of the Development of Popular Printmaking in the East and West

Religious painting, an integral component of Western traditional art, has consistently enjoyed widespread acceptance among people from all walks of life, from commoners to nobles. Early European woodblock prints, which emerged over 700 years after their Chinese counterparts, exhibit striking similarities in terms of composition and form. The earliest extant "Prota Woodblock Paintings" clearly demonstrate the influence of traditional Chinese woodblock prints, evident in the line-drawn and sun-engraved depiction of Christ. In both the East and the West, early woodblock prints served as vehicles for religious dissemination. From a formal perspective, traditional Chinese woodblock prints emphasized the use of lines to capture the characteristics of objects, prioritizing the aesthetic expression of the lines themselves. In contrast, traditional Western woodblock prints employed lines to construct dignified compositions, placing greater emphasis on the physical perception of objective objects [5].

In Western art, printmaking has traditionally been used as a means of book illustration. However, as printmaking gained popularity, artists began to explore its potential beyond book illustration. Many painters began using printmaking techniques to replicate their oil paintings, which they would then print and sell, thus establishing a new artistic practice. The emergence and establishment of independent printmaking workshops further contributed to the recognition of printmaking as an independent art form, with its own unique aesthetic value. This development was closely linked to the growing cultural needs of the urban middle class during that period. In China, during the Ming dynasty, painters such as Chen Hongshou primarily used their paintings as illustrations for books, rarely exhibiting them as independent works of art. However, in the late Ming and early Qing dynasties, the flourishing economy and cultural development led to a golden age for the printmaking industry. Various types of prints emerged, including comic strips, traditional Chinese opera prints, novel illustrations, New Year prints, and literary works (Figure.1).

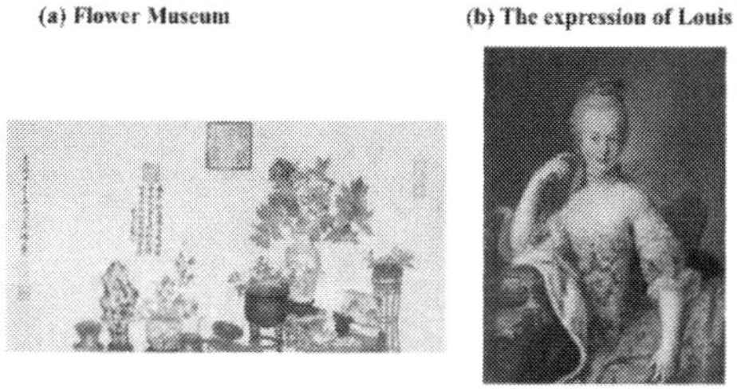

Fig. 1. Comparison of Expressions in Print Flower Museum and Louis XVI.

2.3. The Primary Differences in Popular Printmaking Art between the East and the West

Religious culture holds an extremely important position in Western society, serving as both the overarching backdrop and a profound influence on Western culture. As a prominent component of Western culture, religion exerts a strong theological influence, which is evident in artistic works. Many artistic materials relate to religious genres, and there are numerous works that praise God. In contrast, China is a nation with multiple religious beliefs, lacking the singular religious faith found in the West. In Chinese religion, human talent takes center stage, and the ultimate goal is human happiness rather than divine dignity. This is particularly apparent in Suzhou printmaking, where most works revolve around people's lives, expressing their prayers for peace and happiness, and reflecting their daily experiences. For the Chinese people, religion is seen as a blessing that enhances human life, rather than being the central focus of existence. This difference between Chinese and Western ideological systems is clearly reflected in their respective works of art (Table 1).

Examining the originality of popular printmaking art in both Eastern and Western cultures reveals shared characteristics of authenticity. Despite regional and cultural variations, these art forms fundamentally transcend temporal and spatial boundaries, following a common trajectory. They are rooted in the people, closely connected to the masses, and fulfill practical functions derived from basic life needs. This foundation allows for the integration of local characteristics and the spiritual essence of the masses, combining practicality and aesthetics to create numerous unique artistic images. This fusion serves as an infinite source of inspiration and an artistic treasure for future artistic development (Figure. 2).

Table 1. Comparison of the Originality of Chinese and Western Popular Printmaking Art

Country	Types	Aims	Primary characteristics	Background
China	Chinese opera novels, literary works, New Year paintings, woodcut comics, pictorial posters	The emergence of popular prints with independent aesthetic functions.	The spontaneity of the masses; The themes are mostly selected from the daily life of the general public The popularity of the content being expressed; Regional and Amateur Characteristics	Social prosperity, diplomatic envoys (missionaries) from Western European countries came to China, the flourishing of woodblock craftsmanship, and the strong demand of citizens for popular literature
West	Comics, letters and documents, illustrated posters	-	The production method is simple, the practicality, regional and amateur nature of the work, and the content is popular	Rapid social development, humorous attitude towards life, and the public's demand for popular literature

(a) Water Margin Leaves **(b) The Revelation**

Fig. 2. Comparison between Chen Hongshou's Water Margin Leaves and Doule's Revelation.

2.4. The Influence of European Popular Printmaking on Chinese Woodblock Printmaking

In the past, research on Western missionary painters who came to China has primarily focused on the imperial painters serving in the palace during the Qianlong period of the Qing Dynasty. However, insufficient attention has been given to the influence of Western painting and printmaking on popular woodblock prints [7]. In reality, there is a significant number of woodcuts in folk art that replicate Western copperplate paintings or incorporate Western printmaking styles into popular woodblock prints. A prime example of this can be seen in the fusion of Chinese and Western elements in the Suzhou Taohuawu Wooden New Year paintings during the Qing Dynasty. During the Qianlong and Jiaqing periods, Suzhou's woodblock New Year paintings extensively adopted the European copperplate painting technique, with many large landscape woodblock New Year paintings utilizing woodblock coloring to emulate the effect of copperplate painting. Such artistic forms and expressive techniques are rare in traditional woodblock New Year paintings.

Suzhou printmaking incorporates the forms and perspectives of Western printmaking, utilizing traditional Chinese architecture, characters, and landscapes as subjects of expression. This approach results in a more realistic, three-dimensional, and visually captivating art form that appeals to the public with its natural effect. The presented images are unprecedented, combining traditional Chinese decorative qualities with a more realistic and delicate expression. During this time, Suzhou printmaking required exceptional painting skills. The shapes of buildings, characters, and plants were meticulously portrayed, with great attention to detail. The pursuit of perspective in depicting distance and proximity gave the works a high degree of completion [8]. The original works are rarely found in China, with some printmaking pieces still preserved in Japan and Europe, serving as crucial resources for international research on cultural exchanges between the East and the West.

Suzhou printmaking primarily utilizes wooden boards and relief plates to print outline lines, often accompanied by a lightly colored ink plate to depict shadows and other details. The colors are frequently applied directly with a brush using the hand coloring method. In the later stages of Suzhou printmaking, the size of the works even exceeded one meter, growing increasingly large. Some were single pieces, while others consisted of two pieces that could be joined together. For instance, in the painting "The Changmen Gate of Gusu," a vast scene was divided into two parts, each capable of functioning as a complete picture when separated. The European-style Suzhou printmaking, spanning from the Yongzheng to Qianlong period, showcased the flourishing society, culture, and commerce in Suzhou, as well as the people's fascination with Western painting. This unique style of expression in popular printmaking at the time contributed to a stable and prosperous society, a growing freedom in artistic expression, and a heightened aesthetic appreciation among the public.

From the perspective of regional characteristics, there is a significant time gap between Chinese and Western printmaking, with the latter emerging more than 700 years after the former. However, this delay has not affected the original interpretation of printmaking works, as their mass appeal and popular nature determine their uniqueness. While the comparison of works reveals different appearances, they also incorporate and integrate local cultural characteristics, showcasing an inherent trait. In terms of creative objects, both Chinese and Western printmaking were influenced by the social background and the needs of the common people, characterized by spontaneity and amateurism. The production methods for both involved woodblock engraving, followed by printing and publishing, showcasing strong handmade craftsmanship and simplicity. In terms of genre, both types of printmaking focused on the lives and social conditions of the lower classes, demonstrating popularity and universality. From this, it can be concluded that popular printmaking in both the East and the West reflects the primary characteristics of popular art in their works. They integrate the primary characteristics of the people into printmaking creation, imbuing it with historical significance and collectible value.

From the 17th century AD, printmaking began to symbolize urban populations' taste and identity. For a long time, watermark woodcut has been an important medium in Chinese printmaking, showcasing its unique style and form in different historical periods. Suzhou printmaking, including Taohuawu woodblock New Year paintings, was significantly influenced by Western copperplate prints from the 17th to 18th centuries, giving rise to special content and form over the following 100 years. However, these works are seldom encountered today. On one hand, the rapid changes in the content of New Year paintings led to their inadequate preservation. On the other hand, Chinese literati at that time considered New Year paintings as folk customs and did not give them much attention, resulting in a lack of understanding of this area today.

3. Conclusion

This article provides a comprehensive overview of the materials used in popular printmaking in both the East and the West, including folk stories, legends, folk printmaking, satirical comics, and more. It offers a detailed history, showcases notable works, and provides explanations to better understand the art form. Throughout history, printmaking has played a significant role in disseminating images, starting with the invention of woodblock printing by the Chinese in the 7th century AD. Countless images created through reproduction have been widely spread and preserved as books or images. These images cover a diverse range of subjects, from religious, historical, and political themes to everyday life and the activities of the common people, reflecting the broad appeal and popularity of printed artwork. From the perspective of Suzhou printmaking, it becomes apparent that popular printmaking works from both China and the West possess distinct regional and local characteristics. They share inherent similarities in terms of subject matter selection, expressive content, and technique style to varying degrees. I refer to this convergence as the concept of "originality" discussed in this article.

While most of the public prints we currently observe come from overseas collections, they offer a glimpse into the historical style of that era. It's worth considering whether the influence of Western painting styles in the late Ming and early Qing dynasties not only impacted the artistic forms of Chinese court and folk painters at that time, but also potentially influenced the visual perception habits and needs of the Chinese people. For instance, the emergence of painters deeply influenced by Western painting under the tutelage of foreign painters appointed by the court, such as Leng Mei, Shen Yuan, Tang Dai, and Qiu Ying, could reflect this influence. Similarly, many folk painters, including Ding Yunpeng, Wu Tingyu, and Chen Hongshou, were also influenced by Western painting. They incorporated Western painting concepts and methods into their visual painting languages, which consequently affected the aesthetic perspective and appreciation interests of the people.

The profound influence of Western copperplate painting on Chinese printmaking reveals that Chinese painters studied and absorbed Western painting methods during the late Ming and early Qing dynasties, integrating them with the artistic forms of Chinese painting. The extensive and deep communication between these two traditions over an extended period of time exceeded our expectations. By analyzing this, we can explore the original and historical value behind the developmental trajectory of popular printmaking art. This understanding can then be incorporated into contemporary printmaking creation, contributing to the advancement of the printmaking industry.

References

1. Hui Ma.(2023).The Pre-emergence of Chinese Wood Block Printing—Based on Propagation Medium and Social Transition.Media and Communication Research,4: 040801-.DOI: 10.23977/MEDIACR.2023.040801.
2. zur Nieden Gesa Over Berthold.(2023).Walsh in Europe and Beyond: Dissemination and Reception of English Music Prints in the 18th Century.Eighteenth Century Music,20:229-233. DOI: 10.1017/S1478570623000210.
3. Zhuzhi Liu,Hushinaidi Bin Abdul Hamid Ke Fu.(2023).The development of China Sichuan folk woodcut motifs using reduction cutting print.Art and Performance Letters,4: 040805. DOI: 10.23977/ARTPL.2023.040805.
4. Khoo Flora.(2023).Prints of a New Kind: Political Caricature in The United States, 1789–1828.American Journalism,40:384-386. DOI: 10.1080/08821127.2023.2228662.
5. Sooyun Sohn.(2023).The Influence of Dutch Genre Painting in Emblematic Prints: Jan Luyken'sDes Menschen, Begin, Midden en Einde(1712).Humanities,12: H12020026. DOI: 10.3390/H12020026.
6. Jiongming Xie.(2023).A Review of Chinese Wood Engraving Research.Art and Design,6: 2023.62011. DOI: 10.31058/J.AD.2023.62011.
7. Mazzotti Angelo Alessandro Ilchmann Achim.(2023).A Method for Recognising Oval Forms: The Case Study of a Copperplate Engraving of the Bibliotheca Wolfenbüttel 1705/23.Nexus Network Journal,25:685-712. DOI：10.1007/S00004-023-00653-Z.
8. Henderson Felicity.(2023).Engraving Accuracy in Early Modern England: Visual Communication and the Royal Society.The Seventeenth Century,38:181-182. DOI: 10.1080/0268117X.2022.2116200

Exploring the reasons for the rise and fall of Taoism from the perspective of historical development: taking several key periods as examples

Juncheng Ding[a], Xin Luo*

The Masters School 49 Clinton Avenue, Dobbs Ferry, New York;[2]Zhejiang University 866 Yuhangtang Rd, Hangzhou 310058, P.R. China

Abstract: The paper delves into the historical development of Taoism, analyzing its rise and fall across various Chinese dynasties. It begins with the Eastern Han dynasty, emphasizing Zhang Ling's role in establishing Taoism as a significant religious force. The paper highlights the strategic expansion of Taoist influence under Zhang Lu in Sichuan. During the South North Dynasty, the focus shifts to Tao Hongjing's efforts in integrating Taoist, Buddhist, and Confucian ideas, thereby creating a comprehensive deity system. The contributions of Ge Hong, especially in alchemy and the concept of 'inner alchemy', are noted in the context of the Danding School. The peak of ancient Taoism is traced back to the Song and Yuan dynasties, underscoring the pivotal support of emperors and the roles of figures like Zhang Zhengsui and Zhang Jixian in promoting Taoism. However, the Ming and Qing dynasties saw Taoism's decline due to the suppression of religious practices and its reduction to a mere cultural aspect for the royal family and aristocracy. The paper concludes by proposing a future path for Taoism, emphasizing the need for adaptation to modern society. It suggests that Taoism should lower barriers to entry and increase its relevance to contemporary life, learning from other religions like Christianity, to sustain its growth and significance in the modern era.

1. Introduction

1.1. East Han: Origin of Taoism

Taoism is an early folk religion native to China. Originating from Taoist thought during the Spring and Fall, and Warring States periods, the overall teachings and concepts revolve around the Huang Lao doctrine, the religion is based on Lao Tzu's Five Thousand Texts of Lao Tzu. The birth of Taoism as a religion was in the Eastern Han Dynasty, with the earliest Taiping Dao and Wudou Mi Dao as the mainstream. After the failure of the Yellow Turban Uprising, Taiping Dao immediately dispersed, giving the dominance of Taoism to Wudou Midao.

The founder of Wudou Midao, Zhang Ling, his appearance determined the rise of Taoism in the Eastern Han Dynasty, and Zhang Ling, who originally lived in Beizhu Mountain, moved to Yunjin Mountain in Jiangxi Province to escape the imperial court's edict, and later changed the mountain's name to Longhu Mountain. At that time, in order refine the elixir of immortality, Zhang Ling's funds soon bottomed out. In search of an income source, he traveled to modern-day Szechuan because he heard that the people in the Bashu area were "simple and pure, easy to educate". Zhang Ling wanted to both accumulate wealth and educate the local residents at the same time. Zhang Ling, invented Fushui to earn money Fushui is a magical method used to cure diseases, he earned a sum of money through this method. Zhang Ling himself did not ask for a fee, but the local residents insisted on giving something, so Zhang Ling had to compromise and let the village give rice, thus having the saying of Wudou Mi Dao (five stones of rice).

"Teacher Zhang Ling righteously refused money and only collected five bags of rice, which made the villagers admire him. It is only like this he is worthy of being a high-ranking person". [5]

In the first year of Emperor Heng's life in the Eastern Han Dynasty (155), Zhang Ling was named "Zhengyi Shi" (Heavenly Master) on that day, and his name was changed to Zhang Daoling. Zhang Daoling confirmed the religious position of Taoism before his ascension to the heavens, and Taoism has been Taoism since then. As a religious leader, Zhang Daoling determined several religious characteristics of Taoism, the ultimate concern for life, what to do after death, the guidance of religious classics, and the practice methods and rituals.

The Heavenly Master after Zhang Daoling is his son Zhang Heng, Zhang Heng as a cultivator can be ranked as supreme, but as of performing Heavenly Master duties, Zhang Heng is far less capable than his father or even his own son, Zhang Lu, in terms of leading the Zhengyi forces. At that time, Sichuan was divided into two regimes, one in Xichuan, led by Liu Zhang, who was then the pastor of Yizhou. The other is in Dongchuan, which is led by Zhang Lu, the leading Hanning Taishou. Zhang Lu

[a]juncheng.ding@mastersny.org; *786051162@qq.com

differs from his predecessors in that he has extraordinary political talent. Zhang Lu immediately attacked Liu Zhang after Liu Zhang killed his mother and brother. After fighting several battles, Zhang Lu's forces gradually grew stronger, but he was unwilling to be bound by the title of Hanning and wanted to claim the title of king himself, and after the failed political coup, since then fell into the bottom of his life.[3]

Zhang Lu is actually quite unique in political management. His administrative jurisdiction was all under the control of the Tianshidao's "Jijiu" and "Dajijiu". Individual areas were all made religious by Tianshi Dao, and Zhang Lu perfected the original organization on the basis of the original religion and added his own innovations. Zhang Lu was eventually captured by Cao Cao, and the Tianshi Dao slowly declined from its peak at that time with Zhang Lu's decline. Although Zhang Lu did not amount to great success at the end of his life, he created the only theocratic regime in Chinese history, and he was the only one.[7]

During the Eastern Han Dynasty, the initial development of Tianshi Dao was sluggish, but in Zhang Lu's hands, because of his political talent, he was able to expand the influence of Tianshi Dao in Sichuan. At the end of the Eastern Han Dynasty, the imperial family's attitude towards Taoism changed from indifference to disgust. Mainly after starting from Emperor Xian of Han, due to the revolt of the Yellow Turban Army, the emperor had to make a move, which lead to great chaos in the world and created a lot of problems for the rise of Taoism. Considering the ruler's attitudes of different rulers, Cao Cao was superior to the Han emperor. Cao Cao used the Mandate of Heaven to get the princes to control Zhang Lu in his own hands. The Heavenly Master is in his hands, and the Heavenly Master Dao has to listen to him. Even though this meant the end for Zhang Lu, still, Cao Cao's operation also preserved the bloodline of Wudou Mi Dao and continued it.

2. South North Dynasty: The reformation of Taoism

During the South North Dynasty, it was a time of chaos and instability. After the development of the four dynasties of "Song, Qi, Liang, and Chen", Taoist talents are also emerging in this era, "If Zhang Daoling started Taoism, then the work of perfection was finally completed by Ge Hong, Tao Hongjing, Lu Xiujing and other later magi during the two Jin and Northern Dynasties."[5] At the same time, Buddhism from the West also planted roots in Chinese soil.

In the Wei and Jin dynasties, this was an extremely turbulent era. Since the decline of the Heavenly Master Dao led by Zhang Lu, various sects have also competed within Taoism. The talents of the Shangqing faction were born one after another. Among them, Tao Hongjing of the Shangqing Dynasty was a prodigy of centuries. With Buddhism from the west and stepping into the Central Plains, Tao Hongjing realized what Taoism lacks [2]. Taoism has not had a complete system of deities since Zhang Daoling founded Taoism. As a religion, Buddhism, with its regular deity system, is easier to spread among the populace, and at the same time, the ultimate concern for life, was something Taoism has not yet discovered. Taking Buddhism as an example, after death, people will fall into the six reincarnations, and the goodness in this life will be used as a blessing in the next life. This ultimate understanding and interpretation of life is the root of religious attraction, but Taoism at this time is like a pile of sand. Starting from the immortal system, Tao Hongjing spent 40 years compiling the "True Spirit Position Karma Map", a masterpiece that integrates all the deities of Taoism. From the moment this book was published, it received support from the government, basically, everyone in the country had a copy of the "True Spirit Position Karma Map", although Taoism had its own immortal system, but it was still more or worse than Buddhism at that time. However, Tao Hongjing's contribution to the cause of Taoism goes far beyond this "True Spirit Karma Map". He also brought reforms to the new Taoist theory, and the originally unrelated Confucianism, Buddhist thoughts and Taoism were synthesized into the new Taoist theory under Tao Hongjing. He pioneered "dual practice of Buddhism and Taoism" and "integration of three teachings". These actions made the already famous Shangqing faction leap to become the same rank as the Taoist leading faction as Tianshi Dao. These theories also contributed to the pluralism of Taoism. However, there is not only Tao Hongjing who has powerful Taoist priests in the Southern and Northern Dynasties, and there is a rising sect in the Jiangnan region, the Danding School. And there is also a powerful faction in the Danding faction, that is, the grandson of the founder Ge Xuan, "Bao Puzi" Ge Hong.

Ge Hong, as a person who can be ranked high in history, he is naturally extraordinary. He inadvertently invented gunpowder while refining alchemical ingredients, but it wasn't his greatest achievement. His contribution to alchemy was unprecedented. Before Ge Hong, all the alchemy techniques were all "outer dan", and many Taoist priests were obsessed with practicing "outer dan" to dissolve and ascend to the heavens, but later many Taoist priests learned to practice "outer dan" and caused countless deaths. Ge Hong used the technique of refining "Outer Dan" to develop a method of refining "Inner dan", which retained as Taoism's status as a formal religion, and "Inner dan" cultivation has since become the foundation of life cultivation, and since then all sects have used "Inner dan" as the cornerstone. In addition to the "Inner dan" cultivation, Ge Hong also has a book "Bao Puzi". In this book, Ge Hong put forward a supreme idea that made Taoism famous.[9]

In the book, Ge Hong loudly shouts out the most forceful sentence in Taoism: ----- 'My life is in my hands, not the gods, and I will become god and last for billions of years! [5]

This sentence solemnly expounds Taoism's claim on the ultimate care of life. The main factor in the existence of a religion is what people can get from that religion. Christianity is going to heaven, Buddhism is becoming a Buddha, or escaping into the six reincarnations. The "benefits" of these religions to people are virtually unverifiable, and they all exist in the afterlife. However, this is the charm of Taoism, as long as you can strictly follow the Taoist cultivation method, you do not worry about what happens after death, because you will not die at all.

In addition to the above magi who have made unrivaled contributions to the basic development of Taoism, there are also legendary figures who have made the Tianshi Dao reach the peak again, that is, the Heavenly Master who is not surnamed Zhang, Kou Qianzhi. Kou Qianzhi was born into a famous nobleman. When he was young, he met a man, Cheng Gongxing, who took Kou Qianzhi into the being a Taoist, and because of a mistake, Kou Qianzhi missed the opportunity to become immortal. After Kou Qian descended the mountain, he began to build his own Northern Tianshi Dao. Kou Qianzhi was aware of the status of Taoism in the Northern Wei Dynasty at that time, so he brought himself closer to the emperor through Cui Hao, a dignitary, thus achieving his goal of being the "master of the emperor". Through the battles of Emperor Taiwu of Wei sending troops to attack Daxia, directly bringing the Tianshi Dao to its peak, Emperor Taiwu of Wei also made Taoism the state religion.

In year 440, officially change the name of the Dynasty to Taiping Zhengjun, officially announced Taoism as the national religion " [1]

Kou Qianzhi even promoted the world-shaking Buddha extermination event at that time, and under the influence of Cui Hao and Kou Qianzhi, Emperor Taiwu of Wei decided to launch a Buddhist extermination. But Buddhism itself has a unshirkable responsibility for this incident. Because the Buddhists built temples on a large scale and spent too much money, the emperors at that time were thrown into poor status due to this excessive use of wealth. The problem of having a high degree of merit led to the eradication of Buddhism.

3. Song, Yuan Dynasties: The peak of ancient Taoism

After the Southern and Northern Dynasties, the Taoist system and religious components have been perfected, like most things in the world, once stable, it is the beginning of prosperity. The status of Taoism during the Song Dynasty began with Song Zhenzong in the Northern Song Dynasty, and its status became higher and higher, and the peak of Taoism was under the rule of the Yuan Dynasty.

Since Chen's reign, the status of Taoism in the Song Dynasty has become even higher. The emperor at that time, Song Zhenzong, had the advantage in the struggle against the Liao state, but he himself was too cowardly. So, a peace treaty was signed with the Liao State. After the "Alliance of the Yuan", Song Zhenzong used religion to justify himself, the most convenient being Taoism. He made a big speech, which was concise and clear, that is, the heavenly immortals sent the heavenly book to Song Zhenzong, saying that the current suffering is temporary, and if you continue to make efforts, the bright future can be expected. Song Zhenzong used this set of rhetoric to improve his people's morale, but when it came to the origin of this immortal, it was related to the Heavenly Master Dao, which also had to do with Zhang Zhengsui, the current Heavenly Master, who revitalized the Tianshi Dao in the Song Dynasty. It is said that this immortal was originally the ancestor of the Zhao family, named Zhao Xuanlang, but he was also one of the suns that was shot down by Houyi, and then he folowed Zhang Daoling and became a Dan furnace. As soon as this news appeared, Zhang Zhengsui was distressed for a long time, and then he eventually went down the mountain to resolve this issue. Zhang Zhengsui also cleverly used the story of Song Zhenzong to hold conferences around the country, so that everyone had admiration for Taoism. At that time, the admiration for Taoism had a heavy atmosphere, allowing Tianshi Dao to directly ascend to the top. After the death of Emperor Zhenzong of Song, the status of Tianshi Dao in the Song Dynasty still maintained its peak, and several generations of Heavenly Masters were given the honorific title of "Sir" by the emperor. Especially Song Huizong, the emperor had a unique love for Taoism. At that time, the Heavenly Master, Zhang Jixian Master, could be said to be the Heavenly Master who was summoned by the emperor the most times in history. Because of Song Huizong's love, Zhang Jixiani also continued the good tradition of being named "Sir" and was named "Mr. Void Jing". However, it was also because of this love that when the Jin soldiers invaded, the Northern Song Dynasty was caught off guard, and Song Huizong also handed over military power to an unknown Taoist priest. Later, the Song army suffered heavy casualties, and Song Huizong was also captured.[10]

The status of Taoism in the Northern Song Dynasty remained on the rise until the Northern Song Dynasty was expelled to the south by the Jin State.[6] During the Southern Song Dynasty, Taoism was actually in a lukewarm state, but there were also active Taoist advocates. At that time, the Heavenly Master was already the 35th generation Zhang Ke Great Heavenly Master, and although his position in history was not very important, he promoted the development of Northern Taoism. The Mongols realized the power of religion during their own conquests to the West. Having seen the religious attitude of Westerners, the Mongols also wanted to master this power. So Kublai Khan sent a Wang Yiqing Taoist to the south to communicate with Zhang Tianshi. Finally, when the Yuan army finally defeated the Song Dynasty, the true spring of Tianshi Dao came.

The original Fuqi school had three major sects, the Tianshi Dao of Longhu Mountain, the Shangqing Sect of Maoshan, and the Lingbao Sect of Gezao Mountain. Originally, the other two mountains pressed the Tianshi Dao so much it could not develop, but since the Song Dynasty, the Tianshi Dao has slowly developed its advantages, and by the Yuan Dynasty, the Tianshi Dao directly dominated the three sects. In the middle of the Yuan Dynasty, the Fuqi faction slowly merged into one to form a huge faction, "Zhengyi". At the same time, in the far north, the Quanzhen sect founded by Wang Chongyang gradually gained fame.[8]

Wang Chongyang originally lived in the tomb of the living dead at the foot of the Junan Mountain, and in 1163, Wang Chongyang left the place for the Shandong

Peninsula. In Shandong, Wang Chongyang made a name for Quanzhen, and there were seven more disciples under him, later known as the "Seven Sons of Quanzhen", and the most famous of them was Mr. Qiu Shuji. In 1219, Qiu Zhiji led 18 disciples to embark on a two-year long march of more than 20,000 kilometers at the invitation of Genghis Khan. The relationship between Qiu Zhiji and Genghis Khan became closer and closer, and even Qiu Zhiji's title changed directly from "Sir" to "Qiu Shenxian". Genghis Khan finally gave Quanzhen several benefits, was exempted from all taxes, and ordered Qiu Shuji to take charge of all the monks in the world. Returning to Quanzhen's Ancestor Wang Chongyang, Wang Chongyang realized that today's Taoist theory was deeply flawed, so he extracted many elements from Buddhism and Confucianism. Zhang Tianshi's family made great contributions to the Yuan Dynasty, but only the Heavenly Master was named a "Zhenren", and Wang Chongyang received much better treatment in comparison, each of the seven sons of Quanzhen was a Zhenren, and Wang Chongyang was named a "Zhenjun". The Yuan Dynasty began to make a effect on the status of Quanzhen, but after the debate between Buddhist and Dao, the Quanzhen Dao was short-lived. The Quanzhen Dao collapsed after that, but the Quanzhen Taoists did not stop there, and they seized more than 480 Buddhist temples. Kublai Khan could not let Quanzhen go unchecked like this, so the status of Taoism in the hearts of the Yuan royal family plummeted. However, the popularity of Tianshi Dao was not affected in the slightest, and under the 90-year rule of the Yuan Dynasty, after Zhang Lu, the dream of Tianshi Dao revitalizing was also achieved. Since the Yuan Dynasty, the title of Heavenly Master is not only a title, but for the first time in history, the Master's position has had substantial political significance. South of the Yangtze River, all disputes over Taoist affairs had to go through Zhang Tianshi first, and he was regarded as a first-class official. In the late Yuan Dynasty, the power of the Zhengyi faction reached its peak in history. The Zhengyi faction, which included many sects, also became a hegemon in the Jiangnan region. It basically perfectly reproduces the scene of Zhang Lu back then, Zhengyi sect is now as bright as the midday sun.[11]

4. Ming, Qing Dynasties: From peak to downfall

Taoism during the Ming Dynasty was not actually the prosperous era that Taoists expected. Under Zhu Yuanzhang's rule, having seen the power of religious terror, he decided to suppress all religions in his territory, especially Taoism. All Taoist priests, were forced to live in Taoist temples, a move that undoubtedly cut off the financial resources of most Zhengyi Taoists, and the government also controlled the number of Taoist priests, and people under a certain age were not allowed to become monks. On the surface, Zhu Yuanzhang instructed the Heavenly Master to take charge of all the Taoists in the world, but he himself set up a special judicial department, the Daolusi Division, which was the hand in charge departments of the all Daoists in the world. Even the law is extremely harsh for the Taoists

But in the Ming Dynasty, Taoism still played a role in history, that is, the forty-third generation of Heavenly Master, Zhang Yuchu Heavenly Master. He compiled many famous Taoist classics, such as the Ten Rules of Daomen, and he also led the compilation of the famous Orthodox Daozang. This book contains many aspects of Taoism, from ideas and history to magic and alchemy. This book is no less important in the history of Taoism than Lao Tzu's Tao Te Ching. And bad luck will not haunt the Heavenly Master all the time. During the Yongle period, after Zhu Di took the throne, Mr. Zhang Yuchu won the favor of this imperial master, but he also shouldered a heavy task, that is, to find Emperor Jianwen. At the same time, Zhu Di also asked Zhang Yuchu to find Zhang Sanfeng. Zhang Sanfeng made a name for himself in the Ming Dynasty with his own no-end style. Zhang Sanfeng's ability is world-famous in the country, and even the hot-tempered Zhu Di is very tolerant of him. At that time, Zhang Sanfeng made a prophecy that Wudang Mountain would one day prosper, and Zhu Di also fulfilled this prophecy and pulled hundreds of thousands of people to build the Wudang Taoist Temple. Zhang Yuchu and Zhang Sanfeng's temper, personality, and behavior are unrelated, but they have a perfect fit for each other. Zhang Yuchu is the face of Taoism, the image of facing everyone, and Zhang Sanfeng is the image of a hermit. This is why the two seem to be at odds, but they actually complement each other. It is a pity that Taoism has not had such a powerful talent since these two.[12]

In 1647, the Qing army had already conquered the Central Plains, and the last trace of the Ming Dynasty was extinguished with the Chongzhen Emperor. Also, a foreign invasion, the Manchus did not care about Taoism at all. The Yuan Dynasty was the peak of Taoism, when there were talents such as Wang Chongyang and Quanzhen Qizi, and after the Ming Dynasty, only Zhang Yuchu and Zhang Sanfeng took the shot, and in the Qing Dynasty, it was a state of rest. There is no breakthrough in doctrinal theory, only a slight modification, fried cold rice, but everything has a turnaround. When the foundation of the Great Qing was laid, the emperor found that Taoism was not as weak as he thought, and the foundation of the Great Qing was not as strong as he imagined, so he used the old routine and recruited the Heavenly Master to the dynasty. Giving the Heavenly Master official position, thinking about continuing to control them. The Qing dynasty's attitude towards Taoism has always been disrespectful. In the previous dynasties, the object of respect of various emperors in Taoism was even if they did not like it. In the Qing Dynasty, Jing slowly became "use", and finally reduced to "play". Although the Qianlong Emperor finally raised the position of Heavenly Master to the third grade, the glory of Taoism was gone.

5. Conclusion: Use historical experiences to brace for future

Taoism has also experienced great ups and downs throughout history. In the Eastern Han Dynasty, Taoism was just beginning to emerge, and it was all operated by Zhang Daoling and Zhang Lu, laying the foundation, and the Wudou Mi Dao has since made a name for itself in the Central Plains. During the Southern and Northern Dynasties, the improvement of Taoism and subsequent sects and reforms also appeared. Tao Hongjing and other Daoist priests of the Shangqing school have made great contributions, and the Taoist immortal system genealogy "True Spirit Position Karma Map" compiled by Tao Hongjing himself provides a standardized worship goal for the common people, and Buddhism from the west has also caused certain harm to the development of Taoism. With the passage of time, Taoism also ushered in its peak, and Taoism, which laid the foundation in the Song Dynasty, was released in the Yuan Dynasty. Zhang Zhengsui and Zhang Jixian and others contributed to the Heavenly Master Dao more than to have a good relationship with the royal family. Taoism has always been a religion that relied heavily on rulers, and it was these two heavenly masters that kept Taoism in a high position in the eyes of the rulers of the Song Dynasty. In the Yuan Dynasty, these Mongol invaders also realized the power of religion, so they also chose to promote Taoism to implement religious rule. This is also the first time that the name Zhengyi has appeared in history. Taoism in the late Yuan Dynasty reached its historical peak. In the Ming Dynasty, the importance of Taoism slowly declined, and after Zhang Yuchu and Zhang Sanfeng, there were no Taoist talents. During the Qing Dynasty, Taoism also became the plaything of the royal family and aristocracy, and since then Taoism has been in decline.

Throughout the history of Taoism for 2,000 years, there is a constant law, that is, the rise and fall of Taoism largely depends not on its own ability, but on the attitude of the ruler. From the favor of Emperor Taiwu of Wei to the snub of Yongzheng, the journey of Taoism has never been in his own hands, which is also a major weakness of Taoism. Because the teachings and concepts of Taoism have not changed drastically in 2,000 years, they have only been applied to a small number of people since ancient times, which is why it is difficult for Taoism to continue to flourish. If Taoism wants to flourish in the future, it must develop new religious methods, reduce the requirements for belief, and not demand too much feedback from believers. For example, in Buddhism, Buddhists only need to live a clean life to have a good fate in the next life, but Taoism has extremely high requirements for the ultimate care of life (ascending to immortals) and requires hard practice, and Taoism is much worse at this level. If the threshold for ascension can be lowered and feedback can be given more timely, perhaps the number of believers will also increase. In order to escape the fate of being controlled by the rulers, Taoism also needs to spread its popularity, learn Christianity, hold weekend classes or summer camps, winter camps, etc. Enhance the presence of Taoism among the general public, because the government of the current economy will no longer promote a religion for its own liking, like the previous rulers. But Taoism has more room to develop in the future than other existing religions.

Taoist culture is not about material or fame, it is about the true values in life, respect, and the great Dao is enough" [4]

From this point of view, the concept of Taoism will be more in line with the concept of contemporary people, after the founding of the People's Republic of China, the development and future continuation of Taoism need to test their own ability. Second, in accordance with the Taoist culture's principle of "knowing the common and tolerant," they should be good at learning the strengths of other families, including learning from the successful experience of Western studies on Taoist culture, so as to constantly enrich themselves; at the same time, in order to meet the needs of modern social life, they should also interpret the main Taoist classics and catechism as much as possible in line with the spirit of modernization, so that Taoist culture can be understood and accepted by more people.

References

1. Chen Zhiwei. (2009). A Study on the Development of Taoism During the Northern Dynasties. Huaxia Culture Forum (1), 8.
2. Lin Guoni. (2013). Research on the Compilation of Taoist History During the Sui, Tang, and Song Dynasties. Journal of Jishou University (Social Sciences Edition), 34(4), 108-113.
3. Liu Lin. (1981). On the Transformation and Development of Taoism During the Eastern Jin and Northern and Southern Dynasties. Historical Research (5), 21.
4. Qing Xitai. (2001). Preliminary Discussion on the Development of Taoist Culture in the 21st Century. Religious Studies (4), 4.
5. Yin Mengfei. (2007). A Comprehensive Reading of Taoist History. Shaanxi Normal University Press.
6. Zhu Yunpeng. (2000). A Discussion on the Development of Taoism in the Northern Song Dynasty. China Taoism (4), 4.
7. Britannica, T. Editors of Encyclopaedia. "Wang Che." Encyclopedia Britannica, January 1, 2022. https://www.britannica.com/biography/Wang-Che.
8. Owusu-Addo A, Yao D W J. Visualising the Historical Development and Belief System of Taoism[J]. Scholars Journal of Science and Technology, 2022, 3(1): 491-502.
9. Wang Y. The rise and fall of imperial China: The social origins of state development[M]. Princeton University Press, 2022.
10. Li X, Hou W, Liu M, et al. Traditional thoughts and modern development of the historical urban landscape in China: Lessons learned from the example of Pingyao historical city[J]. Land, 2022, 11(2): 247.
11. Yu G, Gan H, Guo Y. Location and Fortune: An Exploration of the Buddhism and Daoism Roles of Geomancy in the Song Dynasty[J]. Religions, 2023, 14(7): 859.

12. Lu P, Zhang Z, Liu C, et al. Unification conditions of human civilization patterns: based on multi-agent modeling of early Chinese history (770 BC to 476 BC) [J]. Archaeological and Anthropological Sciences, 2022, 14(10): 205.

Research on the Construction of Cultural Parks in the Jing-Jin-Ji Region Based on Foreign Models: A Study on the Development of Ice and Snow Tourism Routes

Jingyi Wang[1,a], Yueyu Wang[1,b], Jie Xiang[2,c], Kejin Liu[3*]

[1]Cultural Industry Management in the Business School of Beijing Institute of Fashion Technology, Beijing, China
[2]Accounting at the Business School of Beijing Institute of Fashion Technology, Beijing, China
[3]Assistant Professor of Cultural Industry Management in the Business School of Beijing Institute of Fashion Technology, Beijing, China

Abstracts: National cultural park is an innovative initiative for the protection and development of natural and cultural heritage resources in the new era, reflecting the core strategy of cultural heritage protection and development of representative cultural resources. It is not only an important carrier for the protection of natural and cultural heritage, but also a new model for promoting the development of cultural industry. Based on their own national conditions and experiences, countries have developed distinctive national park management models, including the native recreation value orientation of the United States, the sustainable club economy of Europe, the public supremacy of private ownership of land in the United Kingdom, and the synergistic community-neighborhood development of developing countries in Asia and Africa. In view of the heritage resources brought by the Beijing Winter Olympics, this study explores the idea of ice and snow tourism routes centered on Beijing, Yanqing and Zhangjiakou, and proposes the principles of sustainable development, mutual benefit and symbiosis, and public supremacy, which is committed to constructing a development model integrating culture, tourism and ecology.

1. Introduction

In the context of the 21st century, national cultural parks have become one of the programs emphasized and promoted worldwide. Each country has its own unique national park management model, which not only protects natural and cultural resources, but also promotes social development and tourism prosperity. This paper will explore different national cultural park management modes including the United States, Europe, the United Kingdom, as well as Asia and Africa, etc. By comprehensively analyzing the park management practices in foreign countries, it explores the feasibility of constructing a snow and ice tourism route with Beijing, Yanqing and Zhangjiakou as the core.

2. Research Background

As an innovative initiative for the protection and development of natural and cultural heritage resources in the new era, the national cultural park is not only an important carrier for the protection of natural and cultural heritage, but also a new type of cultural industry development model. In recent years, the government of China has attached great importance to the construction of national cultural parks.In July 2019, the consideration and adoption of the Program for the Construction of National Cultural Parks of the Great Wall, the Long March, and the Grand Canal marked the entry of the construction of national cultural parks into a substantial stage [1].These policies not only clarify the management mechanism and spatial layout of the national cultural parks, but also emphasize the key tasks in the areas of protection and inheritance, research and excavation, improvement of environmental support services and facilities, as well as cultural and tourism integration. In foreign countries, it is also common to pay attention to cultural heritage and park construction, and these successful cases provide valuable experience for the construction of national cultural parks in China.

3. Second, the typical characteristics of foreign national park management mode

3.1 Native recreation value orientation: the American wilderness idea guides the top-down management model

The U.S. national park model is based on the idea of "saving natural resources from being damaged by human activities for the sake of national interests", so the U.S. national parks adopt the wilderness path, i.e., the segregation of nature and society. Its large tracts of pristine wilderness have unique recreational potential, which

[a]973216853@qq.com; [b]2257592463@qq.com; [c]xiangj0111@163.com; [*]20190030@bift.edu.cn

makes the U.S. take the original ecological recreation as the value orientation. In order to protect the wilderness landscape, the U.S. has established the form of national parks, which are managed from the top down and isolate nature from society to provide recreational opportunities for the public[2].

For example, the Yellowstone National Park in the United States has a full-time Resource Operations Coordinator for resource operations, as well as employees, volunteers, partners, and foundations who serve as "guardians" to ensure the smooth operation of the park. The U.S. National Park Service has embodied the recreational and educational value of its wilderness through the management of the largest area of wilderness, while ensuring that the wilderness is accessible to visitors.

3.2 Economic Sustainability: The Tourism Economic Model of Cultural and Political Integration in Europe

In the construction of European national parks, the model of cultural and political integration has successfully combined natural protection with cultural heritage protection, providing tourists with rich cultural experiences while also protecting the natural ecological environment inside the park. Secondly, in the process of cultural park construction, emphasis is placed on the organic combination of culture and natural environment. Drawing on the experience of European cultural park construction, China can strengthen multi-party cooperation in park management structure. Similar to Europe, the construction of domestic cultural parks also requires the joint participation of the government, local communities, businesses, and stakeholders. This multi-party management model can effectively formulate policies that are conducive to the sustainable development of cultural parks and provide technical support for park ecological protection.

Most of the national parks in Europe tend to learn from the American model, and implement more strict protection. In the construction of national parks in Europe, the park management structure has taken a series of measures to protect the natural environment and cultural heritage in the parks, and at the same time, local communities, enterprises and stakeholders are also involved in the management. Multi-party management not only formulates good policies for national cultural parks, but also provides technical support for their ecological protection.

The French National Park of the Cévennes is a typical example, where the park's management organization works closely with local communities to develop cultural activities and protect cultural heritage. Thus, most national parks in Europe develop models of cultural and political integration that successfully combine nature conservation with sustainable development[3].

In terms of economic sustainability, the construction of domestic cultural parks can learn from the European model and actively develop the cultural tourism industry. In the construction of European national parks, cultural activities and the protection of cultural heritage have promoted the development of local tourism, bringing considerable economic benefits to the local economy. Therefore, in the construction of cultural parks, China can focus on the development of cultural tourism resources, promote the development of related industries, improve the level of local economic development, and achieve the economic sustainability of cultural parks.

3.3 Private land ownership and public primacy: a conservation model for rural residential landscape ecology in the UK

The construction model of national cultural parks in the UK emphasizes the importance of the entertainment dimension in cultural and tourism development. Compared to other European countries, most of the national parks in the UK are located in the suburbs of cities, corresponding to the fifth category protected areas of the International Union for Conservation of Nature (IUCN). This layout makes it easier for the park to approach densely populated areas, making it convenient for tourists to visit and explore. In the development goals of parks, entertainment factors are given top priority, emphasizing the provision of rich and colorful tourist experiences, attracting tourists, and promoting the development of local tourism industry. The construction model of national cultural parks in the UK emphasizes private ownership of land and ecological protection. Almost all national parks in the UK are privately owned, including numerous farms and villages. Nevertheless, under the principle of private ownership of land in the UK, ecological protection remains the primary task of national park construction. This model requires close cooperation between park management agencies and private landowners to protect the natural environment and biodiversity within the park, ensuring its sustainable development.

The UK has implemented a model different from that of other European countries, in which the recreational dimension is placed at the top of the development objectives of the national parks. Therefore, the national parks correspond to IUCN category V protected areas and are mostly located in the suburbs of cities. Almost all the land in the UK national parks is privately owned, including a large number of farms and villages. Under the principle of public ownership of private land in the UK, ecological conservation is the first priority for national parks[4].

The Loch Lomond National Park Authority management model emphasizes cooperation and communication with local communities, stakeholders and visitors. The United Kingdom has adopted a unique model in the development of national cultural parks, emphasizing the principles of private land ownership and public supremacy. In addition, the management model of the Lomond Lake National Park Authority emphasizes cooperation and communication with local communities, stakeholders, and tourists. This cooperation model not only involves the management process of the park, but also includes the planning and development of the park. By collaborating with local communities and stakeholders, park management agencies can better understand local cultural traditions and development needs, and formulate development strategies that are more in line with the actual situation. Through the establishment and management of the national park system, the UK has successfully balanced economic development and ecological protection and realized the goal of sustainable development.

The unique model adopted in the construction of national cultural parks in the UK has played an important role in cultural and tourism development, providing a balance between economic development and ecological protection in the UK. This model places the entertainment dimension in the first place of the park's development goals, while emphasizing the principles of private ownership of land and public supremacy. Through cooperation and communication with local communities, stakeholders and tourists, the benign interaction between economic development and ecological protection has been achieved.

3.4 Community Neighborhood Synergistic Development: System-oriented Models in Developing Countries in Asia and Africa

Developing countries in Asia and Africa have explored different management models according to their own national conditions when establishing national park systems. For example, Vietnam's national park management model has gone through three stages: provincial administrative management, state-owned enterprise management, and parastatal enterprise management[5]. With the obvious trend of decentralized management, Vietnam has created a public-private coexistence management model for national parks, which is characterized by the following features: the government owns the land; national parks' sources of income include admission fees, franchise licenses, and taxes related to tourism income; and the government, private enterprises, and consortiums are the main management bodies.

Third, the foreign model of China's national cultural park construction inspiration and suggestions

The construction and management of national cultural parks and national parks involves a variety of organizations and strategies. National parks should not only maintain the ecological environment and natural landscape, but also take into account regional cultural heritage, education, recreation and economic development. China can learn from the United States to protect the wilderness as the core, through the maintenance of natural ecology at the same time, strengthen the excavation and inheritance of local culture, so that the cultural tourism experience and cultural education organic combination. In the construction of parks, we can learn from the European model of cultural and political integration, and incorporate the community, private enterprises and joint ventures and other stakeholders into the park management system to form a win-win cooperation pattern. With reference to the British principle of private land and public supremacy to enhance public participation, the maintenance of recreational rights, while actively encouraging the public to give feedback and suggestions on the construction of national cultural parks, to enhance the sense of participation and satisfaction of the public.

4. Beijing-Hebei Ice and Snow Cultural Tourism Route Research Envisioning and Planning

The Beijing Hebei region has abundant ice and snow resources and profound cultural heritage, with enormous potential in the ice and snow tourism market. By planning ice and snow cultural tourism routes, regional tourism resources can be further explored and integrated, promoting the deep integration of ice and snow tourism with cultural, sports and other industries, forming ice and snow cultural tourism routes with regional characteristics. Tourists can provide richer and more colorful tourism experiences, promote the coordinated development of tourism in the Beijing Hebei region, and enhance regional tourism competitiveness.

The planning and implementation of ice and snow cultural and tourism routes aims to create distinctive ice and snow tourism brands, attract more tourists to experience, promote the prosperity of the tourism market, and help promote the coordinated development of the tourism industry in the Beijing Tianjin Hebei region. The ice and snow cultural tourism route will integrate the historical, folk, and cultural elements of the two regions, providing tourists with an opportunity to deeply understand the culture of the Beijing Hebei region, which is of great significance for promoting cultural prosperity and social progress in the Beijing Tianjin Hebei region. In addition, the development of ice and snow cultural tourism routes can enhance the competitiveness of tourism in the Beijing Hebei region. Create unique ice and snow tourism products to attract more tourists to experience and increase the market share of tourism.

The comprehensive path for the construction of Beijing-Hebei Ice and Snow Culture and Tourism Route should be a "culture-tourism-ecology" trinity development model. A systematic management and operation mechanism should be formed through top-level design, legal protection, management innovation, win-win cooperation and public participation. Combining the special culture of Beijing and Zhang, we will empower ice and snow tourism from the perspectives of culture, economy, fashion, etc., to achieve sustainable development of the Winter Olympic legacy, utilize natural resources, stimulate the development of the surrounding economy, promote the synergistic development of the city and the region, and the progress of social civilization, as well as to provide tourists with richer and higher-quality tourism services.

5. Conclusion

Whether in the United States, Europe, Asia or Africa, each country has its own unique model and experience in cultural and natural heritage protection and ecological residential landscape construction, which can provide inspiration for the construction of national cultural parks in China. For example, the United States established national parks with a top-down management model; Britain has a profound historical and cultural heritage and has accumulated rich experience in the protection of cultural heritage and the restoration of historic buildings. The National Cultural Park of China can learn from its practice, dig deep and inherit the regional history and culture, and enhance the cultural value of the park; Many European countries pay attention to community participation in the protection and inheritance of cultural heritage, and encourage local residents to actively participate in the organization and promotion of cultural activities. China's national cultural park can also learn from its practice in the construction process, strengthen community participation, inherit and carry forward regional culture. Some African countries have rich experience in ecotourism development, which focuses on protecting the natural ecology and local culture, while promoting the development of tourism. In the process of construction, China's national cultural park can learn from its experience, develop ecological tourism, and realize the positive interaction between cultural heritage protection and tourism development.

With the concept and practice of national cultural parks, national cultural parks not only play a crucial role in maintaining national cultural confidence and promoting traditional culture, but also become an important platform for promoting local development and stimulating cultural innovation. Based on the reference and thinking of the series of planning of the National Culture Park, through the comprehensive integration of cultural heritage, tourism resources and ice and snow sports facilities in the region, they are connected with each other to create a comprehensive experience area integrating the Winter Olympic culture, regional characteristics and the spirit of ice and snow sports, and then promote the comprehensive upgrading of the regional tourism economy.

The "culture-tourism-ecology" trinity development model provides us with a structural idea. Under this model, the snow and ice tourism in Beijing and Hebei will be integrated into the cultural park system, forming a snow and ice industry chain with outstanding characteristics and optimized structure, taking the Olympic heritage as the core, and promoting the in-depth integration of snow and ice tourism and cultural tourism through high-standard planning, so as to provide strong support for the harmonious development of culture and nature conservation, the overall revitalization of the local economy, and the popularization of the national snow and ice sports.

Acknowledge

Source of the Project: General Project of Social Science Planning of Beijing Municipal Commission of Education "Research on Strengthening the Urban Cultural Space Construction in Beijing by Leveraging Winter Olympics Cultural Resources" (Project No.: SM202110012011).

Reference

1. Peng, J.; Xiao, H.; Wang, R.; Qi, Y. The Impacts of Establishing Pilot National Parks on Local Residents' Livelihoods and Their Coping Strategies in China: A Case Study of Qilianshan National Park. *Sustainability*2022, *14*, 3537. https://doi.org/10.3390/su14063537
2. Deng, Z. (2016) Three Principles of the Establishment of National Park System and Their Implications for China's Practice. *Open Journal of Business and Management*, 4, 401-407. doi: 10.4236/ojbm.2016.43042.
3. Barry Mackintosh, Harold Ickes and the National Park Service. Olympic National Park: Twenty Years of Controversy. *Journal of Forest History*29. No.22(Oct 2021):78-84. https://doi.org/10.2307/4004916
4. Pablo Alonso González, Alfredo Macías Vázquez. Between Planning and Heritage: Cultural Parks and National Heritage Areas. *European spatial research policy*, 2015-01-27
5. Holger Preuss, Anke Plambeck. Utilization of Olympic Stadiums: a conceptual stadium legacy framework. *International Journal of Sports Marketing and Sponsorship*, 2020-11-02

Research on the media field of tourism culture communication under the background of omnimedia

Meng Li*

Guilin University of Aerospace Technology

Abstract: Tourism culture is an intuitive presentation of local culture. Tourism culture communication is an important part of mass communication. Influenced by the subject, object and media carrier of communication, tourism culture communication has formed the characteristics of content diversification, communication fragmentation and audience differentiation. 'Mass communication ecology ' puts forward: ' From the perspective of McLuhan 's communication ecology, media ecology is the core of communication ecology. In the sense of cultural anthropology, McLuhan regards communication as a civilized phenomenon in the overall sense. He is committed to expounding the psychological and ecological characteristics of contemporary media from the cultural and historical characteristics of media. Therefore, from the perspective of communication ecology theory, studying the field of tourism culture communication media under the background of all media can construct the subject and object of tourism culture communication and analyze the influencing factors of tourism culture communication.

1.Tourism culture communication subject

1.1 The main body of communication with mass communication as the core element

In the theory of communication, the original meaning of communication is newsletter, communication, disseminate and so on, as in modern society. The most common and active mass communication activities, communication refers to the use of appropriate media by communicators, using a social activity in which information is transmitted and communicated to the recipient in a certain form. In this process of communication activities. It contains a variety of social relations, including communicators and communicators, recipients and recipients, communicators and recipients, communicators. With the media and so on, mass communication activities are actually the interaction of various social relations in communication, in which communication. The communicator, the media and the receiver are the elements that constitute a complete communication behavior (Li Ying 49)[4].

Subject communication and object communication together constitute the dissemination of tourism culture. Many scholars regard the relationship between the subject and object of communication as a binary opposition to distinguish and study, but in the era of all media, with more and more diverse communication carriers and more and more complex communication environment, in fact, it is difficult for us to distinguish the relationship between tourism culture communication and binary opposition. At present, more attention should be paid to the status of the audience. Based on the perspective of mass communication, the relationship between the subject and the object of communication should be established as the interaction between communication and acceptance.

Tourism culture reflects the regional culture, which is composed of history, geography, policy, folklore, society, economy and other factors. Robert Macintosh, an American scholar, first proposed the concept of cultural tourism. In a broad sense, he believes that as long as tourists can learn new history, tradition and contemporary life and thought from tourism, they can be regarded as cultural tourism (Liu Yang 20)[5].Tourism culture has the characteristics of inclusiveness, comprehensiveness, regionality, integrity, interactivity and experience.

At present，we should not only pay attention to the main body of tourism culture communication, but also pay attention to the main body of tourism culture communication. The subject of tourism culture communication refers to the creator, disseminator and recipient of tourism culture, which is based on the mass communication in the real social environment and the network mimicry environment. Habermas understands society as composed of life world and system (Zhi Tingrong 35)[6]. The main body communication of tourism culture is a ' social + media ' communication system that integrates tourism and cultural symbols in the life world. In the process of communication, it emphasizes the role and influence of the media on tourism culture and pays attention to the feedback of the audience.

*2021073@guat.edu.cn

1.2 The main types and characteristics of tourism culture communication

From the perspective of communication, the communication subject of tourism culture can be summarized as the vertical communication of time and the horizontal communication of space. Specifically, the horizontal communication of time can be understood as 'inheritance ', while the horizontal communication of space can be understood as 'sociality '. The core of 'inheritance ' is to emphasize the cultural inheritance of tourism culture based on the change of time and not restricted by time. The essence of 'sociality ' is the group attribute and social style of tourism culture.

The ' inheritance ' of tourism culture should be divided into two parts. Tourism, as an entertainment and leisure activity in life, is essentially a cultural exchange and cultural communication activity (Zou Wei 12)[7].The process of tourism is accompanied by cultural exchanges and communication activities, which is the effective dissemination of content. The inheritance of culture is continuous development and innovation, and tourism is a carrier of cultural inheritance. Therefore, the ' inheritance ' of tourism culture has two attributes of content and carrier, so it is comprehensive.

Tourism activities run through the whole history of human beings. Tourism culture is the yearning and pursuit of spiritual civilization on the basis of realizing material civilization. From a sociological point of view, modernity is different from non-modern society from an economic point of view, which is manifested in superior infrastructure conditions, reasonable arrangements for work, and the cultivation of modern mind (Li Baihua 8)[8]. The " sociality " of tourism culture is a concrete expression based on the " inheritance " of tourism culture, and it is a concrete expression of the interaction and integration of tourism activities and social fields.

When tourism culture exists as a disseminator, its characteristics are contemporary, innovative, regional and group. The times and innovation are the frontier characteristics of the development of tourism culture. The spread of tourism culture will be affected by the times and the changes in the content, mode and carrier of communication. Innovation will be accompanied by the influence of the times to optimize the content of tourism culture communication, change the mode of tourism culture communication, and put forward the carrier of tourism culture communication. Regionality and group are the basic characteristics of tourism culture. Regionality presents the characteristics of tourism culture communication. Group is the group attribute of tourism culture, and it is the main body communication with the same regional cultural characteristics.

2.The object of tourism culture communication

The object of tourism culture communication exists in two aspects: material activities and spiritual activities. Material activities are embodied in social life, and spiritual activities are embodied in value pursuit.

2.1 The object of communication in material activities

In a society with little change, culture is stable, and there are few new problems. Life is a traditional way(Fei Xiaotong 83)[9]. Chinese society has been in a stable and prosperous state for a long time. Tourism culture has naturally become an important part of public social life. The material activities of tourism culture communication and social life have also become a kind of communication object. In the process of communication, social life exchanges information with tourism culture and transforms it into a concrete objective world. It emphasizes the close relationship between social life and tourism culture, and establishes the realistic principle that social life reflects the dissemination of tourism culture, and social practice is the main expression of social life.

If lifestyle and production practice are manifested in specific forms, social practice is the overall presentation of social life. Social practice is mainly reflected in certain social interaction and social relations, which is the essential reflection of social life (Xu Qi, Deng Li 108)[10]. Social practice is reflected in many aspects such as nature worship, survival and development, production and life, which undoubtedly directly reflects the spread of material activities of tourism culture.

2.2 The object of communication in spiritual activities

The spiritual activities of tourism culture communication are reflected in the pursuit of value. Tourism culture is the specific expression of social activities. However, in the process of communication, we should not only pay attention to the object of communication in material activities, but also pay attention to the object of communication in spiritual activities. Specifically, the object of communication in spiritual activities is the pursuit of value, including the construction of tourism culture brand, the expression of cultural history and the dissemination of tourism core value.

In many people 's view, tourism culture brand is the product of the new era, but in fact, it is not difficult to find that it has already formed, such like Guilin landscape culture, Mongolian nomadic culture, northeast shaman culture and other cultural brands with natural, regional, religious and other attributes. The construction of tourism brand culture plays an important role in the inheritance and protection of regional culture. Most of the world 's outstanding scenic spots and places of interest are successful in the embodiment of regional culture. Scenic spots without regional cultural support are difficult to survive for a long time(Zhou Shujing 15)[11]. Therefore, the construction of tourism culture brand has become an inevitable requirement in the dissemination of tourism culture.

The expression of cultural history is the responsibility and mission of tourism culture communication. Any kind of tourism contains the yearning and worship of nature, the cognition and recognition of culture. There are a large number of ethnic groups in China, and there are great differences in customs and folklore among each ethnic group. Through the development of tourism economy, the promotion of ethnic characteristic culture can be realized, and the diversified development of culture can be promoted(Yang Junshu 133)[12]. The cultural and historical expression in the process of tourism culture communication is an intuitive presentation of carrying forward Chinese excellent culture and strengthening cultural self-confidence in the new era.

The dissemination of tourism core value is divided into two levels: narrow and broad. The narrow level is the basic cognition, experience feedback and brand culture promotion of tourism cultural products. The broad level is based on the in-depth discussion on the basis of the narrow level, including cultural identity, cultural sharing and cultural dissemination.

3.The interpretation of the media carrier of tourism culture communication from the perspective of McLuhan 's media theory

McLuhan suggests, to draw attention to our environment, to the ground of our being-together, and the habits it forms (Roden D R 1)[1]. In the ' Journalism and Communication Theory ' edited by Liu Hong and Luan Yimei, the media carrier is subdivided into paper media, electronic media and new media. Although this distribution introduces the style characteristics of the media carrier in detail, the current era is developing rapidly and the media carrier is constantly updated and improved. More attention should be paid to the sociality, times and inheritance of the media carrier in the all-media era. Therefore, this paper summarizes the media carrier of tourism culture communication as traditional media, new media and integrated media. Traditional media refers to paper media and electronic media, new media refers to Internet media, and fusion media refers to the fusion media of traditional media and new media.

'Traditional media ' and ' new media ' are a relative concept. The research on the development of traditional media that what are talking about must be after the development of new media is relatively formed. The relevant research of new media will be compared with traditional media. Only in the face of the impact of ' new media ', will there be a revolutionary thinking on the development of ' traditional media '(Hu Xueqian 9)[13]. The concept of " media convergence " originated from Poole 's " free technology, " which describes the trend of electronic technology to break the boundary of communication form and move towards integration. This is recognized by many scholars as the origin of the concept of media convergence(Hu Xueqian 10)[13]. McLuhan 's ecological thought of communication emphasizes the core role of the media. It is an effective way to sort out the media of tourism culture and optimize the carrier and content of communication by expounding the contemporary media from the cultural and historical characteristics of the media.

3.1 Sociality of traditional media

Media, that is, information, is not a simple description of the definition of media. This theory is one of McLuhan 's core ideological contents. It is a summary and summary of the development process of media, reflecting the relevance between media and social development, and emphasizing the important position of media(Yang Fubo 87)[14]. In today 's rapid change of information, the media's social value is still can't be ignored

In the in-depth research and analysis of media theory, McLuhan divides the media into cold media and hot media according to the clarity of information provided by the media, the integrity of content, the certainty of goals, and the ability level and degree of reception of recipients of information dissemination (Bian Ning 13)[15]. However, McLuhan 's classification of hot and cold media does not have a consistent standard, and there is a contradiction in logic. Therefore, some people say that the classification of ' hot and cold media ' itself does not have much scientific and practical value. What is important is its enlightenment: different media act on people in different ways, and the psychological and behavioral reactions caused by them also have their own characteristics. These factors should also be taken into account in the study of media(Bian Ning 14)[15].

Human communication begins with face-to-face communication. The rise of traditional media makes mass communication have the depth and breadth of information dissemination. Tourism culture communication is the main product of mass communication. The sociality of traditional media to tourism culture communication is reflected in two aspects: historical value and cultural value.

The historical value is reflected in the printing revolution and radio technology, which makes the mass communication of traditional media possible. Whether it is the simple communication mode of paper media, the linear communication of radio media or the rich function of TV media, it has a direct impact on the communication of tourism culture in this period, which greatly strengthens the dependence and consciousness of the audience on the media.

Cultural value is reflected in the coordination of social and ideological understanding of tourism culture in the process of communication. The dissemination of tourism culture is the process of creative transformation of the ideological achievements of traditional culture and natural culture. It is also the process of cognition and dissemination of various ideological cultures and conceptual forms in the history of various ethnic groups. Tourism culture can realize the function of coordinating social relations and maintaining social order in the process of dissemination. At the same time, there will be many ideological understandings in the process of dissemination of tourism culture, including the concept of ' community of destiny ', the concept of ' cultural identity ', etc., which are the concrete embodiment of carrying forward Chinese traditional culture and strengthening cultural self-confidence.

3.2 The contemporaneity of new media

In his preface to " Understanding Media, " McLuhan begins: ' This book first looks at some general situations of the media, and then examines the origin and development of various extensions separately '. He sets an equivalent replacement formula for the concept of ' media '. The so-called ' media ' is equal to the extension of human beings. In McLuhan 's view, technology has its necessity for the extension of human beings, and it will also have inevitable consequences for the human body. Extension is to cope with the stimulation and pressure brought by the external environment. All technologies are the extension of the strength and speed of the body and nervous system. Moreover, unless the strength and speed increase, the new extension of the human body will not occur, and it may also be abandoned if it occurs ' (Chen Zhiyi, Hu Yiqing 39).[16]

McLuhan intuitively expounds the direct reflection of media change. In the 1960 s, Kluhan first proposed the concept of " Global Village " in his typed report " Report on Understanding New Media. " He believes that with the development of electronic media technology, the earth will gradually become a village, and human beings will eventually return to the tribal ' global village '(Du Fangwei 205).[17]

Both the ' media extension ' theory and the ' global village ' theory McLuhan emphasized the era of media, that is, the era of media change. The new media communication of tourism culture is the optimization of the era communication carrier of traditional cultural products, and it is the manifestation of tourism cultural products adapting to the era transformation of media field. In this process, it deeply describes the content of tourism culture, deepens the core of tourism culture, and improves the quality of tourism culture.

3.3 The inheritance of media convergence

Most of the early research on the media in the United States focused on the content and influence of the information conveyed by the media, while McLuhan inherited and expanded the idea of Innis to link media technology with the history of human civilization, emphasizing the progress of media technology. The degree of influence on the development of social culture and social civilization clearly explains that the application of media technology has a more profound and thorough impact on people and society than the content carried by the media(Gao Huilin 110)[18]. Today, with the continuous change of technology, new media communication has become the mainstream of the times, but still cannot ignore the influence of traditional media, which is the embodiment of the inheritance of media.

The birth of converged media is the inheritance of traditional media and new media. There is no doubt that converged media has fully penetrated into every corner of the real society and affected people 's lives (Wang Record, Gao Smart 85)[19]. Under the influence of media, tourism culture has become one of the best beneficiaries. Traditional media has changed the limitations of face-to-face communication of tourism culture. New media media has improved the convenience of tourism culture in traditional media communication. The emergence of media has presented tourism culture more intuitively and comprehensively, increasing the depth and breadth of tourism culture communication.

4.Influencing factors of tourism culture communication

Any kind of cultural brand will be affected by subjective and objective factors in the process of communication. Subjective factors are reflected in policies, regions, concepts, etc., which directly affect the subject of communication. Subject constraints, multiculturalism, audience categories, etc., have an impact on the object of communication, which is also the objective factor of cultural brand in the process of communication.

4.1 The influencing factors in the main body of communication

Region, policy and concept are the core factors that affect the main body of tourism culture communication. Region, policy and concept have both similarities and differences. Region is the generalization of natural environment, policy is the presentation of national environment, and concept is the expression of human environment. The three interact and are interrelated. Both Han culture and minority cultural environment are influenced by natural environment, so they also present different tourism cultural characteristics and brands. It is in this national cultural environment that the human environment of local customs and consciousness is formed. The influence of region, policy and concept on the subject of tourism culture communication is intuitive.

4.2 Influencing factors in the object of communication

Subject restriction, multiculturalism and audience category are the key factors affecting the object of tourism culture communication. Subject restriction, multiculturalism, audience category scores in different fields. Subject restriction refers to the restriction of the object of tourism culture communication on the content and carrier of communication under the influence of region, policy and concept. Diversified culture refers to the impact of various cultures on the dissemination of tourism culture under the mutual integration and mutual influence of various cultures ; the audience category is to emphasize the pertinence and differentiation consciousness in the process of tourism culture communication. The influence of subject restriction, multiculturalism and audience category on the object of tourism culture communication is specific.

4.3 Influencing factors in the media carrier

Media carrier is the main factor in the process of tourism culture communication. The arrival of the all-media era has greatly changed the way audiences obtain information. Different audiences obtain information through different media carriers. Tourism culture is influenced by content creation, consumer perspective and concept in media communication. The content creation of tourism culture in the era of omnimedia has changed the simple and intuitive way of information dissemination of traditional media, but strengthened the innovation of content. ' Creation ' is creation and ' fresh 'is freshness, which not only emphasizes the creative characteristics of tourism culture content but also emphasizes the timeliness of content dissemination. The consumer perspective is the direct interpretation of marketization. Tourism culture is benefited by market demand. Therefore, consumers have become the target object of tourism culture communication, and the consumer perspective is the target content of tourism culture media communication. The media carrier of tourism culture communication is also influenced by the concept. The concept emphasized here is different from the expression of the humanistic environment of the main influencing factors of tourism culture communication, but a direct interpretation of the single subject and lack of channels of media carrier communication.

5.the path of tourism culture communication

Information dissemination is an important factor affecting social development and historical progress at any time, and tourism is the practice of the public 's pursuit of spiritual life and material life. In the all-media era, the dissemination of tourism culture has the characteristics of more obvious cross-regional, higher requirements for innovation and communication, and stronger requirements for continuity (Bian Zhiyao, Yang Libin 61)[20]. Strengthening cultural identity, deepening core quality and optimizing communication carrier are the continuous and effective communication paths of tourism culture in the all-media era.

5.1 Strengthen cultural identity

The report of the 20 th National Congress of the Communist Party of China points out that we should take the consciousness of the Chinese nation community as the main line, unswervingly follow the correct path of solving ethnic problems with Chinese characteristics, adhere to and improve the system of regional ethnic autonomy, strengthen and improve the party 's ethnic work, and comprehensively promote the cause of national unity and progress. Promoting Chinese cultural identity is of great significance for casting a strong sense of community of the Chinese nation. ' The problem of cultural identity has been solved, and the identity of the great motherland, the Chinese nation and the road of socialism with Chinese characteristics can be consolidated (Zhou Yu, Liao Xiaoqin 55). '[21] Tourism is the exchange of political thought, economic development, natural worship and spiritual pursuit. Culture is the crystallization of mass spiritual culture and material culture, with the attribute of communication. Tourism culture communication is a very important form of cultural exchange at present. Strengthening the recognition of tourism culture is an important way to promote the mutual exchange, mutual learning and mutual influence of Chinese excellent traditional culture, and also an effective action to carry forward and protect Chinese excellent traditional culture.

5.2 Deepen the kernel quality

Improving culture and tourism integration efficiency is an important way to promote the high-quality development of cultural tourism (Fei L, Huaiguo R ,Xinglong Z e0277063)[2]. With the progress and rapid development of China 's contemporary economic and social progress, whether the tourism project has the characteristic cultural heritage and charm has become the core element of the majority of tourists in the selection of travel destinations. At the same time, those tourism projects and scenic spots with distinctive cultural characteristics, high-quality cultural tastes, and diversified cultural expressions are being sought after by the government, capital, and tourists, and are increasingly becoming the darling of domestic tourism destinations (Zhou Rong 41)[22]. On the basis of mass communication, Katz put forward the theory of ' use and satisfaction ', which guides communicators to pay more attention to the audience, including audience needs, audience feelings and audience feedback, and takes whether to meet the needs of the audience as the basic standard to measure the effect of communication. To optimize the path of tourism culture communication, it is necessary to deepen the core quality of tourism culture, taking the audience as the starting point and the foothold, but this does not mean comprehensive marketization and commercial operation, but emphasizes the brand establishment and quality improvement of tourism culture, and fully implements ' tourism + culture ' into the whole process of publicity, use and feedback of tourism products.

5.3 Optimize the media

In the era of omnimedia, should pay more attention to the influence of digital transformation on the carrier of tourism culture communication. The digital transformation of Internet platform, network paper currency, VR, AR video and so on has an impact on the content, mode and carrier of tourism culture communication. In the era of all media, tourism culture communication should create three-dimensional communication channels and integrate resources in an all-round way. It should not only pay attention to the technological change of new media, but also not ignore the authoritative role of traditional media. Everaging digital intelligence technology to bolster brand technological sophistication and communication (Iakovaki E, Konstantakis M 1509)[3]. Tourism culture communication should pay special attention to personalized creation, pay attention to the impact of media changes on society, culture and economy, constantly optimize the media, enrich the content of communication, pay attention to interactive participation, pay attention to audience feedback, and put forward communication strategies.

6. Conclusion

The all-media era is the era of technology empowerment. The dissemination of tourism culture should keep up with the pulse of the times, pay attention to the construction of the subject and object of communication and the feedback of the audience, and make full use of the characteristics of the new media, such as fast communication speed, many audiences and wide influence range. Under the background of economic globalization, we should optimize the media as a means to enhance the personalized creation of tourism culture and the establishment of tourism culture brand. Under the background of cultural diversity, we should strengthen the cultural identity of tourism culture, deepen the core quality and improve the service quality, so as to realize the inheritance and protection of Chinese excellent traditional culture.

Reference

1. Roden D R .Review: What Marshall McLuhan can teach us in the age of digital media[J].America,2023,228(1) : 1.
2. Fei L ,Huaiguo R ,Xinglong Z .Spatio-temporal evolution and influencing factors of culture and tourism integration efficiency in Shandong Province, China under high-quality development.[J].PloS one,2022,17(12):e0277063.
3. Iakovaki E ,Konstantakis M ,Teneketzis A , et al.Analyzing Cultural Routes and Their Role in Advancing Cultural Heritage Management within Tourism: A Systematic Review with a Focus on the Integration of Digital Technologies[J].Encyclopedia,2023,3(4):1509.
4. Li Ying. Research on the communication ecology of folk art [D]. Southeast University, 2015 : 49.
5. Liu Yang. Research on the coordinated development of cultural tourism and urban economy [D].Northwest University, 2016 : 20.
6. Zhi Tingrong. Mass Communication Ecology [M]. Hangzhou : Zhejiang University Press, 2004 : 35.
7. Zou Wei. The evolution and characteristics of tourism culture communication mode in the digital era [D]. Hunan Normal University, 2021 : 12.
8. Li Baihua. Research on the spread of Shaman symbols in Changbai Mountain tourism culture [D].Jilin University, 2019 : 8.
9. Fei Xiaotong. Local China [M]. Beijing : People 's Publishing House, 2015 : 83.
10. Xu Qi, Deng Li. Natural ecology, ethnic inheritance and social life-the integration of traditional ecological culture in Guizhou [J].Guizhou ethnic studies, 2023,44 (03) : 108.
11. Zhou Shujing. Research on brand image design in tourism culture [D].Qingdao University, 2022 : 15.
12. Yang Junshu. Tourism culture communication and tourism economic development [J].National circulation economy, 2023 (10) : 133.
13. Hu Xueqian. Dynamic Analysis and Dilemma Reflection on the Development of Traditional Media Convergence in China [D].Zhonghua Agricultural University, 2021 : 9-10.
14. Yang Fubo. A Study on McLuhan 's Media Theory [D]. Jilin University, 2007 : 87.
15. Bian Ning. A preliminary study on the dual aesthetic value of McLuhan 's media theory [D].Liaoning University, 2018 : 13-14.
16. Chen Zhiyi, Hu Yiqing. On McLuhan 's " media is the extension of man " -Revisiting the classical theory of media ecology [J].News reporter, 2023 (05) : 39-40.
17. Du Fangwei. On the theory and reality of McLuhan 's ' global village ' [J]. Journal of Higher Education. 2015 (17) : 250-251.
18. Gao Huilin. A study on the philosophy of new media technology based on McLuhan 's media view [D]. Dalian University of Technology, 2020 : 110-111.
19. Wang Record, Gao Smart. Media Convergence and Public History [J]. Journal of Henan Normal University (Philosophy and Social Sciences Edition), 2021, 48 (05) : 85.
20. Bian Zhiyao, Yang Libin. Tourism culture communication mechanism in ethnic minority areas-Taking Guangxi as an example [J].Social scientists, 2020 (12) : 61.
21. Zhou Yu, Liao Xiaoqin. The connotation, structure and realization path of Chinese cultural identity - - Also on strengthening the consciousness of the Chinese nation community [J].Journal of North University for Nationalities, 2023 (04) : 55.
22. Zhou Rong. The development and external communication of tourism culture in western China-in the context of the Belt and Road [J].Social scientists, 2022 (07) : 41.

Cultural Dialogues in Artistic Expression: Case Studies in Cross-Cultural Artistry

Yue Wang*

Shandong Normal University, Jinan, China

Abstract: This article provides a comprehensive exploration of the dynamic and multifaceted interactions between cultures and artistic expressions, with a strong emphasis on the profound significance of cross-cultural artistry. Through a series of illuminating case studies, it vividly illustrates how artists representing diverse cultural backgrounds engage in intricate and meaningful dialogues through their creative works. The in-depth analysis conducted throughout this study not only underscores the pivotal role of art but also highlights its extraordinary power as a transformative medium for promoting cross-cultural understanding and fostering effective communication among different societies and communities.

1. Introduction

Art has perennially transcended the confines of geography, serving as a universal language that bridges cultural divides and nurtures the exchange of ideas and perspectives. In this article, we embark on a captivating journey into the realm of cross-cultural artistry, where artists hailing from diverse origins converge to forge works of art that encapsulate intricate cultural dialogues. Through a compelling series of case studies, we embark on an exploration that unveils the manifold ways these dialogues breathe life into artistic expression. The profound influence of cross-cultural interactions on the global art landscape takes center stage, illustrating their capacity to reshape and redefine artistic expression within our increasingly interconnected and globalized society. The tapestry of cross-cultural artistry is woven with threads of innovation, fusion, and inclusivity. It is a testament to the richness of human creativity and the boundless possibilities that emerge when cultures intersect and collaborate [1]. As we delve deeper into this world, we will uncover the artistry's ability to transcend boundaries, foster mutual understanding, and inspire a shared appreciation for the diverse cultural tapestry that envelops our world. This exploration illuminates not only the challenges but also the opportunities that cross-cultural artistry presents, positioning it as a dynamic force in shaping the artistic landscape of our global community.

2. Cultural fusion and synthesis

2.1. Hybrid Aesthetics

Cross-cultural artistry often leads to the development of hybrid aesthetics, where elements from multiple cultures intertwine to form new, unique artistic expressions. This fusion enhances the visual and emotional impact of the artwork, creating a deeper connection with the audience.

In the realm of hybrid aesthetics, artists become cultural alchemists, blending diverse artistic elements into a harmonious whole. This creative process involves the seamless integration of visual, auditory, and thematic elements from different cultures. For example, an artist might incorporate traditional Japanese ink painting techniques into a contemporary Western canvas, resulting in a masterpiece that resonates with viewers on multiple levels [2].

The power of hybrid aesthetics lies in its ability to evoke a sense of familiarity and novelty simultaneously. Audiences encounter the known and the unfamiliar within the same artwork, sparking curiosity and appreciation. This fusion transcends geographical and cultural boundaries, making the art accessible to a global audience. As viewers engage with these hybrid creations, they embark on a journey of discovery, exploring the intricate layers of cultural narratives woven into the artwork.

2.2. Bridging Narratives

Artists engage in the act of narrative bridging, weaving together stories, myths, and histories from diverse cultures. This process not only preserves cultural heritage but also serves as a means of storytelling that resonates with global audiences.

Narrative bridging is akin to creating a tapestry of tales from around the world. Artists draw inspiration from the rich storytelling traditions of different cultures, seamlessly intertwining narratives that might have originated continents apart. For instance, a painter might fuse Greek mythology with Indigenous folklore, crafting a visual narrative that speaks to themes of human connection and the universal quest for meaning.

*Corresponding author's email: 2482516799@qq.com

These bridging narratives not only preserve the essence of cultural storytelling but also facilitate cross-cultural understanding. They serve as universal threads that connect individuals from various backgrounds. Through these narratives, artists become cultural ambassadors, conveying messages of unity, diversity, and shared human experiences [3]. Audiences, regardless of their cultural origins, find common ground in the narratives, fostering a sense of empathy and appreciation for the stories of others.

2.3. Symbolism and Universality

Certain symbols and motifs used in cross-cultural art transcend linguistic and cultural boundaries. These symbols take on universal meanings, enabling artists to convey profound messages that resonate with viewers worldwide.

Symbolism in cross-cultural art is a language of its own, transcending words and cultural contexts. Artists harness symbols and motifs that hold inherent meanings across cultures, allowing them to communicate universal themes. For instance, the lotus flower, a symbol of purity and enlightenment in Asian cultures, can be integrated into an artwork with profound implications for audiences globally. The beauty of symbolism lies in its ability to evoke emotions and convey messages without the need for translation. It serves as a bridge between the artist's intent and the viewer's interpretation. As audiences encounter these universal symbols, they embark on a journey of emotional and intellectual exploration, delving into the layers of meaning embedded in the artwork. Symbolism in cross-cultural art acts as a unifying force, reminding us of the shared human experience and the common emotions that bind us all [4].

These expanded sections provide a deeper understanding of the concepts of hybrid aesthetics, narrative bridging, and symbolism in cross-cultural artistry. If you would like further elaboration or have specific points to include, please let me know, and I can continue to refine the content.

3. The Role of Cross-Cultural Collaborations

3.1. Cross-Cultural Artistic Collaborations

Collaborations between artists hailing from diverse cultural backgrounds offer a fertile ground for the cultivation of rich dialogues. These collaborations transcend geographical boundaries, bringing together unique perspectives and experiences. Within this creative crucible, artists fuse their cultural influences, resulting in artworks that resonate with a profound sense of interconnectedness. These collaborative endeavors become a testament to the power of art to bridge divides and engender mutual understanding. As brushes meet canvases and ideas intertwine, the boundaries that once separated cultures blur, giving birth to a new realm of artistic expression that transcends the limitations of any single culture.

3.2. Cultural Exchange through Exhibitions

Cross-cultural art exhibitions represent dynamic and enriching platforms for the exchange of culture and the celebration of diversity. These exhibitions, often hosted within the hallowed walls of galleries and museums, serve as vibrant showcases where the creations of artists become cultural ambassadors, embarking on journeys that transcend geographical boundaries and span generations. With each brushstroke, sculpted form, and carefully curated piece, these exhibitions carry with them the profound narratives and heritage of their creators, inviting viewers to embark on immersive voyages of cultural discovery [5].

Within the confines of an art exhibition, the gallery space transforms into a microcosm of global culture. Visitors encounter a tapestry of artistic expressions that traverse continents, eras, and artistic movements. It is a unique opportunity for international audiences to engage with and immerse themselves in the rich stories, traditions, and artistic languages of the world. As they wander through the meticulously arranged displays, spectators are encouraged to explore the nuances, symbolism, and techniques unique to each culture.

These exhibitions serve as windows into the intricacies of different cultures, fostering a deeper and more profound appreciation for the beauty of diversity. Viewers are not merely passive observers but active participants in a cross-cultural dialogue facilitated by art. They are encouraged to delve into the historical contexts, social landscapes, and cultural narratives that have shaped each artwork. In doing so, they gain valuable insights into the unique perspectives and identities of various cultures, transcending surface-level understanding.

Furthermore, cross-cultural art exhibitions offer a space for artists to engage in dialogues that extend beyond words. Through their creations, artists communicate not only with their immediate audience but with the world at large. These exhibitions facilitate an exchange of ideas, values, and worldviews, encouraging viewers to reflect on the shared human experience that unites us all.

In essence, cultural exchange through art exhibitions is a testament to the power of art to bridge gaps, create connections, and promote cross-cultural understanding. It is a celebration of the rich tapestry of our world's cultures, an invitation to explore the multifaceted facets of human creativity, and a reminder that art has the potential to transcend boundaries and foster a more interconnected and harmonious global community. Through the lens of art, we glimpse the beauty of our collective cultural heritage, and in doing so, we strengthen the bonds that unite us as one human family.

3.3. Education and Cultural Sensitivity

Cross-cultural artistry transcends the boundaries of mere creation; it delves deep into the realms of education and cultural sensitivity. Artists who embark on the path of cross-cultural exploration often find themselves on profound journeys of research and study. These journeys take them into the heart of cultures far removed from their own, immersing them in the rich tapestry of traditions, symbols, stories, and artistic expressions.

The educational aspect of cross-cultural artistry is a powerful catalyst for cultivating cultural sensitivity and awareness. It serves as a reminder that art is not created in isolation but is shaped by the historical, social, and cultural contexts from which it emerges. Artists who engage in this form of artistic expression recognize the need for profound respect and empathy [6]. They understand the importance of acknowledging the intrinsic value of each culture's contributions to the world of art.

This educational journey not only transforms the artists themselves but also extends its profound influence to their audiences. When artists immerse themselves in the study of foreign cultures, their artworks become more than visual representations; they become bridges between worlds. These works prompt viewers to see art as more than a visual feast; they become windows into the hearts and minds of those who have crafted it. It is in this educational and culturally sensitive approach that cross-cultural artistry takes on its true transformative power.

Audiences, too, are enriched by this educational journey. As they engage with artworks born of cross-cultural exploration, they are encouraged to view art as a vehicle for cultural understanding and connection. They are invited to explore the diverse narratives and perspectives woven into each piece, fostering a deeper appreciation for the intricacies of human culture. In this way, cross-cultural artistry becomes a catalyst for reshaping perspectives, dismantling stereotypes, and nurturing a global community that is profoundly enriched by the tapestry of cultures it embraces.

In conclusion, cross-cultural artistry, with its educational and culturally sensitive dimensions, transcends the realm of artistic creation. It becomes a transformative force that not only empowers artists to create with respect and empathy but also invites audiences to engage with art as a means of fostering cultural understanding and unity in our diverse and interconnected world.

4. Challenges and Opportunities

4.1. Navigating Cultural Sensitivities

The realm of cross-cultural artistry, while a valuable avenue for creative exploration, demands a highly nuanced approach to navigate the intricate web of cultural sensitivities. Artists embarking on cross-cultural dialogues must tread carefully, being acutely aware of the imperative to respect the cultural contexts from which their inspirations are drawn. At its core, this challenge hinges on the delicate equilibrium between appreciation and appropriation.

Respecting cultural contexts necessitates a profound level of commitment to research, understanding, and engagement with the traditions, symbols, and narratives inherent to the cultures in question. Artists must embark on a journey of discovery, immersing themselves in the rich tapestries of these cultures [7]. This entails a dedication to studying the historical significance and context of the elements they seek to incorporate into their work. The importance of this respect cannot be overstated; it forms the bedrock of ethical cross-cultural artistic expression.

Missteps in this regard can have far-reaching consequences, potentially leading to unintentional cultural insensitivity, misappropriation, or even causing offense. It is incumbent upon artists to approach cross-cultural artistry with humility, demonstrating a genuine commitment to understanding and honoring the cultures with which they engage. By doing so, they can forge meaningful connections that transcend borders and create art that authentically resonates with the diversity of our world [8].

4.2. Cross-Cultural Misunderstandings

Within the realm of cross-cultural artistry, the specter of misunderstandings often looms as a persistent challenge. Artistic expression, by its very nature, is open to interpretation, and when cultures converge, meanings can easily become entangled and misconstrued. These misunderstandings may arise from disparities in cultural contexts, historical backgrounds, or even language barriers.

Artists venturing into this multifaceted landscape must be prepared to embrace the potential for constructive dialogues that promote mutual learning. When cross-cultural misunderstandings inevitably occur, they should be viewed as opportunities rather than obstacles. These instances offer artists a chance to engage in profound conversations with their audiences, transcending the boundaries of culture and language.

Such dialogues can lead to heightened cultural awareness, increased empathy, and a deeper understanding of the intricate tapestry of different cultural perspectives. Artists are encouraged not only to be receptive to feedback but also to actively seek it out. By acknowledging the potential for misunderstandings and engaging in open, empathetic conversations, artists can contribute to a climate of mutual learning and growth that enriches their art and fosters a more interconnected world.

4.3. Global Reach and Impact

The realm of cross-cultural artistry opens doors to remarkable opportunities, chief among them being the potential for global reach and impact. When artists engage in cross-cultural dialogues, they position themselves to communicate with audiences that extend far beyond geographical and cultural boundaries. This expansive reach is underpinned by the universal language of art, capable of touching hearts and minds irrespective of individuals' backgrounds and origins.

The impact of cross-cultural artistry transcends the mere realm of aesthetics; it possesses the power to enrich cultures and contribute to greater societal awareness. Through their creative works, artists become conduits for introducing audiences to the nuances and intricacies of diverse cultures. In doing so, they embark on a journey of breaking down stereotypes, fostering a profound sense of global interconnectedness, and nurturing cultural appreciation. The significance of this global impact cannot be overstated. It often leads to a heightened sense of shared humanity among individuals from various walks of life and regions of the world. The transformative power of art, as a unifying force, becomes evident as it transcends borders, languages, and belief systems. This phenomenon underscores the continued importance of cross-cultural artistic endeavors as a means of promoting understanding, cooperation, and unity in our increasingly interconnected and diverse world.

In summary, cross-cultural artistry's ability to transcend boundaries and create a global impact serves as a testament to the profound influence of art on our shared human experience. It reinforces the idea that art knows no borders, fostering a sense of unity and interconnectedness among people from all corners of the globe.

5. Conclusion

Cross-cultural artistry, as illuminated in this exploration, stands as a testament to the boundless potential of human creativity. It transcends geographical, linguistic, and cultural boundaries, uniting artists from diverse backgrounds in dialogues that have the power to reshape artistic expression. The journey through the intricate tapestry of cross-cultural artistry has revealed profound facets, from the fusion of cultures in hybrid aesthetics to the act of narrative bridging and the universal language of symbolism. These elements have not only enriched art but have also deepened its connection with global audiences.

Cross-cultural art exhibitions, the vibrant showcases of this rich tapestry, serve as cultural ambassadors on a global stage. Within the walls of galleries and museums, they offer audiences immersive experiences that transcend mere observation. Each artwork becomes a vessel carrying the narratives and heritage of its creator's culture, inviting viewers on journeys of cultural discovery. These exhibitions provide invaluable opportunities for international audiences to engage with the diverse stories and traditions of the world, fostering a deeper appreciation for the beauty of our shared human heritage.

The role of education and cultural sensitivity in cross-cultural artistry extends beyond artistic creation. It is a transformative journey for artists, one that immerses them in the intricate web of foreign cultures and traditions. This educational aspect reshapes artists, instilling in them profound respect, empathy, and an understanding of the value of each culture's contributions to the world of art. Moreover, it extends its influence to audiences, inviting them to view art as more than a visual feast. Art becomes a window into the hearts and minds of those who have crafted it, fostering a deeper appreciation for the intricacies of human culture.

While cross-cultural artistry presents its share of challenges, including the delicate navigation of cultural sensitivities and potential misunderstandings, it offers unique opportunities. Artists who engage in cross-cultural dialogues find themselves poised to communicate with audiences that transcend geographical and cultural boundaries. The universality of art allows it to touch hearts and minds, promoting cultural understanding and interconnectedness. It reinforces the idea that art is a unifying force, a universal language that transcends borders and fosters a sense of shared humanity.

In conclusion, cross-cultural artistry's transformative power extends far beyond the canvas and the gallery walls; it enriches our global society. It reinforces art's status as a universal language, a powerful means of fostering cultural understanding, and an enduring testament to our shared humanity. The impact of cross-cultural artistry is indelible, leaving a lasting mark on the tapestry of our interconnected world, where diversity is celebrated, and dialogues continue to reshape the vibrant landscape of artistic expression.

Reference

1. TING, Caroline PIRES, and Ilya A. KANAEV. "Analogical Reasoning in Artistry: A Cross-cultural Examination of the Artist's Engagement with Matter." THE THIRD WORLD CONGRESS ON ANALOGY. 2023.
2. Casetta, Sophia D. "The Artistry of Mediation: A Look at Mediation's Effectiveness for Resolving Cross-Cultural Disputes Through the Leonardo da Vinci Conflict Between France's Louvre Museum and Italy's Uffizi Gallery." Pepperdine Journal of Communication Research 11.1 (2023): 6.
3. Kuralbayevich, Saparov Rinat. "The Artistry and Physiology of Ballet: Unraveling the Harmony of Movement and Expression." Best Journal of Innovation in Science, Research and Development 2.8 (2023): 24-26.
4. Adair, Stephanie. "Politeness as Social Artistry." The Philosophy of (Im) politeness. Cham: Springer International Publishing, 2021. 33-53.
5. Bennett, Kurt. Shipwright Artistry: Cultural Transmission of British Colonial Ship Design and Construction during the Eighteenth and Nineteenth Centuries. Diss. Flinders University, College of Humanities, Arts and Social Sciences., 2021.
6. Chitrabongs, Chittawadi. "Curartistry: Curating Everyday Artistry in Bangkok." Nakhara: Journal of Environmental Design and Planning 21.1 (2022): 208-208.
7. Yates-Lu, Anna. "Plotting the course: artistry, celebrity and kugak in South Korea." Celebrity Studies 12.2 (2021): 250-266.
8. Schrag, Brian, and Julisa Rowe, eds. Community Arts for God's Purposes:: How to Create Local Artistry Together. William Carey Publishing, 2020.

An Experimental Analysis on Degree Adverb "Hen" of Yuanjiang Dialect Xiang Chinese

Zhang Fen[1,*], Gong Qi[2,a]

[1]South China Business College Guangdong University of Foreign Studies, College English Department, Guangzhou, Guangdong, China
[2]Jinan University, College of Foreign Studies, Guangzhou, Guangdong, China

Abstract: This paper examines the phonetic properties of the degree adverb "hen" in Yuanjiang dialect (YJD hereafter) with empirical data from local people. Three sets of parameters, i.e. fundamental frequency (F0), duration and tone value (T-value), were analyzed. The degree adverb "hen" in YJD can be used as not only an adverbial but also a complement, and the sound of "hen" varies with syntactic functions and semantics. The results show that "hen" as an adverbial can be read as both "[xei^{45}]" which means "very" and "[xei^{21}]" which implies nearly no practical meaning, and that "hen" being a complement is uttered as "[xei^{41}]", indicating the meaning of "very" but carrying higher degree and stronger intonation than "[xei^{45}]". According to phonetic experiments, the sound change of "hen" in YJD lies in the change of tone value without transforming the initial consonant and vowel. Such phonetic phenomenon of "hen" in YJD is neither literal and colloquial readings nor tone sandhi, but a polyphonic phenomenon caused by internal inflexion.

1.Introduction

Yuanjiang County, located in the northeast of Hunan Province, belong to Yiyang city. There are three main dialects in the county: YJD, Chishan dialect and Nanda dialect. This paper will focus on YJD. The adverbs of degree in YJD can be divided into two categories: one is "hen (very)" class of degree adverbs; the other is the "ji (extremely)" class of degree adverbs.[1] In terms of syntactic function, the degree adverbs of "hen (very)" class in YJD are usually used as an adverb, while the degree adverbs of "ji (extremely)" class are often used as a complement. From the semantic point of view, "hen (very)" class degree adverbs are roughly equivalent to "hen (very)" in Mandarin, and "ji (extremely)" class degree adverbs mostly represent unlucky things, negative verbs or verbal words. This paper will mainly discuss the usage and pronunciation of the degree adverb "hen" in YJD specifically, and then conduct an experimental analysis of its tones with the aid of Praat.

2.The Usage of "hen" in Yuanjiang Dialect

In YJD, the adverb of degree "hen" is not only written but also spoken. From a semantic standpoint, "hen" itself is a neutral word, but the pattern "[xei]+X" as a whole can directly express the speaker's either positive or negative emotions. From the perspective of syntactic function, "hen" can be used as both an adverb and a complement. As an adverbial, "hen" can modify adjectives, verbal words, and locational words, and it can also be used with negative adverbs "[pu]"or "[mau]", both expressing the meaning of "no" or "not". When used as a complement, it is mainly used in the "X+[tə]+[xei]" format.

2.1 As a degree complement

Just as "hen" in Mandarin Chinese, "hen" as a complement in YJD is mainly used in the format of "X+[tə]+[xei]", in which X could be adjectives, verbs, and some phrases.[2] For example:

(1) [xau tə xei] (as good as gold)
(2) [kuai tə xei] (very beautiful)
(3) [p'a tə xei] (be very scared)
(4) [kau ɕin tə xei] (enjoyed a lot)
(5) [iəu min tɕ'i tə xei] (have a great reputation)
(6) [iəu i ȵi tə xei] (make a lot of sense)

As shown above, [xau] (good) and [kuai] (beautiful) in example (1) and (2) are adjectives; [p'a] (scare) and [kau ɕin] (enjoy) in example (3) and (4) are verbs; [iəu mintɕ'i] (have a reputation) and [iəu iȵi] (make sense) in example (5) and (6) are verb-object phrases. In spite of the same meaning of both patterns: "[xei]+X" and "X+[tə]+[xei]", the pattern "X+[tə]+[xei]" gets much stronger intonation to express higher degree. For example, the degree of [mɔ̃ tə xei] (have hands full) is higher than [xei mɔ̃] (very busy).

2.2 As a degree adverb

In YJD, the degree adverb "hen" can modify both monosyllabic and disyllabic adjectives. For example:

(7) [xei in] (very overcooked and mushy)
(8) [xei mei] (very depressed and low-spirit)
(9) [xei ɕi tɕi] (very careful)
(10) [xei k'a p'i] (very stingy)

*Corresponding author's mail: 258232505@qq.com; [a]jamesgq36@163.com

As noticed, [in] (mushy) and [mei] (depressed) in example (7) and (8) are monosyllabic adjectives; and [ɕi tɕi] (careful) and [k'a p'i] (stingy) in example (9) and (10) are disyllabic adjectives. As indicated by example (7) (8) (9) and (10), "hen" works as adverbial, modifying either monosyllabic or disyllabic adjectives to form the pattern of "[xei]+X".

The degree verb "hen" of YJD can also modify not only mental verbs and a few volitive verbs but also verb-object phrases. For instance,

(11) [xei ŋai] (love very much)

(12) [xei uei] (be very good at)

(13) [xei pa tɕia] (care for the family very much)

(14) [xei iau mie tsɪ] (have great honour)

In example (11), [ŋai] (love) is a verb relating to mental activities; in example (12) [uei] (be able to) is a volitive verb. In example (13) and (14), [pa tɕia] (care for the family) and [iau mie tsɪ] (have the honour) are verb-object phrases. As shown in example (11) (12) (13) (14), "hen" works as adverbial to modify verbal words.

The degree adverb "hen" in YJD could modify both simple and synthetic locational words too. For example,

(15) [xei liẽ] (very front)

(16) [xei au] (very back)

(17) [xei tau liẽ] (very front)

(18) [xei au pei] (very back)

As shown above, "hen" as adverbial works to modify both simple locational words like "[liẽ] (front)" or "[au] (back)" and compound locational words like "[liẽ tau] (the front)" or "[au pei] (the back)" to form expressions [xei liẽ] and [xei liẽ tau], [xei au] and [xei aupei] to express the front location or back location respectively. What should be noticed is that the simple locational words in YJD should appear together with degree adverbs; however, compound locational words could be used alone without degree adverbs. In other words, in YJD, we couldn't say "[xati ueitsɪ pai tə liẽ]" , but we can say "[xati ueitsɪ pai tə tauliẽ] (His seat is arranged at the front.)" .

In YJD, "hen" could be used with negative adverb "[pu]" or "[mau]", including mainly four patterns: "[pu]/[mau]+[xei]+X","[xei]+[pu]+X", "[xei]+V+[pu]+C" and "[xei]+V+[pu]+C+O". For instance,

(19) [pu xei tɕ'yn] (not vey stupid)

(20) [pu xei ŋai] (do not love very much)

(21) [mau xei fa xẽ] (do not work very hard)

(22) [mau xei kɔ̃ tɕin] (be very particular about)

(23) [xei pu xɔ̃ sɪ] (ill at ease)

(24) [xei pu tən uei] (very insensitive)

(25) [xei k'ã pu kuã] (disapprove very much)

(26) [xei k'au pu tɕy] (very unreliable)

(27) [xei kɔ̃ pu tɕ'i ua] (to talk in vain)

(28) [xei lən pu tɕy tɕ'i] (easily lose one's composure)

In the pattern of "[pu]+[xei]+X", X could be adjectives or verbs, as example (19) and (20); in the pattern of "[mau]+[xei]+X", X could be predicate-object verbs as example (21) and (22). And in the pattern of "[xei]+[pu]+X", X could be mental or volitive verbs as example (23) and (24). In comparison, the pattern of "[xei]+[pu]+X" embodies higher degree than the pattern of "[pu]/[mau]+[xei]+X". To be specific, the degree of [xei pu xɔ̃sɪ] (ill at ease) is higher than [pu xei xɔ̃sɪ] (do not fell at ease).

As shown in example (25) (26) (27) and (28), both patterns of "[xei]+V+[pu]+C" and "[xei]+V+[pu]+C +O" ought to transform "[pu]" into "[tə]" to express relatively positive meaning, namely [xei k'au pu tɕy] into [xei k'au tə tɕy], and [xei lən pu tɕy tɕ'i] into [xei lən tə tɕy tɕ'i]. However, such corresponding is not absolutely balanced. For instance, in YJD, there is no saying of [xei mɔ̃ tə in], generally speaking, to express higher degree of "very busy", we say [mɔ̃ tə xei] (have hands full).

3.The Pronunciation of "Hen" in YJD

In YJD, the degree adverb "hen" which has three pronunciations: [xei^{41}], [xei^{21}], [xei^{45}][3-4] could functions as an adverbial or a complement. Moreover, the pronunciation of "hen" changes with different grammatical functions and semantic meanings. As an adverb, "hen" could be pronounced with two different tones: one is "[xei^{21}]" which represents no significance; the other is "[xei^{45}]" which means "very". As a complement, "hen" pronounced as "[xei^{41}]", whose intonation is stronger than as adverbial.

3.1 Hen [xei^{41}]

In YJD, "hen" could work as a complement, which in this case is similar to Chinese Mandarin grammatically. When pronounced as [xei^{41}], "hen" is often used in the pattern of "X+[tə]+[xei]". Despite the same meaning of the pattern of "[xei]+X", "X+[tə]+[xei]" represents higher degree. For example,

(29) [tɕi tə xei] (in a rush)

(30) [mɔ̃ tə xei] (have hands full)

(31) [sai tə xei] (very sunburned)

From examples (29), (30) and (31), it is obvious that the degree expressed by "[mɔ̃tə xei]", "[tɕi tə xei]" and "[sai tə xei]" is higher than "[xei mɔ̃]", "[xei tɕi]" and "[xei sai]" respectively. What's more, the intonation of "hen [xei^{41}]" is increased by stressing the degree of core words like "[mɔ̃]", "[tɕi]" and "[sai]".

3.2 Hen [xei^{21}]

When "hen" is pronounced as [xei^{21}] in YJD, it embodies little degree meaning with stronger adverbial function. Here, "hen" shouldn't be stressed. In this case, "hen [xei^{21}]" is similar to the usage of "hen" which indicates "no practical significance"[5] in Chinese Mandarin. Consider the following two examples:

(32) [xa ko tsa lən xei lau sɪ] (He/She is very honest.)

(33) [tɕin tsau tso tsɪ kau tɕy iəu xei to ts'ai] (There are many dishes on the table today.)

As shown in example (32), the expression of "[xei lausɪ] " in YJD is not to emphasize the degree of "[lau sɪ] (honest) but to affirm the fact of being honest ". In other words, "hen [xei^{21}]" here does not mean "very", but just play an adverbial role. Therefore, the expression of "[xei lau sɪ] (honest)" in certain context expresses the same meaning of "[lau sɪ] (honest)" in YJD. Just as example

(32), "[xei]" in example (33) modifying the adjective "[to] (many)" only serves to reinforce the intonation. Accordingly, the degree of "[xei to] (many)" is equivalent to "[to] (many)". In short, when "hen" is pronounced as [xei^{21}] in YJD, it mostly plays a adverbial role instead of strengthening the degree of following adjectives, so "hen [xei^{21}]" as an adverb in YJD functions grammatically but not semantically.

3.3 Hen [xei^{45}]

In YJD, while "hen" is pronounced as [xei^{45}], it means "very". Being an adverb, [xei^{45}] may be used not only to modify mental verbs, verb-object phrases, adjectives and nouns of locality but also with negative adverbs "[pu]" or "[mau]". Take the following five sentences as examples:

(34) [xei ɕiɔ̃] (miss very much)

(35) [xei iəu liẽ] (very wealthy)

(36) [xei ŋ̍i] (very hot)

(37) [xei tau liẽ] (very front)

(38) [xei pu xɔ̃ sɪ] (ill at ease)

As indicated by the above five examples, "hen" as adverbial is used to intensify the degree of the following words such as mental verbs like "[ɕiɔ̃] (miss)" in example (34), verb-object phrases like "[iəu liẽ]" (be of wealth) in example (35), adjectives like "[ŋ̍i] (hot)" in example (36), nouns of locality like "[tau liẽ] (the front)" in example (37) and negative adverbs like "[pu] (not)" in example (38). The pronunciation and usages of "hen [xei^{45}]" appears most frequently in YJD.

To sum up, in YJD, the pronunciation of "hen" varies with syntactic functions. As a complement, it is pronounced as [xei^{41}]. As an adverb, there are two pronunciations: [xei^{21}] and [xei^{45}]. It is noteworthy that the degree adverb "hen" as an adverbial in YJD may imply differently when it pronounces as [xei^{21}] or [xei^{45}]. Take the expression of "[xei lau sɪ]" into account again: when "hen" is pronounced as [xei^{21}], just as what we have discussed above, the meaning of "[xei lau sɪ]" is similar to "[lau sɪ]" without the change of degree, which implies the meaning of "honest"; while "[xei lau sɪ]" may mean "very honest" when "hen" is pronounced as [xei^{45}], hence the much higher degree of "[xei lau sɪ]" than "[lau sɪ]".

4.An Experimental Analysis of "Hen" in YJD

The dialect investigated in this paper is YJD in Hunan province, China. The data are mainly from field investigation and the author's daily accumulation. In YJD, the degree adverb "hen" has three pronunciations, namely [xei^{41}], [xei^{21}] and [xei^{45}]. The difference among the three pronunciations lies in the change of tone value. In Chinese dialects, tone is an inherent level of sound that can distinguish meaning. Tone is mainly determined by pitch.[6] Pitch is correlated to the fundamental frequency (F0) which determines the pitch of a syllable.[7]

This paper aims to conduct phonetic experiments on the degree adverb "hen" in YJD by using Praat, and then thoroughly analyze the duration and pitch of "hen" in different contexts, so as to obtain the tone value of "hen" according to the T-value calculation formula by Shi Feng[8] and the five level tone mark proposed by Zhao Yuanren[9]. The T-value is calculated as follows:

$$T=[(lgX-lgmin)/lgmax-lgmin]\times 5 \qquad (1)$$

where max refers to the maximum F0, min refers to the minimum F0, X refers to the fundamental frequency value of the measuring point in the pitch curve, and T refers to the value between 1-5. There is also a certain correspondence between the T-value and the five-level tone value, that is, the T-value between 0-1 can be regarded as the 1st level, the T-value between 1-2 can be regarded as the 2nd level, the T-value between 2-3 can be regarded as the 3^{d} level, the T-value between 3-4 can be regarded as the 4th levels, and the T-value between 4-5 can be regarded as the 5th level.

4.1 The Citation Tones in YJD

In YJD, there are 5 tones: Yinping 34, Yangping 13, Shangsheng 41, Qusheng 21, Rusheng 45.[10] Firstly, Praat was used to record the five tones of YJD, and each tone was pronounced ten times with different characters, as shown in the following Table 1:

Table 1 The citation tones in YJD

Citation Tones	Tones Types				
	Yiping 34	**Yangping 13**	**Shangsheng 41**	**Qusheng 21**	**Rusheng 45**
1	tɕy (pig)	tɕy (divide)	tɕy (host)	tɕy (live)	tɕy (orange)
2	pi (compel)	pi (skin)	pi (compare)	pi (quilt)	pi (pen)
3	tɕin (gold)	tɕin (musical instrument)	tɕin (well)	tɕin (near)	tɕin (energy)
4	iəu (excellent)	iəu (oil)	iəu (have)	iəu (again)	iəu (pomelo)
5	ti (low)	ti (title)	ti (bottom)	ti (ground)	ti (lose)
6	i (clothes)	i (move)	i (chair)	i (easy)	i (benefit)
7	mən (mosquito)	mən (door)	mən (fierce)	mən (dream)	mən (stuffy)
8	tɕi (chicken)	tɕi (drunk)	tɕi (squeeze)	tɕi (stand)	tɕi (rush)
9	pau (bag)	pau (float)	pau (be full)	pau (hug)	pau (newspaper)
10	pin (ice)	pin (bottle)	pin (cookie)	pin (illness)	pin (funeral)

Then, the Praat is used to observe the pitch curve for each pronunciation, and five data are evenly selected for each tone from the pitch curve after the head is removed and the tail is pinched. At last, all of the data are logged into an Excel spreadsheet. Thus, the maximum F0 and minimum F0 are determined, as shown in the following Table 2. By analyzing Table 2, it is found that the maximum F_0 is 475Hz, and the minimum F_0 is 101 Hz.

Table 2 The maximum and minimum F_0 in YJD

Tone types	Maximum F_0	Minimum F_0
Yinping	309.6	174.8
Yangping	214.6	141.6
Shangsheng	271.3	126.4
Qusheng	251	101
Rusheng	475	186.9

4.2 The Duration and Spectrogram of "Hen" and T-values

In YJD, when "hen" is pronounced as [xei[41]] as a complement, it mainly applies in the pattern of "X+[tə]+[xei]", take "[tɕi tə xei] (in a rush)" and "[mɔ̃ tə xei]" (have one's hands full) as examples. The following Picture 1 and Picture 2 show the duration and spectrogram of "[tɕi tə xei]" and "[mɔ̃ tə xei]" separately.

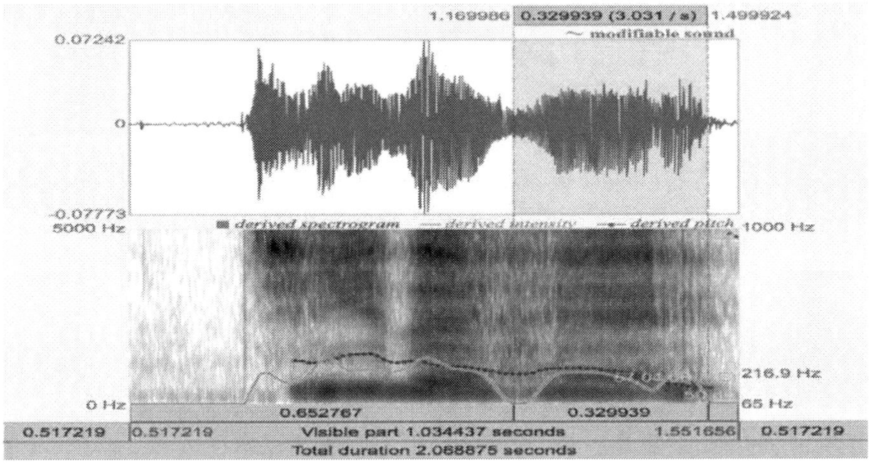

Picture 1 The duration and spectrogram of "[tɕi tə xei]"

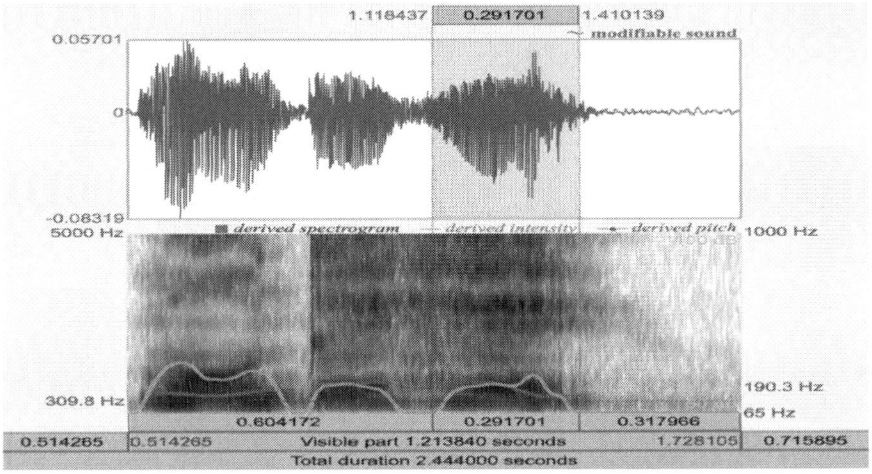

Picture 2 The duration and spectrogram of "[mɔ̃ tə xei]"

From the above Picture 1 and Picture 2, we can see the duration of "hen" of "[tɕi tə xei]" is approximately 0.33 seconds, and the duration of "hen" of "[mɔ̃ tə xei]" is 0.29 seconds. The following Table 3 shows the F_0 and duration of five sample points of "[xei[41]]".

Table 3 The F_0 and duration of "hen [xei[41]]"

Examples	Sample 1/Hz	Sample 2/Hz	Sample 3/Hz	Sample 4/Hz	Sample 5/Hz	Duration/s
[tɕi tə xei] (in a rush)	241.2	255.4	231.5	174.7	150	0.329939
[mɔ̃ tə xei] (have hands full)	201.4	224.2	213.9	213.7	164.1	0.291701

In YJD, when "hen" is pronounced as [xei21], it plays an adverbial role, but does not mean much practical meaning. At this time, "hen" would not be stressed. The following Picture 3 and Picture 4 show the duration and spectrogram of [xei lau sɿ] (honest) and [xei to ts'ai] (many dishes) respectively. According to Picture 3 and Picture 4, both duration of "hen" are about 0.2 seconds. The following Table 4 shows the F_0 and duration of five samples of "[xei21]".

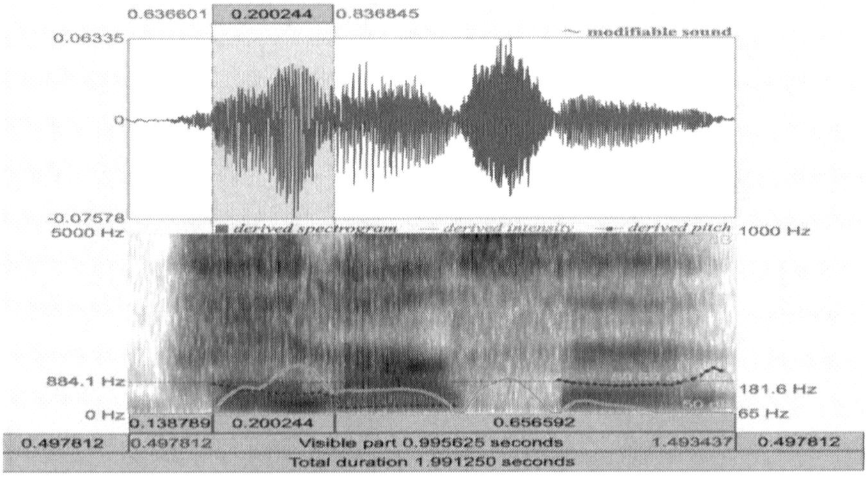

Picture 3 The duration and spectrogram of "[xei lau sɿ]"

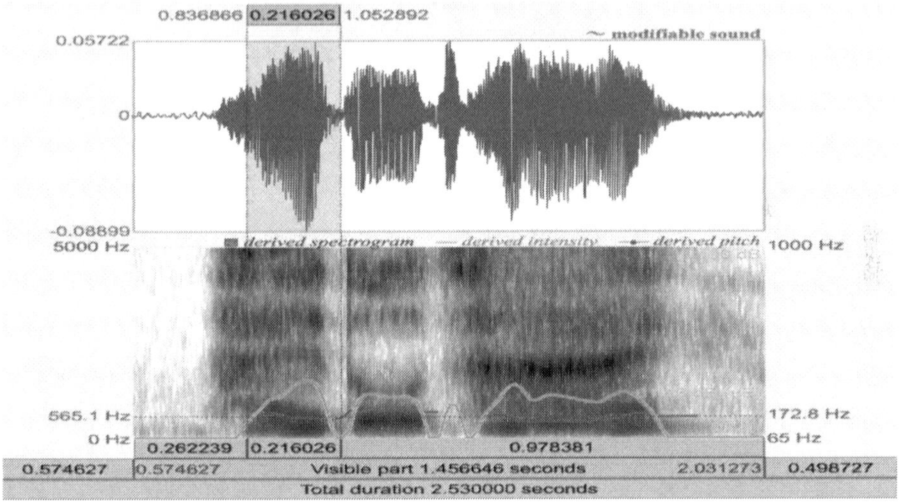

Picture 4 The duration and spectrogram of "[xei to ts'ai]

Table 4 The F_0 and duration of "hen [xei21]"

Examples	Sample 1/Hz	Sample 2/Hz	Sample 3/Hz	Sample 4/Hz	Sample 5/Hz	Duration/s
[xei to ts'ai] (many dishes)	202.1	183.7	169.2	163	158	0.216026
[xei lau sɿ] (honest)	201.5	169.7	166.4	162	153.6	0.200244

In YJD, "hen" as an adverbial would be read as [xei45] with highest frequency, which indicates the meaning of "very". The following Picture 5 and Picture 6 show the duration and spectrogram of "[xei tən zɿ] (very sensible)" and "[xei po] (very white)" respectively. From Pictures 5 and Picture 6, both duration of "hen" is 0.2 seconds. And the following Table 5 shows the F_0 and duration of [xei45] of five samples.

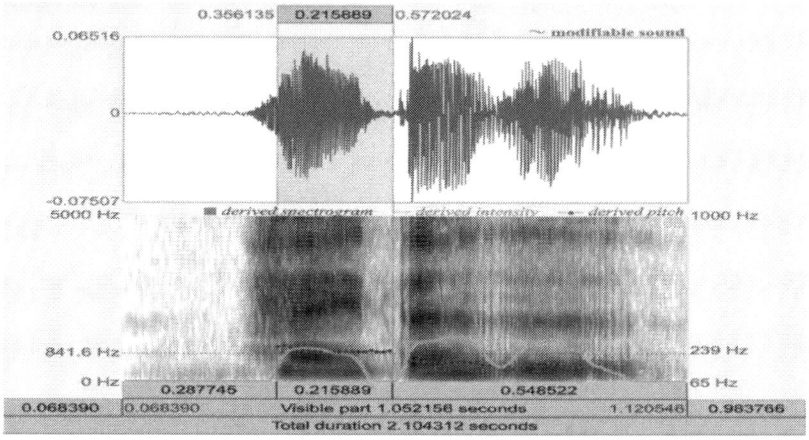

Picture 5 The duration and spectrogram of "[xei tən zɪ]"

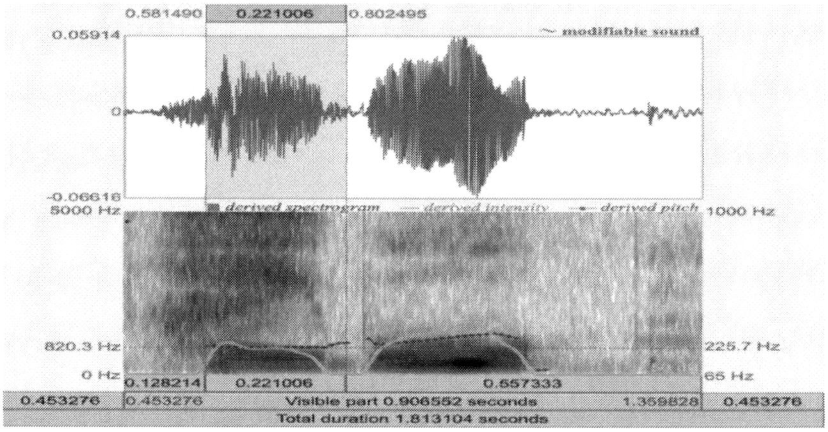

Picture 6 The duration and spectrogram of "[xei po]"

Table 5 The F_0 and duration of "hen [xei^{45}]"

Examples	Sample 1/Hz	Sample 2/Hz	Sample 3/Hz	Sample 4/Hz	Sample 5/Hz	Duration/s
[xei tən zɪ] (very sensitive)	267.1	235.1	232.2	232.5	231.5	0.215889
[xei po] (very white)	264.8	241.4	247	245.8	242.4	0.221006

4.3 Experimental Results

Based on the above experimental data, it can be determined that maximum F0 is 475 Hz, and the minimum F0 is 101 Hz, so that the T value of "hen" can be calculated according to the T-value calculation formula, as shown in Table 6:

Table 6 The T-value of "hen"

Examples	Sample 1	Sample 2	Sample 3	Sample 4	Sample 5	Duration/s
[tɕi tə xei]	2.8	3	2.68	1.78	1.27	0.33
[mɔ̃ tə xei]	2.2	2.6	2.4	2.4	1.6	0.29
[xei lau sɪ]	2.23	1.67	1.61	1.52	1.35	0.2
[xei to ts'ai]	2.24	1.92	1.66	1.54	1.54	0.2
[xei tən zɪ]	3.14	2.73	2.69	2.69	2.68	0.216
[xei po]	3.11	2.81	2.87	2.87	2.83	0.221

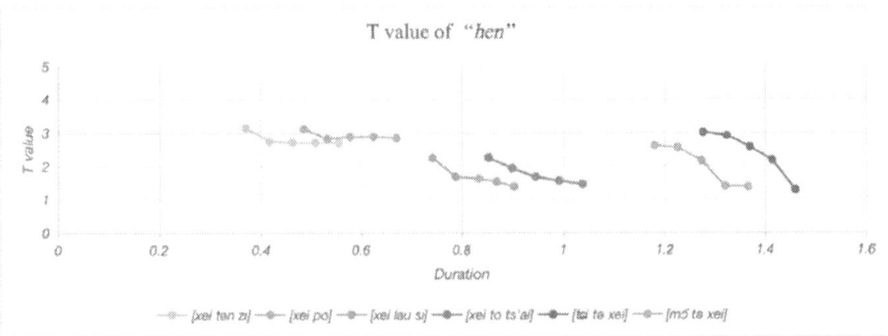

Picture 7 The tone curve of "hen"

According to the above Picture 7, "hen" in YJD has three tones: shangsheng 41, qusheng 21 and rusheng 45, among which the shangsheng is falling, the starting point slightly higher than 3, the end close to 1, recorded as 41; the starting point of qusheng is a bit higher than 2, and the end point is close to 1, denoted as 21; The starting point of rusheng is slightly higher than 3, and the end is higher than 2 and close to 3, almost flat, recorded as 43, a bit different from tone value of 45, which need further study and explanation.

5.Conclusions

Through the collection of data and the analysis of phonetic experiments, this paper finds that degree adverb the pronunciation of "hen" in YJD changes in different contexts. The three pronunciations of "hen" in YJD could cause the variations in meaning and syntactic function. It is well-known that literal and colloquial readings which is a particular phonetic phenomenon of Chinese characters would not lead to the changing of semantics and syntactic functions.[11] Therefore, the sound change of "hen" in YJD seems not to be the phenomenon of literal and colloquial readings. What's more, the tone change of "hen" in YJD is not the result of tone sandhi which can be triggered by adjacent tones like pre-syllable or post-syllable.[12] This paper holds that the degree adverb "hen" in YJD is a polyphonic character, which is a grammatical phenomenon of internal inflection. From the perspective of Chinese dialects, internal inflection is formed by taking advantage of the change of tone and duration to express some specific grammatical meanings[13] , which could be applied to explain the case of degree adverb "hen" in YJD appropriately.

These findings are valuable for further understanding of the grammatical features and phonetic variation of YJD in Hunan Province. Further researches should focus on the usage and rule of pronunciations of "hen", and compare YJD with other dialects to further reveal the differences and similarities between dialects.

Acknowledgments

This Paper is supported by General College and University Research Project of Guangdong Province, China. (2022WQNCX117)

References

1. Xu, H. (2001) Yiyang fanyan yufa yanjiu (Grammatic Studies of Yiyang Dialect).Hunan Education Press, Changsha.
2. Xu, W.L. (2022) Chengdu buyu "hen" de lishi fazhan ji kua yuyan kaocha (The Diachronic Development and Cross-linguistical Investigation of "Hen" as Degree Complement). Journal of Zaozhuang University, 39(01):41-49.
3. Zeng, W. (2010) Hunan yiyang fanfyan de ji ge chengdu fuci (Severel Degree Adverbs of Yiyang Dialect in Hunan Province). Modern Chinese, 11:80-82.
4. Cui, Z. H. (1998) Yiyang fanyan yanjiu (The Study on Yiyang Dialect). Hunan Education Press, Changsha.
5. Tang, C.Y. (2019) The Rise of Degree Adverb "Hen" and the Decline of Degree Adverb "Shen" in Modern Chinese. Journal of School of Chinese Language and Culture Nanjing Normal University, 95(03):174-182.
6. Shi, M. H., Chen, Y. Y. (2022) Qingzhuo tongdiao in Shuangfeng Xiang Chinese: Evidence from phonetic experiments. Studies of the Chinese Language, 411(06):721-735+767-768.
7. Yip, M. (2002) Tone. Cambridge University Press, Cambridge.
8. Shi, F., Xia, Q. S. (2022) The Principles of Sentence Focus in Mandarin Chinese. Linguistic Science, 21(06):580-594..
9. Chao, Y. R. (1930) A System of Tone Letters. Le Maître Phonétique, 45: 24-7.
10. Zhang, F. (2015) An OT Analysis of the Yiyang Tone Sandhi. Jinan University, Guangzhou.

11. Xu, R.Y. (2022) The Literal and Colloquial Readings of Finals in Zhuquan Tuhua Dialect in Jiahe County, Hunan Province. Dialect, 44(04):422-429.
12. Zhang, Q., Ma, Q.W. (2023) The Prosodic Domain of Tone Sandhi in Yantai Dialect. Linguistic Science, 22(01):44-55.
13. Foadi, R. A. , Zarytovskaya, V. (2019). To the Question of Internal Inflection of the Roots in Arabic and Russian (inflected analysis of the root structure).DOI:10.18500/1817-7115-2019-19-3-268-275.

Feng Zhi's Spatiotemporal View of "Spirit of engagement through Landscape" in His Sonnet Collection

Yingying Zheng*

School of Humanities, Southeast University, MA, China

Abstract. In the time of national crisis, Feng Zhi's experience of displacement made him deeply feel the close connection between group experience, historical events and individual life. The unresolved spiritual depression prompted him to persistently seek a positive way of entering the world in his ordinary life and natural landscape. He was inspired by the nature of "wilderness", "path", "mountain and river", etc., and then "fed back" his thoughts to nature, consciously extending his life experience in his poetry collection.

1.The "Wanderer's Discourse" in the War Era

Under the background of the outbreak of the Anti-Japanese War, Feng Zhi and his family were forced to move south, which caused his spiritual transformation. In the context of survival in the Anti-Japanese War, Feng Zhi, like other Chinese intellectuals of the same period, encountered national disaster and national trauma. The difference is that he was obsessed with finding poetic meaning, digging poetic thoughts, and expressing individual life experience in his ordinary daily life experience and the surrounding landscape. He immersed himself in the great rest of all things, and permeated the realistic feelings of feeling the times and worrying about the world in the philosophy of his Sonnet Collection. He used philosophy as the foundation of poetry, and humanistic feelings as the latitude and longitude of poetry, integrating sensibility and rationality, expressing his philosophical concern for himself, reality and the era.[1] Therefore, readers may need to put it in the realistic context of war in the reading process.

The first poem implies the war discourse, using the scene of insects resisting danger to metaphorize the creation of eternity in a moment, that is an "unexpected miracle"[1]. Just as the individual life in the Anti-Japanese War was destroyed in glory and lived forever in nirvana; the second poem uses the verses of "trees shedding leaves and flowers in autumn, cicadas and moths shedding their shells and the scores of songs leaving their voices"[1] to answer "what can fall from us, we let it turn into dust". In the context of the war era, the poet uses the verses to express the great nation's shedding of its impurities in the war and obtaining new life through such a difficult transformation; the seventh poem "has the same warning in our hearts, has the same destiny on our shoulders" and "sea water is divided into river water" reminds people of the situation of the war era, where the life safety of people is greatly threatened, the quality of the whole nation as a life community becomes more prominent, and the responsibility of saving the nation from peril is shared by everyone; the eighth poem reveals the poet's spiritual aspiration in the war situation, "wanting to cling to the peng bird and fly, to talk with the peaceful stars ...... they often learn how to run, how to fall, to arrange the star order in the world, and then throw themselves into the sky like light." The verses convey the poet's hope that people can bravely resist the aggression, find the way of national liberation, and still have the bright wish; and the tenth to fourteenth poems choose five great cultural spirits as the spiritual idols of eulogy, and have dialogues with Cai Yuanpei, Lu Xun, Du Fu, Goethe and Van Gogh, respectively corresponding to the themes of "enlightenment, fighting, hardship, transformation, salvation"; the 21st to 23rd poems have a series of specific images, all of which have the image of "rain", "listening to the storm in the gale" "listening to the deep night rain" "one day the rain clouds suddenly disperse"[2] The verses all imply the theme of facing the hardship and longing for the brightness, which is in line with the poet's spiritual journey in the Anti-Japanese War.

From these specific verses, it can be seen that Feng Zhi's poetry creation is always connected with the reality of the Anti-Japanese War, combining Rilke's modern poetry spirit and the reality of China's Anti-Japanese War[3], forming a "wanderer's discourse" different from the mainstream discourse at that time.[3] Feng Zhi has translated Rilke's famous "Ten Letters to a Young Poet", in which the importance of everyday life to the poet is this pithy statement: "So you should avoid those universal subjects and return to what your own daily life presents you; You write of your sorrows and wishes, of your passing thoughts, of your belief in a certain beauty - with deep, quiet, modest sincerity, with the things around you, the shadows in your dreams, the objects in your memories. If you feel that your daily life is poor, don't complain about it; Or blame yourself, blame you are not enough to be a poet to call the treasure of life; For there is no poverty for

*2539796802@qq.com

the creator, nor is there a barren place that is irrelevant."[4] To some extent, Feng Zhi was inspired by Rilke's conception of the poetics of daily life.

2.In the Landscape of Kunming, expressing the Spirit of "Entering the World"

In the initial escape, the natural scenery that Feng Zhi felt was unfamiliar and alienated. He quoted Du Fu's poem:"I travel in different mountains and rivers, suddenly in another world" in "Chengdu Prefecture" to express his wandering mood of "falling to the end of the world" at that time.[5] He wrote "the familiar things are getting farther and farther away, and the unfamiliar scenes are unfolding in front of me one by one, everything seems to be fleeting. " [6] This reveals his inner anxiety and strangeness. It was not until he arrived in Kunming that Feng Zhi had the opportunity to get close to nature, and was able to balance the contradiction between spirit and reality in his ordinary life. He wrote in the postscript of "Landscape" that "in the most depressed years of the Anti-Japanese War, I relied on the simple wilderness to provide me with unlimited spiritual food. When the general phenomena in the society tended to rot day by day, any small grass on the field ridge, any tree on the hillside, had given me many inspirations."[7] He gained a new life experience from nature, shining with brilliant poetic thoughts. But he was neither completely intoxicated with the pleasant scenery of the four seasons, nor did he only emphasize the suffering and sorrow brought by the war.

Even when he got a stable life, the deep concern for the national destiny made it difficult for him to follow the Taoist thought of "wandering freely" to transcend the world and enjoy the peaceful and beautiful life. The war made him feel more deeply that the individual life was inseparable from the era environment and the national future, and this was in line with Du Fu's spirit across a thousand years. Feng Zhi's creation and research of Du Fu focused on taking Du Fu as the standard, drawing from Du Fu the spiritual strength and ideological motivation that the era lacked. It was also from Du Fu that Feng Zhi found a way to reconcile the conflict between the era and the individual: "There is no transcendence, no detachment, only persistence: persistence in nature, persistence in life." And his Sonnet Collection is imbued with his ideological proposition of "overcoming this era and overcoming himself".

In addition, it is worth noting that the landscape depicted by the poet in his poetry is not focused on the regional writing of Kunming scenery, but more on the unnamed scenery, close to the generalization, and its implied thought is far in the vague universe. For example, in "A Disappeared Mountain Village", "we walk into any forest, or a grassland, and always feel that they are mostly like this in the prehistoric era. Human history has evolved for thousands of years, but they are outside of humanity. They do not change, thousands of years as one day. Silently facing eternity."[8] It can be seen that the landscape here is different from the ancient people's feelings of landscape or the leisure of playing in the mountains and waters, but becomes the synonym of "world" and "universe", carrying the poet's thinking of reality and life with an indefinite meaning.

Other spatial images related to natural landscape also reflect his natural view of "entering the world through landscape". The first poem of the collection uses a small insect's "resistance to danger" to show the value of the individual; the second poem uses a tree's life and death transformation in autumn to symbolize the change of life; the third poem uses the towering eucalyptus tree's sacredness and solemnity to show the loftiness of life; the fourth poem uses the humility and dignity of the mouse ear grass by the road to reflect the attitude of life; the fifth poem uses the connection between islands to imply the relationship of life; the sixth poem uses the cry of a village child or a peasant woman to express the sorrow of the whole universe. From this we can see that Feng Zhi pays more attention to the unchanging nature of landscape, placing the small self in the vast world, "observing it with its unchanging ones", and perceiving the essence of life, just like Su Shi's state of mind of "floating and floating, what is it like, a sand gull in the world".

3.The Spatial Consciousness of "Road" and "Dream" from "Thatched Cottage" to "Wilderness"

3.1 A group of highly repetitive images

The images in Feng Zhi's Sonnet Collection are repetitive, such as "wilderness", "thatched cottage", "dream" and "road" appear many times in the collection. The author counts the images with high repetition in the poetry as follows: 1. "Wilderness" and similar images: "The Cry of the Wilderness", "The Path of the Wilderness", "We Sometimes Spend an Intimate Night " have three "wilderness" images, "We Stand on the High Mountain Top" has three "plain" images, and "Our Life is Like the Wilderness Outside the Window" in "We Sometimes Spend an Intimate Night" has a "wilderness" image, which is vague but profound, symbolizing the vague and intangible life, and can also be understood as the vast universe; 2. "Road" images such as: "Lu Xun" (the grass by the road), "We Stand on the High Mountain Top" ("which road", "path"), "The Path of the Wilderness" (six "road" images), "We Sometimes Spend an Intimate Night" (one "road" image), "We Walk a Small Road Every Day" (two "road" images); 3. "Dream" images such as: "An Old Dream", "How Many Faces, How Many Voices" (three "dream" images), "Deep Night and Deep Mountain", "The Desk is Laid with Utensils" all have "dream" images; 4. The humanistic image "thatched cottage" appears many times in "We Sometimes Spend an Intimate Night" and "We Listen to the Storm in the Gale", on the one hand, it represents the universality of the place, on the other hand, it is also the symbol of the poet himself as the place where he settles down. These categories of images appear repeatedly in the collection, not by chance, but by the concentration of the author's thoughts. "We stand on the high mountain top and turn into a boundless distant view, into a vast plain in front of us, into the crisscrossing paths on the plain." ("We Stand on the High Mountain Top") The images of "mountain top" and "plain" reflect the author's view of integrating himself into the natural landscape, turning natural scenery into human life, and human experience and emotion into nature.[9] Nature affects people, and people get inspiration and comfort in nature. It can be said that the circular and repetitive thought journey in the poetry is also the author' s dream of turning back and forth.

3.2 The poetic thoughts shown by the order of the collection

Feng Zhi's spatial concept of creating Sonnet Collection is also reflected in the arrangement of the poetry. The collection is not arranged according to the chronological order, but according to the theme that echoes each other, forming a complete cycle of life experience. Feng Zhi's poetry is different from Bian Zhilin's meticulous carving, his poetry is more inclined to be non-logical, and is created from the past life experience of consciousness and subconsciousness.

Sonnet Collection is a collection of poems that explores the theme of human survival. There are 27 poems in total, which can be divided into several parts according to the content. The beginning and the end of the collection (the first and the 27th) echo each other, implying the uncertainty and contingency of survival, as well as the poet's acceptance of life: "We are ready to receive deeply".[10] The second to the eighth are a group of poems that reflect the state of human existence. The poet uses natural images to metaphorize the process of human life: "We arrange ourselves in this era, like the trees in autumn", "We arrange ourselves in nature, like the metamorphosed cicadas and moths", "We arrange ourselves for the future death". These poems express the way of human survival in nature, how to experience the changes of seasons like trees, how to experience metamorphosis and rebirth like cicadas and moths, and how to face the inevitability of death. The poet shows his insight and comprehension of the law of life in these poems. The third and the fourth are the concretization of the second, respectively taking the eucalyptus tree and the mouse ear grass as examples, depicting the growth and withering of the trees. The fifth is the response to the third, using cicadas and moths as symbols, describing the transformation and rebirth of human beings: "A loneliness is an island, and they all become friends. When you pull my hand, it's like a bridge on the water. When you smile at me, it's like a window opening suddenly on the opposite island." The sixth, seventh, and eighth are poems about death, revealing the sorrow, crisis, and turmoil brought by death, consuming one's life, and the poet reminds people to be sober and cherish life: "Cherish this fate". The ninth to the fourteenth are a group of poems that face the secular world, expressing the poet's criticism and transcendence of the secular, which is a further deepening of the previous survival theme. The fifteenth to the twenty-sixth are a group of poems that explore the various relationships between man and nature, past and future. The poet shows his multi-dimensional thinking and feeling of life here.

From this classification, we can see that the author arranges the order of the collection according to his own creative theme classification and re-creation, rather than simply according to the writing time. Therefore, taking the writing theme as the path, selecting the representative poems with the images of wilderness and road, we can reflect the author's mood changes that he wants to convey to a certain extent. The following will take the second "There are Eucalyptus Trees", the sixth "The Cry of the Wilderness", the sixteenth "We Stand on the High Mountain Top", the seventeenth "The Path of the Wilderness", and the twenty-sixth "We Walk a Small Road Every Day" as examples to analyze the author's spatial consciousness of integrating into the landscape and experiencing the change of mind. Among them,

"There are Eucalyptus Trees" uses rich images, such as autumn wind, jade tree, music, palace, tower, body of the living, noise of the city, shell, field, soil, humanistic and natural spatial elements are ingeniously integrated. Among them, "tree" is a core image, which not only symbolizes the author's vitality and creativity, but also reflects the author's thinking on the relationship between man and nature, man and society. The "tree" in the collection is not isolated from the noise and customs of the city, but is closely connected with human life. It stands on the vast wilderness, experiencing the changes of seasons and the baptism of wind and rain, and also guides people to move forward, seek the meaning and value of life.[11] This reflects the poet's spirit of "entering the world through landscape". He does not advocate using landscape as a refuge from reality, but advocates cultivating a positive personality through landscape, facing the difficulties and challenges in life, and also reflects his sincere attitude towards life.

Feng Zhi's poetry also shows his concern for the times and his sympathy for the people. He uses "wilderness" as a metaphor for the times in "The Cry of the Wilderness", depicting the crying and tears of the "village children" and "peasant women", expressing his intolerance and indignation for the suffering of the people, but he does not sink because of this, but strengthens his faith and ideal. In "We Stand on the High Mountain Top", he shows a high-spirited mood, blending "we" with the natural scenery, both being a part of nature and a creator of nature, reflecting his ecological concept of mutual symbiosis between man and nature.[12] In " The Path of the Wilderness", he uses the two images of "wilderness" and "road" to express his exploration and discovery of life. He thinks that "wilderness" is both the natural wilderness and the spiritual wilderness, and "road" is both the road trodden by pedestrians and the imprint of memory. He seeks the mystery of survival in nature, and also seeks the meaning of life in his mind. "We Walk a Small Road Every Day" is a daily life poem by Feng Zhi. He proposes a paradox in this poem, that is, the things we are most familiar with may be the things we know the least, they may hide deep and strange connotations, waiting for us to discover. He thinks that the terrible thing is not the blandness and monotony of life, but the numbness and dullness of the mind. We should use the eyes of discovery and the desire for novelty to change our life and ourselves.

The collection contains the spatiotemporal view of "entering the world through landscape". In that special era, Feng Zhi did not choose to directly express the suffering and sorrow of the war, but chose to write the reality and ordinariness of the world through the landscape of the world, showing a kind of poetry style full of humanistic feelings and warm and intimate.

Reading Feng Zhi's poems, we feel his thoughts like "feeling the scent of a rose."At this point, we may understand why, under the dark clouds of the war in the 1940s, Feng Zhi had such a deep passion for daily life and such a deep feeling for all things natural, because all these are deeply related to his life. He wrote "CAI Yuanpei", "Lu Xun", "Du Fu" with deep admiration, and he dedicated sincere praise to an ordinary soldier, a tree, a plant of grass, or a small insect. "Deep in the great rest of all things"[13], he saw from those great or ordinary things the tenacity and consciousness of individual life, saw the sense of self-determination and the spirit of courage to take responsibility, and this is perhaps the most urgent need of a nation in distress. Therefore, Feng Zhi, who wrote the Sonnets, did not, like Dai Wangshu, He Qifang, Bian Zhilin and other poets, eagerly "join in a certain big rhythm", banished the exquisite personal lyricism before and integrated into the chorus of The Times; Nor do poets like Mu Dan and Do Yun-seop present a painful state of split soul in the struggle between self and times, reality and metaphysics. In contrast, Feng Zhi may choose a middle way, that is, he does not give up the personalized philosophical contemplation while paying attention to the real suffering, and the personalized philosophical contemplation also contains the attention to the real suffering, and the two are perfectly integrated into a daily poetics realm. War and everyday life, war and poetry, war and intellectuals, these are probably the questions that every poet who lived in the context of the war of the 1940s had to face.

References

1. W. Yunxia. The Poetics of Daily Life in the Context of War: Reading Feng Zhi's Sonnets [J]. Journal of Wuhan University (Humanities Edition),145-152 (2011). [in Chinese]
2. F. Zhi. "A Brief Explanation of Goethe's Thirteen Poems", The Complete Works of Feng Zhi, Vol. 8 [M], Hebei Education Press, 147 (1999). [in Chinese]
3. S. Denggao. Transformation and Integration of life: An Interpretation of Life Consciousness in Feng Zhi's Sonnets [J]. Journal of Inner Mongolia Agricultural University (Social Sciences Edition),207-208 (2012). [in Chinese]
4. Rilke, "Ten Letters to a Young Poet", The Complete Works of Feng Zhi, vol. 11, Hebei Education Press, 288-289 (1999).[in German]
5. T. Chaojia. From the abstract "landscape" to the deep digging of nostalgia: An interpretation of Feng Zhi's thought transformation [J]. Journal of Wuhan University of Science and Technology (Social Science Edition),574-580 (2019). [in Chinese]
6. L. Changhua. From Romantic Myth to poetic philosophy: Feng Zhi's narrative poems of Myth and Legend and the Sonnets [J]. Modern Chinese Literature Research Series,139-146 (2011). [in Chinese]
7. Y. Zhi. Comparison of Time and space Experience between Feng Zhi and Du Fu's Poems [J]. Modern Chinese Literature Studies Series,230-253 (2006). [in Chinese]
8. C. Wei. Western Landscape Concept and Feng Zhi's Landscape and Sonnets [J]. Modern Chinese Literature Research Series, 80-89 (2011). [in Chinese]
9. W. Youxin, Long Yongqian. Hidden and Beyond the traditional roots of Feng Zhi's Sonnets [J]. Literary Review, 165-170 (2009). [in Chinese]
10. T.S. S. Eliot: The Metaphysical Poet. Collected Essays on Eliot's Literature, Baihuazhou Literature Publishing House, (22) 1994. [in England]
11. J. W. Goethe, Theory of colours: Narrative part. In F. Zhi, Goethe and Du Fu (Vol. 8, p. 184). [in German]
12. B. Spinoza, Ethics. In J. Hampshire, The feast of thought, Kyushu Press (2005). [in Dutch]
13. X. Zhixi. Poetry and Thought: An Interpretation of Feng Zhi's Three Sonnets [J]. Modern Chinese Literature Studies Series, 91-106 (1992). [in Chinese]

Recreating Fantasy: Fan culture in fan-made merchandise and advertising on Chinese social media

Ruiyang Zang*

Tisch School of the Arts, New York University, New York, NY 10012, United States of America

Abstract. Fandom has long been recognized as a dynamic and participatory culture. In the context of Chinese social media Weibo, this study investigates the fan-made merchandise and advertising landscape within the pop culture fan community, and explores how fan producers and consumers interact in the creation, promotion, and acquisition of fan-made merchandise by delving into the intricacies of product design, advertisement composition and its impact on audience feedback. With data collected from text analysis, the result of regression and statistic results show that fan producers exhibit a strong preference for merchandise featuring specific character images, emphasizing the ornamental aspects of their creations. Advertisement posts on social media serve as platforms for artistic self-expression, while the consumers prioritize concise product information. This dynamic interaction fosters collaborative value creation in the modern fan community, offering participants a chance to modify and add onto the original content as well as construct their own identity.

1.Introduction

As early as 1990, Fiske suggested that audiences are not passive consumers but resistant readers and consumers who adapt culture. The participation mode of fans in popular culture is not static; they never just sit back and passively receive information. They actively create and export value on existing texts. With the development of networks and productivity, fans have more room for expression. Whether it is due to the convenient environment of resource aggregation, the pursuit of identity in virtual communities, or more accessible technology, unlike the traditional static mode of participation, fans today are eager to utilize their own creativity to reproduce the cultural products they are passionate about [1].

For fans of pop fiction works, usually animes, comics, games and novels (hereinafter "ACGN"), there are countless ways to engage in cultural reproduction, from the most typical virtual forms of cross-media creation, including fan arts, fan fictions, fan games and so on to cosplay events and large conventions taking place in offline communities. Many fan studies have focused as well on the psychology of fan creators, participation patterns, the uniqueness of medium in fan creations, and even the dynamic of fan communities in a sociological sense, examining in depth the interactions between fans on a linguistic, textual, and value level. However, the form of the physical economy within fan communities – merchandise designed, produced and sold by fans, and purchased by fans – seems to be an unexplored area.

In fact, the size of the market for fan-made merchandise is substantial. In May 2023, the 29th Comicup, the largest anime convention in China, which featured goods exclusively from fan creations, drew more than 300,000 creators and consumers to the event. Similar events that focus primarily on the sales of fan creations also include Comiket in Japan, with a history of more than 40 years. Besides self-published print works, the merchandise sold at the convention is often small and cheap objects with fan-created illustrations, sold at or near cost. The conventions clearly reflect the duality of the identity of the fans in them – as both producers and consumers. However, since profit is not the primary goal of the fans, such activities are not considered commercial; the physical exchange of money and goods actually constitutes a way of exchanging values and ideas.

Fans' enthusiasm for merchandise does not spring up in a sudden. While the characters and plots of the works are completely fictional and intangible, what does a physical object beyond the screen and paper mean? From an inward perspective, merchandise maintains and derives the experiences fans have in their works into reality, leaving traces of their fantasies in their lives and fulfilling their imaginations; from an outward perspective, merchandise has its aspect of fashion [2]. It is a means for fans to establish and show off their own identity. As the Troika study puts it, fandom is a relationship between an individual and an object [3]. Consumption of merchandise expresses one's fandom, which indicates who they are, so the existence of peripheral merchandise is crucial for fans to have a recognizable identity [4].

Combining these two aspects, the act of consuming merchandise is completely self-centered, but the situation is slightly more complicated for the producers of fan merchandise. On the one hand, since profit is not the main

*Corresponding author's mail: rz2077@nyu.edu

objective, fan producers, unlike officials, do not need to rack their brains to cater to popular tastes when designing goods. Just as creating fan arts, they can produce from their own interests and use production as a channel for self-expression, leaving their own unique imprint on the merchandise. On the other hand, due to the existence of production costs, they cannot completely free themselves from sales concerns, and appropriate strategies to attract consumers are still necessary.

To fulfill such a demand, advertising of fan merchandise was born. Fan producers post on social media showcasing the items they will be selling, and then spread them with the power of the community to increase exposure. With the growth of the fan peripheral economy and iterations of social media affordance, this type of advertising has evolved into a unique form and been integrated as part of fan culture. Unlike typical commercials, they constitute communication. Producers output their preferences and ideas in advertisements, and every choice and decision serve their need for expression while pursuing better diffusion.

The purpose of this study is to explore how fan culture is reflected in the way fans think, act, and value by observing the tendencies of fan producers as a group in making decisions on the design of merchandise, crafting advertisements, and feedback on social media as a form of communication.

2.Weibo as the platform of observation

Weibo, initially released in 2009 as a product of the Web2.0 era, has become one of the most popular and commonly used social platforms in China, with nearly 600 million monthly active users. Not only serves as a mainstream platform for information sharing by those from official agencies to individuals, Weibo has also built a virtual community with its characteristics of remarkable immediacy and interactivity [5]. While Weibo carries the basic affordance of repost, comment, and likes, its functions of tagging, topic and subscription allow users with the same interest to get into contact with each other in a common cyber space, especially enhancing the sense of belonging and dependence of subcultural groups with weak discourse power and limited member connections in reality. Therefore, Weibo makes the habitat of ACGN fans. By April 2020, there are 2.92 pan-ACGN-fans who discuss their beloved works on their homepages or in exclusive topics, follow their favorite fan artists, appreciate their works and interact with them on Weibo, constructing the energetic dynamic of the community.

The mechanics of posting, browsing and display of Weibo fit the needs of ACGN fans. The current version of Weibo supports sending up to 18 images per post. In the preview of a single post on the user's screen, some of the content will be folded in order to reduce the length, but the first 9 images will be shown in the form of nine squares, and regardless of the image-text ratio in a post, images always take a larger screen area than text does. This layout gives fan arts, usually in anime style, plenty of room to play to their strengths. Fanart creators are given more space to show their works, and the general audience is able to view clearer and more eye-catching creations. When Li talks about the application of anime design in advertising, he mentions the novelty and uniqueness of the picture language, as well as the wide imagination space and rich interest it offers, which means the accentuated images not only have an innate appeal to the ACGN fans built around visual content, but also becomes the appropriate promotion platform for merchandise [6].

The result is the common occurrence of advertisements of fan-made merchandise on Weibo, taking the advantage of its both depth and width in communication. Fan artists make their works into a variety of products, posting for promotion and sell them, which is often called "paid exchange" by participants, on a small scale within the fan community, As not only followers would be notified instantly for new posts, but posts would also be pushed to the home page of other users with similar interests by the algorithm, posting on Weibo is effective in increasing the exposure of the merchandise with the concentrated fan groups and the easy display, communication and diffusion.

The highly active ACGN fan community and a large number of fan-made merchandise promotion posts on Weibo provide rich, real and up-to-date samples. Therefore, Weibo is chosen as the platform to conduct observation for this research.

3.Research design

3.1 Method

This research adopts the content analysis as the primary method to study the original fan-made merchandise advertisements on Weibo, including aspects of design of products in the advertisement, composition of the advertisement itself, and the feedback received after posting, so as to explore the choices and values of fans as producers. In the context of the Weibo ACG fan community, the concepts have unique connotations. Therefore, constructs and corresponding operationalizations in this research are stated below.

3.2 Variables

In this research, the preferences of fan producers will be investigated in product design and advertisement composition, each aspect containing three features as variables. Also, the feedback each advertisement post gained is also quantified to estimate the relation between the communication effect and choices producers made on the advertisement. Table 1 shows the concepts functioning as variables in the research and their definition.

Table 1. Variables and definitions

Product Design	Image Feature (Figure/Concept) The characteristic of the illustration used on the merchandise. Divided as concrete figures as the subject, or abstract signs and concepts and scenes as the subject.
	Refinement (Raw/Refined) The part of design completed through technical processing during mass production, not included in the original illustration, but can significantly improve the appearance of the merchandise. E.g., surfaces coated with laser film to obtain bright visual effects.
	Practicality (Practical/Non-practical) The function of the merchandise. Divided into low practicality as merchandise with mere decorative functions and high practicality as including uses beyond.
Advertisement Composition	Preview Format (Assemblage/Sole Image) Whether the image preview of the post preview is presented as multiple small pictures combined to form a complete larger picture, or the pictures are independent of each other.
	Graphic Design (With/Without) Whether the pictures of the advertisement involve a certain level of visual design, such as considerations on font, composition, color, shape and decoration.
	Text Length (Short/Long) In addition to the name and necessary descriptions, whether the advertisement includes more than 50 characters of promotional text.
Feedback	The number of reposts, comments and likes the post receives. The index reflecting the effective impact the advertisement achieves on the audience.

3.3 Data sources

The advertisement posts examined in the research are all collected from Weibo, and are limited to the advertisements of merchandise sold on Comicup 29 conference (CP29) for the following reasons: 1) Large database. According to the conference official, CP29 has a total of about 87,000 fan merchandise on sale. 2) Stability. Its related traffic has become static after 5 months. 3) Homogeneity. The time, context, and distribution of goods tend to be similar, eliminating distractive factors beforehand. 4) Basic exposure. The heat of the conference has a positive impact on the advertising posts marked with relevant tags, and they serve more effectively in studying feedback with a certain level of exposure.

On this basis, in order to further eliminate the interference caused by the uneven or low popularity of the IP, in data collection, random sampling is done among the 4 most popular IPs in CP29. According to the official booth map, the IPs with the most booths at the exhibition are Ensemble Stars! (about 475 booth numbers), Arknights (about 340 booth numbers), Final Fantasy (about 246 booth numbers) and Haikyuu!! (About 163 booth numbers). Finally, 970 merchandise and their advertisements are included as samples in the research and coded according to the above operational definitions.

3.4 Analysis models

The research starts with descriptive statistics on Product Design and Advertising Composition, the number and frequency of each decision by fan-made merchandise producers is statistically recorded and visualized into bar charts to compare and interpret the tendency of choice.

For the aspect of Feedback, three indexes of feedback - reposts, comments and likes - are weighted according to their status of importance from 3 to 1, to quantify the total feedback value an advertisement post receives. After the linear regression model is used to examine and exclude the influence brought by the number of followers of the poster's account, the value will be associated with the choices studied in the first two aspects. Based on the type of data collected for each aspect, linear regression models for Product Design and compare means for Advertising Composition, will apply to explore the relation between the choice of the fan-made merchandise producer and the feedback gained.

4.Results

4.1 Product design

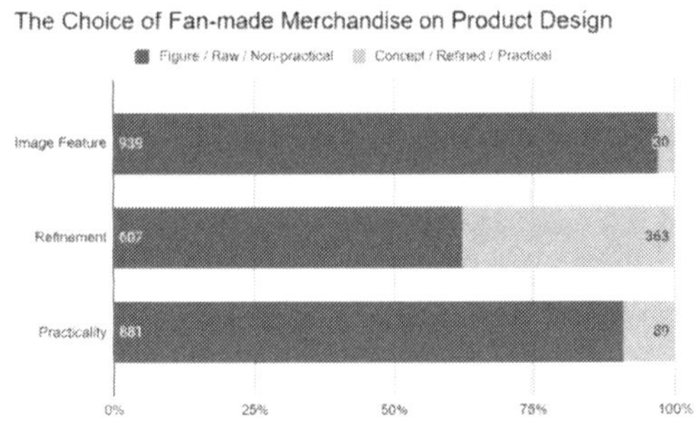

Fig. 1. The Choice of Fan-made Merchandise on Product Design

Part 4.1 calculates and compares the proportion of merchandise under each choice of Product Design by looking at the statistical data of merchandise, and establishes the basis for summarizing the common habits and preferences of the fan-made merchandise producers as a whole. Fig. 1 shows that most of the fan products in the sample are printed with specific figures and have no practical use. More than half of the merchandise are not processed, highlighting the art itself, but there are still a certain percentage of merchandise that choose to add technological refinement to achieve better visual effects.

4.2 Advertisement composition

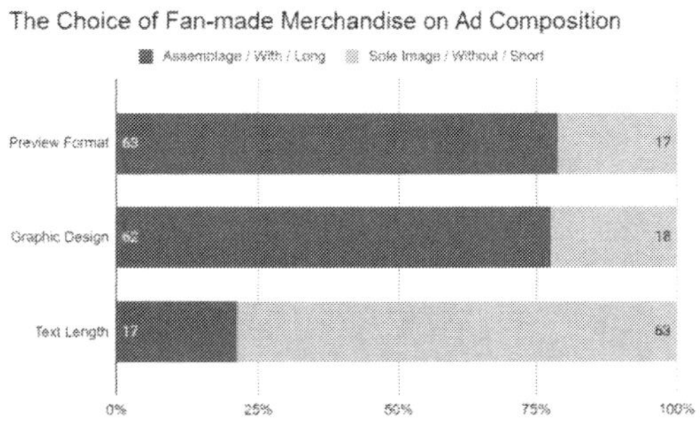

Fig. 2. The Choice of Fan-made Merchandise on Advertisement Composition

Part 4.2 calculates and compares the proportion of advertisement posts under each choice of Advertisement Composition with the aim to make a sketch of the preferred and commonly used strategy fan producers adopt when promoting their merchandise. Fig. 2 shows that over 75% of advertisement posts in the sample takes the format of Assemblage for preview, have a certain extent of graphic design and uses short text.

4.3 Feedback

4.3.1 Feedback vs. Number of fans

Table 2. Regression Analysis of Feedback value vs. Number of fans

Regression Statistics	
Multiple R	0.4419187587
R Square	0.1952921893
Adjusted R Square	0.1849754225
Standard Error	1109.739037
Observations	80
Significance F	0. 000040641114464
Coefficient	0.01694375554
P-value	0.00004064114497
Lower 95%	0. 009190627795
Upper 95%	0.02469688329

First, in order to confirm the influence of the number of fans that the poster's account owns on the response of the advertisement post, a scatter plot is made according to the number of fans of each poster recorded and the feedback value obtained by weighted calculation, and the regression line is calculated. As shown in Table. 2, although R^2 is only around 0.195, representing less than 20% of the actual data matches the line, but as p = 0.05, coefficient = 0.0169, there is still a weak positive correlation indicated between variables, that is, the number of fans has a slight positive effect on the feedback parameters of posts.

Therefore, in order to further study the separate relations between Product Design, Advertisement Composition and Feedback in the environment excluding disparity caused by the number of fans, all samples are divided into groups by the interval of number of fans (n), including n≥100000, 100000>n≥10000, 10000>n≥5000, 5000>n≥1000, 1000>n≥100 and n<100, to counteract as much as possible the interference of number of fans. Among them, only 6 samples exist in the group of n>=100000, and only 3 samples exist in the group of n<100. The two groups are thus not taken into following research for the data insufficient to form a universal conclusion.

4.3.2 Feedback vs. Product design

For the aspect of Product Design, the research starts with exploring whether the three elements of "Figure", "Refined" and "Practical" are more conducive to bringing positive effects to the feedback of advertising posts, that is, in the real context, whether the three choices of design can arouse more audience's attention and interest on the post.

The corresponding choices made in each sample are denoted as 1, and the opposite is denoted as 0. After calculating the mean of the corresponding choices in the merchandise displayed in each advertisement post, the data is mapped into a scatter plot, and the relation between each choice and Feedback Value is computed using multiple regression.

This process is repeated for each group, aiming to arrive at a consistent pattern.

Table 3. Regression Analysis of Feedback value vs. Product Design in group 100000>n≥10000

Regression Statistics			
	Figure	Refinement	Practicality
Multiple R	0.3661993304		
R Square	0.1341019496		
Adjusted R Square	-0.1906098193		
Standard Error	1423.04339		
Observations	12		
Significance F	0.7483271806		
Coefficient	-11865.20508	909.1105779	-965.466155
P-value	0.7257174658	0.6702534867	0.776655513
Lower 95%	-87156.30679	-3834.827237	-8552.6498
Upper 95%	63425.89663	5653.048393	6621.71749

https://doi.org/10.1051/shsconf/202418502014

Table 4. Regression Analysis of Feedback value vs. Product Design in group 10000>n≥5000

Regression Statistics			
	Figure	Refinement	Practicality
Multiple R	0.6039514463		
R Square	0.3647573495		
Adjusted R Square	0.0471360243		
Standard Error	559.3593202		
Observations	10		
Significance F	0.4031111961		
Coefficient	-960.1945246	990.725786	-972.7400519
P-value	0.3816405756	0.3412733216	0.6106891806
Lower 95%	-3449.239114	-1355.211684	-5406.460295
Upper 95%	1528.850065	3336.663256	3460.980191

Table 5. Regression Analysis of Feedback value vs. Product Design in group 5000>n≥1000

Regression Statistics			
	Figure	Refinement	Practicality
Multiple R	0.3910984018		
R Square	0.1529579599		
Adjusted R Square	0.01921447984		
Standard Error	234.4375737		
Observations	23		
Significance F	0.3569094945		
Coefficient	-186.9960238	88.26407729	454.986228
P-value	0.5493130202	0.6751321991	0.2200847822
Lower 95%	-828.9782756	-345.7328852	522.2610397
Upper 95%	1528.850065	-1316.413203	323.0930666

Table 6. Regression Analysis of Feedback value vs. Product Design in group 1000>n≥100

Regression Statistics			
	Figure	Refinement	Practicality
Multiple R	0.3468790896		
R Square	0.1203251028		
Adjusted R Square	0.0003694350265		
Standard Error	144.9394439		
Observations	26		
Significance F	0.4100673032		
Coefficient	370.9698501	-0.05249893873	198.6721666
P-value	0.2306787192	0.9996620498	0.1950933088
Lower 95%	-253.1156194	-254.2011758	-109.6459849
Upper 95%	995.0553197	254.0961779	506.9903181

As shown in Tables 3-6, the P-values for all groups remain greater than 0.05, and R^2 appears to be low, no correlation between the variables can be inferred from this model, and the Feedback in the research sample tends not to be affected by the choices made in terms of Product Design.

4.3.3 Feedback vs. Advertisement composition

In order to examine the effect of advertisement composition on its feedback, in each group, the means of the Feedback Value under the corresponding choice are taken respectively for comparison.

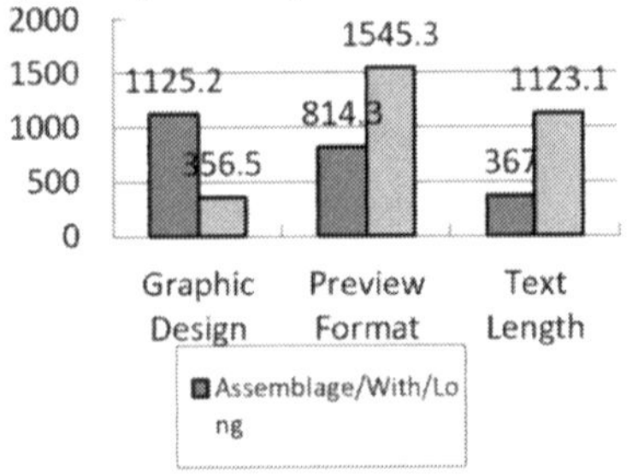

Fig. 3. Feedback Value vs. Advertisement Composition in group 100000>n≥10000

Fig. 3 reveals that in this group, choices of Assemblage and Short text show marked advantage in the resulting Feedback. However, the audience seems insensitive to the use of graphic design as it does not lead to more active responses than those without graphic design.

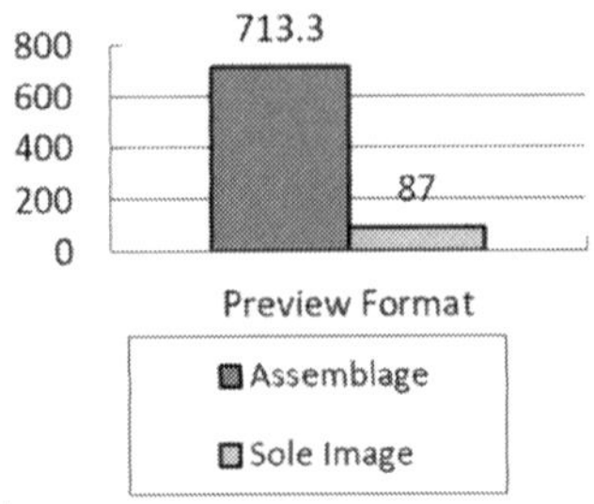

Fig. 4. Feedback Value vs. Advertisement Composition in group 10000>n≥5000

This group does not include choices of Without for Graphic Design and Long for Text Length, so only Preview Format is examined. See Fig. 4.

In this group, Assemblage exhibits a clear attraction to feedback compared to Sole Image.

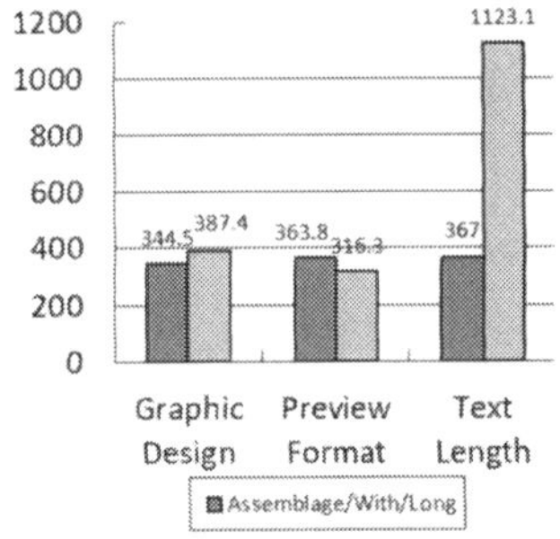

Fig. 5. Feedback Value vs. Advertisement Composition in group 5000>n≥1000

In this group, as Fig. 5 shows, the choices regarding Preview Format and Graphic Design have an almost balanced impact on Feedback Values, with Assemblage and Without graphic design typography slightly lower than their counterparts. At the same time, the association between Short text and higher Feedback Values remains significant.

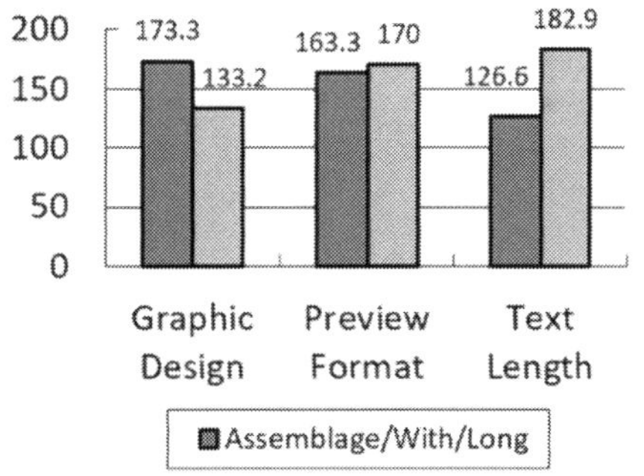

Fig. 6. Feedback Value vs. Advertisement Composition in group 1000>n≥100

In this group, Fig. 6 shows that Assemblage tends to exceed Sole Image to a limited extent in gaining feedback, while the results for choices of Graphic Design are almost even. Short texts still show remarkable advantages over long texts.

In the majority of cases, Assemblage and Short text are more successful in capturing the audience and prompting them to provide effective feedback, whereas well-designed image layouts do not show clear appeal, and even slightly lag behind those advertisement posts without graphic design.

5.Discussion

From the results of the study, it is clear that fan producers have certain tendencies in general when it comes to product design. Explicit character images are favored over abstract conceptual motifs. This is different from the pattern identified by previous researchers for the relationship between fan level and preference for explicit/invisible signals [7]. Cultural re-creators, often seen as high fan levels, do not favor the subtle visual cues that are supposed to highlight their uniqueness and differentiation over mainstream fans. This divergence perhaps stems from the differences in the types of merchandise. While previous studies have focused on official merchandise, such as T-shirts, the results of Practicality show that fan-made merchandise consists mainly of low-cost badges, plastic pendants, and postcards that are not practical. Although they share the function of being carried around and marking identity, fan merchandise emphasizes more on the ornamental nature of the items. In the process of printing and shaping the art fan producers create into reality, the touchable objects take on the role of a medium, giving substance to an otherwise unbodied and intangible creation. Materialization is undoubtedly welcomed by both groups. It does more than satisfy consumerist fetishism; it deepens the satisfaction fans derive from the original fan art work. By giving digital fan art real-life significance in a more direct way, it recognizes the passion and output of fan artists, and for fan consumers, purchasing it allows them to acquire a copy or a part of their favorite fan art work. Therefore, the production of fan merchandise is a re-creation of the value of the fan art itself, above the cultural reproduction by the fan art of the original text.

Precisely because the mind of the fan merchandise producers is projected onto their goods, the character-centered design reflects the way they approach the work. More interested in specific characters than in transforming and recreating representative elements that condense the whole work or plot, their passion for the work is further refined, falling on one or a few individual characters, and then, by manifesting their love for the character, they express their fandom. With the Cool Japan strategy in the 1980s, the trend of consuming "characters" took shape in the merchandise market. The "character economy" centered on virtual visual images rose to prominence and soon became the mainstay of the toy market of ACGN IPs [8]. By the time that culture has matured and consumerism has become the background sound of the times, fans are skilled at finding the characters they resonate with the most in their work, adoring and pursuing them as if they were picking out potato chip flavors in a supermarket aisle. As the fan works are considered to be interpretation of the original text, fans are choosing a more personalized perspective to interpret the work, not looking top-down at the whole picture, but focusing on a particular character, a cross-section of the work, devoting more attention to them and creating more value from them [2]. Fans break down, transform and repurpose the original text in character according to their own ideas, resulting in new content [9]. When each piece of merchandise with a printed individual character is assembled, they in turn reorganize the work with fresh significance, completing deconstruction and reinvention in a modernist way.

In this sense, the adoption of refinement in fan merchandise is tied to the motivations of the producer. The refinement allows the merchandise to be more visually appealing than with merely the original pattern. The choices made by the producers reveal whether or not they have a desire to go further than self-expression in terms of aesthetics. More than half of the merchandise in the research is free of refinement, preserving the original appearance of the fan art, reflecting the fact that most producers are satisfied with the message conveyed by the art itself. At the same time, a notable percentage of producers chose to strive for excellence, which means that for a large number of producers, "production" itself is also a part of conveying fandom's passion.

Then, from the results of advertisement compositions, the respective habits of the producers and consumers are summarized. The vast majority of producers put great amounts of effort into nice-looking layouts and using stylized embellishments to enhance the visual impact of their ad posts, even though they actually have little effect on the gain in feedback. It seems that the audience for this endeavor is the producers themselves, not the consumers. This breaks with the political construct of traditional advertising. The producers use numerous decorative symbols to fill the pages of their promotional images, but none of them are signifiers in the sense that Kettemann mentions – they do not convey a meaning to the viewers to stimulate an impulse for them to consume [10]. Their meaning actually arises for the producers themselves. They represent a refined, aesthetically pleasing, well-designed artistic pursuit that the producer wants to possess as their own identity. It is to this end that they put in the labor of production to exchange. They are the ones who buy the values in the advertisements. By contrast, real consumers care little about the ingenuity of advertising posts. Only one kind of information here passes between producers and consumers through advertising: the fact of the goods themselves. The consumer's need for that knowledge is so simple, direct and exclusive – they prefer a broad preview image in the form of an assemblage that can be captured at a glance on the homepage of Weibo, and text as brief as possible, except for the necessary description. The most prominent function of ad posts for fan merchandise is to evoke attention, not to add value. The meaning that the public usually seeks in ordinary commercial advertisements has been fulfilled by the fandom, and the posts themselves have become non-utilitarian derivative creations, allowing the producers the freedom to express themselves in them, while the consumers are attracted by the no more than the quality of the goods [1].

Around fan merchandise, the community builds a mutually beneficial communication. Producers and consumers build their identities and interpret themselves in their own ways through the use of commodities, while at the same time satisfying and maintaining each other's needs. Consumers have the right to make their own choices, and the lack of publicity stunts is relatively fair to the different producers. Their interaction is a process of collaborative value creation.

6.Conclusion

This study explores the energetic ACGN community and the fan culture behind it through fan-made goods and their advertisements on Chinese social media. Through quantitative analyses of product design, advertising composition and its impact on feedback, it provides an attempt to interpret the behavior of fan producers and consumers in this unique cultural landscape. Fan producers show a clear preference for product design. Concrete character images are prioritized over abstract, generalized symbols, and the focus tends to favor decorative goods over utilitarian items. Re-imagining and reinterpreting characters is central to the creative expression of fan producers. On the other hand, the motives of the advertisements are distinct from the traditional ones. While fan producers put a great deal of effort into designing visually appealing advertisements, it is found that consumers primarily seek concise information about the product itself. The major function of advertising posts is to attract attention and increase exposure instead of selling meanings, which sets them apart from typical commercials. Consumers express their preferences by choosing goods that resonate with them, while fan producers invest their creative energies in producing unique designs and advertisements, which ultimately become a platform for self-expression where both parties mutually benefit from each other's efforts to re-create value based on works of pop culture, forming a vibrant social model.

While serving as an illuminating glimpse into the real economy in fan culture, the study focuses primarily on an objective analysis of conclusive data and phenomena. Possible future investigations into the subjective thoughts and motivations of fan producers and consumers could reveal more about the behavioral logic behind their decisions about fan merchandise, thus helping to understand the distinctive ACGN culture. Meanwhile, there are more potential topics to be explored in the field, such as whether fans in different regions change their attitudes toward fan merchandise due to differences in copyright laws, community morals, or cultures may be able to help construct a corner of fandom ethnography.

Modern fandom culture has a wide variety of practices, with fans responding enthusiastically to the original works while their unique creativity continues to rewrite the texts and give them new connotations, and they themselves construct, communicate, and continually refine their own identities in the process. It is an attempt to dissolve the capitalist shackles that have long surrounded the creation and exchange of value with affinity, and purely and non-utilitarianly use their labor to realize and bring to others the meaning of production itself.

References

1. Y. Chen. Acad Forum. 37, 2, 4 (2014)
2. E. Affuso, A. Santo. Film Crit. 42, 2, 72-87 (2018)
3. Troika. The Power of Fandom Report (2017), Available online at: https://issuu.com/siwanseok/docs/fandom_report_062317_11am.
4. A. Santo. Sartorial Fandom: Fashion, Beauty Culture, and Identity. 67–83 (2023)
5. W. Xiao, Y, Wang. Today. Mass. Media. 22, 8, 2 (2014)
6. H. Li. Mod. Bus. 11, 277-279 (2010).
7. D.C. Smith-Glaviana, J.E. Lee. Fash. Text. 9, 1, 18 (2022)
8. R. Han. Dongyue Trib. 35, 1, 6 (2014)
9. N. Lamerichs. Productive Fandom: Intermediality and Affective Reception in Fan Cultures. 11-34 (2018)
10. B. Flath, E. Klein, B. Kettemann. Advertising and design: Interdisciplinary perspectives on a cultural field. 45–60 (2014)

Media and Culture: An In-Depth Academic Discourse

Yuan Gao[1,a], Hao Yuan[2,b], Xiangyue Zhang[3*], Yiyuan Li[4,c], Tong Shen[5,d]

[1]The University of Sydney, Sydney Australia
[2]Nuova Accademia di Belle Arti, Milan, Italy
[3]University of Nottingham, Nottingham, United Kingdom
[4]Goldsmiths, University of London, London, United Kingdom
[5]University of Leeds, Leeds, UK

Abstract. The intersection of media and culture is a dynamic and multifaceted domain that has captivated the attention of scholars, critics, and practitioners alike. This comprehensive academic paper delves into the intricate relationship between media and culture, exploring how media both reflects and shapes cultural norms, values, and identities. It examines key theories, historical perspectives, and contemporary manifestations of this nexus while also addressing the ethical dimensions and future directions of this crucial discourse.

1. Introduction

The intricate interplay between media and culture constitutes a dynamic and complex relationship that profoundly impacts our society. Media, spanning a wide array of platforms, from traditional print to the ever-evolving digital landscape, engages in a continuous dialogue with culture. On the other hand, culture, with its multifaceted tapestry of beliefs, practices, and traditions, reciprocally influences media, shaping narratives, representations, and societal norms. This scholarly pursuit embarks on a comprehensive journey to delve into the depths of this intricate connection, aiming to illuminate the profound impact that media has on culture, and conversely, how culture molds and informs the media landscape.

The examination of this symbiotic relationship is crucial for understanding how media serves as a reflection of cultural values, a vehicle for cultural preservation, and a catalyst for cultural change. As we navigate this exploration, we will uncover the ways in which media both mirrors and shapes our collective consciousness, influencing our perceptions, behaviors, and our very sense of self. This endeavor underscores the enduring relevance of this discourse in an ever-evolving globalized society, where media and culture continue to evolve in tandem, shaping the narratives that define our world.

2. Theoretical Frameworks

2.1 Cultural Imperialism

Traditional The concept of cultural imperialism represents a foundational theory in the examination of media's relationship with culture. It asserts that powerful media conglomerates, often originating from dominant cultures, possess the capacity to exert significant influence over the cultures of other nations, ultimately resulting in the erosion of indigenous traditions and identities. This theory, originally formulated and championed by scholars such as Herbert Schiller, offers profound insights into the impact of global media, particularly Western media, on the cultural landscapes of various societies.

Central to the notion of cultural imperialism is the idea that media content produced by economically and technologically advanced nations, such as the United States, tends to flood the global media marketplace. This content, which includes television programs, films, music, and digital media, is often characterized by its high production values, sophisticated storytelling techniques, and extensive marketing campaigns. As a result, it gains widespread popularity and consumption across diverse regions and cultures.

The consequences of this widespread consumption are far-reaching. Proponents of the cultural imperialism theory argue that the predominance of Western media content leads to the homogenization of cultures worldwide. Indigenous traditions, customs, and distinct cultural identities can become marginalized or overshadowed by the pervasive influence of Western values, lifestyles, and narratives.

One prominent example of this phenomenon is the global dominance of Hollywood films and American television shows. Hollywood's ability to produce blockbuster movies with broad appeal has led to the worldwide dissemination of American cultural values and norms. As audiences around the globe consume these narratives, they often encounter portrayals of Western ideals, lifestyles, and consumerism. This can result in the emulation of Western cultural practices, which may displace or erode local customs and traditions.

Moreover, the economic power and reach of dominant media conglomerates allow them to shape global media markets and dictate what content is available to audiences.

E-mail: [a]2482516799@qq.com; [b]2360919540@qq.com; [*]757122973@qq.com;
[c]wellington589125@gmail.com; [d]asderty67rtyasd@gmail.com

This can limit the diversity of voices and perspectives in the media landscape, further reinforcing the influence of Western cultural narratives.

Critics of cultural imperialism theory argue that it oversimplifies the complex interplay between media and culture. They contend that audiences have agency and can interpret and adapt media content in diverse ways, sometimes incorporating elements into their own cultural practices without eroding their indigenous identities. Additionally, the rise of digital media and online platforms has provided opportunities for cultural exchange and the promotion of non-Western voices and perspectives.

Nonetheless, the concept of cultural imperialism remains a critical lens through which to analyze the power dynamics within the global media landscape. It underscores the need for careful consideration of the impact of media on cultural identities and the importance of preserving cultural diversity in an increasingly interconnected world.

2.2 Cultural Studies

Cultural studies, as an influential field within the broader context of media and culture, takes a nuanced and comprehensive approach to understanding the intricate relationship between media and cultural dynamics. Pioneered by notable scholars like Stuart Hall and Raymond Williams, cultural studies have provided invaluable insights into how media functions as both a reflector and a shaper of cultural meanings, norms, and social structures.

Complex Examination of Media Representations: At its core, cultural studies delve deep into the complex tapestry of media representations. It scrutinizes not only what is portrayed but also how it is portrayed, recognizing that media messages are laden with implicit meanings and ideologies. By analyzing the narratives, symbols, and discourses within media content, cultural studies researchers seek to unveil the underlying cultural codes and ideologies that inform and shape these representations.

Reinforcing and Challenging Norms: Cultural studies recognize that media can either reinforce prevailing cultural norms and power structures or challenge them. For instance, media can perpetuate stereotypes and uphold dominant narratives that maintain existing hierarchies. Conversely, media can be a site of resistance, where marginalized voices and alternative perspectives find expression, contesting established norms and ideologies. This duality underscores the complexity of media's role in shaping culture.

Power Dynamics and Cultural Hegemony: Cultural studies also pay close attention to power dynamics and cultural hegemony. It acknowledges that media can be a site where dominant cultural groups exercise control over the narratives and representations that circulate in society. Stuart Hall's concept of "encoding" and "decoding" media messages illustrates how audiences can interpret media content differently, either aligning with the intended message or subverting it, based on their cultural context and positioning within society.

Intersectionality and Diversity: Cultural studies emphasize the importance of intersectionality, recognizing that individuals inhabit multiple social categories (e.g., race, gender, class) that intersect and influence their experiences of media and culture. This perspective highlights the need to consider the diverse ways in which different groups engage with and are represented in media, as well as the power dynamics that shape these interactions.

Media Literacy and Critical Engagement: Cultural studies advocate for media literacy and critical engagement with media content. It encourages audiences to question, deconstruct, and critically analyze media messages rather than passively consuming them. This critical perspective empowers individuals to become active participants in the cultural conversation, challenging problematic representations and advocating for more inclusive and socially just media[8].

3. Media as a Mirror of Culture

Media serves as a reflective surface that captures and projects the intricate tapestry of values, beliefs, and ideologies embedded within the culture it operates. This function is manifest in the diverse content, intricate narratives, and nuanced portrayals that media generates. A prime example of this dynamic interaction can be observed in television shows and films, which frequently serve as powerful conduits for representing and dissecting societal issues, challenging or reinforcing gender roles, and illuminating the depth of cultural rituals. These media forms, therefore, offer a lens through which audiences can not only recognize but also critically interrogate their own cultural realities.

Television shows, as an integral part of contemporary media, have long been recognized as a mirror reflecting societal values and norms. Whether it's the portrayal of family dynamics in a sitcom, the exploration of political issues in a drama series, or the satirical commentary in a late-night talk show, television provides a canvas upon which the cultural landscape is painted. For instance, a series centered on a diverse group of friends may not only reflect the cultural diversity of its audience but also challenge preconceived notions about inclusivity and acceptance.

Similarly, the realm of cinema is replete with examples of how it both mirrors and shapes culture. Films have the power to capture the zeitgeist of a particular era, offering a window into the prevailing societal attitudes and concerns. They can also challenge the status quo, as seen in movies that push the boundaries of gender roles or offer alternative perspectives on historical events. For instance, a film that portrays a strong, independent female protagonist can not only reflect changing gender dynamics but also inspire conversations about feminism and empowerment[7].

Moreover, the depiction of cultural rituals in media is a potent reflection of a society's heritage and traditions. Whether it's a documentary showcasing religious ceremonies, a fictional narrative set during a cultural festival, or even a travel program exploring culinary traditions, these portrayals serve as a mirror that allows viewers to gain insights into diverse cultural practices. Audiences can appreciate the richness and diversity of global cultures while also questioning their own assumptions and biases.

In essence, the media's role as a mirror is a dynamic and multifaceted one. It not only reflects the values, beliefs, and ideologies of a culture but also has the potential to shape and influence them. Audiences, in turn, have the agency to engage critically with the content presented to them, using it as a tool for self-reflection, cultural exploration, and societal progress. This reciprocal relationship between media and culture underscores the profound impact that storytelling and representation have on our collective understanding of the world.

4. Ethical Considerations

4.1. Perpetuation of Stereotypes

The influence of media in reinforcing stereotypes and misrepresenting diverse cultural groups is a complex and pervasive issue. In many instances, media depictions can oversimplify the richness and complexity of different communities, reducing them to caricatures or one-dimensional portrayals. For example, certain racial or ethnic groups have often been subjected to harmful and reductive stereotypes in the media. African Americans may be portrayed solely as criminals or athletes, overlooking the vast diversity of their experiences and contributions to society. Similarly, Asian characters may be pigeonholed into roles that emphasize exoticism or reinforce the model minority myth, neglecting the wide spectrum of their individual stories and achievements.

These stereotypical portrayals not only perpetuate harmful biases but also contribute to the marginalization and discrimination faced by these communities in real life. They can lead to prejudiced attitudes, reinforce existing biases, and hinder efforts to promote diversity, equity, and inclusion in society. Moreover, the impact of such portrayals extends beyond individual perceptions. They can influence public policies, shape cultural attitudes, and affect how institutions interact with these communities. Therefore, it is crucial for media creators and consumers alike to be aware of these harmful stereotypes and advocate for more accurate, respectful, and inclusive representations that reflect the true diversity of cultures and communities[2].

4.2. Reinforcement of Biases

The influence of media in reinforcing stereotypes and misrepresenting diverse cultural groups is a complex and pervasive issue. In many instances, media depictions can oversimplify the richness and complexity of different communities, reducing them to caricatures or one-dimensional portrayals. For example, certain racial or ethnic groups have often been subjected to harmful and reductive stereotypes in media. African Americans may be portrayed solely as criminals or athletes, overlooking the vast diversity of their experiences and contributions to society. Similarly, Asian characters may be pigeonholed into roles that emphasize exoticism or reinforce the model minority myth, neglecting the wide spectrum of their individual stories and achievements.

These stereotypical portrayals not only perpetuate harmful biases but also contribute to the marginalization and discrimination faced by these communities in real life. They can lead to prejudiced attitudes, reinforce existing biases, and hinder efforts to promote diversity, equity, and inclusion in society. Moreover, the impact of such portrayals extends beyond individual perceptions. They can influence public policies, shape cultural attitudes, and affect how institutions interact with these communities. Therefore, it is crucial for media creators and consumers alike to be aware of these harmful stereotypes and advocate for more accurate, respectful, and inclusive representations that reflect the true diversity of cultures and communities[1].

4.3. Exploitation of Cultural Differences

In the relentless quest for profit, media entities have occasionally demonstrated a propensity to not only sensationalize but also overtly exploit cultural differences. This inclination can manifest in various ways within the media landscape, and its consequences are multifaceted.

One prevalent manifestation of this phenomenon is the commodification of cultural traditions and practices. Cultural events or ceremonies that hold deep significance for particular communities may be reduced to mere spectacles for the sake of attracting viewership or readership. Such reductionist portrayals not only undermine the cultural richness and complexity but also contribute to the trivialization of traditions that deserve respect and understanding[3].

Furthermore, the pursuit of sensationalism and commercial gain can lead to cultural insensitivity. Media outlets, in their zeal to capture attention, may inadvertently or intentionally perpetrate stereotypes, caricatures, or misrepresentations of cultures. This insensitivity can perpetuate biases and reinforce prejudiced attitudes, thereby hindering genuine cultural understanding and empathy.

In some instances, the media's relentless drive for sensational coverage can result in the objectification of individuals from particular cultural backgrounds. People may be portrayed as exotic curiosities rather than as individuals with their own agency, experiences, and stories. This objectification further devalues the lived experiences of individuals and reinforces harmful power dynamics[6].

The distortion of cultural practices for commercial gain is another dimension of this complex issue. Media entities may manipulate or exaggerate cultural practices to make them more palatable or entertaining to a broad audience. In doing so, they risk misrepresenting the true essence and significance of these practices, potentially leading to misconceptions and misappropriations.

Addressing these ethical challenges necessitates a concerted effort by media professionals, regulatory bodies, and society at large. By fostering responsible reporting practices, promoting cultural sensitivity, and encouraging media literacy among consumers, it is possible to counteract the harmful effects of commodification and exploitation of cultural differences in the media landscape[5].

5. Future Directions

As we stand at the crossroads of technological advancement, it becomes increasingly evident that the interplay between media and culture is on the precipice of profound transformation. The emergence and rapid development of cutting-edge technologies, such as virtual reality (VR), artificial intelligence (AI), and immersive storytelling, promise to revolutionize how culture is not only represented but also experienced through media.

Virtual Reality (VR):

Virtual reality is poised to offer audiences immersive experiences that blur the boundaries between the real and the virtual. With VR, individuals can step into different cultural landscapes and historical settings, fostering a deeper understanding and empathy for diverse cultures. It has the potential to transport users to distant locations, allowing them to participate in cultural events, rituals, or experiences in a more visceral and authentic manner.

Artificial Intelligence (AI):

Artificial intelligence is reshaping how media content is generated, curated, and personalized. AI algorithms can analyze user preferences and behaviors to tailor content recommendations, exposing individuals to a wider array of cultural perspectives and narratives. Additionally, AI-driven content creation tools can facilitate the production of culturally diverse media, enabling creators to explore and celebrate cultural richness.

Immersive Storytelling:

Immersive storytelling techniques, such as augmented reality (AR) and mixed reality (MR), are enriching narratives by integrating digital elements into the physical world. Cultural heritage sites can come alive with augmented historical reconstructions, and storytelling can extend beyond traditional media formats to engage audiences in culturally immersive experiences[4].

Furthermore, the democratization of media production and distribution through digital platforms continues to empower individuals and marginalized groups to challenge dominant narratives and assert their cultural voices. Social media, online publishing, and user-generated content platforms enable people from diverse backgrounds to share their stories, perspectives, and cultural expressions with a global audience. This democratization has the potential to counterbalance traditional media's historical underrepresentation of certain cultural groups. In this ever-evolving landscape, it is essential for media professionals, content creators, and cultural institutions to adapt and harness the potential of these emerging technologies thoughtfully and ethically. As these technologies become more accessible and pervasive, they hold the promise of fostering cross-cultural dialogue, promoting cultural appreciation, and providing platforms for marginalized voices to be heard.

6. Conclusion

In conclusion, the intricate and symbiotic relationship between media and culture is a multifaceted domain that lies at the heart of academic exploration. It is evident that media serves not merely as a reflection but also as a dynamic force that actively shapes cultural landscapes. This influence extends far beyond mere entertainment and news consumption; it reaches deep into the core of our identities, our values, and our comprehension of the world around us.

As we contemplate the future, it is evident that media's evolution will continue to be a driving force in cultural transformations. The rapid advancement of technology, the proliferation of digital platforms, and the democratization of content creation all herald an era where the impact of media on culture will be even more pronounced.

In this evolving landscape, we must remain vigilant to both the opportunities and challenges that lie ahead. While media can amplify diverse voices, foster cultural exchange, and facilitate global understanding, it can also perpetuate stereotypes, deepen divides, and manipulate perceptions. Ethical considerations and responsible media practices will be paramount as we navigate this ever-changing terrain.

This academic endeavor reaffirms the enduring relevance of the media-culture discourse in our modern, globalized society. It underscores the importance of continued scholarly investigation and critical reflection to comprehend and harness the power of media as a cultural force. As we move forward, this discourse will serve as a guiding light, helping us navigate the intricate interplay between media and culture, ensuring that it remains a force for positive cultural evolution and societal progress.

References

1. da Silva, Jaime A. Teixeira. "How to shape academic freedom in the digital age? Are the retractions of opinionated papers a prelude to "cancel culture" in academia?." Current Research in Behavioral Sciences 2 (2021): 100035.
2. Anyim, Wisdom O. "Use of academic social networking sites among lecturers in state universities." Journal of Media, Culture and Communication (JMCC) ISSN: 2799-1245 1.01 (2021): 1-13. Anyim, Wisdom O. "Use of academic social networking sites among lecturers in state universities." Journal of Media, Culture and Communication (JMCC) ISSN: 2799-1245 1.01 (2021): 1-13.
3. Al-Husain, Raed. "Statistical analytical study of the impact of social media use on students academic achievement and its relationship to some economic and social characteristics." Journal of Management Information and Decision Sciences 25 (2022): 1-26.
4. Stokes, Jane. How to do media and cultural studies. Sage, 2021.
5. Deacon, David, et al. Researching communications: A practical guide to methods in media and cultural analysis. Bloomsbury Publishing USA, 2021.
6. Moores, Shaun. Media and everyday life in modern society. Edinburgh University Press, 2019.
7. Shuter, Robert. "Introduction: New media across cultures—prospect and promise." Journal of International and Intercultural Communication 4.4 (2011): 241-245.

https://doi.org/10.1051/shsconf/202418502015

8. Yates, Simeon, and Eleanor Lockley. "Social media and social class." American Behavioral Scientist 62.9 (2018): 1291-1316.

Exploring the Influence and Potential of New Media on Traditional Cultural Communication

Haotian Wei*

CHASS, University California Riverside, California, 92507, The United States

Abstract. This paper delves into the dynamic relationship between new media and traditional cultural communication, aiming to shed light on their impact, competitive advantages, and audience dynamics. It begins by unveiling the evolving landscape of new media platforms, highlighting the challenges faced by traditional cultural communication, and underscoring the positive influence wielded by new media in this context. Subsequently, the study scrutinizes the competitive edges inherent in new media platforms, encompassing their expansive reach, cost-efficiency, and heightened interactivity. The article also navigates through the shifting demographics of traditional cultural communication's audience, focusing on the preferences and heightened engagement of the younger generation. In conclusion, the findings of this research are synthesized, culminating in a forward-looking proposal for the future evolution of traditional cultural communication. The digital age brings with it the risk of oversimplification and misrepresentation. Traditional cultural elements may be distilled into bite-sized, easily digestible content, potentially diluting their depth and significance. Additionally, there is the challenge of discerning authentic cultural representation from appropriation and commercialization.

1.Introduction

With the development of the Internet and the increasing maturity of new media technology, traditional culture is facing new opportunities and challenges in the digital era. The rise of new media platforms provides new ways and means for the dissemination and inheritance of traditional culture. This paper aims to explore the influence and role of new media on traditional cultural communication, and analyze its unique competitive advantages and audience characteristics [1]. This paper analyzes the rapid development of the Internet and new media, the dilemma of traditional cultural communication, and the positive impact of new media on traditional cultural communication [2]. With the popularization and use of new media platforms such as social media and online videos, traditional culture has been more widely disseminated. At the same time, traditional culture faces the limitations of time, space and content differences in the digital age, which is difficult to resonate with young people. Therefore, the rise of new media platforms provides new opportunities for the dissemination of traditional culture. This paper will focus on the influence and role of new media on the dissemination of traditional culture. Traditional culture is a treasure of a country and a nation, and inheriting and carrying forward traditional culture is of great significance for cultivating and inheriting the national spirit and enhancing cultural self-confidence. As a new way and means of traditional culture dissemination, new media platforms can better attract young people to participate in the inheritance and development of traditional culture. Through in-depth study of the influence of new media on the dissemination of traditional culture, we can provide new ideas and methods for the inheritance and development of traditional culture. This paper will focus on the following questions: how does new media affect the dissemination of traditional culture, what is the competitive advantage of new media platforms, and what is the impact of new media communication on the audience of traditional culture? This paper aims to analyze the influence and role of new media on traditional cultural communication, explore the competitive advantages of new media platforms, and analyze the audience characteristics of traditional cultural communication. This article will first introduce the influence and role of new media on traditional cultural communication, including the rapid development of new media platforms, the dilemma of traditional cultural communication, and the positive impact of new media on traditional cultural communication. Second, it will analyze the competitive advantages of new media platforms, including the expansion of dissemination, cost reduction and enhanced interactivity. Then, the audience characteristics of traditional cultural communication will be explored, including the preferences and increased participation of young people. Finally, the research results of this paper will be summarized and the future development of traditional culture communication will be proposed.

*Corresponding author's mail: hwei029@ucr.edu

https://doi.org/10.1051/shsconf/202418502016

2.Representative Products

New media platforms such as Douyin, B Station, Xiaohongshu, etc. provide a broad stage, enabling traditional cultural programs, documentaries, dramas and other content to achieve new empowerment through digital means. According to statistics, as of June 2021, there are 1,557 representative items of national intangible cultural heritage in China. In order to help explore the cultural and market value of intangible cultural heritage and help the dissemination of intangible cultural heritage, the Douyin platform has launched programs such as "Intangible Cultural Heritage Partners" and "Seeing Craftsmanship", through strengthening traffic support, official training, live broadcast base services, etc., so that intangible cultural heritage can be seen by more people, while bringing more employment opportunities and generating more income for intangible cultural heritage inheritors. Which was once on fire at Station B, through entering the thousand-year-old porcelain capital Jingdezhen, into the life of porcelain makers to understand the history and development of porcelain, and adding popular elements that young people like to see in documentaries. In a novel way, the audience will be presented with the historical stories and changes of various porcelain such as Doucai porcelain, Lang kiln red, blue and white porcelain, and Linglong porcelain. In the current era of short videos on Internet platforms, traditional operas such as Peking Opera, Kunqu Opera, and Huangmei Opera have also ushered in a new renewal. Many creators combine popular elements with traditional opera, and use the influence of new media platforms to inherit and promote traditional culture. From the rave reviews of "Chiling" to the tens of billions of broadcasts of "Wanjiang" to the popularity of "Wujiapo 2021", the combination of national tide and opera has made the traditional national essence shine on the Internet. This type of work has attracted the love of netizens, especially young people, on social platforms. For contemporary people, traditional opera has many constraints such as time and place, and the content is quite different from modern culture, which is difficult to resonate with the younger generation. Nowadays, the Internet and social media have broken the barriers of time and space, and the novel combination of modernity and tradition also allows the audience to feel the charm of traditional culture. New media has gradually become a window for audiences to understand traditional culture, forming a matrix of traditional arts such as opera art through diversified communication channels, expanding the audience from square inches under the stage to thousands of screens.

3.Competitive Advantages

Compared with traditional marketing methods, new media marketing has a larger scope of communication. New media platforms such as social media (Facebook, Instagram, Twitter, LinkedIn), video sharing sites (YouTube, TikTok), blogs and online news sites have been widely popularized and used worldwide. These platforms are capable of attracting billions of users every day, and through social media platforms, diversified communication methods can be used to reach more potential target groups. Secondly, the cost of new media marketing is lower. Compared with traditional advertising, new media platforms such as social media and online video have lower advertising costs, and creators can produce and disseminate content at a relatively low cost, so that more people can participate in cultural promotion and dissemination. In addition, new media has higher interactivity, its rise and development is not limited by time and space, effectively connecting traditional culture and new media, creating highlights and showing its value, and attracting users to discuss and participate. Based on this, information such as audience response, audience size and engagement can be tracked [3]. This enables creators to better understand their audiences, optimize content based on data, and strategically adjust to better communicate traditional culture. The advent of the epidemic has caused an unprecedented impact on the tourism industry, and museums are also facing problems such as no one to visit the exhibition. This has promoted the process of digital development of museums from another angle, and some museums have got rid of difficulties through online live exhibitions, etc., helping cultural dissemination on the basis of publicizing themselves to improve the popularity of museums, and showing the audience the history and culture behind popular science exhibits [4]. According to survey statistics, the two live broadcasts of the Gansu Museum reached 900,000 people online at the same time, and the live broadcast of the collection of the Suzhou Museum reached 1.93 million views, which is equivalent to its offline passenger flow for three months. On the other hand, the "digital +" industry is also another idea for museums to develop under the situation of Internet new media [5]. Many museums have opened cloud viewing channels on websites, clients, and WeChat mini programs, so that visitors who cannot go out due to the epidemic can freely view exhibitions through the Internet, media and other platforms. Digitize the museum's artifacts and collections with digital artifacts and create an online antiquities database that allows people to browse and search the museum's collections. Provide guided tours, introductions, historical information queries and other functions to help visitors better understand the content of the collection. On this basis, AR technology is combined to provide immersive experience, enhance the sense of interaction and user experience satisfaction. The marketing model under the new media situation breaks the time and space barriers of cultural communication and provides users with more convenient channels; compared with the relatively single and boring viewing method offline, the experience mode of digital and virtual reality undoubtedly attracts people's attention to a greater extent [6]. As a carrier of cultural dissemination and inheritance, the new media platform has played an irreplaceable role in the development of traditional culture in the current era, showing amazing advantages.

4.Audience

New media technologies make it possible to combine traditional culture with innovation. Cross-border cooperation in art, music, poetry, film and other fields has promoted the development of cultural innovation. On September 28, 2022, Shanghai Library launched the promotion of virtual ambassador Luo Tianyi, and virtual singer Luo Tianyi attended the opening ceremony and performed the chant "The Book of Poetry, Qin Feng, Yingyi". As a traditional culture that has existed and circulated in China since ancient times, after combining this trendy method loved by young people, chanting shows the audience the charm of chanting and the breadth and depth of traditional culture, and also attracts a large number of audiences to participate in the inheritance and development of traditional culture [7]. In the recent popular animation work "Chang'an 30,000 Li", a masterpiece of the successful combination of traditional culture and new media animation. "Chang'an 30,000 Li" unfolds the description of Sheng Tang from the perspective of Gao Shi, the film content is introduced by 48 ancient poems, and modern animation means are used as the medium to present the romantic imagination in the poets' hearts with 3D production technology and other audio-visual modern means combined with modern means. The combination of science and technology and culture greatly allows the audience to feel the romance of culture and the flourishing Tang Dynasty atmosphere of Chang'an [8]. Compared with the slightly boring poems in books, the means of new media animation undoubtedly have unique advantages in showing artistic conception and attracting people's attention. When the poem "All the ancient sages were lonely, only the drinker left his name" came out, the audience could see that above the Nine Heavens Palace, the palace door was wide open, and countless poets and sages in the hall who left a brilliant mark in the long river of history raised their glasses and drank bitterly with Li Bai and others [9]. This intuitive visual impact is undoubtedly in line with people's aesthetic imagination, and can also greatly arouse the emotional resonance of the audience. This plays a vital role in promoting the spread of traditional culture in the new era, from the elderly to children, as long as you walk into the theater, you can intuitively feel the impact of culture and experience its charm and essence.

5.Future Development

Use new media to create interactive educational platforms to make it easier for the younger generation to access traditional culture. For example, online courses, games, virtual reality experiences, etc., present traditional culture in a way that attracts the interest of young people. It is encouraging people to share their understanding and pay attention to the feelings and experiences of the audience. Use new media platforms to promote dialogue and exchange between different cultures [10]. This helps traditional culture to gain more attention worldwide and promote cultural integration and development. Leveraging actual cultural carriers like porcelain and tea, companies have a remarkable opportunity to engage with their audience and craft a distinctive brand identity. By harnessing the power of social media platforms, they can embark on a journey to not only enhance brand recognition but also cultivate a sterling reputation that resonates with consumers. Porcelain, with its rich history and timeless allure, can serve as a captivating focal point for companies seeking to establish a unique brand image. Businesses can create visually stunning content by sharing exquisite porcelain pictures on social media platforms. These images can capture the intricate details, craftsmanship, and elegance of porcelain creations. Through these visual narratives, companies can communicate their commitment to quality and aesthetics, reinforcing their brand's identity as one synonymous with sophistication and refinement. Moreover, the production process of porcelain presents a captivating story waiting to be told. Companies can leverage the power of videos to showcase the artistry and dedication that go into crafting porcelain masterpieces. By offering behind-the-scenes glimpses into the intricate steps involved in porcelain production, businesses can foster a deeper appreciation for the craftsmanship behind their products. This transparency not only humanizes the brand but also builds trust with consumers who value authenticity and heritage. Tea, as a cultural symbol and beloved beverage, presents another avenue for companies to connect with their audience. On social media, companies can curate content that explores the world of tea – its origins, varieties, brewing techniques, and cultural significance. Sharing informative and engaging posts about tea allows companies to position themselves as experts in the field, elevating their brand's authority and credibility. Additionally, companies can use social media as a platform to promote tea-related experiences, such as tea tastings, workshops, and cultural events. These interactive activities not only create opportunities for consumer engagement but also foster a sense of community among tea enthusiasts. By organizing and sharing such events, companies can establish themselves as facilitators of cultural experiences, further enhancing their brand's reputation. Beyond the content itself, the way companies engage with their audience on social media is crucial. Prompt and personalized responses to inquiries, comments, and messages demonstrate a commitment to customer satisfaction and build a positive brand perception. Consistency in posting content and maintaining an active online presence also reinforces the brand's reliability and relevance. Moreover, companies can collaborate with influencers and experts in the fields of porcelain and tea to expand their reach and credibility. These partnerships can lend authenticity to their brand, as influencers and experts can vouch for the quality and cultural significance of the products. In conclusion, the fusion of culture and commerce on social media offers a compelling opportunity for companies to establish a unique brand identity and bolster their reputation. Through captivating visuals, storytelling, and engagement strategies, businesses can harness the allure of porcelain and tea to create a brand that resonates with consumers on both a cultural and commercial level. By nurturing these connections and consistently delivering on their brand promise, companies can not only enhance recognition but also foster a lasting positive reputation in the hearts and minds of their audience.

6.Conclusion

The impact of new media on traditional Chinese culture is a multifaceted and intricate issue that requires a comprehensive exploration. This phenomenon can be more effectively dissected and understood by delving into various dimensions, such as the role of new media in cultural communication, innovation, audience participation, and more. These aspects collectively contribute to a positive impact on several vital facets of traditional Chinese culture. One of the noteworthy impacts of new media is its role in enhancing cultural self-confidence. In an era where globalization and cultural exchange are prevalent, new media platforms provide a means for China to assert its cultural identity on a global stage. Through the dissemination of traditional values, practices, and art forms via new media channels, there is a resurgence of cultural pride and self-assuredness among the Chinese population. This newfound confidence stems from the realization that traditional culture holds a unique and invaluable place in the world. Furthermore, new media has proven to be a powerful tool for attracting a larger audience to traditional Chinese culture. Traditional cultural forms, such as ancient art, literature, and performing arts, once limited in their reach, can now be accessed by a global audience. Online platforms and social media have democratized cultural consumption, allowing people from diverse backgrounds to engage with and appreciate traditional Chinese culture. This broader audience base ensures that these cultural treasures do not fade into obscurity but continue to thrive and evolve. In addition to attracting a larger audience, new media plays a pivotal role in promoting traditional Chinese culture to the world. The digital age has dismantled geographical barriers, enabling cultural exchange and dialogue across borders. Traditional Chinese festivals, customs, and practices can now be shared with an international audience, fostering cross-cultural understanding and appreciation. Through platforms like streaming services and social media, cultural enthusiasts worldwide can partake in celebrations like the Spring Festival, explore the depths of Chinese philosophy, and admire the intricacies of ancient Chinese calligraphy. Another significant impact lies in the realm of cultural diversity. New media platforms have facilitated the preservation and revitalization of various regional and ethnic cultures within China. The ability to share and celebrate diverse cultural practices has led to a deeper appreciation of the nation's rich tapestry of traditions. Moreover, it has encouraged intercultural exchange within China, promoting unity and harmony among its diverse population. However, it is essential to acknowledge that the advent of new media also presents new challenges to traditional Chinese culture. In conclusion, the impact of new media on traditional Chinese culture is profound and multifaceted. It has ushered in a new era of cultural communication, innovation, and audience participation, bolstering cultural self-confidence, expanding the global audience, promoting cultural heritage, and fostering diversity. While new media provides incredible opportunities for the dissemination of traditional culture, it also demands vigilance in preserving its authenticity and depth. To harness the power of new media fully and ensure the prosperity and inheritance of traditional culture, a holistic understanding of this complex relationship is paramount.

References

1. Carr, C. T., & Hayes, R. A. (2015). Social media: Defining, developing, and divining. Atlantic journal of communication, 23(1): 46-65.
2. Hennig-Thurau, T., Malthouse, E. C., Friege, C., Gensler, S., Lobschat, L., Rangaswamy, A., & Skiera, B. (2010). The impact of new media on customer relationships. Journal of service research, 13(3): 311-330.
3. Van Aelst, P., & Walgrave, S. (2004). New media, new movements?. The Role of the Internet in Shaping the 'Anti-globalization'Movement, Cyberprotest, Routlege, London, 87-108.
4. Mansell, R. (2004). Political economy, power and new media. New media & society, 6(1): 96-105.
5. Dietz, S. (2016). Collecting new-media art: Just like anything else, only different. In New Collecting: Exhibiting and Audiences After New Media Art (pp. 57-71). Routledge.
6. Ruthmann, S. A., & Hebert, D. G. (2012). Music learning and new media in virtual and online environments (Vol. 2, pp. 567-583). New York: Oxford University Press.
7. Gill, R. (2002). Cool, creative and egalitarian? Exploring gender in project-based new media work in Euro. Information, communication & society, 5(1): 70-89.
8. Weber, S., & Mitchell, C. (2008). Imaging, keyboarding, and posting identities: Young people and new media technologies. Youth, identity, and digital media, 7: 25-47.
9. Peppler, K. A. (2010). Media arts: Arts education for a digital age. Teachers College Record, 112(8): 2118-2153.
10. Thurlow, C. (2007). Fabricating youth: New-media discourse and the technologization of young people. Language in the media: Representations, identities, ideologies, 213-233.

Gender Disparities in Self-Presentation on WeChat Moments

Xinyuan Zhang*

China Agricultural University, International College, Tsinghua East Road, Haidian District, Beijing, China

Abstract: This study delved into the relationship between gender and self presentation in WeChat Moments, and analyzed gender patterns and differences through questionnaire data. Using Erving Goffman's drama theory, self presentation in WeChat Moments is viewed as an online performance, in which users play their own roles and carefully manage their online image. WeChat Moments serve as an inclusive space where users of all genders can express themselves and participate in social networks. Research has found that regardless of gender, both male and female users actively participate in posting behavior on WeChat Moments. Although male posting frequency is slightly higher, this difference is not statistically significant. The survey also found that gender has no significant impact on the composition of personal social networks and unique content creation in WeChat Moments. This study provides important insights into the role of gender in social media usage and self presentation, enriching our understanding of digital social platforms.

1. Conceptual interpretation

The self image presentation and management of WeChat Moments refers to individuals shaping their image through publishing content, commenting and interacting, and taking certain measures to manage their image to achieve specific goals when using WeChat Moments. This concept mainly includes two aspects: self positioning and image shaping and management. Self positioning refers to an individual's determination of their position and role on social networks through posting content on WeChat Moments and interacting with others (Kr ä mer&Winter, 2008)[5]. Image shaping and management refers to presenting and managing one's self-image in WeChat social media by publishing text, images, emoticons, and other means, as well as setting permissions, controlling publication content, and responding to comments (Siibak, 2009)[7].

The concept of self image presentation and management in WeChat Moments is the application of drama theory in modern social media environments(Brake,2012)[1]. People use WeChat circles of friends to position roles and shape and manage their own images, which is consistent with the view that people use different symbols and behaviors to play roles in social occasions advocated by the "dramaturgy".

The study's questionnaire data provides insight into the intricate relationship between gender and self-presentation on the well-known social media site WeChat Moments. Through an analysis of several facets of users' views and behaviour, we hope to identify gendered patterns and differences in the digital sphere.

WeChat Moments are actively used by respondents, male and female, according to the data on posting frequency. The average number of posts made by male respondents was marginally higher than that of female respondents; however, this difference is not statistically significant. This implies that, despite minor differences, all genders use the platform for communication and self-expression.

The WeChat Moments friend circles of individuals were examined in detail by the questionnaire. The statistics makes it clear that respondents, both male and female, keep in touch with roughly the same number of friends on the network. Moreover, the percentage of strangers in their friend groups is likewise very similar for both genders. This implies that gender may not have a major impact on the makeup of a person's social network on WeChat Moments.

The data paints a complex picture of the percentage of unique content in Moments posts. On the site, both male and female respondents generate and distribute content; but, on average, male respondents submit a little bit more unique content. However, the difference is not substantial and does not imply a significant gender-related disparity in content creation. (Pang, H, 2020)[6]

This highlights that both genders are active contributors to the content shared on WeChat Moments.

Overall, the conceptual interpretation of the questionnaire data underscores the notion that WeChat Moments serves as a space for self-expression and interaction for both male and female users. While subtle differences in posting frequency and original content creation exist, they do not indicate pronounced gender-based disparities in self-presentation on the platform. Instead, the data suggests that WeChat Moments provides an inclusive digital stage where individuals of all genders engage in shaping their online personas and connecting with their social networks.

*Corresponding author's email: zxyzxy48@126.com

2. Literature review

Numerous studies have explored how gender influences individuals' usage patterns on social media platforms. It has been consistently observed that women are more inclined to share personal content, such as photos and videos, while men tend to use social media for work-related reasons (Pang, H, 2020)[6]. This pattern is consistent with women's traditional roles as nurturers and caregivers, who frequently use social media to stay in touch with one another (Haferkamp et al., 2012)[3]. On the other hand, cultural norms surrounding masculinity may have an impact on men's attention to work-related content (Krämer & Winter, 2008)[5].

There has been curiosity in the reasons behind self-presentation on social media platforms. According to Haferkamp et al. (2012)[3], female students, in particular, are more likely to use WeChat for peer comparison and may place more value on presenting a positive self-image. This implies that women may be more motivated by the need for social approval and to uphold particular cultural standards of femininity.

Gender roles and societal conventions have major influences on how people behave online. Women may use the platform to express themselves more freely due to their motivation for peer support and social contact (Hou et al., 2017)[4]. On the other hand, men may conform to traditional standards of guarded self-presentation due to the impact of social notions of masculinity. These gender-based expectations can significantly influence how individuals present themselves on social media platforms.

The concept of "Dramaturgy" was first proposed by Goffman in his book "The Presentation of Self in Everyday Life". The dramaturgy is a theory that explains the interaction behavior of human society. It compares social behavior to drama. People play roles in the interaction, and use different symbols and behaviors to shape their own image in order to leave an impression on others or achieve a certain goal. In this opinion, people often adopt different role-playing and behavioral styles based on different social situations, in order to better adapt and respond to different situations and needs. Goffman believes that Dramaturgy is an inevitable behavior in people's daily lives, which involves shaping their self-image, others' impressions and evaluations of themselves, and confirming social roles and status. By creating dramas, people can not only better understand and adapt to society, but also gain more social resources and opportunities (Goffman, 2002)[2].

Erving Goffman's theory of dramaturgy has been used as a framework to understand online identity construction (Zhu & Li, 2021)[9]. It suggests that individuals adopt different roles and behaviours in response to social contexts and goals. Applying this theory to WeChat Moments, we can view users' self-presentation as a form of online performance, where college students act out their roles and carefully manage their online personas (Zhu & Li, 2021)[9]. Incorporating these insights from existing research, our study aims to contribute to the understanding of gender disparities in self-presentation on WeChat Moments.

3. Introduction of survey methods and questionnaire combined with theoretical analysis

The survey begins by collecting demographic data, with a focus on respondents' gender, which is central to our investigation of gender disparities in self-presentation. We find that male and female respondents engage with WeChat Moments actively, with male respondents reporting slightly more frequent posting on average. That being said, there is no statistically significant difference. This result is consistent with earlier studies that show that people of all genders use social media sites actively (Krämer & Winter, 2008)5[5].

WeChat Moments friend circles of respondents are surveyed to learn more about their traits. Respondents who are male and female keep similar numbers of friends, and the percentage of strangers in their social circles is similarly similar. This suggests that gender may not have a substantial impact on the makeup of social networks on WeChat Moments, which is in line with previous research (Yang & Seo, 2022)[8].

The questionnaire also looks at how much of Moments posts are original. Although respondents who are male tend to report posting somewhat more original content, the difference is not statistically significant. This suggests that users of both genders are actively contributing to the information published on WeChat Moments, which supports the notion that the platform provides a space for people of all genders to express themselves.

We used an independent samples test to determine the significance of the observed differences between respondents who were male and female. These tests' outcomes, which include t-tests and Levine's test for equality of variances, are shown. Further information about the extent of gender disparities can be obtained from effect size computations using methods like Cohen's d, Hedges Correction, and Glass Delta.

By combining the survey methods with theoretical analysis, we aim to contextualize our findings within the broader framework of gender disparities in self-presentation on social media platforms. The theoretical underpinnings, drawn from previous research, help us interpret the questionnaire data and provide meaningful insights into the online behaviour of male and female users on WeChat Moments.

The questionnaire is as follows:

Table 1. Group statistics

	What is your gender?	Number of cases	average value	standard deviation	Standard error of the mean
How often do you post on Moments?	male	37	4.11	1.524	.250
	female	69	3.64	1.414	.170

How many friends do you have in your circle of friends?	male	37	2.38	.828	.136
	female	69	2.52	1.079	.130
What is the proportion of strangers (including friends you have never met in real life) in your circle of friends?	male	37	2.41	1.066	.175
	female	69	2.17	1.150	.138
What is the scope of your circle of friends you are allowed to view?	male	37	2.57	1.068	.176
	female	69	2.77	1.178	.142
What proportion of the content you publish in Moments is original content?	male	37	1.84	1.214	.200
	female	69	1.62	1.152	.139

Table 2. Independent samples test

		Levine's test for equality of variances		average equal to t-test						
		F	Significance	t	degrees of freedom	Significance (two-tailed)	Average value difference	Standard error difference	95% confidence interval lower limit	95% confidence interval upper limit
How often do you post on Moments?	Assuming equal variances	.737	.393	1.589	104	.115	.470	.296	-.117	1.057
	Does not assume equal variances			1.553	69.123	.125	.470	.303	-.134	1.075
How many friends do you have in your circle of friends?	Assuming equal variances	3.818	.053	-.704	104	.483	-.143	.204	-.547	.261
	Does not assume equal variances			-.762	91.317	.448	-.143	.188	-.517	.231
What is the proportion of strangers (including friends you have never met in real life) in your circle of friends?	Assuming equal variances	.215	.644	1.013	104	.313	.231	.229	-.222	.685
	Does not assume equal variances			1.036	78.708	.303	.231	.223	-.213	.676
What is the scope of your circle of friends you are allowed to view?	Assuming equal variances	.550	.460	-.863	104	.390	-.201	.232	-.662	.260
	Does not assume equal variances			-.889	80.177	.377	-.201	.226	-.650	.249
What proportion of the content you publish in Moments is original content?	Assuming equal variances	.591	.444	.898	104	.371	.215	.239	-.260	.689

Table 3. Independent sample effect size

		Standardized quantity a	point estimate	95% confidence interval lower limit	95% confidence interval upper limit
How often do you post on Moments?	Cohen d	1.453	.324	-.079	.725
	Hedges Correction	1.463	.321	-.078	.720
	Glass Delta	1.414	.333	-.072	.735
How many friends do you have in your circle of friends?	Cohen d	1.000	-.143	-.543	.257
	Hedges Correction	1.007	-.142	-.539	.255
	Glass Delta	1.079	-.133	-.532	.268
What is the proportion of strangers (including friends you have never met in real life) in your circle of friends?	Cohen d	1.122	.206	-.194	.606
	Hedges Correction	1.130	.205	-.193	.602
	Glass Delta	1.150	.201	-.200	.601
What is the scope of your circle of friends you are allowed to view?	Cohen d	1.141	-.176	-.575	.225
	Hedges Correction	1.149	-.175	-.571	.223
	Glass Delta	1.178	-.170	-.570	.231
What proportion of the content you publish in Moments is original content?	Cohen d	1.174	.183	-.218	.583
	Hedges Correction	1.182	.182	-.216	.578

Glass Delta	1.152	.186	-.215	.586

a. Denominator used when estimating effect size.
Cohen's d uses pooled standard deviation.
The pooled standard deviation plus an additional adjustment factor are used in Hedges correction.
The sample standard deviation of the control group is used by Glass Delta.

4. Conclusions

According to the Independent sample effect size test in Table 3, both male and female respondents are actively involved in posting on WeChat Moments, according to the analysis of the questionnaire data, while there is a minor trend for male respondents to post more frequently overall. It is imperative to highlight, nonetheless, that this difference is not statistically significant. This result emphasizes how inclusive WeChat Moments are, since people of all genders actively engage in conversation and self-expression.

According to the research, the proportion of strangers in the friend circles of both male and female respondents is similar, and both genders keep a similar number of friends on WeChat Moments. This implies that there are no appreciable gender differences in the social network composition on the site. Users can interact with a wide variety of people on the network, regardless of their gender.

Although respondents who are male tend to report posting somewhat more unique content, this difference is not statistically significant. The information debunks the myth that there are differences in content creation depending on gender since it shows that both male and female users actively submit original content to WeChat Moments. The content shared on the network is significantly shaped by users of both genders.

The results of our study provide important new understandings of gender dynamics in WeChat Moments digital self-presentation. It seems that the website offers a welcoming environment where people of all genders may express themselves and connect. Gender-based inequities are not implied by the slight variations in posting frequency and unique content production that have been identified. Rather, they showcase the variety of ways people of all genders engage in self-presentation on the internet.

Future studies in this field should examine how age, culture, and online networks interact to further shape how people present themselves online as social media usage continues to grow. Comprehending the intricacies of digital self-expression necessitates sophisticated methodologies that take into account personal incentives, cultural standards, and changing gender roles that impact virtual conduct.

In conclusion, by demonstrating that WeChat Moments promotes a varied and inclusive atmosphere, our study advances knowledge regarding gender differences in self-presentation on the platform. Even though there are small differences, the information indicates that WeChat Moments function as a virtual platform where people—male or female—actively create their online identities and engage with their social networks. These findings encourage a more nuanced and inclusive perspective on gender and online self-presentation, ultimately enriching our comprehension of the intricate digital landscape.

References

1. Brake, D. R. (2012). Who do they think they're talking to? Framings of the audience by social media users. International journal of communication, 6, 21.
2. Goffman, E. (2002). The presentation of self in everyday life. 1959. Garden City, NY.
3. Haferkamp, N., Eimler, S. C., Papadakis, A. M., & Kruck, J. V. (2012). Men are from Mars, women are from Venus? Examining gender differences in self-presentation on social networking sites. Cyberpsychology, Behaviour, and Social Networking, 15(2), 91-98.
4. Hou, J., Ndasauka, Y., Jiang, Y., Ye, Z., Wang, Y., Yang, L., ... & Zhang, X. (2017). Excessive use of WeChat, social interaction and locus of control among college students in China. PloS one, 12(8), e0183633.
5. Krämer, N. C., & Winter, S. (2008). Impression management 2.0: The relationship of self-esteem, extraversion, self-efficacy, and self-presentation within social networking sites. Journal of media psychology, 20(3), 106-116.
6. Pang, H. (2020). Examining associations between university students' mobile social media use, online self-presentation, social support and sense of belonging. Aslib Journal of Information Management.
7. Siibak, A. (2009). Constructing the self through the photo selection-visual impression management on social networking websites. Cyberpsychology: Journal of psychosocial research on cyberspace, 3(1), 1.
8. Yang, T., & Seo, S. (2022). An Exploratory Study on Chinese Females' Social Media Self-Presentation: A Case Study of WeChat. Asian Journal for Public Opinion Research, 10(3), 230-253.
9. Zhu, Y., & Li, W. (2021). An Analysis of Self-Presentation in the Post-90s Micro-Social Field from the Perspective of Drama-Simulator Theory. In 2021 5th International Seminar on Education, Management and Social Sciences (ISEMSS 2021) (pp. 98-101). Atlantis Press Top of Form

Research on Influencing Factors of Users' Sharing Intention in Health Science Popularization Short Videos

Shaoyang Li*

School of Economics and Management, Nanjing University of Science and Technology, Nanjing, China

Abstract. With the rapid development of the short video industry, various vertical fields of short videos have also emerged, and the medical and health field has received widespread attention. Famous doctors, public hospitals, and health institutions have joined short video platforms to publish health science popularization short videos and spread health knowledge. To improve the dissemination of health information, this study combines elaboration likelihood model and information ecology theory to construct a factor model of users' willingness to share health science popularization short videos to help spread Health Science Popularization Short Videos.

1. Preface

<The 52nd Statistical Report on the Development of China's Internet> pointed out that as of June 2023, the number of online video users in China has reached 1.044 billion, accounting for 96.8% of the total number of internet users. Among them, the number of short video users is 1.026 billion, accounting for 95.2% of the total number of netizens. With the rapid development of the short video field, various vertical short videos have also emerged, and the health field has attracted much attention.

In the dissemination of health science popularization short videos, the sharing behavior of health science popularization short videos is a very important part. On the one hand, information sharing between users is the most effective way of content dissemination, which can greatly reduce the cost of dissemination, allowing health science popularization short videos to spread exponentially and generate a fission effect. On the other hand, with the further expansion of user scale, social communication software and short video software close to the upper limit of user scale began to seek new development directions. Social communication software represented by WeChat and short video software represented by Tiktok showed a trend of cross-border development. In the context of cross-border integration, health science popularization short videos can also be further disseminated through social channels. However, the vast majority of research on health information sharing behavior is limited to generalized social media contexts, ignoring the differences between different social media platforms. As a rapidly emerging social media platform in recent years, few studies have specifically focused on the sharing behavior of users towards health education short videos on short video platforms. Therefore, this paper takes the Tiktok short video platform as the research object to explore users' willingness to share short videos of health science popularization on the Tiktok platform, hoping to help popularize health information knowledge, break the digital divide, further improve the health literacy of the whole people, promote the healthy lifestyle action of the whole people, and achieve the health of the whole people.

2. Literature review

2.1. Health information sharing

Wang defined health information sharing in his research on online health information as the process of information exchange through online communication and interaction, in which health information is transmitted from one party to another[1]. It can be seen that health information sharing behavior has its uniqueness. It is not only an interaction with users and health information sources, but also an interaction with other users. It has its unique social attributes, and users' health information sharing behavior is naturally influenced by various factors. Jin pointed out that the willingness of users to disseminate health knowledge on social media is mainly based on trust in information sources and platforms, rather than trust in information content [2]. Berger found that public health information that can cause anxiety is more likely to spread on social networks. In terms of social factors, Liu studied elderly people in rural China and explored the impact of social factors on their health information sharing behavior. The results showed that social support from families and social embeddedness of elderly people were the decisive factors for rural elderly people to engage in health information sharing behavior, while social support from friends had no significant impact on their health information sharing behavior [3].

*Corresponding author's mail: leeyang2020@163.com

2.2. Elaboration likelihood model

The elaboration likelihood model originates from social psychology, which explains how information processing affects a person's information decision-making process. The elaboration likelihood model suggests that individuals evaluate information through two different information processing pathways based on differences in individual information content and information processing abilities: the central pathway and the peripheral pathway. When an individual's motivation and abilities are sufficient, they evaluate information through central cues related to information quality. When an individual's motivation or abilities are insufficient, they tend to make judgments based on overall impressions and intuition, Process information through peripheral paths [4]. The central path requires more cognitive effort from the information receiver, requiring them to carefully evaluate the information using central clues such as argument quality. The edge path requires less cognitive effort and relies more on the intuition of the information receiver. The information receiver uses edge clues that can be obtained without excessive thinking, such as perceived reputation, attractiveness, and perceived source credibility, to evaluate information. Compared to the central path, the information processing of the edge path appears to be simpler, more direct, and more intuitive. Attitude changes caused by the central path will be more lasting and easier to predict than those caused by the peripheral path.

The detailed possibility model provides an ideal theoretical framework to explain how individuals form their cognition and attitudes. Although these two paths may seem somewhat exclusive, scholars have pointed out that they are poles on the cognitive processing continuum, indicating the level of mental effort an individual puts into evaluating information. People in a highly cognitive state are more likely to carefully evaluate the information they are exposed to, therefore, central cues have a greater impact on them. People in a low cognitive state, on the other hand, lack the corresponding motivation or ability and are more susceptible to peripheral cues such as source credibility. Generally speaking, two pathways jointly affect an individual's processing of information, but the degree of influence on information processing varies depending on the individual's ability and motivation .

2.3. Information ecology

The theory of information ecology was proposed by Western scholar Horton, who introduced the ecological theory of natural sciences into the field of information. Starting from a systemic perspective, he defined the information ecology as the relationships generated by the flow of information within an organization from an ecological perspective. Information, people, information technology, and information environment are important factors in the information ecosystem. Among them, information is the foundation of the information ecosystem and is not transferred by human will; Human beings are the core factor of the information ecosystem, using information as a carrier for communication activities, and are the center of all information activities, controlling the information activities in the information ecosystem; Information technology is a means of information circulation that helps information flow within the ecosystem; The information environment is the external condition for the interaction between information and information people, which has a certain impact and constraint on the information exchange between people or organizations; The various ecological factors are interrelated and reach equilibrium within a certain information space. The information ecosystem, as an interactive system between individuals and information, has strong interrelationships. The various elements of the information ecosystem are interrelated, and when one element changes, the entire system can be affected. When studying the information ecosystem, it is not necessary to study the changes in a single element, factor, or link in isolation. It is necessary to consider the coordinated connection and development of various elements.

3. Research hypothesis

3.1. Information factors

The quality of health science popularization short videos refers to the value and persuasiveness of health science popularization short videos disseminated on short video platforms. Previous studies have shown that the quality of online news may affect users' attitudes towards sharing news on social media. A news that is easy to understand and clear in content can help users form a positive attitude and share it with their family and friends on social media without worrying about potential content risks[5]. For health science popularization short videos, it can be considered that their content quality characteristics include timeliness, readability, and interactivity. Users may have a positive sharing attitude towards health science popularization short videos with strong timeliness, readability, and interactivity. Source authority refers to the degree to which users of health science popularization short videos believe that the creators of health science popularization short videos are professional and trustworthy. From the perspective of information recipients, due to the diversity and complexity of online health information, individuals are more inclined to believe in health information published by professionals or authoritative institutions. Chao found in his research on user sharing of health debunking information that source authority is an important basis for users to share health debunking information, and health debunking information published from government accounts is shared more frequently[6]. The following assumptions are proposed based on the quality characteristics of comprehensive health science popularization short videos and the characteristics of the source of health science popularization short videos:

H1: The timeliness of health science popularization short videos positively affects users' attitudes towards sharing health science popularization short videos.

H2: The readability of health science short videos has a positive impact on users' attitudes towards sharing health science short videos.

H3: The interactivity of health science popularization short videos positively affects users' attitudes towards sharing health science popularization short videos.

H4: The authority of the source of health science popularization short videos has a positive impact on users' attitudes towards sharing health science popularization short videos.

3.2. Capability factors

In The elaboration likelihood model, individual ability is an important factor affecting the way individuals process information. Individuals with strong abilities are more inclined to process information through central pathways. In the context of electronic health information, the ability is reflected in good electronic health literacy, and users with high electronic health literacy tend to use central pathways to process health information. For example, Wang found that individuals with low cognitive abilities rely more on the quality of arguments in peripheral and central cues to receive debunked news, while individuals with high cognitive abilities rely more on the readability of information in central cues to receive debunked news[7]. Therefore, users with high electronic health literacy may be more inclined to process health information based on the path of the health science popularization short video center, while users with low electronic health literacy may be more inclined to rely on the edge path of information source authority to determine their attitude towards sharing behavior. Therefore, the following assumptions are proposed:

H5a: The electronic health literacy of users positively regulates the impact of the timeliness of health science popularization short videos on their attitudes towards sharing health science popularization short videos.

H5b: The electronic health literacy of users positively regulates the impact of readability of health science short videos on their attitudes towards sharing health science short videos.

H5c: The electronic health literacy of users positively regulates the impact of interactive health science short videos on their attitudes towards sharing health science short videos.

H5d: The negative regulation of electronic health literacy among users affects the authoritative source of health science short videos and their attitudes towards sharing health science short videos.

3.3. Motivational factors

The user's sharing motivation includes altruism and reciprocity. Oh investigated some common characteristics and motivations of people answering health-related questions on the social Q&A website Yahoo, and found that their sharing behavior is driven by altruism [8]. Liu found in his research on health information sharing among elderly people in rural areas that their health information sharing behavior is driven by reciprocal motivation, especially under the influence of collectivist culture. Due to the limited opportunities for elderly people in rural China to access health services, providing mutual information support has become an important way to maintain and consolidate social relationships among the elderly. Zhang Weiwei found that a sense of reciprocity is an important factor in promoting long-term participation of users in online health communities. The sense of reciprocity increases users' sense of association and belonging to online health communities. When other community members seek help, they are willing to share their knowledge in the community to help other community members. Therefore, the following assumptions are proposed:

H6: Altruism positively affects users' willingness to share health science short videos.

H7: Reciprocity has a positive impact on users' willingness to share health science short videos.

3.4. Platform factors

Algorithm recommendation refers to the degree to which a platform pushes health science popularization short videos that meet the needs and interests of users. Unlike traditional film and television experiences, recommendation technology enables short videos to cater to the fragmented content consumption characteristics of the Internet era, making content transmission and reception more efficient, and users easier to receive information. At present, algorithm recommendation plays an increasingly important role in various information platforms, especially short video platforms. Compared to traditional information recommendation methods, the content recommendation mechanism based on personal preference characteristics links users and information, making the push of information "thousands of people and thousands of faces". Personalized recommendation information can affect user experience, thereby strengthening dependence on related apps. According to information processing theory, an individual's ability to process information is limited, and their interests and needs are the main factors affecting attention. Information that is consistent with the topic of interest to the user is more likely to attract their attention, thus having a greater chance of being shared. A good algorithm recommendation mechanism can also enhance users' sense of belonging to the platform and promote the dissemination of platform information.

In the context of this study, convenience of functions refers to the degree to which the platform provides convenient and fast information sharing services when users share health science short videos. Convenient and efficient sharing services can reduce user sharing costs, thereby promoting their willingness to share. However, if users spend too much time, effort, or resources on sharing behavior, it can suppress their willingness to share. When exploring the influencing factors of health information sharing willingness and behavior, Wu found that users' self-efficacy in sharing health knowledge on WeChat is reflected in their confidence in the technology, content, and self sharing ability used by WeChat. Mastering technology is one of the main motivations for users to choose to receive and forward information. He suggested that designers of social media platforms fully consider the ability of users at different levels to accept technology, Design a relatively simple user interface to facilitate user operations[9].Based on this, the following assumptions are proposed:

H8: The algorithm recommendation has a positive impact on users' willingness to share short videos of health science popularization.

H9: The convenience of functions has a positive impact on users' willingness to share short videos of health science popularization.

3.5. Attitude

Attitude has been proven to be an important factor in knowledge sharing behavior, and health science short videos can be seen as a manifestation of health knowledge. Wu integrated planned behavior theory, usage and satisfaction theory, and social cognition theory together and found that the willingness to share health information is significantly influenced by attitude, subjective norms, and self-efficacy. Users who hold a positive attitude towards health information sharing are more likely to engage in sharing behavior on WeChat, and attitude is a key factor affecting their willingness to share health information[9]. Based on this, the following assumptions are proposed:

H10: The user's attitude towards sharing health science short videos has a positive impact on their willingness to share health science short videos.

Based on the detailed possibility model and information ecology theory, an empirical model of the willingness of health science popularization short video users to share is constructed, as shown in the following figure 1:

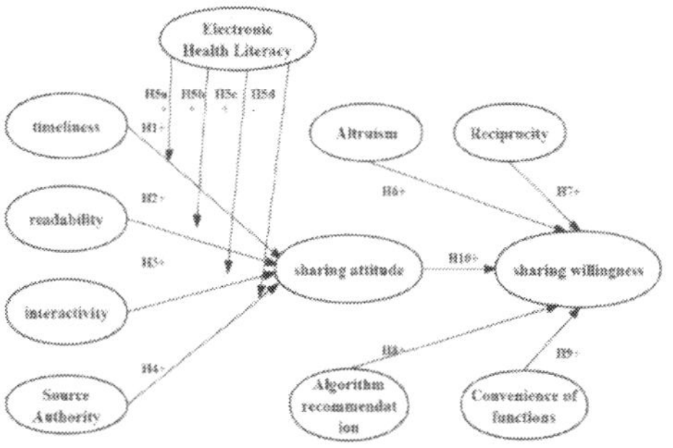

Figure 1 A Model of Factors Influencing the Sharing Intention of Health Science Popularization Short Video Users

4. Questionnaire design and distribution

The questionnaire for this study mainly consists of two parts. The first part is a survey of general statistical factors of users, including gender, age, and education level. The second part is the measurement of relevant variables, which is the main content of the questionnaire, including 11 potential variables. Except for the 8 measurement items of electronic health literacy, each item has 3-4 measurement items. The Likert 5-level scale is used, where 1 represents very disagree, 2 represents disagree, 3 represents average, 4 represents agree, and 5 represents very agree. The relevant variables specifically include the timeliness and readability of health science popularization short videos The interactivity of health science popularization short videos, the authority of the source of health science popularization short videos, the level of electronic health literacy of users, altruism, reciprocity, functional convenience, algorithm recommendation, as well as the sharing attitude and willingness of users towards health science popularization short videos, have all been measured based on existing literature and adjusted appropriately.

QuestionStar is a comprehensive platform for questionnaire design and publication. In this study, QuestionStar was used to design a questionnaire on the factors influencing user sharing willingness. The questionnaire was then distributed on social media from October 15, 2023 to November 2, 2023. The questionnaire is released by means of link or poster QR code, and the release channels are Baidu Post Bar, WeChat Friends Circle and Tiktok Platform. The multi-channel and multi platform release can ensure the diversity of groups, so as to draw more comprehensive and accurate conclusions and analysis. In the end, a total of 383 questionnaires were collected through various channels in this study, with 362 valid questionnaires and an effective rate of 94%.

5. Data analysis and hypothesis testing

5.1. Descriptive statistics

The distribution of survey subjects in this survey is shown in Table 1. From the results of descriptive statistical analysis, it can be seen that all participants in this questionnaire survey were 180 males and 182 females, with a relatively balanced sample gender. The age distribution proportion of the surveyed subjects basically follows a normal distribution. In terms of education, among the surveyed individuals, vocational education accounted for 34.8% and undergraduate education accounted for 51.9%, indicating a relatively high overall cultural level.

Table 1 Demographic factor analysis

Index	Classification	Number	Proportion
gender	man	180	49.7
	women	182	50.3
age	under 17	17	4.7
	18-25	150	41.4
	26-35	86	23.8
	36-45	56	15.5
	over 46	53	14.6
qualification	Junior high school and below	18	5.0
	senior high school	30	8.3
	college degree	126	34.8
	Graduate degree	188	51.9

5.2. Reliability and validity testing

Reliability refers to reliability, and conducting reliability testing is mainly to ensure that multiple measurement results for the same target can be consistent, stable, and reliable. The most commonly used methods for reliability analysis include test-retest reliability, half selected reliability, and Cronbach's α Coefficient method. The test-retest reliability method requires the same group to complete the same set of scales at different times, and to conduct correlation tests on the two results to estimate the stability of the scale results. However, the online distribution method is difficult to ensure that the group filling out the questionnaire twice is the same. Therefore, the half reliability method has a high overall requirement for the questionnaire. Currently, the most widely used reliability test method is Cronbach's α The coefficient method is also the method used in this article. Currently, for the questionnaire Cronbach's α There is no unified standard for coefficient requirements, but based on feedback from most users, Cronbach's α If the coefficient is above 0.9, then the reliability of the scale is good. A range of 0.8-0.9 indicates good, and a range of 0.7-0.8 indicates that the corresponding results are still acceptable. As shown in Table 2, the Cronbach's values for each variable in this model are α The coefficient is basically above 0.8, and the overall Cronbach's α The coefficient value is 0.921, indicating good reliability of the questionnaire. The measurement indicators of validity are mean variance extraction (AVE) and combined reliability (CR). Average variance extraction (AVE) is a statistical measure used to test the internal consistency of structural variables in statistics. Combination reliability (CR) reflects whether all questions in each latent variable consistently explain the latent variable. Based on the results of AVE and combination reliability (CR), it can be used to represent the aggregated validity of the latent variable within the factor. Table 2 shows the results of the AVE and CR indicators of the model. Generally speaking, AVE above 0.5 and CR above 0.7 indicate high convergent validity. The average variance extraction (AVE) and combined reliability (CR) of this study were all above 0.6 and 0.8, indicating good overall convergent validity.

Table 2 Reliability and validity testing

Variable	Cronbach's α coefficient	AVE	CR
Short video timeliness	0.839	0.637	0.839
Short video readability	0.832	0.627	0.834
Short video interactivity	0.797	0.544	0.826
Source Authority	0.826	0.614	0.827
Convenience of functions	0.828	0.625	0.833
Algorithm recommendation	0.870	0.693	0.871
Electronic Health Literacy	0.912	0.574	0.914
Altruism	0.828	0.623	0.831
Reciprocity	0.839	0.637	0.841
User sharing attitude	0..833	0.647	0.834
User sharing willingness	0.852	0.656	0.851

5.3. Relevant hypothesis testing

This study used SPSS and SPSSPRO software to plot the paths between various latent variables, and imported experimental data obtained through questionnaire surveys into the structural equation model diagram to calculate the path coefficients. The results are shown in Figure 2:

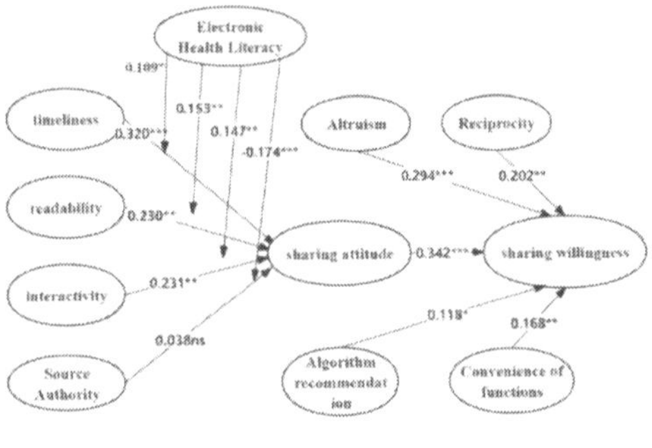

Figure 2 Model data analysis results

6. Summary and Outlook

The main conclusions of this article are as follows:

The information aspect of health science popularization short videos mainly includes timeliness, readability, interactivity, and source authority. Empirical research has found that timeliness, readability, interactivity, and user attitudes towards sharing health science short videos have a significant positive impact, which in turn affects user willingness to share. There is no relationship between the authority of the source and the user's attitude towards sharing health science short videos. One possible explanation is that when users actually watch short videos, due to the infinite up scrolling design and full screen playback method, they can deeply immerse themselves in the experience of short videos. Users in a state of flow may not pay attention to the relevant information of health science short video creators. The electronic health literacy of users can positively regulate the timeliness, readability, and interactivity of health science short videos on their sharing attitudes. This indicates that users with high-level electronic health literacy pay more attention to the intrinsic factors of information when sharing, and the quality of health science short videos is an important factor in promoting the dissemination of health science short videos.

The motivation level mainly includes altruism and reciprocity. The research results indicate that altruism, reciprocity, and user willingness to share health science short videos have a significant positive impact. When health science short video sharers believe that the health information they share is useful to the sharing audience, they will increase their willingness to share health science short videos. In addition, the sharing behavior of users towards health science popularization short videos is also driven by reciprocity. Sharing health science popularization short videos with others can, on the one hand, facilitate discussions with others and enhance the sharer's understanding of the correctness of the short video content; On the other hand, both parties can exchange their own health information to enrich their health knowledge reserves; In addition, communication of information often accompanies emotional interaction. During the process of communicating with the sharing object, the sharer can feel the sharing object's care for the sharer, thereby alleviating the sharer's health anxiety. This emotional comfort is the reward for the user's sharing behavior.

At the level of short video platforms, it includes functional convenience and algorithm recommendation. The convenience of functions and algorithm recommendation have a significant positive impact on users' willingness to share health science short videos on short video platforms. The more convenient it is for users to share health science short videos, the more willing they are to share them. If the operation of sharing health science short videos is relatively cumbersome, according to social exchange theory, users tend to expand benefits and reduce costs in interpersonal interaction. Users may give up sharing behavior due to high cost costs. In terms of algorithmic recommendation, personalized algorithmic recommendation mechanisms can provide users with personalized recommendation content based on their interests and preferences, which is an important factor in promoting users to use and even become addicted to short video platforms. Excellent algorithm recommendations on the platform can enhance users' sense of belonging to the platform, and they are more willing to participate in platform interactions, such as commenting, bookmarking, or sharing their favorite short videos.

Last, The Electronic Health Literacy Scale is a fairly mature scale that has been applied in multiple countries and regions since its development by Norman. However, subjective evaluations of electronic health literacy may not reflect the actual level of electronic health literacy. On the other hand, although Norman's measurement items on electronic health information have good reliability and validity, the current network environment is developing rapidly, and the integration of network and life is further improving. Digital technology is gradually entering public life, and there is a need to develop scales that are more suitable for contemporary electronic health practices. In addition, the themes of health education are diverse, but specific themes were not distinguished in this study. Therefore, in future research, the themes of health education can be further refined to gain a deeper understanding of the factors that affect users' willingness to share health education short videos.

References

1. Manafo E, Wong S. Journal of Nutrition Education and Behavior, 44(2012).
2. Jin X-L, Yin M, Zhou Z, et al. Information Processing & Management, 58 (2021),.
3. Liu M, Yang Y, Sun Y. Health Communication, 34(2019).
4. Petty R E, Cacioppo J T, Petty R E, et al. Springer New York, 1986.
5. Zhang Y, Song S. Proceedings of the 2020 Conference on Human Information Interaction and Retrieval[C]. Vancouver BC Canada: ACM, 2020.
6. Chao F, Wang X, Yu G. Internet Research, 2023.
7. Wang X, Chao F, Yu G, et al. Computers in Human Behavior, 130(2022).
8. Oh S. Journal of the American Society for Information Science and Technology, 63(2012).
9. Wu X, Kuang W. International Journal of Human–Computer Interaction, 37(2021).

Translating advertisements from Chinese to English: Strategies and methods

Rong Jiang*

School of Foreign Language, Communication University of China, Nanjing, Nangjing Jiangsu, China

Abstract: This study explores the strategies and methods of translating advertisements from Chinese to English. It adopts a functional approach to translation studies, encompassing the Skopos theory and equivalent translation theory. The translation strategies are divided into semantic, structural, language, and rhetorical levels. At the semantic level, the use of literal translation, liberal translation, and semantic conversion is employed to convey both the literal meaning and intended meaning of the advertisements. At the structural level, supplementary translation, condensed translation, and the division and merging of sentences are utilized to adjust the structure to meet the translation requirements. At the language level, extensive use of adjectives, frequent use of imperative verbs, and personal pronouns are employed to highlight features, prompt actions, and establish connections. At the rhetorical level, the use of puns, simulation, personification and exaggeration is employed to enhance interest, convey messages, and imbue products with human-like qualities. By employing a functional approach and various translation strategies, advertisements can be effectively translated, capturing the interest and resonance of the target audience. However, this study has certain limitations in terms of sample selection and research scope. Future research can further explore additional translation strategies and methods to improve the effectiveness and quality of advertisement translation.

1.Functional approach to translation studies

The paper's chosen method for Translation Studies is the functional approach, which encompasses Skopos theory and Equivalent translation theory as its two main aspects.

1.1 Skopos theory

Skopos theory is a translation theory proposed by German scholar Vermeer in the 1970s. Vermeer freed translation research from the constraints of the original text centered theory, believing that translation must follow the principles of purpose, coherence, and fidelity, with the principle of purpose being the primary principle, which states that "any translation behavior is determined by the purpose of translation, that is, the purpose of translation determines the means of translation" (Munday 2012: 122) [1].

When it comes to advertising translation, the ultimate goal is to promote products and services to potential consumers and generate economic benefits. To achieve the best advertising effect, translators can follow Skopos theory and employ appropriate translation methods that align with the characteristics of the products and services they are promoting. This will enable them to effectively convey the intended message to the target audience and maximize the impact of their advertising efforts.

1.2 Equivalent translation theory

The Equivalent translation theory, which was introduced by the American translator Eugene A. Nida in the early 1940s, holds that translation should focus on functional equivalence rather than simply adhering to the form and structure of the source language[2]. In this theory, Nida pointed out that "translation is the use of the most appropriate, natural, and equivalent language to reproduce the information of the source language from semantics to style". Nida's definition of translation indicates that it involves not only lexical equivalence, but also semantic, stylistic, and formal equivalence. Translation conveys information that includes not only surface lexical information but also deep cultural information. The "dynamic equivalence" proposed by Nida includes four aspects: lexical equivalence, syntactic equivalence, discourse equivalence, and stylistic equivalence. Among these aspects, Nida believes that "meaning is the most important, followed by form".

Therefore, Nida's equivalent translation theory emphasizes the importance of achieving functional equivalence in translation, taking into account not only the lexical meaning, but also the cultural nuances, style, and intended function of the source text[3].

In advertising translation, the theory of equivalent translation is useful in guiding translators to choose appropriate translation strategies and ensure that the

*Corresponding author's mail: jiangrong@cucn.edu.cn

translated text can achieve similar advertising, promotional, and sales effects in the target language, while considering the expression and functional requirements of the original text and the language habits and cultural background of the target language. By doing so, the translated text can be more readable and acceptable, effectively achieving the goals of advertising translation, promotion, and sales.

2.Translation strategies

The importance of advertising translation lies in its direct impact on the dissemination effect and efficiency of advertising. Advertising is one of the most important means in commercial marketing, with the aim of promoting the sale of products or services. The translation of advertisements involves transforming the information, language, and culture of advertisements into a form that the target audience can understand and accept, which is crucial for the successful dissemination of advertisements. Therefore, selecting appropriate translation strategies is crucial for the effectiveness of advertising communication[4].

2.1 Semantic level

In terms of semantics, advertising translation requires accuracy, attractiveness, alignment with the target culture and brand positioning, while also striving to preserve the original ad's creativity and personality. Translators need to fully grasp the semantic meaning of the original ad, apply appropriate translation strategies and techniques to ensure that the translated semantics remain consistent with the original ad and achieve the desired effect.

2.1.1 Use of literal translation

The use of literal translation in advertising translation helps to maintain the original flavor, preserve the vocabulary and sentence structure of the source text, and accurately convey the advertising message[5]. It also aims to retain the creativity and personality of the original ad, ensuring that the translated ad maintains the same style and expression, thus enhancing its effectiveness and impact.

(1) ST: 谁跑得最长, 谁笑得最好。

TT: He laughs best, who runs longest.

The example 1 is a tire advertisement. In the target text (TT), the translator preserves the original advertisement's expression style and sentence structure through a literal translation method, ensuring that the advertisement maintains a similar style in the target language. This helps maintain the coherence and consistency of the brand image.

Additionally, the use of literal translation emphasizes durability and endurance. The translation of "who runs longest" conveys the concept of durability and reliability, implying that the promoted tires have durable and reliable performance to support long-term usage. This aligns with the advertisement's objective of emphasizing product durability and long-lasting effects to attract potential consumers' attention.

Furthermore, the literal translation retains the original advertisement's metaphors and emotive power, enabling the translated advertisement to convey the same emotions and effects. The literal translation conveys the implicit connection between "running the longest" and "smiling the best," allowing readers to make corresponding associations in their minds, thereby increasing the advertisement's appeal and impact.

2.1.2 Use of liberal translation

In advertising translation, translators often use the method of liberal translation to evoke emotional resonance in the audience, making it easier for them to develop an interest in the product or service. At the same time, it helps to adapt to different cultural backgrounds and ensures that the advertising message is accurately understood and accepted by the target audience. The use of liberal translation gives translators greater creative space, enabling them to express the advertising content in a more appealing and personalized manner. Through liberal translation, advertising can establish memory and recognition in the target market, enhancing the consistency and recognition of the brand image on a global scale.

(2) ST: 黑妹牙膏, 强健牙龈, 保护牙齿。

TT: Do not show me any other， but show me Black Sister.

In the ST of example 2, The original phrase “黑妹牙膏”, refers to a specific brand of toothpaste, and a literal translation into English may not accurately convey the specific meaning and cultural background of the brand. In the TT, through the use of liberal translation, the translator transforms it into "show me Black Sister" to convey the brand name and theme, which is more likely to resonate with English readers. Moreover, "Show me Black Sister" has a unique expression in English that may evoke readers' interest and curiosity on a subconscious level, making it more likely to capture their attention to the product.

(3) ST: 创新不断，才能时刻超前。

TT: To stay ahead you must have your next idea waiting in the wings.

The example 3 is an advertisement promoting Audi cars. By using liberal translation, the advertisement can effectively convey the core values and philosophy of the Audi brand in a way that is more easily understood by English readers. The phrase “创新不断” in the ST is translated as "have your next idea waiting in the wings". This translation captures the essence of the brand's pursuit and emphasizes the importance of continuous innovation and staying ahead. It aligns better with the language and cultural background of English readers, while maintaining the appeal and effectiveness of the advertisement. Such a translation enables the advertisement to resonate more easily with English readers, stimulating their interest and attention towards Audi vehicles.

2.1.3 Use of semantic conversion

The use of semantic conversion method can help advertisements convey information more naturally within the cultural context of the target language. Certain English words may not have a direct equivalent in Chinese or may have subtle differences in meaning across different cultural backgrounds[6]. Through semantic conversion, one can select vocabulary and expressions that align better with the target language readers' understanding and habits, making the advertisement more easily comprehensible and acceptable.

(4) ST: 蚊子杀、杀、杀。

TT: Mosquito bye, bye, bye.

The example 4 is a mosquito repellent advertisement. By employing semantic conversion, the TT successfully conveys the essence of the original Chinese advertisement to the English-speaking target audience. Instead of a straightforward translation like "Mosquito kill, kill, kill", the creatively adapted phrase "Mosquito bye, bye, bye" effectively captures the concept of eliminating mosquitoes in a more engaging and emotionally resonant manner. This approach fosters a stronger connection with the audience and reinforces the intended message of the advertisement. As a result, the advertisement becomes more relatable and memorable to English readers, ensuring effective communication of the product's benefits and features. Furthermore, the repetition of "bye, bye, bye" adds a rhythmic and playful tone to the translation, making it more engaging and memorable for the audience. This type of expression is more likely to grab the attention of English readers and leave a lasting impression.

(5) ST: 吸烟请到吸烟区。

TT: No smoking except in the designated smoking area.

The example 5 is a public service advertisement slogan in an airport waiting room. The ST aims to inform everyone that smoking is prohibited in the waiting room and smokers should use the designated smoking area. However, a direct translation of the ST as "The passengers who smoke, please go to the smoking area" not only fails to convey the message of smoking prohibition but also seems to encourage passengers to smoke. In order to accurately convey the intended meaning, the translator employed semantic conversion in the TT and translated the original text into a highly authentic English expression.

2.2 Structural level

In Chinese-to-English advertising translation, there are certain cases where the original text may contain additional information or details that need to be supplemented in the translation process to ensure that the translated text conveys the same meaning and effect as the original. Supplementary translation can enhance the attractiveness and persuasiveness of the advertisement, making the translation more culturally and linguistically relevant to the target audience[7]. Furthermore, there are instances where it is necessary to condense and streamline the information from the original text within a limited space. Through condensed translation, lengthy sentences or paragraphs can be compressed into concise and clear expressions, retaining the key information while ensuring the conciseness and appeal of the advertisement. Additionally, there are times when it is necessary to divide or merge sentences from the original text to adapt to the grammar structure and expression conventions of the target language. The division and merging of sentences as a translation method can make the translated text more in line with English grammar norms, while improving readability and fluency. Overall, these structural changes in translation methods can help ensure the accuracy, fluency, and persuasiveness of advertising translation. They can adapt to the characteristics and cultural backgrounds of the target language while maintaining the original intent, making the advertisement more attractive and impactful, thereby achieving the desired promotional effect.

2.2.1 Use of supplementary translation

The use of supplementary translation is a method of adding and supplementing translation content to meet the needs of the target language audience. Due to the different expressions, language habits, and ways of thinking between Chinese and English, in the process of advertising translation, in order to make the translation more in line with the pragmatic habits, context, and cultural background of the target language, the translator needs to add some sentences, phrases, or words to enable the target language audience to more accurately understand and accept the meaning of the translation.

(6) ST: 溪口千层饼采用传统工艺，制作精细，质地松脆，清香可口。

TT: Xikou Qiangceng Cake, with numerous clear sheets in it, is finely made in a traditional way. It is tasty and crisp.

The underlined part in the ST of example 6, "千层饼," was not translated literally as "thousand and sheets cake," but instead, the translator chose to use transliteration, rendering it as "Qianceng." This approach preserves the original sound and essence of the Chinese name. Besides, the translator employed supplementary translation to provide additional information about the cake----"with numerous clear sheets in it", which can arouse the interest of foreign readers and entice them to try it. By using supplementary instructions, the translator was able to effectively convey the seductive message of the original text to a foreign audience.

(7) ST: 拥有力莱纤维，就拥有最优美舒适的丝袜。

TT: Lilion, the finest yarn that makes your stocking look beautiful and feel smooth.

In the Example 7, the translator provides additional information and details for the term "力莱" in the ST to ensure that the translated text conveys the same meaning and effect as the original. "力莱" is a specific product or brand name that may not have a direct equivalent in English. By offering supplementary translation, the translator can provide readers with more information about the product, enabling them to understand its features and value. This approach enhances the accuracy and completeness of the translation, while also boosting the attractiveness of the advertisement, as readers can access more specific and relevant information that is likely to draw their attention to the product's advantages. Furthermore, the translator assists readers in better understanding the connection between "力莱"and the most beautiful and comfortable stockings, aiming to engage the target audience and increase their interest and identification with the product.

2.2.2 Use of condensed translation

Advertising is often limited by space or time constraints, so using condensed translation helps ensure that the advertising message is conveyed within the given limitations[8]. By simplifying and compressing the language expression, more core information can be delivered within the limited space while maintaining clarity and impact. Through condensed translation, the advertising message can be condensed into a more attractive and memorable form, aiding the audience in better remembering the content. By distilling the information to its core essence, the primary purpose and intention of the advertisement can be communicated more effectively, without relying excessively on specific cultural or linguistic details.

(8) ST: 12 型手扶拖拉机具有结构简单，耐用可靠，操作灵活，马力大，重量轻，通用性能好等优点，并备有乘坐装置，可以坐着耕作。

TT: Model-12 two-wheel tractor is recognized for its simple structure, reliability, long service life, easy operation, ample output, light weight and versatility, and is equipped with a riding installation.

In the source text (ST) of example 8, the underline parts "备有乘坐装置"and"可以坐着耕作" have the same meaning. Therefore, the translator applied a condensed translation method in the TT, omitting the latter phrase while retaining the key information, achieving a concise and impactful effect in the translation. By condensing the translation, the translator streamlined the expression within the limited space, eliminating redundancy and repetition from the original text, resulting in a more concise and compelling advertising message.

Through condensed translation, the TT becomes more concise and to the point, making it easier for readers to accept and understand. It effectively conveys the core message within a limited space, making the advertisement more impactful and attention-grabbing. Furthermore, it improves the readability and fluency of the advertisement, ensuring compliance with English grammar norms.

2.2.3 Division and merging of sentences

The division and merging of sentences are crucial in the process of translating Chinese advertisements into English. Chinese sentences are often longer than their English counterparts, and breaking them down into shorter units enhances readability and comprehension. Additionally, English grammar and expression may differ from Chinese, so dividing sentences into smaller units allows for better adaptation to English structure. On the other hand, Chinese information may be spread across multiple sentences, whereas English often consolidates related information into a single sentence. By merging sentences, the advertising message can be conveyed more clearly, avoiding redundancy and ensuring a concise and impactful advertisement. This process also ensures grammatical correctness and fluency, as Chinese and English have differences in word order, vocabulary choice, and grammar rules. By appropriately dividing and merging sentences, advertisements become more readable, engaging, and able to deliver a clear message within a limited timeframe.

(9) ST: 新款手机拥有强大的处理器和高清屏幕，带给您更流畅、更震撼的用户体验。

TT: The new phone features a powerful processor and a high-definition screen. It brings you a smoother and more immersive user experience.

In the source text (ST) of example 9, it both conveys that the new phone possesses a powerful processor and a high-definition screen and emphasizes the enhanced smoothness and immersive user experience it brings. In the target text (TT), the translator uses the method of sentence division. The first sentence highlights the primary features of the new phone, while the second sentence further underscores the advantages of user experience. By dividing the sentences, each sentence can focus on presenting particular information, making it more prominent and engaging. Simultaneously, it aids in conveying information clearly, avoiding confusion, and improving readability. Readers can more easily comprehend and retain the key points of the advertisement. By breaking down long sentences into shorter, easily comprehensible segments, each sentence can convey a distinct idea, avoiding information overload. This approach ensures that the information remains organized and coherent.

2.3 Language level

Language plays a crucial role in advertising translation. It serves as the primary tool for conveying advertising messages[9]. Through accurate, clear, and engaging language expression, advertising translation effectively communicates the features, advantages, and value of products or services, capturing the interest of potential customers and motivating them to take action. Additionally, language possesses the power to evoke emotions. Appropriate language choices and expressions can resonate with readers or listeners, making the advertisement more compelling and influential. The use of effective language expressions and marketing techniques can capture the audience's attention, stimulate their desire to make a purchase, and prompt them to take action, thus achieving the commercial objectives of the advertisement. Therefore, in advertising translation, it is crucial to focus on language selection, expression, and the application of marketing techniques.

2.3.1 Extensive use of adjectives

The inclusion of a greater number of adjectives in advertising translation offers several advantages. It enables the highlighting of product features, creating a more impactful impression on the target audience. Secondly, it establishes emotional connections with the audience, increasing the likelihood of a positive response. Thirdly, adjectives facilitate comparison and contrast, setting the product apart from competitors. Lastly, the use of descriptive adjectives enhances brand recall and recognition, fostering greater brand loyalty and awareness. Together, these benefits synergistically enhance the overall effectiveness of advertising translation.

(10) ST: 柴油机体积小，重量轻，运转平稳。

TT: Diesel engine has small volume, light weight and stable running.

In the ST of the example 10, it uses the adjectives "小" "轻" and "平稳", and the translator also emphasizes these three aspects in the translation. In the target text (TT) of, the adjectives of "small", "light" and "stable" serve the purpose of capturing potential customers' attention and generating interest in the product. By employing vivid and captivating adjectives, advertisements can differentiate themselves from competitors and grab the target audience's focus. These adjectives offer brief descriptions that enable potential customers to comprehend the product's features and benefits. Therefore, utilizing adjectives effectively helps consumers form initial impressions of the product, stimulating their curiosity and motivating them to explore and make a purchase.

2.3.2 Frequent use of imperative verbs

The frequent use of imperative verbs in the English translation of advertisements serves to emphasize actions and provide direct instructions to readers or audiences, urging them to take specific actions[10]. Imperative verbs play a vital role in guiding and influencing consumer decision-making within the context of advertisements by explicitly prompting the audience to act.

(11) ST: 地毯商店举办地毯展销，提供各种手织地毯，欢迎前来参观稀世珍品----中国精美华丽的地毯。

TT: A Carpet Display and Sale Sponsored by a Carpet Shop offers a variety of hand-knitted woollen carpets. Come and visit an exotically luxurious world of Chinese charm and beauty.

In the target text (TT) of example 11, the translator adds imperative verbs "come" and "visit" in the underlined part to encourage audience participation and interaction. By urging them to come and visit, it establishes a sense of engagement with the audience, fostering a stronger connection between products and consumers. This interactive approach prompts the audience to actively engage with the advertisement, leading to increased product awareness. In addition, it creates a clear and direct tone that can stimulate their interest and initiative, motivating them to engage in purchasing, participating, or trying out the product.

2.3.3 Skillful use of personal pronouns

In advertising translation, the use of personal pronouns such as "you" or "we" establishes a personalized connection with the audience, allowing potential customers to feel involved and enhancing the appeal of the advertising message. This personalized approach creates a direct sense of closeness. Additionally, the use of personal pronouns individualizes the advertising message, making it more targeted. By treating potential customers as individuals, it generates a sense of importance and relevance, which contributes to increasing the effectiveness of the advertisement. Furthermore, when personal pronouns are used in advertisements, it becomes easier for people to relate them to themselves, creating emotional resonance. This strengthens their attention and interest in the advertising message, encouraging a more active response to the call-to-action.

(12) ST: 为您的家人每天提供七种重要好处，只需享用美味的达能酸奶。了解以下好处，看看您如何帮助您所爱的人过上更健康的生活方式!

TT: You can give your family seven important benefits every day just by serving delicious yogurt, Dannon Yogurt. To see how you can help your loved ones live a healthier lifestyle, take a look at the benefits below!

In the TT of the example 12, the translator retained the personal pronoun "您"from the ST, and the second-person pronouns "you" and "yours" are repeatedly used in the TT. It reads as if a friend is warmly introducing Dannon yogurt to consumers and their family, creating a sense of familiarity. By using personal pronouns, this yogurt advertisement is able to stimulate consumers' active participation. This direct interaction with consumers encourages them to take action or experience the product.

2.4 Rhetorical Level

The application of rhetorical devices is a common translation strategy in advertising translation. Rhetorical devices can provide advertisements with more vivid, unique, and creative expressions, thus enhancing their attractiveness and impact. Through the use of devices such as puns, simulation, and personification, advertisements can leave a deep impression on readers or viewers, enhancing their memorability and credibility[11]. Moreover, rhetorical devices in advertising translation help to convert the original text's creativity and expression into equivalent expressions in the target language. By flexibly employing corresponding rhetorical devices, translators can effectively convey advertising messages to target audiences, overcoming language and cultural barriers. Additionally, rhetorical devices can endow advertisements with distinctive personality and style, helping brands establish a unique, interesting, and standout image. By skillfully utilizing rhetorical devices, advertisements can showcase brand creativity, intelligence, and distinctive characteristics, thereby enhancing brand awareness and loyalty.

2.4.1 Use of puns

(13) ST: 道路不沾水,司机更安全; 司机不沾酒,道路更安全。

TT: The driver is safer when the road is dry; The road is safer when the driver is dry.

The example 13 is a traffic promotion advertisement. The ST contains two meanings: Roads are free from water, making drivers safer; Drivers do not get drunk, making roads safer. In the target text (TT), the translator uses the rhetorical device of pun: the word "dry" carries a semantic pun. In the first sentence, "dry" refers to the absence of water, indicating dry road conditions. In the second sentence, "dry" implies that the driver abstains from alcohol. In this context, "dry" is translated as "no water" and "no alcohol," respectively, retaining the parallel form of the original text.

2.4.2 Use of simulation

In advertising translation, the use of the simulation approach is frequently employed, with the most common being the simulation of proverbs from the target language to translate the original advertisement. Proverbs serve as commonly used expressions in the target culture, enabling resonance and connection with the target audience, thereby enhancing the cultural affinity of the advertisement. Moreover, proverbs often carry emotions and wisdom, capable of triggering emotional resonance in the target audience, making the advertisement more appealing and impactful. Additionally, proverbs are typically concise, refined, and easy to remember, enabling them to leave a lasting impression in the minds of the target audience, thereby enhancing the advertisement's memorability. By utilizing proverbs or idioms from the target language, advertisements can effectively convey information, establish brand identity, and foster a strong emotional connection with the target audience.

(14) ST: 车到山前必有路,有路必有丰田车。

In this example 14, the ST contains two declarative sentences: Where there is a car, there must be a road; Where there's a road, there's a Toyota. In the TT, the translator emulated the English proverb "Where there is a will, there is a way" to translate the ST into English as: "Where there is a way, there is a Toyota." By simulating the English proverb in the translation, the brand can showcase its uniqueness and creativity on the international stage, contributing to brand shaping, promotion, and enhancing brand image and reputation. Therefore, employing this translation method of simulation helps effectively convey the meaning and emotions of the original advertisement in cross-cultural communication, improving its comprehensibility and memorability while showcasing the brand's distinctiveness and charm in the international market.

2.4.3 Use of personification

In Chinese-to-English advertising translation, utilizing personification can help simplify complex product features and information into a more easily comprehensible and relatable form. By personifying the product or service and portraying it as an entity with human characteristics and behaviors, it becomes more accessible for potential customers to understand and remember the relevant information. Consequently, the conveyed message becomes clearer, more succinct, and facilitates purchase decisions. Moreover, personification adds a human touch to the product or brand, allowing consumers to establish a stronger emotional connection by associating themselves with the depicted human traits, desires, and emotions. Additionally, by personifying the product or brand, a distinctive and captivating brand image can be crafted. This image enhances the product or brand's vividness and memorability in consumers' minds, thereby fostering brand loyalty and identification.

(15) ST: 她工作，你休息。

TT: She works while you rest.

The example 15 is an advertisement promoting a washing machine. It employs personification, personifying the washing machine. The phrase "she works" contrasts with "you rest," creating two contrasting scenes: the washing machine can help consumers share the household chores, while consumers can leisurely enjoy life. By personifying the washing machine as "she," the translator implies the machine's effort and dedication during its work, aligning with the consumer's life, and enhancing the consumer's emotional identification with the product. By describing the washing machine with human characteristics as "she," the message directly conveys that the washing machine provides convenience to consumers while allowing them to relax, making the advertisement easier to understand and remember. Additionally, by personifying the washing machine as a hardworking woman, the advertisement portrays a reliable, diligent, and caring brand image, which increases consumer trust and affinity towards the brand.

2.4.4 Use of exaggeration

Exaggerated translation can stand out among a sea of advertisements, capturing the attention of potential consumers. It can grab their eyeballs and pique their curiosity about the ad content. By employing exaggerated adjectives, adverbs, and phrases, the translation can leave a lasting impression of the product or service in consumers' minds. Through the use of an exaggerated linguistic style, the advertisement can differentiate itself, establishing the brand's uniqueness and personality, thus building brand recognition and fostering consumer identification[12].

(16) ST: "葵花"电扇，清凉无限。

TT: "Sunflower" fan, fans away the sun.

The example 16 is a fun advertisement. The ST uses the exaggerated phrase "清凉无限"to describe the immense power and excellent cooling effect of the fan. The translator, with a rich imagination, employs a unique and exaggerated approach in the TT, translating "清凉无限" as "fans away the sun" ----sweeping away the scorching sun. This translation evokes the idea that the "Sunflower" fan can provide an incredibly comfortable cooling sensation during the sweltering summer days, emphasizing the powerful cooling effect of the product. By using such an exaggerated expression, the "Sunflower" fan leaves a distinct impression, establishing the brand's uniqueness and personality, contributing to brand recognition and consumer identification.

3.Conclusion and limitation

The utilization of a functional approach and diverse translation strategies can lead to the successful translation of advertisements, effectively captivating the attention and connection of the intended recipients. Nevertheless, it is important to acknowledge the limitations of this study, specifically regarding sample selection and research scope. Future research endeavors should aim to delve deeper into additional translation strategies and methodologies, with the objective of enhancing the efficacy and caliber of advertisement translation.

Acknowledgments

This work was partially supported by the Research Project of Communication University of China, Nanjing titled "Reform of College English Teaching Model Based on Educational Digital Transformation" (JG202321)

References

1. Ai Zhen. *A Study on Translation Strategies of Advertising Text Guided by Skopos Theory.* Journal of Jiangsu Normal University (Educational Sciences Edition) 5(1): 90–93, (2014)
2. Liao J. *Research on "Precise Translation" of Commercial Advertising Based on Big Data*[J].Journal of Physics Conference Series, (2021)
3. Feiran Li, Hainv Xu. *A Reception-Theoretic Approach to the Advertising Translation Criterion*[J].Overseas English, (2019)
4. Mahdi A *A Functional Analysis of The Translation of Advertising Headlines in Terms of Translatorial Action Theory*[J].(2021)
5. Li Gang, and Li Bing. *The Language Characteristics and Translation Strategies of Business Advertising English.* Guangzhou: Guangdong World Book Publishing, Inc. (2013)
6. Cai L.*The Strategy of English to Chinese Translation of Advertisements from the Perspective of Nida's Functional Equivalence Theory*[J].Region - Educational Research and Reviews, (2022)
7. Damaskinidis G, Kostopoulou L.*Intersemiotic Translation of Subliminal Messages in Brand Logos*[J].International Journal of Semiotics and Visual Rhetoric, (2021)
8. Munday, Jeremy. *Introducing Translation Studies: Theories and Applications.* London – New York: Routledge.(2002)
9. Zhaozhong Peng. *Advertising Translation and the Perspective of Advertising in Translation.* Beijing: Chemical Industry Press. (2019)
10. Shi Lei. *Advertising Translation Studies from the Cultural Perspective.* Shengyang: Liaohai Publishing Press. (2018)
11. Wang Lin, and Guangni, Chen. *The Application and Translation Strategies of Puns in Advertising Discourse.* Journal of Inner Mongolia Agricultural University (Social Science Edition) 55(13): 356–357, (2011)
12. Orazbekova I, Rustemova A, Tleugabylova Z. Techniques of Russian-Kazakh advertising translation[J].Eurasian Journal of Philology: Science and Education, (2022)

The Operation Logic of Traditional Culture Enabling Tea Brand Marketing: Take CHAGEE as an Example

Zixin Chen[1, *], Siyu Fu[2], Xintong Huang[3]

[1] Nanjing Foreign Language School, Jiangsu 210008, China
[2] GDPU Undergraduate School of Medical Business, Guangdong Pharmaceutical University, Guangdong 510006, China
[3] Huafu International (HFI), Guangdong 510630, China

Abstract. The research background of this paper is to focus on the globalization and diversification of the market, and many brands intend to integrate culture into their products for marketing. At the same time, by the end of 2023, the stores of new tea brands can reach up to 5 billion. Currently, China's milk tea industry has entered China and entered the era of new tea drinks. This paper to the overlord CHAGEE the brand as a research entrance, the traditional culture can assign tea brand marketing logic study the subject, the research method is used to the process tracking method and 4P theory, through the two methods to the operation of traditional culture risks and the analysis, found that the brand using traditional culture can assign brand marketing method, and at the end to the brand in the use of traditional culture marketing to provide relevant Suggestions. This study has guiding significance for the future development of the related milk tea beverage industry.

1. Introduction

This study focuses on the globalization and diversification of the market, and many brands consciously integrate culture into their products for marketing. Meanwhile, by the end of 2023, the stores of new tea brands will reach 500,000 [1]. Now China's milk tea industry has entered the era of new tea drinking. This study is very meaningful for how to use the brand and the traditional culture to build the brand and product marketing; This study mainly focuses on the example of the CHAGEE brand, The operation logic of using traditional culture to empower the tea brand marketing; Using the literature analysis method to search and read the relevant materials and literature, The advantage of this approach is that it can well analyze the risks and relative countermeasures of other brands in adopting the traditional culture, Benefit to the conduct of the research; The ultimate research goal of this study is how to make the brand better use the traditional Chinese culture to empower marketing, By the way, The 4P theory was used to analyze the selected cases.

2. Case Analysis

2.1. Background

"CHAGEE" is a tea brand of China-fashion Enterprise Management (Yunnan) Co., LTD. As a new Chinese tea brand, it originated from —— Yunnan, the hometown of world tea. The brand name comes from the well-known allusion to *Farewell My Concubine* and uses the traditional Chinese culture of Peking Opera Huadan Facebook as the brand Logo. The brand's main Oriental culture and tea inheritance will use tea brewing and milk of raw milk, at the same time including pure tea fresh tea, and other kinds of drinks, innovation to build a new Chinese tea, on behalf of Chinese tea become the Oriental symbol, from opera inheriting Chinese culture, focusing on opera, inheriting innovation of tea culture. New tea drink refers to the use of superior tea, supplemented by different extraction methods of concentrate as raw material, adding fresh milk and other ingredients into the drink [2]. The brand was first launched on June 1,2017 and opened its first store in Kunming, Yunnan Province on November 17 of the same year. The brand not only uses traditional culture in the brand concept, but also adds elements of Chinese traditional culture in products and stores to design so that consumers can feel the charm of traditional Chinese culture in —— vision, touch, smell, and taste in all aspects. At the visual level, "CHAGEE" uses the pattern of Chinese cultural elements and the design logo of facial makeup in the product packaging, and uses the seal script handwriting to design the font. At the tactile level, the offline store uses the outer ring design of the ancient architecture of Oriental beauty where the natural texture of logs can be detected by hand. In terms of smell, "CHAGEE" uses the fragrance machine under the store to spread the tea fragrance to the whole space, creating a tea fragrance atmosphere full of Oriental beauty. In terms of taste, the use of raw leaf tea soup and fresh milk brewing brings consumers the most direct enjoyment of Oriental beauty. In recent years, "CHAGEE" has also adopted traditional Chinese cultural elements in

*Corresponding author's mail: Cecilia.chen25@nflsbca.com

its marketing. The brand co-branded famous photographers, in a modern way to tell the traditional culture, using a variety of traditional cultural elements to create a brand image with strong Oriental color.

2.2. 4P for Theoretical Analysis

The 4P theory was first proposed by Professor Jerome McCarthy, an American marketing scholar in the 1960s, namely product (Product), price (Price), promotion (Promotion), and channel (Place). The proposal of this marketing theory has produced a milestone change in modern marketing [3]. Cultural marketing is one of the marketing methods with humanism as the core. Enterprises take the cultural value of products as the carrier to meet and guide the spiritual and cultural orientation of consumers, thus generating a sense of cultural identity and reducing the anxiety and distance caused by the difference in values [4]. Cultural marketing refers to the appropriate marketing means, which is guided by the cultural values and spiritual and cultural needs of consumers, combined with product characteristics and enterprise ideas and goals [5]. "CHAGEE", as a new tea brand, has not yet reached the wide popularity of "xi tea" or "Nai Xue tea" in the market, but it also shows a lot of potentials. The increasing development of the economy has led to the improvement of people's living standards and the change in consumption thoughts, thus leading to the development of the tea industry [6]. With the continuous improvement of the social supply level, the competition among enterprises is becoming increasingly fierce, and the focus of operation has gradually shifted from improving the material function of products to the spiritual category of culture and personality conveyed by the brand and the product itself [7]. At the same time, for the question of what Chinese cultural elements, scholar He Jiaxin defines it as derived from Chinese traditional culture or closely related to Chinese culture; can be recognized by most Chinese people, consumers will immediately associate with Chinese culture. In the process of internationalization, the good application of Chinese cultural resources can bring associative differences to cross-cultural consumers [8].

"CHAGEE" pays great attention to characteristics and differentiation in product design (product), to attract more consumers' attention. For example, with a drink named "Boya Xian" out of the circle, they deeply excavated the essence of Chinese culture, and through the combination of modern tea, successfully created a unique combination of allusions and modern tea "national style" brand image. For people with similar cultural values, the higher the familiarity with cultural elements in the material field, the easier to obtain relevant cognitive [9]. In addition to focusing on cultural characteristics, it also provides a variety of product choices. In addition to traditional fresh milk tea, there is a variety of fruit tea, sugar-free options, low-calorie drinks, and nutrient-rich tea drinks to meet the needs of different consumer groups. This diversified product line not only expands its potential customer base but also enables every consumer to feel that this is a brand that can be customized according to personal taste and health needs. In terms of quality, "CHAGEE" is not willing to be left behind. The brand emphasizes the use of high-quality raw materials and exquisite production techniques, such as "ecological tea mountain original leaves straight mining", "sunshine pasture quality milk" and "ecological orchard-fresh fruit direct delivery", which are its main quality assurance. From the perspective of price (price) competitive pricing, the average price of "CHAGEE" is within the range of 15-20 yuan. Such a price positioning is within the relatively competitive range and can attract more young consumers. To further boost sales, the brand will also issue coupons through social media or public accounts, or hold limited-time discounts as a pricing strategy. Pricing is the key to the success of the enterprise. Pricing is conducted according to the different psychological characteristics of consumers [10]. In terms of location (place) selection, it is mainly concentrated in areas where young people are frequently active, such as near universities, business districts, or shopping centers. In addition, the brand also operates through e-commerce platforms and its website to cover a wider range of consumers. In terms of promotion (promotion), "CHAGEE" makes extensive use of social media platforms, including Weibo, WeChat, and TikTok, to expand its brand influence. It also actively seeks cooperation and co-branding with popular culture, local features, or other brands to attract different groups of consumers and to further consolidate its market position.

In general, through its unique products, and reasonable price positioning, "CHAGEE" has successfully created its own national style tea drinking world with selected locations and ingenious promotion strategies in the tea market.

3. The Risk of Traditional Culture Empowering Brands

When the brand uses traditional culture, the research and investigation of traditional culture are not deep enough, and a series of behaviors such as fabricating and disrespecting the contents of traditional culture appear, to mislead consumers, and distort and harm traditional culture.

The excessive consumption of traditional culture in the marketing process and the neglect of consumers' demand for products will affect the overall image of the brand and the sales of the product. At the same time, it will lead to a wrong understanding of Chinese brands by the outside world, resulting in a large negative social impact, which is not conducive to the later development of the brand and does not conform to the main development trend of the current society.

At present, the main means of marketing in society is traditional culture, and brands using traditional culture marketing are everywhere in the market. It is inevitable that many homogenized products caused by insufficient innovation will appear and cause aesthetic fatigue in consumers.

4. Responses

For "CHAGEE", integrating traditional culture into their products and brand stories can create unique value, but it also comes with a series of risks. It has proposed corresponding countermeasures for the risks they may face.

4.1. Cultural Misunderstanding

When "CHAGEE" integrates traditional cultural elements into the brand, there is a risk of misunderstanding and offense. This may be due to not understanding the deeper meaning of culture, or because branding activities are seen as commercializing or abusing traditional culture. This can damage a brand's reputation and lead to dissatisfaction and negative reviews from consumers. It can take the following measures to respond to this: in-depth research and understanding of cultural elements, seeking help from cultural consultants or experts to ensure respect for cultural traditions; conducting sensitivity training to ensure that employees understand cultural differences and sensitivities; actively listening to consumers Feedback, promptly apologizing and correcting any cultural misuse.

4.2. Market Saturation

2022 Maituan Tea Drinks report stated that "The first-tier cities are becoming saturated and the lower-tier markets are developing steadily." First-tier cities in China. The tea market has become very saturated, with various brands competing for the same consumers [11]. When all brands try to leverage traditional cultural empowerment, it can lead to an oversaturated market that makes it difficult to distinguish the differences between different brands. It can take the following responses to this: To stand out in the market, tea brands need to continue to innovate and provide unique products and experiences. They can look for different cultural elements to avoid duplication with competitors and create a personal traditional cultural style that is unique to the brand. In addition, brands can seek cooperation with other industries to provide consumers with a more comprehensive cultural experience, thus attracting more attention. For example, the collaboration between "CHAGEE" and Sanxingdui closely follows current events pays attention to the latest historical archeology, and demonstrates the precise positioning of the brand to consumers. At the same time, co-branding with products in different fields, such as the recent cooperation with the novel IP *Tomb Raiders*, has also set off a boom.

4.3. Cultural Sensitivity Combined with Localization

Traditional cultural elements may trigger different reactions in different countries and regions. Some cultural elements may be popular in some places but may cause controversy or discomfort in others. Tea brands need to consider how to adapt to the cultural sensitivities of different markets. It can take the following countermeasures: "CHAGEE" should conduct targeted market research for each city in each country to understand the cultural sensitivities of different regions and adjust their marketing strategies accordingly. They can choose to use different cultural elements in different markets to adapt to the needs of local cultures. In addition, build local partnerships to better understand and respect local culture. "CHAGEE" is also very dynamic in the Southeast Asian market. For the longer-term development of the brand, "CHAGEE" can consider integrating it with local culture, which will help increase local consumers' favorability of the "CHAGEE" brand.

4.4. Cultural Fatigue

"Traditional elements need to be inherited, but not blindly appropriated", a large number of national fashion brands have emerged may cause consumers to feel that the brand has fallen into the trap of "cultural appropriation", placing too much emphasis on cultural elements and ignoring product quality and innovation [12]."Aesthetic fatigue" is a popular aesthetic term in the context of popular culture. In the special environment of popular culture, its connotations are constantly enriched and enriched, which has attracted the attention of many literary and artistic workers on this phenomenon [13]. Countermeasures can be taken to deal with this: balance the combination of traditional cultural elements and brand uniqueness; Not only focusing on culture but also emphasizing product quality, sustainable marketing, and marketing innovation. For example, CHAGEE's best-selling product "Bo Ya Jue Xian" quotes traditional allusions and promotes high-quality national trends, rather than simply citing patterns and using traditional culture as a short-lived selling point; regularly updates brand stories and elements to maintain consumption The reader's freshness towards a brand.

In general, empowering brands with traditional cultural elements is a challenging but promising strategy. To mitigate risk and ensure success, "CHAGEE" needs to deeply research and understand culture, build relationships with community partners, comply with regulations, balance cultural elements, establish brand uniqueness, and maintain engagement and transparency with consumers. Only in this way can brands make full use of the value of traditional culture while respecting and protecting these precious cultural heritages.

5. Conclusion

This paper studies the operation logic of traditional culture-empowered brand marketing by taking "CHAGEE" as an example, using the process tracking method and a few cases comparison method to explore the risks and coping methods of CHAGEE's marketing means of using traditional culture-empowered brands in the current market, and analyzes its marketing means with 4p theories. It can make some references for many brands that use traditional culture marketing at present, and improve the influence of brands themselves. With the continuous development of China's economy, traditional culture has also been paid attention to, and more and more brands have adopted traditional culture for marketing, which is the traditional culture to empower the brand itself. In the current era of rapid development. Cultural marketing should adapt to the background of The Times and have the courage to innovate in order to better promote brand development. Secondly, in terms of operation culture, it is necessary to pay attention to the core of the culture itself and carry forward the excellent traditional Chinese culture to the world while making good use of traditional Chinese culture to help brand building.

Authors Contribution

All the authors contributed equally and their names were listed in alphabetical order.

References

1. IMedia Consulting. Survey and Analysis Report on the Development Status and Consumption Trend of China's New Tea Drinking Industry in the first half of 2022, https://baijiahao.baidu.com/s2id=1734972705788071080&wfr=spider& for=pc, 2022-06-07
2. Yongxin Phoenix Tea. 2020 11 China New tea industry development status and consumption trend survey and analysis report (2020).
3. Chen Qiumei.5E Marketing: A new perspective using 4P combination Theory. China Circulation Economy, (2): 76–80 (2011).
4. Philip, K.: Marketing Revolution 3.0. China Machine Press (2011).
5. Conglin, Z.: The application of cultural symbols in international marketing: A case study of "CHAGEE" (2023).
6. Li, L.: Analysis of the characteristics of new tea consumption market and industry development strategy. Journal of Anhui Normal University (2021).
7. Haifeng, Q.: Symbol marketing. Shanghai University of Finance and Economics Press (2006).
8. Jiaxun, H.: Globalization of Chinese Brands: A brand Strategy integrating "Chinese Elements" -- A case study of Li Ning. Journal of East China Normal University (Philosophical and Social Sciences Edition), 45 (04), 124-129+155-156 (2013).
9. Johnson, G., Scholes, K., Whittingtonr, W.: Exploring corporate strategy: text & cases .8th Edition. Upper Saddle River: Prentice Hall Press, 122 (2008).
10. Yu, C.: The Application strategy of Chinese cultural elements in the international marketing of new consumer brands: a double case study of Huaxizi and Bubblemart. Master's thesis. Beijing Foreign Studies University (2023).
11. Meituan Food and Kamen released the Tea Beverage Development Report (2022).
12. Wenyong, W.: Discussion on the abuse of traditional Elements in Modern Design. Design, (02), 180-181 (2013).
13. Zhenyu, H.: Research on aesthetic fatigue from the perspective of popular culture (2019).

Analysis of "Justice Online" Mobile Game Based on Creative Communication Management Theory

Huiyao Fu*

School of foreign language, North China Electric Power University, Beijing, 102206, China

Abstract. 2023, China's mobile game market competition is very fierce, and an open world 3D martial arts action MMO mobile game - "Justice Online" mobile game was officially launched on 30 June, and quickly stood out in a crowd of hand tour. Based on the creative communication management theory, this paper analyses the creative communication strategy of "Justice Online" mobile game from the participants of creative communication and the path of realization, and thinks about the inspiration of its success, so as to provide a reference for the game marketing communication.

1.Introduction

1.1 Research background and significance

According to the data of the 51st statistical report on China's Internet development, as of December 2022, the scale of China's online game users reached 522 million, accounting for 48.9% of the overall Internet users. It can be seen that in 2022 China's online game industry presents a stable development trend. The favourable policies continue to be released, supporting the stable development of the online game industry. The above data shows that China's Internet environment actually provides strong support for the development of the hand game industry. However, with the development of the Internet, people's requirements for mobile game have gradually improved, and the competition in the hand travel market has become more intense.

This year, there is a hand tour in the competition to kill, it is "Justice Online".

After more than four years of efforts by the project team of more than five hundred people, the mobile game "Justice Online" was officially open beta on 30 June this year. "Justice Online" mobile game in the first 12 days on the line, the number of reservations has reached as many as 40 million, on the line but a week "Justice Online" has topped the App Store best-seller list. As of 23rd August, "Justice Online" handbook has been on line for nearly two months, and the heat has slightly subsided, but it still resides in the 14th place in the list, and the second place in the TikTok game list, which is enough to prove that its publicity efforts are great and the effect is good. Therefore, this topic is based on the theory of creative communication management, focusing on the three core concepts of creative communication, i.e. "digital living space", "life service provider" and "lifer". The concept focuses on the three core concepts of "digital living space", "life service provider" and "lifer", and analyses the creative communication elements of "Justice Online" mobile game around the realization path of creative communication, and puts forward the author's own thinking, which is a practical application and supplement to the theory of creative communication management, and is of certain reference value to the marketing and communication in the digital era.

1.2 Overview of Research Status

1.2.1 Overview of Creative Communication Management Theory

In 2008, Professor Chen Gang of the School of Journalism and Communication of Peking University first put forward the Creative Communication Management Theory (CCM). 2012, the book Creative Communication Management Theory - Marketing Revolution in the Digital Era was published by Mechanical Industry Press. The theory defines the Internet environment in which people are now living as a new type of digital living space, in which the relationship between enterprises and consumers in the traditional marketing environment has undergone a certain transformation into the relationship between life service providers and lifers. In order to adapt to this change, the marketing communication model is bound to change, from then on into the era of creative communication management. Over the past ten years, this nascent theory has grown with the development of the Internet, and many researchers have used the theory to conduct case analyses and re-innovate it with new ideas and suggestions, injecting it with a constant stream of new vitality.[1]

*Corresponding author's mail: huiyaofu@gmail.com

1.2.2 Related research on the application of creative communication management theory

Creative communication management theory was born in the Internet era, it exists for a relatively short period of time, the actual research on this theory is not a lot of research, and most of the existing research is the use of case studies to make strategic analysis of a brand's publicity, and most of these studies focus on the entity enterprise, film and television works of the publicity and marketing.

For example, Peng Guanyu published "Research on Corporate User Communication Marketing Based on Creative Communication Management Theory--Taking NIO as an Example" (2020) [2], the author combined with creative communication management theory, in-depth analysis of NIO's marketing publicity from the perspectives of communication management, creative communication, communication contact, and core communication element, etc., based on the analysis proposed the construction of the user communication matrix, and finally summed up the analysis of NIO's user communication strategy, and analysed the marketing of NIO's publicity in comparison with that of the traditional automobile enterprises. Finally, it summarises the analysis of NIO's user communication strategy and analyses the success of NIO's publicity compared with the marketing of traditional automobile companies.

"Research on the Creative Communication Strategy of <Nezha: I am the destiny>" (2020) by Liu Limin [3], the author analyses from the perspectives of the three types of meme of hotspot attention type meme, lifers-made type meme and theme dissemination type meme and the four types of creative communication triggering strategies of own communication resources trigger, paid communication resources trigger, available communication resources trigger, and star social communication resources trigger. The study analyses the success and shortcomings of creative communication and finally proposes optimization strategies.

The above two studies are the application and supplementation of creative communication management theory, and both analyse the marketing strategy of the case in a more complete manner, and put forward suggestions on how to better use creative communication management theory for marketing and publicity, which are of reference significance to this paper.

1.2.3 Mobile phone network game marketing research

At present, China's research on mobile games is mostly focused on the development of the industry and product development, but not much research on mobile phone network game marketing and publicity, the use of creative communication theory research is even more lacking.

"Research on the communication strategy of mobile online game--Taking Tencent Mobile Games as an example" published by Zhang Tiantian (2015) .[4] The article combines the theories of communication and marketing, analyses the case of Tencent Mobile Games from the perspective of integrated marketing communication, gives in-depth thoughts from the perspectives of the communication condition, communication elements, successes and limitations, and finally puts forward suggestions on mobile game communication strategies based on this.

"Analysis on the creative communication strategy of the mobile game Evolver (2018)" [5] is a rare study based on creative communication management theory to analyse mobile game marketing, the author analyses from the three angles of communication elements, meme and communication triggering, and more comprehensively and aptly applies the creative communication management theory to the communication case of the mobile game Evolver, and finally also puts forward a unique thinking for the above analysis.

The above research is a specific analysis of mobile game communication and guidance, hand tour communication related research has reference value, but about the hand tour communication strategy research is still a lot of room for development, the mobile games developing in recent years have achieved a certain degree of success in the marketing and communication. As well as the research object of this topic, "Justice Online" mobile game was officially launched on 30 June, only on-line for less than two months but has made considerable achievements, but because of the shorter time related research is almost blank.

1.3 Research Methods

1.3.1 Case study method

With "Justice Online" mobile game as a typical representative and research object, I through in-depth experience of the game, and join the relevant social media exchange groups to communicate with other players, summed up and summarised "Justice Online" mobile game in the characteristics of creative communication, and combined with my own thinking on the creative communication to put forward a new revelation.

1.3.2 Questionnaire Survey Method

When analysing the "lifers" in the creative communication of "Justice Online" mobile game, i.e. the players of the game, I plan to use the questionnaire survey method to portray the characteristics of the players, and conduct a survey on the gender, age, occupation and geographic location of the "lifers" of the game, so as to outline the approximate image of the players. We will investigate the gender, age, occupation, geographic location, etc. of the game's "lifers" and outline a general image of the players.

2.The participants of the creative communication of "Justice Online" mobile game

2.1 The living space of the Song Dynasty Martial World

The game worldview set by the "Justice Online" mobile game is an fictional Northern Song Dynasty Jianghu, and the large map where players live includes two types of living spaces, realistic adaptations and completely fictional ones, such as Bianjing, Hangzhou, Yanmen Pass, Medicine King Valley, and Immortal Island, and so on. The digital living space is a positive semantic space that is continuously created by many information entities that eventually together constitute semantic content. On the one hand, this space is an extension of real life. The space of Bianjing and Hangzhou in "Justice Online" mobile game is the Northern Song Dynasty world which is perfected based on real-life information (e.g. Qingming Shanghe Tu), allowing players to travel back in time to enjoy the beautiful scenery of the Northern Song Dynasty thousands of years ago. On the other hand, this space is different from real life. In the worldview of "Justice Online" mobile game, spaces such as the Medicine King Valley and the Immortal Island have been fictionalised on the map of the Northern Song Dynasty, and different schools of martial arts have been developed in these places. Each player chooses a school of martial arts to join in learning the skills of spells after entering the game, which is impossible to realise in real life. The digital living space must allow for a strong sense of immersion and immersiveness. The open world of "Justice Online" mobile game provides players with a lot of life games that are similar to real life (such as cooking, fishing and farming), and the fictional game instances and other gameplay are also justified by the complete and grand worldview it builds, coupled with technologies such as artificial intelligence npcs that can chat freely, making it easy for players to form the sense of immersion of living in the Jianghu of the Great Song Dynasty! Thus, it can trigger emotional resonance.

2.2 The lifers in the Great Song Dynasty Martial World

The gamers of the "Justice Online" mobile game are living in the Great Song Jianghu as disciples of the Zi Zai Men. According to the questionnaire survey I conducted, the users of "Justice Online" mobile game are mostly concentrated in young people aged 19 to 29, and MMO games like "Justice Online" mobile game are undoubtedly most attractive to this part of the population, and the stimulating and bloodthirsty game instances and competitive gameplay requirements for the manoeuvres are also the most suitable for this category of people. However, "Justice Online" mobile game also launched a casual pension game to meet the needs of young people and middle-aged people who do not like the combat gameplay. "Justice Online" mobile game launched the "different paths, same destination" mode, each player can just choose the most suitable and favourite way to play, do not need to charge a lot of money and do not need to spend a lot of time to get a good game experience. Combined with the geographical distribution and occupation of the users, most players are living in first-tier cities and have a certain income, but their time is not necessarily very abundant, and this mode of "not forcing the time investment and not forcing fund input" perfectly suits their game demand points.

2.3 Song Jianghu's life service provider

The developer of the game, NetEase Lei Huo Studio, is the service provider of this digital living space. Lei Hugo Studio provides strong technical support for the digital living space constructed by "Justice Online" mobile game, maintaining its daily operation as well as version updates. At the same time, the official WeChat account of "Justice Online" mobile game, "Xiao Han", is also considered as a life service provider, which undertakes a variety of publicity functions such as absorbing players' opinions in a timely manner, providing players with feedback on updates, and even gossip and other promotional functions, with a witty and humorous tone, sincere and earnest attitude to trigger the emotional resonance of the players, improve the game to make it more in line with the needs of the players, so as to strengthen the user viscosity.

3.The realisation path of creative communication of "Justice Online" mobile game

3.1 Finding communication elements (meme)

Meme is the core communication element of creative communication, which is the carrier of communication as well as the point of realising creativity. It is a kind of cultural unit based on content, which unites the topics that interest the lifers and are easy to attract attention and discussion, and will be continuously enriched and spread in the interaction after it is put into the digital living space. Meme generally has four characteristics: clear singularity, shareability, extensibility, and participatory experience. In the creative communication of "Justice Online" mobile game, hotspot attention type meme, lifers-made type meme and theme dissemination type meme are used.

3.1.1 Hotspo attention type Meme

The hotspot concern type meme refers to the combination of the content of the communication of the lifers and the hotspot events, relying on the high attention of the hotspot events to attract the attention of the lifers and their participation, so as to achieve the purpose of the marketing communication of the lifers.

3.1.1.1 Chinese Traditional Festivals

Chinese traditional festival is undoubtedly a very hot spot that can attract attention, and "Justice Online" mobile game, as a Chinese traditional style mobile game, also naturally attaches great importance to Chinese traditional festivals. For example, during the Qixi Festival period this year, "Justice Online" mobile game launched a series of activities related to Qixi Festival, players can do exclusive tasks with their "love affair", but also with their favourite characters to spend a sweet Qixi Festival drama. The magpie bridge built in the manor by players on their own initiative has gained 85,000 likes after it was released on Jitterbug, which proves that "Justice Online" mobile game has successfully used the meme of the Chinese traditional festival as a hotspot concern.

3.1.1.2 AI chat npc

With the development of technology in recent years, AI is getting more and more attention and has become an extremely hot topic, "Justice Online" mobile game integrates AI technology into the game, and puts a certain number of npc that can carry out AI chatting on each map, and they will reply to the player's information according to their own character. Like Bianjing City, there is an NPC called Yu Qian Qian, her setting is a big lady, so her tone when she talks to the player is more domineering, the tone is upward. Many people therefore like to play "Justice Online" mobile game. What's more, a player called "Luo Binghe" through the AI chat function "fall in love" with Yu Qian Qian, the video released in the TikTok and gaining 200,000 likes.

3.1.2 Lifers-made type Meme

Lifers-made type meme refers to the fact that in the digital living space, the content created by a large number of lifers themselves can cause other lifers to pay attention to a wide range of participation, and even gradually be influenced and assimilated in the process of participation, and then consciously or unconsciously participate in the reproduction and extension. The topic initially created by a large number of lifers has become a meme that is sufficient for marketing communication, and the life service providers then combine it with their own marketing communication content, thus achieving the purpose of rapid dissemination by attaching to the meme created by the lifers.

The UGC (user-generated content) ecosystem of "Justice Online" mobile game is very prosperous, and the development is getting better and better, we can refer to the data on TikTok: as of 9 September, short videos about "Justice Online" mobile game has gained 11.5 billion times of playback, and the videos topics of funny characters' face, manor building, strategy and so on have tens of millions of playback. The content created by players, such as a funny face, a beautiful manor, or even eavesdropping on the npc chat video, can easily harvest 500,000 likes. The official TikTok account of the "Justice Online" mobile game leaves a funny comment under the videos to make the players laugh, helping the rapid spread of its marketing content.

3.1.3 Theme dissemination type meme

Theme dissemination type meme refers to the life service provider's extension of various additional activities and information on the relevant theme, and seeks to deliver the relevant theme to life in-depth through systematic activities and information release. Instead of relying on certain events or topics for marketing, this type of meme directly creates a theme and related activities and information to achieve communication. The core theme plus related activities and information is the basic structure of the theme dissemination type meme.

There is a major theme of "Justice Online" mobile game, which is "Breathing Jianghu", and all the activities and information are based on this major theme. Under the major theme, there are many branches of the small theme, these small themes will change with each update, season change. For example, in the 24th August update, the "Justice Online" mobile game updated a new map "Xian Ju Yuan", based on this launched a small theme "Strange fate of Xian Ju Yuan", a series of activities, such as beach comb, and cross-border communications with small animals, etc., but also supplemented with a lot of new information on the topic has also been added. As of 9 September, the topic of "Strange fate of Xian Ju Yuan" had received more than 20 million views.

3.2 Triggering Creative Communication

In the digital living space, different communication resources have different ways of presenting content, speed of publication and amount of information. Life service providers have to choose appropriate communication platforms to send meme according to specific marketing communication objectives and programmes, triggering the core of creative communication, i.e. collaborative creativity. In this regard, "Justice Online" mobile game has done well in the three triggering strategies of own communication resources triggering, paid communication resources triggering and special star social communication resources.

3.2.1 Own communication resources trigger

In all kinds of creative communication, own communication resources are the starting point and the end point. Life service providers should always start their marketing campaigns in their own communication resources. Like in the App Store, the competition is very fierce, how to design marketing strategy to attract players is an important issue that every game has to consider. The slogan of ""Justice Online" mobile game is "Martial arts open world, breathing Jianghu", which succinctly points out the main content and gameplay of the game, and also attracts people's attention with interesting and vivid descriptions. The combination of video, pictures and text in the detail page presents all the special and novel gameplay (such as single-player ai game instances, highly intelligent npcs, etc.) of "Justice Online" mobile game, which is highly attractive to most gamers.

3.2.2 Paid communication resources trigger

Paid communication resources trigger mode refers to the life service provider to first use paid communication resources to attract the attention of the living people, and then with other online and offline promotional activities to further stimulate the living people's extensive discussion, triggering the replication of meme and synergistic creativity. NetEase, as one of China's largest game makers, has decided to use its "money power" to promote its "Justice Online" mobile game, which has been one of its key projects in recent years, after its launch this year. Whether it is TikTok, bilibili or WeChat, QQ are not short of "Justice Online" mobile game of publicity ads. However, the nature of the platform is not the same, putting the publicity advertisement is also different. In video platforms like TikTok and bilibili,"Justice Online" mobile game chooses to cooperate with accounts with high visibility and influence to produce some game-related high-quality works and create explosive topics, so as to achieve the dissemination and replication of communication elements. On the other hand, in social platforms like WeChat and QQ, the promotional advertisements placed are relatively simple and rough, such as popping up an advertisement of " 'Justice Online' mobile game will be re-launched on 30 June" when the screen is opened, or popping up an advertisement of " 'Justice Online' mobile game gameplay subvert the tradition" in the friends circle to attract the attention of potential players in the most direct way.

3.2.3 Special star social communication resources

In the creative communication trigger mode, stars are a very striking phenomenon. In the digital living space, stars and their social media (such as celebrity weibo) are an inseparable whole, and together they exist as communication resources that can be paid for and utilised by life service providers. This is different from the traditional sense of celebrity endorsement, which is no longer a hard push, but a communication message that is integrated into the life service provider's social media through daily communication with the lifer on the celebrity's social media. At this point, in addition to the identity of the star, they are more like a neighbour who can be consulted and trusted, constantly sharing new products and new needs with the lifers and driving them into collaborative creativity. In addition to NetEase's powerful "money power", the star team of "Justice Online" mobile game is very influential, and it has created a powerful national style group based on the content of the game: there is the author of "Justice Online" Wen Ruian, a martial arts consultant Zhao Wenzhuo, a singer of genre songs Hu Yanbin, and there is a tea culture consultant Zhang Zhifeng, etc. This powerful and comprehensive national style group has been formed to provide the best service to the people of China and provide a powerful boost to the marketing and publicity of "Justice Online" mobile game.

3.3 Activating Lifers for Collaborative Creativity

Today's digital living space provides a big stage for life service providers and lifers to realise collaborative creativity, changing the traditional marketing and communication activities from one-way communication by enterprises and passive acceptance by consumers to the co-creation of life service providers and lifers. The essence of collaborative co-creativity is creativity centred on the participation, sharing, experience and interaction of lifers, and the often-used method is to provide a creative frame after sending the meme, to re-aggregate the wisdom of lifers and to copy, forward, extend and spread the meme according to the rules of the creative frame, so as to realise the purpose of creative communication.

After sending various communication elements on various platforms, the "Justice Online" mobile game builds a topic with "Justice Online", which is its creative frame, and other lifers publish game-related creative content under this topic and creative frame, which is the process of realising synergistic creativity.

4.The revelation of creative dissemination of "Justice Online" mobile game

The "Justice Online" mobile game can achieve such a shocking good result of over 2 billion Yuan in one month on line, which is inevitably inseparable from the success of its creative communication. It is a cliché for life service providers to seriously dig into the psychology of players and do a good job of service. There is another very novel feature of the creative communication of "Justice Online" mobile game, that is — the personality of the enterprise IP.

The life service provider and the lifers live together in the digital living space. People usually only focus on the life service provider should continue to improve the technology to provide a more comfortable digital life experience, but did not think that the life service provider should also have their own "personality" as the lifers. I believe that, rather than a cold technical service provider, the user will definitely prefer a service provider who has its own personality, who can communicate back and forth, and who even has a great sense of humour. The creative communication of "Justice Online" mobile game is almost ahead of most of the corporate publicity in this regard.

So how to do a good job of corporate IP personification? I have distilled two points.

4.1Shape a distinct personality

Every lifer in the digital living space has his or her own personality, and life service providers should have one too. The most important thing to shape a distinct personality for enterprise IP is to work on the promotion copywriting, meme and other places that can reflect the personality. Take the official WeChat account of "Justice Online" mobile game as an example, it calls itself "Xiang Han", and the text and emoticons it sends out are mainly in a cute style, it has changed the game's official cold announcement style and started to be a "simp" of its customers. This not only strengthens the old players' love for the game, but also attracts new players to join, which is a good way to achieve the purpose of communication.

4.2 Spiritual core support

Without the support of a strong spiritual core, any more fancy character is just a castle in the air, and does not have the charm that can really attract people. The excellent traditional spiritual values, such as family and country sentiment, chivalry and righteousness, etc., contained in the game are the unique kernel that supports the character of "Xiao Han". This kernel exists in the hearts of almost every Chinese person, and can constantly attract more people to discover, understand, and join "Justice Online" mobile game. Without such a strong spiritual core, the gorgeous Song Dynasty Jianghu constructed by "Justice Online" mobile game will no longer exist, and how can we talk about publicity?

5.Conclusion

The development of creative communication management theory is relatively short, and domestic related research is relatively limited, this study is a practical application and supplement to the creative communication management theory. This paper takes "Justice Online" mobile game as the research object, and analyses the creative communication strategy of "Justice Online" mobile game with the theory of creative communication management as the theoretical basis. The success of "Justice Online" mobile game is not only due to its diverse and free gameplay, but also due to the fact that it sends out meme that are easy to be copied, extended and spread on the right platform, thus successfully triggering synergistic creativity and realising creative communication. This paper mainly focuses on the analysis of the creative communication strategy of "Justice Online" mobile game, but does not cover the part of communication management. Creative communication management theory is a pioneering revolution of new marketing communication in the digital era, which deserves to be studied and researched by more people. In addition, this paper is just a preliminary idea for life service providers to have their own IP personalities, and the research is not deep and thorough enough. Solving the problem of how to better help life servicers to achieve IP personification is valuable and meaningful for all future marketing communications of enterprises.

Reference

1. Chen Gang. Creative Communication Management [M]. China Machine Press,2012.
2. Peng Guanyu. Research on Corporate User Communication Marketing Based on Creative Communication Management Theory--Taking NIO as an Example[J]. Advertising Panorama (Theoretical Edition),2020(01):41-50.
3. Liu Limin. Research on the Creative Communication Strategy of <Ne Zha: I am the destiny> [D]. Jiangxi University of Finance and Economics: 2020.DOI:10.27175/d.cnki.gjxcu.2020.000893.
4. Zhang Tiantian. Research on the communication strategy of mobile online game——take the Tencent Mobile Games as an example [D]. Xiangtan University :2015
5. Jiang Wen. Analysis on the creative communication strategy of the mobile game Evolver [D]. Northeast Normal University:2018.

Nation and World: The Marketing Model of Internationalization of Local Brands –A case study of Genshin Impact

Qingyun He[1], Xiaosi Li[2], Xinhao Liu[3,*]

[1]Changzhou Senior High School of Jiangsu Province, 213004 Jiangsu, China
[2]Faculty of New Media, Guangdong Baiyun University, 510450 Guangdong, China
[3]Psychology, Menlo College, 94027 California, America

Abstract. The research background of the paper is that the Genshin Impact has become very famous in recent years. The game made $4 billion in revenue in just two years after its launch. The game's worldwide popularity has attracted a lot of attention. Thus, this paper wants to find out the producer uses which kind of methods to attract such many players and gain a large amount of profit. The paper uses a literature review and case analysis as research methods. By using these two methods to research, this paper finds that the producer of the game Genshin Impact uses lots of market strategies to attract players. Also, this research wants to explore how the game Genshin Impact successfully integrates traditional Chinese culture and promotes traditional Chinese culture to overseas players. The conclusion is producer of Genshin Impact uses different market strategies to attract players and help promote traditional Chinese culture to overseas people.

1.Introduction

This study focuses on exploring what marketing strategies Genshin Impact has used to become a popular game in many countries around the world. The study of this topic allows learn useful marketing methods to attract consumers to gain profits. Of course, by analyzing the marketing strategy behind it, one can know what kind of marketing is effective today and can open the market to the world. This can also lay a foundation to learn this kind of marketing techniques in the future. This study is mainly based on how the domestic game Genshin Impact became a popular game all over the world.

This article analyzes what kind of marketing and content creation the game uses to attract players. Through real cases, it shows how it is marketed, disseminated, planned, and finally becomes a circle of the game. It is known that good games focus on the core. Studied the mechanism of Chinese culture in the creation and dissemination of the game, Genshin Impact as the main research object, emphasizing the importance of meaning form, publicity atmosphere, gaming, and audience interaction. Also, Literature analysis is used to search and read relevant materials and literature. The advantage of this method is that it can well analyze how the public views the success of this game, what they think the future development of this game will be, and what needs to be improved. This method is conducive to the research.

The ultimate goal of this research is to understand the marketing strategy and means used by the game Genshin Impact, and hope that other domestic games can learn from it and then apply it to their own games, so as to help more domestic games enter the world market. In order to achieve this goal, this paper uses two learning methods to elaborate on how to carry out research.

2.Background

"Genshin Impact" speeded up the process of industry products. After the game industry entered the era of product king, the Matthew effect on the product side intensified, emphasizing the logic of explosive products, accelerating the development process of the industry product from the aspects of art, technology, narrative, music, gameplay, etc., and raising the threshold of product research and development investment, but also improving users' understanding and aesthetic appreciation of high-quality games, and increasing the requirements for game quality [1].

Especially in the young category, the phenomenon of quality comparison between various products is particularly obvious. Study the rare cases of the products released on all platforms of Genshin Impact, including mobile games, PC, console, and cloud games, and achieve excellent commercial performance on all major platforms, truly release the value of "all-platform", user level is the basis of game performance, based on high-quality game content, cross-platform can obtain more user growth [2].

The biggest feature of the open world is its open world. Players can freely explore, challenge missions, and carry out various activities in this world. The game

*Corresponding author's mail: xinhao.liu@menlo.edu

is divided into seven countries with different elements. Each country has its own terrain and architecture. At the same time, there are many treasures and puzzles waiting for players to dig and solve. At the same time, the development of the game plot is also non-linear. Players can experience and complete different tasks and events according to their own wishes and needs without any restrictions.

There are more than 30 characters with different characteristics in the character system game, and each character has its own unique skills, weapons, and attributes. At the same time, each character has his or her own story. Players can learn about their past and growth experiences by collecting story fragments and completing tasks. Players can choose their characters according to their own needs and preferences, and even give full play to their greatest strength through in-depth cultivation. At the same time, the creation and design of each character are unique. Whether it is clothing, hairstyle, voice, or behavior, it has distinct personality and characteristics. This is also one of the reasons why the protagonist and plot of the Genshin Impact are deeply loved by players.

The game design of the Genshin Impact of the game design is very exquisite and meticulous. The addition and design of various elements, as well as the setting of the open world and mission plot, have greatly stimulated the curiosity and exploration of players. The swimming pictures and sound effects are also excellent, from the rich and detailed environment to the action performance of the character.

The user group of Genshin Impact is mainly composed of the following types of people:

Core players: the "family rice" of Mi HoYo manufacturers, including Mi Guard, is the core player group of the game.

Two-dimensional players: including console players and Zelda's "cloud players" It also includes ordinary passers-by players.

Pan-two-dimensional crowd: including ordinary passers-by players, as well as some specific two-dimensional enthusiasts, such as console players, painting enthusiasts, etc. These user groups have different behaviors and needs in the game Genshin Impact, including players' extraction and cultivation of characters, the pursuit of appearance and preferences, and the game plot and the world—exploration, etc.

3.Restore the international concept of Genshin Impact

Genshin Impact is among the world's hottest video games today. While the game has most Japanese invention characteristics from big swords, giant robots, characters with rainbow-colored and spikey hair, huge eyes, and a fixation on women endowed in maid-like outfits, the video game is Chinese. It was officially released in 2020, and it is the first video game from China to be recognized internationally. Unlike other video games from China, Genshin Impact has generated the most revenue from other countries.

3.1 Internalization ideas of Genshin Impact

This video game is calculatingly showcasing different cultures, different from a typical design because most video games adhere to Western styles. In this role-playing video game, the protagonist must seek their lost sibling through a journey traversing seven regions, which displays and imitates the cultures and landscapes of seven countries in reality. Deliberately showcasing cultural diversity deviates from the traditional dos of the gaming industry, an excellent idea to internalize the video game. The success of the game across the world and the respect for different cultures showcased on online platforms have proven how effective this strategy is.

3.2 Literature review

In the literature review, the research will focus on the mobile game market and the game culture. It also examines the existing literature on problems that developing and maintaining the game may encounter. This will help identify any information that may be useful or needed to answer any research questions. The development of the Genshin Impact and other mobile games has been motivated by the internet, engineering, mathematics, psychology, mass communication, science, and technology. The video gaming industry is rapidly becoming a significant force in the entertainment and business world. According to Shliakhovchuk and Muñoz Garcia, today, video games have become "sophisticated tools inhabiting and disseminating racial, gender and cultural meaning." [2].

In the article "*Research on the Communication Effect and Creation Mechanism of Chinese Culture in Game Media in the Internet Era- Taking Genshin Impact as an Example*", Tang Yingqi and other scholars studied the connotation of Chinese culture gamification, the creation of communication atmosphere and the form of Chinese culture gamification, taking the game Genshin Impact, which has a good communication effect at home and abroad, as the main research object through literature review and case analysis. And the audience subject of Chinese cultural games and so on. However, the content of the marketing means of the game is not much involved, this paper will start with the marketing strategy and marketing means and carry out research on the Genshin Impact [3].

Role-playing video game like Genshin Impact portrays how real-life experiences can blend with virtual ones to show the realities of different cultures. Genshin Impact can considerably break through its current cultural and entertainment functions. It may influence and change people's social life [4]. Therefore, video gaming has the advantage of influencing culture diffusion. Researchers and scholars are analyzing mobile and online video game market models and competitive environments. Since the Genshin Impact was launched, internationalization has been the main direction of the game's operation strategy. The Genshin Impact has attained a better position in the gaming industry, making most of its income from other countries. The gaming industry has expanded over the years, where researchers base most of their theoretical research.

Internalization has been researched and has evolved a lot over the years. With the development of online and mobile games, more disciplines are engaged in the gaming industry. They have also improved social interaction among people from different countries and cultures [5]. Internalization also provides an excellent opportunity for entrepreneurial ventures, which helps promote the game internationally. Challenges that may arise due to internalization are confronted by entrepreneurial enterprises, local governments, international organizations, and large corporations. The competition of Genshin Impact in the global market is improved by economic liberalization, which helps global players enjoy better services. Mi HoYo's success included the companies.

Genshin Impact has been the gaming god that has withstood the gaming industry pressure. It has a high consumer stickiness, shown by its outstanding quality, extreme popularity, and subdivisions in the available games. After the launch of the Genshin Impact, the company that developed this game witnessed a unicorn business a year later. Therefore, this game has greatly impacted the company. According to Chang et al. game culture research has proved that Genshin Impact has paved a new path in the gaming world due to its anime-styled game theme. This has caused culture diffusion since Genshin Impact was accepted in the gaming market and facilitated traditional culture output. The Genshin Impact is set to deeply break through the current entertainment and cultural functions and influence social life.

The best matrix researchers can use is the SWOT analysis to identify the strengths and weaknesses of the Genshin Impact since it would help them access generous funding and precedence in overseas markets. The developers of the Genshin Impact should also emphasize advancing the game to be of better quality and promote a two-dimensional culture [5]. Due to the development of more games of the same caliber as the Genshin Impact, they should also focus on different competition strategies to help the game retain and achieve a better position in the gaming industry. Most research findings show that the gaming industry is thriving in international markets since it has abundant funds, talented teams, they have dynamic capabilities, and good market entry strategies. The Chinese have now accepted online and mobile games into their culture after the Genshin Impact acceptance by other nations. This game has been used to spread the Chinese culture to international markets and has impacted these markets and the Chinese culture. Therefore, the gaming industry has a hand in promoting different cultures.

Conclusively, the primary solution to achieving high-quality development in the gaming industry is creating the primary publishing position of precise games. Genshin Impact is a game that aims to prioritize technology since it has clear goals that are evident in the game. It creates awareness for other game developers where they learn the development strategies online games undergo in a new light. It also provides them with future prediction progress for the gaming industry in general. Therefore, the internalization of the Genshin Impact promotes market and development strategies for the gaming industry worldwide [6]. Mi HoYo, the company responsible for the Genshin Impact development, is a successful gaming company because it is committed to developing quality games, has a unique range of gaming products, and has no desire to make quick profits. Therefore, the invention of Genshin Impact has gained its reputation in the global market with the ongoing competition in the wide range of gaming products.

Scholar Yin Jiacheng studied in the article "*On the Sea and Spread of Chinese Mobile Games -- Taking Genshin Impact as an Example*" that in order to promote the sea and spread of Chinese mobile games, first of all, mobile game manufacturers should establish the concept of taking more social responsibilities and implement the concept; Secondly, relevant departments need to continuously improve policies and build a long-term supervision and guidance mechanism for the game industry based on China's national conditions; In addition, mobile game manufacturers can also combine the excellent music and art culture of the Chinese nation and actively link with the national cultural industry. However, the content of other marketing means used by game developers is not much involved, so this paper will start with other marketing means to study [7].

In the article "*Research on Traditional Chinese Culture Communication Mode of Domestic Games -- Taking Genshin Impact as an Example*", scholars Zhang Jing Lan and Yao Jia studied the open-world role-playing game Genshin Impact developed by Mi HoYo as an example and explored the strategies of domestic games to spread traditional Chinese culture by analyzing the process of Genshin Impact communication to traditional Chinese culture. However, the content of other marketing means used by game developers is not much involved, so this paper will start with other marketing means to study [8].

In the article "*Research on Cross-cultural Communication from the Perspective of Participatory Culture -- A Case Study of the Chinese game Genshin Impact*", scholar Tang Jie studied the role of participatory culture in cross-cultural communication of Genshin Impact and explored the practical path of using participatory culture to carry out cross-cultural communication, so as to help cross-cultural communication. First, grasp the target audience and build community connections. However, the content of other marketing means used by game developers is not much involved. This paper will start with other marketing means [9].

In the article "*Exploration of the Path of Cultural Export of Domestic Games from the Perspective of Cultural Confidence -- Taking Genshin Impact as an Example*", scholars Chen Yu and Li Zhaokun studied that from the perspective of cultural confidence, the game Genshin Impact, by integrating the common ideas of the East and the West, triggers the emotional resonance of players, and to a certain extent crosses the cultural gap, which not only makes more and more people begin to understand and like Chinese culture, but also helps them to understand and like Chinese culture. And it is also of great significance to enhance the soft power of cultural export. However, the content of other marketing means used by game developers is not much involved, so this paper will start with other marketing means to study [10].

3.3 Marketing strategies

Genshin Impact's Impact creators, Mi HoYo, have employed regional and global marketing strategies leveraging content creators and influencers from different countries to promote the game. Another marketing strategy is celebrating different cultural festivals in the game, making it engaging and relevant to different players [1].

Conclusively, Genshin Impact is an excellent example of an internalization concept with a unique game design, cultural references, and community-building efforts. The game has fostered a worldwide global base and intelligently marketed different cultures, unlike other video games that usually lean more on the Western style.

4.Case analysis

"Genshin Impact" at the core of the game experience based on the mechanism of an open-world adventure game, including facets of the ecological environment is reflected in realistic ecological and freehand brushwork in traditional Chinese painting two kinds, namely the contains of natural and geographical feature reduction, also includes the interpretation of the cultural characteristics of the social custom, order, rules and so on.

The worldview in the game is not completely disconnected from the world. It is a "mirror" of the real world and social rules, a free space where virtual and real coexist. In addition, the open world fu players a high degree of autonomy and freedom, the player can according to the sequence and methods of the expected independently explore the game world of vast, interact with the elements in the game, and trigger the corresponding random events, promote the development of the plot.

The game uses traditional Chinese culture to create its unique atmosphere, which is a very innovative attempt and a good model for other games in China. It also has beautiful and vivid graphics to create an immersive feeling for the player.

4.1. Analysis of causes

First, high-quality game production, "Genshin Impact" is developed by the Chinese game company Mi HoYo, with its excellent art design, game mechanics, and exquisite music design, so that players are immersed in it.

Second, free play mode, "Genshin Impact" uses free download to play, in-game purchase mode of operation, but the purchase content is not necessarily a necessary condition to promote the progress of the game.

Third, diversified role and element system, the "Genshin Impact" game mechanism includes multiple elements and different characters, they come from different countries, have different clothes, and different ways of fighting, players can form their own diversified team through diverse roles to face different situations of combat.

Fourth, excellent operation and publicity team. The popularity of a game is not limited to the excellence of the game itself, but more about the publicity and operation before and after the release of the game.

Fifth, excellent combination of traditional Chinese culture, even if the "Genshin Impact" is not related to reality, players can always find some of the traditional festivals and architectural styles of real countries in the game.

Overall, the success of "Genshin Impact" combines high-quality game production, play mode, and perfect integration with traditional Chinese culture, which all contribute to the success and popularity of the game in a short period of time.

5.The logic of the marketing process around national culture

The core game experience of Genshin Impact is based on the mechanism of its open-world adventure game, in which the description of the ecological environment is embodied in two ways: realistic ecology and freehand ecology, namely, the restoration of natural and geographical styles, and the interpretation of social customs, order, rules, and other cultural characteristics.

The presentation of Chinese elements in map scenes, the restoration of natural scenery, and the expression of humanistic spirit in architectural art are not only valuable in presenting external scenes but also in infiltrating the spiritual core of Chinese culture into game storylines. The combination of Eastern scenes and the Chinese humanistic spirit in the game can enable overseas players and audiences to better and deeper perceive Chinese cultural temperament.

When people see news and promotional videos from other countries, they may realize that this is a highly purposeful input of ideology and ideological viewpoints; Many people may also realize that foreign film and television works are essentially an expansion of cultural values in other countries, a global cultural distribution.

The characteristics of the game itself, de ideological and eliminate the mentality of vigilance. Games are mainly related to self-entertainment, self-experience, and self-happiness, reflecting a strong subjectivity. Many people do not consider it as an output channel for information and opinions, and its ideological tendencies and ideologies are also obscured in entertainment.

6.Conclusion

The results of the research are that this report mainly explains from different angles how the game Genshin

Impact is spread around the world as a game developed by Chinese people. So it can further draw the conclusion that the report mentions the market strategies that the game Genshin Impact uses to attract players from all around the world and spread the Chinese traditional culture to people from various cultures. This study provides a lot of valuable reference significance for future research in this direction and mainly affects the future development direction of domestic games.

In the future, it will more focus on the ability to find and analyze more strategies from the game Genshin Impact to conduct in-depth research, which can help other kinds of Chinese games to know what strategies they should use to attract foreign players and spread to the world. The article was to explore the game in the spread of Chinese cultural issues, does not provide a clear solution or suggestion. The inclusion of suggestions on how to overcome these problems will make the article more practical. Some ideas and arguments can be developed further. For example, the integration of games with Chinese culture can further explore how to ensure the authenticity and depth of cultural elements.

Authors Contribution

All the authors contributed equally and their names were listed in alphabetical order.

References

1. B. Dooley, P. Mozur, Wor N. Vid. (2022), URL: https://www.nytimes.com/2022/03/16/business/genshin-impact-china-japan.html
2. E, Shliakhovchuk, A, Muñoz Garcia, Edu Sci: The & Pra, 20, 40-58 (2020)
3. Y.Q. Tang, Comedy World: China, 4, 0145-0147 (2023)
4. M. J. Adams, British J Chinese Stu, 2, 188-208 (2022)
5. X. Cai, Y. Chen, Y. Mao, L. Cai, In Int Con Com Sci and Edu, 6, 460-470 (2022)
6. X. Chang, T. Zhen, Y. Wang, Inter J Edu Hum, 8, 147-150 (2023)
7. J.C. Yin, Chinese Sci Tec J Data Eng Tec, 5, 4 (2022)
8. J.L. Zhang, J.Yao, Com Cop 14, 82-86 (2023)
9. J. Tang, Com Copt, 6, 89-92 (2023)
10. Y. Chen, Z.K. Li. J Y. Che. Uni. 6, 54-59 (2022)

TikTok Influencers: How age affects popularity

Yingjia Ma*

Vassar College, Poughkeepsie, New York, 12604, United States

Abstract. TikTok has become one of the most popular social media apps today, its user-generative nature allows anyone to upload videos onto the platform with the potential to become famous. This gives rise to TikTok influencers, and content creators with a large number of followers on TikTok. This paper offers a qualitative study on how the age of TikTok influencers affects their popularity through a literature review and TikTok content analysis. The research result reveals that younger TikTok influencers are more popular than older TikTok influencers. This difference in popularity is a result of the different nature of their video content and ways of presentation. Compared to older influencers, younger influencers tend to have greater content diversity, better technological skills to generate videos with more captivating effects and presentation style, and higher compatibility with TikTok's user demographics. Furthermore, due to the generation gap between young and old people, the predominately young social media users tend to discriminate against older content creators on the platform, causing them to have more difficulties in gaining popularity.

1. Introduction

TikTok is a short video-sharing app that has gained soaring popularity in recent years. According to a study by Iqbal, TikTok's global impact is extremely far-reaching as it has close to 1 billion active users monthly [1]. The type of content on TikTok, just like other social media platforms, is undoubtedly diverse. Its user-generative nature enables everyone to be the director of their content and to share it with people from all over the world. Because of how accessible and easy it is to upload videos on TikTok, many people dedicated themselves to becoming TikTok influencers.

TikTok influencers are an indispensable part of the TikTok ecosystem. They ensure the liveliness of the community and make TikTok a platform where e-commerce businesses thrive. They generate huge profits every day for TikTok, and other companies that leverage TikTok for marketing, as well as themselves. Thus, there has been rising scholarly interest in TikTok influencers lately. While most scholarly works have focused on TikTok influencers as a new marketing strategy, very few research have explored the age of TikTok influencers in relation to their popularity.

From 19-year-old most viral TikToker Charli D'amelio to 92-year-old "granfluencer" Grandma Droniak, there are numerous examples of successful TikTok stars from a range of ages. Are younger TikTok influencers more popular than older TikTok content creators? If so, what are some of the causes behind this phenomenon? What social implication does this observation have?

To address these questions and the lack of study on how the age of TikTok influencers affects their popularity, it would be worthwhile to conduct research comparing the difference in levels of popularity between younger TikTok influencers and older TikTok influencers. In this research, younger TikTok influencers are defined as having an age of 18 to 30 and older TikTok influencers as those 50 and above. This paper will examine factors that contributed to the differences in popularity level between young TikToker and senior TikToker by deeply analyzing their content types and form of presentation. The research method used would include both a literature review and qualitative social media analysis. Specific TikTok videos that represent the younger influencers and those that are created by older influencers would be compared and contrasted based on the type and form of these chosen content, and detailed interpretation would be provided. Finally, a study like this would yield valuable social implications in areas such as popular culture, digital engagement, and mental wellness. It further reveals the generational divide in digital engagement and leads to the proposal of better ways to create an inclusive digital space for people of all ages.

2. Understanding TikTok

Before diving into the analysis of influencer content, the paper will first give an introduction to TikTok. TikTok is a short-video app first launched by the Chinese company ByteDance, which was also known to be the developer of Musical.ly, a similar app that merged with TikTok after it was released [2]. Though TikTok is just one of the many social media apps, as a new platform, it differs drastically from its predecessors such as Instagram,

*Corresponding author's mail: yingjiama@vassar.edu

YouTube, and so on. Some of its unique features and characteristics including the in-app recording and editing, short video length, automatic scrolling, and video re-creation made content creation ever so easy, inspiring numerous innovations and digital trends. TikTok's typical 15-second video feature and equal promotion on the For You Page, give anyone the opportunity to be liked by millions of strangers all over the world, a very attractive idea to young people who are playful and looking for new excitement [3]. According to data from Marketing Charts, young users aged from 16 to 24 take up the biggest portion of TikTok user demographics in the United States [4]. Since TikTok is an app that is entirely made up of user-generated content, its user demographics indicate that the platform is skewed towards younger audiences. Not only is most of the content created for younger netizens but also created by younger influencers. This is obvious when people identify the most popular TikTok influencers and their age.

As of 2023, the most popular TikTok influencer is Charli D'amelio, who has nearly 150 million followers on the platform. This 19-year-old girl rose to fame on TikTok by dancing to trending songs. The second famous TikToker is 25-year-old Bella Poarch with over 90 million followers and whose lip-syncing videos became the most liked video ever on TikTok. However, some of the most famous senior influencers such as Grandma Dronaik only has 11 million followers, which is about ten times less than that of Charli D'amelio. The fact that all the top TikTok stars are relatively young seems to demonstrate that the lower the age of the TikTok influencer, the more popular they are likely to be. To further prove this hypothesis, the paper will examine specific TikTok videos from young and old influencers to determine whether that is true and to explore the reasons behind such a result.

3. Popular young TikTok influencers

3.1 Video content genre and message conveyed

Just like its predecessor Musical.ly and as its brand name indicates, one of the most popular genres on TikTok is dancing. Usually, someone would first upload an original dance to a trending song, and then a lot of TikTok users would try to learn the choreography and post their own covers on the platform. Though called dancing, these dance videos mostly only involve the movement of the upper body with a lot of hand and arm movements, and the dancer could just remain in one place to complete the entire choreography [5]. Due to these seemingly easier dancing rubrics and the shorter length of these dances, it is easy for anyone to quickly grasp the dance within a few minutes. Thus, it became popular among young people, who could post a dance cover and feel good about themselves just by sparing a few minutes.

The currently most popular TikTok star Charli D'amelio started her TikTok career by posting viral dance videos. While Charlie has branched into posting other types of TikTok videos as a celebrity now, her most popular videos are still her dance videos back in 2020 during her earlier stage of TikTok exploration. Charlie is an excellent dancer, but she always presents herself as someone who is real and goofy so her followers can relate to her well [6]. In her dance videos, she mostly appears solo but sometimes brings in her friends and family members to dance with her. She often wears athleisure clothes such as yoga pants, crop-tops, hoodies, and shorts. Her bright smile, effusive expressions, clean make-up, and fit body emanate confidence and energy. Charlie's uplifting dance, casual outfits, and unrestrained expressions portray her as a popular yet relatable teenage girl whom everyone wants to be friends with. TikTok content creators like Charlie can gain so much following on the app because she made the majority of TikTok users, teenagers, and young adults, aspire to be as cool as her.

Besides dancing, another trending content that is frequently adopted by young TikTok influencers is the POV, or point of view videos. The hashtag POV has over 980 billion videos under it, proving its popularity. The POV videos in general feature the content creator re-enacting a scene by pretending to be someone else. The audience is invited to feel like they are present and witness the scenario that is depicted in the video. TikToker Julietteweg is famous for her POV videos. She frequently embodies the "pick me girl", which is an internet slang for young girls who act in a certain way for others' attention and especially with the goal of impressing boys. In her video "POV the pick me girls eat lunch with the boys," she pretends to be a girl who is superficially nice to her female friends but begs for attention when she is around men. She speaks in a sharp high-pitched voice, keeps applying makeup, and insults her girlfriends for their appearance. As the "boys" come over, she greets them with a big smile, pulls one side of her clothes off the shoulder, and pretends that she only eats healthy food. Her vivid acting skills along with her realistic high school campus background attracted thousands of people to her comment area. Many echoed her accurate portrayal of the "pick me girl" and expressed how they could relate to this simulation.

POV creators like Julietteweg are extremely successful at making viewers feel that these incidents occurred in their lives even though they might not have experienced this in reality [7]. The POV content is a brilliant idea that has infinite potential since there are so many similar experiences that people share in their daily lives. These common experiences give rise to all kinds of POVs scenarios for young people to criticize and make fun of things that happen in life. It is again, the realness and relatability of these POV videos that draw people in and make them stay. The POV videos on the social media platform TikTok create a hyperreality space for teenagers and young adults to complain about incidents in life and release social pressure without any real-world consequences.

3.2 Video type and form of presentation

Viral TikTok videos among younger influencers take on various forms. Cervi's study introduced that the two main forms of TikTok videos are duets and challenges [5]. People make duet videos when they either perform the same action as the original video or film their reaction to the original piece, adopting a split-screen effect by having their video side-by-side to the original piece. This presentation enables viewers to see both the original video and the influencer's reaction, giving them a chance to see if their favorite influencer has the same opinion on the trending TikTok as them or not. It is also entertaining to see the duet person's exaggerated reactions and be amused by their scathing remarks. Besides, creative content creators also make duets where they perform the same action as the original video but turn it into something new. For instance, yandani.sing is a young boy whose most popular videos are him singing in duets with a singer of the original song cover. The boy would sing in harmony with the original singer and turn the song cover into something even more beautiful than the initial cover.

TikTok challenges is another form of video where young people join in the trend to film their own dance covers or physical challenges. To join a dance challenge, the dancer just needs to record a video using the trending dance soundtrack and the video will be collected into the archive of that sound. Dance challenges are often filmed with a focus on the upper body in a mundane location such as the bedroom [6]. The informal settings of the filming environment invite people to create content no matter where they are, encouraging video quantity and diversity. Besides dance challenges, physical challenges are also always trending. To be specific, the hashtag couples challenge is trending now. Many people hashtag the topic of couples' challenges to carry out a series of physical movements with their partner. Based on a trending couple challenge video, people would follow the same movement instruction by filming their practices, the moments of success, and failure.

4. Viral senior TikTok influencers

4.1 Video content and message conveyed

Though elderly people are often believed to be less tech-savvy than younger people, some of them managed to navigate social media proficiently and gained a large number of following on TikTok. Recently, the TikTok "granfluencers," which refers to older content creators, have caught public attention [8]. These grandparent influencers tend to post content that is educational, practical, and fun. 93 years old Grandma Droniak is a TikTok influencer with 11 million followers. She frequently posts videos following the latest TikTok trends such as GRWM, get ready with me, showing her putting on make-up, picking an outfit, and doing fun activities. She also posts videos of her complaining about her relationships such as her video for her ex-boyfriend. When Grandma Droniak talks, she always sounds carefree and confident. She would also use a lot of internet slang such as "slay" and "toxic" as well as curse words. Despite people usually associating elderly people with being frail, conservative, and technologically challenged, Grandma Dronaik exhibits none of those characteristics. Her grasp of popular culture, careless attitude, and good taste in fashion drew many viewers to her channel. Many young people enjoyed her videos and support her sassy demeanor because they feel connected to her as if she is not an elderly person but a friend of their age.

Similar to Grandama Dronaik, there are other older TikTokers who made an effort to present themselves in a positive light to combat age stereotypes [9]. One of them is Antisue. 62-year-old Antisue is a singer, and her page is filled with song covers. Nevertheless, what makes Antisue stand out from thousands of other TikTok singers is that she covers the latest Kpop songs. From Black Pink's Pretty Savage to Wayv's Love Talk, Anitsue sings these songs passionately wearing sexy leopard print dresses. Though Kpop music is popular nowadays, they are not mainstream music in the West. It is hard to associate Kpop song covers with 60-year-old white women like Antisue, who would be expected to have limited knowledge and appreciation for Korean popular music. However, Antisue's enthusiastic song covers and her youthful presence surprised many young people and incentivized them to follow her account. Additionally, Antisue not only energetically embraces popular Gen-Z culture, but also dresses herself confidently, challenging the aging stereotypes such as being feeble and orthodox.

Moreover, Grandadjoe is a grandpa TikToker who is famous for his videos on life hacks. In one of his videos, he teaches young people how to make tasty sandwiches in the way he used to make them during food rationing and wartime. Another video of his is a cooking tutorial on homemade fries and pan-fried meals. These videos are highly practical and fascinating as they introduce young people to things that don't exist now but are common back in the day. By watching these videos, young people could gain more understanding of older people and appreciate their way of living.

4.2 Video type and form of presentation

In terms of video presentation form, older TikTok influencers generally adopt basic TikTok features such as incorporating title captions, audio, songs, and replying to the comment effect. For instance, Anitsue often uses the title caption to inform the viewers about the songs that she will be performing in her video so that people could be better informed. Grandma Dronaik's beloved TikTok feature is lip-syncing. Lip-syncing is a distinctive feature on TikTok that pairs a video with a soundtrack, which allows users to re-create the original video or sound [2]. In one of Grandma Dronaik's video, she lip-synced the audio "the bitch is back" while changing her clothes to a fancy blouse to surprise her followers with a new upload. She also leverages the reply to comments feature to engage with her viewers and to create new content. To be specific, she quoted one previous comment asking her if she has a boyfriend by clarifying humorously that she doesn't have one and doesn't want one.

5. Young and old TikTok influencers' popularity comparison

5.1 Video content

The diversity of content is a key factor that contributed to the success of younger TikTok influencers. Though younger TikTok influencers are known for their entertaining and prank-filled videos, they also create videos on more serious topics related to social issues [1]. From dance challenges to educational and activist videos, young people offered the viewers numerous options to engage with. Their videos are more aesthetic and energetic, often featuring pretty girls and boys and their youthful bodies. On the other hand, senior influencers' videos are more monotonous. Due to their limited physical mobility and exposure to popular culture, their videos tend to focus on mundane topics such as family, age, and advice. Their videos also tend to be more practical. Common videos are advice on relationships and cooking. These types of videos might require viewers to make more effort to watch than the fun and call-to-action videos created by younger influencers.

5.2 Presentation style

Furthermore, younger TikTok influencers' video content are more popular because they tend to have the skills to better navigate TikTok features to create videos in a variety of forms. To elaborate, young influencers are often more tech-savvy, so they are able to adopt various TikTok effects and features that older influencers find difficult to use. For example, younger influencers frequently use TikTok features such as duets, green-screen, filters, AI voices, whereas older TikTok content creators tend to only adopt the most simple and basic features such as captions in video and their own voices. The cool effects that young influencers use make their videos more eye-catching and entertaining to watch. Besides, they are better at forming relationships with other TikTok creators of their age on the platform and creating all kinds of collaboration videos to further attract fans to their pages.

5.3 Negative social stereotypes

Finally, negative social stereotypes also caused senior influencers' videos to be less popular than young TikTokers' videos. One example of discrimination against older people is the "OK, Boomer" trend on TikTok. It is a slogan used by Millennials content creators to complain and make fun of Baby Boomers, people who were born between the end of the 1940s to the mid-1960s. The "OK, Boomer" video usually features a scenario where a Millennial would be rude to their parents or older relatives when these adults try to discipline them by responding "OK, Boomer" to irritate them. This trend was supported by many young people on TikTok because they are annoyed by the generational gap between them and older people, who are often out of touch with modernity and maintain conservative beliefs [10]. The hashtag "Ok Boomer" has over 4 billion views, and all the videos exhibit a high level of spite and ridicule targeting not only the baby boomers but elderly people in general. The trend was also echoed by Millennials who sided with Gen-Z users to advocate for the disapproval of Baby Boomers [11]. Such a phenomenon reveals how negatively older people are affected by ageism on this platform. Because of the malice and judgement that young people have towards older people, it is rather difficult for senior influencers to be accepted and supported on TikTok, which directly affects their level of popularity.

6. Conclusion

Both the research data and TikTok content comparison above prove that younger influencers are more popular on the platform than older influencers due to differences in their content and ways of presentation as well as their compatibility with TikTok's user demographics. Despite being less popular in general, many older TikTok influencers demonstrated a strong desire to combat ageism stereotypes by creating numerous entertaining videos, engaging with younger audiences, and learning the internet culture and latest technologies on TikTok. Some senior influencers managed to gain millions of followers by uploading engrossing content in unique ways of presentation. They have especially won the hearts of many younger audiences, who were moved by their effort to embrace popular culture and progressive ideas. TikTok as a creative digital platform has the potential to bridge the generational gap between young people and older people, dissolving misunderstanding and encouraging communication. If younger influencers could collaborate with older influencers in content creation on TikTok, they could spread positivity on aging to the larger society, improving communication and understanding between people of different ages.

References

1. J, McLean., C, Southerton., & D, Lupton. Social & Cultural Geography, 24, 1–19, (2023).
2. K, E, Anderson. Library Hi Tech News, 37, 7–12, (2020).
3. P, J, & J, A. CARDIOMETRY, 24, 896–902, (2022).
4. J, M, Vaterlaus, & M, Winter. The Social Science Journal, 60, 1–20, (2021).
5. L, Cervi. Theatre, Dance and Performance Training, 12, 198-204, (2021).
6. M, Kennedy. European Journal of Cultural Studies, 23, 1069–1076, (2020).

7. B. L., Elvira, R, Firdaus, & A, Setijowati. International Journal of Innovative Science and Research Technology, 8, 102-107, (2023).
8. R., Ng., & N, Indran., The Gerontologist, 62, 1196–1206, (2022).
9. R., Ng., & N, Indran. The Gerontologist, 62, 1207–1216, (2022).
10. B, A, Meisner. Leisure Sciences, 43, 56-61, (2021).
11. J, Zeng & C, Abidin. Communication & Society, 24, 1-23, (2021).

Social Comparison on Social Media Platforms: A media and communication Perspective

Yue Qiu*

Faculty of Arts and Social Science, University of Sydney, Sydney, NSW, 2006, Australia

Abstract. Many existing studies of social comparison focus on the psychological component, but the reality of users' lived experiences is that most users incorporate multiple platforms into their communication practices in order to access the people and networks they desire to influence. This paper delves into the phenomenon of social comparison on social media platforms, examined through the lens of media and communication studies. Particularly emphasized is the role of algorithmic curation and the emergence of social media influencers as modern benchmarks of success and aspiration. This paper endeavors to offer a comprehensive understanding of the intertwined dynamics of technological affordances, socio-cultural catalysts, and psychological impacts in the realm of digital social comparison. Finally, the paper reflects on potential strategies to navigate this complex terrain, aiming to strike a balance between digital engagement and mental well-being. The overarching aim is to foster a digital environment that, while enabling connection and expression, also ensures the psychological well-being of its users.

1.Introduction

In the era of digitalization, the landscape of human interaction and self-presentation has been significantly transformed. Social media platforms, as one of the chief harbingers of this change, have not merely altered the way individuals communicate but have deeply influenced self-perception and societal values. There is no doubt that social media platforms are exerting a significant influence on interpersonal and sociocultural patterns of interaction. Specifically, social media platforms introduce new possibilities for managing personal networks and social activities. One finds a fascinating, albeit complex, the interplay of technology and human behaviour shaping an environment rife with social comparison. The Straits Times has reported that social media exacerbates feelings of inferiority among young people. The abundance of posts showing personal excellence can trigger feelings of inferiority or inadequacy in young people, especially for those who are unable to separate the world of social media from their real lives [1]. Young people tend to rely on social media to gain self-worth and build their self-image.

Festinger's theory of social comparison posits that individuals inherently assess their own abilities and attitudes by juxtaposing themselves against others, especially in the absence of objective standards or when faced with uncertainties about their own standing in a particular domain [2]. While the intrinsic human tendency to compare oneself with others has historically been restrained to local or community interactions, or through conventional media, the rise of social media has supercharged this phenomenon, expanding its scale, scope, and implications. Festinger's theory finds new resonance in this digital context; with a deluge of information but lacking clear objective standards on what constitutes 'success' or 'happiness', users find themselves incessantly measuring against the varied metrics of social media—likes, shares, comments, or even the perceived lifestyles of other platform users.

Given the relevance of social media platforms to a variety of social functions, an extensive body of experimental research from the perspective of social psychology has documented detrimental effects on social media users' mental well-being from exposure to social media posts. For example, Vogel et al. found that individuals with a higher inclination for social comparison orientation who engage in this behaviour on Facebook may experience a range of negative psychological outcomes, including lower self-perceptions, decreased self-esteem, and poorer emotional well-being compared to those with lower social comparison orientation who engage in similar online activities [3]. This finding underscores the potential negative consequences of excessive social comparison on social media platforms like Facebook. Similarly, individuals with a higher frequency of online comparisons tend to have higher levels of depressive symptoms, increased levels of addiction to social media, more negative self-perceptions, and a greater number of maladaptive social media behaviours [4].

Historically, such comparisons might have been limited to face-to-face interactions or through traditional media. However, today, the unceasing stream of updates, life highlights, and achievements presented on social media serve as a comparative backdrop, frequently intensified by algorithmic curation. Social media

*Corresponding author's mail: yqiu2736@uni.sydney.edu.au

platforms, while enabling unprecedented global communication and serving myriad social functions, have also ushered in profound implications for individual and societal mental well-being. This essay aims to unpack the multi-faceted dimensions of social comparison on social media platforms, emphasizing the symbiotic relationship between technology—its affordances and algorithms—and the socio-cultural phenomena, particularly the rise of social media influencers.

2.Affordances in shaping social comparison

The notion of affordances is essential for understanding the complex relationship between social comparison and platform features. Affordances have been widely used by scholars in media and communication studies to describe human-technology interactions. Broadly, technological affordances refer to the capabilities and functions a particular technology provides to its users [5]. That is, platforms are designed to contain various technological features that allow users to engage with the digital environment and provide users with opportunities for self-disclosure and self-expression. For example, the functions of social media platforms allow users to curate and present their lives through sharing, posting, and updating content in different forms. Importantly, the technological affordances do not constrain users' online behaviour, however, they do configure the environment in a way that shapes users' engagement [6].

Different platform features showcase how affordances are integrated into the architecture of social comparison. Lee found that when people frequently use Facebook to compare themselves to others, they tend to expect positive reactions or responses from others when they post content on the platform [7]. In other words, individuals are more looking forward to receiving likes, comments, or other positive feedback when they share something on social media platforms. The likes, comments and shares that users receive on social media are a feedback mechanism. Users often seek validation and social approval through these interactions. Similarly, many social media platforms provide metrics such as follower counts, likes, and viewer numbers, which serve as benchmarks for comparison. Users may compare their metrics with those of others, leading to self-esteem issues and a sense of competition. These features trigger social comparisons, as users may measure self-worth and popularity based on the number and quality of interactions their posts receive. Essentially, the architecture of the platform matters, and the architecture of social comparison is shaped by affordance.

By utilizing the technological affordances of creating highly curated content on social media platforms, users are able to construct online identities by presenting and performing in a self-conscious way [8]. In particular, users have the ability to filter and select the content they like to display on their accounts for others to view [9]. For example, self-representation on social media takes place through customizing users' personal homepage using various digital tokens such as nicknames, avatars and fronts to express themselves. Personal profiles present a rich set of information about users themselves, including achievements, viewpoints, daily activities, personalities, relationship status, habits, etc.

Moreover, social media users who produce content vary their self-presentation strategies in patterned ways, based on the platform-specific features [10]. For example, features like "Stories" on platforms such as Instagram and Snapchat can amplify comparison by offering real-time glimpses into people's daily lives. However, this filter and selectively present aspects of the self may not be the full picture of others' lives, since people tend to show the best side of themselves on social media [9]. Thus, when users position themselves as an observer who is watching other people's life, they only see a partial representation. People then compare their unfiltered, real lives to the idealized versions they see on social media, leading to feelings of envy or inadequacy. Social comparison behaviours come into play when users constantly compare themselves to others based on their online identities which are only partial representations.

Social comparison can also be facilitated depending on different platforms. Lewin and colleagues studied the relationships between different types of social comparison and the problematic use of Facebook, Instagram, Snapchat, TikTok, and Twitter. The result indicates that when people often compare their abilities to others on all these five platforms, they tend to use these platforms despite continue to use the platform would impair their daily functioning and psychological distress [11]. On the other hand, the problematic use of Facebook, Instagram, and Snapchat is less when people frequently compare their opinions with others [11]. This suggests that people who engage in a greater comparison of abilities are more likely to seek opportunities for comparison in all places, and social media would present an easy opportunity to engage in the behavior of social comparison, while the dimensions of comparison differ depending on the platform.

Technological affordances can be one of the factors that account for this difference in terms of their range of interpersonal connections and audiences of content across platforms. For Goffman, individuals have multiple identities, and the way individuals present themselves depends on the social context in which they live [12]. People construct their identities based on where they are and who they are with [9]. In the realm of social media platforms, the user online identity and the generated content are delivered based on characteristics and functions that vary across different platforms, enabling a variety of public and private communication pathways [6]. Users may perform a public online identity that differs from their private selves across the platforms. Facebook, Instagram, and Snapchat primarily focus on personal social connections and sharing moments, emphasis on private connections with friends and acquaintances. Within these platforms, people tend to opt for online identities that are relatively similar to their offline personas performing in front of acquaintances, and seeking for consistency [8]. Whereas TikTok and Twitter have a broader user base, which includes not only close tie relationships but also a wide range of users, such as celebrities and influencers. Users can discover and engage with content from accounts they don't personally know. This broader reach makes interactions on these platforms relatively more public by default.

In contrast, online identity and self-representation can be constructed in a way that is less constrained by the interpersonal relationship and require less consistency with their offline identity within the platforms that are considered public space of social interaction [13]. Nevertheless, users might still treat other users' self-representations on these public platforms as if they were the actual and authentic representations of themselves. This dissonance due to differences in the technological affordance of platforms as well as self-representation can lead to social comparison when others perceive the public persona as authentic and compare themselves to it.

Despite the technological affordances of platforms allowing individuals to build online identities, it is not sufficient to explain the cause of the formation of social comparison. Nagy and Neff criticize that the previous notion of technological affordance mainly focuses on what users can do with technology and how technology shapes sociality, while ignoring the affordances as dependent on users' actions, awareness, and perceptions [14]. They introduce the term 'imagined affordances' which highlights that users' interactions with technology are constructed through users' perceptions, expectations and emotional experiences of platforms [14]. Initially, users have expectations or imagination of the technological artifact as it has a certain function or property. The designers rely on the users' imagination to develop the affordance that can fulfil the users' expectations. Hence, imagined affordances are not simply technologies that only determine what the users passively use on the platforms. Rather, it encompasses an active action of platform users and designers to enable everything that is happening on the platforms. As a result, social comparison on social media platforms is not passively experienced by the users, but the users choose to compare themselves with others based on the content they are viewing. That is, technology only facilitates the behavior of social comparison.

3.Algorithmic facilitation

Social media algorithms act as directors of the digital stage, highlighting content that is deemed attractive and masking content that is not. These complex rules determine which posts are amplified and which are weakened in a user's push, acting as gatekeepers to a user's digital social exposure. Algorithms prioritise content that generates a lot of interaction - often content that is emotional, sensational or enviable - which inadvertently encourages a culture of comparison.

Since functions and features are built within the design of the platforms, social media platforms through their design and algorithms, play a substantial role in shaping individual behavior, including the tendency toward social comparison. Algorithms may unintentionally reinforce social comparison. For the majority of platform users, the algorithm is hidden under the enormous technological structure [14]. Algorithms are designed to show users content that aligns with their interests and beliefs. without being aware of how algorithms work and influence their content feed, users may be more susceptible to social comparison without understanding why they are seeing certain content. For instance, platform algorithms such as TikTok deliver trendy content based on engagement metrics like likes, comments, and shares on platforms. When platforms consistently show content that receives high engagement, it can create a skewed perception of reality. Users may believe that everyone else is leading more exciting lives or is more successful, leading to feelings of inadequacy. Understanding the properties, affordances, and designs common to social media platforms provides a valuable framework for working out the logic of social comparison.

Social media platforms are engineered to capture and retain user attention; they achieve this through meticulously designed features and algorithms that exploit psychological tendencies. The 'like' button, personalized feeds, and content recommendations are not arbitrary fixtures but are deliberate choices aimed at optimizing user engagement. The algorithms that power these features are adept at learning what content keeps users scrolling, often prioritizing material that incites emotional responses, including content that fosters social comparison. This is because emotional engagement, whether positive or negative, drives more prolonged interaction and deeper platform immersion. For example, when users encounter posts depicting idealized lifestyles or 'highlight reels' of others, it can trigger a comparison against their own lives, an activity that the platform algorithms have learned to promote subtly through content curation based on prior user engagement.

Social media platforms, through their design and algorithms, sculpt the digital environment to which individuals are exposed. As users navigate their feeds, they are not simply consuming content; they are engaging with a system designed to capture their attention and to draw them into comparison. The intricate relationship between user behaviour and algorithmic reinforcement creates a loop whereby social comparisons can be a driver of social media content consumption and production. As users respond to content that elicits comparisons, platform algorithms learn and subsequently surface more such content, creating a feedback loop that perpetuates and intensifies attention to social comparisons. The propensity for social comparison is thus not merely a by-product of user interactions but a phenomenon intricately woven into the fabric of these platforms. In this way, social media platforms, through their algorithmic design, are not passively carrying content, but actively shaping the social dynamics they carry. The result is a digital ecosystem that exploits the human psyche and fuels social comparisons, leading to negative outcomes such as lower self-esteem and increased anxiety among users.

4.Influencers and the escalation of social comparison

Except for the technological constrain that are innate in the platforms, influencers also play a pivotal role in shaping perceptions, values, and behaviors on social media. In the ecosystem of social media, influencers are the apex dwellers whose lifestyles, opinions, and endorsements shape the dynamics of social interaction and self-perception among users. Influencers, armed with their curated content, exemplify this phenomenon, presenting an idealized portrayal of life that is often far removed from the everyday experiences of their followers. Their meticulously edited images and videos project a standard of beauty, success, and happiness that appears unattainable to the average person. This disparity between the influencer's online facade and the personal reality of users is a fertile ground for social comparison. Users, especially younger ones, are prone to scrutinizing and contrasting their lives to the polished narratives presented by influencers, which can lead to feelings of inadequacy and dissatisfaction with one's own life.

Influencers with curated and idealized online personas, set aspirational standards. Their impact on the issue of social comparison is multi-dimensional. Social media influencers emphasize their connection and commonality with their followers by constantly sharing their emotions, thoughts and the things that happened in their life, regardless it is regular and banal, so that they are viewed as more identifiable, similar to users themselves than celebrities [15]. According to the social comparison theory, people tend to compare themselves to others who are alike [1]. While users have a perceived closeness and similarity toward influencers, many influencers curate a version of their life that might seem perfect or aspirational [16]. While many provide positive content and authentic interactions, the selective sharing of their lives – luxury travels, impeccable fashion, flawless skin – can distort perceptions of reality for their followers. Consequently, constant exposure to the users can inadvertently set benchmarks that seem normative but are often unattainable, intensifying feelings of inadequacy among users.

Moreover, the interactive nature of social media allows encourages constant engagement with influencer content. Influencers frequently engage with their audiences through methods that give the illusion of a personal connection and create a sense of digital intimacy, such as responding to comments or sharing details about their personal lives [17]. Likes, comments, shares, and the ability to follow someone's life in real-time create an illusion of proximity and personal relationship with the influencer. This pseudo-relationship lays the groundwork for upward social comparison, where users measure their own worth against the seemingly superior life of the influencer. The danger of this comparison is twofold: it is not only with a person who may have an entirely different set of life circumstances but also with a carefully crafted persona that may only partially reflect reality. The psychological impact is significant as it can exacerbate feelings of low self-esteem and foster a negative body image among followers. The prevalence of such comparisons can lead to a pervasive sense of underachievement and the belief that one's own life pales in comparison to those idolized online.

The role of influencers in driving social comparison on social media platforms cannot be understated. By setting often unrealistic standards for lifestyle, appearance, and success, they inadvertently become benchmarks against which ordinary users measure their own lives. This incessant evaluation against an influencer's highlight reel can warp one's self-image and ambitions. In striving to mirror the opulence and appeal of influencer lifestyles, individuals may engage in detrimental behaviors such as excessive spending or unhealthy dieting, which further entrenches the negative cycle of comparison. As influencers continue to dominate the social media landscape, the challenge becomes finding a balance between inspiration and intimidation, ensuring that the aspirational content does not morph into a source of distress for the impressionable audience they command. The psychological impact is compounded by the sheer volume of influencer content that users are exposed to daily, which can normalize the exceptional and make the extraordinary seem mundane, thus escalating the propensity for social comparison.

5.Conclusion

Social comparison has been vastly amplified in the digital age, particularly through the prism of social media platforms. Through a comprehensive media and communication lens, it is evident that the technological affordances and algorithmic designs of these platforms play a significant role in perpetuating social comparison. Social media, by its very structure, facilitates instantaneous access to highlights of people's lives, often filtered and embellished, leading users to inadvertently juxtapose their everyday lives against these optimized portrayals. Beyond technological intricacies, the phenomenon of social media influencers serves as another catalyst.

Several recommendations are proposed to mitigate the adverse effects of online social comparison. Firstly, platforms could implement educational modules to inform users about the potential pitfalls of constant comparison, promoting a more informed and critical consumption of content. Additionally, social media platforms can take responsibility by offering resources, such as access to mental health professionals or self-help modules, for users who may feel overwhelmed or impacted by online comparison. Furthermore, rather than merely emphasizing popular content, algorithms could be designed to showcase a more diverse range of posts, including those that portray everyday life and its challenges, fostering a balanced view of reality on platforms. Finally, influencers could be encouraged to share and discuss the reality behind their curated feeds. This transparency can help in grounding perceptions and ensuring followers understand the line between online personas and offline realities.

In sum, while the age of digital media offers boundless opportunities for connection and expression, it also harbours challenges that society must navigate judiciously. The ubiquity and design of social media platforms mean that almost everyone, at some point, might find themselves comparing their lives to what they see online. By understanding the technological and sociological

https://doi.org/10.1051/shsconf/202418503008

drivers behind online social comparison, stakeholders can collaborate to create a more balanced and psychologically healthy digital ecosystem.

References

1. A. Qing, & C. H. Won, Social media use can trigger feelings of inferiority or inadequacy among young: Experts (2021), Available online at https://www.straitstimes.com/singapore/social-media-use-can-trigger-feelings-of-inferiority-or-inadequacy-among-young-experts.
2. L. Festinger, Human Relations (New York), 7(2), 117–140. (1954).
3. E. A. Vogel, J. P. Rose, B. M. Okdie, K. Eckles, & B. Franz, Personality and Individual Differences, 86, 249–256. (2015).
4. M. Gomez, D. Klare, N. Ceballos, S. Dailey, S. Kaiser, & K. Howard. International Journal of Human-Computer Interaction, 38(10), 938–948. (2022).
5. T. Bucher, & A. Helmond. The SAGE Handbook of Social Media, 233–253, (2018).
6. D. Boyd. *A networked self: Identity, community, and culture on social network sites* (Taylor & Francis Group, Z. Papacharissi, 2010)
7. Lee, S. Y. Computers in Human Behavior, 32, 253–260 (2014).
8. A. E. Marwick, & D. Boyd, New Media & Society, 13(1), 114–133. (2011).
9. A. E. Marwick. A Companion to New Media Dynamics, 355–364, (2013).
10. L. Scolere, U. Pruchniewska, & B. E. Duffy. Social Media + Society, 4(3), (2018).
11. Lewin, K. M., Ellithorpe, M. E., & Meshi, D. Personality and Individual Differences, 199. (2022).
12. E. Goffman. *The Presentation of Self in Everyday Life* (Doublebay. 1959).
13. J. van Dijck. Media, Culture & Society, 35(2), 199–215. (2013).
14. P. Nagy, & G. Neff, Social Media + Society, 1(2), (2015).
15. S. Tian, S. Y. Cho, X. Jia, R. Sun, & W. S> Tsai. The Journal of Product & Brand Management, 32(7), 1046–1062. (2023).
16. J. Reade. New Media & Society, 23(3), 535–553. (2021).
17. T. Raun. Convergence, 24(1), 99–113. (2018).

The influence of Xiaohongshu female bloggers on female values

Luyi Qian*

Department of Communication and Media, University of Liverpool, Liverpool, L3 5TR, United Kingdom

Abstract. The social media industry in China is diverse, among which an app with a significant female user base is Xiaohongshu. This article discovers that female users' values are easily influenced by bloggers through an in-depth analysis of the accounts of three different types of female bloggers on the platform (dress-sharing bloggers, fitness bloggers, and shopping-sharing bloggers) and paying attention to their fan characteristics. This article finds that the values of female users are easily influenced by bloggers. On one hand, these mainstream popular videos can not only influence users' thoughts but also give them help and motivation. This article investigates the phenomena of Xiaohongshu users across a range of age groups and concludes that Xiaohongshu will significantly alter women's shopping demand and aesthetics. These images and videos will aid female followers in establishing a proper value if the Xiaohongshu bloggers are able to provide accurate and authentic information. On the other side, material provided by bloggers that is not wholly useful might have a negative impact on women's values.

1.Introduction

As we-media becomes increasingly popular, people start turning to bloggers rather than journalists for information because they believe bloggers are more like them and are therefore more reliable [1]. In comparison to conventional media, social media platforms are more advanced and have a wider range of effect, which also help to drive the economy and are more effective at spreading information. Research have shown that men and women prefer various social networks and have different interests in all aspects. It is obvious that women frequently communicate online more effectively than males [2]. Additionally, it implies that women are more impacted by the media than males, and that they are more open to the themes that bloggers convey.

On the other hand, it also means that the concept of women can be easily changed. In China, Xiaohongshu has a large number of female users, 83.31% of Xiaohongshu's active users are between the ages of 18 and 34, and 90.41% of them are female [3]. Female bloggers can use this platform to display themselves in the form of images and videos, such as daily dressing, body management and shopping sharing, many of which exaggerate their appearances to appeal to female viewers. Some bloggers flaunt their incredible wealth or unique physical types. The proliferation of videos has had a subtle impact on changing the behavior of female viewers. This has a positive aspect in that some users try to better themselves in an effort to pursue a better life or beauty. While some users may use it to improve themselves and strive for a better life or beauty, these material possessions are out of reach and can not be achieved in the short term. This unrealistic goal will change women's values and their vanity, especially when adolescent women are still in the value-shaping period.

The author pays attention to the impact of female bloggers in Xiaohongshu on the values of female users amid the flood of social media communications. In order to analyze how bloggers shape the values of female users, the author shall group bloggers into three broad categories. The three categories of fashion display (Outfit of the Day), fitness exercise and shopping sharing are the most popular forms of Xiaohongshu. The research purpose of this paper is to make more reasonable and safe use of these social media to prevent female viewers from experiencing anxiety, jealousy, and other negative emotions after receiving a large number of messages, to make Xiaohongshu a platform that can encourage women.

2.The influence of bloggers

These three categories of bloggers are directly linked to users' daily lives. Women frequently focus on information regarding fashion, shape, and shopping in the hopes of finding more helpful advice from bloggers. This implies that bloggers will probably become their followers' main source of information. Bloggers can give advice on all aspects of life, and some long-term followers may even imitate their behavior, and if bloggers can not make sure that their content is helpful to followers, there will be negative consequences. When bloggers misguide their followers, the minor negative impact is the loss of money or the trust of fans, meanwhile, the serious negative impact is the harm to women's values such as stimulating women's vanity or appearance anxiety. Female adolescents in particular

*Corresponding author's mail: Luyi.Qian22@student.xjtlu.edu.cn

have more regular media habits. Also, young females have not yet developed their own values and judgment, and the content posted by bloggers will be an important reference for them.

By using their fans to promote them, bloggers may quickly become more well-known. Additionally, the content that bloggers provide can be shared with local female communities, where it can swiftly gain traction and impact.

2.1 Dress sharing bloggers

Many female bloggers on the Xiaohongshu platform provide videos of their daily outfits as well as information on clothing brands for readers to view or purchase. Because of the strong user demand and the fact that many women do not know what is appropriate to wear or do not have the time to put their own clothing together, this sort of blogger also makes up the majority of bloggers on the Xiaohongshu. Users are eager to emulate the fashion decisions made by some bloggers as they have become trendy.

2.1.1 The impact of dress sharing bloggers

Finding bloggers who wear similar or the same kind of clothes as them in the Xiaohongshu is an established method among women who want to emulate their favorite bloggers. The influencer's ensembles may not all be to the followers' tastes or standards of beauty, they may be generally drawn to the person's sense of style, leading them to hunt for further postings and outfits [4]. Furthermore, some white-collar women at work do not have a lot of time to match the clothes to wear every day, referring to the blogger's clothing may facilitate daily work collocation. Clothing bloggers can offer female users a lot of alternatives to assist users in discovering the correct style. With the rapid growth of internet shopping, many businesses will cooperate with bloggers to promote their products in a euphemistic way. Influencers on social media have emerged as significant marketing tools because of their incredibly personable and customized product reviews [5]. This indicates that not all the stuff that bloggers publish is what they truly wish to endorse. Additionally, when the promotion covers the nature of advertising, dishonest behavior may occur, as in the case of a blogger introducing poor-quality apparel to their audience. In contrast, many bloggers have their clothing sizes tailored to have a better impact, while regular consumers may only purchase clothing in accordance with a fixed size, which has a totally different effect from the blogger. Women frequently compare themselves to similar peers as well as unrealistic media representations of women, which negatively affects their perception of their bodies and causes them to fall short of these idealized representations [6]. When the user notices that the results are not as excellent as the blogger suspects that their appearance might be good enough, their confidence will be reduced by the misleading size. The blogger is more of an 'imaginary friend' than a brand promoter [7]. Contrary to conventional insertion adverts, bloggers' recommendations and sharing frequently result in higher sales, and users who share items through bloggers may receive some sort of discount, which is advantageous to all three parties. However, users who imitate the blogger's dress for a long time will lose their aesthetic judgment, and as fashion trends change frequently, they will be forced to follow them and end up looking unoriginal.

2.1.2 Cause of impact

The reason that bloggers have such a large following among females is that they speak in a more approachable and relatable manner than celebrities do, and they have a wide range of styles that are appropriate for both weekend casual wear and business attire, which many people may use as inspiration. Xiaohongshu bloggers may also use the comments section to gather fan preferences, which will help them make their upcoming videos more audience-relevant. The primary cause of the detrimental effects is the closed-door collaboration between bloggers and companies, which makes it difficult for followers to discern if the material that bloggers post is sponsored. This implies that consumers are more likely to trust incorrect information posted by bloggers, that bloggers' service is not as professional as that of some online retailers, and that the features of Xiaohongshu stores are inferior to those of well-known e-commerce sites.

2.2 Fitness bloggers

The Xiaohongshu fitness bloggers frequently discuss or teach their own fitness techniques because an overwhelming number of women are highly concerned with their physical appearances and figures. Fitness bloggers frequently publish recipes for weight reduction and make videos about exercise. The motivation to work out at home and improve one's physical condition is the aim shared by the majority of fitness bloggers. However, many bloggers will lose too much weight to get the "perfect body" in an effort to attract more attention.

2.2.1 The impact of fitness bloggers

Nevertheless, a lot of each person's body status depends on individual hereditary variances, while a few bloggers may unduly pursue the body's shapes through medical beauty procedures to pride themselves on their figures. A wide range of Xiaohongshu's bloggers are skinny and attractive, and many of fans follow the fad of slimming bloggers' guides and recipes. If these diets and courses are effective, they can encourage healthy weight reduction and aid in the physical fitness of more women. However, if some extreme weight loss methods such as extreme or unbalanced diet will affect health, similar news has emerged in an endless number of women to lose weight and lead to endocrine disorders or even more serious physical damage. After following the blogger's exercise to lose weight, appearance anxiety begins when women feel they are unable to live up to the physical ideal that the bloggers portray. On social media, bloggers enjoy displaying their best selves and happy feelings. This gives their followers the impression that their lives are constantly going perfectly and that their appearance is flawless. The continuous feed of these photos and videos causes women to start analyzing and criticizing themselves, which leads to face anxiety. This sort of anxiousness will trigger a lot of unpleasant feelings, especially among young people. Adolescents are constantly exposed to information about appearance through social media, which is likely to reinforce their comparison of appearance and heighten anxiety about being judged by the outside world [8]. It is easy for teenagers to become obese or insecure about their appearance during their development, and they need to establish the right healthy body awareness. Many teenagers in China admire thin bodies because women in the mainstream media are slender. Xiaohongshu bloggers who blindly pursue extremely thin bodies distort the aesthetic concept of young women. Professional fitness bloggers who discuss their weight reduction techniques might encourage youngsters to get in shape from a practical standpoint rather than aimlessly seeking an extreme physical appearance.

2.2.2 Cause of impact

Women are under a lot of strain in today's culture, particularly with regard to beauty. Some employers also take into account if a female employee looks beautiful during the interview. People have very high standards for their bodies, which makes many women think about exercise and weight loss. The popularity of weight reduction material has increased as more and more women who lack the time or are unable to visit the gym resort to online instructors for guidance. As a result, Xiaohongshu's weight loss content has been increasing. In addition to providing online fitness classes and giving many women the strength to endure, Xiaohongshu is linked to a large number of professional fitness bloggers who can assist women in an efficient manner. Due to the growing demand, a growing number of individuals are creating online fitness classes in an attempt to gain popularity. However, since the platforms are unmonitored, some of the information may be inaccurate, which has several detrimental impacts.

2.3 Shopping sharing bloggers

The majority of the female bloggers in Xiaohongshu will introduce the recently purchased goods in a daily way, most of which are luxury goods. Numerous bloggers have a propensity to flaunt their riches, which is greatly inflated and exceeds that of average customers. Fans may use the shopping material that is shared with them as a guide for purchases, and ladies can pick more suited goods thanks to blogger suggestions.

2.3.1 The impact on shopping sharing bloggers

Sharing high-end luxury items will frequently result in more likes and comments. Female users will be more easily attracted by such videos, and many users will comment to express envy and praise. As a result of the positive reaction to these videos, more and more bloggers started showcasing their high-end items in Xiaohongshu, including some who were devoted to sharing their luxury shopping. Under the brainwashing of such videos, some young women have a shopping demand for luxury goods. Compared to conventional celebrities, online celebrities are more powerful, persuasive, and influential [9]. Fans desire to emulate bloggers by purchasing the same luxury things they do because they admire or trust them, which leads to impulsive and early spending. Nevertheless, when followers do not have enough economic conditions to support these requests, they will often suffer from inferiority and loss. According to press sources, some women are prepared to steal or borrow things to finance their buying. Sharing certain high-end goods is perfectly acceptable, although since Xiaohongshu users are of all ages, even mature women struggle to discern the veracity of videos and control their impulses. These videos will plant a seed and lead to inappropriate consuming views in adolescent females. There will be strong negative feelings if they are unable to match the purchasing power and riches of bloggers.

2.3.2 Cause of impact

People's cognition is restricted when the network is underdeveloped, and they are only able to comprehend the lives of those in their immediate vicinity. The media's widespread distribution has made it possible for individuals to observe other lives, which either inspires positivity and the desire for a better life in many, while it causes jealousy or even poor self-esteem in others. Many women have a strong interest in shopping, and via the sharing of Xiaohongshu bloggers, they might become familiar with items or shopping techniques that they had never heard. These videos receive a lot of hits and are shared more extensively because extravagant bloggers can make their female fans happy. These fans aspire to live the same lifestyle as the bloggers. Bloggers are more likely to get attention and praise through the envious psychological state of their suitors. The advice offered by bloggers will be highly valued when followers think that the bloggers have improved their own quality of life. This further increases the level of confidence that readers have in this type of blogger since many readers mistakenly believe that wealthy bloggers would never defraud their followers in order to get personal gain.

3.Suggestion

The power of the media is enormous, and people can not imagine that just a few short words can influence the values and ideas of others. This is a double-edged sword. It can help users influence the public more effectively when people utilize it appropriately. Additionally, certain inappropriate information will harm the user's psyche. In fact, Xiaohongshu is a very effective platform with a sizable female user base, which gives it significant power. If this platform is effectively exploited, it will have a significant impact on Chinese women's values. Given how diverse Xiaohongshu is as a social media platform, they must exert greater control over the accuracy or usefulness of some information. None of the three types of bloggers' posts stated above are intrinsically good or harmful if the content is appropriate.

Bloggers who post outfits should keep an eye on the fabric's quality and act honestly while endorsing them. As long as they refrain from sharing clothing just to promote a certain outfit, they might assist users in finding clothes and looks that suit them. Contrarily, fitness bloggers should have a diversity of body types; they are not required to be skinny. Even people with obesity can become fitness bloggers. Sharing their own methods in the process of healthy exercise to let more people participate in exercise is also the meaning of fitness bloggers. The Xiaohongshu platform will also implement a series of regulatory policies, such as removing exercise methods that have no scientific basis (such as dieting or not eating fat). The platform may evaluate certified personal trainers and provide scientific texts or videos to assist users in maintaining a healthy weight. Bloggers who offer shopping-related information should distribute it selectively and refrain from overshow casing pricey items. Instead, they could start by recommending followers better products or by making some remarks rather than making a single display of riches. When a customer feels jealous of a celebrity or model in advertising, their jealousy is not motivated by hatred but rather by the desire to work toward becoming a better version of themselves [10]. Bloggers should use this psychology to transform jealousy into an incentive to encourage their followers to improve their lives.

Female users of Xiaohongshu should exercise their own discretion as social media users. They should not blindly follow the advice or promotion given by bloggers. For instance, people should utilize their bodies as a guide while viewing shared videos of casual attire and primarily concentrate on the style that suits them rather than adhering to the most recent trends until the clothing actually fits them. Women who want to improve their appearance also need to exercise with the right diet and scientific advice. They should learn to recognize expert female bloggers as fitness references, and at the same time, rather than seeking thinner weight blindly, they can visit the hospital to seek the opinion of licensed medical professionals. Finally, when it comes to shopping with the correct morals, women need to think about whether the items they purchase are for their genuine requirements or only to indulge their vanity. They should act in accordance with their abilities, and if they want to seek better, they should put in a lot of effort and develop themselves in order to realize their ambitions.

4.Conclusion

Xiaohongshu is a broad platform that helps women see more possibilities, which not only helps women in their daily lives but also shapes their values. This indicates that Xiaohongshu's platform requires expert oversight since if there is misleading information, many female groups would be misled. The three categories of bloggers mentioned above all have various weaknesses therefore people should consider how to improve the current platform even better. By reminding female users not to follow their favorite bloggers blindly, my research hopes to assist social media sites like Xiaohongshu in better policing the content of bloggers. There is nothing wrong with using Xiaohongshu for clothing matching, fitness, or shopping information. These bloggers' posting is helpful for reference. However, it can not demonstrate that every piece of information is accurate and worthwhile, therefore women should use their own discretion when deciding whether or not to utilize the Xiaohongshu. In actuality, values are related to determining the veracity of internet content. Women who possess the right values will resist being readily persuaded by external factors. As a result, when using Xiaohongshu, users should not only read a blogger's posts but also do additional searches or look for relevant information on other platforms. After Xiaohongshu is adequately controlled, women will be able to use this social platform with security and self-assurance. Females can instill positive ideals without having to worry about the veracity of the video material. For instance, in terms of physical well-being, bloggers support a diversity of bodies since they may still be attractive even if the weight base is rather high. Women prioritize their health over their physical looks, and in such a setting, they will develop and gain greater self-assurance.

Social media platforms should be sources that help people get more information and provide them with more convenience. Users' judgment will be impacted by the information they find because its veracity can not be guaranteed. Women require more safety since they are already more inclined than males to believe what they see online. The material on Xiaohongshu has to be more engaging and expert because it caters to a lot of female consumers. In the foreseeable future, women will benefit more from Xiaohongshu's assistance.

References

1. B. Castillo-Abdul, L. M. Romero-Rodríguez, & J. Balseca, 11 (2021)
2. K. Lokithasan, S. Simon, N. Z. B. Jasmin, & N. A. B. Othman, IJMTSS, 2 (2019)
3. J. Guo, *Global Media and China*, 7 (2022)
4. K. Sokolova, H. Kefi, J. Retail. Consum. Serv. 53 (2020)
5. X. Duan, *Global Media and China*, 5, 228-246. (2020)

6. V. Seekis, G. L. Bradley, A. L. Duffy, Psychol. Women Q. 44 (2020)
7. H. Reinikainen, J. Munnukka, D. Maity, V. Luoma-Aho, J. Mark. Manag. 36 (2020)
8. H Yang, JJ Wang, GYQ Tng, S Yang. 7 (2020)
9. R. Ladhari, E. Massa, H. Skandrani, J. Retail. Consum. Serv. 54 (2020)
10. J. A. Lee, M. S. Eastin, J. Interact. Advert. (2020)

SHS Web of Conferences **185**, 03010 (2024) https://doi.org/10.1051/shsconf/202418503010
ICLCC 2024

Visual rhetoric in advertising of China's new tea beverage industry, using HEYTEA as an example

Yufei Ye*

School of Literature, Communication University of China, Beijing, 100020, China

Abstract. In recent years, China's tea market has undergone immense transformations, giving rise to a diverse range of novel products collectively known as new tea beverages. This market trend has led to intense competition, compelling brands to employ innovative advertising strategies to captivate consumers. This study focuses on the well-known Chinese new tea beverage brand "HEYTEA" as a case study. It employs the theoretical framework of visual rhetoric to analyze visual rhetoric in new tea beverage advertisements from two dimensions: visual image and rhetorical techniques. In terms of visual image, advertisements effectively convey messages through a rich array of visual elements, attracting target audiences and enhancing their overall impact. On the other hand, within the domain of linguistic visual rhetoric, advertising copy emphasizes the use of words, sentence structures, and rhetorical devices to accentuate product features, thereby stimulating consumers' sensory experiences. The objective of this research is to explore the value of visual rhetoric in new tea beverage advertising.

1.Introduction

Since 2010, with the growth in consumer demand for diversified beverages and changes in consumption patterns, China's tea industry consumption market has gradually witnessed the emergence of a new type of tea beverage product distinct from traditional teas and bottled ready-to-drink teas. These products have broken through the boundaries of traditional tea production and consumption, offering features such as healthy ingredients, innovative designs, and on-site preparation. They meet the needs of the younger generation of consumers in the new era, leading to rapid industry development [1].

New tea beverage advertisements are a derivative form of advertising designed to cater to the new tea beverage market, with their primary function remaining as marketing. In the common case, consumers are often influenced by advertising marketing and no longer rely solely on product quality as their purchase criterion; they also consider the overall discourse of the advertisements [2]. Therefore, in order to stand out in a highly competitive market, various brands have begun actively establishing advertising marketing channels to attract potential consumers and enhance brand loyalty.

Furthermore, according to the "2022 China Catering Gourmet Awards" list released by the Chinese dining data research and evaluation organization New Catering Big Data (NCBD), HEYTEA ranks first as the "Most Popular New Tea Beverage Brand [3]". Therefore, this paper will take HEYTEA as an example and explore how the advertising image of such widely recognized brands is constructed, using the framework of visual rhetoric theory.

1.1 Vision

Vision is a fundamental human capacity for understanding the world. In the era of new media, it has become the primary way people gather information. Visual information, in this context, is composed of various visual symbols, including lines, light, colors, and other elements. These symbols serve as a medium for conveying diverse types of information [4].

1.2 Rhetoric

Rhetoric originally referred to the use of language techniques, with its research primarily focused on language or textual symbols in the past. Nowadays, research on rhetoric has become increasingly comprehensive and profound, finding applications across various industries. Within the field of advertising, rhetoric provides a framework for advertising strategies [5]. In recent years, visual communication based on new media has rapidly evolved, and the concept of "reading images" has become a widespread cultural pursuit. People are more inclined to accept information predominantly conveyed through visual symbols, which play a significant role in communication. Presently, the practice of conveying messages primarily through visual elements, supplemented by language, text, sound, and other symbols, is referred to as visual rhetoric [6]. Choosing appropriate symbols and modes of expression for conveying meaning is crucial in effectively

*Corresponding author's mail: yufei_ye@cuc.edu.cn

communicating the desired message from advertisers to consumers. The application of visual rhetorical methods has increasingly come to the forefront of this process. Enhancing advertising's communicative effectiveness through the utilization of visual symbols poses a critical question that necessitates contemplation within marketing strategies.

HEYTEA's digital advertisements on various new media platforms effectively exemplify the techniques of visual rhetoric. They intricately incorporate visual images based on seasonal ingredients, holidays, and trending topics, coupled with a diverse array of visual and linguistic rhetorical methods. This enriches the expressiveness of the advertisements, simultaneously serving as a reflection of the advertiser's marketing intentions. These efforts effectively implant marketing content into the consumer's psyche.

2.Visual images in HEYTEA's advertisements

Advertisements encompass a variety of information. Yet from the perspective of visual symbols, they primarily revolve around tangible human figures, objects, and relatively abstract brand images. Within this context, human figures featured in advertisements can be categorized into advertisers themselves (such as product developers or manufacturers) and individuals external to the advertisers (such as product endorsers or consumers). Similarly, objects within advertisements can be classified into products (including logos and manufacturing processes) and supplementary items employed in product promotion.

HEYTEA's advertisements predominantly start with object imagery, positioning the promoted beverages as the visual focal point. These advertisements incorporate numerous supplementary elements, utilizing corresponding content formats to effectively convey information to the target or potential audience, achieving precision in their promotional impact. Notably, the design of supplementary object imagery closely aligns with popular topics, such as Chinese culture or cyberpunk, seamlessly blending elements of current trends with promotional content to cater to the aesthetic preferences of the consumer base. This strategy enhances the "memorability" of the advertisements, facilitating efficient delivery and dissemination of the intended message.

3.Image vision rhetoric

As mentioned earlier, HEYTEA's advertisements primarily focus on object imagery. Within the process of constructing advertising imagery through visual rhetoric, the image of the promoted beverages serves a "presentation" function. It either conveys partial information about the product's producer or service provider or highlights the outstanding aspects of the product or service [6]. On the other hand, auxiliary object imagery beyond the product serves a "symbolic" function, which involves the "transfer of characteristics from one object to another." From a semiotic perspective, these "presentation" and "symbolic" functions correspond to the visual rhetorical methods of "metaphor " and "metonymy," respectively.

Metaphor and metonymy are two fundamental rhetorical devices characterized by the use of one thing to represent or imagine another [7]. Whether metaphor or metonymy, they are not limited to external ornamentation or useful patterns; they are fundamental forms of perceiving the surrounding environment. For example, humans rely on visual perception as an essential guiding form during exploration and expression. In such cases, visual metaphor and visual metonymy may come into play [8]. Visual metaphor involves using another thing to understand and experience what is currently captured visually [9]. Visual metonymy, on the other hand, is essentially about image reference, emphasizing the use of a visual element to refer to another thing associated with it [10].

Taking a HEYTEA advertisement released during the Spring Festival as an example, the visual symbol of the " 福 (Good Fortune)" character sticker on the right employs visual metonymy to metaphorically represent the Chinese New Year, aligning with the timing of the advertisement (Spring Festival). The prominent text " Spring Festival Limited Edition" on the left reinforces the information that the beverage is available for a limited time during the Spring Festival. At the top, the peeled longan, used as the primary visual symbol, serves as a metonym for fresh ingredients. The central image of the "Longan Bubble Tea" product within the advertisement visually demonstrates the use of high-quality ingredients and presents an enticing appearance.

4.Language vision rhetoric

Language-based visual rhetoric refers to rhetorical practices that employ language and textual symbols as a means of achieving optimal visual effects [11]. Various rhetorical techniques, including word choice, sentence structure, and figures of speech, can be employed to create vivid rhetorical effects. Roland Barthes coined the term "anchorage" in *Rhétorique de l'image (1964)* to describe the use of text within images, where textual elements serve to "anchor" or fix relevant meanings to the visuals. In HEYTEA advertisements, copywriting often effectively amplifies the product's aroma, taste, flavor, and other characteristics through rhetoric, establishing a strong correspondence between images and text. This correspondence contributes to the dissemination of persuasive messages aimed at stimulating consumer desire among the advertising audience. In the following sections, the analysis of visual rhetoric within copywriting is the key point, focusing on aspects such as word choice and grammar.

4.1 Various types of words

4.1.1 Internet slang and creative language

Internet slang and creative language play a significant role in HEYTEA's advertising copy, particularly through the use of homophonic transcriptions and metaphorical associations. For instance:

"8137, use HEYTEA to massage away your troubles!" (8137, 用喜茶给眉头做个马杀鸡！)

In this first advertising slogan, numerical homophones are employed. "8137" phonetically resembles "don't be disheartened" in Chinese, and "马杀鸡" (mǎ shā jī) creatively translates to "massage," drawing a humorous and playful connection, making it lively and engaging.

"As time flies by, I 'zi' care about you." (任时光匆匆，我紫在乎你。)

The second sentence utilizes Chinese characters' homophonic qualities, where "紫" (zǐ) phonetically resembles "只" (zhǐ), cleverly incorporating the beverage name into the advertisement. This approach effectively leverages color-related words to evoke visual image, making the ad vivid and enhancing its communicative impact.

"Three-in-one, a brilliant plan to extinguish the heat." (三招合一，灭火妙计成。)

In this case, "灭火" (miè huǒ), which translates to "extinguishing the fire," metaphorically suggests that the beverage's refreshing quality can relieve the summer heat. HEYTEA's target audience primarily consists of intellectually vibrant and imaginative young individuals. The use of metaphorical and associative language helps capture the attention of a younger demographic, thereby achieving the goal of promoting the product.

4.1.2 Frequently employing imagery-rich vocabulary

For instance:

"Natural peach aroma, sweet and enticing, with a soft and velvety texture." (自然桃香，清甜诱人，口感软糯。)

"Crackling and bursting, exploding with succulence." (噼里啪啦，爆炸多肉。)

Each word corresponds to a psychological auditory or visual image, as well as related experiences, capable of evoking various psychological sensations [11]. For example, terms like "清甜" (qīng tián - sweet and clear), "软糯" (ruǎn nuò - soft and glutinous), and "噼里啪啦" (pī lǐ pā là - crackling and bursting) in the examples respectively serve to trigger olfactory, gustatory, and auditory perceptions. When the audience comprehends these words, they naturally draw upon their existing experiences to stimulate psychological sensations.

HEYTEA's advertisements are predominantly disseminated on self-media platforms, and in order to facilitate online transmission and communication, they employ a variety of creative and diverse rhetorical techniques in their language.

4.2 Flexible syntax

4.2.1 Variation in sentence structures and tones

There is a diversity of sentence structures and tones in HEYTEA's advertisements. For instance:

"How much mango? So refreshing and generous, busy relieving your greasiness." (有多芒？又清爽、又多料，忙着解腻。)

" It is SUPER fragrant! " (嘎嘎香！)

Here, the advertisement employs a variety of sentence structures, including affirmative and negative sentences, declarative and interrogative sentences, and exclamatory sentences, among others, to create a complex and engaging narrative [12]. This approach allows for more effective communication in the organization of advertising discourse.

4.2.2 Reconfiguration of sentence length and organization

The advertisements by HEYTEA exhibit a combination of sentence structures, both in terms of sentence length and organization. For instance:

"Red apricots weigh down the branches, half-ripe and yellow; next door, waiting for the season. Golden peaches send fragrant breezes in waves, hanging on branches, facing each other. "(红杏压枝黄半熟，邻墙，候时。金桃送风几阵香，挂枝，相望。)

At a micro level, these sentences interweave structured and fragmented elements, creating a rhythmic and engaging reading experience [13]. However, when considered as a whole, the paragraph maintains consistent sentence structures, such as the contrasting " red apricots " (红杏) and " golden peaches " (金桃) and the parallelism between "next door" (邻墙) and " hanging on branches" (挂枝) in Chinese. HEYTEA's advertising copy often combines both structured and fragmented sentences, achieving a harmonious synergy that enhances the overall aesthetic appeal.

"Switching from addition to subtraction, simplifying complexity, returning to the original intention, confronting the true essence of cherries, one's mindset also finds tranquility. 'Full Bottle Cherry' arises from this."(换加法为减法，化繁为简，回归初心，直面车厘子本味，心态也随之放平，"满瓶车厘肉" 便由此而来。)

"No more words, just more flesh." (没别的，就多肉。)

These examples illustrate different visual effects conveyed by HEYTEA's advertising slogans for the same product. In terms of sentence structure, longer sentences offer richer and more intricate descriptions. Using longer sentences in advertising can effectively convey the brand's philosophy. Conversely, shorter sentences feature simple structures, fewer words, and convey less information. Advertising needs to showcase the most valuable information within limited space, and the use of short sentences demonstrates strong "conciseness."

4.3 A variety of rhetoric devices

4.3.1 Depiction: Enhancing the Sensory Appeal of the Product

"The subtle aroma of red oil peaches combines with the sweet and sour freshness of hibiscus plums, enveloped in the delicate fragrance of jasmine flowers, offering a layered experience of crispness, freshness, and sweetness."(淡淡的红油桃香气与芙蓉李的酸甜沁爽，包裹住清雅茉莉花香，脆、鲜、甜层层递进。)

Depiction is a rhetorical device used to vividly describe the sensory qualities of objects, such as their colors, smells, and more. It allows for the concrete and sensory portrayal of objective phenomena [12]. In the food industry's advertising, marketing relies solely on ad copy, leaving the audience unable to directly experience the taste, aroma, and appearance of the food. Language-based visual rhetoric can be interchanged with other sensory rhetoric to create various sensory impressions. In the process of rhetoric, people often utilize connections between the senses to reproduce sensory experiences through visual images. Therefore, in addition to using images, combining vivid depictions allows consumers to more directly assess whether a product is worth purchasing. In the example sentence, the depiction of peaches, plums, and floral tea enhances the descriptive imagery, making it vivid and engaging.

4.3.2 Transference: Infusing Novelty into the Product

"The subtle sweetness, a hint of bitterness, and assertive sourness blend seamlessly, creating a harmonious fusion."

Transference, consciously applying words applicable to one thing to describe another, comes in various forms. One common form is transferring emotions by using words describing human emotions to characterize other objects [13]. In the example sentence, "assertive," originally describing a person's personality, is used to emphasize the novel experience brought about by the sour taste, connecting the sensory phenomenon with a psychological sensation. HEYTEA incorporates the concept of 'inspiration' into its marketing, aiming to provide consumers with a sense of novelty. By utilizing transference, it transforms mundane descriptions, amalgamating connections between objects, thereby stimulating associations and generating fresh experiences.

5.The Impact of Visual Rhetoric on Advertising Effectiveness

Firstly, visual rhetoric endows advertisements with striking visual appeal. Within the context of new tea beverage advertising, visual rhetoric stands out due to its uniqueness and creativity, guiding the audience's gaze towards the content of the ad. By employing vivid images, rich colors, engaging compositions, and other elements, advertisers can capture the visual attention of the audience, making them more inclined to delve deeper into the information conveyed by the advertisement.

Secondly, visual rhetoric exerts a positive influence on the persuasiveness of advertisements. Advertising is an art of persuasion, and to some extent, more persuasive advertisements stimulate greater consumer motivation. Vision is the subjective sensation obtained through the encoding, processing, and analysis of external environmental stimuli by the visual system. It is estimated that over 80% of external information is acquired through vision. In contemporary culture, high levels of visuality highlight the significance of visibility and visual pleasure, making visual factors a central element of modern culture and a crucial means of creating, representing, and conveying meaning [14]. Consequently, new tea beverage brands like HEYTEA, often employ unique visual imagery and visual rhetorical elements to trigger emotional responses in the audience and arouse their interest, thereby embedding the persuasive function of the advertisement deep within the audience's emotional cognition.

Most importantly, visual rhetoric involves the skillful selection and arrangement of various visual components used in communication, aiming to maximize the effectiveness of advertising [15]. By adeptly employing diverse visual rhetorical strategies, advertisements can vividly showcase the features, advantages, and purposes of products. Furthermore, visual rhetoric allows for a more expressive conveyance of the emotions and meanings contained within an advertisement. Building upon this, brands can not only elicit emotional responses and resonate with the audience through visual elements but also, to a certain extent, mask the persuasive nature of the advertisement, enhancing its entertainment value [16].

Summarizing the analysis of HEYTEA's advertisements, it becomes evident that advertisers actively utilize visual rhetorical techniques to evoke sensory experiences of new tea beverages while stimulating consumers' imaginative faculties. Visual rhetoric enriches the visual image and conveys meanings in new tea beverage advertisements, simultaneously enhancing the effectiveness of visual elements and textual content. This not only augments the visual appeal and memorability of the advertisements but also strengthens the effectiveness of conveying information. By eliciting sensory experiences and emotional resonance in the audience, visual rhetorical methods imbue advertisements with deeper significance, establishing a potent visual and emotional connection for the brand.

6.Conclusion

This study reveals that potential consumers, when purchasing new tea beverages, take into consideration not only product quality but also the overall discourse of advertisements. Consequently, the successful marketing of new tea beverage advertisements relies not only on the product itself but also significantly on the use of visual rhetoric in advertisements. Various forms of visual rhetorical methods play an indispensable role in constructing the visual image of advertisements.

Moreover, this study suggests that as competition intensifies in the new tea beverage market, brands should promptly grasp and align with the characteristics and styles of outstanding brand advertisements within the industry. This will help maintain the freshness and distinctiveness of advertising marketing. Such an approach contributes to fostering the diversified development of the new tea beverage advertising market, catering to the needs of various consumer groups, and enhancing brand market share.

In conclusion, the success of new tea beverage advertising relies heavily on the application of visual rhetoric, offering brand advertisements opportunities for innovation and differentiation. In the future, researchers can delve further into the effectiveness of various types of visual rhetorical methods in advertising and explore how to better meet the needs of the audience, thereby promoting further development in new tea beverage brand advertising marketing.

References

1. J. F. YIN. CHINA TEA. (08), 1-6, (2021).
2. Mokshin, S. Purp. Represent. 9(SPE1), e916, (2021).
3. F. F. YU. Mark. Circ. (11), 31-33, (2023).
4. M. YING., & Y. LUO. Contemporary Commun. (06), 22-24, (2007).
5. Tevi, A., & Koslow, S. J. Advert. Res. (1), 58, 111-128, (2018).
6. Y. CHEN. Advert. Panor. (03), 83-87+113, (2007).
7. T. LIU. Journal. Mass Commun. (12), 33-46, (2018).
8. Y. GAO. J. Sun Yat-sen Univ. (Soc. Sci. Ed.). (05), 66-74, (2012).
9. T. LIU. J. Soc. Sci. Hunan Normal Univ. (06), 140-148, (2017).
10. T. LIU. Nanjing J. Soc. Sci., (10), 10, (2018).
11. R. D. CHEN. J. Hubei Norm. Univ. (Philos. and Soc. Sci.). (01), 47-53, (2005).
12. W. D. CHEN. Introduction to Rhetoric (pp.139+241). Shanghai: Shanghai Educational Publishing House, (1997).
13. X. J. WANG. Chinese Rhetoric(pp.100-103). Beijing: Beijing Publishing House, (1983).
14. J. W. LI. Mod. Commun. (J. Commun. Univ. China). (09), 141-144+156, (2019).
15. B. Q. FENG. J. Beijing Inst. Technol. (Soc. Sci. Ed.). (06), 3-7, (2003).
16. Y. HAN. Journal. Commun. (01), 104-105+108, (2022).

Brand Strategy Impact Study of SKIMS and the Potential Brand Trajectory Post AI Integration

Yanxi Zhang*

Design Department, School of Visual Arts, New York, 10010, The United States

Abstract: This paper delves into SKIMS' strategic positioning in the contemporary fashion industry, emphasizing its robust Direct-to-Consumer model that enables genuine consumer engagement. The brand's utilization of celebrity endorsements, especially its founder, Kim Kardashian, facilitates a compelling blend of global recognition and authentic consumer connections. Central to SKIMS' success is its ability to cater to modern consumer preferences for personalization and diversification, effectively distinguishing itself from competitors like Victoria's Secret. SKIMS exhibits a unique synergy that accentuates its industry dominance through strategic influencer collaborations and a pronounced digital presence. However, inherent challenges emerge, notably the potential pitfalls of relying heavily on celebrity-driven branding and navigating product diversity in a saturated market. The allure of celebrity endorsement provides immediate brand benefits but could pose long-term vulnerabilities given the unpredictable nature of celebrity dynamics. A transformative insight from this paper is the pivotal role of Artificial Intelligence (AI) in modern marketing for SKIMS. AI's predictive capabilities bolster SKIMS' inventory management and consumer engagement, promoting real-time adaptability in marketing strategies. Thus, while SKIMS showcases a blend of strategic insight and technological integration, it must also address the inherent challenges of the evolving fashion landscape. In essence, SKIMS' journey offers valuable lessons for brands navigating the complexities of modern consumerism and market dynamics.

1.Introduction

In the contemporary era, marked by rapid development, human society is transforming profoundly, transitioning from the information age to the communication age. This transformation has metamorphosed the very nature of human identity as humanity has moved from the purely physical to the digital realm. And the advent of the communication age has given rise to a new profession - "influencers." These individuals possess a powerful influence that effectively changes the dynamics of traditional social media platforms. Their influence radiates horizontally, transcending the confines of conventional social networks to reach a global audience. As these digital celebrities rise to prominence on various online platforms, and due to the internet's borderless nature, their followers transcend geographical and cultural boundaries. As a result, people's social networks are expanding and diversifying due to shared passions and interests. The presence of influencers acts as a catalyst in fostering a sense of community among like-minded people attracted by the charisma of these digital celebrities, thus expanding the outreach and resonance of online communities. This rapidly evolving sociocultural evolution has spawned dramatic changes in the business world, and mastering the strategic balance between tradition and innovation has become the key to contemporary business success. In marketing, the emergence of "influencers" heralded a new era in online marketing campaigns. Influencers leverage their unique and wide-ranging fan base to offer an attractive prospect for companies in industries that match their fan base - optimizing advertising by partnering with these online celebrities to promote their products and services peer-to-peer to their target groups. This symbiotic relationship brings about a paradigm shift in how marketing is done, elevating the endorsement of influencers to an indispensable channel for brand messaging. Influencers are uniquely positioned to pinpoint their target demographics due to their unique appeal, friend-like rapport with their fans, and influence over their fan base. By partnering with influencers, brands can increase their visibility and stimulate product sales [1]. However, the transformative impact on marketing is not limited to influencers. Represented by the emergence of ChatGPT, the rapid advancement of artificial intelligence has brought about dramatic changes in the marketing space. AI has gone through multiple iterations in just a year and a half, giving rise to many AI-focused companies that have sprung up in the market. This revolutionary technological advancement has ignited a vigorous debate among people from all walks of life, sparking discussion about the upheaval that the emergence of AI could bring to life. This booming craze has inspired active participation in AI research and development from all walks of life. The wide-ranging impact of AI extends far

*Corresponding author's mail: Jzhang44@sva.edu

beyond the marketing radius, as people from diverse backgrounds are making serious efforts to utilize the potential of AI to improve traditional ways of doing things and try to tread new paths for human development through practice. This revolutionary innovation has also raised some questions: Can AI be used to reduce the workload of humans? Can people use the supercomputing power of AI to do things that will move industries forward? Skims, a renowned fashion brand established by Kim Kardashian, who is globally acknowledged as an influential figure, primarily focuses on a contemporary line of lingerie, loungewear, and shapewear. The brand's primary approach to marketing involves collaborating with influencers to promote and directly market their products through the official Skims website. This paper aims to examine the influencer-led branding strategy of Skims, analyzing its strengths and weaknesses, exploring the impact of influencers on the brand, and discussing how the integration of AI into the branding strategy might have differed from previous approaches and whether it would have yielded better or worse outcomes.

2.Direct-to-Consumer Model

The Direct-to-Consumer (DTC) model entails brands engaging directly with consumers, circumventing traditional intermediaries such as department stores or retail brokers. Unlike conventional online brands, they focus on a singular product or a narrow range of interconnected products, often emphasizing product or business model innovation. With a robust and dedicated customer base, these brands are carving out a significant presence in the market[1]. This approach affords brands enhanced control over their brand narrative, fortifies customer relations, and generally boosts profit margins. The author has observed that the avant-garde fashion brand SKIMS has adeptly incorporated various aspects of the DTC model into its marketing strategy. For instance, establishing its official website for direct product sales mitigates potential profit losses or traffic diversions that might arise from product representation by other suppliers. In doing so, not only can it engage directly with its target audience, but it can also exert better control over product presentation and brand image. However, diverging from typical DTC brands that solely rely on direct sales, SKIMS synergizes its strategy with influential marketing, capitalizing on the immense social media clout of its founder, Kim Kardashian. This hybrid approach is a potent marketing strategy that blends the advantages of direct consumer engagement with the far-reaching impact of influencer marketing, positioning SKIMS distinctively in a saturated market space. SKIMS taps into the influential power of its founder and other internet celebrities, directing the original traffic from these celebrities - the fans - straight to its official platform. Subsequently, through organic promotion from its loyal fan base and feedback on its social media, SKIMS attracts the fans of their fans, friends, and others, employing grassroots promotional methods. This enhances the potency of the DTC model and fosters a sense of intimacy among the fans.

3.Celebrity Endorsement and Influencer Collaborations

In the advertising sector, celebrities function as commodities and workers, serving as messages and messages. Their presence in advertising campaigns aims to leverage their media recognition, popularity, and persona to amplify brand awareness. Early theorists on celebrity believed that celebrities were not innately born but were societally produced within dialectic relations with audiences. To audiences, a celebrity is understood as "a person known for their knownness." The value of creating a celebrity lies in garnering widespread attention, converting such notoriety into a form of sociocultural currency or celebrity capital. Driessens defines celebrity capital as "media visibility accumulated through recurrent media appearances or broad recognizability" that can be transferred across social domains. Concepts derived from Bourdieu lay the foundation for understanding how celebrity can be converted into other forms of capital and resources. Hence, celebrity is a process of cultural production, not merely fame [2]. Celebrity Endorsement and Influencer Collaboration model hinges on the association between well-known personalities and brands, aiming to boost brand visibility and credibility. Historically, brands have deployed celebrity endorsements to instill trust in their products and create aspirational consumer connections. The digital age has expanded this model to encompass influencer partnerships, wherein individuals with a solid social media presence endorse or partner with brands. While these influencers might not always be traditional celebrities, their perceived authenticity and close relationship with their audience grant them influential power over purchasing decisions. The author observes that SKIMS doesn't solely rely on the foundational celebrity status of its founder, Kim Kardashian, but also seamlessly weaves influencer collaborations into its promotional arsenal. While traditional endorsements can sometimes be insincere or transactional, SKIMS' amalgamation of high-profile celebrities with micro-influencers strikes an authentic chord with its audience. The outcome is a blended marketing strategy, where the robust recognition from celebrity endorsements is fortified with the genuine engagement and trust brought about by influencer collaborations. This meticulous merger empowers SKIMS to adeptly navigate the intricate matrix of modern-day consumer trust and brand loyalty.

3.1 Wide Product Range

The concept of "personalization" has gradually taken center stage in marketing in recent years, occupying a critical position. Companies must proactively understand customer needs and assist them, aiming to achieve this "personalization." As the market evolves, consumers are no longer tethered solely to the traditional act of buying. Beyond the product, they consider the supplementary services accompanying the product sale and the emotional value the product offers. Consumers select fashion goods based on their spending capacity and personal style, necessitating fashion companies to discern how to deliver unique products and experiences. Many fashion firms have responded to this trend by expanding their product portfolio, becoming increasingly "multi-style brands " [3]. This method seeks to capture a broader market segment by catering to diverse consumer needs and reducing dependence on a singular product line. Such diversification enhances market penetration, nurtures consumer loyalty, and bolsters the brand's resilience against market fluctuations. This paper identifies its congruence with this model by examining SKIMS' marketing strategy. SKIMS does not confine its offerings to a narrow category but spans a diverse range from shapewear to loungewear, catering to various price points and, thus, meeting different consumer needs. This strategy undeniably succeeds. SKIMS addresses the heterogeneous conditions of its target audience by providing a varied product line for consumers of diverse spending capacities. This tactic has been pivotal in reinforcing the brand's market position and resonating with consumers. Coupled with the immense influence of its founder, the outcome is a harmonious blend of brand association with a prominent figure and a product range that effectively aligns with varied consumer needs, allowing SKIMS to retain a competitive edge in a saturated market.

3.2 Limited Edition

The "Limited Edition Series" has emerged as an essential marketing strategy in the fashion domain, notably within the streetwear and luxury brand sectors. By launching a finite number of specific collections or products, companies leverage the principles of scarcity and exclusivity to amplify consumer demand and urgency. Intentionally producing limited quantities of a particular series imbues a sense of urgency in brands, urging consumers to purchase lest they miss out on coveted items. This model enhances the brand's perceived value and cultivates a unique relationship between the brand and the consumers, making each product acquisition feel like a distinctive experience. This paper notes that launching such products typically leads to heightened consumer expectations, allowing brands to create buzz and excitement in the market more efficiently. This bolsters the brand's perceived value and appeal and can lead to these products being resold at higher prices in the secondary market. Such promotional mechanisms with set limits encourage browsing by customers. Some may visit web pages offering such sales and make impulse purchases. Promotions make consumers succumb to impulsive buying as they elevate positive emotions and alter the consumer's reference pricing standards, impacting their purchasing intent [4]. When evaluating SKIMS' marketing approach, the author observes that while SKIMS primarily harnesses the strength of its extensive product range, it has also integrated elements of the "Limited Collection" within its strategy. By occasionally launching exclusive series or collaborating with well-known personalities, SKIMS capitalizes on the allure of limited supply to stimulate customer spending. This blended approach ensures that while SKIMS caters to a broad consumer base, it retains the charm of exclusivity, strategically positioning itself to appeal to the masses and niche audiences craving exclusivity. This nuanced blend further solidifies SKIMS' competitive edge in a saturated market, reinforcing its position. SKIMS effectively navigates the intricate dynamics of modern consumer behavior through this balanced approach. SKIMS employs the Direct-to-Consumer model, amplifying its direct engagement with consumers and enhancing its control over the brand narrative. Furthermore, the brand harnesses the power of celebrity endorsements and influencer collaborations, presenting a robust fusion of global recognition and genuine consumer engagement. It strategically utilizes well-known celebrities and micro-influencers to craft a dynamic marketing mix. In conjunction with these strategies, the extensive product range of SKIMS signifies its acknowledgment of the modern consumer's desires for personalization and diversification. By catering to diverse consumer preferences, the brand solidifies its market position, resonating with a broad spectrum of consumers and fostering loyalty. Additionally, SKIMS occasionally ventures into the "Limited Edition Series," capitalizing on the consumer allure of exclusivity and scarcity, creating a sense of urgency and desirability. This analysis suggests that SKIMS's success in the contemporary market is not merely by chance. The brand meticulously amalgamates a variety of marketing strategies, ranging from direct consumer engagement and impactful collaborations to product diversification and limited edition offerings, positioning itself adeptly within a competitive landscape. This multifaceted approach, coupled with the significant influence of its founder, Kim Kardashian, ensures that SKIMS remains relevant, resonant, and robust in its market presence. The author concludes that SKIMS exemplifies the potency of strategic marketing in navigating the intricate nuances of today's consumer landscape, achieving a harmonious balance between mass appeal and niche exclusivity.

4.Advantages

4.1 Inclusive Size Range

In the dynamic landscape of the fashion industry, one of the pivotal factors for a brand's triumph is its ability to address diverse consumer needs. When dissecting brands within the lingerie and shapewear sector, a significant differentiation becomes evident regarding inclusivity, especially size range. SKIMS has a pronounced edge when placed alongside prominent brands like Victoria's Secret. This paper highlights SKIMS' considerable success in inclusivity, offering an expansive size spectrum ranging from XXS to 5X, with ten available size options [5]. Such an approach amplifies the brand's core philosophy – "a solution for everybody"- and furnishes it with a broader consumer base. The implication is the more individuals who find sizes suitable for them in the SKIMS product range, the more likely they are to gravitate towards the brand. Conversely, Victoria's Secret has faced critique for its lack of size inclusivity, with further controversies related to misogynistic culture revelations. While recent efforts have been made to diversify its product range, its sales figures remain markedly reduced compared to its zenith [6]. The result of such comparative analysis underscores the paramountcy of inclusivity in the contemporary market. SKIMS' strategy of providing an inclusive size range not only resonates with a vast audience but also positions the brand as a vanguard in catering to the manifold needs of modern consumers. The author posits that SKIMS demonstrates a competitive advantage over its peers in size inclusivity, showcasing an acute comprehension of modern-day consumer demands.

4.2 Fast adaptation and innovation

Product innovation has emerged as a definitive criterion for brand differentiation in the evolving domain of lingerie and shapewear. It also serves as a litmus test for a brand's genuine commitment to heeding the voices of its customers. For a nascent fashion label, it becomes imperative for market researchers to undertake exhaustive investigations into consumer needs, understanding prevailing preferences in terms of styles, colors, design aesthetics, and fabric choices. By analyzing this data, there should be robust dialogues with in-house designers to predict and align with emerging trends. It's about discerning the varied perspectives from which consumers choose a brand and crafting a tailored narrative for one's offerings [7]. A salient strength of SKIMS lies in its avant-garde "Solution" series, which exhibits acute sensitivity to consumer feedback. This brand continually refines its products, perpetually recalibrates its positioning, and routinely refreshes its collections to mirror contemporary societal demands and fashion inclinations. Such proactive approaches equip SKIMS to cater to diverse body types, challenges, and aesthetic preferences. By ceaselessly rejuvenating its product mix and adapting to burgeoning fashion sensibilities, SKIMS has staked its claim as a trailblazer in the industry. Its ability to frequently reshape and introduce novel offerings remains in astute alignment with consumers' shifting tastes. The author concludes that SKIMS, through its pledge to product innovation, effectively positions itself as a visionary leader in the industry, securing a competitive edge over some traditional stalwarts.

4.3 Global Accessibility

In the lingerie sector, having widespread global acceptance and resonance with consumers can directly influence a brand's market share. Through its influencer marketing strategy, SKIMS capitalizes on its founder's vast global influence, achieving rapid and effective promotions. However, only some ventures promoted by Kim Kardashian, even with her immense international following, perform the same success as SKIMS. The efficacy of such a promotional model hinges on the harmonious interplay of three modules: the influencer, the brand, and the consumer. These modules must be intertwined and aligned to ensure effective communication with the consumer, initiating a ripple effect. The unity between the influencer and the brand dictates the promotion's success. Fans aspire to emulate influencers, and when an influencer seamlessly aligns with a brand, fans evaluate if the brand matches their ideal self [8]. Given this perspective, this paper posits that the global influence of Kim Kardashian and her profound alignment with SKIMS is a pivotal reason for its worldwide distribution and appeal. In contrast to traditional competitors like Victoria's Secret, one of SKIMS' significant advantages is its adeptness at leveraging digital platforms and e-commerce. With the founder, Kim Kardashian, having established her prominence via the internet under her guidance, SKIMS astutely capitalizes on online marketing and the advantages of contemporary global shipping, ensuring seamless access and purchase options for consumers across varied geographies. This expands the brand's audience base and maintains its unique relevance in an era dominated by digital consumerism. Furthermore, collaborations with international influencers and celebrities bolster SKIMS' global influence, transcending geographical and cultural nuances. The modern fashion landscape, particularly in the lingerie and shapewear area, demands a tripartite focus on inclusivity, adaptability, and global accessibility to achieve success and maintain relevance. Under the aegis of its founder, Kim Kardashian, SKIMS has demonstrated a significant understanding of these tenets. Its commitment to an inclusive size range, ensuring a broad spectrum of consumers find representation, starkly differentiates it from contemporaries like Victoria's Secret. Moreover, its enthusiasm for adapting to ever-changing consumer needs, evidenced by its innovative "Solution" series and quick-to-evolve product offerings, solidifies its position as a leader attuned to present-day demands. Moreover, the brand's global accessibility, backed by strategic influencer marketing and a solid digital presence, emphasizes its adeptness in navigating the digital age, securing a wide-reaching consumer base. The unique synergy between the brand and its influencer and the potent leverage of digital platforms underlines SKIMS' ascendancy in the industry. Collaborations with international personalities further amplify its reach beyond regional boundaries, eroding cultural divides. Through an in-depth analysis of these facets, this paper concludes that SKIMS has strategically positioned itself at the forefront of the industry, capitalizing on a keen comprehension of modern consumer preferences and expectations. Its robust blend of inclusivity, innovative agility, and digital savviness is a blueprint for success in contemporary fashion.

5.Disadvantages

5.1 Over-reliance on Celebrity Endorsement

In the competitive arena of lingerie and shapewear, brands employ varied strategies to distinguish themselves from their peers and foster consumer loyalty. As previously alluded to, one of the principal strategies of SKIMS hinges on celebrity endorsement, with the brand's meteoric rise inextricably linked to the formidable influence of its founder, Kim Kardashian. While such a strategy has endowed the brand with instant recognition and a distinct consumer base, this paper discerns that this strategy manifests potential vulnerabilities when juxtaposed with brands adopting a more diversified marketing approach. According to research by Bharati, influencers, in contrast to brands themselves, are susceptible to accumulating an abundance of negative press over time. Such adverse publicity can dissuade consumers from committing to a purchase even before having a firsthand experience with the product. Concurrently, a demographic victimized by the negative news associated with an influencer might spontaneously deter others from patronizing products endorsed by said influencer, consequently impacting sales adversely. Another salient risk to be acknowledged is the propensity for the influencer to become entangled in scandals, subsequently casting a pall over the brand they represent [9]. In essence, this over-reliance on a singular association, although beneficial in the short term, exposes the brand image to the erratic public perceptions of Kim Kardashian within the celebrity realm. Any negative news or contentious actions involving Kardashian could tarnish the brand's reputation. SKIMS' emphasis on aligning predominantly with a single celebrity might alienate potential consumers who find no resonance with Kardashian's image or those who approach celebrity-driven consumerism skeptically. In summation, while SKIMS has reaped immediate dividends from its celebrity-centric modus operandi, its strategy exhibits potential frailties concerning sustained effectiveness in the long run.

5.2 Product Diversity and Over-Saturation

Within the vast domain of lingerie and shapewear, myriad brands relentlessly innovate to establish their niche, accentuating a diversified product range to cater to customer demands. As this paper juxtaposes SKIMS with other contemporary brands within the same category, certain latent shortcomings become palpable, notably in Product Diversity and Saturation. Concerning Product Diversity, although SKIMS prides itself on selections tailored predominantly around the vision of its celebrity founder, Kim Kardashian, with some of its most renowned skirts cherished for accentuating feminine contours, this specificity might simultaneously serve as its potential vulnerability. Competitors in the market proffer a more extensive array of products, addressing a spectrum of consumer requirements, both functional and aesthetic. The author underscores that while SKIMS' specific product focus stands as its distinctive selling point, it might concurrently curb its allure for a broader audience, especially when set against brands that offer abundant choices in design, materials, and functionality. The pitfall of Over Saturation looms large. Propelled by celebrity-driven marketing and extensive media coverage, the brand risks pervasive overexposure. Such omnipresent promotions might engender consumer aesthetic fatigue or foster perceptions of the brand as a "fashion item" devoid of unique functionality. Moreover, SKIMS launches many diverse products at a breakneck pace, a strategy aimed at stimulating impulsive purchases and optimizing sales for individual items. Due to the rapid turnover of product choices, such brands can incentivize consumers to shop repeatedly, discard their old items more frequently, and purchase new apparel, leading to potential environmental concerns [10]. In summation, while SKIMS derives substantial advantages from its branding, the challenges emanating from Product Diversity and Saturation necessitate meticulous strategizing. Navigating the intricate terrain of lingerie and shapewear, brands continually adapt and strategize to maintain relevance and dominance in the market. This paper has critically assessed the strategies employed by SKIMS and juxtaposed them with prevalent trends and practices within the sector. Two overarching themes are pivotal in this discourse: the implications of an over-reliance on celebrity endorsement and the challenges associated with Product Diversity and Saturation. The allure of celebrity endorsement, especially with a figure as iconic as Kim Kardashian, bestows SKIMS with a unique edge. However, as this paper has highlighted, the very essence of this strength could metamorphose into a potential vulnerability. The volatility of celebrity reputation and its subsequent impact on a brand that is profoundly interwoven with the celebrity's persona warrants caution. While the immediate returns on celebrity-driven branding are evident, the long-term ramifications, dictated by the unpredictability of celebrity dynamics, underscore the need for a diversified branding strategy. Furthermore, while specificity and uniqueness have granted SKIMS a distinct market positioning in the realm of product offerings, the broader landscape demands adaptability and diversification. The author emphasizes that a brand's strength in a saturated market stems from its unique adaptability and capacity to address the myriad demands of an evolving consumer base. Compounding by aggressive marketing and rapid product churn, Saturation could lead to consumer fatigue and consequential environmental concerns. In light of these insights, it becomes evident that while SKIMS enjoys significant advantages emanating from its unique positioning and branding, it concurrently grapples with challenges that demand nuanced, forward-thinking strategies. For sustained success and longevity in the market, brands must balance leveraging their strengths and continually reassessing and recalibrating their system in response to the dynamic market landscape.

6.Integration with AI

6.1 Predictive Analysis and Inventory Management

Within the vast landscape of contemporary marketing, Artificial Intelligence (AI) emerges as a beacon of transformative potential, notably exemplifying its prowess in areas like predictive analysis and inventory management. The notable efficiency of AI in handling big data significantly alleviates the workload of marketers. Its unparalleled capability to gather and synthesize massive volumes of information assists in translating raw data into tangible, actionable strategies and methodologies. AI's insights from immense datasets equip marketers to seize opportunities and ascertain market trends quickly [11]. Grounded in AI, predictive analysis is critical to deciphering intricate patterns within colossal data repositories. AI offers SKIMS profound insights into impending fashion market tendencies by scrutinizing historical sales figures, consumer purchasing behaviors, and market inclinations. Such foresight forecasts market shifts and ensures an agile response to these fluctuations. The outcomes derived from big data analytics enable SKIMS to align its product design, launch timings, and other pivotal decisions harmoniously with consumer demands, optimizing sales while curtailing the build-up of unsold inventory. Moreover, the intervention of AI in inventory management stands unmatched in efficiency. Its anticipatory analytics aid in the reasonable estimation and superior control of stock levels, averting the pitfalls of overproduction and consequent stockpiling, which could culminate in wastage. Additionally, it facilitates tracking the provenance of materials, ensuring ethical and sustainable procurement [12]. Thus, SKIMS can tailor its inventory to mirror demand fluctuations by harnessing real-time data analytics. This precision can drastically mitigate scenarios of overstock and stockouts, ensuring prudent resource utilization and wastage reduction. In essence, by tapping into the predictive capabilities of AI, SKIMS stands poised to carve a distinctive competitive edge. AI's potential to cultivate an inventory management system that resonates with market dynamics and consumer preferences is evident. Consequently, the amalgamation of AI with SKIMS' ethos may indeed chart a transformative trajectory in the fiercely competitive fashion paradigm.

6.2 Optimized Marketing Campaigns

Artificial Intelligence (AI) offers the remarkable capability to comprehensively and adeptly process vast datasets, facilitating an intricate comprehension of consumer behavior, inclinations, and engagement dynamics. By harnessing these analytical insights derived from data, SKIMS is equipped to meticulously tailor its marketing initiatives to align seamlessly with its target demographic's explicit requirements and anticipations. AI empowers marketers to deliver bespoke services to consumers by analyzing past user data and proactively customizing and recommending products that individuals will likely resonate with [13]. The campaigns birthed from this strategy transcend the realm of generic advertising, morphing into personalized narratives that foster profound resonance with consumers, enhancing engagement levels and promoting brand allegiance. AI-propelled algorithms possess the understanding to evaluate the efficiency of diverse marketing channels, discerning which mediums yield the optimal return on investment for SKIMS. Such discernment ensures that advertising reaches the intended audience with precision and curtails potential oversaturation or wastage in the promotional process [14]. These revelations contribute to the reasonable allocation of marketing funds, ensuring amplified visibility and engagement while circumventing unnecessary expenditures. Additionally, the real-time reactivity inherent in AI capacitates SKIMS to recalibrate its marketing strategies dynamically. If a specific campaign facet underperforms or a shift in consumer sentiment is observed, AI mechanisms can swiftly detect these discrepancies, prompting immediate adjustments. This agility safeguards the contemporaneity and potency of SKIMS' marketing endeavors. By enhancing campaign strategies anchored in genuine consumer insights and adaptive real-time responsiveness, SKIMS stands poised to reposition its engagement and sway within the fashion marketplace. In light of the elucidated insights, this paper underscores the revolutionary potential of Artificial Intelligence (AI) within the multifaceted domain of modern marketing, particularly in the context of SKIMS. When focusing on predictive analysis and inventory management, AI emerges as a catalyst for enhancing efficacy, enabling SKIMS to navigate the complex terrains of market dynamics seamlessly. By leveraging AI's vast analytical capabilities, SKIMS can anticipate market shifts and aptly calibrate its inventory, ensuring timely product launches and waste reduction. Furthermore, from the perspective of optimized marketing campaigns, AI becomes instrumental in formulating nuanced strategies that genuinely resonate with consumers. By ensuring personalized and data-driven narratives, SKIMS can foster deeper connections with its target audience, reinforcing brand loyalty. The utility of AI extends beyond mere campaign customization; its potential in real-time monitoring and agility in strategy adjustments emphasizes AI's value as an invaluable tool for adaptive marketing. By meticulously evaluating various promotional channels, AI aids SKIMS judiciously allocating resources, maximizing visibility, and minimizing unproductive expenditures. To encapsulate, the incorporation of AI into SKIMS' operational and marketing framework can not only enhance its internal efficiencies but also amplify its external consumer engagements. The analytical might of AI, combined with its predictive proficiencies, positions SKIMS favorably in the fast-evolving fashion domain, equipping it to remain relevant and influential. With AI as its strategic ally, this paper posits that SKIMS is poised to redefine its trajectory in the fashion industry, paving the way for a more data-driven, consumer-centric, and adaptive future.

7.Conclusion

In synthesizing the extensive exploration of SKIMS' positioning within the contemporary fashion landscape, this paper observes multiple dimensions of its strategic success and the challenges it encounters. Central to its achievement is SKIMS' adept embrace of the Direct-to-Consumer model, the strategic harnessing of celebrity endorsements, and its attuned response to the modern consumer's preferences, especially in the realms of personalization, diversification, and exclusivity. By intertwining these elements, SKIMS has constructed a brand narrative that resonates powerfully with a diverse consumer base. However, beneath this triumphant facade lies a mosaic of challenges. The brand's profound association with the persona of its founder, Kim Kardashian, while serving as a potent brand enhancer, also emerges as a potential point of vulnerability, given the unpredictability of celebrity reputations. Additionally, the difficulties of product diversification in a saturated market present a double-edged sword. While a diversified product portfolio could resonate with a broader audience, it could engender consumer fatigue and environmental ramifications. Furthermore, the pivotal role of Artificial Intelligence (AI) in SKIMS' marketing and operational strategy needs to be improved. AI augments SKIMS' predictive prowess in inventory management and refines its consumer engagement through personalized marketing campaigns. This integration of technological advancement underscores SKIMS' commitment to innovation and adaptability, hallmarks of a brand that aims to stay ahead of the curve. Nevertheless, the balance between leveraging inherent strengths and recognizing emerging challenges will shape SKIMS' future trajectory. While the brand presently thrives on its unique synthesis of strategies and tools, the evolving dynamics of the fashion industry, coupled with the unpredictable nature of celebrity branding and the challenges of product saturation, necessitate a continual reassessment of strategies. This paper asserts that SKIMS' journey symbolizes the broader challenges and opportunities within the fashion industry. SKIMS provides invaluable insights for brands seeking relevance and resilience in a competitive, rapidly evolving market by navigating this intricate nexus of brand identity, technological innovation, and consumer expectations.

References

1. Kim, N.L., Shin, D.C. & Kim, G. (2021) Determinants of consumer attitudes and re-purchase intentions toward direct-to-consumer (DTC) brands. Fash Text 8: 8.
2. Brooks, G., Drenten, J., & Piskorski, M. J. (2021). Influencer celebrification: How social media influencers acquire celebrity capital. Journal of Advertising, 50(5): 528-547.
3. Gazzola P, Pavione E, Pezzetti R, Grechi D. (2020) Trends in the Fashion Industry. The Perception of Sustainability and Circular Economy: A Gender/Generation Quantitative Approach. Sustainability. 12(7): 2809.
4. WiranataA. T., & HanantoA. (2020). Do Website Quality, Fashion Consciousness, and Sales Promotion Increase Impulse Buying Behavior of E-Commerce Buyers? Indonesian Journal of Business and Entrepreneurship (IJBE). 6(1): 74.
5. SKIMS. (2023). Size Guides. https://skims.com/pages/size-guides
6. Sapna Maheshwari, Vanessa Friedman (2021).Victoria's Secret Swaps Angels for 'What Women Want.' Will They Buy It? New York Times Magazine. 45(1): 34.
7. Bharati Rathore. (2019). Chic Strategies: Revolutionizing the Industry through Innovative Fashion Marketing. International Journal of New Media Studies: International Peer Reviewed Scholarly Indexed Journal. 6(2): 23–33.
8. Belanche, D., Casaló, L. V., Flavián, M., & Ibáñez-Sánchez, S. (2021). Understanding influencer marketing: The role of congruence between influencers, products and consumers. Journal of Business Research, 132: 186-195.
9. Bharati Rathore. (2019). Chic Strategies: Revolutionizing the Industry through Innovative Fashion Marketing. International Journal of New Media Studies: International Peer Reviewed Scholarly Indexed Journal. 6(2): 23–33.
10. Diantari, N. K. Y. (2021). Trend Cycle Analysis on Fast Fashion Products. Journal of Aesthetics, Design, and Art Management. 1(1): 24-33.
11. Silva, E. S., Hassani, H., & Madsen, D. Ø. (2020). Big Data in fashion: transforming the retail sector. Journal of Business Strategy. 41(4): 21-27.
12. Bharati Rathore. (2019). Artificial Intelligence in Sustainable Fashion Marketing: Transforming the Supply Chain Landscape. Eduzone: International Peer Reviewed/Refereed Multidisciplinary Journal, 8(2): 25–38.
13. Bharati Rathore. (2019). Artificial Intelligence in Sustainable Fashion Marketing: Transforming the Supply Chain Landscape. Eduzone: International Peer Reviewed/Refereed Multidisciplinary Journal, 8(2): 25–38.
14. Bharati Rathore. (2019). Fashion Sustainability in the AI Era: Opportunities and Challenges in Marketing. Eduzone: International Peer Reviewed/Refereed Multidisciplinary Journal. 8(2): 17–24.

Discovering the Impact of Chinese Social Media Influencers on Generation Z Consumer Behaviour

Zimo Shi*

Institution of Education, University College London, London, N1C 4DD, United Kingdom

Abstract. The influence of Chinese social media influencers on Generation Z's consumer behavior has become increasingly pronounced, with the advent of COVID-19 further magnifying their impact on digital consumer trends. Generation Z places a remarkable level of trust in these influencers, driven by their relatable personalities, specialized knowledge, and interactive engagement. Moreover, following these influencers serves to fulfill Generation Z's intrinsic need for social identity while fostering a deep sense of attachment. Nevertheless, this rapidly evolving landscape also presents its own set of challenges, including the potential for influencer-related scandals and an imperative demand for transparency and authenticity. Effectively navigating this environment necessitates that companies and influencers develop a profound understanding of Generation Z's unique characteristics and preferences. This understanding forms the basis for crafting tailored marketing initiatives that resonate with this generation. The key to success in influencer marketing lies in maintaining content authenticity and building trust with Generation Z when endorsing products. By diligently employing these strategies, businesses and marketers can adeptly target Generation Z consumers, nurturing enduring brand loyalty and attachment that transcends digital trends.

1.Introduction

In the fast-paced and ever-changing landscape of the digital age, the behaviour of consumers worldwide is undergoing a profound transformation, primarily catalyzed by the emergence of social media influencers. This sweeping trend isn't limited by geographical boundaries, and China, a nation known for its technological prowess and vibrant online communities, is no exception to this paradigm shift. These digital trendsetters, often referred to as Key Opinion Leaders (KOLs), have not only captured the attention of the younger generation but have also become potent forces in shaping the consumption patterns and choices of Generation Z (Gen Z). Born between the mid-1990s and early 2010s, Generation Z is positioned as the vanguard of the future of society. They have a unique set of characteristics and preferences, largely shaped by their upbringing in the digital age. This generation's deep affinity for technology, social media and online engagement defines their consumer behaviour in unprecedented ways. It is in this digital realm that the influence of Chinese social media influencers on their purchase intentions has become a fascinating and far-reaching phenomenon. This paper seeks to illuminate the interrelationship between these influencers and their Gen Z audience. By conducting an exhaustive review of existing literature, it intends to delve into the diverse and intricate ways in which Chinese social media influencers impact the purchasing decisions of Gen Z. Moreover, it aims to uncover the connections between pertinent social media influencers and their Gen Z followers. Beyond this, the paper will briefly investigate the obstacles encountered by both consumers and brands within this ever-evolving landscape and offer suggestions to shape the future of influencer marketing.

2.Literature review

2.1 The Rise of Chinese Social Media Influencer Marketing

To comprehend the influence of Chinese social media influencers on Generation Z consumer behaviour, people must first acknowledge the rapid rise and widespread popularity of these influencers. The COVID-19 pandemic brought about a dramatic shift in the global retail landscape. During the lockdown of countries, traditional physical stores were no longer a choice for individual consumers, and purchasing goods on digital platforms became the new norm [1]. This shift has resulted in the emergence of a new type of digital celebrities known as social media influencers or Key Opinion Leaders (KOLs). Meanwhile, social media platforms are rapidly evolving into pivotal touchpoints for digital marketers seeking to connect and engage with consumers [2]. Without questioning, the prevalence of social media has transformed it into a central area of interest for businesses and brands, and those individuals who engage with social media platforms represent potential customers for these businesses and brands [3]. To harness the considerable

*Corresponding author's mail: zimo.shi.21@ucl.ac.uk

marketing opportunities presented by social media platforms, a significant proportion of firms choose to collaborate with influencers for the purpose of endorsing and evaluating their products [4]. Social media influencers became active during the COVID-19 period and are significantly influencing online consumption, especially in the Chinese social network. Companies have the ability to utilise the influential capabilities of individuals to enhance brand recognition and establish a strong position within the market. Consequently, influencers engage in the practice of posting a product on their social media platform, for which they receive money from the respective business [5]. The content shared on various platforms can take many formats, including videos or written material, as long as they are capable of being spread. In China, platforms like Weibo, WeChat, Douyin and Red have created a thriving ecosystem for content creators to amass large followings. These platforms have their own loyal users, with WeChat, in particular, is emerging as the most comprehensive social media platform in China, with 1.3 billion monthly active users as of the end of June 2023 [6]. China's population is more than 1.4 billion, which means that WeChat's reach is even more than 90%. Because of this large consumer base, all major social media have undergone significant changes in recent years to accommodate diverse content formats to increase user engagement. These platforms not only allow influencers to share content but also use big data algorithms to make content recommendations and interactions with different groups of people, thus promoting brand awareness and user stickiness more efficiently. When influencers mention a brand or product in their posts and make recommendations, their posts are simultaneously disseminated to millions of potential consumers to ensure maximum exposure of brand and product information [7]. In addition, Chinese social media influencers often form strategic partnerships with brands to provide a wide range of content, including product reviews, tutorials, and lifestyle endorsements. Chinese social media influencers are able to seamlessly integrate branded content into their narratives, making it appear organic and genuinely engaging to their Chinese social media influencers are able to seamlessly integrate brand content into their narratives, making it appear organic and truly engaging to their fans, which further enhances their allure. With this in mind, the influence of Chinese social media influencers on Gen Z can't be ignored.

2.2 Understanding Gen Z as Consumers

The exponential progress of digital technology has had a profound influence on nearly all aspects of everyday lives to Generation Z. Gen Z was born into digital nativism in the digital age between 1995 and 2010. they used mobile devices frequently and were exposed to social media for long periods of time. This upbringing has profoundly shaped their worldview and consumer behaviour. This consumer group relies on social media for learning, entertainment, and shopping, but is more thoughtful in their interactions with social media. Individuals frequently engage with influencers on social media platforms through actions such as like, publishing, subscribing to channels, and sharing influencers' content with their network. When members of Generation Z encounter influencers whom they like, they exhibit a desire to acquire further information on the goods or products endorsed by these influencers. This inclination stems from their aspiration to emulate and replicate the actions and choices made by these influential figures [8]. Individuals between the ages of 18 and 24 in China constitute around 15% of the population and are seen as the next engine of domestic consumption development. Furthermore, 70% of this generation Z is persuaded to buy through social media sites. Influencers play a crucial role in the growing tendency of young Chinese purchasing items through social media [9]. The report by Euromonitor also predicts that Generation Z will be the largest consumer group by 2030. Notably, Chinese Gen Z, like global Gen Z, values authenticity, transparency, and affinity. Compared to gorgeous celebrities, Gen Z are more likely to trust influencers on social media, because they're like friends. Thus, they feel more comfortable commenting and interacting on influential posts than celebrities, who are people they cannot identify with [7]. They seek genuine connections and are attracted to influencers who share their personal experiences, challenges and successes. They actively build their online presence and value the ability to connect with like-minded people. This interconnectedness extends to their purchasing decisions, with many Gen Z young people relying on online reviews, recommendations and feedback when making choices. Building trust and connections on Chinese social media is the foundation of influencers' influence on Gen Z consumers.

2.3 The Appeal of Chinese Social Media Influencers to Gen Z

Chinese social media influencers are attracted to Gen Z for a number of reasons. Firstly, they have a more approachable image. Since 2016, Douyin has become one of the most popular apps in China. Almost everyone has downloaded and viewed the short videos, and Douyin breaks away from the traditional TV adverts that Gen Z tends to distrust, and instead seeps into social media content, making Gen Z more willing to watch their product promotions. Frequent interactions and sharing allowed them to build a close connection with their audience. For example, personal experiences, product usage, daily photos and videos are shared and exchanged almost in real time between influencers and followers through social media platforms. Influencers are usually portrayed as Gen Z-aged and real and relatable, making their endorsements more persuasive. They are more like regular people with specific expertise or friends who live around consumers rather than traditional celebrities with distance. They build their online presence around authentic, relatable experiences. This authenticity particularly resonates with Gen Z, who value the transparency and sincerity of influencers. As a result, Gen Z is more likely to trust influencers' perspectives and believes that their opinions are real and credible. Secondly, the content produced by these influencers tends to match the interests and aspirations of Generation Z. Whether it's fashion, beauty, technology or lifestyle, influencers cater to the diverse needs of this demographic. An influencer usually builds niche expertise, positioning themselves as an authority in a particular field. Some micro-influencers (10k-100k followers) may not have a very large number of followers, but they are still popular because of their relevance and authenticity [8]. Nano-influencers with less than 1000 followers had a higher engagement rate (7.2%) than macro-influencers who have more than 100k followers. Thus, the impact influencers have is not caused by the number of followers, but by specialisation. This specialisation deepens their connection with audiences with similar interests, leading to increased engagement and in turn a more pronounced impact on Gen Z's consumer behaviour. Finally, their engaging content formats, such as live-streaming and interactive challenges, resonate with Gen Z's preference for immersive experiences. In China, the live-streaming market has spread at a phenomenal rate over the previous few years. According to revenue reports from giant internet companies such as Alibaba, the total transaction value of Taobao live streaming reached 500 billion RMB from March 2020 to March 2021. Studies point out that live streaming embedded in e-commerce, such as platforms like Taobao and Jingdong, can provide consumers with more accurate and comprehensive information, helping them make better purchasing decisions [5]. Influential people as often chosen to be anchors in live-streaming and the content is highly engaging. They are able to have a strong interaction with consumers while selling products, a process that can enhance consumer engagement, satisfaction and pleasure. Therefore, benefiting from the well-developed Internet and convenient communication channels, Chinese influencers are taking advantage of Gen Z's fear of missing out on trends to influence Gen Z's consumption and even people of all ages to a certain extent.

2.4 Creating FOMO (Fear of Missing Out)

The "Fear of Missing Out" (FOMO) phenomenon is a potent tool harnessed by Chinese social media influencers. They create a sense of urgency and desirability around products or experiences, instigating a fear that if Generation Z doesn't act quickly, they will miss out on the latest trends. This fear drives impulse purchases and promotes consumerism, which directly impacts Generation Z's spending habits. The "limited-time offers" and "exclusive discounts" promoted by these influencers intensify the FOMO effect. In China, major platforms have promotions almost once a month. Chinese New Year, Valentine's Day, Douyin 618, Double Eleven, and so on, there are endless gimmicks surrounding every consumer, and the mechanism of each promotion is different. Taking beauty products as an example, each brand will come up with its top products for the promotion, and the samples given away vary from event to event, or the makeup tools included change. In order to stay on top of the trends, Gen Z usually checks social media and compares products and prices over and over again. The role of influencers is to be the first to share new trends or products at the time of each promotion, attracting followers to consume them [8]. The fear of missing out (FOMO) serves as a driving force for Generation Z to engage in current trends and avoid experiencing feelings of exclusion [9]. While FOMO increases anxiety, it also motivates them to increase their purchase intentions and even impulse purchases.

3.Influence mechanism

How will influencers continue to enhance and exert influence over customers' purchasing behaviors? According to Bawa et al., it is crucial to comprehend the relationship between consumer purchase intentions and consumer behaviour, which can be used to forecast the purchasing process. In other words, purchase intentions is a factor in the purchase decisions [10]. Spears & Singh define it as "an individual's conscious plan to make an effort to purchase a brand". Research conducted by Xu & Pratt indicates that consumers tend to gravitate toward influencers who share similar lifestyles, personality traits, and behavioral preferences. Consequently, harnessing the expertise of influencers for product marketing yields a positive impact on consumers' intentions to make a purchase.

3.1 Credibility and Professionalism

Due to the value of information converted by influential content on social media, purchase intention increases when the level of trust is elevated. Furthermore, this informative content by influencers is likely to enhance the credibility of brand posts among their followers, leading to a greater inclination to make a purchase. This can be attributed to the perception that influencers possess expertise in their respective domains, enabling them to effectively sway their followers through their opinions and experiences regarding particular products and services associated with their profession [10]. Generation Z in China, accustomed to the vast amount of information available on the Internet, tends to look to influencers as reliable guides in times of information overload. These influencers provide carefully curated content and informed opinions that simplify complex choices and help consumers make decisions.

3.2 Social Identity

The function of social identity is of utmost significance in shaping the impact of Chinese social media influencers on Gen Z consumers. Social media not only provides these young people with more than just a sharing platform but also allows young people to experience new modes of self-expression and have the opportunity to build and continually develop their sense of identity. As a result, Chinese Gen Z typically seek to connect with influencers who share their values, interests, and aspirations. These influencers become symbolic figures representing a particular lifestyle that resonates with the audience. This alignment creates a sense of shared social identity, leading followers to believe that influencers reflect their own beliefs and aspirations. For example, influencers who like to wear make-up may attract followers who also love to travel but like to wear make-up but are not proficient at it. Thus, recommendations and endorsements made by influencers are not seen as mere marketing messages, but rather as guidance from people who identify with their identity and preferences. This psychological connection promotes trust and credibility, making Gen Z consumers more receptive to influencers' product recommendations and thus increasing purchase intention. Social media platforms in China prominently display the number of followers, likes, comments and shares an influencer's content has received. Once one sees that their favourite content matches others, this public display of recognition acts as social proof that the influencer's views are endorsed by a large number of peers. This is when Gen Z feels part of a larger community [11]. This sense of security comes from the feeling that one belongs to a social, emotional, or political body, or a community of united emotional bonds.

3.3 Emotional Attachment

Emotional attachment may be understood within the framework of attachment theory, whereby it represents a distinct form of emotional bonding between an individual and a certain objective or entity. Bowlby's definition of attachment includes an enduring psychological connection between individuals, that is, the desire to be close to and connected to the other to whom one is attached. Many researchers have determined that when customers follow influencers, they form emotional relationships with them. Over time, this emotional attachment influences consumers' judgments, decisions and purchasing decisions through experience. This is why marketing often chooses influencers who are attractive, skilled, and have a positive image to promote their products, as this may lead to a deeper emotional connection, which in turn leads to consumers developing an emotional attachment to a brand. Therefore, brands will consider the feelings of Gen Z consumers when choosing influencers, and these feelings will in turn influence Gen Z's purchasing decisions [12].

4.Challenges of Influencer Marketing

4.1 Transparency and credibility

There are some difficulties that arise when doing influencer marketing. Firstly, for Gen Z consumers, they are afraid of being lied to. Since Gen Z makes good use of the internet, Gen Z is more aware of firms' influencer marketing techniques, so consequently, they hold the expectation that both brands and influencers show transparency. They know that influencers are paid by the company and as long as the brand and the influencers are honest about it, they don't mind. However, due to the dividends that come with promoting bandwagons as a method, many influencers do not personally try the product and find it useful before recommending it to consumers, but instead hypocritically memorise the advertisement words required by the brand to lure consumers into placing an order by unscrupulous practices. Often, these disgruntled consumers will take these brands to task via social media. As a result, the brand's reputation will be greatly affected.

4.2 The scandal of influencers

When a brand engages in a partnership with an influencer, this influencer's reputation is fundamentally associated with the inherent worth and reputation that the brand has worked hard to develop. When influencers are caught in scandals or in trouble, consumers are no longer willing to trust following the influencer. Hence product sales suffer, and the brand as a whole is negatively impacted. For example, Li Jiaqi, a very famous and successful Chinese e-commerce anchor, conducts live commerce on Taobao every day. The products he recommends are carefully screened and he personally negotiates the price mechanism with the brands for all the consumers so that they can enjoy affordable prices and high-quality products [13]. In doing so, he has gained the trust of the majority of Chinese consumers. However, in September 2023, he refuted a comment made by a consumer in his live commerce. In the comment, the consumer gave feedback that a 79RMB (around 8.8GBP) eyebrow pencil from a local Chinese brand was too expensive, and after reading the comment, Li Jiaqi said, "Expensive? The price has been the same for so many years. Don't talk nonsense. Sometimes people should look for their own reasons, after so many years, have people worked hard enough." Such comments instantly angered all the consumers in the livestream, who thought Li Jiaqi was standing on the level of a capitalist accusing the bottom consumers of not being able to afford the products he recommended. After the public outcry festered, he quickly issued an apology. However, this apology did not quell the public's anger, and the number of his Weibo followers dropped by about 2 million. Most importantly, the brand's eyebrow pencils were also thrust into the limelight. After the incident, the brand's sales plummeted because people found out that the price per gram of the eyebrow pencil was more than 900RMB, equivalent to the price of 2 grams of gold.

5.Conclusion

As a result, Chinese consumers are beginning to rethink whether Chinese beauty brands are over-promoting the true value of their products. One shopper exposed a 919RMB makeup brush set from the brand as being made of synthetic fibre bristles, which are considered cheap and of poor quality. The revelation garnered more than 240 million views in just a few hours, further fuelling the public's derision of the once-proudly domestic beauty brand. As the incident continued to fester over the following week, the brand eventually issued an official apology, which topped 460 million views within hours. The post said the incident left them "overwhelmed" and said the apology was made "with the utmost sincerity and trepidation." Despite the brand's efforts, the disappointment of consumers has been irreversible. As a demonstration of this, the slightest carelessness in an influencer's comments can cause huge financial damage to a brand. In brief, Chinese social media influencers have exerted a substantial influence on the consumer behaviour of Gen Z. The spread of COVID-19 has accelerated the shift to digital platforms, giving social media influencers a stronger role in shaping consumer behaviour. Gen Z tends to trust influencers due to their approachable image, specialised knowledge and high interactivity. In the process, their need for social identity is also fulfilled while attachment is attached to these influencers. However, this dynamic environment also poses challenges for consumers and brands, such as the risk of influencer scandals and the need for transparency and authenticity. To successfully navigate this environment, companies and influencers need to understand the unique characteristics and preferences of Gen Z in order to design targeted marketing programmes for this generation. Influencer marketing will be more successful if there is maximum scope to ensure content authenticity and gain Gen Z's trust when recommending products. By employing these strategies, companies and marketers can effectively target Gen Z consumers and build long-term brand loyalty and attachment.

References

1. Bagozzi, R. P., Gopinath, M., & Nyer, P. U. (1999). The role of emotions in marketing. Journal of the Academy of Marketing Science, 27(2): 184–206.
2. Bawa, K., & Ghosh, A. (1999). A model of household grocery shopping behavior. Marketing letters, 10: 149-160.
3. Dinh, T. C. T., & Lee, Y. (2022). "I want to be as trendy as influencers"–how "fear of missing out" leads to buying intention for products endorsed by social media influencers. Journal of Research in Interactive Marketing, 16(3): 346-364.
4. Evans, N.J., Phua, J., Lim, J. and Jun, H. (2017). "Disclosing Instagram influencer advertising: the effects of disclosure language on advertising recognition, attitudes, and behavioral intent", Journal of Interactive Advertising, 17(2): 138-149.
5. Goldring, D., & Azab, C. (2021). New rules of social media shopping: Personality differences of U.S. gen Z versus gen X market mavens. Journal of Consumer Behaviour, 20: 884–897.
6. Guan, C., & Li, E. Y. (2021). A note on influencer marketing in social media. International Journal of Internet Marketing and Advertising, 15(2): 124-128.
7. Jin, S. A. A., & Phua, J. (2014). Following celebrities' tweets about brands: The impact of twitter-based electronic word-of-mouth on consumers' source credibility perception, buying intention, and social identification with celebrities. Journal of advertising, 43(2): 181-195.
8. Leung, F. F., Gu, F. F., Li, Y., Zhang, J. Z., & Palmatier, R. W. (2022). Influencer marketing effectiveness. Journal of Marketing, 86(6): 93–115.
9. Ling, A., Subramaniam, T., & Eleena Nordin, N. (2023). A study on factors influencing live streaming shopping among generation Z in Ipoh, Perak. International Journal of Management Studies and Social Science Research, 04(06): 64–74.
10. Lou, C., & Yuan, S. (2019). Influencer Marketing: How Message Value and Credibility Affect Consumer Trust of Branded Content on Social Media. Journal of Interactive Advertising, 19(1): 58–73.
11. Spears, N., & Singh, S. N. (2004). Measuring attitude toward the brand and purchase intentions. Journal of Current Issues & Research in Advertising, 26(2): 53–66.
12. Sun, Y., Wang, R., Cao, D., & Lee, R. (2022). Who are social media influencers for luxury fashion consumption of the Chinese Gen Z? Categorisation and empirical examination. Journal of Fashion Marketing and Management, 26: 603–621.
13. Xu, X., & Pratt, S. (2018). Social media influencers as endorsers to promote travel destinations: an application of self-congruence theory to the Chinese Generation Y. Journal of travel & tourism marketing, 35(7): 958-972.

Analyzing Kylie Cosmetics' Marketing Strategies and Charting its Future Path

Chutong Feng*

Grey College, Durham University, 0191 334 5900, United Kingdom

Abstract. This investigation derives into evaluating the current marketing strategies of Kylie Cosmetic, one of the well-known celebrities originated cosmetic brands started in 2015 and now values over 1.7 billion US dollars. The brand first specialized in selling lipsticks and progressively developed other cosmetic products for expansion. The performances of Kylie Cosmetic are intimately associated with Kylie Jenner, a reality star with over hundred million followers on social media, and its effective use of social media marketing as the main channel of communication. However, Kylie Cosmetics has been gradually outcompeted by its competitors with declining sales while competitors doubled in years. This situation is more noticeable in recent years as the taste and preferences rapidly change in the cosmetic market. This research will explore opportunities and areas for improvement for Kylie Cosmetic to remain competitive in the highly intense cosmetic market by comparing the brand to its several top competitors, especially Fenty Beauty, a cosmetic brand that is highly similar to Kylie Cosmetic.

1.Introduction

Cosmetic/beauty and personal care market in the U.S has grown to reach a market size of USD 91.34 billion in 2023, and is expected to continue expanding to USD 104 billion in 2028. With the huge potential to grow, the market attracts new entrants to enter, including celebrities, which increasingly escalates the level of competitiveness in the beauty market. According to data provided by Trade Algo, a market research platform, over 50 celebrities and influencers, such as tennis prodigy Naomi Osaka and singer Lady Gaga, have launched cosmetic, haircare and skincare brands in only the past three years. Kylie cosmetic, founded by Kylie Jenner, a member of the Kardashian family, had been rated as one of the fastest-growing beauty brands ever as it took less than two years for Kylie to reach an estimated $630million sales since the launch of Kylie's $29 lipsticks in 2015 [1]. Undeniably, the immediate financial returns are intimately associated with her identity as a notable celebrity figure, which gives the brand prior competitive advantages (i.e brand awareness, customer loyalty). With such a high start-out, Kylie cosmetic is projected to rake in $1 billion in lifetime sales by 2022, anticipated by a well-known fashion-industry trade journal, known as the "Bible of fashion".

2.Cosmetic market

Kylie cosmetic started in 2015 by launching the collection of three liquid lipsticks with corresponding lip liners in one ready-to-go kit and followed by introduction of other cosmetic products majoring face, eyes, eyebrows and noses to broaden the product line. The recent new products include matte lip crayons, gloss drip, classic matte palette, high gloss and tinted butter balm. The recent collections are gloss glow, kris collection and birthday collection. Birthday collections, together with holiday collection, valentine collection, Christmas collection and Halloween collection are all annual collection series available yearly, with new design and new product in different years. Besides these regular collections, Kylie cosmetics collaborate and partner with her Kardashian sisters, friends and internationally renowned fashion brands to introduce co-branded products. For instance, Kylie x Kendall, Kris collection, Koko collection, Kourtney collection, Kylie x Jordyn and partnership with Kim's brand KKW. Kylie Cosmetics also partners with luxury clothing brand Balmain to target new customers. These partnerships severely bring exposure and natural attention for Kylie cosmetics in terms of brand awareness. Introducing new products satisfies customer's needs for other cosmetic products to complete their make-up. Kylie Cosmetics' official website includes products for lips, face, eyes and eyebrows with apparently more products in the lips section. Kylie cosmetic introduced a variety of lip related products other than liquid lipsticks, for instance, lipsticks, lip glosses, lip balms, lip blushes, lip shine lacquers, lip crayons, lip liners and lip care to satisfy all different preference and demands of its customers. In comparison, less products are listed under face, eyes and eyebrows. What's noticeable is that Kylie Cosmetics does not provide foundation or any relevant products.

*Corresponding author's mail: chfe2023@cis.edu.sg

2.1 Price

All lips relevant products are priced between $23-$27 dollars, similar to most of its competitors (Perfect Dairy, Huda Beauty) and with more products available as its competitors mostly only provide lipsticks or lipgloss. However, in terms of face, eyes, and eyebrows products, Huda Beauty and Perfect Diary have more options for customers to choose from and offer foundation [2]. Kylie cosmetic adopts product bundle pricing, which a bundle of lips collection is more cost-effective than purchasing only one lipsticks. The original price for the set will be canceled with the discounted price listed beside to assist clients in seeing the difference between the current price and the original pricing, as well as the amount of savings they will receive. For newly signed-up customers, Kylie cosmetic provides discounts for them when they create an account on the official websites - 15% off via using particular code on their next order which incentives newly signed-up customers to place an order to use the discount.

2.2 Promotion

Kylie cosmetic's marketing strategies differ from the traditional marketing strategies by heavily focusing on social media communication and advertising other than traditional promotion methods. With over 4.7 billion social media users, accounting for nearly 60% of the world population, social media have become an essential platform for information exchange and further development of globalization. Kylie Jenner as the fourth most followed account on instagram had successfully converted her popularity into actual sale revenue by possessing competitive advantage over its competitors. Majority of Kylie cosmetics orders are sourced from direct websites selling online. The official website requires customers to first create an account with limited personal information (email and password) needed only. This severely shortens the purchasing process. Acknowledging customer emails enables Kylie Cosmetics to contact new customers for information updates, launching of new products, providing personal discount codes and introducing products. A discount code will be sent to a newly signed-up account with organized product categories available below for customers to directly browse interested products. However, for gmail users, promotional materials will be automatically categorized into the 'promotion' section if not actively opened to check and cause miss of information for customers. Within the eight different social network channels Kylie Cosmetic are on, Instagram solely obtains 63.57% of the social media traffic. This is because thee target audience for Kylie cosmetics is primarily young women who are rapidly updated and notified with the latest fashion and beauty taste. Over 52% of Kylie cosmetics' customers are composed of young and mature females aged between 18 to 34. Similarly, over 60% of instagram users are aged between 18 to 34, reported by statista. With over 27.5 million followers, Kylie cosmetic uses its official account on instagram to soon communicate, engage and update their main targeting customers about new information regarding their brand. Instagram provides bloggers with user-friendly functions, such as instagram stories, highlights, posts and tagged posts. Kylie cosmetics showcase the latest collection using stories and organize stories into highlights that are easier for customers to access while interested. Posts allow the Kylie cosmetic to insert links that direct transfers the users to the official website for further information by shortening the steps till purchase. In addition, the official website posts behind-scene stories and Kylie Jenner herself using all Kylie cosmetics to complete her makeup in order to educate, interest and engage with the customers. Besides, the official account often posts ordinary people trying on their products, using plain folks to showcase that the cosmetic product is of appeal and value to everyone. Apart from using the official account to secure and update the existing customers, Kylie Jenner uses her personal instagram account to promote Kylie cosmetic products whenever a new product or collection is launched to expose the brand to more potential customers. For example, Kylie together with Kendall, sisters in the Kardarshain family, launches a collective collection 'Kylie x Kendall'. With nearly 700M followers collectively, this collection was sold out in nearly eight hours after being introduced. This has been proved successful according to the data provided on statista as over 60% of the cosmetic and beauty users in the U.S are aware of the brand. Kylie Jenner is a key character in the Kardashian family, with over hundred million fans on social media, she solely experiences great social media traffic and attention, so does her sisters. Several collections partnering with other members of the Kardashian family drew lots of public attention on social media via posting to announce the collaboration and free media coverage. For instance, when Kylie first started Kylie cosmetic by introducing the lip kit set, she shared the origin reason for starting the brand - her lack of confidence and insecurity about her lips. The public was previously having a controversial discussion regarding the change in her lips as most people suspect that she had a lip filler surgery to pump up her lips. Kylie introduced the lipkit set during the public discussion and gained significant attention. With Kardashian family members as the main channel to expose Kylie cosmetics to the general social media users, Kylie Cosmetics also collaborated with nano and micro-influencers to build buzz outside of the Kardashian following, particularly among a more diverse audience.

2.3 Place

Kylie Cosmetic is basically operated online via official website as it does not have an offline physical store until March 2023, the first Kylie Cosmetic store opened in Sydney airports. Cosmetic products directly sell through its official website from business to customers without partnering with any e-commerces and retailers such as beauty collection stores. In this way, Kylie Cosmetic directly controls customer shopping experience and its relationship with their customers. However, with limited purchasing channels, potential customers overseas may find it difficult to purchase products from Kylie Cosmetic via its official website [3].

3.Revenue

Despite generating skyrocket sales revenue throughout the years, direct selling through official websites of Kylie cosmetics and Kylie Skin have significantly reduced by almost 80% in the US, so as the sales revenue generated, since the start of 2017, according to the graphical presentation by ecommerceDB. While the sales revenue generated by Fenty Beauty, one of the top competitors of Kylie cosmetics, started by Rihanna, singer with over 150 million followers on instagram had doubled in 2022, stated in the end of year report of LVMH. Reflected by the reduction in sales revenues and amount of online order placed, Kylie cosmetic is gradually outcompeted by its main competitors in the cosmetic market with less purchase made by customers [4].

4.Competitor (SWOT) Analysis

Fenty Beauty is a cosmetic brand that is multidimensionally similar to Kylie Cosmetics in that it was founded by a globally influential celebrity and generates constantly increasing sales revenue yearly. During its first month, Fenty Beauty outsold Kylie Cosmetics by a wide margin. Fenty Beauty is currently valued at roughly $17 billion, while Kylie Cosmetics is valued at $1.2 billion following the acquisition of a controlling share by Coty, Inc. Comparing Kylie Cosmetic to Fenty Beauty allows discoveries for unserved areas, competitiveness and area for improvement in terms of strategies.

4.1 Strengths (Internal):

As the second-highest-selling singer, Rihanna, the originator, has a large and loyal fan base, which will naturally bring public attention to the brand and drive sales. With her contagious and positive image as a singer, fans believe every message given, so her supporters are likely to be converted into brand customers. Fenty Beauty values inclusiveness and diversity. The goal statement of the brand is to include women everywhere. The business has included the theme of diversity into the majority of its ads. With relevant notion widely promoted in the U.S, Fenty Beauty correspond with the general preference in the market. This effective brand message brings the brand more customers aligned with its brand values. Fenty Beauty discovered a gap in the beauty industry: people of colour had long been excluded. They had a difficult time finding a color that suited their skin tone. The business first released its Pro Filt'R foundation in 40 colors to accommodate diverse skin tones, but it quickly expanded the collection to 50 shades. The foundation now comes in 59 different hues. Fenty Beauty's other products also come in a variety of hues. The brand's diverse product line boosts its competitiveness and distinguishes it from other beauty companies, allowing it to win over many consumers, particularly people of color who struggle to find the perfect shade.

4.2 Weaknesses

The goal statement of the brand, "so that women everywhere would be included," highlights women's inclusion. However the male group are left unmentioned in its goal and yet men accounts for around 26% of visits to its websites. Advertisements and marketing campaign fails to communicate with its male customers, which unmatched its brand message of inclusiveness. Another demographic that Fenty Beauty has not served is those who were satisfy with the current shades on the market prior to the brand. Fenty Beauty makes a concerted attempt to live up to its dedication to diversity and inclusion, but it falls short of making its other advantages obvious.

4.3 Opportunities

Fenty Beauty recently collaborates with YouTube, Instagram and TikTok influencers to expose its products to customers out of the fanbase. Gen Z as the brand's top targeting group, tends to "use social media to seek inspiration" while shopping, the brand may explore cooperating with more influencers in the future. After the pandemic, customer's purchasing preference and habitats have alter from pose-covid period as a consequence of economic instability and inflation [5].

4.4 Threats

The present cosmetic market is highly competitive with endless new entrants and competitive rivalry. Other famous celebrities such as Kylie Jenner and Selena Gomez also owns a cosmetic brand and even earns a price advantage as compared to Fenty Beauty. After the introduction of Fenty Beauty, other cosmetic brands such as L'Oreal, Huda Beauty, and Estee Lauder soon caters to the current notion of inclusiveness and diversity by expanding the shade range of their current product. This pose a threat to Fenty Beauty's revenue as it is no longer the only cosmetic brand that offer various foundation shades [6].

5.SWOT Analysis for Kylie Cosmetic

5.1 Strengths

Kylie has a large number of fans on her social media sites. She has nearly 200 million Instagram followers. She uses this platform to show off her cosmetic abilities, clothing, travels, and her daughter Stormi. She engages with her fans and always delivers on their desires. She even has an Instagram account dedicated to her beauty company [6]. She has nearly 25 million followers on her account. Her brand's growth and success are aided by her name and familiarity. She always tweets sneak peaks of her new beauty collections as well as photos of herself wearing her products. Her followers are fascinated by her cosmetics and rituals. In addition, the collaboration with her Kardashian sisters and international fashion brands brings huge exposure of her brands to the public. Kylie Cosmetics started selling a set of lipkit and progressively introduced cosmetic products for other face areas. Kylie Cosmetics provides various types of cosmetic products ranging from lips, face, eyes and eyebrows, especially lips products. Kylie Cosmetics releases over 10 different types of lips products for customers to choose from according to their preferences. In 2023, Kylie Cosmetic introduced innovative functional cosmetic products, such as the new 8 hour wear and lasting color lip formula that serves customers who care about being clean, convenient and quality.

5.2 Weaknesses

Kylie Cosmetic is only available on its own official website and at Sydney Airport. According to Statista market insights, offline purchasing channels occupied over 75% of cosmetic revenues. With limited physical opportunities for potential customers to try-on, the brand is less exposed to the general cosmetic customers. In addition, for customers out of the U.S, especially in Asian countries, shipping and contacting will be even more difficult online, causing a worse-off shopping experience [7].

5.3 Opportunities

Kylie Cosmetic post education makeup tutorials of Kylie Jenner solely or together with the other Kardashian sisters. Kylie cosmetics do collaborate with nano and micro influencers but not other mega influencers or celebrities to expand her clientele. Kylie Cosmetic may organize video filming of Kylie Jenner together with cosmetic mega influencers, with one questioning and one answering. This video format can also respond to the public suspicions that the brand is not professional enough as the originator started it in her seventeens [8].

5.4 Threats

The rapid growth rate of the cosmetic market attracts new entrants and urge existing brands to continuously innovate to remain competitive in the market. In comparison to its top competitors, Kylie cosmetic specialize in introducing lips relevant products but fall short of other cosmetic products such as foundation to satisfy other cosmetic demands of its customers [9]. Other competitors, such as huda beauty, perfect diary, although have lesser lips product range but experience price advantage than Kylie Cosmetic [10].

6.Conclusion

To sum up, Kylie Cosmetics as one of the fast grown beauty brands has a detailed marketing strategy, especially promotion and marketing, it involves and adopt the latest social media marketing, influencer marketing in effective manners to expose and promote the brand to the public. It's official website, one of the two purchasing channels, is constantly upgraded with new techenologies to better serve its customers with awesome and unforgettable online shopping experience that is user-friendly. In addition, the brand connect and engage with every single customers that signed up on its official websites for information update and shopping experience feedback. Besides, with eight social media channels, Kylie Cosmetic get in touches with social media users rapidly and receives customer's feedback for improvements. This also enables that not only its signed-up customers on its official website receives information updates, but also all the social media followers and users. Kylie Jenner, the originator, also regularly post tutorial videos, share her makeup process and notice the public for launching of new products. All those aspects are contributors to the current achievements of Kylie Cosmetic. However, what's concerning is the constant downwarding sales revenue trend since this start of 2017. A major reason analysed via the competitor analysis conducted is its lack of differentiation, effective brand message and quality concern in compared to its top competitor Fenty Beauty. Nevertheless, Kylie Cosmetic do have lots of opportunities to grow by introducing innotive products to cater to customer's needs after the global pandemic, continue expand its product range, develop sustainable responsibilities, and reposition its core brand value to target a broader customer base besides its fans. By satisfying customer needs and discovering unique selling point to differentiate its brand from other competitors, Kylie Cosmetic increases its competitiveness within the intense cosmetic market. With leveled up competitiveness, sales revenues will potentially be increased with the increase in loyal customer base.

References

1. J Cosmet Dermatol. (2021) Changes in purchasing patterns in the beauty market due to Post–COVID-19. Literature review, 34: 492.
2. Similarweb. (2023) kyliecosmetics. https://www.similarweb.com/website/kyliecosmetics.com/#overview
3. Statista Dominique Petruzzi. (2023) Cosmetics industry in the U.S. - statistics & facts. https://www.statista.com/topics/1008/cosmetics-industry/#topicOverview
4. EcommerceDB, (2023) eCommerce net sales development of kyliecosmetics.com. https://ecommercedb.com/store/kyliecosmetics.com

5. Statista Alexander Kunst. (2023) Kylie Cosmetics brand awareness, usage, popularity, loyalty, and buzz among cosmetics and make-up users in the United States in 2022. https://www.statista.com/forecasts/1340107/kylie-cosmetics-cosmetics-and-make-up-brand-profile-in-the-united-states
6. Xu, X. (2023) Influencer Marketing with Social Platforms: Increasing Brand Awareness and User Engagement. Journal of Education, Humanities and Social Sciences, 19: 228–234.
7. Höfer, L.(2021) The Impact of Social Media Marketing on Customers' Purchasing Intention in the Cosmetics Industry, Journal of Module university, 21: 1 - 64.
8. Yifei Yang, (2023) Analysis the influence of "web celebrity" phenomenon on young consumer's perception in the perspective of new media -- taking cosmetic industry as example. Journal of Humanities, 56:204.
9. Voyado Elevate. (2023) How is Generation Z shopping? https://www.apptus.com/blog/generation-z-online-shopping-habits/
10. Rahmani, Devani Alisyia. (2019) The advertisement language in persuasive captions of jeffreestar cosmetics and kylie cosmetics instagram accounts. Digital Library. 45: 1-9.

Sam's Club Current Situation Analysis and Recommendation in China

Ruiyi Deng*

International College, Beijing University of Agriculture, Beijing, 100028, China

Abstract. With the development of China's economy, retail and warehousing have a very objective market. As Sam's club, which has been deeply engaged in China for many years, this will be a good opportunity. However, competition in China's retail market is still fierce. Today, China's local retail enterprises have fired the first shot in the price war against Sam. This paper uses economic knowledge to analyze the market situation of Sam's club in China, including but not limited to swot, pestle and market positioning analysis. Through the analysis of economics, this paper clarifies the advantages and disadvantages of Sam in the principality market. In addition, it also clearly pointed out the challenges and opportunities faced by Sam's Club in China. In the case that competitors have started to compete in the price war, this paper gives suggestions that are more in line with China's national conditions. This will greatly help Sam's Club to understand China's national conditions and develop new market strategies.

1.Introduction

Sam's Club is a large warehouse membership store in the world. It is a member store of Walmart. It has more than 800 stores in the world. The first store opened in Midwest, Oklahoma in April 1983. Sam has a history of nearly 40 years. On August 12, 1996, the first Sam's Club opened in Shenzhen. At present, Sam's has opened several stores in China, which are located in Beijing, Shanghai, Shenzhen, Guangzhou, Fuzhou, Dalian, Hangzhou, Suzhou, Wuhan, Changzhou, Zhuhai, Tianjin, Xiamen, Nanjing, Changsha, Nanchang, Chengdu, Shenyang, Nantong, Ningbo, Kunshan, Chongqing and Huizhou. In recent years, Sam's Club has become the "Internet celebrity place" where many people come to check in. As the "number one player" of China's paid members-only retail, and a supermarket mainly providing high-quality goods, Sam's has a complete set of members-only business model. Zhu Xiaojing, president and CEO of Walmart China, once said in an interview, "Sam's success is not because it is a member store, nor because it charges membership fees. Good at forward-looking insight into consumer needs; Focus on How to serve consumers better and more effectively than others."

2.Marketing Analyze

2.1 Market Segmentation

Sam's Club is a high-end members-only store owned by Walmart in the United States. The competitive response is not necessarily to lower prices, as segmentation patterns of brand loyalty and price-sensitive consumers suggest that in some cases existing consumers can raise prices in response to low-cost consumers [1]. Therefore, its target market is the middle class. Through the paid membership system of behavioral standards, Sam selects accurate high net worth customers. With the rise of the middle class in consumption upgrading, more and more urban new middle class pursue a better quality of life, and "high quality" has become the primary consideration for these people when shopping. Therefore, Sam takes advantage of Walmart's global sourcing characteristics, ensuring high quality through selection while lowering prices. At the same time, the warehousing model gives the middle class a clean and pleasant shopping experience [2].

2.2 Target Market

Since there are many supermarkets in the middle class, Sam's large-scale purchase method not only reduces the purchase cost, but also transforms Sam's target market into families. The binding of the main and secondary cards also helps the family to shop. In addition, Sam is mostly in the supermarket, so it is necessary to drive to go shopping, which is also the reason why Sam decided to target the couples in the family. Couples can bring children and seniors to experience free tastings, while cheap roast chicken and croissants also increase the stickiness of customers.

2.3 Market Positioning

The advantages of Sam's Club over domestic supermarkets are differentiated products, services and

*Corresponding author's mail: 202021011052@bua.edu.cn

quality. The number of SKUs in traditional supermarkets is generally about 30,000. In order to meet the needs of middle-class families, Sam controls the number of SKUs at about 4000 all the year round, which strictly controls the quality of goods. The core secret: the single-item strategy. Provide members with a limited number of items that are most popular with them. [3] In addition, if a product has many identical products in the market, it will also be replaced unless Sam can upgrade the quality of the product to be differentiated or provide more competitive products. This means that Sam's advantage lies in the distinctive single products, a large number of packaging, as well as preferential prices and high quality.

3.Pestle Analysis

3.1 Political Environment

Sam's Club, a high-end members-only store owned by the US company Walmart, was banned from importing goods from Xinjiang on December 24, 2021, after it removed Xinjiang products from its shelves and the US signed the Uyghgur Forced Labor Prevention Act, which banned US companies from importing goods from Xinjiang. Especially tomato, cotton, polysilicon and so on. This has led to a great deal of discontent among Chinese consumers, with many customers demanding refunds. According to the 2021 White Paper on American Business in China, China, as the world's largest and fastest growing market, is a strong attraction for American companies, mainly due to the huge size and potential growth of the Chinese market. [4] The US 'heterodoxy and political interference in China's national conditions have triggered tensions in Sino-US relations, which will be the biggest challenge for US companies operating in China. The most fatal thing is that Sam, as an American company, did not understand China's importance to the "One China" principle. In this storm, Sam's Club only gave an explanation: "The goods from Xinjiang are out of stock, and they will be put back on the shelves when they are available." As for members' card return requirements, some offline physical stores even indicate that "once the card is returned, it will not be allowed to handle it in the future" unreasonable warning. In recent years, due to the impact of the epidemic, the competition among middle class supermarkets is very fierce, and Sam's Club is accelerating its expansion. Such treatment will cause Sam's Club to have serious negative public opinion and its reputation will be questioned.

3.2 Economic Environment

The improvement of economic level directly drives the improvement of residents' consumption power. In 2015, the retail sales of consumer goods in China reached 30,093.1 billion yuan, and in 2019, the total retail sales of consumer goods reached 3,809.87 billion yuan, with an average annual growth rate of about 10%. In 2020, due to the impact of COVID-19 in various industries, the total retail sales of consumer goods fell to 39,198.1 billion yuan. [5] During the continuous COVID-19 pandemic, the global economy has been hit hard, and only China has bucked the trend and is the only major economy to achieve positive growth. This is undoubtedly a good signal for Sam, who is rooted in China. Retail has great market potential, and the middle class, as the main force of consumption, can still play an excellent role during the pandemic. This shows that Sam's target market is very popular, and the economic environment is very strong. According to the Research Report on the Development Status and Consumption Behavior of China's Warehouse Member Supermarkets Industry in 2021-2022, 58.4% of consumers know and have been to warehouse member supermarkets, more than 80% of consumers in first-tier, new first-tier and second-tier cities are willing to apply for membership cards, and nearly 80% of consumers in third-tier cities are willing to apply for membership cards.[6] In 2021, the market size of the warehouse member supermarket industry will reach 30.43 billion yuan, with a year-on-year growth of 12.3%; In 2022, the market size of China's warehouse member supermarket industry is expected to reach 33.50 billion yuan, with a year-on-year growth of 10.1%. It can be said that such an economic situation is the breeding ground for warehouse membership stores. In the warehouse member stores, Sam's reputation and service quality in China are much better than those of other competitors. Since the opening of the first Sam's Club in Shenzhen in 1996, it has been operating in mainland China for 26 years. Currently, Sam's has 27 stores in mainland China. Compared with other warehouse member stores, Sam's Club has been open for the longest time in mainland China, and its membership system is relatively mature and stable. According to the Survey Report on Consumption Driving Force of Sam's Club, in terms of purchasing intention of middle and high-end consumers in China, product quality has become the first choice for consumers to purchase.

3.3 Social Environment

With China's rapid economic growth relative to other countries and huge consumer population, this has become a huge attraction for foreign department retailers, which have already saturated their domestic demand. The first to occupy the territory, the first to have a fixed consumer group, is to seize the opportunity. Ellickson argues that grocery stores compete by offering more variety, which requires investing in distribution centers and improving quality by raising fixed costs rather than marginal costs. With the post-80s, post-90s and post-00s becoming the main purchasing power, this sentence has been confirmed. With the influx of a large number of Internet marketing information, the excellent quality of Sam's Club stores has been promoted and the popularity of "punching in" Sam shopping, Sam's sales have reached their peak. Sam's member stores have already opened 37 stores in 23 cities in China, with six more to open in the second half of 2023.[7] For Sam's own brand Member's Mark, Sam's roast chicken, hemp potato and durian thousand layers have all become must-buy products. For example, the jujube clay cake that has been sold in the store for more than ten years, and 25,000 Sam's homemade steamed buns are sold every day. Data shows that 60 percent of Sam's Club sales come from the food section. As the trend of clocking fades, the excellent quality of other products has left huge customers.

3.4 Technical Environment

With the increasing emphasis on fresh food and the improvement of the DC system, Walmart has gradually implemented and improved the warehouse distribution system, that is, the order data of the store directly reaches the DC, and the goods of each supplier are also sent to the DC according to the requirements, and the DC completes the distribution. This improves the accuracy of goods arriving in stores and completes Walmart's digital control of fresh goods. [8] Through the connection between the cold chain distribution end and the store data system, the whole process data monitoring of fresh goods is finally realized. From suppliers, to DC, to logistics, and finally to store sales, the whole flow process is recorded in the form of data. That is to say, the warehousing, transportation, sales and loss of a single commodity can be completely analyzed and predicted. The moving selling speed of a single product, the response speed of suppliers, the loss of each link, etc., can finally be turned into digital reports and trend analysis to help the operation department make decisions quickly and further improve human efficiency. At the same time, in recent years, data, VR technology, AI robot, face recognition and other technical means have been improved, which makes the logistics and online sales of goods have been improved iteratively. The Development Report of China's Department Store Retail Industry 2021-2022 shows that the top 85.4% of enterprises have launched online business. Naturally, Sam's Club did not miss out, giving full play to its logistics advantages and bringing excellent experience to users through 2h extremely fast delivery.

3.5 Law Environment

In September 2006, the Law Governing the Promotion Behavior of Retailers was promulgated. It stipulates that any retailer selling in China must follow the rules. So far, the state has repeatedly issued supportive policies for new retail and e-commerce. In 2021, the "14th Five-Year Plan" e-commerce development Plan said: by 2025, China's high-quality development of e-commerce has achieved remarkable results. New forms and models of e-commerce have flourished, the core competitiveness of enterprises has been greatly enhanced, and online retail has continued to lead consumption growth. A high-quality digital lifestyle has basically taken shape. By 2035, e-commerce will become an important driving force for the sharp rise of China's economic strength, scientific and technological strength and comprehensive national strength. This means that in these four years, Sam's development will be supported by policies, which will be a good signal.[9]

4.Swot Analyze

In this paper, by comparing Hema Fresh with Sam's Club, which chooses the middle class as its target market in China, the dilemma of Sam's Club and its future development direction are analyzed.

4.1 Strengthen

Sam's Club has the largest number of stores, with 27. Among them, Beijing and Suzhou have three stores each, which are the cities with the largest number of stores; Shanghai, Ningbo and Shenzhen have two each. Although the first store opened late, Hemaseng already has seven stores in China, including four in Shanghai and one each in Suzhou, Nanjing and Beijing. However, in terms of geographical location, Sam's Club has obvious geographical advantages. Sam's Club has formed a pattern with Beijing, Shanghai and Shenzhen as the core, radiating to the three northeastern provinces in the north, radiating to the Guangdong-Hong Kong-Macao Greater Bay Area in the south, and continuously extending inland through major provincial capitals. Although Hema has chosen Shanghai and Suzhou with high income and price, Sam has already seized the market earlier. The membership system increases the loyalty of customers, and the prepaid consumption mode determines the strong loyalty of customers. Even with the attraction of other factors, it is difficult to change the consumption location of fixed customer groups [10].

4.2 Weakness

Backed by Alibaba's resources, Hema Fresh can accurately select the most popular categories, brands and single products through big data, so it has a great advantage in consumer demand. Moreover, Hema X's product replacement rate is significantly higher than that of Sam's Club and Costco. In terms of product packaging, specifications and selection, because it is a local enterprise, the products sold by Hema X are more in line with the purchasing habits and demands of Chinese consumers.[11] However, Sam's Club is at a disadvantage in localization, with only one or two products with the highest cost performance in each category, which is not in line with Chinese consumption habits. At the same time, although the unit price for large packaged goods is lower, it can save money for members. However, in China, where shopping malls have a high coverage rate, large packages of goods are very difficult for families with only two or three members. Take Shanghai as an example. According to the data of the seventh population census of Shanghai in 2021, more than 60% of households in Shanghai are 2 or 3 people, and the average number of people in each household is 2.32. Such market positioning largely limits the sales [12].

4.3 Opportunities

One of Sam's characteristics is to vigorously develop its own brands, which is also an important source of its profits. By eliminating intermediaries such as distributors and agents, warehouse member stores can take goods directly from manufacturers, so profits are higher. Among the more than 3,000 kinds of SKUs in Sam's Club, more than 700 kinds of SKUs are owned by private brands, accounting for 23% of the number, but accounting for 30% of the sales. This is Sam's advantage point. The private brand of Hema fresh is not only sold in Hema fresh, but also sold in other formats of Hema fresh and Hema MINI, so it is not possible to form the stickiness of consumers to hema fresh through the private brand. This will be the strongest card for Sam to compete in the middle market, while the high profit of its own brand can maintain Sam's popular products to attract customers at a low price. Take Member's Mark imported beef, which has always been highly sought after, as an example. Due to the limitations of cutting technology and transportation, such high-end steaks are very rare in the channels of ordinary supermarkets. Sam not only delivers the steaks to the store with full temperature control through the self-built transnational cold chain system; It can also bring breakthrough price advantages with strong bargaining power. Sam also builds multi-channel shopping methods according to different consumption scenarios. People have continuously upgraded offline stores and created interactive areas such as Sam's Restaurant Bar, Sam's Kitchen, health management center and Sam's Cloud Home to create more inspiration for members' lifestyle, which are very rare among other competitors. At the same time, Sam vigorously develops its e-commerce business, develops its mobile App "Sam's Club Store", and provides delivery services including "one-hour fast delivery", to meet the immediate needs of members when they are unable to reach the store. In addition, Sam App delivery scope covers most parts of the country [13].

4.4 Threat

On August 1, 2023, Hema took the lead in pricing Sam's best-selling durian thousand-layer cake at 99 yuan, 30 yuan cheaper than Sam. Sam countered by lowering the price to 98.9 yuan. On August 8, Hema's fresh durian cake was priced at 89 yuan, but Sam still fought. With several price cuts, Hema fresh hit the "moving mountain price" label. As a Chinese local enterprise, it uses the classical story of Chinese tradition. Every Chinese knows the spirit of Yugu moving mountains. Subsequently, a series of fresh with the price of moving mountain discount, hema fresh harvest a party praise.

After this battle, Sam's Club's crisis emerged. The overlap rate between Hema and Sam's users reached 43.1%, which means that nearly half of Sam's users also installed Hema, and the two users overlapped highly. If the brand is not localized enough, it will be at a disadvantage in front of the marketing of Chinese feelings relying on the Internet. [14] At the same time, the competition for the middle class has become a bidding war. In 2022, more than 680 traditional supermarkets will close their doors, including once-famous retailers like Aeon, Yonghui and Carrefour. But one trend is that the market size of warehouse membership supermarkets in China has grown by 10.1%. In the face of such a huge market and severe competition, Sam's Club faces challenges. [15] At the same time, as Sam chooses more suburbs, if there is not enough passenger flow support, the terrible vacancy rate will be Sam's primary enemy.

5.Conclusion

Based on pestle's market analysis, this paper argues that China's cultural and political ideas should be respected and the one-China principle should be adhered to. On November 17, 2018, the Italian luxury brand Dolce & Gabbana released a video involving insults to China, and its designer apologized without regret. Although they believe that the Chinese people will forget the incident, according to the company's financial report of the same year, in 2019 alone, Dolce & Gabbana reported a profit of 156 million euros, 16 million euros lower than the previous year, due to the impact of greater China. Dolce & Gabbana's sales in China continued to decline from 2020, and it almost lost the country's entire luxury market. Therefore, as an American enterprise, how to balance Chinese culture is a very important part. Only by respecting customers can we bring profits. In the Swot analysis, Sam's Club still has some difficulties in the competition with Hema Fresh. Although Hema Fresh has deeply cultivated Chinese culture and introduced many products that meet the needs of Chinese people. However, there is still a great shortage of seasonal fruits and vegetables. If we can open up channels to purchase fresh Chinese food materials such as lotus seeds and water chestnut, it will be more popular. Walmart can take advantage of global procurement to ensure the freshness of food ingredients to the greatest extent. In addition to launching specialty products, in order to compete for middle-class customers, it can also start from a new track. Price is not the only criterion. Sam's Club already has food, flowers and other areas, which can carefully select several kinds of food in the dining bar. Building a multi-functional area can also be Sam's selling point. It is not easy to eat, drink and play in the warehouse supermarket. Sam chose to go to the suburbs more, which is not in line with the shopping habits of Chinese people. People do not want to go there just for shopping. Especially for the intermediary class, membership fees are not what guarantee customer loyalty. Remoteness is a big pain point, which is why there is a high degree of overlap with Hema users. Willing customers to buy, especially with a family, to eat and play will be Sam's focus. More importantly, with the development of the Internet today, Sam's Club should also promote itself more through social media influencers. Loyal users will have a chance to speak up for the brand only if more of them are promoted on social media.

References

1. Frank, Richard G. and David S. Salkever. (1992). "Pricing, Patent Loss and the Market for Pharmaceuticals." Southern Economic Journal 59(2): 165-179.
2. Cascio W F. (2006) Costco to Wal-Mart's Sam's club. Academy of Management perspectives, 20(3): 26-37.
3. Courtemanche C, Carden A. (2014) Competing with Costco and Sam's Club: Warehouse club entry and grocery prices[J]. Southern Economic Journal, 80(3): 565-585.
4. Anon (2023) 'You've Got to Set Your People Up to Succeed' An interview with Tim Simmons, chief product officer of Sam's Club. Vol. 101. WATERTOWN: Harvard Business School Publishing Corporation.
5. Zhou Qi. (2023) Analysis of Sam's Club Store Operation Mode under the background of new retail. Trade Show Economics, 6: 92-94.
6. Gandara, M. (2020) Sam's Club store during COVID-19.
7. McGaw, J. (2019) Sam's Club testing program to reduce members' health care costs. Central Penn Business Journal.
8. Bai P H. (2019) Walmart increases "fresh". Times Economics and Trade, 22: 101-102.
9. Anon (2014) Sam's Club. 31 (19), 83–.
10. He Liyin. (2014) The multi-dimensional stickiness of Sam's Club. New Marketing, 11: 36-39.
11. Courtemanche, C. & Carden, A. (2014) Competing with Costco and Sam's Club: Warehouse Club Entry and Grocery Prices. Southern economic journal. [Online] 80 (3), 565–585.
12. Du Weiwei, Liu Wensheng. (2023) SWOT analysis of Warehouse member stores: Based on the comparison of Sam's, Costco's and Hema's X member stores. China Business Theory, 8: 62-64.
13. Grabowski, Henry and John Vernon (1992). "Brand Loyalty, Entry, and Price Competition in Pharmaceuticals after the 1984 Drug Act," Journal of Law and Economics, 35: 331-350.
14. LU X Y. (2021) Research on the development of paid membership system in retail industry under new retail: Taking Sam's Club as an example. Modern Marketing: Next, 6: 78-79.
15. Tu Yanling. (2006) Discussion on the current Implementation status and improvement Scheme of local Membership System. Science and Technology Information, 03: 87-91.

How Social Media Marketing Impacts Darry Ring (DR)

Hongyu Yu*

Shanghai Weiyu Highschool, Shanghai, 200126, China

Abstract. This essay analyzes to what extent does social media marketings the profit model, competitive advantage, target audience, product, and social media strategy of Darry Ring (DR), a Chinese jewelry brand that specializes in engagement and wedding rings. DR claims to be the world's first brand that requires ID verification before purchasing a ring, and limits each customer to buy only one ring in their lifetime. DR's slogan is "One True Love in a Lifetime", and its mission statement is to promote the value of true love and commitment in the modern society. The essay shows that social media marketing helps DR to enhance its brand image, increase its brand awareness, and retain its customers. Social media marketing also helps DR to differentiate itself from other jewelry brands, and to create a loyal community of true love advocates. The essay concludes that social media marketing has a significant impact on DR's business performance and success.

1.Introduction

DR (Darry Ring) is a Chinese jewelry brand that specializes in engagement and wedding rings. It claims to be the world's first brand that requires ID verification before purchasing a ring, and limits each customer to buy only one ring in their lifetime. DR's slogan is "One True Love in a Lifetime", and its mission is to promote the value of true love and commitment in the modern society.[1] DR has expanded its market to several countries, including the United States, France, Japan, and Vietnam. Social media marketing is one of the key strategies that DR uses to communicate with its target audience, build its brand image, and increase its sales. This essay will analyze how social media marketing affects DR's profit model, competitive advantage, target audience, product, and social media strategy. Darry Ring (DR) has embarked on an ambitious journey, extending its market reach across multiple countries, including the United States, France, Japan, and Vietnam. In this global expansion effort, social media marketing stands out as a pivotal strategy through which DR connects with its target audience, cultivates its brand image, and bolsters its sales figures. This essay aims to delve into the profound impact of social media marketing on DR's profit model, competitive edge, target demographics, product portfolio, and overall social media strategy. First and foremost, DR's adoption of social media marketing has ushered in substantial changes in its profit model. By leveraging platforms like Facebook, Instagram, Twitter, and more, the company can engage directly with potential customers. This engagement often translates into increased conversion rates, as social media provides a convenient channel for customers to inquire about DR's products, place orders, and share their experiences. The result is a boost in sales and profitability for the company, exemplifying the transformative power of social media marketing. Furthermore, DR's commitment to social media has amplified its competitive advantage. In a saturated market, standing out is essential, and an active and well-crafted social media presence is a formidable asset. DR's regular posting of high-quality images and content showcasing their exquisite jewelry has not only attracted more followers but also positioned the brand as a trendsetter in the jewelry industry. This distinctive image helps DR maintain an edge over competitors by fostering brand loyalty and attracting a discerning clientele. In terms of target demographics, social media marketing allows DR to refine its approach and tailor content to specific audiences. Through data analytics and insights garnered from these platforms, the company can better understand the preferences, habits, and demographics of its followers. Armed with this information, DR can create content and products that resonate with its target audience, thereby strengthening its market position and customer base. DR's product portfolio has also evolved with the aid of social media marketing. By actively listening to customer feedback and monitoring social media conversations, the company can adapt its offerings to meet changing consumer demands. This adaptability ensures that DR remains relevant in a dynamic marketplace and continues to introduce products that captivate its audience. Finally, DR's social media strategy itself has undergone refinements over time. Regularly analyzing engagement metrics, tracking the success of different content types, and experimenting with new approaches allows the company to fine-tune its strategy for optimal results. This continuous improvement ensures that DR remains agile and responsive to the ever-evolving landscape of social media platforms.

In conclusion, social media marketing has proven to be a linchpin in Darry Ring's expansion and success on

*Corresponding author: agraytfk84981@student.napavalley.edu

the global stage. Its influence extends to DR's profit model, competitive prowess, target demographics, product development, and social media strategy. By harnessing the power of social media, DR has not only connected with a vast and diverse audience but has also positioned itself as a dynamic and innovative leader in the jewelry industry.

2.Profit model

DR's profit model is based on selling high-quality diamond rings at a premium price. According to its official website [2], the average price of a DR ring is about $2,000, which is higher than the average price of a diamond ring in the US market ($1,500). DR's profit margin is also higher than the industry average (10%), as it claims to use only natural diamonds with GIA and NGTC certificates [3]. DR's profit model relies on creating a strong brand identity and reputation that can justify its high price and attract loyal customers. Social media marketing plays a vital role in achieving this goal, as it allows DR to showcase its unique value proposition, share its customer testimonials and love stories, and interact with its potential and existing customers. Social media marketing also helps DR to reduce its advertising costs, as it can leverage the power of word-of-mouth and user-generated content to spread its brand awareness and influence. The company's financial statement has been strong due to their effective branding and promotion strategy. The revenue reaches 1.5 billion RMB in 2018, 1.665 billion RMB in 2019, 2.464 billion RMB in 2020. The gross profit is 273 million RMB in 2018, 264 million RMB in 2019, 563 million RMB in 2020. Compared with other jewelry brands like "I Do", DR is a lot more profitable than competitors. However, comparing their annual reports year to year, the trend is not looking good. [4,5] The profitability has been decreasing since 2021. Also, the public's opinion on the brand has been worsening. Here quotes a comment by a popular account: "DR isn't selling true love, they are selling true stupidity."[6] It's clear that DR needs to transform their social media marketing strategy, and they are doing so currently. They have already created content-making accounts on Xiaohongshu, a newly emerging social media platform in China, and gained more than 200000 fans and 1000000 likes now [7].

3.Competitive advantages

DR's competitive advantage lies in its differentiation strategy, which focuses on creating a distinctive brand image and offering a unique customer experience. DR differentiates itself from other jewelry brands by emphasizing its true love verification system, which requires customers to provide their ID and personal photo before buying a ring [3]. This system is designed to ensure that customers are serious about their relationship and commitment, and that they will not buy another ring from DR for another person. DR also differentiates itself by providing personalized design service from its Paris design center, which creates limited edition rings that reflect the romance of Paris [2]. Furthermore, DR differentiates itself by providing a true love agreement, which is a handwritten document that expresses the couple's promise to each other and their commitment to work together for a better world [8]. Social media marketing enhances DR's competitive advantage by highlighting these features and benefits, and by creating a sense of exclusivity and community among its customers. Social media marketing also allows DR to monitor its competitors' activities and strategies, and to respond quickly to any changes or threats in the market.

4.Target audience

DR's target audience is mainly young urban professionals who value true love and marriage, and who are willing to pay a high price for a quality product. According to a report by McKinsey & Company, China's urban middle class is expected to grow from 430 million in 2020 to 780 million in 2025, representing 55% of the total population. This segment has a high disposable income, a strong desire for consumption, and a preference for premium brands. DR's target audience also includes overseas Chinese who live in countries where DR has established its presence, such as the US, France, Japan, and Vietnam. These customers share similar cultural values and aspirations with their counterparts in China, and they are also influenced by the local trends and preferences. Social media marketing helps DR to reach and engage with its target audience effectively, as it can use different platforms and channels to cater to their needs and interests. In today's interconnected world, businesses are constantly seeking innovative ways to connect with their customers on a global scale. One such approach is leveraging the power of social media marketing. DR, as a forward-thinking company, has recognized the immense potential of this strategy in bridging the communication gap with its diverse customer base in different regions of the world. In the vast landscape of social media platforms, DR has strategically chosen to utilize WeChat and Weibo to engage with its Chinese customers. WeChat, often referred to as China's "app for everything," serves as a versatile communication channel. DR uses it not only for disseminating product information but also for building a sense of community among its Chinese clientele. Weibo, a microblogging platform, provides a platform for DR to share real-time updates and engage in conversations with its Chinese audience, thereby enhancing brand loyalty. [9] For the American market, DR has harnessed the power of Facebook and Instagram. Facebook, with its extensive user base, allows the company to target a wide range of demographics and interests. Instagram, known for its visually appealing content, enables DR to showcase its products in an aesthetically pleasing manner. Through these platforms, DR can tailor its marketing messages to resonate with the specific preferences and behaviors of its US customers. In the Japanese market, where cultural nuances and preferences play a significant role, DR has established its presence on Line and Twitter. Line is immensely popular in Japan and offers features such as stickers and personalized communication, allowing DR to establish a more intimate connection with its Japanese customers. Twitter, on the other hand, facilitates real-time interactions and feedback, enabling DR to stay attuned to the dynamic Japanese market. In Vietnam, DR has embraced Zalo and TikTok as its preferred social media channels. Zalo is a messaging app that dominates the Vietnamese market and offers a seamless platform for customer engagement. TikTok, known for its short-form videos, allows DR to tap into the creativity of its Vietnamese customers and create viral marketing campaigns that resonate with the local culture. One of the key advantages of social media marketing is its ability to segment the target audience effectively. DR leverages this feature to tailor its messages and offers based on demographics, psychographics, behavior, and location. By analyzing user data and preferences, DR can create highly personalized content that speaks directly to the needs and desires of its customers in each market. In conclusion, DR's strategic use of various social media platforms has allowed it to foster meaningful connections with its customers around the world. Whether in China, the United States, Japan, or Vietnam, the company adapts its communication approach to align with the unique characteristics and preferences of each market. Through social media marketing, DR not only communicates with its customers but also builds lasting relationships that drive brand loyalty and business success. This global outreach strategy exemplifies the importance of embracing the digital age to connect with a diverse and dynamic customer base.

5.Product

DR's product is mainly engagement and wedding rings made of natural diamonds. DR offers various collections of rings that suit different tastes and occasions. [4] For example, it has the Love Mark collection that features classic solitaire rings with six-prong or four-prong settings, the Love Palace collection that features round solitaire rings with pavé settings, the Heart collection that features heart-shaped rings with halo or twisted settings, and the Just You collection that features round side-stone rings with star or sky themes. DR also offers limited edition rings that are designed by its Paris design center, such as the Believe Promise ring that features a round halo ring with a cross-shaped band, and the My Heart Halo ring that features a round halo ring with a heart-shaped band. DR's product is influenced by social media marketing in several ways. First, social media marketing helps DR to collect customer feedback and insights, which can be used to improve its product quality and design. Second, social media marketing helps DR to showcase its product features and benefits, and to demonstrate its product value and quality. Third, social media marketing helps DR to create a buzz and excitement around its product launches and promotions, and to generate word-of-mouth and referrals.

6.Social media marketing strategy

DR's social media strategy is based on four main objectives [5]: awareness, engagement, conversion, and loyalty. To achieve these objectives, DR uses a variety of social media platforms and tools, such as blogs, videos, live streams, podcasts, webinars, e-books, infographics, quizzes, surveys, contests, coupons, hashtags, influencers, and user-generated content. DR's social media strategy follows a four-step process: listen, create, communicate, and measure. In the listening stage, DR monitors the social media conversations and sentiments about its brand, product, competitors, industry, and target audience. It uses tools such as Hootsuite, Sprout Social, and Brandwatch to track and analyze the relevant keywords, hashtags, mentions, reviews, ratings, and trends. In the creation stage, DR produces and publishes high-quality and relevant content that showcases its brand story, value proposition, product features and benefits, customer testimonials and love stories, and social responsibility initiatives. It uses tools such as Canva, Adobe Spark, and Animoto to create attractive and engaging visuals, such as images, videos, animations, and slideshows. In the communication stage, DR interacts with its target audience on various social media platforms and channels. It uses tools such as Buffer, CoSchedule, and Loomly to schedule and manage its posts and campaigns. It also uses tools such as Mailchimp, HubSpot, and ActiveCampaign to send personalized emails and newsletters to its subscribers and customers. In the measurement stage, DR evaluates the performance and effectiveness of its social media marketing activities. It uses tools such as Google Analytics, Facebook Insights, and Instagram Insights to measure the key metrics and indicators, such as reach, impressions, clicks, likes, comments, shares, views, followers, leads, conversions, sales, and ROI. Social media marketing has a significant impact on DR's brand awareness, reputation, customer engagement, and sales performance. According to a report by Kantar Group [6], DR ranked first among all jewelry brands in China in terms of brand power index, which measures consumers' familiarity, favorability, and loyalty to a brand. DR also ranked second in terms of brand value, which reflects the financial potential of a brand based on its market share, growth rate, and profitability. The report attributed DR's success to its effective use of social media to create emotional connections with consumers and differentiate itself from other jewelry brands. Social media marketing also helps DR to reach and attract its target audience, which is mainly composed of young, urban, affluent, and educated men who are looking for a unique and meaningful way to express their love and commitment. By posting content that resonates with this group's values, aspirations, and preferences, DR can influence their purchase decisions and increase their willingness to pay a premium price for its products. For example, DR often posts stories that emphasize the importance of true love, fidelity, and marriage, as well as the challenges and joys of proposing and getting married. [10] Nevertheless, social media marketing enables DR to interact and communicate with its customers and potential customers more directly and frequently. By responding to comments, questions, feedbacks, and complaints on social media platforms, DR can enhance its customer service quality, satisfaction, and retention. By encouraging customers to share their own stories and experiences with the brand on social media platforms, DR can generate positive word-of-mouth referrals, testimonials, and reviews that can boost its credibility and trustworthiness. By launching campaigns, contests, events, and promotions on social media platforms, DR can stimulate customer participation, involvement, and loyalty. By analyzing data and insights from social media platforms, DR can monitor customer behavior, preferences, trends, and feedbacks more closely and accurately.

7.Conclusion

Over the years, DR has been reinforcing its brand image of "true love" by various marketing strategies, including social media marketing strategy. One of the most significant success is the "One true love in a Lifetime" marketing campaign, which demonstrated DR's market position in the Jewelry industry and the brand image of "each male customer can only purchase one engagement ring in his lifetime". During this process, social media marketing played an important role. Social media marketing has a significant impact on DR's profit model, competitive advantage, target audience, product, and social media strategy. Social media marketing helps DR to build its brand image, increase its brand awareness, engage with its target audience, sell its product, and retain its customers. Social media marketing also helps DR to differentiate itself from other jewelry brands, and to create a loyal community of true love advocates. DR's social media marketing strategy is based on four main objectives: awareness, engagement, conversion, and loyalty. DR uses a variety of social media platforms and tools to achieve these objectives, and follows a four-step process: listen, create, communicate, and measure. For DR, social media marketing has laid a great foundation of brand recognition and customer loyalty. Now what they need to do with social media is to transform their original marketing strategy from maintaining the status to try and attract more Gen-Z customers on short video platforms like Tiktok, Xiaohongshu and Weibo. Currently, it can been seen that DR has started its transformation. They have reduced their interactions with the audience in traditional social media platforms like Weibo and Wechat. Ever since the beginning of 2021, they have been inviting content creators on Xiaohongshu for promotion of their products instead of posting contents on Weibo. However, it can't be 100% guaranteed that this will succeed since the change just begun. Only time will tell the effectiveness of doing so.

References

1. Tang, Jinshen, Si Chen. (2015) The Future Improvement of Darry Ring and its" only" Marketing Strategy." Journal of marketing strategy, 23: 439.
2. Darry Ring. Id Verification Ring for One True Love in a Lifetime. (2023) Darry Ring | ID Verification Ring for One True Love in a Lifetime. us.darryring.com/.
3. Ruijie Zhang. (2014) "Darry Ring: One ring a lifetime, One lifetime one ring." Travel age, 12: 92-93.
4. Dr Jewelry Collection. (2023) Darry Ring, DR Jewelry Collection, Darry Ring, us.darryring.com/jewelry/shop.
5. Xiong Yan, Chen Jiawen. (2016) "The marketing model of jewelry brands in the context of SoLoMo - a case study of Dai Rui Jewelry's Weibo marketing." Journal of Gemstones and gemology, 18: 59-66.
6. Kantar Brandz. (2021) Chinese Global Brand Builders 2021." Kantar BrandZ Chinese Global Brand Builders. www.kantar.com/campaigns/brandz-downloads/kantar-brandz-most-valuable-chinese-brands-2023. Accessed 10 Sept. 2023.
7. DR Co., LTD. (2023) Giant tide Information network. static.cninfo.com.cn/finalpage/2022-04-22/1213028258.PDF.
8. DR Co., LTD. (2023) Summary of the 2022 Annual Report of DR Co., LTD., DR Co, 28 Apr. 2023. file.finance.sina.com.cn/211.154.219.97:9494/MRG G/CNSESZ_STOCK/2023/2023-4/2023-04-28/9149334.PDF.
9. DR Diamond Ring. (2023) "Selling True Love" Business Going Bad?, m.thepaper.cn/baijiahao_20033828.
10. Darry Ring's Official Account. Darry Ring. www. user/profile/5a6ff20411be1020bfcbc774. Accessed 12 Sept. 2023.

A Comprehensive Analysis of Chanel's Advertising Strategy

Jingchu Liu*

Comm and Media Studies, Fordham University, NY 10023, America

Abstract. This research delves into the profound impact of CHANEL's advertising strategies, recognizing them as a pivotal element in shaping the brand's identity and influencing consumer behavior. CHANEL, a globally acclaimed luxury fashion brand, is renowned not only for its distinctive style and impeccable craftsmanship but also for its iconic advertising campaigns. The study's primary objectives encompass several critical aspects. First and foremost, it seeks to unravel how CHANEL's advertising strategies contribute to the establishment and perpetuation of brand recognition and awareness. By examining the visual and thematic elements of CHANEL's advertisements, we aim to discern the underlying mechanisms that maintain the brand's prominent position in the luxury fashion sphere. Furthermore, this research aims to explore the tangible influence of CHANEL's advertising strategies on market share and sales performance. Analyzing sales data and market trends in correlation with advertising campaigns will shed light on the direct impact these strategies have on the brand's economic success. In addition, the study endeavors to elucidate how CHANEL's advertisements resonate with their target consumers, ultimately affecting purchasing decisions and fostering brand loyalty. By delving into consumer perceptions, preferences, and the emotional connections forged through advertising, we aim to uncover the intricate dynamics between CHANEL's messaging and consumer behavior. Lastly, this research delves into the broader societal and cultural implications of CHANEL's advertising strategies. It seeks to unravel how these strategies both reflect and shape contemporary societal and cultural trends.

1.Introduction

CHANEL, as a globally renowned luxury fashion brand, is known not only for its distinctive style and exquisite craftsmanship but also for its memorable advertising strategies. Advertising serves as a vital component of brand identity, shaping perceptions of the brand. However, in the ever-evolving landscape of media and consumer behavior, understanding the impact of CHANEL's advertising strategy has become paramount. It not only molds the brand's image but also has far-reaching effects on market share, sales performance, and consumer purchasing decisions. This research aids in brand management. A deep understanding of the effectiveness of CHANEL's advertising strategies enables the brand to better plan and optimize its advertising tactics, enhancing brand recognition and market share. Secondly, the study of how advertising strategies influence consumer behavior provides valuable insights to meet consumer demands and establish brand loyalty. Furthermore, the research can contribute to societal and cultural understanding. Analyzing how advertising reflects and shapes contemporary societal and cultural trends helps people gain a deeper understanding of the place and impact of luxury and fashion in people's lives. To delve into the impact of CHANEL's advertising strategy, this research poses the following critical questions: How do CHANEL's advertising strategies shape and maintain brand recognition and awareness? What is the influence of advertising strategies on CHANEL's market share and sales performance? How do CHANEL's advertisements attract and affect the purchasing decisions and brand loyalty of their target consumers? How do advertising strategies reflect and shape contemporary societal and cultural trends? In this study, people will conduct a comprehensive analysis of Chanel's advertising strategy, which includes a variety of aspects. First, the author will take an in-depth look at the various components that make up Chanel's advertising strategy, including the content of the advertisements, the choice of communication media channels, the brand positioning strategy, and the methods used to communicate these advertisements to the target audience. Subsequently, the author will critically assess the competitive advantages of these advertising strategies for Chanel and what different advantages these advertisements can bring to Chanel. In addition, the author will explore the intricate interplay between advertising and target audience segments, examining how these strategies shape consumers' perceptions of the Chanel brand and influence their purchasing behavior. Then, the author will investigate their products, the different products corresponding to different advertisements, and their final results. Finally, the author hope to reveal intriguing connections between Chanel's advertising strategies and current social and cultural trends, thus enriching people's understanding of the

*Corresponding author's mail: jliu449@fordham.edu

broader social impacts that advertising carries. Through this holistic research approach, the author hopes to reveal the multifaceted impact and significance of Chanel's advertising strategy in today's dynamic market environment.

2.Chanel's advertising revenue model

Chanel employs a sophisticated advertising revenue model that is strategically crafted to elevate its worldwide brand recognition. This esteemed luxury fashion brand makes substantial investments in advertising and brand promotion, utilizing a diverse array of channels. These encompass television advertisements, placements in renowned magazines, high-profile fashion shows, impactful social media campaigns, and its official website. Through these meticulously curated avenues, Chanel effectively disseminates its iconic brand imagery and showcases its exquisite range of products to a global audience. [1] Chanel's fashion shows are legendary in the fashion world, and they are meticulously designed to be extravagant, memorable events that go beyond simply showcasing clothing collections. One notable example is Chanel's Spring-Summer 2019 fashion show [2] held at the Grand Palais in Paris. The event featured a life-sized replica of a cruise ship named "La Pausa," which was the name of Gabrielle Chanel's villa in the South of France. The runway was transformed into a cruise ship deck, complete with a pool, lounge chairs, and even lifeguards. This immersive setting not only highlighted the nautical theme of the collection but also paid homage to Chanel's personal history. Such attention to detail and creativity in their fashion show settings not only captivate the audience but also generate extensive media coverage and social media buzz, reinforcing Chanel's brand image of sophistication and innovation. Celebrity endorsements and collaborations with prominent figures further elevate Chanel's visibility and cultural relevance. The company also leverages digital channels for advertising, such as its official website and mobile applications. One noteworthy example is the iconic Chanel No. 5 perfume campaign [2] featuring actress Nicole Kidman in 2004. Kidman's association with Chanel added a touch of Hollywood glamour to the brand and drew considerable attention. In terms of collaborations, Chanel partnered with renowned fashion designer Karl Lagerfeld for decades. Lagerfeld's creative direction and influence on Chanel's collections played a pivotal role in keeping the brand at the forefront of high fashion. His collaborations with prominent figures in the fashion industry, such as models like Cara Delevingne and Lily-Rose Depp, brought a fresh and youthful perspective to Chanel's image. Chanel's mobile applications, like the "Chanel Fashion" app, enable users to explore collections, watch fashion videos, and stay updated on the latest trends, enhancing the brand's accessibility and engagement with a tech-savvy audience. Furthermore, in the age of digital marketing, Chanel has adeptly embraced modern communication channels. The brand's official website serves as a digital hub, offering an immersive experience where customers can explore the latest collections, view runway shows, and access behind-the-scenes content. Chanel's mobile applications [3], available on smartphones and tablets, provide on-the-go access to fashion insights, allowing users to stay connected with the brand's offerings and events effortlessly. By expertly integrating these digital channels into its advertising strategy, Chanel maintains a strong online presence, ensuring its accessibility and relevance in the digital age.

3.CHANEL's advertising strategy

CHANEL's advertising strategy sets itself apart from numerous other brands within the luxury fashion and beauty sector by blending a distinctive combination of elements. One key aspect is the brand's unwavering commitment to timeless elegance and sophistication. This approach is exemplified by their consistent use of high-quality visuals that highlight the brand's enduring style. For instance, CHANEL's iconic No. 5 fragrance[4] campaigns often feature renowned actresses like Nicole Kidman or Audrey Tautou in visually stunning and emotionally resonant advertisements. These ads focus on the enduring allure of the fragrance, emphasizing the timelessness of CHANEL's products. Another notable element is CHANEL's strategic use of celebrity endorsements. While other brands may feature celebrities in their campaigns, CHANEL's choice of celebrities tends to align closely with the brand's image of sophistication and refinement. An example is CHANEL's collaboration with Keira Knightley, who personifies the brand's elegance and grace in their advertising. CHANEL's distribution strategy is also distinctive. The brand deliberately maintains an aura of exclusivity by limiting product availability to select boutiques and high-end department stores. This stands in contrast to some competitors who may adopt a wider distribution approach. Moreover, storytelling is a prevalent theme in CHANEL's advertising, with a focus on its rich heritage and iconic status. For example, the brand's short film "The One That I Want"[5] featuring Gisele Bündchen not only showcases CHANEL No. 5 but also delves into the brand's history and the enduring appeal of its products. Consistency in brand image is a hallmark of CHANEL's advertising. The brand's signature double-C logo and the use of black and white are consistently present across campaigns, reinforcing brand recognition. This stands in contrast to certain competitors who may experiment with different visual styles and aesthetics over time. In adapting to the digital age, CHANEL has embraced social media and online advertising to reach a broader and younger audience. For instance, their #ChanelFallWinter hashtag campaign on Instagram effectively engaged younger consumers during fashion events. Lastly, CHANEL's history of advertising innovation, such as being one of the first to create a branded fragrance, sets it apart from competitors. This innovative spirit continues with initiatives like virtual fashion shows, which became essential during the COVID-19 pandemic.

4.Chanel's audience

Chanel's audience is a richly diverse tapestry of individuals hailing from various backgrounds, united by their mutual admiration for the brand's exceptional fusion of enduring sophistication and haute couture. Within this multifaceted community, a fascinating array of demographics and interests coexist, underscoring Chanel's status as a brand that defies limitations and appeals to a broad spectrum of enthusiasts. [6] Fashion enthusiasts, regardless of age, are magnetically drawn to Chanel's offerings. Be it the graceful lines of their clothing, the allure of their accessories, or the artistry of their fragrances, Chanel's sophisticated and iconic designs are like a siren's call to those who covet high fashion. For them, Chanel represents an embodiment of their style aspirations, a gateway to the world of ultimate chic. Luxury collectors form a substantial and discerning part of Chanel's audience. To them, Chanel products are not just beautiful possessions but prized investments and status symbols. Their pursuit of limited-edition Chanel pieces and timeless classics isn't driven solely by desire but also by a keen eye for enduring value. The realm of Chanel is also graced by the presence of celebrities and social elites. Chanel's ubiquitous presence on red carpets and its coveted collaborations with A-list stars have solidified its status as the brand of choice for the glitterati. By being worn by the famous, Chanel's prestige is perpetually enhanced. Acknowledging the shifting tides of the digital age, Chanel has taken deliberate steps to engage with a younger generation of consumers. Through meticulously crafted digital marketing campaigns, captivating social media narratives, and innovative product launches, the brand has skillfully bridged the generational gap. Millennials and Gen Z, with their affinity for both heritage and contemporary style, have embraced Chanel as a symbol of their evolving tastes. In the corporate world, professional women seeking attire that exudes style and empowerment find Chanel's designs to be the epitome of sophistication. Chanel collections often feature pieces that effortlessly transition from boardroom to soirée, offering versatility alongside impeccable tailoring. In sum, Chanel's audience is a kaleidoscope of fashion enthusiasts, astute luxury collectors, high-profile celebrities, digitally savvy younger generations, and empowered professional women. Each of these facets converges on Chanel, attracted by its enduring elegance, iconic status, and ability to harmonize tradition with the ever-changing winds of fashion. Chanel's timeless relevance in the world of luxury fashion is a testament to its ability to resonate with a wide and diverse audience.

5.Chanel's advertising campaigns

are a breathtaking tapestry of their diverse product offerings, meticulously crafted to encapsulate the brand's unwavering commitment to timeless elegance and luxury. At the forefront of these captivating advertisements are Chanel's haute couture and ready-to-wear fashion collections. [7] These collections, which include an array of meticulously designed dresses, impeccably tailored suits, luxurious coats, and stylish blouses, often take center stage in high-profile campaigns across both traditional print media and the dynamic digital landscape. Chanel's fashion advertisements are an embodiment of sophistication, an open invitation into a world where style is synonymous with everlasting grace. Among Chanel's most iconic and coveted product categories are its handbags, featuring timeless classics such as the Chanel 2.55 and the Classic Flap Bag. These exquisite accessories are elevated to star status in Chanel's advertising, celebrated for their flawless craftsmanship and enduring allure. Chanel's handbag campaigns extend a seductive invitation to consumers, tempting them to indulge in the epitome of chic sophistication. Chanel's fragrances, with Chanel No. 5 standing as a revered global icon, find their rightful place in the brand's advertising repertoire. These fragrance campaigns are nothing short of olfactory journeys, transporting viewers into realms of sophistication, romance, and irresistible allure. They do more than evoke emotions. they forge a profound and indelible connection between consumers and the brand, making Chanel fragrances an essential part of one's personal identity. The brand's extensive line of cosmetics, ranging from makeup essentials to skincare and beauty products, enjoys its share of the spotlight. Chanel's cosmetic advertisements frequently feature models or celebrities, their radiant beauty highlighting the brand's commitment to enhancing natural allure. These campaigns inspire confidence and align consumers with Chanel's dedication to making them look and feel their best. Chanel's jewelry collections, adorned with exquisite rings, necklaces, earrings, and bracelets, are portrayed as symbols of unparalleled elegance and refinement. These campaigns tantalize consumers with a sense of desire, expertly embodying the brand's unwavering dedication to timeless sophistication and understated luxury.[13] Chanel's watches, known for their precision, artful craftsmanship, and enduring style, grace advertisements that emphasize not only their technical excellence but also their inherent elegance. Each timepiece is portrayed as an embodiment of enduring sophistication, designed not just to keep time but also to make a lasting impression. Chanel's footwear, sunglasses, accessories, and skincare products each have their moments in the spotlight. These campaigns are uniquely tailored to reflect Chanel's unwavering commitment to quality, innovation, and, above all, timeless style. They seamlessly weave into the larger narrative of Chanel, where each product is a vessel of elegance, style, and luxury. In the realm of Chanel's advertising, every product transcends the status of mere commodity; it becomes an emblem of a refined and sumptuous lifestyle. Each product is thoughtfully and strategically integrated into the rich tapestry of storytelling and heritage that Chanel is known for. This approach not only entices but also fortifies Chanel's image as a brand that endures as an aspiration, one rooted in the very essence of sophistication and grace. Chanel's advertising campaigns are a mesmerizing blend of sophistication, elegance, and storytelling that have defined the brand's image as an iconic symbol of luxury. At the heart of Chanel's advertising lies an unwavering commitment to timeless elegance, which is a hallmark of the brand. Whether it's haute couture fashion, fragrances, or accessories, Chanel's advertisements consistently radiate a sense of enduring beauty that transcends fleeting trends and resonates across generations. [11] One of Chanel's signature approaches to advertising is its strategic use of celebrity endorsements. The brand frequently collaborates with A-list celebrities and influential figures, infusing its campaigns with an extra layer of prestige and glamour. For instance, the enduring association of Chanel No. 5 [8] with Hollywood legends like Marilyn Monroe and Nicole Kidman has solidified its status as an iconic fragrance. Iconic imagery [9] is another cornerstone of Chanel's advertising. Symbols like the Chanel No. 5 perfume bottle and the double-C logo are omnipresent in their campaigns, serving as visual anchors that reinforce the brand's heritage and global recognition. These symbols resonate deeply with consumers, signifying a world of luxury and sophistication. Chanel's advertising doesn't just sell products; it tells compelling stories. The brand expertly weaves narratives that connect each product to the rich tapestry of Chanel's history and values. These stories create an emotional connection with consumers, inviting them into the world of Chanel and making them feel like they are part of the brand's legacy. High production values are a defining feature of Chanel's ads, whether they appear in print or as captivating video campaigns. The use of top-tier photography and cinematography adds to the overall sense of opulence and refinement, reinforcing the brand's image as a paragon of luxury. Chanel also leverages the exclusivity of its products in its advertising strategy. The brand often emphasizes limited availability and its selective distribution network, further enhancing the allure of Chanel products as coveted treasures. In the digital age, Chanel has adapted its advertising approach to include a robust online and social media presence. The brand engages with a broader and younger audience through platforms like Instagram and YouTube, seamlessly blending its timeless elegance with modern digital strategies.[15] Furthermore, Chanel's history is marked by a spirit of innovation, demonstrated by its pioneering role in advertising. From being one of the first brands to create a fragrance to embracing virtual fashion shows, Chanel consistently pushes boundaries, ensuring it remains at the forefront of the luxury fashion and beauty industry.[14] Therefore, Chanel's advertising is a mirror reflecting the brand's core values—timeless elegance, luxury, and a storied heritage. Beyond promoting products, it encapsulates the essence of the Chanel lifestyle, creating a sense of aspiration and desire that has cemented Chanel's place as an iconic name in the world of luxury fashion and beauty. In summary, CHANEL, a globally renowned luxury fashion brand, is celebrated for its distinctive style and impeccable craftsmanship, bolstered by iconic advertising strategies that shape brand identity and profoundly influence market share, sales, and consumer behaviors [10].

6.Conclusion

This research holds vital implications for effective brand management, offering insights into CHANEL's advertising strategies that can optimize brand recognition and market presence while fostering consumer loyalty. By scrutinizing the multifaceted impact of CHANEL's advertising approach, this study addresses crucial questions about how these strategies perpetuate brand awareness, impact market share and sales performance, influence consumer purchasing decisions, and reflect contemporary societal and cultural trends. A comprehensive analysis delves into the various components comprising CHANEL's advertising strategy, including content, communication channels, brand positioning, and methods of engaging the target audience. This investigation underscores competitive advantages such as an unwavering commitment to timeless elegance, strategic celebrity endorsements, narrative storytelling, and consistent brand image. The exclusivity of CHANEL's distribution strategy further differentiates the brand from competitors. In the digital age, CHANEL adeptly harnesses digital channels, with its website and mobile applications providing immersive experiences, ensuring continued relevance and accessibility. The audience drawn to CHANEL is diverse, encompassing fashion enthusiasts, luxury collectors, celebrities, millennials, and professional women who appreciate the brand's enduring elegance and versatility. CHANEL's advertising campaigns feature a wide array of products, from haute couture to fragrances, cosmetics, jewelry, watches, and accessories, each portrayed as a symbol of sophistication and luxury intricately woven into the brand's narrative. Key elements of CHANEL's advertising include strategic celebrity endorsements, iconic imagery, emotionally resonant storytelling, high production values, and exclusivity, all contributing to CHANEL's identity as an enduring symbol of luxury that invites consumers into a world of timeless beauty and grace. In sum, CHANEL's advertising represents a harmonious blend of sophistication, elegance, and innovation, consistently encapsulating timeless elegance that resonates across generations, transcending mere product promotion to offer consumers an invitation into a world of enduring beauty and grace. The future of CHANEL advertising is poised to embrace digital innovation and sustainability. CHANEL will likely continue to strengthen its online presence, using social media, immersive experiences, and personalization to engage with tech-savvy consumers.[12] Ethical and sustainable messaging may play a prominent role, reflecting changing consumer values. CHANEL's rich heritage and storytelling will remain central, while inclusivity, diversity, and collaborations could expand its reach. The brand will adapt to shorter content formats and interactive shopping experiences to cater to evolving consumer behavior while maintaining its signature elegance and sophistication.

References

1. Chang, Yi-Wei Eva. (2022) Space exploration inspiration for fashion styling and design in six decades since 1960: A review. Acta Astronautica ,198: 767-776.
2. Ofori-Okyere, Isaac, and Emmanuel S. Asamoah. (2015) Celebrity endorser selection strategies as effective marketing communications tool in the automobile industry–A review paper on related literature." International journal of business and marketing management 3: 1-15.
3. Ren, Ruijuan, and Jiangbo Liao. (2016) Processing Objets Trouves: A Review of Appling Collage Thinking and Techniques in Fashion." Asian Culture and History 8: 160-160.
4. Jones, Andrea. (2017) Chanel and Chanel No. 5: A Global Marketing and Advertising Strategy." University of Victoria, Business Journals, 17: 890.
5. Picardie, Justine, and Cassandra Harwood. (2010) Coco Chanel: The Legend and the Life. Ha Business Journals, 67: 459.
6. Cattani, Gino, Mariachiara Colucci, and Simone Ferriani. (2016) Chanel's creative trajectory in the field of fashion: The optimal network structuration strategy. Multidisciplinary contributions to the science of creative thinking 16: 117-132.
7. Kim, Hye-Shin. (2000) Examination of emotional response to apparel brand advertisements." Journal of Fashion Marketing and Management: An International Journal 4: 303-313.
8. Bulmer, Sandy, and Margo Buchanan-Oliver. (2006) Visual rhetoric and global advertising imagery." Journal of Marketing Communications 12: 49-61.
9. Kim, Hye-Shin. (2000) Examination of emotional response to apparel brand advertisements." Journal of Fashion Marketing and Management: An International Journal 4: 303-313.
10. Knoll, Silke, Martin Eisend, and Josefine Steinhagen. (2011) Gender roles in advertising: Measuring and comparing gender stereotyping on public and private TV channels in Germany." International Journal of Advertising 30: 867-888.
11. Laczkó, Dorka, and Elisabeth Putz. "Breathing N° 5: StorytellingStrategy of Chanel: The Impact on Generation Źs Brand Perception." (2023).
12. Cao, Yujia. "Research on Digital Transformation Based Luxury Brands Marketing Strategy." Proceedings of the 6th International Conference on Economic Management and Green Development. Singapore: Springer Nature Singapore, 2023.
13. Parashar, Ashwina. "INSIGHTS INTO LUXURY BRAND MANAGEMENT THROUGH A CASE STUDY OF CHANEL."
14. LeeJa, S. U. H. "Chanel's Modern Fashion Culture which changed the Women of the Ancient Regime into the Modern Citizen." *Korean Review of French History* 49 (2023): 75-108
15. Liu, Yifan. "Analysis on Chanel Group Digital Marketing Strategies." *Journal of Education, Humanities and Social Sciences* 16 (2023): 155-159.

Research on the Impact of Perfect Diary Brand Strategy

Guoqi Pan*

School of Film and Television and Media, Shanghai Normal University, Shanghai, 200030, China

Abstract. The arrival of the new media era has brought new publicity ideas to enterprises, enriched marketing methods and channels, and allowed brand and product information to be delivered to consumers in a more comprehensive and rapid manner, thereby achieving more efficient and comprehensive marketing. Effect. Through digital means, brands can better find target audiences, provide personalized interactive experiences, and achieve precision marketing. Among them, social media platforms are the main platform for Perfect Diary brand communication. Perfect Diary can be said to be a successful example of social media marketing. Through short videos, grass planting notes, combination of pictures and text, and social marketing, it has been widely used on Douyin, Kuaishou, Xiaomi, etc. Conduct all-round publicity on social media such as Red Book and WeChat to cater to the viewing habits and consumption habits of the younger generation on social media, communicate more directly with users, understand consumer psychology and needs, provide products that meet user requirements in a timely manner, and fully penetrate The social media ecology of the younger generation establishes deeper connections with consumers through social media.

1.Introduction

The advent of the new era of domestic products has provided a broad space for development of domestic cosmetics brands. At a time when national trends are prevalent and people are pursuing a better life, consumers are particularly fond of domestic cosmetics, which also provides a good environment for Perfect Diary. In the new media environment, although short-term explosive publicity will bring exposure to the brand, homogeneous content and excessive publicity will also make consumers tired. The popularity of a single product cannot guarantee the longevity of the brand. People should focus on long-term maintenance on social media rather than short-term promotion, deeply explore consumer needs, innovate content creation, and focus on the sustainable development of the brand. [1] This article is based on the new media environment and takes the marketing strategy of "Perfect Diary" as the research object to analyze why Perfect Diary can succeed. This article introduces Professor Chen Gang's creative communication theory and creative communication management theory to analyze Perfect Diary's brand strategy from aspects such as Perfect Diary's profit model, marketing strategy based on 4I theory, Perfect Diary's audience and products, and social media communication meta-forms. In order to provide certain reference value and significance for other domestic cosmetics brands in marketing strategy formulation, content management, communication channel management, etc.

2.Perfect diary profit model

Perfect Diary is an Internet brand focusing on beauty and skin care. Its profit model mainly includes the following aspects:

2.1 Product sales

Perfect Diary sells its products through its own online mall, offline stores and cooperative channels. They offer a variety of beauty products, such as facial masks, makeup, etc., and constantly launch new products to meet consumer needs.

2.2 Brand cooperation

Perfect Diary cooperates with other brands to jointly launch co-branded or limited edition products, and attract more consumers' attention and purchases through brand cooperation.

2.3 Social media marketing

Social media marketing: Perfect Diary actively carries out marketing activities on social media platforms, cooperates with Internet celebrities and KOL (Key Opinion Leader) to promote products, and uses the influence of social media to attract more users and increase product sales.

*Corresponding author's mail: guoqi@ldy.edu.rs

https://doi.org/10.1051/shsconf/202418503017

2.4 Membership system

Perfect Diary has established a membership system to encourage users to purchase products through member points, coupons, etc., and provides member-exclusive activities and benefits to increase user stickiness and repurchase rates [2].

2.5 Data operation

Perfect Diary analyzes user behavior and preferences through big data, conducts refined operations and personalized recommendations, and improves sales conversion rate and user satisfaction.

2.6 International expansion

Diary began to expand internationally, enter overseas markets, sell products through online and offline channels, and develop more consumer groups. In general, Perfect Diary achieves profitability through product sales, brand cooperation, social media marketing, membership systems, data operations and international expansion. At the same time, they also focus on product quality and user experience, and continuously improve their brand image and market competitiveness [3].

3.Perfect Diary's marketing strategy based on the 4I theory

The 4I marketing theory was proposed by Don Schultz, a marketing professor at Northwestern University in the United States in the 1990s. The 4I theory is one of the classic theories of marketing, including four aspects: interest, interests, interaction, and individuality. [4] The emergence and rapid development of the "her" economy have given a huge boost to the beauty industry, and competition in the beauty market has become very fierce. Perfect Diary uses its own competitive advantages and marketing strategies to make the brand stand out among so many competitors.

3.1 Interest marketing

3.1.1 Interesting packaging

Interest marketing is to guide consumers to identify with the concept, product functions, and value of a product or brand through consumer identification, and value identification is the key factor that promotes consumer purchases. Perfect Diary's innovation in product packaging is unique, and the packaging and meaning perfectly match each other. It is not only interesting, but also full of positive energy, and has been recognized by consumers. For example, Perfect Diary and McDull launched a joint collaboration full of fun and surprises. The lipstick is designed as a macaron-colored business card packaging. The unique flat transparent design changes the traditional lipstick round tube packaging, making Perfect Diary more recognizable, and each lipstick corresponds to an anime character in McDull. The McDull pig packaging of the eyeshadow palette has captured the hearts of many girls. The appearance uses McDull cartoon image and cappuccino rose pattern to interpret the charming and hazy beauty. The eyeshadow palette uses pure medium-low saturated cappuccino rose warm pink color, [5] which is highly suitable for Asian women's skin color. In addition, Perfect Diary also gives away hair clips and McDull sippy cups for girls in the same color, successfully expanding its consumer base into the animation industry.

3.1.2 Interesting short films

In addition to interesting packaging, Perfect Diary also launched with McDull with the theme of "Workplace is a Show". In the jointly planned short film, Perfect Diary invites McDull and May, Ah Hui and other members of the Springfield Huahua Colleague Association to come to the Perfect Diary office building to experience the working life of professionals, and gives them exclusive workplace personalities to spend time together. [6] Perfect Diary encourages every migrant worker to, like McDull and his colleagues, regard the workplace as a show and boldly express themselves through makeup, face workplace life with an optimistic and cheerful attitude, and discover those shining and independent women hidden in daily life. Traits. Perfect Diary combines animated IP images with makeup products and integrates them into product packaging and short film creation. It can be seen that Perfect Diary has grasped the true meaning of Interest marketing.

3.2 Interests marketing

3.2.1 Material interests

The prices of Perfect Diary meet the interests of consumers. Since the brand's target audience has strong demand for beauty products, but the financial strength is slightly insufficient, Perfect Diary adopts a low-price strategy. Most products are priced between 19 and 200 yuan. For those born after 1995, For new consumption forces, it is within their affordable consumption range. When big-name lipsticks are priced at 200 to 300 yuan, Perfect Diary is priced at 60 to 70 yuan. It is a high-quality, big-name alternative that is very timely. Consumers also evaluate Perfect Diary's products as "worth buying" and "high quality and low price" [7].

3.2.2 Non-material interests

The brand meaning of Perfect Diary is that beauty has no limits. The brand advocates that the younger generation should not be constrained by external labels and strive to break through themselves. The brand values conveyed are consistent with the younger generation's pursuit of individuality, freshness, and the courage to play and try. The younger generation is consuming It pays more attention to brands that are consistent in spiritual connotation and can represent self-assertion. Therefore, consumers not only buy products, but also their attitude towards life [8].

Perfect Diary taps into traditional Chinese culture and combines culture with products. It has an innate cultural background of national fashion and national confidence, which is consistent with the current value orientation of young consumer groups. Let consumers feel national confidence and patriotism when purchasing products. Chinese beauty market has long been dominated by foreign brands. The emergence of Perfect Diary makes customers feel proud when purchasing products, and generates a sense of identity and confidence in the country and national culture. As a result, they have a sense of identity with brand products and are more willing to use the brand and product promotion.

3.3 Interactive marketing

3.3.1 Creative interaction in the public domain

Any Internet company is inseparable from one core issue - traffic. Only with traffic can the next step of conversion be carried out, and "traffic" represents the public's focus. For Internet companies, traffic is the market, traffic is users, and traffic is business opportunities. Public domain traffic, such as Taobao, JD.com, Douyin, Xiaohongshu and other large traffic platforms, all traffic needs to be purchased, and it is getting more and more expensive. The "paying to buy" here refers to advertising promotion and ranking promotion. wait. With exposure, users' focus (browsing behavior) will naturally come. Perfect Diary has 6.27 million Douyin fans. Most of the content it publishes is product creative videos, which can capture users' pain points and needs, thereby gaining fans' comments and attention [9].

3.3.2 Create private IP

Private domain traffic refers to traffic that is independently owned by a brand or individual, is free of charge, can be used repeatedly, and can reach users at any time. For example, WeChat public account, official website, Weibo, etc., Perfect Diary has created the IP "Xiao Wanzi" to act as customer service and beauty consultant, establishing warm two-way communication with users, which is different from other mechanized operation models. Perfect Diary transforms Xiaowanzi from a pure customer service image into a close friend image, prompting users to have a better impression of the brand. Establishing a WeChat group is an extremely effective way of community interactive marketing. By adding friends, users can join the group. Xiao Wanzi can share valuable content in the group, such as how to apply eyeliner, how to apply contouring and highlighting, and distribute some benefits. [10] Let users have no idea of leaving the group, form effective communication with users, and gain user trust. This can further manage retention and stimulate repurchase.

3.4 Individuality marketing

The brand spokesperson of Perfect Diary is Zhou Xun. Perfect Diary selects its spokesperson from the perspective of fans, because fans are mostly young women, and girls can break boundaries and dare to explore. Such a personality is in line with the future development philosophy of the new generation of women. The aesthetics and concepts of Perfect Diary are both advanced. The cooperation between Perfect Diary and Zhou Xun means that Perfect Diary, like her, will not be limited to a certain framework. It can always break the inherent impression and discover the infinite possibilities of life. Perfect Diary wants to Zhou Xun is undoubtedly the most perfect candidate to convey the brand proposition of "beauty without limits" to young women around the world [11].

4.Perfect Diary audience

4.1 Audience purchasing behavior

The audience of Perfect Diary is mainly young women aged 18-35, who have high spending power and purchase intention. While pursuing fashion and beauty, they pay more attention to natural and comfortable makeup experience. Its audience is mainly concentrated in first-tier cities and some second-tier cities. Consumers in these cities pay more attention to quality, cost-effectiveness and personalized experience. The positioning of Perfect Diary is very young, and the color, packaging and promotion of the product are full of novel elements and concepts. Therefore, the main audience of Perfect Diary is consumers who pursue novelty and innovation. For example, Perfect Diary teamed up with the Forbidden City to launch a joint national-style lipstick; Perfect Diary teamed up with China's National Geographic to get inspiration from China's four natural landscapes and launched joint cosmetics "Red Danxia", "Fundai Plateau" and "Blue Lake", "Glowing Terraces" four themed eyeshadows. Perfect Diary teamed up with Discovery Channel to create an "Explorer Twelve Color Eyeshadow Palette" full of wildness and creativity, inspired by the design and color matching of the four major wild animals.

In addition, with the development of the "her economy", women's pursuit of beauty continues to increase. When purchasing, the audience of Perfect Diary usually conducts research and understands product information in advance, and makes decisions after comparing products from multiple brands. With the popularity of online consumption, they are more inclined to purchase products online and will take advantage of various preferential activities to obtain more discounts. Perfect Diary's audience is mostly in-depth users of various social platforms, that is, digital natives. Perfect Diary is mainly targeted at the younger generation of digital natives. These young people are accustomed to obtaining information through the Internet and social media. They are the main market for the Perfect Diary brand and focus more on social interaction and cross-border innovation. They will actively use and share their experience of beauty products through social media, and will also recommend products to their friends and family.

4.2 Potential needs of the audience

The audience of Perfect Diary pays more attention to product quality, brand image and service experience in their potential future needs. They want a personalized skin care and cosmetics experience, and they also want to be able to use different cosmetics on different occasions to meet the needs of different occasions.

5.The perfect diary product

5.1 Beauty products

Perfect Diary focuses on makeup and cosmetics, creating rich and professional makeup items. It first entered the market with foundation, but found that the response was not very good, so it switched to lipsticks and eyeshadow palettes, which are now the flagship products of Perfect Diary, and it has caught on to the fame of co-branded brands. Initially, it occupied the market with a small and beautiful single product, starting with "little black lid liquid foundation", and later launched various eye shadow palettes and gradually attracted the attention of consumers. Perfect Diary product categories are subdivided into: base makeup products, lip makeup products, eye makeup products, makeup tools, and makeup remover products.

5.2 Hot items

Perfect Diary frequently releases popular items, such as the "Small Heel" lipstick, which was jointly developed by Perfect Diary and "Lipstick Master" Li Jiaqi. After 76 versions of formulas, more than 100 versions of color screening and as many as 3,000 real-person interviews The final carefully polished product after trial use. With its unique and high-end appearance design and the spiritual connotation of female independence, this product has won enthusiastic support from consumers as soon as it was launched. In addition, Perfect Diary uses the colors of morpho butterflies and blooming flowers in the spring garden to decorate the early spring with pink and purple colors. It launches the "Business Card" lip gloss secret series and the "Butterfly" fairy purple palette, using two classic products to create a clear makeup look. Encounter spring romance. Perfect Diary integrates imagination into makeup, and specially invites celebrity makeup artists to launch makeup tutorials. Using Zhao Lusi, the brand's youth spokesperson, as the inspiration for makeup, she created butterfly fairy purple makeup and shy girl makeup, which moved countless fans.

6.Perfect diary social media communication meta-form

The book "Creative Communication Management - Marketing Revolution in the Digital Age" was written by Professor Chen Gang. Creative Communication Management theory believes that the Internet has built a new digital living space. In the digital living space, the relationship between enterprises and consumers in the traditional marketing communication environment has transformed into the relationship between life service providers and living people. This change has led to a revolution in the marketing communication model, and marketing communication has since entered the era of creative communication management. Creative communication management emphasizes that enterprises must carry out management innovation, set up a special communication management department to manage communication, and on this basis, carry out creative communication. The core element of creative communication is the communication element. Relying on the element of communication and using various forms to trigger people in the digital living space to continuously share and collaborate on creativity, we can jointly and continuously create positive and influential content about corporate products and brands [12].

The communication element can be a relatively simple phonetic structure composed of words or phrases, or it can be a sound or a picture. It is suddenly triggered under specific conditions through different media and spreads instantly and out of control. As a corporate communicator, people need to use communication elements to resonate with consumers, thereby promoting collaborative creation and dissemination among consumers.

6.1 Hot-spot communication elements

Perfect Diary is good at using hot communication elements to promote product advertising on social media platforms, such as Douyin, Xiaohongshu, Kuaishou, Bilibili, etc. In July this year, Perfect Diary used the Chinese Valentine's Day "Love Poems" gift box as a letter, inviting lovers to write their affectionate love poems together to express their love in a heart-warming atmosphere, including eye shadow, lipstick, loose powder and other products. This Chinese Valentine's Day, Perfect Diary has integrated the design of romantic love poems into its products, using the name of love poems to encourage lovers to bravely express their love and boldly pursue the true love in their inner world. The extremely romantic communication element and creative expression of love also make consumers happy to share the product after receiving it [13].

6.2 Life-making communication element

Anti-media is an important feature of the Internet. Relying on digital technology, various information dissemination and communication activities in human real life can be virtually restored or even amplified on the Internet. This form of communication has created a new type of digital living space. Perfect Diary mainly adopts a pyramid advertising strategy on Xiaohongshu. Its advertising targets cover top bloggers, celebrities, KOLs, waistline influencers, and amateur bloggers. In terms of advertising ideas, [14] Perfect Diary adopts a large-scale advertising strategy. The main idea is to use top bloggers and celebrities to build brand reputation and endorsement, and to use KOLs and waist bloggers to complete large-scale planting. Finally, through a large number of Amateur bloggers superimpose their voices to complete customer testimonials. A product or a topic gradually spreads on social media platforms under the recommendation of different people, and the effect gradually amplifies.

6.2.1 Arouse attention and discussion through the planting of top bloggers and celebrities

As a new brand, the first thing to do when it is launched is to attract consumers' attention and establish itself, so planting through top bloggers and celebrities is the best and most direct way. Relevant data shows that more than 60% of users are willing to buy the same style from celebrities, because celebrity endorsements have a certain endorsement effect. At that time, Perfect Diary found celebrities such as Zhu Zhengyan, Angela Chang, and Ouyang Nana to promote it, and finally achieved explosive exposure in a short period of time. On August 22, 2018, the official account of Perfect Diary released "The first spokesperson of Perfect Diary is here! Guess who he is? "'s notes, announcing that traffic star Zhu Zhengting will be the spokesperson. In the following week, the official account released a large number of notes containing information about Zhu Zhengting, and the number of likes for this series of notes reached thousands. This wave of publicity for spokesperson Zhu Zhengting has also successfully brought sufficient exposure to the brand.

6.2.2 Guide consumers to purchase through KOL and waist celebrity color testing

Although the planting effect of leading bloggers and celebrities is very good, their investment costs are also relatively high. Therefore, after arousing user attention and discussion, it is necessary to find another way to further enhance the impact of grass planting on users. [15]. At this time, Perfect Diary selected KOLs and waistline influencers to launch the campaign, and asked them to do various color trials and guides to complete the planting process. For example, when Perfect Diary promoted the "Explorer Twelve Color Animal Eyeshadow" series of products, it invited many bloggers with millions of fans to post related product sharing posts in the early stage, and they all gained a lot of attention. In terms of communication content, Perfect Diary mainly focuses on "new product introduction", "color test effect" and "use experience". During the hot discussion stage, Perfect Diary will invite a large number of waist experts to spread the word, creating a "hot discussion" atmosphere.

6.2.3 Through the sharing of user experience by amateur consumers

Because amateurs themselves do not have charisma and marketing power, amateur advertising cannot directly promote transactions. But a large number of amateurs can also create an atmosphere where the products are selling well and being used by many people.

At that time, Perfect Diary chose to place a large number of amateur bloggers on Xiaohongshu to create a sense of immediate product sales, which also successfully allowed the brand to effectively form a superposition of brand reputation.

In the end, driven by many amateur bloggers, more and more ordinary Xiaohongshu users began to spontaneously purchase products, post notes, etc. In this era where everyone is a communicator and creator, creative fans themselves Pick up the available audio and video production tools and participate in the collaborative creativity of brand building, truly achieving the effect of collaborative creation and communication among consumers.

6.3 Thematic communication communication element

Perfect Diary uses online live streaming to drive product sales and strive to monetize traffic. Perfect Diary uses online live streaming to promote new products and conduct live makeup tutorials on Taobao. Compared with browsing and purchasing products online, online live broadcasts are more interactive. Consumers can better understand the functions and effects of the products through the anchor's trial and explanation. Perfect Diary evaluates product performance and compares it with other similar products through live broadcasts by merchants, users and celebrities on the Xiaohongshu App, [16] intuitively summarizing their consumption experience and guiding consumers to consume. Realize the perfect diary Weibo and Douyin screen-swiping mode through live video broadcast on Weibo and Douyin. In addition to setting up live broadcasts on the official account on Douyin, Perfect Diary also cooperates with KOLs at all levels to conduct live broadcasts. When cooperating with top KOLs, Perfect Diary chose a dedicated live broadcast to monetize traffic and convert the brand's commercial value. As a new marketing method currently adopted by fashion companies, live broadcast marketing has the characteristics of low cost and high profit, and is a highly cost-effective marketing method. Perfect Diary takes advantage of the live broadcast format to take advantage of the Internet and attract a large number of consumers.

Since the founding of Perfect Diary, it has been making continuous efforts to explore beauty and is committed to integrating thousands of beautiful colors into makeup aesthetics. Since 2019, Perfect Diary has launched creative co-branded products with the British Museum, the Metropolitan Museum of Art, Discovery Channel, Honor of Kings, etc. On the occasion of the Mid-Autumn Festival in 2020, it also co-branded with China Aerospace to create an animal eyeshadow jade rabbit plate full of imagination of the interstellar world, and to pay tribute to the women who have made great contributions to China's aerospace industry. In April 2023, on the occasion of the brand's 6th anniversary, Perfect Diary launched a joint cooperation with the National Ballet of China to integrate ballet aesthetics into the design of makeup products, explore the fusion of art and color, and bring a new ballet limited series. This time, the brand launched a new limited-edition "ballet" stiletto lipstick to help women create high-end makeup looks; it also teamed up with the National Ballet of China to bring an attitude film, showing the confident and elegant ballet spirit with dancers' postures. Perfect Diary continues to break through the boundaries of cross-border cooperation, creates creative beauty products full of surprises, [17] and achieves multiple upgrades in product technology, cultural connotation, and creative design to meet the diversified beauty needs of young consumers.

7.Conclusion

"Perfect Diary" relies on social media to achieve brand fission, making "Perfect Diary" stand out among domestic beauty brands. At the same time, Perfect Diary leverages the influence of brand spokespersons to enhance brand awareness and appeal. When choosing artists to collaborate with, the brand values most things such as word-of-mouth, personal labels and past endorsement results. The personal labels of the artists who collaborate with the brand reflect the brand image that the brand hopes to create at this stage. As a cutting-edge domestic beauty brand, Perfect Diary has always impressed consumers with its rich cosmetics products, fast product launches and emphasis on social media marketing. The artists that Perfect Diary has cooperated with in the past are mainly young actors or new generation singing and dancing artists. , are all artists popular among young people, making Perfect Diary's brand image very young. Suitable spokespersons and internet celebrities can help the brand better establish emotional connections with the target audience.

However, in the context of the new media environment, the marketing strategy of "Perfect Diary" still needs to be improved, and the advantages of social media can be used to improve the brand's marketing strategy. Perfect Diary can adopt a comprehensive digital strategy, including data analysis, social media management, content creation and other aspects to analyze and manage fan portraits and comments to understand user psychology and needs. After the brand has gained popularity, marketing should be appropriately reduced to avoid user resentment. We should focus on research and development and product quality, open channels for user opinions, and allow users to participate in product research and development to ensure the continued success of the brand in the new media era. . Through the all-round digitization of new media, we can identify the target group, establish a private domain traffic pool through WeChat, and use "Xiao Wanzi" to digitally segment community consumers in an all-round way, and then adopt targeted marketing strategies. Taking advantage of social media, it is not difficult to promote a single product. What is difficult is how to maintain the vitality of the brand for a long time and make Internet celebrities become popular. The cultural value of products is a good way to enhance the stickiness of social media users. On the basis of people having a certain similar cultural background and value recognition, communication elements continue to spread. People are looking for something graspable and graspable on social media. Copiable elements can be propagated again. Perfect Diary can increase the international popularity of its own products by cooperating with international natural and cultural organizations, giving beauty products a higher level of cultural significance, and laying a solid foundation for them to enter the international market.

References

1. Zhang Hengshan. (2015) Digital publication marketing strategy based on 4I principles. Publishing and Distribution Research, 10: 50-52.
2. Qin Suxiang, Huang Dandan & Li Qingmei. (2021). Analysis of the marketing strategy of domestic beauty "Perfect Diary" from the perspective of 4I theory. Modern Marketing (Xueyuan Edition) 12: 115-118.
3. Shen Hong. (2012). Communication elements of creative communication and advertising creative communication. Advertising View (Theoretical Edition) (04): 47-58.
4. Chen Gang. Shen Hong. Ma Che et al. (2012) Creative Communication Management: Marketing Revolution in the Digital Era. Machinery Industry Press, Beijing.
5. Liu Yuchen. (2020). Analysis of the creative communication strategies of domestic cosmetics brands in Xiaohongshu APP - Taking Perfect Diary as an example. Editor, 04: 182-183.
6. Chen Maobo. (2021). How "Perfect Diary" makes new media marketing strategies more perfect. Today's Fortune 23: 80-83.
7. Wang Zhuohui. (2020). The rise of domestic beauty brands: Analysis of "Perfect Diary" marketing strategy. Media Forum 04: 143-148.
8. Peng Mengjie, Xie Zhen & Zheng Jinhua. (2021). Research on cross-border joint marketing strategies of national fashion and cosmetics brands - taking the "Perfect Diary" brand as an example. Liaoning Vocational and Technical College of Economics. Journal of Liaoning Economic and Management Cadre College, 06: 27-32.
9. Du Shen, Dong Xiao, Guo Jia & Zhang Yu Huizi. (2022). Perfect Diary to retain China's beauty. Fashion Beijing 01: 24-25.
10. Li Ting & Shi Dan. (2022). Perfect Diary: Without R&D, the highlights will eventually fade. Business School 01: 61-63.
11. Cao Yanan. (2020). Perfect Diary joins hands with Zhou Xun, the methodology of new brand spokespersons has changed. Sales and Marketing (Marketing Edition) 11: 58-60.

12. Lujian & Zhang Duanmin. (2020). Analysis of marketing strategies of online self-created cosmetics brands—taking Perfect Diary as an example. Modern Marketing (Later Issue) 07: 77-79.
13. Li Chenyu. (2022). Perfect Diary: Marketing should shape the brand and promote product innovation. International Brand Observation 07: 12.
14. Li Chenyu, Wei Baotao, Wang Shuang, Wang Huirong & Fei Nanqian. (2022). Over 90% of the market value has evaporated in one year. Can Perfect Diary create perfection again with innovation? International Brand Observation 07: 11.
15. Wang Mohan & Xue Xue. (2020). New media promotes the marketing and development of domestic beauty product brands - taking the "PERFECT DIARY" brand as an example. Marketing Industry, 22: 1-2.
16. Appel, G., Grewal, L., Hadi, R. et al. (2020) The future of social media in marketing. J. of the Acad. Mark. Sci. 48: 79–95.
17. Giandomenico Di Domenico, Jason Sit, Alessio Ishizaka, Daniel Nunan. (2021) Fake news, social media and marketing: A systematic review, Journal of Business Research, 124: 329-341.

Analyzing the Strategic Impact of Zara's Branding Strategies on Consumer Engagement and Market Position

Siying Liu[1,*], Yingshun Huang[2], Qianhui Pan[3]

[1]College of Foreign Languages, Huaihua University, Hunan, 418000, China
[2]The Grier School, PA Tyrone, 16686, the United States
[3]Shanghai Guanghua Cambridge International School, Shanghai, 201319, China

Abstract. Zara is well-known in China as a leader in fast fashion brands. The brand has a large market share among apparel brands and consistently earns big profits. However, as a result of the pandemic, changes in buying patterns, and the growth of indigenous Chinese brands, the development of many overseas fashion companies in China has slowed, besides ZARA. Based on this context, this article explores the Zara fashion brand's traditional strategy, including its profit model, competitive advantages, product functions, and marketing model. At the same time, a SWOT analysis model is established to help evaluate the brand's strengths and weaknesses. The article proposes creative ideas, integrates the general environment, and uses social networks, media, and other technologies in order to carry forward the brand's advantages, make the brand self-reform, and bring the brand as a whole closer to Chinese consumers, which can empower the brand. The suggestions that are provided in this article can fulfill the demands of local customers and maintain sustainable long-term brand growth.

1.Introduction

In the current situation of rapid economic and social development, people's living standards have gradually improved, the national consumption level is also higher and higher, people will spend more money in to dress themselves to get material and spiritual satisfaction. And China as the world's largest country in terms of population there is a huge consumer market, the major well-known clothing brands are locked in the Chinese clothing market, they all hope to achieve a certain market share. And these brands generally have their own advantages, according to different brand strategy for different target groups, their clothing style also follow the trend, can be very good to meet the masses of the pursuit of fashion. Among them, Zara as the clothing industry's leading brand is the most representative, 1it is with a unique brand strategy to quickly occupy the market, so that consumers are increasingly keen on this fast food mode of fashion clothing. [1] In recent years, China's clothing industry has developed rapidly, the local clothing brands have gradually matured and can be connected with the world's leading brands, but due to the lack of experience in brand operations, brand marketing appears very weak, the development of the brand is also therefore stagnant. In order to solve the current development status quo, China's clothing brands can be combined with their own actual situation selective reference Zara's marketing strategy. The current era of the environment has created a fast fashion brand, and fast fashion as a controversial field, the study of its brand has a typical, by analysing the development of the brand in the public consumption psychology, brand image construction, brand strategy implementation and so on to help the construction of the theory, in the development of the brand presents the characteristics of the problem also has the value of the research. [2] The external environment of brand communication is different from that of the early stage of fast fashion development, from the change of brand image construction and consumer demand, to the updating of product design, to the use of new media, fast fashion has made positive changes to cope with the development of the times, and by analysing the above contents, we can summarize the laws in the process of brand development, optimize the brand operation according to these laws, and improve the related problems so that a good cycle can be formed. Improvement to form a good cycle. Fast fashion has three characteristics: fast speed of new products, low price and keeping up with the fashion trend, it is through the feedback and imitation of the elements of the fashion show, and make them affordable, so that its design and the relationship with the mass consumer market is closer. Fast fashion through diversified marketing to enhance market sales, has a good market adaptability, the clothing market demand changes quickly, just in line with the characteristics of fast fashion, which attracts a large number of young people's favourite. [3] According to the characteristics of the fast fashion field, this paper takes Zara as an example to analyse how to better implement brand strategy. This paper takes fast fashion clothing brand Zara as the background, based on Zara's brand strategy research, through analysing Zara's strengths and

*Corresponding author: ebrown51523@student.napavalley.edu

weaknesses in the Chinese market can understand the challenges and characteristics of the clothing industry, and ultimately for the development of China's fast fashion clothing brands to provide inspiration and constructive advice. This paper will understand the current development status of Zara by reviewing the literature and information related to the Zara brand, and analyse the characteristics of the current fast fashion field by introducing the concept of fast fashion led by Zara, and study Zara's profitability model, competitive advantages, audience, product itself and promotion and marketing, so as to summarise the communication pattern and method mode of Zara brand, and then analyse China's fast fashion brand. The article will analyse the problems encountered in the development of China's current apparel industry and put forward relevant strategies for improvement based on Zara's experience. The whole article will be unfolded through the idea of putting forward the problem - analysing the problem - solving the problem.

2.Profit Model

Zara is one of the world's most successful fast-fashion chains. With around 80% contribution of Inditex in 2009, it has become the world's third fashion retailer following the steps of H&M and Gap. There are nearly 2000 shops and 500 Zara Homes in 2023 around the world [4], Zara gained great knowledge in how to provide a style that complements the public needs, manages its prices at a reasonable limit, and distributes high-quality clothes efficiently. This was all made possible due to the following business methods: Vertical integration; Rapid product replacement; Zero Spending on Brand Advertising.

2.1 Vertical Integration

Zara's vertical supply chain allows the company to dominate the process of designing, manufacturing, sourcing, and distribution to retail stores. This allows the company to lower risk by flexibly managing any process before distribution. The company begins the integration with designing with quality instead of spending money on product advertisement and establishing brand recognition. All designs of the products come directly from Zara's designers. Moreover, the balance in fabric supply and manufacturing of the product itself contributes to the company's success. Zara has most of their products manufactured while others are retailed. All products are manufactured in Zara's main site in Spain. Most of the products are shipped from the "A Coruña depot", and all stocks are not held for long periods and are sent out to all the Zara stores twice a week. International deliveries, on the other hand, are delivered to the border of Spain, while the logistic provider in charge of that country takes over the distribution to the stores. Afterward, the ideas and design of a product came from the designer. The designer gets the idea of what product to design next utilizing its sales from stores and customers' feedback and comments. [5] The success of Zara is caused by the dominant control in every aspect of the business process, from design to distribution. By having total control of the process, Zara can quickly adapt to the fast-changing fashion trends and customer preferences, which provides the company with customer demands. This allows Zara to create fashionable clothes within a short period. All the functions of the business work together to produce new collections and designs which are updated and completed every week, this shows the constant production and revision which assures good quality products. Zara shop managers report to designers in La Coruña daily on what has and has not sold. This report is used to determine if a product is to be kept or altered, and whether new lines are to be created.

2.1.1 Zara's Supply Chain

Zara's supply chain is separated into four different sections: design, manufacturing, distribution, and sale. All four steps will be repeated as a cycle to allow Zara to produce high-quality and plentiful amounts of products. In short, this system is designed for short production cycles, quick response to demand, and reduced number of markdowns. First of all, all designers make their designs in the company's main office in Inditex Spain, and the final design will be reviewed quickly for later process. The main role of management in Inditex is to determine apparel designs and manufacturing locations. Afterward, the finished designs will be transferred to three different locations to be manufactured. The 20% of products made in Asia vary in quality due to the cheaper cost; however, the 60% of products produced in-house and in North Africa/Europe have better quality due to higher cost. Next, after the production of the apparel, the products are sent directly to distribution. It is usually distributed in a distribution center where it holds frequent shipments on small scales. All of these lead to a quick response rate for the company which can successfully transfer the distributed products to decentralized stores for sales.

2.2 Rapid Product Replacement

The fashion clothing Zara produces reaches a wide variety of consumers, from kids to adults, at a high production efficiency. Zara's supply chain allows the company to import new apparel to stores at least two a week. To be more specific, after a product is designed, it only takes about 10 to 15 days for the product to reach nearby stores. And this whole process of identifying consumer needs for imported products will take no longer than 30 days. By catching up with fashion trends simultaneously with customers, Zara can have more opportunities to sell products at its full price than selling at a low discount. In contrast to other companies where they try to predict future trends, which causes slow production speed, Zara uses the pull system, a system that produces and distributes in line with the consumers' wants and needs. Zara's constant trend research allowed the company to follow the hot topics accurately. Two methods that Zara collects consumers' preferences and popular styles is by encouraging employees at a Zara store to document consumer preferences on their personal digital assistant. Another way is to give out surveys and collect data from social media, 24 hours active, to understand consumers' fashion sense. Ultimately, this information will be passed on to the analysts to work out new ideas and designs within 24 hours. The benefit of having rapid product replacement is that their working capital requirements are reduced because production is always happening.

2.3 Zero Spending on Brand Advertising

Zara has used almost no advertising or endorsement throughout its entire existence. Preferring, instead, to invest a percentage of its revenues in opening new stores instead. Zara has a very unique approach to marketing compared to its competitors. It spends a meager 0.3 percent of sales on advertising compared to an average of 3.5 percent by competitors. [6] The brand's founder, Amancio, has never spoken to the media nor has they in any way advertised Zara. This is indeed, a truly successful brand where customers appreciate and desire the brand truthfully, and are strongly driven by the brand experience rather than brand popularity. Instead of advertising, Zara displays the stores as the key elements of its marketing strategy. By choosing to be in the most prominent and populated locations in a city, Zara ensures high customer traffic for its sales. Its window displays, where they showcase the most outstanding pieces in the collection, are also an important communication tool designed by its specialized team. A lot of time and effort is put into the window displays since it showcases the company's style and work ethic. Moreover, Zara's work ethic is reflected in its employees who are required to wear Zara "uniforms" to reflect socio-economic differences in the regions they are located. This shows the focus of the mass market with attention to consumer needs.

3.Target Market

Defining the target audience is important in figuring out the right marketing technique. Hence, this section is to drill into the specific demographic of Zara's consumers. Generally, Zara's target age distribution is between adults aged 18-40, including both men and women. Zara's target market is largely focused on Millennials and Gen Z, who are both fashion-conscious and tech-savvy. Zara was quite successful in their target audience, earning an e-commerce revenue of $6.7 billion USD in the year of 2021 [7]. Zara's customers are mainly middle-aged adults, aged 21-30, which is increasingly high compared to the general population's adults aged 20-30. Moreover, Zara's fashion clothing tends to skew more towards female consumers than male in the US with 69% female shoppers and 31% male shoppers. The Zara Kids line taps into their parents who are looking for stylish yet affordable kid's clothing.

4.Market Analysis

Market analysis is crucial in determining the capabilities and opportunities of a company. This paper will look into brief pros and cons of the company's strategies and methods of distributing products and marketing. The SWOT analysis is used widely by analysts, where it examines the strengths, weaknesses, opportunities, and threats. Each category goes into detail on the specific topics that ultimately analyze the company's performance. On the other hand, the 4Ps is a "marketing mix" that allows companies to achieve their targets more efficiently. It is divided into product, pricing, plan and distribution, and promotional and advertising. The last section will be focused on a comparison of Zara with another major fast-fashion brand–H&M, which is extremely different in its methods of production and distribution.

4.1 SWOT Analysis

SWOT, is a method of analyzing a company's competitive situation and is one of the basic analysis methods of marketing. By analyzing it, the company is able to conduct an in-depth and comprehensive analysis of its competitive advantages and position its competitive advantages before formulating development strategies.

4.1.1 Strengths

Zara has high-efficiency production and allows new trendy fashion items to be displayed in stores as soon as possible to follow consumer needs. As mentioned before in this paper, the high production rate allows Zara to market without relying on star endorsement and brand advertisement. Zara produces low-price items that are accessible for most consumers, especially the youth. Its unique approach to making fashion affordable, offering high-end fashion with high quality at a low price. attracted a lot of young fashionistas by providing a similar style to the bigger, more expensive fashion brands. Zara has unique and numerous styles. Mainly relying on the company's supply chain, Zara has managed to have more available time to manage a research team on customer preference through social media and email surveys. The flexible styles allow the company to attract people with a broad range of fashion interests.

4.1.2 Weaknesses

Zara has lower quality products compared to expensive brands. In April 2012, Greenpeace sourced 141 samples from 29 countries and regions around the world and found that ZARA's clothing contained the most harmful substances. Zara has an overly extended scale, in terms of franchised stores. The performance statistics of Zara stores located in major cities are doing well. Yet, the store located in more rural areas might not operate in expectation. The second and third-tier places with Zara stores are threatening the company greatly. Also, due to following popular trends, Zara has a bad for for plagiarism. For instance, ZARA copied illustrations from a New York designer, Adam J. Kurtz, which led to hot discussion and debate from the original artist. Moreover, it was found that Zara has also copied bigger brands like Louis Vuitton, Saint Laurent, Stella McCartney, and other brands in their design.

4.1.3 Opportunity

Zara has increased the development of artificial intelligence (AI technologies). The rapid development potentially assisted the designing stage of the vertical integration. To be more specific, activities like clothing styling, clothing color matching, garment sampling, and virtual fitting can all be done by AI instead of relying on manpower. Zara can also rely on the increase of commonwealth because as the economy continues to develop, Zara can have more opportunities in its target audience purchase abilities. As the Information Era proceeds, Zara can eventually reply more on e-commerce. With the rapid development of technology around the world, Zara can use social media to promote its products with quicker connections and direct feedback from consumers. This avoids wasting time on connecting with consumers individually.

4.1.4 Threats

Due to the lack of brand identification, Zara might suffer from a decrease of consumers. As time changes, people's consumption choices might vary too, since a lot of youngsters value brand fame and recognition a lot more than before. Therefore, the loyalty of customers is normally not high. As shown in Table 1, Zara has strong competitors in this industry. Since Zara produces a variety of clothes, from men's wear, women's wear, to children's wear, its competitor comes from all sorts of big and small clothing retail stores. Moreover, though Zara is known for their low price fast-fashion items, its competitor H&M produces efficiently with almost 20-30% lower prices than Zara. [8] It is also worth the mention that the growth of Shein, founded in Nanjing in 2008, has become the largest fast-fashion retail store by 2022. The prices of Shein's clothing are extremely low, a lot cheaper than Zara's, and since Shein mainly operates online, therefore, the business thrived during COVID times.

Table 1. SWOT content

SWOT	Content
Strength	Efficient production Affordable high-end products Varies and exceptional designs
Weakness	Low-quality products Overly extended scale Plagiarism
Opportunity	Development of AI Increase in income E-commerce
Threats	Lack of brand identification Strong competitors

4.2.4 Ps

In order to determine the marketability of a product, companies have to hold 4 Ps analysis, also known as the "marketing mix". The four Ps are separated into: product, pricing, place, and promotion.

4.2.1 Product Strategy

The products from Zara vary greatly. It is commonly known to sell retail fashion and fast-fashion items; however, it also provides consumers with other choices like shoes, purses, accessories, etc. Moreover, Zara Home, founded in 2003 with about 400 stores opened worldwide [9], gives customers furniture choices. Zara is a well-known fast fashion brand with a total sale of $13 billion USD, therefore, granting them the 3rd largest international fast-fashion brands. The company values unique and high-quality design at a low price, which means that the production and distribution process has to be very efficient. In addition, the company's efficiency in its supply chain and design process, allows Zara to differentiate from other competitors. In many other cases, their low price has become a symbol for many fast-fashion companies.

4.2.2 Pricing Strategy

Most consumers will be able to afford products from Zara due to its affordable pricing and variety of clothing styles. On the other hand, this might mean that the company might be putting in too much supply cost in order to satisfy customer values. If more Zara stores began to experience a decline in profit, Zara should consider increasing their product prices, so it is more expensive for ordinary customers. This is definitely achievable because their products are still considered high-end fashion.

4.2.3 Place and Distribution Strategy

Choosing a sustainable place to distribute Zara apparel is really important because it can affect financial performance since the company does not rely on any brand advertisement. Zara started their small expansion by establishing some stores in Portugal and India. Then it soon spread throughout the world, with around 2000 stores in cities and suburbs. Granted, Zara then became one of the top fast-fashion brands. Besides from physical store expansions, Zara has also managed to create online outlets, making its products more accessible. Online channels are a great way to market to the younger generations who spend a lot of time on social media. This method ultimately creates a better connection between the brands with a wider range of consumers by keeping a strong online presence.

4.2.4 Promotional and Advertising Strategy

Zara's approach to this factor is truly unique. When other companies are spending tons on marketing through TV commercials and celebrity endorsements, Zara relies on inexpensive but high-efficiency methods by utilizing social media frequently. For instance, if Zara wants to do any promotion of new apparel, all it is required to do is to make a Facebook post, then 31 million followers would immediately tune into the announcement.

5.Product

5.1 Feature

Para's product approach can be succinctly summed up in three points: cutting-edge design, quick iteration, and relatively low price. [10] ZARA has a very powerful team of new product designers with a sensitive and accurate understanding of fashion. The designers watch fashion shows and star parties all the time so that they can get inspiration from fashion shows in Milan and Paris, identify popular fashion trends, and imitate the fashion of the trend. Furthermore, ZARA releases new clothing into stores in just 2 weeks. Zara offers the public the latest fashion at incredibly quick speed and relatively affordable costs in contrast to traditional production techniques, which have a production cycle of 4 to 12 months, has won over many fans [11].

5.2 Brand current situation

Take Zara's Chinese market as an example. It makes sense that the demand for apparel will rise as domestic per capita consumption levels rise and people's purchasing power dramatically rises. Nevertheless, figures show that Zara's market share and number of outlets have dramatically declined in recent years. Therefore, it is conceivable that price increases are the primary means through which brand income grows.

The author believes that this phenomenon is significantly related to the consumption downgrade caused by the decrease in income of some customers after the new coronavirus epidemic in 2020. [12] Zara's products pay more attention to design. In order to reduce costs, they do not have good control over the quality of clothes. According to the content released by the quality department, the wool content in a casual Zara pair of pants is nearly half less than the label and is replaced by relatively cheap acrylic and polyester. The phenomenon of reducing the labelled content and replacing it is also very common at Zara. A Zara employee said that the price of cotton has soared in recent years and that the cost of ordinary materials is low. Substituting materials and reducing content can bring greater profits to the company. The major consumer groups currently, however, place greater value on product quality than brand in recent years. More and more people are paying closer attention to picking items with greater cost performance and better quality, especially in light of circumstances like the pandemic and high-rate inflation. In the garment sector, consumer choice is particularly noticeable. This highlights Zara's shortcomings in terms of product quality, which have an impact on clothing sales.

5.3 Suggestions

In response to this phenomenon, the author gives several suggestions. First of all, improving product quality is a must at present. Brands should strengthen the selection of product raw materials and product quality testing. For brands, this means more market research is needed. Brands need to collect the quality of materials provided by different raw material suppliers in different countries for more stringent screening and analysis and take into account the efficiency and cost of logistics transportation generated in the supply chain. On the basis of not significantly increasing the cost, select fabrics that are relatively more durable, comfortable, and cost-effective. In addition, the final product quality inspection should also be strengthened to reduce consumer complaint rates. Increasing after-sales service can also help provide consumers with brand loyalty and retain customers. In addition, on the basis of improving quality, brands should continue to innovate in clothing design to expand brand advantages and attract consumers to purchase. Therefore, the author recommends that brands use social media, combined with digital technology, to analyse the degree of discussion on social media topics. Gain insights into hot trends, combine current hot topics and discussion points, and design clothes that are more in line with the needs of local consumers. In China, a large portion of the consumer population commutes and works. In 2023, 'urban core' will have become a hot topic of discussion among young people. The number of interactions for this keyword on social media, like 'red book, is more than 40,000. Among the clothing previously put on Zara's shelves, only a relatively small amount of clothing meets the needs of this group of consumers. Therefore, the author recommends increasing the number of clothing designs and shelves in this part.

6.Market Campaign

6.1 Advertisement

Regarding advertising and marketing: Zara invests very little in traditional advertising and marketing. Traditional fast fashion brands spend about 3%–4% on advertising every year, while Zara's investment is 0-0.3%, which is almost negligible. This greatly reduces marketing costs and is a strong brand advantage. Savings on advertising costs have almost become another source of profit for it.

6.2 Physical stores

It is worth mentioning that Zara usually opens its stores in high-end business districts and bustling transportation hubs. Although the cost of opening a store in these places is high, But Zara always leaves a spacious space in the store to create a relaxed and pleasant shopping environment for customers. In terms of store layout, watches and clothing in Zara stores are generally not stacked according to product type, but watches, trousers, leather bags, and accessories are put together. Make it easy for customers to buy a whole set of things at once.

Combined with the psychological feelings of consumers, although many people will hang out on bustling commercial streets, not everyone can afford luxury stores. Therefore, when they see Zara stores with lower prices for comparable products and nice decorations in shopping malls, people are more willing to go in and make purchases. The superior geographical location and unique in-store display make Zara extremely attractive without advertising. However, the author still suggests that Zara can increase advertising on social media during the annual discount season to attract more consumers and reduce inventory accumulation while controlling costs.

7.Conclusion

Zara can stand out among many fast-fashion brands. Its success lies in its precise control of brand positioning. It keeps up with trends and consumer needs, embodying the concept of customer demand as the center. Its relatively efficient and complete supply chain system allows it to quickly follow market changes and adjust brand strategy and product supply, laying the foundation for the brand's success. Being highly sensitive to changes in consumers' psychological needs, a series of measures have been taken to further improve the brand's influence. Reasonable revenue and expenditure arrangements greatly reduce production costs and increase brand profitability. In order to further improve brand effectiveness and increase revenue, brands should make some improvements to their own shortcomings while giving full play to their own strengths, for example, by discussing brand quality issues. In addition, it should be combined with current trends, rational use of new media technology, brand innovation, and enhancing brand image. Brands should always pay attention to society's discussion topics about the brand in order to understand society's evaluation of the brand. Social media is an important medium for understanding how your brand is perceived by the outside world. Brands should strengthen their monitoring of social media comments and be good at using advanced digital algorithms to help brands monitor social media discussions in order to propose reasonable countermeasures. In addition, you can also use social media to build a sense of interaction between customers and the brand through comments, likes, votes, etc., to help increase brand stickiness and enhance customer brand loyalty. Brands should not only market their products but also let customers feel the goodwill of the brand in a more sincere way, so that customers are more willing to recommend the brand to more people, achieving positive and natural brand promotion! The author believes that only brands that keep pace with the times and have humanistic sentiments can achieve a better future through marketing!

Authors Contribution

All the authors contributed equally and their names were listed in alphabetical order.

References

1. Gross, A. M., Wolters, P. L., Dombi, E., Baldwin, A., Whitcomb, P., Fisher, M. J., ... & Widemann, B. C. (2020). Selumetinib in children with inoperable plexiform neurofibromas. New England Journal of Medicine, 382(15), 1430-1442.
2. Pinto, E. B., & Fernandes, G. (2021). Collaborative R&D the key cooperation domain for university-industry partnerships sustainability–position paper. Procedia Computer Science, 181, 102-109.
3. Linden, A. R. (2016). An analysis of the fast fashion industry.
4. Statista. (2023) Zara Stores https://www.statista.com/statistics/674434/number-of-zara-stores-worldwide-by-region/ .
5. Palladino, A. P. (2010). Zara and Benetton: Comparison of two business models.
6. Mahardika, P. D., & Santika, W. (2021). Strategies For Creating Competitive Advantage Through Product Development, Design and Quality (Case Study on the ZARA Brand in Badung Regency). American Journal of Humanities and Social Sciences Research (AJHSSR), 5(1), 279-284.
7. Ghiasi, S. (2023). TikTok as a communication platform for brands.
8. Duoyan, H. (2021). Research on ZARA strategy from the perspective of SWOT analysis method. In 2021 6th international conference on social sciences and economic development (ICSSED 2021) . pp. 201-205.
9. Dobre, Baron, O. (2015). The business model of the largest retail chains. Annals of the University of Petroşani. Economics, 15, 17-28.
10. Han Yiqiang (2018) Research on Management Strategy of "Fast Fashion" Brand: Taking ZARA for Example. Journal of Jiangsu Vocational and Technical College of Economics and Trade. 04: 28-31.
11. Gao Xing. (2010) Discussing the Brand Competitiveness of ZARA Clothing Products. Journal of Shandong Textile Economy. 08: 28-40.
12. Sun Hao, Mao Zhonggen,Wang Zehao. (2020) Consumption downgrade: False Images and Their Warnings. Journal of economics and management. 34(03): 19-26.

Analysis of the Marketing Strategy of HEYTEA

Kunhuan Li*

School of Sports Engineering, Beijing Sport University, Beijing, 100000, China

Abstract. The aim of this paper is to study HEYTEA's marketing strategies, exploring its path to success and its impact on the market. Through a detailed analysis of HEYTEA's development history and marketing practices, the unique strategies and innovative initiatives of HEYTEA in market competition are investigated. The research adopts two methods, literature review and case analysis, combined with relevant data and information, to comprehensively analyze HEYTEA's marketing strategies from multiple dimensions. The research findings indicate that the key to HEYTEA's success lies in its strategic collaborations with other brands and co-branding activities. Through partnerships with well-known brands, HEYTEA has expanded its consumer base and enhanced its brand image. Additionally, the constant product innovation and introduction of new beverages have been crucial factors in attracting consumers. HEYTEA's continuous adaptation to meet the demands of young consumers for personalized and trendy drinks has been instrumental in its success. The conclusion of the study is that HEYTEA's marketing strategies have achieved success with predominantly positive effects. HEYTEA has gained consumer favor and obtained a competitive advantage in a highly competitive market through collaborations with other brands and product innovation. It is recommended that HEYTEA continues to focus on innovation, strengthen digital marketing, and expand its international market efforts to maintain its leading position and achieve sustainable development in the future.

1.Introduction

In the modern business landscape, effective marketing strategies play a crucial role in driving the success and growth of a brand. With the rise of the digital era, companies are exploring innovative approaches to reach and engage with their target audience. HEYTEA, a renowned Chinese tea brand, has emerged as a prominent player in the highly competitive beverage industry through its unique marketing strategies and new media integration. HEYTEA was born in 2012 as a small street-side shop in an alley. Initially, it was called "Huang Cha" and had the English name "ROYALTEA." Despite its small size, HEYTEA continuously introduced innovative and attractive products at a time when modern-style milk tea had not yet emerged. As a result, it had already formed a certain consumer base. In 2016, the company decided to abandon the original name and rebranded itself as HEYTEA, which means "inspiration tea." Today, HEYTEA has grown into a large-scale business, with its headquarters being ShenzhenMeixi Catering Management Co., Ltd. Thanks to HEYTEA's bold innovations, its corporate culture resonates well with the young consumer demographic, leading to widespread acceptance and admiration [1]. This paper aims to analyze the marketing strategies employed by HEYTEA and examine how the brand leverages new media platforms to enhance its market presence. By delving into the various aspects of HEYTEA's marketing approach, people can gain valuable insights into the company's success and understand the implications for other businesses in the industry. The significance of this study lies in exploring HEYTEA's marketing strategies, which have proven instrumental in its rapid growth and popularity among consumers. Understanding the underlying principles and tactics employed by HEYTEA can provide valuable lessons for marketers, entrepreneurs, and industry professionals seeking to create impactful marketing campaigns. The paper will follow a structured approach to analyze HEYTEA's marketing strategy, focusing on key elements such as product differentiation, aesthetic design, co-branding collaborations, and integration with digital marketing channels. Additionally, this analysis will highlight the company's utilization of advertising, digital marketing, public relations, and discounts as communication tools within its integrated marketing efforts. By examining HEYTEA's marketing strategy and its integration with new media platforms, people can gain insights into the effective utilization of various marketing channels to attract and engage consumers. This analysis will provide a comprehensive understanding of how HEYTEA's marketing strategies have contributed to its brand recognition, customer loyalty, and market competitiveness. The subsequent sections of this paper will delve into the specific marketing activities and collaborations undertaken by HEYTEA, providing a detailed examination of its advertising techniques, digital marketing campaigns, and discount strategies. Through this comprehensive analysis, the researchers aim to uncover the key factors driving HEYTEA's marketing

*Corresponding author's mail: 2020011046@bsu.edu.cn

success and draw relevant implications for industry practitioners. In conclusion, this paper will shed light on HEYTEA's marketing strategy, highlighting its integration with new media platforms and the effectiveness of its various marketing collaborations. By analyzing the company's approach, marketers and businesses can gain valuable insights into successful marketing tactics in the beverage industry and adapt them to their own contexts. Ultimately, this analysis aims to contribute to the existing body of knowledge on marketing strategies and provide practical guidance for businesses aspiring to achieve similar success in the market.

2.Competitive edge

Competitive advantage refers to the advantage that a company obtains in the market relative to its competitors, enabling it to stand out and achieve success. Here are the competitive advantages that HEYTEA possesses in the market competition: HEYTEA's products have a great taste and high-quality ingredients. Traditional milk tea beverages often use cheap tea powder and milk powder as ingredients. However, HEYTEA abandons these unhealthy ingredients and uses fresh tea leaves and fresh milk as the tea base for its products. Additionally, HEYTEA innovatively combines salty and creamy cheese to create a "tea-based with cheese topping" healthy beverage. HEYTEA quickly gained popularity among young customers with its product innovation, high-quality and healthy ingredients, and rich flavor. The offline stores are stylish and minimalist, providing a completely new experiential environment. HEYTEA embraces the current trend of fashionable minimalism and designs its stores based on its brand philosophy of "cool, inspiration, Zen, and design." The stores are equipped with comfortable waiting and leisure areas for customers, creating landing points for customer entertainment, socializing, and even work. Customers can engage in daily social interactions, gatherings, and work activities within the stores. HEYTEA empowers the business through store space design and redefines the scene experience in the tea beverage industry. Enthusiasm for cross-industry collaborations and the launch of co-branded products. Since its establishment in 2017, HEYTEA has collaborated with over 50 brands, spanning a wide range of industries, including cosmetics, cultural and creative products, fashion, daily necessities, and the internet. This approach caters to the characteristics of young customers who are fond of novelty. By leveraging the brand influence of both collaborating parties, HEYTEA brings together complementary consumer groups and generates increased brand discussion and buzz [2].

3.Marketing mode

Therefore, the next step will be to analyze further how HEYTEA integrates its marketing strategy and its new media marketing strategy with other marketing collaborations. The key to integrated marketing is to determine a unified theme for the company, coordinate the use of various communication channels, and leverage the advantages of different communication tools to achieve higher profits. It can be seen that HEYTEA maintains a central theme and objective across almost all marketing channels. Direct statements such as "Bring authentic quality tea drinks and brands that inspire joy to more users" can be seen on the official accounts of every new media platform. Surprisingly, during the data collection process, it was discovered that almost all of HEYTEA's marketing activities and products can be summarized into two keywords: differentiated product and aesthetic and inspired design. The four main communication tools in integrated marketing include advertising, digital marketing, public relations, and discounts. Through investigation, it can be seen that HEYTEA is very adept at using co-branding to spread social topics and gain new fans and amplified effects through interactions with other brands. Taking HEYTEA's recent co-branding activity as an example, this analysis will examine the efforts made in the process of integrated marketing from the perspectives of the four communication tools. Let's start with a brief introduction to the co-branding case. HEYTEA collaborated with a popular Chinese game called "Genshin Impact." Genshin Impact is currently one of the most popular games in China, and HEYTEA aimed to attract more new consumers through this collaboration. In just 10 days, HEYTEA sold 1.4 million cups of beverages during the co-branding campaign. The first communication tool is advertising. HEYTEA decorated some special theme stores for the co-branding campaign, where game characters were displayed on the walls, attracting more game enthusiasts to take photos. In return, HEYTEA's beverages were added to the hands of the game characters. Regarding digital marketing, HEYTEA has always been focused on promoting its brand on online platforms. HEYTEA promotes activities and new beverages on multiple platforms simultaneously and even launches fan creation contests to increase engagement. On Douyin (TikTok), HEYTEA promotes beverages through short videos within one minute, using popular internet memes and recommended music. On Bilibili (B Site), HEYTEA attracts netizens with 3-10 minute store exploration vlogs and themed videos on replicating beverages at home. On Xiaohongshu (Little Red Book), HEYTEA invites numerous KOLs (Key Opinion Leaders) and KOSs (Key Opinion Shapers) to taste the beverages in advance and share their experiences. On Weibo, HEYTEA provides real-time updates on the latest sales information and lottery activities. The data exported from TikTok's backend shows the 15 most popular videos from this co-branding campaign. Surprisingly, none of these videos were posted by HEYTEA itself but were created by invited internet celebrities. In some smaller activities within the co-branding campaign, it is worth mentioning that HEYTEA attracted all game fans to its private domain platform through interactive quizzes and rewarded them with in-game items. From these examples, it can be seen that HEYTEA employs multiple communication tools in its integrated marketing, including advertising, digital marketing, public relations, and discounts. The following analysis will delve into

HEYTEA's specific strategies in these areas and its collaborations with other marketing efforts. Advertising: HEYTEA promotes its co-branding campaigns through store decorations and posters. For example, in the collaboration with the game "Genshin Impact," HEYTEA decorated special theme stores and displayed game characters on the walls to attract the attention of game enthusiasts. Additionally, HEYTEA combined game characters with their beverages on vertical posters to increase the appeal of their advertisements. Digital Marketing: HEYTEA places great emphasis on promoting its brand on online platforms. They simultaneously promote activities and new beverages on multiple platforms, and organize fan creation contests to generate more discussions. For example, on Douyin (TikTok), HEYTEA promotes their beverages through short videos with internet memes and popular music. On Bilibili (B Site), they release store exploration vlogs and videos showcasing how to replicate their beverages at home to attract netizens. On Xiaohongshu (Little Red Book), HEYTEA invites KOLs and KOSs to preview their beverages and share their experiences. On Weibo, HEYTEA provides real-time updates on the latest sales information and conducts lottery activities. Public Relations: HEYTEA engages in co-branding activities with other brands to generate social topics and gain more fans and amplified effects. Such collaborations help HEYTEA attract new consumers. For example, HEYTEA collaborated with the popular game "Genshin Impact," which attracted a large number of game enthusiasts' attention and resulted in a significant increase in beverage sales during the campaign. Discounts: HEYTEA offers promotional discounts during specific occasions or events to attract more customers. This strategy helps increasesales and create a sense of urgency among consumers. However, it's important to note that the specific details of HEYTEA's discount strategies were not mentioned in the given information. In summary, HEYTEA integrates its marketing strategy and new media marketing strategy by utilizing various communication tools such as advertising, digital marketing, public relations, and discounts. The co-branding collaborations with popular brands or games, like the "Genshin Impact" partnership, help HEYTEA generate social topics, attract new consumers, and increase sales. HEYTEA also leverages online platforms to promote its brand and engage with consumers through creative and engaging content. By coordinating these different marketing efforts, HEYTEA aims to maintain a consistent theme and objective across all channels while maximizing the impact and reach of its marketing campaigns.

4.Product

When it comes to HEYTEA's marketing, HEYTEA's co-branded model deserves mention. HEYTEA has successfully executed collaborations across various domains, including popular games, Chinese-style TV series, high-end luxury brands, and office software. While these collaborations may initially seem improbable, HEYTEA has managed to achieve them. Based on the information gathered from HEYTEA's official WeChat account and Weibo, the author selected HEYTEA's co-branding marketing activities conducted from January 1, 2019, as the research sample. As of October 30, 2020, HEYTEA has conducted a total of 46 co-branding marketing activities. Among all the co-branding activities, the highest number of collaborations was with food brands, accounting for 39% of the total, with 18 collaborations. This includes 8 collaborations with beverage brands. HEYTEA has collaborated with similar brands, especially with ChaYanYueSe and %Arabica, which are considered similar brands in consumers' minds. The collaboration with ChaYanYueSe, a popular tea brand in Changsha with a "new Chinese-style tea beverage" positioning, was particularly intriguing to consumers, although it may have seemed confusing. Both brands benefited from this collaboration. Firstly, ChaYanYueSe is currently a regional brand, mainly operating in Changsha and exploring the market in Wuhan, while HEYTEA is positioned as a global brand. The two brands only have minimal conflicts in their business presence in Changsha because ChaYanYueSe focuses on cream and tea, while HEYTEA specializes in cheese and tea. Secondly, the combination of ChaYanYueSe's "Chinese style" and HEYTEA's "trendy" aligns with the brand images both brands aim to create. The second highest number of collaborations was with fashion brands. Fashion brands have the most frequent co-branding marketing activities in the market, with successful examples such as Nike and Uniqlo. The third category is furniture brands. As HEYTEA is a tea beverage brand, it naturally evokes associations with cups for consumers. Therefore, collaborations with home furnishing brands, or even directly with cup brands, meet consumer expectations. Additionally, it is worth noting that HEYTEA's co-branding boundaries are expanding. The collaborations have extended beyond personal care products such as body wash and skincare to include games, animation, and even mobile applications. These collaborations with brands that are not directly related to the tea industry help expand HEYTEA's scene range and break industry boundaries. Furthermore, in previous co-branding activities, HEYTEA's logo was prominently positioned, indicating that HEYTEA primarily led the collaborations. However, in recent collaborations with brands like Hema and Wonderlab Milkshake, HEYTEA's logo was placed in a secondary position, suggesting that HEYTEA has become a chosen co-branding partner for other brands. This also indirectly reflects that HEYTEA's brand attractiveness has drawn the attention of other advertisers.[3] Let's begin by examining recent collaborations with popular games. The accompanying product image on the left side of this page showcases HEYTEA's collaboration with the otaku-favorite game, Genshin Impact. As a highly popular game, HEYTEA capitalized on this partnership by offering limited edition drinks and merchandise. Some consumers purchased these drinks solely for the sake of the associated peripheral products. HEYTEA's limited edition drinks stand apart from the ordinary due to their integration of game-inspired elements, which resonates with consumers and justifies their willingness to pay a premium. Despite a supply of 1.4 million units, the products quickly became out of stock, signifying HEYTEA's success in capturing the hearts of gamers. This collaboration has proved so fruitful that HEYTEA recently embarked on a second collaboration with the same game, indicating satisfaction with their previous cooperation. [4] Another notable collaboration involves Fendi, a renowned high-end brand. This year, Fendi and HEYTEA joined forces to launch a collaboration that generated considerable buzz. Some individuals even claimed that HEYTEA was responsible for introducing them to their first cup of Fendi. Together, Fendi and HEYTEA organized an art exhibition titled "Hand in Hand," providing consumers with a limited product experience infused with Chinese Yi characteristics, showcasing respect for craftsmanship and local culture. Prior to the art exhibition, the co-branded cup bodies, coasters, and badges became highly sought-after items among consumers. This collaboration stands as a unique innovation within the tea industry, leveraging the stark contrast between the two brands to generate widespread attention, including trending on social media. The accompanying image of a queue of 200 cups waiting at ten o'clock in the morning on the exhibition day further attests to the public's enthusiastic anticipation and satisfaction with HEYTEA's collaboration. This success aligns with HEYTEA's aspiration to inspire consumers with bold, avant-garde, and fashion-forward tea experiences, reflecting the brand's unwavering ambition. [5] Regarding the acquisition of these insights, they were primarily obtained through social media platforms. HEYTEA boasts a substantial following of 450,000 fans on Xiaohongshu, with each post receiving hundreds or even tens of thousands of likes. This platform has enabled HEYTEA to reach and engage a diverse audience, promoting their collaborations to a wide array of users. Leveraging social media has facilitated rapid brand dissemination, heightened product exposure, provided timely feedback, and fostered brand recognition and customer loyalty. [6] Moreover, marketing on social media has proven cost-effective, allowing HEYTEA to allocate resources more effectively towards the development of new products.

In conclusion, HEYTEA's co-branding strategies, exemplified by its successful collaborations, have enabled the brand to expand its reach, enhance customer loyalty, and position itself as a trendsetter in the tea industry.

5.Social media

This passage is focusing on the mini-program of HEYTEA which name is HEYTEA GO, which is also a kind of social platform. At that time, the biggest pain point for HEYTEA was the long queue time for customers. After the launch of the "HEYTEA GO" mini-program, it achieved integration of ordering, appointments, and delivery. Within 7 months of its launch, "HEYTEA GO" attracted 6 million users through zero-cost promotion, with a repurchase rate reaching 300%.[7] This data reduced the number of people queuing at HEYTEA stores while significantly increasing the order volume and improving operational efficiency. Most importantly, the data accumulated from user interactions allowed HEYTEA to develop a clear user profile and understand consumer preferences. In the early stages, HEYTEA's promotion of the mini-program was simple. They would display a QR code in their stores, encouraging customers to scan and order without having to queue. As the promotion expanded, HEYTEA introduced dedicated "Go Quick Sales" stores specifically for the mini-program service. These stores were small in size and exclusively accepted orders through the mini-program. HEYTEA added a large number of users through this mini-program. How to Personalize Marketing? The author crawled a lot of data on the website for analysis. Based on the data obtained from online crawling of HEYTEA GO, the author believe that HEYTEA should focus on the following two aspects on HEYTEA GO in the future: The sales of succulent grapes are the best, which means that no matter how many new products are launched, HEYTEA should prioritize the marketing of succulent grapes. [8] Young people seek unique and personalized experiences. HEYTEA will introduce the concept of personalized customization, allowing customers to tailor their tea beverages based on their taste preferences. By offering a variety of flavor options, ingredient choices, and sweetness adjustments, HEYTEA will ensure that each customer can enjoy a one-of-a-kind HEYTEA experience. HEYTEA can leverage social media platforms to launch engaging and attention-grabbing marketing campaigns. Through collaborations with popular social media platforms among young people, such as Instagram, TikTok, and WeChat, HEYTEA will share carefully crafted visual content, fun challenges, and user-generated content activities to engage young people and encourage them to share. [9] Additionally, HEYTEA will collaborate with key opinion leaders (KOLs) and social media influencers to become brand ambassadors, further expanding brand influence. Young people seek unique and personalized experiences. The mini-program will introduce the concept of personalized customization, allowing customers to tailor their tea beverages based on their taste preferences and preferences. By offering a variety of flavor options, ingredient choices, and sweetness adjustments, HEYTEA will ensure that each customer can enjoy a one-of-a-kind HEYTEA experience. Partner with popular brands and designers to launch limited-edition co-branded products. Such collaborations will attract young people's attention and enhance the brand's fashionability and uniqueness. [10] Additionally, HEYTEA can collaborate with music, art, and fashion events to host special activities and parties, creating more HEYTEA-related social experiences for young people. HEYTEA stores will focus on creative and interactive designs. These stores will introduce innovative interior decorations and interactive elements such as art installations on walls, projection mapping, and virtual reality technology to capture the interest and engagement of young people. By creating a unique and distinctive store experience, HEYTEA will establish a social space that attracts young people to visit, take photos, and share. Establish a user engagement and reward program to encourage active participation in HEYTEA's activities and social media interactions. By offering incentives such as check-ins, sharing, commenting, and referring friends, users can earn points, discounts, and exclusive benefits. Such programs will inspire young people's involvement and loyalty while increasing their interaction with the HEYTEA brand.

6.Conclusion

The research on HEYTEA's marketing strategies has provided valuable insights into the brand's success and its impact on the market. Through the analysis of HEYTEA's co-branding activities and its evolution from a small street-side shop to a prominent player in the tea beverage industry, several key findings have emerged.

Firstly, HEYTEA's strategic collaborations with various brands, particularly in the food and beverage industry, have contributed significantly to its growth and brand recognition. The partnerships with similar brands, such as ChaYanYueSe and %Arabica, have allowed HEYTEA to tap into new consumer segments and strengthen its brand image. Secondly, HEYTEA's ability to adapt to market trends and introduce innovative products has been a driving force behind its success. By constantly offering unique and appealing tea beverages, HEYTEA has been able to attract and retain a loyal customer base, even in a highly competitive market. The research findings have demonstrated a predominantly positive impact on HEYTEA's brand reputation and consumer perception. HEYTEA's bold rebranding and its alignment with the preferences of the young consumer demographic have propelled its rapid acceptance and admiration. Looking ahead, it is recommended that HEYTEA continues to focus on product innovation and strategic collaborations to maintain its competitive edge. Expanding its co-branding boundaries into new industries and exploring partnerships with global brands could further enhance HEYTEA's brand influence and market reach. Additionally, HEYTEA should invest in digital marketing and e-commerce capabilities to capitalize on the growing trend of online shopping and delivery services. Leveraging social media platforms and implementing targeted marketing campaigns will help HEYTEA engage with a wider audience and strengthen its brand presence.

As the tea beverage market continues to evolve, HEYTEA's future development is expected to be characterized by sustained growth, expanding market share, and increased international presence. By staying true to its core values of innovation, quality, and customer satisfaction, HEYTEA is well-positioned to remain a leading player in the industry and continue delighting tea lovers with its unique and inspiring offerings.

References

1. Shao, Z.Y. (2022) Research on the Optimization of Word-of-mouth Marketing Strategy for HEYTEA. Journal of Donghua University, 56(44): 455.
2. Ji, R.X, Yan, G.D, Liu, Y.A. (2021) Analysis of marketing strategy of HEYTEA based on AHP-SWOT model. Business and Management,11: 56-60.
3. Zhang, Z.C. (2021) Study on joint marketing strategy of HEYTEA. Business Economy, 06: 73-77.
4. Yu, Y.Q. (2020) Research on Marketing Mode Transformation of Chain Catering Enterprises in the New Media Era —— Taking HEYTEA as an Example. Modern Business,30,8-10.
5. Bai,T, Yu,J.(2021) Analysis on the Internet Marketing Strategy of HEYTEA. Today's Wealth (China Intellectual Property),01: 79-80.
6. Tian, G.Y, Zhou, X.Q. (2023) Research on Word-of-mouth Marketing Strategy of HEYTEA. Modern Business, 01: 7-10.
7. Zhang,J.J. (2021) Analysis on the Causes of "Phenomenological" Punching in online celebrity Brand Tea. Time-honored brand marketing, 09: 15-16.
8. Lu, J.H. (2021) HEYTEA: the way to break the circle of new tea brands. International brand observation, 16: 51-54.
9. Zhang, J. (2022) Study on the Optimization of HEYTEA Marketing Strategy. Journal of Lanzhou University of Technology, 45(01): 490.
10. Guo, S.H, Sheng,L.R. (2020) Research on the Marketing Strategy of "HEYTEA" Content. Enterprise technology and development, 10: 199-201.

The Impact and Investigation of Starbucks' Profit Generation Strategies

Qun Zhou*

Dulwich International High School, Suzhou, 215000, China

Abstract. The noticeable proliferation of Starbucks outlets stands as a testament to the company's burgeoning success in the market and its exceptional adaptability within the dynamic beverage industry landscape. In this paper, we embark on an in-depth exploration of various dimensions within Starbucks' intricate marketing strategy, encompassing elements such as brand logo, brand loyalty, target consumer demographics, location selection criteria, pricing methodologies, product promotion tactics, and advertising strategies. As Starbucks continues its relentless global expansion, our comprehensive analysis endeavors to illuminate the multifaceted strategies that the company employs to sustain its preeminence in the fiercely competitive coffee market. The study delves into the ways Starbucks has effectively harnessed the power of its iconic brand logo, masterfully cultivated unwavering brand loyalty among its diverse consumer base, astutely catered to the unique preferences of specific target demographics, strategically handpicked prime locations for its outlets, meticulously positioned its pricing strategies, and innovatively deployed product promotion and advertising techniques. By conducting a thorough examination of these diverse facets that constitute the bedrock of Starbucks' approach, our research seeks to offer invaluable insights into the complex interplay of factors that underlie the brand's enduring prosperity and its enduring appeal on a global scale. As Starbucks' influence continues to expand and evolve, our analysis aims to provide a comprehensive understanding of the dynamics that drive its continued success, making it a compelling case study for both academics and industry professionals alike.

1.Introduction

In recent years, Starbucks has emerged as a compelling global success story, capturing the imagination of not only coffee enthusiasts but also business leaders and strategists worldwide. This phenomenon has elicited widespread attention and engendered thoughtful contemplation among managers, academics, and industry experts alike. The proliferation of Starbucks stores, serving as tangible markers of this success, has become a defining feature of the contemporary social and economic landscape [1]. Starbucks' ascendancy as a market leader has been characterized by its remarkable adaptability within the ever-evolving beverage industry. With a discerning glance at society, one cannot help but notice the steady increase in the number of Starbucks stores. This observable expansion signifies Starbucks' growing influence in the market and its remarkable ability to adapt to the dynamic and competitive beverage industry. This adaptability has not only allowed Starbucks to flourish but has also presented an intriguing case study for those seeking to understand the intricacies of business success in the modern world.

This paper embarks on a comprehensive exploration of Starbucks, delving deep into the intricate facets of its business model and marketing strategies. We delve into the very essence of Starbucks, dissecting its marketing strategy to uncover the underlying principles that have propelled it to the pinnacle of the coffee industry. We scrutinize elements such as the iconic Starbucks brand logo, analyzing its impact and significance in fostering brand recognition and loyalty. Intriguingly, Starbucks has managed to cultivate a remarkably loyal customer base—a phenomenon people investigate in detail. People examine the diverse consumer groups that Starbucks appeals to, dissecting the strategies employed to cater to their varying tastes and preferences. Moreover, the analysis ventures into the strategic importance of location selection for Starbucks stores. People explore how the choice of prime locations has contributed to the brand's prominence and accessibility to a wide and diverse audience.

2.Profit model

With the continuous development of China's economy, many industries and fields in the economic market are approaching saturation. From relying on the incremental economic model brought by the demographic dividend to the flood of seizing the stock economic model, Starbucks coffee has become a leader in the field of competence. How to win the favor of consumers in the increasingly fierce competition, enhance customer

*Corresponding author's email: Scarlett.zhou24@stu.dulwich.org

loyalty, to build brand culture, Starbucks has made a new attempt - by building a sense of brand ritual to achieve the purpose. These include a sense of environmental ritual, visual sense of ritual, auditory sense of ritual, interactive sense of ritual and other multiple shaping strategies [1]. The profit model of Starbucks is very simple. Starbucks stores are generally located in downtown areas where there are shopping malls or office buildings. Such places are places with high traffic. Through the establishment of stores, brush "presence" in front of consumers, improve the brand's own visibility. It can be seen that Starbucks mainly relies on experiential marketing and word-of-mouth marketing to maintain customer relations.

2.1 Brand logo

The Starbucks brand logo is characterized by its uniqueness. The name Starbucks is just as intriguing as its logo. It originates from the American writer Melville's novel "Moby-Dick," where there is a calm and charismatic first mate who happens to be a coffee enthusiast. This connection makes it fitting that Starbucks is a coffee shop. The Starbucks logo features a siren from Greek mythology, a two-tailed sea god resembling a mermaid. The mermaid image in the logo carries a dual meaning of blending the primitive and modern: her face is simplistic, yet she is presented in a modern abstract style, primarily in black and white, with a colorful circle surrounding the outside. This iconic logo was created in 1971 by a young Seattle designer named Teri Heckler, who drew inspiration from a medieval woodcut depicting the sea god. With a minimalist color style, consumers can remember the mark briefly. Now, when consumers see this iconic color, they think of Starbucks. Of course, the Starbucks logo doesn't just appear on stores and coffee cups. In the beginning, Starbucks mainly sold coffee beans, and they printed the logo on everything related to coffee, such as key chains, star cards, or cloth bags. They try to make the brand logo appear in the eyes of consumers as much as possible. The power of Starbucks is not only to "spread" the logo, but also to "gather" people. For many people, the mermaid image in the logo has long become a symbol of American coffee culture. This classic image has been consistently recognizable in any version of the Starbucks logo throughout its history, but few people seem to notice that the mermaid known as the "Starbucks Goddess" is slightly different from the image people take for granted in people's minds - it's a two-tailed mermaid. The mermaid with two tails is indeed not very common in people's visual memory, is it a designer to make its composition more symmetrical and intentional, or the two-tailed mermaid itself has some special meaning [2]? From the beginning, this logo was intended to express "coffee as seductive as a mermaid", to the current green two-tailed mermaid. Starbucks intends to portray the mermaid as a combination of man and nature, a symbol of abundance in ancient civilizations. people can also use such a special mark to let consumers remember their logo. The evolving logo design went through several changes before it was finalized in 1987. The mermaid's green hair color and the stars in the coffee cup symbolize the quality and taste of Starbucks coffee.

2.2 Brand loyalty

In the era of rapid development of socialist market economy, brand competition has become a fierce means of competition between enterprises. Brand loyalty determines the market position of enterprises and directly relates to the operating efficiency of enterprises. Therefore, it is of great practical significance to study brand loyalty for enterprises [3]. When a brand has a certain popularity, it will produce a fixed consumer group. This group of consumer have brand loyalty, which means consumers will prefer this brand goods than others. The customer's understanding of brand loyalty is the customer's trust in the brand, which is the value of the customer. This increases the stickiness between goods and consumers. For example, when consumers approve of Starbucks coffee or Starbucks products, they are more likely to make a second purchase. Consumers will also rely on Starbucks products, which will build consumers' trust in the brand. Starbucks takes advantage of consumer loyalty to maintain the relationship between consumers and products. These customers who are loyal to the brand will most likely recommend their satisfactory products to people around them. Then Starbucks will gain new users, and so on, while building brand loyalty, expand their target group, and bring maximum benefits to the company.

3.Consumer loyalty

Customer loyalty essentially reflects the extent to which customers prefer and rely on a company. It is both a behavioral state and a result of customers' satisfaction with the company. In simpler terms, customer loyalty isn't just about how customers feel psychologically but also about the strength of the connection between their attitude towards a company and their actual patronage behavior. Therefore, measuring customer loyalty involves analyzing both customer behavior and their attitudes [4]. Over the past 50 years, Starbucks has evolved from a small coffee shop into a global leader in the coffee service industry, with a presence worldwide. During its development, Starbucks has progressively identified its target customer groups. Positioning them in the middle and high-end groups with low price sensitivity, such as white-collar workers who love fashion and pursue avant-garde, enthusiasts who have a special fondness for coffee culture, and elites who pursue brand symbolism. Lots of elites, merchants, professors. They always need to on business trip around the world, which means they do not have enough time to know different brand of coffee. During the business trips they may have lots of meeting. Therefore, these people will very busy. They reason why these people enjoy coffee because coffee can refresh people. In this case, coffee can help them keep a good state at work. Look at Starbucks from their perspective, Starbucks have simple, uniform decoration,and their menu as simple as well. The time for these people are limit and when they come Starbucks,they can just order the type which they enjoy before. On the other hand, Starbucks focus on have life and social experience consumers . As the target target audience of Starbucks likes to experience fashionable, high-quality and high-end consumption feelings, and takes coffee shops as a social platform, where they can enjoy delicious coffee and pastries, chat with friends, relax or work. In addition, they often focus on brand image and environmental awareness, and like to establish an emotional connection with brands that are also environmentally conscious and socially responsible. When customers enter Starbucks to buy products, most of the time they will find someone sitting there in a quiet office. This place really help some workers, elites when they have to have a meeting when they may not in the company.

3.1 Location place

Grab the commanding heights: The store is the best advertising Starbucks grab gold shops, willing to spend money, but also know how to enjoy. [5] Starbucks focus on two ways to make decisions where should they set up.First, they want to find the place which is crowed. After Starbucks selects the business district, they will measure the flow of people, determine the main flow line, select the gathering point, and take the location of the gathering point not far away as the location of the store. Because on the main flow line of people, this means that the maximum flow of people passing through the unit time is at the position of the gathering point, indicating that the crowd stays here for a long time. This brings one of the most direct "benefits" consumers walking on the street can see the store at a glance. This place means more people may pass by and they will have more opportunity to go into the Starbucks and buy somethings. Second important factor for Starbucks select the position is covenience. Convenient transportation and the accessibility of the store location are important conditions for consumers to choose. This is the catering industry must consider the problem. The number of parking Spaces, the area of radiation, the number of parking Spaces in the radiation area, the purpose of such consideration is to increase the rate of guests entering the store. When Starbucks opens in a mall, there will be a certain amount of traffic, and the mall will have its own parking space. In this way, there is no need to worry about the flow of people and there is no parking space. If Starbucks is located near a residential building farther from the city center, they may have less foot traffic because there are fewer people in the residential building that they target, and fewer people will drive near the store to buy coffee.

4.Product pricing

A single cup of coffee has garnered an unprecedented level of attention, drawing Starbucks into the debate on profiteering. In this discussion on profiteering, there are diverse opinions from various perspectives. Wang Zhendong, President of the Shanghai Coffee Professional Committee, asserted that the material cost of a 354ml medium-sized latte is less than 5 yuan. In response to this, Starbucks issued a statement regarding its pricing. Starbucks' pricing strategy varies across different countries and is developed over the long term, taking into account the specific conditions of distinct products and markets. In the Chinese market, Starbucks faces unique operating costs and market dynamics that differ from those in other countries. This leads to questions such as, "What should be the appropriate price for a cup of Starbucks coffee?" and "What is Starbucks' pricing strategy?" How should Starbucks' success prompt similar industries in China to rethink? [6] This article mention the price which Starbucks set in Chinese market and provide a question about why Starbucks give different prices in different regions. On the one hand, Starbucks provides a rare leisure environment for Chinese people. The data shows that Chinese and Americans have different spending patterns at Starbucks. 80 percent of Americans don't eat, but grab coffee and leave. Chinese people like to drink and relax in coffee shops. Moreover, many people sit in Starbucks for an afternoon after consumption, as afternoon tea and relaxation, and there are also office crowds. The resulting opportunity cost may be the reason for high domestic prices. On the other hand, the relatively low demand elasticity of domestic Starbucks consumer groups for its products is also one of the reasons for the high pricing of Starbucks in the domestic market. The sensitivity of domestic consumers to a cup of Starbucks coffee is not as high as that of other countries, and enterprises will naturally adjust product prices based on the perspective of profit maximization. From the cost of Starbucks raw material. The cost of coffee beams is low someone may think it is not possible for a cup of coffee price set above 25 RMB. However, people did not focus on the four factors of production. Four factors of production include land, labour, capital and enterprise. First and formost, Starbucks need to find places to grow coffee trees and they will pay the rent or buy the land. One type of cost occurs. Then they need to hire staff to grow, water the plant, and picking coffee beans, processing coffee beans and so on. The second type of cost occurs. When processing coffee beams, they have to use machines to help them. Therefore, they have to pay for machines. When everything is ready for production, the store will be built. The company also needs to open a shop, decorate, including coffee machines, chairs, tables, cabinets and so on. There's a division of labor, so there's a need to hire. The final price of coffee takes into account all the costs of production. Starbucks is also a well-known brand, so there will be brand premium, and the added value of this brand should also be added to the cost, which indicates that the cost accounting method is no longer fully applicable to Starbucks.

4.1 Product positioning

The middle class's higher income levels enable them to afford a more elevated level of consumption. As a result, Starbucks' investment in the domestic market is naturally different from its approach in other markets like the United States. Apart from roasting high-quality coffee and promoting its unique coffee culture, ensuring a flawless customer experience has become another primary objective for Starbucks. These factors have transformed Starbucks into a cherished "coffee companion." During this time, coffee has become both a reason and a pretext for people to gather. Starbucks uses the coffee label to amalgamate cultural elements, allowing its customers to find solace and a connection to themselves [7]. Brand positioning serves as the cornerstone of a brand's strategy. It strives to create a lasting image for the brand, shaping its distinctive characteristics and setting the direction for future brand development. In the context of brand positioning theory, it involves the enterprise specifying a particular market position based on consumers' perceptions, understanding, and attention towards the brand. This strategy aims to cultivate specific product characteristics and brand images in consumers' minds, catering to their preferences and needs [8]. From the above mentioned Starbucks provides them with a comfortable environment, such as afternoon tea, talking to work, holding a simple meeting, etc. Looking at the whole coffee circle, only Starbucks should be able to provide them with such an environment. Why the elite love Starbucks so much. From the above mentioned Starbucks provides them with a comfortable environment, such as afternoon tea, talking to work, holding a simple meeting, etc. Looking at the whole coffee circle, only Starbucks should be able to provide them with such an environment. The matching sofa chair and round table, the unified color, is now the pursuit of young people's comfort and simple style. Nowadays, the three words "Starbucks" are synonymous with the elegant bourgeois life. The companies themselves agree that they are selling not just coffee, but experiences. Starbucks is dedicated to ensuring that every customer experiences both tangible and intangible rewards. This is why a cup of coffee, which costs only a few yuan to produce, can be sold for nearly 30 yuan. However, this pricing doesn't seem like excessive profit to Starbucks customers. They visit Starbucks not just for the coffee itself, but more so because they are drawn to the café's unique ambiance and atmosphere. They come to enjoy not only the taste of the coffee but also to seek a deeper connection and fulfillment in their spiritual lives.

5.Product promotion

Starbucks has its own loyalty Card, the Starbucks Rewards Card. If you buy a Starbucks Rewards Card, it will include some discounts, such as buy one, get one free, birthday coupons, Starbucks delivery and so on.If people bring their own coffee cup to Starbucks, they will get a discount. Bring the own cup to Starbucks and save $4, or order online and get a discount, but both are smaller. Starbucks gives consumers the impression that they never discount. This aspect establishes the brand of Starbucks as a brand that does not fight price wars and attracts customers through quality.

6.Advertisement

Starbucks doesn't advertise? people believe this is the first reaction of many people when they see this news. If you think about it, it seems to be true. People can see McDonald's, KFC, Coca-Cola, Pepsi and other consumer brands on TV and video sites bombarded with general advertising (in this case, hard advertising), it seems to be rare to see Starbucks advertising [9]. Why he doesn't like advertising? It starts with Starbucks' brand concept. Schultz believes that in this ever-changing world, the strongest and most enduring brands are those that are built in people's hearts - that's the brand that's truly sustainable. Such a brand has a solid foundation, because it empowers people's spirit, not all by bombarding them with advertising. Starbucks has always considered itself more than just coffee, but a "third space" separate from work and home. In this "third space," people are the most important [10]. There is a saying inside Starbucks: "People don't live in the coffee business, people live in the coffee business." They believe that coffee is just a concept [11]. Why do so many people buy Starbucks even though they don't advertise it externally? Through the inquiry of people around them, the researcher found that they learned that Starbucks is from people around them [12]. This is also a way of publicity, to recommend their own good products to people around, so that Starbucks can expand its consumer base. In simpler terms, Starbucks does engage in advertising, but its advertising is exceptionally clever. It leverages the unique traits of the Chinese market, as well as the participation of its partners and members, to disseminate its message [13]. Starbucks recognized that most of its customers weren't necessarily coffee experts, so its objective was to persuade them that it offered genuine coffee and leave them with the impression that they were savoring top-quality coffee [14].

7.Conclusion

One of the key takeaways from our analysis is the pivotal role played by Starbucks' iconic brand logo. Its ubiquitous presence has not only established a strong visual identity but has also fostered a sense of trust and recognition among consumers worldwide. This brand logo, coupled with Starbucks' unwavering commitment to quality, has helped forge enduring brand loyalty. Furthermore, the exploration highlights Starbucks' exceptional adaptability to evolving consumer preferences and the diverse demographics it caters to. By customizing its offerings to suit specific target demographics and strategically selecting prime locations for its outlets, Starbucks has been able to consistently attract a broad spectrum of consumers. The pricing strategies employed by Starbucks, although often perceived as premium, have been carefully positioned to align with the perceived value of their products, further reinforcing their brand image. Starbucks' innovative product promotion and advertising techniques, including seasonal campaigns and community engagement, have consistently resonated with consumers, creating a sense of connection beyond just coffee. As Starbucks continues its global expansion, the lessons gleaned from our analysis offer valuable insights for both academia and industry professionals. It underscores the importance of brand identity, loyalty, adaptability, and strategic positioning in sustaining success within a highly competitive market. In essence, Starbucks' journey is a compelling case study in how a brand can navigate the complexities of the beverage industry and emerge as a global leader. As it continues to evolve and grow, Starbucks' enduring prosperity serves as a testament to the power of a well-crafted marketing strategy and an unwavering commitment to meeting the diverse needs of its global consumer base.

References

1. Wu Chunxiao, Yang Mei, & Feng Mingliang. (2014). A study on Starbucks' business model. Modern Business 11: 01.
2. He Qi. (2020). A Brief discussion on Starbucks brand ritual marketing strategy. News Communication 17: 84-85.
3. Li X. (2022). A Study on the Two-tailed mermaid symbol of Starbucks Based on Western Context. Creativity and Design 02: 45-52.
4. Ding J. (2015). Research on brand loyalty based on Customer value. Chinese market 14: 72-73.
5. Zhou Guanming. (2015). Analysis on factors influencing customer loyalty -- A case study of Starbucks. Economic and Trade Practice, 11: 40-41.
6. Wang Xinlei. (2015). Why are Starbucks, 7-11 and other restaurant companies keen on honeycomb layout? Sales & Marketing (Channel Edition), 10: 14.
7. Lai Xiu-feng. (2016). Analysis and reflection on Starbucks pricing. China Collective Economy 21: 62-63.
8. Chiler. (2017). Starbucks's pricing strategy and benefit analysis in China. Journal of Jilin university. 56: 33.
9. Zhishu. Pricing strategy. Modern business, 13: 35-37. (2021).
10. Lin L. (2015). Starbucks without advertising. Modern Corporate Culture (First Part) 12: 78-79.
11. Sisson, D. C., & Bowen, S. A. (2022). Reputation management and authenticity: A case study of Starbucks' UK tax crisis and "Spread The Cheer" campaign. Journal of Communication Management, 21(3): 287-302.
12. Thompson, C. J., & Arsel, Z. (2022). The Starbucks brandscape and consumers'(anticorporate) experiences of glocalization. Journal of consumer research, 31(3): 631-642.
13. Macdonald, K. (2019). Globalising justice within coffee supply chains? Fair Trade, Starbucks and the transformation of supply chain governance. Third World Quarterly, 28(4): 793-812.
14. Vishwanath, V., & Harding, D. (2023). The Starbucks Effect. Harvard business review, 78(2): 17-17.

AUTHOR INDEX

EDP Sciences – Web of Conferences
17, Avenue du Hoggar
Parc d'Activité de Courtabouf
BP 112
F-91944 Les Ulis Cedex A
France

ISBN 978-1-7138-9557-2

CURRAN ASSOCIATES INC.
proceedings.com